Urban and Regional Economics

The International Library of Critical Writings in Economics

Series Editor: Mark Blaug
Professor Emeritus, University of London
Consultant Professor, University of Buckingham
Visiting Professor, University of Exeter

1. Multinational Corporations
   Mark Casson
2. The Economics of Innovation
   Christopher Freeman
3. Entrepreneurship
   Mark Casson
4. International Investment
   Peter J. Buckley
5. Game Theory in Economics
   Ariel Rubinstein
6. The History of Economic Thought
   Mark Blaug
7. Monetary Theory
   Thomas Mayer
8. Joint Production of Commodities
   Neri Salvadori and Ian Steedman
9. Industrial Organization
   Oliver E. Williamson
10. Growth Theory (Volumes I, II and III)
    R. Becker and E. Burmeister
11. Microeconomics: Theoretical and Applied (Volumes I, II and III)
    Robert E. Kuenne
12. The Economics of Health (Volumes I and II)
    A.J. Culyer
13. Recent Developments in Macroeconomics (Volumes I, II and III)
    Edmund S. Phelps
14. Urban and Regional Economics
    Paul C. Cheshire and Alan W. Evans
15. Modern Public Finance (Volumes I and II)
    A.B. Atkinson

Future titles will include:

Exchange Rate Economics (Volumes I and II) *Ronald MacDonald and Mark Taylor*
Development Economics (Volumes I, II, III and IV) *Deepak Lal*
The Economic Value of Education *Mark Blaug*
The Philosophy and Methodology of Economics *Bruce Caldwell*
General Equilibrium Theory *Andrew Mas-Colell*
International Finance *Robert Z. Aliber*

Urban and Regional Economics

Edited by

Paul C. Cheshire

Professor of Urban and Regional Economics
University of Reading

and

Alan W. Evans

Professor of Environmental Economics
University of Reading

An Elgar Reference Collection

Published by
Edward Elgar Publishing Limited
Gower House
Croft Road
Aldershot
Hants GU11 3HR
England

Edward Elgar Publishing Company
Old Post Road
Brookfield
Vermont 05036
USA

British Library Cataloguing in Publication Data

Urban and regional economics. – (International library of critical writings in economics, no. 14). – (An Elgar reference collection).
1. Regional economics
I. Cheshire, Paul C. *1941–* II. Evans, Alan W. *1938–* III. Series
330.9

Library of Congress Cataloguing in Publication Data

Urban and regional economics/edited by Paul C. Cheshire and Alan W. Evans.
p. cm. – (The International library of critical writings in economics; 14) (An Elgar reference collection)
Includes index.
1. Urban economics. 2. Regional economics. I. Cheshire, P.C. II. Evans, Alan W. III. Series. IV. Series: An Elgar reference collection.
HT321.U275 1991
330.9173′2–dc20 91–16965
CIP

Printed in Great Britain at the University Press, Cambridge

ISBN 1 85278 181 5

Contents

Acknowledgements

The editor and publishers wish to thank the following who have kindly given permission for the use of copyright material.

Academic Press, Inc. for article: L.A. Rose (1989), 'Urban Land Supply: Natural and Contrived Restrictions', *Journal of Urban Economics*, **25** (3), 325–45.

W. Alonso for his own article: (1960), 'A Theory of the Urban Land Market', *Papers of the Regional Science Association*, **6**, 149–57.

American Economic Association for articles: B. Chinitz (1961), 'Contrasts in Agglomeration: New York and Pittsburgh', *American Economic Review*, **51** (2), 279–89; J.R. Harris and M. Todaro (1970), 'Migration, Unemployment and Development: A Two-Sector Analysis', *American Economic Review*, **60** (1), 126–42.

Cambridge University Press for article: I.R. Gordon (1985), 'The Cyclical Sensitivity of Regional Employment and Unemployment Differentials', *Regional Studies*, **19** (2), 95–110.

Carfax Publishing Company for articles: A.W. Evans (1972), 'The Pure Theory of City Size in an Industrial Economy', *Urban Studies*, **9**, 49–77; E. von Böventer (1975), 'Regional Growth Theory', *Urban Studies*, **12**, 1–29; P.C. Cheshire (1979), 'Inner Areas as Spatial Labour Markets: A Critique of the Inner Area Studies', *Urban Studies*, **16** (1), 29–43; M. Neutze (1987), 'The Supply of Land for a Particular Use', *Urban Studies*, **24** (5), 379–88; J.S.L. McCombie (1988), 'A Synoptic View of Regional Growth and Unemployment: I – The Neoclassical Theory', *Urban Studies*, **25**, (4), 267–81.

Committee for Economic Development for article: C.M. Tiebout (1962), *The Community Economic Base Study*, Supplementary Paper 16, chapter 6, 57–60.

D.C. Heath & Co. for article: A. Anas and L.N. Moses (1978), 'Transportation and Land Use in the Mature Metropolis', in C.L. Leven (ed.), *The Mature Metropolis*, 149–68.

Duke University School of Law for article: O.A. Davis and A.B. Whinston (1961), 'The Economics of Urban Renewal', *Law and Contemporary Problems*, **26**, 105–17.

National Institute of Economic and Social Research for excerpt: A.J. Brown *et al.* (1967), 'Regional Multipliers', appendix to 'The Green Paper on the Development Areas', *National Institute Economic Review*, **40**, 33.

Pion Ltd. for article: M. Chisholm (1987), 'Regional Development: the Reagan–Thatcher Legacy', *Environment and Planning C: Government and Policy*, **5**, 197–218.

Regional Research Institute, West Virginia University for article: R.L. Moomaw (1983), 'Spatial Productivity Variations in Manufacturing: A Critical Survey of Cross-Sectional Analyses', *International Regional Science Review*, **8** (1), 1–22.

Regional Science Research Institute, University of Pennsylvania for articles: P. Blackley (1984), 'A Hedonic Approach to the Decentralization of Manufacturing Activity', *Journal of Regional Science*, **24** (4), 541–57; C.L. Leven (1985), 'Regional Development Analysis and Policy', *Journal of Regional Science*, **25** (4), 569–92.

Scottish Economic Society for articles: N. Kaldor (1970), 'The Case for Regional Policies', *Scottish Journal of Political Economy*, **17**, 337–48; J. Twomey and J. Taylor (1985), 'Regional Policy and the Interregional Movement of Manufacturing Industry in Great Britain', *Scottish Journal of Political Economy*, **32** (3), 257–77.

Southern Economic Journal for article: C.M. Tiebout (1957), 'Regional and Interregional Input–Output Models: An Appraisal', *Southern Economic Journal*, **24**, 140–7.

University of Chicago Press for articles: C.M. Tiebout (1956), 'A Pure Theory of Local Expenditures', *Journal of Political Economy*, **64**, (5), 416–24; L.A. Sjaastad (1962), 'The Costs and Returns of Human Migration', *Journal of Political Economy*, **70**, (5), Supplement, 80–93; J.R. Moroney and J.M. Walker (1966), 'A Regional Test of the Heckscher–Ohlin Hypothesis', *Journal of Political Economy*, **74**, 573–86.

Every effort has been made to trace all the copyright holders but if any have been inadvertently overlooked the publishers will be pleased to make the necessary arrangement at the first opportunity.

In addition the publishers wish to thank the Library of the London School of Economics and Political Science and The Alfred Marshall Library, Cambridge University for their assistance in obtaining these articles.

Introduction

Both urban and regional economics are late comers as fields of specialist knowledge in economics. There are individual examples of notable work by earlier economists, for example, Haig's study of the New York metropolitan region published in 1926, or even von Thünen's (1826) classic study of the location of agricultural land uses, a pioneering piece of applied economic research. Nevertheless the study of the economics of towns and the economics of regions by people who might describe themselves as urban economists or regional economists really dates from the 1950s.

Although both urban and regional economics are based on the study of spatial relationships, the similarity in birth dates of the two subjects is to a large extent coincidental since they came into existence for different reasons. Urban economics was born out of transport economics. It was realized that, to obtain solutions for the kind of urban transport problems created by widespread car ownership, it was necessary to understand why urban activities located where they did and how these locations would change if new roads were built or the urban transport system changed in any way. This relationship between transport and land use is brought out in a paper by Anas and Moses (1978), the first of the Readings, in which they discuss the effects of transport changes on the structure of large cities and urban regions, both in the past and in the future.

The scope of urban economics widened over time as economic analysis was applied to other urban problems. The analysis of the determinants of location, particularly residential location, expanded into analyses of the problems of urban renewal and slum clearance in the 1960s. The financial problems of the cities spawned a literature on local government finance. The race riots in US cities in the late 1960s led to the analysis of the consequences of racial discrimination in housing and employment, just as high unemployment in British cities in the 1970s, and *their* riots in the early 1980s, stimulated the study of urban labour markets and the decentralization of employment.

The shift in the nature of urban economics has resulted in a convergence of the interests of urban economists with those of regional economists. Regional economics was born primarily out of macroeconomics. Although examples exist of earlier work which with hindsight we can classify as 'regional economics', particularly work on interregional location theory by Weber (1909), Lösch (1954) and others, the subject as such developed with a burst of activity in the late 1950s and 1960s. At that time Keynesian economic policies appeared to have provided a permanent solution to the problem of high national unemployment, but, whilst national unemployment rates could be held at a low level, the levels of unemployment in some regions appeared to be permanently and unacceptably high. With this perspective, the regional problem was viewed initially as a macroeconomic problem, with the region being viewed as a smaller version of the national economy. Over time, however, the understanding of regional detail, of locational and other spatial relationships, was perceived as necessary to an understanding and appraisal of regional policy and regional problems, and the scope of regional economics widened.

At the same time the level of national unemployment steadily increased and unemployment became once again, in the 1970s, a national rather than a regional problem. Moreover it was observed that some cities or parts of cities in more prosperous regions had persistently high rates of unemployment, whilst some areas in less prosperous regions seemed to have persistently low levels of unemployment. In the analysis of these kinds of local economic problems the interests of both urban and regional economists coincided.

Urban Economics

Why do cities exist? That is the fundamental question with which urban economic analysis must start. Three conditions must be satisfied. First, agriculture must be capable of producing a surplus over and above what is required to maintain the rural population at subsistence level. This surplus can then be traded with the inhabitants of the cities for the goods and services which they provide. Second, there must be some economies of scale in the production of these goods and services. For if there were no economies of scale, the rural population would produce these goods and services for themselves. If there are economies of scale in the production of a good to be sold to the inhabitants of a rural area then it can be produced at one particular site and distributed over the area. Production will take place at some distance from most of the customers; and the greater the economies of scale in production (and in transport) the more distant the place of production is likely to be. Third, the producers of these goods and services must gain some advantage from being grouped together at a single location, in a town or city, instead of being scattered across the countryside. The advantage may be merely access to a common labour force, or it may be that the producers trade with each other, or the various producers may share a common demand for products or services which are not necessarily needed by the rural community, banking for instance. The advantages to firms of grouping together in one place are called, loosely, agglomeration economies; they provide the economic cement which holds the modern town or city together.

From the beginning, the nature of these agglomeration economies has been explored by urban economists. Haig (1926) discussed them in the papers on the New York economy mentioned earlier, and in the 1950s the New York area was again the subject of research which resulted in a notable series of reports (Hoover and Vernon, 1959; Lichtenberg, 1960; Robbins and Terleckyj, 1960; Vernon, 1960). Chinitz (1961) was involved in not only the New York study but also a study of the economy of Pittsburgh; and in a classic paper (Reading 2) he explores the nature of the economies of these two large but contrasting cities, one, Pittsburgh, being the location for a small number of major steel plants, the other, New York City, having a far more diversified economy producing a range of different goods and services with, apparently, no dominant large plants.

Earlier work on agglomeration economies, such as that referred to above, tended to be descriptive and analytical. During the 1970s and 1980s the nature of agglomeration economies were explored using increasingly sophisticated econometric methods to identify and quantify the economic advantages of the large city to the firms that locate there. In the paper reprinted here as Reading 3, Moomaw (1983) critically surveys this work and advances it a further stage.

If cities come into existence because agglomeration economies make it advantageous for firms to locate in them, the next obvious question is what limits their size. In the world, and, indeed, in any country in the world, there are fewer large cities than there are smaller ones. There tends to be an urban hierarchy in each nation, in which the number of settlements in any size class increases as the size class considered gets smaller.

One particular explanation of this urban hierarchy has found favour with geographers. The cities, towns and villages are viewed as central places selling goods and providing services to the surrounding populations in their 'market areas'. The larger the settlement, the larger the market area it serves so that the market areas of the smaller settlements 'nest' in the market areas of the larger, the smaller places selling the more frequently purchased goods and services. A recent survey of central place theory is given by Berry and Parr (1988).

Whilst central place theory has been seen as a plausible explanation of the urban hierarchy in predominantly agricultural areas, it has not appeared to be a satisfactory explanation for the existence of an urban hierarchy in industrial economies. In these economies firms do not sell their products only to some surrounding area, but nationally and even internationally. The larger cities seem to be economic entities whose economic activity is, to a large extent, virtually independent of their location within the economy. Economic explanations for the existence of an urban hierarchy in an industrial economy, such as that by Evans (1973a) in Reading 4, therefore tend to be based on the idea of a balancing of the economic advantages of agglomeration against the economic disadvantages of the concentration of activities in small areas – congestion and pollution, high labour costs and high land costs. The various theories of city size were surveyed some years ago by Richardson (1973a), whilst the economic theory has been surveyed more recently by Henderson (1988).

Incorporated into the economic theories of city size, there is always a theory of urban land costs and land use in which proximity to the city centre is desired by both firms and households, the former because of access to customers, suppliers, and services, the latter because of access to workplaces and services. The higher demand for sites nearer to the city centre causes rents and land costs to be highest at the centre and to decrease with increasing distance from it. Moreover, the larger the city the higher land costs are likely to be at the centre, both for demand reasons – the agglomeration economies will be greater in the larger city, and for supply reasons – the cost of travel from the edge of the city is greater. The theory is a development of early theories of agricultural location and land use, of which von Thünen was the pioneer. Von Thünen analysed the case in which various types of agricultural land use are located around an urban area which is the market for their produce. In the hands of Alonso (1960, Reading 5, 1964a) and Wingo (1961) this was fashioned into a theory of the allocation of urban land uses around a city centre and in the following decade Muth (1969), Mills (1972), and Evans (1973b) developed the theory to provide a thorough understanding of the pattern of residential location in large urban areas.

Stripped to essentials, it is a theory of residential location in a monocentric city in which households trade off journey to work costs, which increase with distance from the centre, against housing costs, which decrease with distance from the centre; hence the name usually applied to this group of theories – the trade-off theory of location. In this basic form the theory is mathematically tractable and, for this reason, if for no other, it has become the basis for much mathematical work in urban economics. This can be said to have begun with the work of Solow (1973), Mirrlees (1972), and Dixit (1973) on optimal location, and the early work in this area, the so called New Urban Economics, was reviewed by Richardson

(1977) and Henderson (1977), with new work appearing in journals such as the *Journal of Urban Economics* and *Regional Science and Urban Economics*.

An implication of the trade-off theory of location is that just as land costs decline with distance from the city centre and are higher at the centre of the larger city so wage costs should also behave in the same way. Workers would tend to require higher rewards for working at or near the centre of a large city since they either have to spend more on their journeys to work, if they live towards the edge of the city, or pay higher housing costs, if they live towards the centre. This idea was first mooted by Moses (1962) and pursued by Muth (1969), Evans (1973b), and Ravallion (1979) among others, but it is not strongly supported by the empirical evidence. It would appear that the higher costs of a central workplace location are often balanced by other advantages such as shorter working hours and proximity to shops and entertainments, and the data available is insufficient, and insufficiently accurate, to allow the urban wage gradient to be confidently identified. It is clear, however, that wages are higher in the very largest cities as the London allowances invariably paid in Britain bear witness.

The urban economic analysis reviewed so far has tended to consider the urban area as a single economic entity. Indeed this is true of much of urban economics; the city is treated in the same way as the firm is treated in the theory of the firm or the nation in national income analysis or international trade. Moreover, as tends to be usual in economic analysis, most early work was devoted to the analysis of the city in long run equilibrium. Urban problems occur, however, when the city is not in long run equilibrium and these problems may become evident only in parts of the city. In Britain and the United States, these parts have been the inner areas; in most of continental Europe and in many other parts of the world the problem areas have often been on the urban periphery.

Concern with the economic problems of urban areas has therefore led urban economics to consider both the problems associated with change and the ways in which the different parts of the city interrelate. In the developed economies the problems of the cities have seemed to be associated with the decentralization of both population and jobs. In the less developed economies the problems have been associated, in contrast, with growth; intensification of agriculture has produced a flow of migrants from the rural areas to the cities and massive urban growth has occurred, apparently ahead of the industrialization which might have been expected to cause it. The problems of third world city growth and rural–urban migration have spawned an extensive literature (see, for example, Yap, 1977; Henderson, 1988; Kelley and Williamson, 1984; Richardson, 1981). The model set out by Harris and Todaro (1970; Reading 6) has had the most influence. In this model wage rates in urban areas, particularly in what are called the formal sectors, tend to be much higher than the incomes that can be obtained in rural areas, because both government and multinational firms tend to be under pressure from outside to pay what are regarded as adequate wages. Migrants are therefore willing to move to the cities to try to obtain a higher paid job, accepting the risk of a long spell of unemployment since the chance of the former compensates for the latter.

As we have already said, the recent problems of unemployment in the cities of the developed economies certainly do not arise from urban in-migration. Indeed their problems since about 1960 have been associated with the decentralization of both jobs and residents. During the 1970s it was sometimes argued that unemployment in the inner cities was due to the decentralization of employment, particularly manufacturing industry, so that, as the jobs left, the people were left without jobs. However it was demonstrated by, among others, Foster and Richardson (1973) and Steinnes (1982), that, if anything, the residents were moving out ahead of the jobs, so that other factors were involved. The decentralization of industry not only from the city centre to the suburbs but away from the cities to more rural areas has been extensively analysed, for example by Fothergill and Gudgin (1982), Scott (1982) and in the volumes of papers edited by Leven (1978) with respect to the United States, and by Evans and Eversley (1980), with respect to Britain. Here we reproduce one of a recent series of studies by Blackley (1984; Reading 7) in which econometric techniques are used to evaluate the importance of the various possible causes – decreasing importance of agglomeration economies, high central city taxes, changing production technologies requiring large sites, transport improvements, and changing location of the labour force.

Even if the decentralization of industry does not precede the decentralization of the population, changes in industrial structure could still cause local unemployment problems. If a firm in an inner suburb closes down would this not cause a higher level of unemployment in that part of the city? If an office development replaces it, would there still not be unemployment because of a mismatch between the skills needed for the new jobs and the skills possessed by the unemployed? And might racial discrimination prevent some residents following the jobs to the suburbs even when others can and do?

The last of these questions was the particular concern of American economists at the end of the 1960s (see, for example, Kain, 1975). The other questions have been studied by British economists since concern rose over the level of inner city unemployment in the mid 1970s (Metcalf and Richardson, 1980; Evans and Richardson, 1981) and a paper by Cheshire (1979; Reading 8) surveys the findings in relation to the inner city problem. The fundamental question is the extent to which the large urban area can be considered as a set of smaller labour markets or as a single labour market. If it is the latter, and that seems to be the conclusion, the effects of a disturbance such as a factory closure would be rapidly spread over the whole labour market so that the increase in unemployment would not be concentrated in the vicinity of the factory but thinly spread as an increase in unemployment over the whole area.

In recent work on this topic Australian evidence has suggested that peripheral settlements may suffer high unemployment rates which are not dispersed over the rest of the urban area because of their relative inaccessibility (Vipond and Beed, 1986). Other research has looked at the way in which, since the younger and more skilled are more likely to migrate than the older and less skilled, differences in the rates of migration by different groups between urban areas, are likely to lead to structural differences between urban areas in the medium term (Cheshire, 1979; Evans and Richardson, 1981; Topel, 1986).

As problems of urban unemployment are seen as problems in the adjustment of the whole urban labour market to change in one part of it, so urban land problems usually arise because of the need to adjust land use to new economic circumstances. Throughout the economic analysis of the city discussed earlier it is assumed, implicitly or explicitly, that the land market operates efficiently and that land is always used by the activity which can pay the highest current rent. Such an assumption has been customary in discussions of rent and land use since the time of Ricardo. Since the early 1970s, however, this assumption has been increasingly questioned, and the economic functioning of the land market has been analysed rather than assumed. The process began with a resurgence of interest in Marxian theories of land rent, particularly among geographers, led by Harvey (1973), which questioned the neutral role assigned to landowners by conventional economic theory, arguing, in effect, that land owners could choose to hold their land off the market if this appeared to be in their long term interests. Conventional analysis has since provided a number of reasons why land may not be supplied for the use offering the highest current rent, and three of these explanations – uncertainty about the future, a belief that an alternative use will yield a higher rent in the near future, and the owner-occupiers treating land as, in part, a consumption good – are reviewed by Neutze (1987; Reading 9). Any current use of a site requires a long term capital commitment in terms of buildings. This means that what may be optimal at one point in time will become non-optimal as conditions change. This problem has been extensively analysed in theoretical models of land use called 'vintage' models, because the buildings are of different ages or vintages (see Muth, 1973). The implication, of course, is that so far from all land being employed in the use which would yield the current highest rent, most land is not used in this way because of the buildings and infrastructure which it has inherited from the past.

The fact that this can be a real economic problem is brought out in discussions of the problem of urban renewal. In Reading 10 Davis and Whinston (1961) demonstrate why public intervention may be necessary to clear slum housing. The rent which could be obtained if any single property is redeveloped is held down by the poor state of repair of the remaining properties; as a result, they argue, no properties may be up-graded even though it may be optimal that they all should. In a sense it is evident that Davis and Whinston prove rather too much. Since their paper was written, the process of gentrification has gone on apace in cities in the developed economies, particularly in the English speaking countries where most higher income households had previously lived in the suburbs. Nevertheless, even though redevelopment and rehabilitation may occur 'naturally', the rapid change engendered by the activities of the London Docklands Development Corporation in London's East End indicates that the process can be considerably speeded by public intervention on a large scale.

The final topic in the field of urban economics which we wish to touch on is that of local government finance. Curiously this is one field with which 'mainstream' economists have been concerned over many years, if only because local government activities are often substantially financed by a tax on property – the property tax or the rates. So Alfred Marshall (1920) discussed property taxation, as did Sir John Hicks (1959). The pattern of local government taxation differs between countries, however, as shown in the review by Bennett (1980). Britain, in the eighties, abolished the taxation of housing in favour of a poll tax, whilst industrial and commercial property was taxed at a uniform rate set by central government rather than rates set by each individual local government. The intention was that the residents would not be able to vote for expenditure to benefit themselves leaving most of the cost to be borne by industry and commerce. So the uniform business rate has been retained with a new tax on domestic property introduced in the nineties.

In practice local variations in expenditure were restrained by central government control, but the idea that local expenditure would be financed by local taxation and determined by local votes is one which has been extensively analysed in urban economics. It originates in a paper by Tiebout (1956; Reading 11). Samuelson (1954) had suggested that people had no incentive to reveal their preferences with respect to goods which were consumed publicly. Tiebout responded by hypothesizing that this would not be true if we were considering goods which were public only to the residents of the local government area which paid for them through taxes, and if there were a large number of these local governments. Householders would tend to live under the jurisdiction of the local government which provided the package of services and taxes which they preferred to all others. In the last twenty years or so, the Tiebout hypothesis has been extensively developed and tested against the empirical evidence and found, despite the apparent unrealism of its assumptions, to represent the situation, to some extent at least, in large US cities.

In what direction will urban economics develop in the future? Any answer must be biased by the interests of those replying. The authors of this Introduction would suggest that major areas of development will be in the economics of the land market and in the economics of land use planning; two topics which, considering their importance, have been relatively neglected in the past. The last paper, by Rose (1989; Reading 12) draws together both these topics and demonstrates that the supply of land matters, whether this supply is limited by zoning regulations or by the natural features of the cities' sites, so that the more restricted the supply, the higher the price of land.

Regional Economics

As we said at the outset, regional economics as distinct from urban economics owes its origins to at least two areas of economic analysis. The developing tools of macroeconomic analysis were applied to regions conceived as spaceless subsets of national economies; this aspect of regional economics is summed up by Leven in Reading 22. The limitations of this essentially aspatial analysis came increasingly to be realized, indeed were always emphasized by the more geographically informed school of regional analysts such as Hoover (1948), Isard (1956) or Moses (1958). The second area of economics on which regional economics drew was locational analysis, but the analysis of location beyond the intra-regional scale. The seminal works of this branch of economics were those of Weber (1909), who pioneered the systematic analysis of location at a scale which could be interregional or even international; and Lösch (1954). Lösch developed an economic theory explaining why, in principle, regions would come into existence.

Locational analysis is itself, however, a vast field and constraints on length mean that it is not represented in this collection at all. Accessible accounts of the early development of the field can be found in the often reprinted paper by Alonso (1964b). Lösch's contribution – the seminal work on the definition of nodal regions dependent upon market areas and the tension between economies of scale and transport costs – is well summarized in his own 1938 article. A more pragmatic analysis of why city-regions or Functional Urban Regions are the most appropriate definition for many types of regional analysis (for example, for policy implementation) can be found in Cheshire and Hay (1989). A whole field of study of spatial competition and spatial pricing has developed from the original article by Hotelling (1929) which focused on non-price locational competition. A notable contributor to this literature has been Greenhut (1970, 1975) but others, such as Norman (1981) and Eaton & Lipsey (1982) have made major contributions.

Although some of the Readings selected for this volume analyse aspects of regional economies explicitly introducing concepts from locational analysis (such as Readings 1 and 8) or consciously try to synthesize locational and regional economic ideas to produce something that might properly be called spatial economic analysis (such as the piece by von Böventer,

Reading 18) pure locational analysis is reluctantly omitted. The emphasis in the choice of regional readings is on the analysis of economic processes between sub-divisions of national economies.

Reading 13, again by Tiebout, is on the application of input/output analysis to regions. This has proved to be one of the most widely applied techniques in regional economics. Tiebout warned that data deficiencies and the heroism of the necessary assumptions made the results of regional I/O studies very tentative. His conclusion, more than thirty years ago, that he was not necessarily calling for more research since that would imply a judgement as to the allocation of scarce research resources, seems, with hindsight, somewhat ironic, given that the flow of regional I/O studies since Tiebout's cautious warnings has been almost constant. Some of the problems Tiebout identified have been overcome but the data demands have remained very high indeed and regional I/O studies have remained (frequent) one-off efforts rather than developed into consistent long-term studies. The attractions of the technique remain as, however, do its difficulties.

The Keynesian income multiplier is another method by which regional impacts may be quantified. It has the advantage that its data requirements are very limited compared to those of input/output analysis as the almost back-of-envelope calculation of Brown and his associates (Reading 14) shows. It can also be formally identified with the older export base multiplier as Tiebout shows in Reading 15. The export base multiplier is simply a special case of the Keynesian income multiplier.[1] The multiplier is a simple tool which can and has been made more sophisticated by, for example, Brownrigg (1971) who analysed the effects of direct leakages from the multiplicand and the effect of induced investment, or Sinclair and Sutcliffe (1978, 1982). Its assumptions are ultimately as heroic as those of I/O analysis and its potential power much less, but its data demands are comparatively limited and as Leven (Reading 22) shows, it has been analytically the foundation of much of traditional regional development policy.

Given the relevance of regional economic analysis to the development of regional policy, it is to be expected that much attention has been focused on the analysis of regional growth. At least three major schools of analysis can be identified and each is represented here. The first is the application of neo-classical growth models to regional rather than national economies. The seminal contributions were made by Borts and Stein both in individual contributions and together. Their best known work is of book length however, (Borts and Stein, 1964) and their contribution is not, in our view, done justice by any single short piece. This school of analysis which emphasizes the growth of regional supply is represented by a recent survey article by McCombie (Reading 16). This does have the disadvantage that the approach is represented by a piece which is ultimately sceptical as to its value, despite the objectivity with which the literature is synthesized, but it has the additional advantage that it offers a brief summary of the diffusion approach to analysing the regional growth process, which some might claim was a legitimate fourth school of analysis.

The second school of analysis is the so-called cumulative causation approach to analysing

[1]Tiebout assumes leakages into savings, taxes and imports but group savings and taxes. Thus his income multiplier is $1/[1 - c(1 - m)]$. His base multiplier is derived from the base identity $Y = S + X$ and $S = C - M$. Given $S = cY - cmY$ and constant propensities, then substitution generates $Y = X/[1 - c(1 - m)]$, that is, the base and the income multipliers are identical.

regional growth. The piece we have selected by Kaldor (Reading 17) bears witness to the interrelationship between regional policy and the analysis of regional growth processes; its title is 'The Case for Regional Policies'. Kaldor drew on earlier ideas of regional development and cumulative causation, such as those of Myrdal (1957), as well as his own work on neo-Keynesian economic growth models. His approach makes the rate of growth of demand for regional output (interacting with increasing returns to scale and nationally determined money wages) the key to regional growth rates. Also, as the name implies, it concludes that regions which begin to grow faster than others experience cumulative advantages; hence his conclusion that there is a case for regional policies. This analytical framework is, as Kaldor recognizes, complementary to the export base idea and to regional policy based on stimulating the demand for a lagging region's output. Indeed Kaldor was primarily responsible for the introduction in Britain of the Regional Employment Premium. This was a subsidy on manufacturing labour costs (at its peak – between 1967 and 1969 – worth 9 per cent of labour costs for qualifying employers – see Brown, 1972) in target regions, intended to change their terms of trade and stimulate demand for their manufactured exports. Models of regional growth on the lines initiated by Kaldor and Myrdal have continued to be developed with the work of Dixon and Thirlwall (1975) being perhaps most widely cited. They have been reviewed in a recent article by McCombie (1988b).

The third approach to understanding the processes of regional growth attempts to synthesize these macroeconomic models – which implicitly assume regional economies to be homogeneous points in space with interregional trade and factor flows unaffected by transport or other costs – with market process and spatial analysis. This approach derives from Richardson (1973b) but is represented here, in Reading 18, by a piece by von Böventer that originated as an extended review of Richardson's book. Von Böventer's approach relies even more on spatial factors, such as economies and diseconomies of agglomeration, environmental preferences and diffusion of innovation, than did Richardson's; and relies commensurately less on the relative price effects influencing regional rates of growth of factor supply, central to neo-classical approaches.

Although Richardson's and von Böventer's contribution to understanding regional growth processes remains to be fully developed or satisfactorily tested, it has the attraction of beginning to integrate those elements of what might reasonably be thought of as the minimum necessary relevant areas of theory and to knit together urban and regional economics. As Leven (Reading 22) notes 'the connections between urban and regional analysis and location and migration theory in reality are not completely separable'. Indeed it was the belief that they were inextricably interrelated that provided the starting point for Richardson's critique of traditional approaches. His book on regional growth theory provides a review of migration analysis and the literature on regional capital movements and trade flows which, although dating, is still useful.

These subjects provide the theme of the next set of selected readings. There are two classic articles, one on migration and the other on regional trade, and a more recent one on migration, regional labour supply and regional unemployment differences. Sjaastad's contribution (Reading 19) was simple. He applied the ideas on human capital theory that were then being developed at the University of Chicago to understanding interregional migration flows. His 'regions' were data determined, the individual states of the United States. He was one of the earliest writers to note the importance of the simple fact that net flows were the difference of two much larger gross flows which were not necessarily determined by the same factors. The application of human capital theory to understanding migration is in many ways more helpful than in its better known application to education and training, since migration is subject to somewhat fewer influences and is influenced less by social factors. Not only does it provide a plausible explanation of the age structure of interregional migrants but it provides a plausible explanation of why rural–urban migrants have a younger age profile than migrants between mature urbanized regions.

Later writers, such as Lowry (1966), Vanderkamp (1971) and Miller (1973) explored the question as to whether sub-groups within the gross flows of migrants were motivated by different influences. Human capital theory could provide a plausible explanation of why regions with high inflows of migrants also had high outflows – an apparent paradox which Lowry was the first to comment on extensively. Vanderkamp explored and quantified not only the different motivations of different groups of migrants but also showed that the volume of the gross flows of interregional migrants was sensitive to overall labour market conditions; as aggregate unemployment in the national economy rose, so the flow of interregional migration tended to fall. Since we also know that job mobility falls as aggregate unemployment increases (see Reading 8) this implies that, in so far as mobility is an automatic adjustment mechanism between regional economies it tends to become less efficient as aggregate unemployment rises.

This, indeed, is in many ways the theme of the next selection by Gordon (Reading 20). This synthesizes three areas of regional labour market analysis; regional unemployment differences; the cyclical sensitivity of regional unemployment and employment; and migration. By painstaking logic and a careful sifting of the evidence, Gordon shows that a major source of cyclical variation in the absolute differences between regional unemployment rates – at least in terms of direct causation – is to be found on the supply side. The underlying cause of regional unemployment differences may be on the demand side but short term fluctuations in the variance of regional unemployment rates result mainly from the reduced rate of adjustment of regional labour supply via migration associated with increases in national unemployment rates. Not only does Gordon show that this effect can be quantified, he also shows that one can estimate the proportion occurring in the first year of the total migration ultimately resulting from given regional unemployment differences. In the low unemployment period of the 1950s and early 1960s mobility was such that 98 per cent of the total expected migration occurred within a year; the estimated proportion occurring within a year at the highest level of national unemployment recorded during the period covered by Gordon's analysis was 17 per cent. This implies that by the 1970s and 1980s regional unemployment differences were well away from their 'equilibrium' values. Because of the lagged response of mobility to increases in unemployment, if everything remained as it was in 1980, regional unemployment differences would have continued to rise well into the 1980s.

The final selection on the theme of regional factor flows (the lack of literature on capital flows reflecting the sparsity of data) is a classic article by Moroney and Walker (Reading 21). Although this is an article widely cited in textbooks on regional economics, it is in some ways only incidentally regional. The authors are really interested in testing the Heckscher–Ohlin hypothesis of international trade – that countries specialize in the production of goods (and tradable services) which employ the factors of production in which they are most richly endowed. They test this on data for the southern and non-southern states of the US because, as they argue in section IV of their article, regional tests provide a way round many of the objections and difficulties involved in testing the theory of trade between countries. Their findings are that the hypothesis does not – at least given the rather crude data available – explain absolute patterns of regional specialization, but it is consistent with the changes in regional specialization they observe during the period covered by their analysis. This piece also reveals one of the problems most frequently encountered in empirical studies, that the data available are not necessarily the precise data required, nor is it possible to know the extent to which the failure to find confirming evidence for an hypothesis reflects data deficiencies or the fact that the hypothesis is wrong. Moroney and Walker use data for 20 two-digit industries but there is, of course, variation in the composition of these industries themselves. Even if we accept the basic assumptions involved in their approach it does not follow that, say, 'transportation equipment' reflects the same activities (and so factor proportions) in the south as it does in the non-south. In their analysis of change in specialization this problem is, in practical terms, far less important and this *may* be the explanation of the success of the Heckscher–Ohlin hypothesis in explaining changes rather than levels of specialization.

The final set of readings relate to regional policy. The first, Reading 22, reviews the history of regional development policy in terms of approaches to regional analysis. Leven suggests that there have been three basic approaches, all of which implicitly or explicitly assume away questions of the internal spatial structure of regions, or problems of regional development associated with locational analysis. The first approach goes back to ideas of the export base of regions which originated with Haig (1928). The policy implications of this school of analysis are that one should stimulate export demand. The second school of analysis, he argues, is based on a disequilibrium view of the space economy and is consistent with ideas about the diffusion of information and technical innovation, or with Richardson's or von Böventer's analysis of regional growth. The policy implications according to Leven, are for infrastructure spending, investment (including investment in human capital creation) and perhaps 'infant-industry' style protection. The growth pole solution, associated with Perroux (1950), is also consistent with this diagnosis of regional problems. The third approach Leven identifies is a market analysis of the regional problem deriving from the work of Borts and Stein (1964) which he suggests leads to non-policy.

Leven's final section explores the implications of the decline in manufacturing employment and the shift to services, leading to regional growth simultaneously with manufacturing employment decline; an observation, he suggests, which is at variance with the more simplistic versions of the export-base school of regional analysis. This leads him to consider some of the implications of what has come to be called 'restructuring' or 'economic transition' and to discuss the spatial implications of this process. Leven's conclusion is that this is associated with even more decentralization, although its implications for regional development policy are not yet clear. Indeed, its implications for net decentralization may not be as clear as Leven suggests. While the production of goods – normally identified with 'basic' activities – may continue to decentralize, the growth of the service sector, of service trading and the locational separation out of service-type employment from manufacturing may produce a recentralizing force.

The short piece by Chisholm (Reading 23) focuses on the preoccupations for regional policy of the 1980s. While Leven identifies a market-based diagnosis of regional problems with non-policy, Chisholm relates it to what might be called supply-side regional development policies. This really has more in common with Leven's disequilibrium diagnosis, although Chisholm gives considerable emphasis to a regional factor of production not discussed by Leven, that is, entrepreneurship. Chisholm's formulation of a new basis for regional policy derives from what he sees as a concern for efficiency over equity and the supply side preoccupations of the Reagan and Thatcher years. It is also more representative of a European perspective. Regional policy in the European Community grew in importance as it declined in importance in Britain and the US during the 1980s. One of Leven's subsidiary themes is to explain the problems of self-interest involved in regional policy and how those relate to the different diagnoses of regional problems that he suggests. The growth of regional policy in Europe during the 1970s and 1980s was the counterpart to moves towards European unity (see Cheshire *et al.* 1990). The emphasis of European regional policy shifted from its original focus on funding large-scale infrastructure projects to developing 'indigenous potential' (CEC 1984) using policy instruments which had much in common with those discussed by Chisholm.

The final selection is one example of a large body of literature which attempts to quantify the impact of regional policy. Much of this literature is British, and Moore and Rhodes are the two people most associated with it, although its origins can be traced to the work of Brown (1972). Moore and Rhodes' (1973) contribution used shift-share analysis to try and identify the impact on job creation of the various measures and varying intensity of British regional policy following World War II. Their later work (for example, Moore and Rhodes, 1976, or Moore, Rhodes and Tyler, 1986) employed more powerful regression analysis. They have consistently found that regional policy measures have had a significant influence on job creation, job moves and unemployment differentials, and have evaluated the effectiveness of different measures. Others have contributed to this literature, however, and it is a piece by Twomey and Taylor (Reading 24) which has been selected. This is partly, it must be admitted, on grounds of length, but it has the merit that it examines moves of manufacturing industry between all pairs of British regions, and does not lump together those that benefited from regional policy as a homogeneous, assisted region to be contrasted with the non-assisted region. Apart from allowing for more regional differentiation, this procedure makes it possible to measure the degree of assistance more accurately since, of course, the types of assistance for which different regions and sub-regions qualified varied greatly.

An almost parenthetical conclusion of Reading 20, by Gordon, was that 'regional differences in pressure of demand for labour tended to narrow during the period of active regional policy (1963–75)'. This is consistent with Twomey and Taylor's findings on interregional manufacturing moves. Their conclusion was that both location controls and investment incentives had a significant impact. Their finer level of regional analysis shows also that location controls were the most influential single instrument (Moore and Rhodes, 1976, had concluded that the Regional Employment Premium was the most powerful instrument) but that the majority of regional moves caused by location controls were not to regions that were the targets of assistance but to other 'neutral' regions – chiefly from the South East to East Anglia and the South West. This finding in the context of an ever more open European economy is of considerable significance and may apply to the side effects of controls – such as the effects of land use planning policy on land availability – not intended to have any particular regional effect on economic development.

Perhaps the conclusion with respect to regional policy is that there is a case for it both on efficiency grounds and on equity grounds. The efficiency arguments go back at least to the Barlow Report (1940) in which it was argued that regional unemployment differences, amongst other things, led to a waste of social capital as well as human resources, although in the 1960s a new argument was suggested by Lipsey (1960) that a more even distribution of regional unemployment would lead, other things being equal, to a lower rate of national wage inflation. The case on efficiency grounds becomes stronger as the overall pressure of demand in the economy increases; it is noteworthy that as the British economy revived and national unemployment fell during 1989 and 1990, people started again to talk of the problem of overheating in the South East and the desirability of steering activity to the high unemployment regions. As unemployment generally rises the efficiency argument for regional policy may become weaker – there are underemployed resources everywhere – but, as Gordon's piece shows, the equity argument becomes stronger. A high national level of unemployment impairs the automatic processes of spatial adjustment in the economy. Although there is evidence that the traditional instruments of regional policy had some effect they have, however, tended to fall out of fashion. There is not yet any systematic quantification of the effectiveness of newer, supply-side orientated instruments such as those discussed by Chisholm.

Acknowledgements

The editors of a book of Readings have to make a difficult choice. They can choose to publish 'classic' articles, or examples of the most recent research, or surveys of the field. If they take the first option they lay themselves open to the criticism that more recent research, which questions or develops ideas in the original piece, has been ignored. If they publish examples of recent research they can be criticized on the grounds that such research is likely to deal with an aspect of the topic and, anyway, it may be refuted or outdated by further work in a year or two. Finally, surveys can be criticized on the grounds that the research is being presented to the reader in pre-digested form and, surely, the idea of a book of readings is to encourage students of the field to read some of the original literature. Textbooks are to survey the field.

In the event we have chosen papers of all three types. We hope we have chosen classics which have something for the modern reader, current research which will stand the test of time and does not deal only with a narrow aspect of the topic, and surveys which also contribute to knowledge. We recognize that we cannot please everybody, however, and in an attempt to obviate criticism before selecting the readings in this book, the authors wrote to a number of economists around the world in order to ensure that our choices were not completely idiosyncratic. For various reasons many were unable to help but we must express our indebtedness to the following for their suggestions and comments – Ed von Böventer (University of Munich), Shozo Kuroda (Senshu University), Charles Leven (Washington University, St Louis), John Parr (University of Glasgow), Louis Rose (University of Hawaii), Peter Townroe (University of East Anglia), Jim Taylor (University of Lancaster), Roger Vickerman (University of Kent at Canterbury), and Christine Whitehead (London School of Economics). Finally we would like to thank colleagues Graham Crampton and Stephen Fothergill and a former colleague, George Norman, with whom we freely consulted. Obviously responsibility for the final choice rests with us.

References

Alonso, William (1960), 'A Theory of the Urban Land Market', *Papers of the Regional Science Association*, **6**, Reading 5 in this volume.

Alonso, William (1964a), *Location and Land Use: Toward a General Theory of Land Rent*, Cambridge, Mass: Harvard U.P.

Alonso, William (1964b), 'Location Theory', in Friedman, J. and W. Alonso (eds) *Regional Development and Planning: a Reader* Cambridge, Mass: M.I.T Press. Reprinted in L. Needleman (ed.) *Regional Analysis*, Harmondsworth, Middx: Penguin.

Anas, Alex and Leon N. Moses (1978), 'Transportation and Land Use: the Mature Metropolis', in C.L. Leven (ed.), *The Mature Metropolis* Lexington, Mass: D.C. Heath. Reading 1 in this volume.

Barlow Report (1940), *Royal Commission on the Distribution of the Industrial Population: Report* Cmd 6153, London: HMSO.

Bennett, Robert J. (1980), *The Geography of Public Finance*, London: Methuen.

Berry, Brian J.L., and John Parr (1988), *Market Centres and Retail Location: Theory and Application*, Englewood Cliffs, N.J: Prentice Hall.

Blackley, Paul (1984), 'A Hedonic Approach to the Decentralization of Manufacturing Activity', *Journal of Regional Science*, **24**, (4), November. Reading 7 in this volume.

Borts, G.H. and J.L. Stein (1964), *Economic Growth in a Free Market* New York: Columbia U.P.

von Böventer, E. (1975), 'Regional Growth Theory', *Urban Studies*, **12**, 1–29. Reading 18 in this volume.

Brown, A.J. *et al.* (1967), 'Regional Multipliers', *National Institute Economic Review*, **40**, 33, Reading 14 in this volume.

Brown, A.J. (1972), *The Framework of Regional Economics in the United Kingdom*, Cambridge: C.U.P.

Brownrigg, M. (1971), 'The Regional Income Multiplier: an attempt to complete the model', *Scottish Journal of Political Economy*, **18**, (3), 281–97.

Cheshire, Paul C. (1979), 'Inner Areas as Spatial Labour Markets: A Critique of the Inner Area Studies', *Urban Studies*, **16**, (1), February, 29–43. Reading 8 in this volume.

Cheshire, P.C. and D.G. Hay (1989), *Urban Problems in Western Europe: an economic analysis*, London: Unwin Hyman.

Cheshire, P.C., R. Camagni and J-P de Gaudemar (1991), '1957 to 1992: towards a Europe of Regions and Regional Policy' in Rodwin, L. and H. Sazanami (eds), *Industrial Change and Regional Economic Transformation: the experience of Western Europe*, London: Harper Collins Academic.

Chinitz, Ben (1961), 'Contrasts in Agglomeration: New York and Pittsburgh', *American Economic Review*, **51**, (2), May. Reading 2 in this volume.

Chisholm, M. (1987), 'Regional Development: the Reagan–Thatcher Legacy', *Environment and Planning C: Government and Policy*, **5**, 197–218. Reading 23 in this volume.

Commission of the European Communities (1984), *The Regions of Europe: second period report on the social and economic situation of the regions of the Community*, Luxemburg: Office for Official Publications.

Davis, Otto A., and Andrew B. Whinston (1961), 'The Economics of Urban Renewal', *Law and Contemporary Problems*, **26** (Winter). Reading 10 in this volume.

Dixit, Avinash (1973), 'The Optimum Factory Town', *Bell Journal of Economics and Management Science*, **4**, 637–54.

Dixon, R.J. and A.P. Thirlwall (1975), 'A Model of Regional Growth Differences on Kaldorian Lines', *Oxford Economic Papers*, **27**, 201–14.

Eaton, B.C. and R.G. Lipsey (1982), 'An Economic Theory of Central Places', *Economic Journal*, **92**, (365), 56–72.

Evans, Alan W. (1973a), 'The Pure Theory of City Size in an Industrial Economy', *Urban Studies*, **9** (Feb). Reading 4 in this volume.

Evans, Alan W. (1973b), *The Economics of Residential Location* London: Macmillan.

Evans, Alan W. and David Eversley (1980), *The Inner City: Employment and Industry* London: Heinemann.

Evans, Alan W. and Ray Richardson (1981), 'Urban Unemployment: Interpretation and Additional Evidence', *Scottish Journal of Political Economy*, **23**, (2), June.
Foster, Christopher D. and Ray Richardson (1973), 'Employment Trends in London in the 1960s and their Relevance to the Future', in D.V. Donnison and D.E.C. Eversley (eds), *London: Urban Problems, Patterns and Policies*, London: Heinemann.
Fothergill, Steven, and Graham Gudgin (1982), *Unequal Growth: Urban and Regional Employment Change in the UK*, London: Heinemann.
Gordon, I.R. (1985), 'The Cyclical Sensitivity of Regional Employment and Unemployment Differentials', *Regional Studies*, **19**, (2), 95–110. Reading 20 in this volume.
Greenhut, M.L. (1970), *A Theory of the Firm in Economic Space*, New York: Appleton-Century-Crofts.
Greenhut, M.L. and H. Ohta (1975), *Theory of Spatial Pricing and Market Areas*, Durham N.C.: Duke U.P.
Haig, R.M. (1926), 'Toward an Understanding of the Metropolis, I and II', *Quarterly Journal of Economics*, **40**, (2) and (3), February and May.
Haig, R.M. (1928), *Major Economic Factors in Metropolitan Growth and Arrangement*, vol. 1, New York: Regional Planning Association.
Harris, John R., and Michael Todaro (1970), 'Migration, Unemployment, and Development: A Two Sector Analysis', *American Economic Reviw*, **60**, (1), March. Reading 6 in this volume.
Harvey, David (1973), *Social Justice and the City*, London: Edward Arnold.
Henderson, J. Vernon (1977), *Economic Theory and the Cities*, New York: Academic Press.
Henderson, J. Vernon (1988), *Urban Development: Theory, Fact and Illusion*, New York: Oxford U.P.
Hicks, John R. (1959), 'Unimproved Value Rating – The Case of East Africa', in *Essays on World Economics*, Oxford: Oxford U.P.
Hoover, E.M. (1948), *The Location of Economic Activity*, New York: McGraw-Hill.
Hoover, Edgar M., and Raymond Vernon (1959), *Anatomy of a Metropolis*, Cambridge Mass: Harvard U.P.
Hotelling, H. (1929), 'Stability in Competition', *Economic Journal*, **39**, 41–57.
Isard, W. (1956), *Location and Space-Economy*, Cambridge, Mass: M.I.T. Pres.
Isard, W. (1960), *Methods of Regional Analysis*, Cambridge, Mass: M.I.T. Press.
Kain, John F. (1975), 'Housing Market Discrimination and Negro Employment', in *Essays on Spatial Structure*, Cambridge, Mass: Ballinger.
Kaldor, N. (1970), 'The Case for Regional Policies', *Scottish Journal of Political Economy*, **17**, 337–48. Reading 17 in this volume.
Kelley, Allen C., and Jeffrey G. Williamson (1984), *What Drives Third World City Growth*? Princeton, N.J: Princeton U.P.
Leven, Charles L. (1978), *The Mature Metropolis*, Lexington, Mass: D.C. Heath.
Leven, C.L. (1985), 'Regional Development Analysis and Policy', *Journal of Regional Science*, **25**, (4), 569–91. Reading 22 in this volume.
Lichtenburg, Robert M. (1960), *One Tenth of a Nation*, Cambridge, Mass: Harvard U.P.
Lipsey, R.G. (1960), 'The Relation between Unemployment and the Rate of Change of Money Wage Rates in the UK 1862–1957 – a further analysis', *Economica*, **27**, (105), 1–31.
Lösch, A. (1938), 'The Nature of Economic Regions', *Southern Economic Journal*, **5**, 71–8.
Lösch, A. (1954), *The Economics of Location*, New Haven: Yale U.P.
Lowry, I.S. (1966), *Migration and Metropolitan Growth: two analytical modes*, UCLA: Institute of Government and Public Affairs Series; San Francisco: Chandler.
McCombie, J.S.L. (1988a), 'A Synoptic View of Regional Growth and Unemployment I – The Neoclassical Theory', *Urban Studies*, **25**, 267–81. Reading 16 in this volume.
McCombie, J.S.L. (1988b), 'A Synoptic View of Regional Growth and Unemployment II – The Post-Keynesian Theory', *Urban Studies*, **25**, 399–417.
Marshall, Alfred (1920), *Principles of Economics*, Appendix G, London: Macmillan, 8th edition.
Metcalf, David, and Ray Richardson (1980), 'Unemployment in London', in A.W. Evans and D.E.C. Eversley (eds), *The Inner City: Employment and Industry*, London: Heinemann.
Miller, E. (1973), 'Is Out-Migration Affected by Economic Conditions?', *Southern Economic Journal*, **39**, (3), 396–405.

Mills, Edwin S. (1972), *Studies in the Structure of the Urban Economy*, Baltimore: Johns Hopkins Press.
Mirrlees, James A. (1972), 'The Optimum Town', *Swedish Journal of Economics*, **74**, (1), March.
Moomaw, Ronald L. (1983), 'Spatial Productivity Variations in Manufacturing: A Critical Survey of Cross-Sectional Analyses', *International Regional Science Review*, **8**, (1) June. Reading 3 in this volume.
Moore, B.C. and J. Rhodes (1973), 'Evaluating the Effects of British Regional Policy', *Economic Journal*, **83**, 87–110.
Moore, B.C. and J. Rhodes (1976), 'Regional Policy and the Movement of Manufacturing Firms to Development Areas', *Economica*, **43**, 17–31.
Moore, B.C., J. Rhodes and P. Tyler (1986), *The Effects of Government Regional Economic Policy*, London: HMSO.
Moroney, J.R. and J.M. Walker (1966), 'A Regional Test of the Heckscher–Ohlin Hypothesis', *Journal of Political Economy*, **74**, 573–86. Reading 21 in this volume.
Moses, L.N. (1958), 'Location and the Theory of Production', *Quarterly Journal of Economics*, **72**, 259–72.
Moses, Leon N. (1962), 'Towards a Theory of Intra-Urban Wage Differentials and their Influence on Travel Patterns', *Papers of the Regional Science Association*, **1**.
Muth, Richard F. (1969), *Cities and Housing*, Chicago: University of Chicago Press.
Muth, Richard F. (1973), 'A Vintage Model of the Housing Stock', *Papers of the Regional Science Association*, **30**, (2).
Myrdal, G. (1957), *Economic Theory and Underdeveloped Regions*, London: Duckworth.
Neutze, G. Max (1987), 'The Supply of Land for a Particular Use', *Urban Studies*, **24**, (5), October. Reading 9 in this volume.
Norman, G. (1981), 'Spatial Competition and Spatial Price Discrimination', *Review of Economic Studies*, **48**, (151), 97–111.
Perroux, F. (1950), 'Economic Space: theory and applications', *Quarterly Journal of Economics*, **64**, (1), 89–104.
Ravallion, Martin (1979), 'A Note on Intra-Urban Wage Differentials', *Urban Studies*, **16**, (2), June.
Richardson, Harry W. (1973a), *The Economics of Urban Size*, Farnborough, Hants: Saxon House.
Richardson, H.W. (1973b), *Regional Growth Theory*, London: Macmillan.
Richardson, Harry W. (1977), *The New Urban Economics*, London: Pion.
Richardson, Harry W. (1981), 'National Urban Strategies in Developing Countries', *Urban Studies*, **18**, (3), October.
Robbins, S.M., and Nester E. Terleckyj (1960), *Money Metropolis*, Cambridge Mass: Harvard U.P.
Rose, Louis A. (1989), 'Urban Land Supply: Natural and Contrived Restrictions', *Journal of Urban Economics*, **25**, (3), 325–45. Reading 12 in this volume.
Samuelson, Paul A. (1954), 'The Pure Theory of Public Expenditure', *Review of Economics and Statistics*, **36**, November.
Scott, A.J. (1982), 'Locational Patterns and Dynamics of Industrial Activity in the Modern Metropolis', *Urban Studies*, **19**, (2), May.
Sinclair, M.T. and C.M.S. Sutcliffe (1978), 'The First Round and the Keynesian Regional Income Multiplier', *Scottish Journal of Political Economy*, **25**, (2), 177–86.
Sinclair, M.T. and C.M.S. Sutcliffe (1982), 'Keynesian Income Multipliers with First and Second Round Effects: an application to tourist expenditure', *Oxford Bulletin of Economics and Statistics*, **44**, (4), 321–38.
Sjaastad, L.A. (1962), 'The Costs and Returns of Human Migration', *Journal of Political Economy*, **70**, Supplement, 80–93. Reading 19 in this volume.
Solow, Robert M. (1973), 'On Equilibrium Models of Urban Locations', in J.M. Parkin (ed.) *Essays in Modern Economics*, London: Longman.
Steinnes, D.N. (1982), 'Do "people follow jobs" or do "jobs follow people"? A Causality Issue in Urban Economics', *Urban Studies*, **19**, (2), May.
von Thünen, Johann H. (1826), *Der Isolierte Staat* (Hamburg). Trans. Peter Hall and published as (1966), *Von Thünen's Isolated State*, Oxford: Pergamon.
Tiebout, Charles M. (1956), 'A Pure Theory of Local Expenditures', *Journal of Political Economy*,

64, (5), October. Reading 11 in this volume.
Tiebout, C.M. (1957), 'Regional and Interregional Input–Output Models: an appraisal', *Southern Economic Journal*, **24**, 140–7. Reading 13 in this volume.
Tiebout, C.M. (1962), *The Community Economic Base Study*, Supplementary Paper 16, New York: Committee for Economic Development. Reading 15 in this volume.
Topel, Robert H. (1986), 'Local Labour Markets', *Journal of Political Economy*, **94**, (3), pt.2, June.
Twomey, J. and J. Taylor (1985), 'Regional Policy and the Regional Movement of Manufacturing Industry in Great Britain', *Scottish Journal of Political Economy*, **32**, (3), 257–77. Reading 24 in this volume.
Vanderkamp, J. (1971), 'Migration Flows, Their Determinants and the Effects of Return Migration', *Journal of Political Economy*, **79**, 1012–31.
Vernon, Raymond (1960), *Metropolis 1985*, Cambridge, Mass: Harvard U.P.
Vipond, Joan, and Clive Beed (1986), 'A Sydney and Melbourne Comparison of Intra-Urban Differentials in Unemployment Rates', *Australian Geographical Studies*, **24**, April.
Weber, A. (1909), *Über den Standort der Industrie* (Tübingen). Trans. G.J. Freidrich and published (1929), University of Chicago Press.
Wingo, London (1961), *Transportation and Urban Land*, Washington D.C.: Resources for the Future.
Yap, Lorraine Y.L. (1977), 'The Attraction of Cities: A Review of the Migration Literature', *Journal of Development Economics*, **4**, (3), September.

[1]

Excerpt from *The Mature Metropolis*, 149–68

8 Transportation and Land Use in the Mature Metropolis

Alex Anas and
Leon N. Moses

This chapter deals with the urbanized areas that grew to large size under the influence of nineteenth and early twentieth century technologies of production, transportation, and communication. These areas–New York, Philadelphia, Boston, Chicago, Detroit, and St. Louis are examples–are viewed as mature today because their populations and levels of economic activity are either stable or somewhat declining. At one time, the core areas of these cities were the most dynamic growth centers of the nation. They absorbed huge numbers of immigrant laborers and immense amounts of capital to develop the nation's great manufacturing and service industries. Here, we explain some of the factors that contributed to this growth and the decline that has taken place, and we provide insight into how current social and economic forces are likely to condition future growth, transportation networks, and land-use patterns in the emerging metropolis.

Production, Transport, Communications, and Growth and Decline of the Great Cities

We tend to think of cities as centers of finance, insurance, advertising, education, and cultural activities. However, the cities that developed rapidly during the last century were products of the industrial revolution. Their growth was driven by the rapid development of textiles; iron and steel and related foundry products; animal slaughtering, rendering, and meat and leather production; milling, and so forth. Coal production expanded tremendously to provide electric power for factories, for lighting cities, and for their transportation systems. Banking, finance, and insurance were essential to the expansion of manufacturing. In addition, the growth of cities would not have been possible without electric power, clean water, sewage disposal, and such cheap means of transportation as trains and trolleys. But up until World War I, the main driving force in economic development was manufacturing.

The Period 1850 to World War I

The CBDs of the great ninteenth-century cities tended to be compact; as much as 90 percent of total employment would be found one to three miles from the center. Downtown areas often had subdistricts relatively specialized in finance, retailing, and legal and other services. Land values were high in the core but they quickly declined with distance from the center and from the main routes of passenger transportation; so did population densities. Why did manufacturing establishments become concentrated in relatively few places, thereby contributing to the huge agglomerations of population and economic activity that characterized cities like New York, Chicago, and St. Louis? One reason was that there were scale economies in the production of goods. As a result, there were relatively few plants in many industries. Given that there would be some concentration in production, why did most of it locate in cities rather than spread out over the countryside? The main reason was the scale economies in transportation.

Manufacturing firms tended to be material intensive, requiring more tons of raw materials per ton of finished product than do comparable products today. Immense quantities of raw materials and finished products had to be moved to and from cities and, in the main, these shipments went by water or rail. Areas with natural water tributaries of sufficient depth and width had tremendous economic advantages. Both canal and railway transport are characterized by scale economies, in both line haul and terminal operations. Their rights-of-way were expensive to construct, but once in place, could accommodate large quantities of freight at very low cost. The larger the flotilla of barges, or the longer the trains, the lower was the cost per ton-mile shipped. In addition, because of the high frequency of in-bound and out-bound service, producers who were located near a major terminal area could operate with smaller inventories of raw materials and finished products than could those who were located in outlying areas. These influences channelized shipments along relatively few but expensive-to-construct routes; even some quite large cities were served by only one or two railroads.

Terminal operations of ports and rail yards also exhibited scale economies and there were, therefore, relatively few of them in a city. Firms tended to locate near these terminals, though there were several reasons why they could have achieved certain economies had they chosen to locate away from them and from the central areas of cities. The price of land was much cheaper away from the core. In addition, there were potential savings in wage rates for firms that chose to locate in outlying areas and employ labor domiciled there. These savings would have arisen because such workers could have reduced their money and time costs of travel, and thus have been willing to accept wages lower than those paid at the core.[1] However, such firms would still have had to assemble the raw materials they needed, and arrange for the export of their finished products through the warehousing and transportation facilities of the core area.

Thus, outlying locations would have raised total firm costs by more than the savings in land and labor costs they would have brought. The explanation is that the cost of moving goods inside cities was very high relative to the per ton-mile cost of interregional shipments. More important, it was also high relative to the cost of moving people inside cities. Within cities, freight was transported by a mode that had remained essentially unchanged for hundreds of years, the horse and wagon moving on unpaved city streets: a high-cost, low-scale, undependable operation. On the other hand, people were transported quite early by horse-driven rail lines, and later by electric trolley, both of which were more efficient and less costly than the horse and wagon. As a result of the differential between the cost of transporting people and freight within cities, the savings in space and labor costs associated with outlying locations were less than the increased costs of freight movements they entailed.

Three other influences reinforced these tendencies for dense core development. First, urban firms had to ship goods to each other due to interindustrial linkages; the cost of transporting these goods caused firms to cluster closely. Second, a communications gap existed in the transmission of information within cities. Interregionally, this was done via the telegraph, but the telegraph could not handle efficiently the heavy demands of intraurban communication since it was not adaptable to switchboard-type operations. The principal method of communication between manufacturing firms and between them and banks, insurance companies, and other business services firms, was either through messengers or face-to-face meetings. Inefficient and high-cost communication added to the clustering tendencies of service as well as manufacturing within the compact core area. The high cost of communications was a major factor in the agglomerative tendencies of business services. Third, the incremental cost of providing such municipal or public utility services as water, waste collection, treatment and disposal, and electric power, fell over a considerable range with increases in output, particularly when that output was distributed in a compact, densely settled area. As a result of these three kinds of economies, urban growth increased central-city tax revenues rather than tax rates.

The great overall growth in urban economic activity, and its concentration in the center, caused the core to expand and intrude into the surrounding ring of low-income, poorly maintained housing. As the core expanded, more poor laborers were accommodated by converting single family, middle-income housing into multiple-family units and to boarding houses. Higher-income population groups lived outside this inner area and commuted to the center via horse-driven carriages or rail-guided horse and wagon.[2] Only shortly before World War I did motorized transportation begin to influence the internal structure of cities.

The Truck, Telephone, and Interwar Period

Earlier, we argued that the compact form of the nineteenth-century city was in very substantial measure due to the high cost of carrying out the functions of intraurban freight movement and transfer of information; these costs were radically altered in the interwar period. The reduction in the cost of intraurban goods movement was the result of the substitution of the truck for the horse and wagon, and a very significant improvement in the quality of urban roads. These changes permitted still more manufacturing to be accommodated inside central cities, because it was no longer necessary for industry to cluster as closely to the terminals of the interregional routes as it had been when freight within cities moved by horse and wagon. The introduction of the truck also led to an expansion of the warehousing districts of major cities, and firms did spread out somewhat. The average distance between firms and between firms and ports and rail terminals increased. However, most firms did not leave the central areas of cities. Thus, the truck increased the economic vitality of the core by increasing the supply of lower-priced land for industry.[3]

The expansion of the economic coré into residential areas led middle-income households to move further out, and their housing to filter down to the large numbers of low-wage immigrant workers. Thus, though somewhat decentralized, the expanding manufacturing sector continued to rely on the central-area's terminals for interregional shipments. The continued growth of manufacturing also created a base for expansion in central-city finance, insurance, and other business services.

The telephone and the radio did similar things for the efficiency of intraurban communication. The telephone did not eliminate the need for face-to-face meetings, but business was no longer bound by such communication. Information of a relatively straightforward variety could be transmitted by telephone. It also played a crucial role in improving the efficiency of those face-to-face meetings that were required for strategic, educational, and other purposes through prior staff communication. Through the telephone, information was exchanged much more cheaply than before, and much faster over longer distances. Through the radio, public information of all sorts became available at a much lower cost than before.

The interwar period was essentially replicative of the 1850-1920 era; large cities continued to grow in size and economic power. Except for the Great Depression (whose effects on cities was temporary in terms of the long-run historic dynamics view of this discussion), the population of cities increased, their land values rose, and their areas of settlement widened, pushing agriculture further out. Core areas continued to develop as centers of finance, entertainment, medicine, and education as well as manufacturing. The tax bases of the largest cities grew, and they were able to provide municipal services of high quality. Annexation of surrounding suburbs continued in many cases, and the jurisdictional size of cities increased.

Suburbanization and Decline of Central Cities

The years since World War II, and particularly since the early 1950s, have seen the decline of the large nineteenth-century city and the growth and development of highly dispersed metro areas such as Los Angeles, Phoenix, Dallas, and Houston. To understand the decline of the older cities, we must look to the factors that caused their manufacturing firms and then a variety of their business service industries to move beyond their political boundaries, as discussed further in Chapters 6 and 13. This movement caused core areas and their fiscal bases to decline. It became difficult for them to maintain municipal services such as police protection and education, which reinforced the tendency of firms and households to move to politically independent suburban areas.

The conventionally accepted explanations for central-city decay do not adequately emphasize the primary role of manufacturing decentralization. Rather, they focus on the growth of personal automobile transportation and the federal home-financing policies. Still another explanation attributes the decline to the movement into central cities of blacks as well as poor whites from areas such as Appalachia. The claim is that in-migration of these groups caused the central city middle-income and upper-income groups to suburbanize, which reduced the tax bases of central cities while increasing the need for and cost of many social services. A spiraling process was set up which led to a further out-migration of middle-income and upper-income households. Though there are elements of truth in the above arguments–they are discussed in more detail in Chapter 12–they do not explain the massive suburbanization of basic manufacturing employment in the post-World War II period.

There is no doubt that increased car ownership and greatly improved urban roads drastically reduced the overall cost (including time) of passenger transport from many outlying areas to centers of employment. Effectively, this change increased the supply of residential land. As the car became the major means of shopping and recreational trips, large suburban shopping centers developed, which contributed to the decline of central-city retail activity. *However, the important question is what impact the automobile and the improvement in urban roads would have had on the location pattern of industry if everything else, but especially the cost of transporting goods in cities, had remained unchanged.*

Each previous innovation that had reduced the cost of personal travel–the horse rail, the electric trolley, or the elevated and subway train–caused population to move out to new areas served by the new systems; retail activity followed. With the automobile, a similar but more ubiquitous spreading out of population occurred, but this suburban expansion could not, by itself, have caused the massive outward shift of manufacturing and business services. *In fact, a reduction in the cost of personal travel would have increased the relative attractiveness of the central city and its core areas as a location for commerce and industry.*

Taken by itself, a reduction in personal travel cost would have caused workers to require a higher wage for working close to home, as an alternative to core area employment, than they did before. In addition, such a reduction in costs would have increased the price of land in the outer, relative to land in the inner, portions of the city. This also would have increased the relative attractiveness of core as a location for economic activity. Finally, an opposite effect on which we will have further comments should be mentioned. High-quality suburban roads and low-cost personal transportation did greatly increase the area from which a suburban firm could draw labor at reasonable wage rates.

To understand the suburbanization of manufacturing activity, we must turn to the reduction in the costs of shipping goods by truck between cities and between cities and their supply areas in the post-1950 period. The immense expansion in interstate highways, the building of outer-circumferential routes, and the increase in the size and efficiency of the long-distance truck, all contributed to a radical decentralization of manufacturing. These changes gave firms the freedom to build new efficient plants on lower-priced land, without incurring increased costs of assembling raw materials and shipping finished products. The intercity truck and interstate highway gave firms an efficient and highly dependable form of transportation that did not involve the older congested terminal areas of the core. To compete for the shipment of intercity freight, railroads established modern suburban rail terminals. This contributed still further to the decline of central cities, since even rail-oriented firms could then shift to suburban locations.

Let us now consider the decentralization of those business services–such as banking, insurance, and advertising–that many urban specialists believed must be located downtown and near one another because of their need for face-to-face contact. First, we observe that service sector decentralization often takes the form of a *relative* shift in activity levels. In other words, such activities as banking have expanded in satellite areas, while the industry has expanded relatively little or remained stable in downtown areas. This is different from manufacturing, where many central cities experienced absolute declines while suburban areas were expanding. The expansion of the service industries in suburban areas is partially explained by the fact that some of their functions are really retail in nature and oriented to the household, rather than the business establishment. Thus, savings and loan associations should be expected to evolve in much the same geographic pattern as retailing; the same applies to personal and home insurance offices. Finally, while the large, nationally known firm can borrow funds from a downtown bank, or a bank in any other city for that matter, a bank probably needs a certain amount of personal contact with a small firm before it will grant a loan. It is therefore not surprising that the great growth of smaller manufacturing and other establishments in suburban areas has been accompanied by a growth of commercial banking. Among the things this chapter is emphasizing, is the importance of improved communications on the form and development of urbanized areas, as was emphasized in Chapter 7.

But why, then, could not business services, such as banking, have expanded in downtown areas and relied on modern communications to maintain contact with manufacturing and other firms growing up in satellite areas? This question has several answers. First, land values and construction costs are very high in core areas. Where branch banking was permitted, it was therefore much cheaper to expand by building a branch in a suburban area, depending on intrafirm communications to make certain that all records needed for central evaluation of performance were readily available within the firm. The suburban branch location also gave the bank closer contact with and more knowledge about smaller customers. Thus, suburban branches gave banks a low cost and efficient way of expanding while bringing the side benefit of closer contact with smaller customers. A third reason for the relative decentralization of the business service sector is that improved communications permitted many firms to separate functions geographically, and perform some of them from less centrally located, and less costly, land and buildings. For example, the keeping of insurance records, the maintenance of information on claims, the mailing of insurance bills and settlement checks do not require a downtown location. Here, the typical contact between company and customer is by mail or telephone, and modern communications and computers provide relevant parts of the firm with almost instant access to the central data file no matter where they are located.

The outflow of all this activity caused a deterioration in the quality of public services and secondary waves of decentralization. The concentration of poor and minorities in the central cities, on the other hand, pushed up the demands for services, and revenue-expenditure imbalances became aggravated, as will be indicated in Chapter 12. This led to increased incentive for middle-income groups to leave central cities.

Some Empirical Observations

U.S. census data for six mature metropolitan areas–New York, Boston, Philadelphia, Chicago, Detroit, and St. Louis–illustrate the basic dimensions and extent of central-city decay and suburban development.[a] The number of manufacturing establishments in the New York SMSA has been declining since 1963 and more recently–from 1967 to 1972–at a rate of 11 percent. Boston and Philadelphia show a similar, but much less pronounced trend, while Midwestern cities show gains in metropolitan manufacturing between 1947 and 1972. Central cities in the six SMSAs we are looking at show a consistent decline in number of manufacturing establishments and suburban areas, a marked increase. In 1967-72 the average rate of decline for the six central cities is 18 percent, while all except New York suburbs show an average growth rate of 21 percent. In New York the suburban growth rate was 2 percent but there was a slight decline between 1958 and 1967. All six areas except New York and Boston have tripled or at least doubled suburban establishments since 1947. Only in the New York and Chicago metro areas does the central city still contain a larger number of establishments

[a]The data discussed in this section has been compiled from U.S. Census of Manufacturing and Population publications.

than is found in the suburbs. Data on manufacturing employment are not comparable by date to data on establishments, but do show the same overall trends of suburban expansion and city decline. Rough calculations also show that "mean firm size" is, in most cases, significantly larger for suburban firms and increasing over time. Somewhat surprisingly, it is not increasing much more rapidly than central-city mean firm size.

Of the cities examined, only New York still had more population in the center city in 1970 than did the suburbs, and by a factor of close to two. In the remaining five areas, suburban population is up to several times central-city population, with Chicago having the narrowest difference of only 4 percent, but a suburban growth rate of 35 percent; central-city populations have been declining. The data also show that the nonwhite population has been growing in both suburbs and central cities, but at a faster rate in all six central cities.

With the exception of New York and Philadelphia, all six cities experienced declines in the number of owner-occupied and tenant-occupied housing units between 1960 and 1970. This trend is especially strong in St. Louis where the number of owner-occupied units in 1970 was 8 percent less than in 1960 and the number of tenant-occupied, 17 percent less. This reflects the attrition and abandonment of the central-city stock as well as the gradual accumulation of central-city vacant land. In New York City both owner-occupied and tenant-occupied units increased by 16 and 4 percent, respectively, between 1960 and 1970, probably reflecting the fact that the number of households increased, even though population fell. Some might argue that the increase in occupied units in New York also reflects the continuing cultural-recreational attractiveness of the area. The data also show that although the number of tenant-occupied units in the suburbs of our six cities is smaller (usually about a third of the suburban stock), they are increasing at rates up to two to three times greater than owner-occupied units, reflecting a boom in suburban apartment construction.

Data on retail trade for mature areas reveal that establishments in suburban areas have been increasing, while the number in central cities and CBDs has been declining; within cities, the number of establishments in CBDs has been falling less rapidly than in the rest of the central city. Surprisingly, Chicago was an exception; the decline in the number of establishments in the CBD in the 1967-72 period was greater than in the remainder of the central city. Overall, there has been an increase in the average numbers of employees per retail establishment. This is especially true in suburban areas, where the number of establishments and their size, as measured by employment, have both increased very significantly.

A comparison of the various work-trip categories shows that the mature cities are still significantly centralized, with the number of commuters from the suburbs to the city still being more numerous than the number of reverse commuters from city to suburbs. However, the number of traditional suburban commuters is increasing at low rates of up to 13 percent (down by 6 percent in

Detroit) while the number of reverse commuters is increasing much faster, more than doubling in Chicago between 1960 and 1970, almost doubling in St. Louis, up by more than half in Detroit and Philadelphia, and up 20 percent in New York and 14 percent in Boston. At the same time, the number of work trips within central city is strongly declining in each case, down by up to 34 percent in St. Louis and by 12 percent in New York City. On the other hand, the number commuting from one suburb to another shows a strong increase in each case. Strikingly, the number of trips from both the cities and the SMSA to exurban locations outside the SMSA also is increasing rapidly except in St. Louis, where there has been a strong decline in both; for details see Table 8-1.

These strong trends in reverse commuting patterns are explained by the rapid suburbanization of jobs to suburban and exurban areas. One can safely conjecture that many of the reverse commuters are low-income and minority residents constrained to live in affordable central-city housing, but with a strong motivation to move out closer to their suburban jobs and to better suburban schools and public services. Whether they can do so or not, depends in part on how vigorously the federal government pursues a policy of low-cost suburban housing construction. It also depends on filtering, particularly in the inner suburbs where the housing stock is older. The rise in reverse commuting could therefore be a temporary, short-run adjustment phenomenon. However, some of the reverse commuters may be middle-income and upper-income households, without children, who are attracted to central-city cultural-recreational amenities and work in the suburbs. The number of such reverse commuters might well increase over time.

Data on central-city public employment trends show increases for all cases, except Detroit. Moreover, the rate of increase is generally greater than that for total SMSA population for 1960-70, with the exception of St. Louis, where SMSA population increased more than central-city public employment. The data must be interpreted with care since the underlying process is quite complex and political. However, others have shown that changes in the composition of population caused central-city public employment to rise despite the lessening dependence of suburbanites on center-city services and declines in central-city populations.[4]

Energy, Public Policy, and the Future Metropolis

The rest of the chapter will deal with three forces we believe will have a strong influence on the distribution of population and economic activity, between as well as within, metropolitan areas. These are (1) changes in the rate of growth of population and its composition, (2) change in the relative importance of international trade for the United States and the impact it will have on the competitive position of various areas of the country, and (3) changes in the cost

158

Table 8-1
Changes in Work Trip Patterns in Six Mature SMSAs

Residence	*Place of Work*	*1960*	*1970*	*% Change*
New York				
City	City	2,885,038	2,549,609	−11.6
City	Suburbs	82,865	99,087	+19.5
City	Outside SMSA	63,530	119,690	+88.3
Suburb	City	307,827	335,715	+9.0
Suburb	Suburb	670,314	891,118	+132.9
Suburb	Outside SMSA	20,379	68,548	+336.4
Boston				
City	City	215,994	177,644	−17.8
City	Suburbs	43,596	49,690	+14.0
City	Outside SMSA	6,055	6,365	+5.1
Suburb	City	193,384	196,094	+1.4
Suburb	Suburb	467,224	564,451	+20.8
Suburb	Outside SMSA	28,561	45,410	+58.9
Philadelphia				
City	City	670,761	559,771	−16.5
City	Suburbs	51,960	80,359	+54.7
City	Outside SMSA	7,946	16,361	+105.9
Suburb	City	198,987	212,553	+6.8
Suburb	Suburb	594,542	743,957	+25.1
Suburb	Outside SMSA	45,772	81,753	+78.0
Chicago				
City	City	1,249,641	994,277	−20.5
City	Suburbs	88,855	206,467	+132.4
City	Outside SMSA	11,490	17,614	+53.3
Suburb	City	328,395	355,135	+8.1
Suburb	Suburb	615,896	992,777	+61.2
Suburb	Outside SMSA	25,255	37,639	+49.0
Detroit				
City	City	461,430	320,668	−31.5
City	Suburbs	96,779	161,095	+66.5
City	Outside SMSA	5,741	7,249	+26.3
Suburbs	City	231,274	216,705	−6.3
Suburbs	Suburbs	433,241	694,206	+60.2
Suburbs	Outside SMSA	17,629	28,445	+61.3
St. Louis				
City	City	240,962	158,068	−34.4
City	Suburbs	21,742	42,234	+94.3
City	Outside SMSA	1,546	1,355	−12.4
Suburbs	City	160,017	181,850	+13.6
Suburbs	Suburbs	238,703	426,762	+78.7
Suburbs	Outside SMSA	43,176	10,884	−25.2

of personal and freight transport due to rising energy prices or energy conserving regulatory measures. Since aspects of the first two factors are discussed elsewhere in this volume–mainly in Chapters 2 and 7–we deal with them rather briefly. Most of the discussion here will be concerned with the implications of rising energy prices and costs of travel on long-run trends in land use. A number of issues related to job suburbanization, minority housing, and mass transit policies also will be discussed.

Population Growth and Composition

Changes in the composition of population will have an important impact on the spatial structure of the United States. Population growth is likely to continue to be lower in the next twenty years than it has been in the past. Both rural migration and foreign immigration (with the exception of illegal immigration) have declined in importance in recent years, and most of the large, older cities have not drawn much population in the last fifteen years or so. Though overall population growth is likely to be quite modest in the next two decades, there is likely to be a continuation of existing trends in the composition and distribution of the population. Population and employment are likely to continue to be attracted to selected cities in the South and West. Such limited out-migration of population from rural areas as does occur will probably take the form of a movement to these newer growing regions. In addition, low-income and minority households from the central cities of older regions will probably migrate to the smaller, growing cities of the newer regions (and to some extent, smaller cities of older regions) because of their more favorable employment opportunities.

The size composition of households will probably change, the average number of children per family falling; the trend will not be as great for the poor and minority groups as for the middle-income and upper-income groups so that the former will comprise an increasing percentage of the labor force. Marriages will probably continue to take place later in life, which will contribute to the decline in the average size of household. The above trends have a number of important implications for the mature metropolis. Though the overall population of most of the mature areas will decrease, they will need more housing to accommodate changing household formation patterns. The larger number of smaller households will require more multiple-family dwellings. A very important question concerns where this housing will be constructed. This question is tied to the issue of rising energy prices, increased costs of personal transport, and the effect these are likely to have on the geographic distribution of population and industry in metropolitan areas. These questions are taken up after a brief consideration of the impact of foreign trade on regional growth.

Foreign Trade and Regional Growth

Throughout most of its history, the United States was not very dependent on foreign trade. Most of the nation's capacity was devoted to producing goods and services for domestic consumption; foreign trade was a small percentage of GNP. The nation did absorb huge amounts of capital and labor from the rest of the world but the expansion in plant and equipment these factor increases permitted, were largely devoted to the production of goods for domestic consumption. The situation has changed in recent years; we are dependent on foreign nations for supplies of many raw materials besides petroleum. However, raw material imports do not by any means comprise the full picture. Many nations compete effectively with us in the production of a wide variety of manufactured goods, including those that entail high technology. Foreign sources of supply and foreign markets are likely to have much more influence on domestic locational choices in the future than they have had in the past. Foreign markets will tend to become much more important to U.S. producers than they were in the past. Firms that depend on raw material from abroad or wish to sell in those markets may be expected to be drawn to those coastal areas that provide the best access to them.

These trends will be reinforced by increases in the cost of shipping goods due to rising energy prices and general cost increases as well. Internal areas that enjoy good inland navigation will not suffer from as great a disadvantage as those that are landlocked. However, even the former will probably suffer some reduction in their capacity to attract industry because there is a very good chance that a system of user charges will be imposed on the waterways. When such charges are imposed, it is hoped that they will take the form of tolls at locks rather than fuel taxes. Tolls are to be preferred because there is congestion at locks and especially if they are adjusted for peaks, they would add to the efficiency with which these resources are utilized.

This discussion has suggested that increased reliance on foreign raw materials, balance-of-payments problems, and a much greater need for American firms to compete in foreign markets, will convey a locational advantage on coastal areas. A number of the mature metropolitan areas are in such locations. Cities like New York are likely to receive some benefit from the above forces but the effect is unlikely to be strong enough to reverse the negative trend of recent years.

Energy, Travel Cost, and Future Patterns of Land Use

As we saw in the first part of this chapter, the costs of personal and freight transport act directly on the internal fabric of the metropolis. This is unlike the influences of population growth and foreign trade which have their primary influence on the overall level of activity; their influence on the internal structure of cities is indirect. In this section we consider how changes in energy prices, but especially motor fuel prices, are likely to influence the long-run demand for urban transportation and land and buildings in different parts of metropolitan regions.

Three alternative patterns of long-run development in metropolitan land use and transportation can be identified. One entails a continuation of the trend toward dispersal of population and jobs within metropolitan areas. Some urban specialists have seen this as quite likely, drawing on the recently observed population increases in exurban areas as evidence of the continued strength of the tendency toward a more uniform distribution of population and employment within metropolitan regions. A second alternative is the drawing back of population and jobs into a more centralized pattern that resembles the spatial structure of the nineteenth and traditional twentieth century city. There are public officials and others who see in the rising price of energy a powerful force that will increase the demand for public transportation in the short run, and draw households back to areas that are well located with respect to the main corridors of public transportation in the long run. A third alternative is for increased multinucleation: the formation of distinct and quite dense suburban and exurban centers. This alternative entails the development of relatively few major employment centers in suburban and exurban areas. It implies a greater degree of centralization of jobs and household locations within suburban areas than has been true in the past. It also implies significant increases in public bus transportation and in the number of multifamily dwellings in the vicinity of major suburban nuclei. In this scenario, no single employment center would have as much employment as the CBD of a mature metropolitan area, but together, suburban areas are seen as having two or three times as much employment as the CBD.

We view the last of these three land-use patterns as the most likely. In part, this conclusion is based on an assumption, the same assumption employed by those who believe that jobs and population will return to the traditional employment areas and corridors of travel. The assumption is that the energy crisis is a long-run economic reality and that there will be very large increases in the real price of petroleum and in the real cost of personal transportation in the future. These increases will either be achieved by allowing market prices to approach the true costs entailed in expanding petroleum output or by a variety of public policy devices, such as gasoline taxes or rationing, that work mostly to reduce demand.[5] The long epoch of low-cost energy probably is over. The actual output of petroleum and other forms of energy in all likelihood will increase, but the increases will entail much more costly forms of production, such as offshore drilling at greater and greater depths, and solar energy at high-capital cost, for example.

Our conclusion concerning the development of multinucleated metropolitan areas, is based also on a belief that people will respond to increases in the cost of personal transportation by buying smaller, lighter cars, and reducing miles traveled to and from work. The view of the elasticity of demand for travel implicit in this conclusion conflicts with the popularly held belief that the demand for transportation, and the demand for personal travel in particular, is highly price inelastic. It is quite common to hear the opinion expressed that gasoline prices have risen very considerably, but reliance on the car for work and other trips is essentially unchanged. We disagree with this conclusion on two grounds. First, the real price of personal transportation has not risen very much and, second, it does not properly distinguish between the short-run and long-run elasticity of demand for travel.

As to the former of these objections, Table 8-2 shows that the real price of motor fuel increased only slightly between 1967 and 1977. The increase was only 4.1 percent in real terms. In addition, a number of durable transportation items such as tires and autos fell in real terms. Overall, the cost of personal transportation either fell or rose very slightly in recent years. The evidence from Europe is similar. A recent study reported that the real price of motor fuel reached an all-time low in England in the period 1971-73; it was cheaper in 1976 than it was in 1953, the overall reduction in the postwar years being about 15 percent.[6] The fact that the public has not yet acted to reduce miles traveled and

Table 8-2
Real Percent Change in Components of Travel Cost (1967-April 1977)

	Consumer Price Index April 1977	*Real Change 1967-April 1977*
All items (1967 = 100)	179.6	–
Transportation	176.8	−1.6%
Private	176.3	−1.8%
Automobile, new	140.6	−21.7%
Automobile, used	187.8	+4.6%
Gasoline	187.0	+4.1%
Motor oil	164.7	−8.3%
Tires	137.2	−23.6%
Auto repair and maintenance	201.3	+12.1%
Auto insurance	210.1	+17.0%
Auto registration	142.2	−20.8%
Parking fees	191.6	+6.7%
Public	180.4	+0.4%
Local transit	177.4	−1.2%
Taxi cab fares	187.7	+4.5%
Railroad fares	173.6	−3.3%
Airplane fares	180.7	+0.6%
Intercity bus fares	211.2	+17.6%

Sources: Handbook of Labor Statistics 1976; CPI Detailed Reports, July 1976; CPI Detailed Reports, April 1977. U.S. Department of Labor, Bureau of Labor Statistics.

gasoline consumption, also is due to significant differences between the short-run and long-run elasticities of demand for travel.

It is difficult to quantify all aspects of the cost of personal travel; it is particularly difficult to measure the impact of changes in the quality of service, comfort, or convenience. Nevertheless, econometricians have attempted to measure the elasticity of consumer demand for motor fuel, automobiles, and travel mileage. These studies are severely constrained by the form in which aggregate data are available and by the relative unavailability of disaggregate data. It is possible to draw some inferences about aggregate and per capita consumption. However, the data do not permit drawing strong conclusions about long-run elasticities because these depend on changes in the locational distribution of jobs and homesites as well as on car ownership, and the cost, quality, and availability of alternatives to private transport.

There have been a number of studies in which attempts were made to measure price elasticities of motor fuel demand for both the short and long run. Of particular interest are those by Houthakker and Taylor, Verleger and Sheehan, Houthakker and Verleger, McGillivray, Chase Econometric Associates, and Burright and Enns.[7] Though the studies differ in the data they use, in the assumptions they make, and in the models they employ, their results are remarkably similar. These results are summarized by Burright and Enns who report that the short-run elasticity of demand for motor fuel in the United States is between –0.1 and –0.3, but that the long-run elasticity of demand ranges between –0.65 and –0.85. These differences between the short-run and long-run elasticities are similar to those reported for West Yorkshire, Great Britain, by Bonsall and Champernowne.[8] They report values of –0.5 and –1.4.[b]

Both sets of findings suggest that increases in the real price of personal travel tend to have much more pronounced effects on gasoline consumption in the long than in the short run. However, the studies do not really take account of the possibility that households will in time tend to choose homesites and job locations that reduce the average length of the work trip. It can be argued that most of the models used to estimate long-run elasticities do not provide insight into the impact of changes in the cost of travel on household location patterns. This purpose is better suited by a full urban simulation model. Bonsall and Champernowne have performed such a simulation for West Yorkshire.[c] They state:

> It is interesting to note that the elasticity of mean trip length by car is higher than that of modal choice suggesting that in the long term the population would change their destination rather than desert their cars.[9]

[b]While it is tempting to argue the transferability of elasticities across the Atlantic, it should be recalled there is a hidden income effect. Verleger and Sheehan, for example, compute the income elasticity of the demand for gasoline at about +1. If the mean income in England is lower than that in the United States, then the difference between the two long-run elasticities ought to be discounted.

[c]The authors also find via simulation that a sixfold increase in the price of gasoline is needed to achieve a state where virtually no one chooses to travel by car.

Clearly, if such a response can be expected from the British consumer, the effect should be much stronger in the United States, particularly in cities that do not have public transportation services comparable to those of England.

While Americans are unlikely to abandon their cars, they will almost certainly shift to smaller, lighter cars. These do not lend themselves to one-way work trips of thirty and more miles because they are uncomfortable, and the comfort and convenience part of personal travel cost is likely to increase markedly in the future. The capacity and quality of much of the nation's urban network is very likely to decline in the years ahead. The cost of maintaining roads has risen dramatically in recent years and will probably continue to do so in the future. The funds needed to maintain the quality and capacity of the network are simply not available, and reductions in travel probably mean that still less will be available in the future, at least via conventional sources of revenue, such as motor fuel taxes. Much of the secondary and tertiary road system of the nation is already in poor condition; this condition is now spreading to cities. New York is surely an example of a city which has less highway capacity, and where that capacity is lower in quality than it was ten years ago. The passage of time and weather, the movement of more heavily loaded trucks and the damage they do to pavements, the increased cost of road repairs, and the reduced availability of funds for such repairs, mean that reductions in the quality and capacity of urban streets and highways will become quite common. The real cost of trips will rise because they will be less comfortable and more time consuming. The cost will also rise because of the effect that poor roads have on automobile life and repair expenditures.

If, as we believe, the real price (including comfort, convenience, etc.) of personal travel is going to increase greatly over the next twenty years or so, then the first of the land-use patterns mentioned earlier–a continuation of the trend toward decentralization and increases in the average length of work trip–is the most costly, and therefore the least likely, of the three alternatives. However, acceptance of the argument that the price of personal travel will increase, of itself does not permit judging which of the other two alternatives is most likely. Multinucleation would reduce energy consumption and travel expenditure by reducing average miles traveled, especially for the work trip. A return of households to the principal corridors of public transit might seem to have an equal potential for reducing travel expenditure by substituting public for private transportation, but we do not believe that a significant number of households will responds in this way.

A rise in the price of personal transportation can be expected to bring some segments of the population back to the central city. Enough of the retired, the young, households without children, and those attracted to cultural and recreational activities may return to the central city to contribute to a revitalization of some of its older neighborhoods, though at much lower densities than before. More widespread recentralization in the mature central cities cannot be expected because their infrastructure, and particularly their school systems, are of poor quality, and could not be brought up to the standards of suburban schools without public expenditure of billions of dollars. Widespread recentralization of population in central cities is not possible unless significant numbers of manufacturing and other establishments return to the central city, a shift that is highly improbable.

Elimination of slum housing, clearing of land, and building of industrial parks and commercial malls might well bring some manufacturing and other establishments to central cities, but it is unlikely to bring any significant increase in the number of central-city jobs. An increase in the price of personal transportation and the clearing away of a certain amount of slum housing to make way for industry will certainly not be enough to bring about a rebirth of the economically dominant, nineteenth-century central city. Access to the Interstate Highway System will probably be even more important in the future than in the past because it is the one part of the road network that is likely to be maintained at its current level of quality. Firms that ship and receive goods by truck will still find it advantageous to have a suburban location. Increases in fuel prices may lead to an increase in the cost of shipping goods by truck, relative to rail, and to some diversion of low-value freight to rail. However, this does not argue for a return of manufacturing establishments to central cities, since the most modern rail handling facilities now are in suburban locations. Finally, there is the question of access to the highly skilled and educated part of the labor force. Most of this labor is located in the suburbs and, given the low quality of central-city schools and other infrastructure, it is almost certain to remain there.

Thus, we conclude that reconcentration of jobs and population within suburban areas, and the development of a truly multinucleated metropolitan region within which there are important employment centers and densely settled areas, is the most likely of the three relevant land-use alternatives. Suburban areas will change; there has already been a very significant increase in the number of high-rise apartment houses built in them; this trend will undoubtedly continue; the rate may even increase; whether or not it does, will depend on public policy decisions on transport, housing, and employment. The distribution of commercial and retail establishments in suburban areas probably also will change. Increases in the cost of personal travel may bring the decline of those shopping centers that must draw customers from a very large area in order to be economically viable. There may well be something of a return to a community pattern of shopping much like the pattern of neighborhood shopping of an earlier era.

The conclusions we have reached on central-city recentralization have implications for some issues in public policy that involve mass transit. In many metropolitan areas, Chicago is an example, local and some federal officials feel that it is important to improve and extend fixed-rail systems. However, the construction cost experiences of BART and METRO are a severe deterrent to such plans. The great expense of constructing rail systems has led some federal government officials to search for new ways to finance them; one such scheme is known as value capture.[10] It is based on the assumption that the building of new fixed-rail facilities, or the improvement of old ones, will draw population to transit stations, and lead to the construction of new multifamily dwellings and to substantial increases in land and property values in their vicinity. The idea behind value capture is that such increases can then be taxed to pay for the transit system. The reasoning is not new; highway planners long ago argued that increased land values in the vicinity of highways proved the existence of significant nonuser benefits, and that such benefits should be counted, along with savings in travel time, in project evaluations. The fact that savings in travel time explain a major part of the property value changes and that the inclusion of nonuser benefits in project evaluations involved double counting was often ignored by highway planners. They also ignored possible negative benefits on areas bypassed by a new road, which have relevance for value capture.

Whatever the political and legal obstacles in its way, certain conditions must hold before value capture policy can make economic sense. If transit extensions and improvements do not result in a net increase in central-city employment and population, it is unlikely that there will be any net overall increase in the value of land and buildings, and we have already argued that business is unlikely to expand in central cities to any significant degree. Thus, if the population that is drawn to a transit line comes from within the area, it is almost certain that any increases in land values around transit lines will be matched by decreases elsewhere in the city. If owners of property whose value falls as a result of the building of a transit line and the population readjustments it causes were compensated, there would be little, if anything, left with which to finance the transit system.

There is a role for expanded public transportation. If we are correct in our conclusion that there will be very large increases in the size and number of multifamily dwellings in the vicinity of suburban employment centers, it should be possible to have economically viable bus systems that transport workers from areas of dense settlement to nearby jobs. It may even be possible to design self-financing bus systems that link some of the major suburban employment centers and their satellite settlement areas.

Housing and employment policy for minority and low-income groups, which is discussed in Chapter 14, also is relevant to the kind of spatial pattern that will evolve in metropolitan areas. Earlier, we indicated that there has been a very large increase in the number of reverse commuters. We reasoned that many of these workers are from low-income and minority groups that are constrained to live in the central city by discriminatory housing practices, and because that is where the stock of low-price housing is found. Increases in the cost of personal travel will work a severe hardship on these groups. If a forecast that the number of jobs in suburban areas will continue to increase is correct, the number of such low-income reverse commuters also will increase. The demands of the low-income population for suburban locations will be very strong, not simply because such locations reduce travel time and cost but because they appear to promise access to higher-quality schools and other suburban amenities. If governments cannot act to increase the supply of low-income subsidized housing near major suburban employment centers, there will be a strong tendency for minority and low-income workers to concentrate in inner, older suburbs that have stocks of older housing ready for filtering. The result will be new suburban ghettos, with many of the same old problems such as poor schools, inadequate street maintenance, infrequent garbage collection, and poor hospitals. The development of bus systems that link low-income neighborhoods and important suburban employment centers might reduce the demand for suburban housing somewhat. However, the time and inconvenience of reverse commuting by bus are likely to be very great. The demand for suburban housing by low-income and minority households, therefore, can be expected to increase despite expanded and even subsidized bus transit.

Notes

1. For the basics of spatial wage theory, see Leon N. Moses, "Towards a Theory of Intra-urban Wage Differentials and Their Influence on Travel Patterns," *Papers and Proceedings Regional Science Association*, vol. 9, 1962.

2. Observation of these concentric ring patterns in cities led to an extension of von Thünen concepts in order to explain urban land use. See R.L. Fales and Leon N. Moses, "Land-use Theory and the Spatial Structure of the Nineteenth Century City," *Papers and Proceedings Regional Science Association*, vol. 28, 1972.

3. See L.N. Moses and H.F. Williamson, "The Location of Economic Activity in Cities," *American Economic Review*, May 1967, for a detailed study of industrial decentralization in this period, and the emergence of the truck between 1910 and 1920.

4. R.B. Pettengil and J.S. Uppal, *Can Cities Survive?: The Fiscal Plight of American Cities*, New York: St. Martin's Press, 1974.

5. See, for example, C. Kenneth Orski, "The Potential for Fuel Conservation: The Case of the Automobile," *Transportation Research*, vol. 8, no. 415, 1974.

6. See P.W. Bonsall and A.F. Champernowne, "Some Findings on the Elasticities of Demand for Petrol," *Traffic Engineering and Control*, October 1976.

7. Of particular interest are H.S. Houthakker and L.D. Taylor, *Consumer Demand in the United States: Analysis and Projections*, Cambridge, Mass.: Harvard University Press, 1970; H.S. Houthakker and P.K. Verleger, Jr., "The

168

Demand for Gasoline: A Mixed Cross Sectional and Time Series Analysis," Report to the Energy Policy Project, 1973 (unpublished); R. McGillivray, "Gasoline Use by Automobiles," *Highway Research Record*, 1975; Chase Econometric Associates, "The Effect of Tax and Regulatory Alternatives on Car Sales and Gasoline Consumption," Report for the Council on Environmental Quality, May 1974 (unpublished); P.K. Verleger and D. Sheehan, "A Study of the Demand for Gasoline," Report prepared for Council on Environmental Quality, 1974 (unpublished); and B.K. Burright and J.H. Enns, "Econometric Models of the Demand for Motor Fuel," Santa Monica: The Rand Corporation, April 1975.

8. Bonsall and Champernowne, "Elasticities of Demand for Petrol."
9. Bonsall and Champernowne, "Elasticities of Demand for Petrol."
10. Carl Sharpe, "A Value Capture Policy," *U.S. Department of Transportation Research Studies*, vols. 1-4, 1974.

[2]

CONTRASTS IN AGGLOMERATION: NEW YORK AND PITTSBURGH

By BENJAMIN CHINITZ
University of Pittsburgh

The natural inclination of a scientist when confronted with a new problem is to try to solve it with old tools. When he is finally convinced that the old tools will not do the job, he retreats to his shop to fashion some new tools. The burden of my argument in this paper is that we have reached the stage in regional economics when we must begin to fashion some new analytical tools.

When I say regional economics I have in mind specifically the analysis of the growth and structure of the economy of geographic subdivisions within a national economy. This type of analysis is now being carried on in at least a dozen metropolitan areas throughout the country and in numerous other types of subdivisions, large and small. I have been associated with two such studies: the New York Metropolitan Region Study, which just recently published its final report, and the Pittsburgh Economic Study, which is at its halfway mark, having been initiated in June, 1959, and being scheduled for completion in June, 1962. My observations, as the title of my paper suggests, are drawn from these two immersions in regional economics.

The basic-nonbasic approach to the analysis of a region has been under severe attack from many quarters in recent years. But I think it is fair to say that alternative approaches have differed in degree of refinement more than in kind. Fundamentally, we still go about our business in the same way. We try to identify the autonomous influences operating on the region and chart a network of interdependence between sectors within the region. I have no quarrel with this approach. I find it difficult to frame the problem otherwise. My quarrel is with the limitations of the maps of interdependence which are typically drawn.

I will surely be doing some of my colleagues an injustice with the following generalization but, begging their pardon, I state it anyway: our efforts so far have been almost exclusively devoted to the demand dimension of interdependence. The supply side has been virtually ignored. Let me elaborate.

The basic-nonbasic model is a way of coming to grips with the demand side of interdependence in one fell swoop. The links in the output-income-consumption chain, the links in the output-capital-formation chain, the links in the output-tax revenues-government spending chain, and the links in the output-materials purchased-output (i.e., input-output) chain, are all subsumed under one grand link between the exogenous and the endogenous elements of the system. Sometimes we can get away with this leap over a lot of treacherous ground just as in football a seventy-yard pass from the thirty-yard line occasionally results in a touchdown. To maintain the metaphor, most of us prefer to gain more yardage on the ground before passing into the end zone.

So we move in small steps. We try to chart the flows between our sectors in greater detail. A dollar of output of industry A, we observe, generates a demand for the output of industry C which is not equal to the demand generated for the output of industry C by a dollar of output of industry B. We observe, further, that a dollar of output of industry A generates more or less personal income than a dollar of output of industry B. If we are really keen observers, we might even discover that a dollar paid out to workers in industry A generates demands for consumer goods, housing construction, and government services which are different from the demands generated by a dollar paid out to workers in industry B.

My point is that in the main we improve upon the crude basic-nonbasic approach by a process of flow disaggregation—a process which hopefully will reduce our margin of error. I characterize this activity as the application of old tools to new problems for the obvious reason that input-output relationships, consumption functions, investment functions, and the like are old tools which were fashioned to solve the problems of a national economy. Furthermore, all those tools are used to come to grips with the demand side of the interdependence between sectors in a regional economy.

When I say that the supply side has been ignored, I mean simply that we have not come to grips with the following question: How does the level of activity in industry A in a given region influence the factor supply curves confronting industry B in the same region? Let me hasten to exclude one kind of effort from my indictment. We certainly have tried to incorporate the influence on industry B of the availability of the output of industry A as an input to industry B. Probably the best example of this kind of work is the Isard-Kuenne study of the impact of the Fairless Works. But this is only one of a number of supply relationships which need to be explored and, as far as I can tell, they have not received adequate attention from regional economists.

My former colleagues on the New York Metropolitan Region Study staff could certainly register a strong objection at this point. After all, another term for supply interdependence is external economies and diseconomies, and there is certainly a lot of discussion about them in a number of volumes of the New York study.

But this discussion is limited to two problems: one has to do with intraindustry external economies and diseconomies the other has to do with the influence of the aggregate size of the region on the costs of individual firms. The first problem is too narrowly defined and the second too broadly defined from my point of view.

Nevertheless, I believe, regional economics owes a great debt to the New York Metropolitan Region Study for highlighting these external relationships. It was only after we were confronted with the problem of understanding certain features of the Pittsburgh economy that we at the Pittsburgh Study felt compelled to probe more deeply into the nature of these interindustry effects.

Pittsburgh, as a metropolitan economy, stands in sharp contrast to New York with respect to these three summary variables: size, industrial structure, and rate of growth in recent decades. New York is between six and seven times the size of Pittsburgh. New York has a much more diversified industrial structure. And, while New York has grown at just a bit less than the national rate for the last thirty years, Pittsburgh has grown at less than half the national rate in the same period.

Superficially, all these contrasts fit a familiar pattern. Large areas are more diversified than small areas. Diversified areas exhibit more stability in their growth because their fortunes are not tied to the fortunes of a few industries. In these terms, Pittsburgh's story seems easy to tell.

Unfortunately the matter cannot rest there. Pittsburgh is much more specialized than any large SMA with the exception of Detroit, including many which are no larger than Pittsburgh and many which are considerably smaller. The question, why is it not diversified, therefore, remains largely unanswered. Of course, if we could accept the lack of diversification as inevitable, we might not have to try to understand it. For it is difficult to quarrel with the proposition that the future of such an area can be safely projected once we project the future for its one or two dominant industries. But here we may be caught on the horns of a dilemma. Suppose we project a sharp decline in the dominant industries along with a modest decline in the region's minor industries. True, the dominant industries will retard the growth of the region but in the process they will also decline in relative importance. The region will then become more diversified in its old age, so to speak. What then? Do we correct for the increased diversification? Does it open up new opportunities to the region?

The need to understand the whys and wherefores of diversification should therefore be quite apparent. This has led us to consider the question which I posed earlier: How does the growth of one industry in an area affect the area's suitability as a location for other industries?

But we are not yet ready to assert that the latter question has to be answered. We might avoid it if we could show that different degrees of diversification in areas of comparable size are due simply to the fact that some areas have a variety of locational advantages which makes them attractive to a variety of industries while other areas offer advantages only to a small number of industries. Observe for example the figures in Table 1 for Cleveland and Pittsburgh.

TABLE 1

EMPLOYMENT IN SELECTED MANUFACTURING INDUSTRIES, 1957

	Cleveland	Pittsburgh
Food	14,532	20,459
Textiles and apparel	14,130	3,550
Printing and publishing	14,618	10,042
Chemicals and products	17,959	6,823
Stone, clay and glass	3,260	21,372
Primary metals	46,894	154,215
Fabricated metals	38,378	31,298
Machinery, nonelectrical	52,552	23,534
Electrical machinery	20,746	27,652
Transportation equipment	55,570	11,047
Total	311,471	358,239

SOURCE: Bureau of the Census, *Annual Survey of Manufactures*, 1957.

Pittsburgh is way ahead in glass and primary metals and leads also in food and electrical machinery. Cleveland, on the other hand, is ahead in textiles, printing, chemicals, fabricated metals, nonelectrical machinery, and transporation equipment. On the whole, Cleveland is a much more diversified manufacturing center. But maybe this is just the outcome of the process by which individual industries gravitate to those areas which are best for them. If Cleveland had attracted the 154,215 employees in primary metals, it might still look more like itself than like Pittsburgh in the rest of its manufacturing profile.

I cannot assert positively that this is an unsatisfactory way of approaching the matter, but I can suggest a number of reasons why I find it necessary to go beyond it. For one thing, this approach implies that location of industry is heavily determined by transportation factors or, as we say in our jargon, transport oriented. By this we mean that the location of markets and materials and the transport network determine the geographic distribution of industries. If a lot of industries end up in one place, presto, you have a diversified regional economy.

Nobody believes that the logic of location runs in these terms for the majority of manufacturing industries. My former colleague, Robert

Lichtenberg, of the New York Study, after a painstaking review of factors influencing industrial location classified 50 per cent of American manufacturing as nontransport oriented. P. Sargent Florence has repeatedly emphasized in his writings that transport orientation is a minor influence in location. There is also a fairly general consensus that the proportion of industry which is transport oriented is diminishing as time goes on.

Once we recognize that variations in production costs are important determinants of location, we cannot avoid the consideration of interindustry factor cost relationships. Production costs are not given by nature, except that nature may influence the cost of energy and the cost of plant. These are trivial determinants alongside the influence exerted by the way in which a region's natural advantages are exploited. If we ask why are wage rates higher in one area than another, it is only in rare cases that nature will provide the answer. In most cases the explanation will run in historical terms; that is, in terms of the heritage of each region as it bears on labor supply.

For many purposes it is sufficient to recognize the difference in wage rates, and there is no compulsion to explain why it exists. A firm which is seeking a maximum profit location for a new plant might very well take the wage-rate differential as given—a type of behavior which fits so well the textbook model of a competitive firm. Even so, a conscientious consultant might very well post a warning signal. After all, a plant represents a twenty-year commitment. What is the wage differential likely to be twenty years hence? Be that as it may, it is certainly inappropriate to take wage-rate differentials as given in a twenty-year projection for a region. A static atomistic approach will not do for a problem in aggregate dynamics.

I also find the multiple-locational-advantages theory of diversification unsatisfactory for another reason. It permits us to assess an area's potential for growth only with reference to industries with known locational requirements. But in a projection, it is difficult enough to anticipate the bill of goods, let alone to project the locational needs of the industries which will be producing them. This may suggest that we ought to give up the ghost. Those who have this alternative are blessed. The rest of us have to seek ways to mitigate the curse. One is to develop the concept of a region's capacity for attracting new industries with considerable freedom of location from a transport point of view. If we are to develop such a concept, we need to probe into the region itself more deeply than we do when we locate industries one by one.

I have said enough—perhaps too much—about my reasons for raising these questions. I will now proceed to the main business of this paper, which is to offer some hypotheses about interindustry influences on factor costs. To begin with, I think that the net has to be spread a lot wider than most people assume. I propose to consider all the traditional categories: entrepreneurship, capital, labor, and land, in that order.

Entrepreneurship. This is a production factor which, to my knowledge, no one has tried to price out at different locations. The implicit assumption, I suppose, is that the supply schedule of entrepreneurship is identical at all locations. Our colleagues studying international differences in growth reject this assumption explicitly. I am convinced that we need to reconsider its validity in regional economics.

When you tell a location analyst that a firm is where it is because its founders prefer to live there, he throws up his hands. Such cases, he claims, are outside his domain. Our own experience suggests that for many industries cost is almost invariant with location—or at least there is no "min min" location. Yet we are reluctant to treat such cases as random phenomena because we feel there are significant variations in the cost of entrepreneurship. Moreover, these differences may be large enough to offset other cost differences.

I came to this notion by reflecting on the differences between New York and Pittsburgh, but I hasten to say that area size is only one variable. For a given size of area, the entrepreneurial supply curve is also a function of certain traditions and elements of the social structure which are heavily influenced by the character of the area's historic specializations.

The proposition I offer is this: An industry which is competitively organized—in the neoclassical sense of the term "competition"—has more entrepreneurs per dollar of output than an industry which is organized along oligopolistic lines. The average establishment in the apparel industry, for example, has one-sixth as many employees as the average establishment in primary metals. Furthermore, multi-unit firms account for 82 per cent of the employment in primary metals, while they account for only 28 per cent of employment in apparel. Now you may have as much management per dollar of output in primary metals as you have in apparel, but you certainly do not have as many managers who are also risk-takers and this is my definition of an entrepreneur.

What is the consequence of this? My feeling is that you do not breed as many entrepreneurs per capita in families allied with steel as you do in families allied with apparel, using these two industries for illustrative purposes only. The son of a salaried executive is less likely to be sensitive to opportunities wholly unrelated to his father's field than the son of an independent entrepreneur. True, the entrepreneur's son is more likely to think of taking over his father's business. My guess is, however, that the tradition of risk-bearing is, on the whole, a more potent influence in broadening one's perspective.

I think I have formulated a proposition which can at least theoretically be tested, although I confess that I have not tested it yet. For all I know, this may already be a well-established proposition in entrepreneurial history.

But if an oligopolistic environment has a lower entrepreneurial birth rate, there remains the question of how receptive it is to the in-migration of entrepreneurs. Here, too, I would argue that the competitively organized area has an edge. Receptivity as measured by factor costs we shall discuss under separate headings later on. What I have in mind now is receptivity as it relates to the entrepreneur's "utility function." There is an aura of second-class citizenship attached to the small businessman in an environment dominated by big business. It manifests itself in many small ways, such as the kinds of social clubs he can belong to, the residential areas he will comfortably fit into, the business organizations he can join, and so forth. The ease of entry, to borrow a concept from industrial organization, is considerably greater in an environment dominated—not dominated, to be more exact—by small firm industries. I am not sure that we can satisfactorily test this notion, but I am hopeful.

Capital. Many of the same observations are relevant to regional differences in the availability of capital. Here, too, we are dealing with a factor whose cost is typically assumed to be invariant with respect to location. This is surely not so. It is true that capital is almost perfectly mobile, provided the probability distribution of returns is approximately known. G.M. and U. S. Steel can raise capital almost anywhere with equal ease. But a small firm embarking on a new enterprise will find a much more receptive ear over the home counter than it will over-the-counter in "foreign" places. The cost of transferring confidence may be high enough to give us a capital-supply function which has distance as an important independent variable.

Once we admit of such immobility, it becomes relevant to inquire into differences in local capital supply among areas. Again the industrial organization of the dominant industries strikes me as an important variable. A major source of capital to new firms in general is the undistributed profit and unexpended depreciation allowance of old firms. Now, the surplus capital which accumulates inside large multiplant companies, I would argue, is more mobile interregionally within the company than intraregionally outside the company. A large corporation is more likely to respond to investment opportunities in its traditional activity at other locations than to investment opportunities at home in unrelated industries. The small firm, by contrast, is more likely to make its surplus capital available to other local enterprise in another industry than to a distant enterprise in the same industry. (Actually, I have overstated the case to avoid a complex formulation. All I need to argue is that the marginal rate of substitution between local and foreign outlets is greater [smaller] for the large multiplant firm [small firm]. Given an equivalent array of investment opportunities at home, the surplus capital of the multiplant industry is more likely to "leak" out to other areas.)

The commercial banks, of course, also play a vital role in the initial financing of new business. Are banks in one area more receptive than banks in another area to the demands of new business and, if so, are these differences in attitude shaped by the industrial traditions of the area? I say yes, on both counts. My conviction on this point is based less on deductive than on inductive reasoning. I have been told that this is the case. Having been told, I can think of some fairly good reasons why this might be the case. When banks cater to a competitively organized industry, they are more likely to accept the insurance principle of making money, not on each customer, but on the average customer. If you have U. S. Steel and Westinghouse on your rolls, you do not have to learn to make money on the insurance principle.

In the present state of my knowledge, I am not too optimistic about being able to test these hypotheses empirically. However, I am not prepared to pronounce them as untestable. This is an altogether too easy way out. I believe if we think hard enough, we can spell out some corollaries which, if we dig hard enough, we can subject to empirical test.

Labor. Now we come to what most will assume and I am prepared to concede is the cost factor, which is most sensitive to interindustry influence. Yet, even here, I suspect I will be spreading my net farther than most people would.

First, the wage level. My colleague on the Pittsburgh Study, Mel Bers, is exploring this question in great detail. The presumption that the wage level in the dominant industry influences the wage level in other industries is one which no one can seriously question. I am confident that Bers's research will throw more light on the network of interdependence than anything that has been done so far. Bers is also immersed in the study of the influence of labor organization in the dominant industry on the structure of wages in the region. These two issues are inseparable in his framework.

But there are other influences relating to labor cost and supply which are not generally recognized. Bers found, for example, that the rate of participation of married women in the labor force in the

Pittsburgh region is far below the average for metropolitan areas. When standardized for industry mix, however, it turns out that the rate is as high as you would expect it to be. The question arises, therefore, do these women represent a potential supply or not? Why are not female-labor-using industries attracted by the surplus? Wages aside, there are at least two other factors relating to the character of the dominant industries which influence the outcome.

The first is the dispersion within the region of the plants of our dominant industries. The ratio of central city employment to SMA employment in manufacturing is much lower in Pittsburgh than in any of the large SMA's. Outside the Central City, the gradient in Pittsburgh is also flatter. The reasons are obvious. Our industries could not be piled up one on top of another as in the garment district even if our land were flat. The topography encourages still greater dispersion. But the importance of this for our purposes is that the early dispersion of manufacturing (plus the dispersion of mining) led to a dispersal of population which is also unmatched among our large SMA's. To the extent that pools of female labor are relevant to industrial location, Pittsburgh is at a disadvantage because a greater radius is required to form a pool of a given size. One must bear in mind that the areas in which the plants of the dominant industries operate are not exactly the most desirable as sites for other kinds of industry. (We shall return to this point later on.)

The second point has to do with the work schedule of the man in the family. Steel is a three-shift industry. The typical worker is not assigned to a particular shift for an indefinite period. Instead he works from 8:00 to 4:00 for some time, then 4:00 to 12:00 for some time, then 12:00 to 8:00 for some time. He also has to put in his share of weekends. It is reasonable to suppose that under these conditions the housewife is somewhat less willing to work than under ordinary conditions. Taken together, these factors tend to dissipate some of the labor force advantages we normally attribute to SMA's. And they are consequences of characteristics of the dominant industries.

Land. We normally assume that an SMA is large enough in area to nullify any considerations of site availability as a location factor except for industries with very special requirements like steel and chemicals. In general, I think this is a sensible approach. Nevertheless, I feel compelled to attach some importance to the impact of an industry's operations on the quality of the air and water in the surrounding area. Pittsburgh, as you all know, was notorious until recent years for its smoke and dust. There were three causes for this condition. The principal one was the use of soft coal as fuel in households and industry. A second was the steel industry. And a third was the railroads with their steam engines. All this has changed now and I do not mind using this forum as an opportunity to plug the radical improvement in the quality of Pittsburgh's air. A white shirt will now stay white in Pittsburgh for as long as it will in any city in the country. But it will take some time to work off our reputation. And furthermore, at a time when the reputation was founded in fact, it was bound to exercise a restraining influence on the growth of subsidiary industries in the region.

Intermediate Goods and Services. So much for the primary factors of production. I said earlier that location analysts have paid attention to a dominant industry's impact on the location of other industries which are oriented to the supply of the product of the dominant industry. But agglomeration is nourished more by the availability of a wide range of goods and services created in the first instance by the growth of the dominant industries. Transportation is the classic illustration of this phenomena. One industry attracts the service, and a second industry coming in finds that the service is available at costs which are lower than they would be in virgin territory. The second industry also finds already in existence a whole community of suppliers of business services such as legal, accounting, duplicating, etc.

The question I raise is whether the emergence of these services and their availability to other industries depends on the character of these industries which trigger development in the first instance. I think much depends on the internal organization of these industries. Large firms incorporate many of these services within their own operations because they can achieve scale economies within the firm. They are much more fully integrated and therefore depend less on outside suppliers. On the one hand, this means that, dollar for dollar, their business is less of a stimulus to the creation of a community of independent suppliers. On the other hand, the new entrant is not likely to find that the company is anxious to spread its fixed costs by making its services available to outsiders.

Again, consider the classic example of external economies: transport services. A firm which operates its own truck fleet on an exempt basis is specifically forbidden by the ICC to transport freight as a common carrier. Imagine then that you have two communities of equal size. In one of these, all the firms rely on common carriage. Hence service to and from a wide variety of places is available to all comers. In the other community, every firm has its private truck fleet. True, the roads are built and this helps a lot. But there is no service available to the new firm coming in unless it starts big.

We do know that Pittsburgh is not up to par in employment in ancillary services. This is indicated by a calculation of location quotients based on the 1950 Census of Population. The Duncans in their recent book, *Metropolis and Region,* also found that Pittsburgh had less than the national average per capita employment in service industries broadly defined. Only Detroit among the SMA's of 1,000,000 population or more shared this characteristic with Pittsburgh. It goes without saying, that much of my reasoning is applicable to Detroit as well.

Summary and Conclusions. It should be apparent by now that what I am reaching for is the specification of a function which relates external economies and diseconomies to industry structure, size being held constant. My feeling is that we have been too prone to associate external economies and diseconomies with size. We have been disturbed at not being able to derive a satisfactory correlation between the two. What I have tried to do is explore some of the residual variation around the size function. I recognize the difficulties of adequately formulating and testing these notions. But I do not think we can afford to ignore them because they are difficult if, as I maintain, they are relevant to an understanding of the dynamics of area development.

To come back to my first point: I think we are not using the optimal combination of tools in regional analysis. We know we can do a lot more to refine the methods we use to trap what I have called the demand side of interdependence. We need bigger and better regional input-output tables, regional capital coefficients, regional consumption functions. But we are not equating marginal returns in all directions if we do not, at the same time, push vigorously on the supply side of the problem.

I said we need new tools in regional analysis. I am prepared to modify that statement in favor of this one. We need to make better use of some old tools which we have not yet applied very extensively to regional analysis. We need to work out the regional implications of market organization.

[3]

© *International Regional Science Review*, Vol. 8, No. 1, pp. 1-22, 1983

Spatial Productivity Variations in Manufacturing: A Critical Survey of Cross-Sectional Analyses

Ronald L. Moomaw

College of Business Administration
Oklahoma State University
Stillwater, OK 74078 USA

ABSTRACT This paper examines recent work on productivity variations over space. Labor productivity and labor productivity controlled for capital intensity both vary among regions and across city size. Urbanization and localization economies, as well as those factors that influence national productivity growth, can be expected to influence these differentials. Empirical studies, however, have not gone much beyond the use of total population or employment in a region as a measure of urbanization or localization economies. As the survey shows, much research remains to be done. Two examples of the needed research are (1) a more detailed specification of the determinants of productivity differentials, and (2) the use of more sophisticated empirical techniques.

I. INTRODUCTION

The existence of spatial differentials in labor productivity has implications for regional and urban development and policy that have just begun to be explored. Moomaw (1980) and Peterson and Muller (1980) argue that the relationship between wage and productivity levels may be important in understanding the regional redistribution of manufacturing. Miller (1980a) suggests that firms should take these differentials into account in their location decisionmaking. Fogarty and Garofalo (1978, 1980) show that the productivity advantages of large cities are offset to some extent by the higher wages that must be paid. Given that these higher wages reflect net disamenities and higher living

Larry Ledebur provided significant assistance in the development of this paper. Juliana P. Moomaw, as she so frequently has, helped to eliminate obscurities. Suggestions made by anonymous referees led to many significant improvements. This research was supported by funds from the Economic Development Administration, U.S. Department of Commerce, provided to the Urban Institute. Additional work on the paper was supported by the Office of Business and Economic Research, College of Business Administration, Oklahoma State University. The views in the paper do not necessarily reflect those of its sponsors.

costs, they reflect a real cost to society that is an offset to the productivity benefit. Thus, to understand the net efficiency advantages of large cities, it is helpful to use a net productivity concept, which is essentially the value of increased output in large cities less the increased wage costs. Yezer and Goldfarb (1978) incorporate externalities into a similar analysis. Rather than concentrate on such studies, however, this paper reviews the literature on the existence of productivity variations among regions and urban areas.

Evidence suggests that substantial differences in labor productivity exist among the manufacturing sectors of the various regions of the United States. Peterson and Muller (1980) compare value added per production worker in 1975 in selected central cities in different Census Divisions. Using the South Atlantic as a base, value added per worker ranges from 81 in New England to 114 in the West. In inner suburbs, defined as the central county of the Standard Metropolitan Statistical Area (SMSA) less the central city, the range of variation is more extreme — 100 in the South Atlantic to 181 in the Southwest.

Interregional and interurban productivity differentials derive in part from differences in industry structure and, as Peterson and Muller caution, must be interpreted with care. Industry mix, however, accounts for only a portion of spatial productivity variation. Regional and state productivity indexes purged of industry mix effects (American Productivity Center 1980; Miller 1980a and 1980b) also reveal spatial productivity differentials.[1] Manufacturing productivity according to these measurements is greatest in the West, followed by the North Central and Northeast Regions, respectively. The South, with the lowest productivity, is the only region below the national average.

Regional averages tend to mask significant intraregional differences in productivity. When Census Divisions are compared, the Pacific and the Middle Atlantic have the highest productivity indexes. The three Southern Divisions and the Mountain West have the poorest productivity performance. All divisions, with the exception of the Pacific, contain states with below-average productivity levels. The South Atlantic and East South Central are the only divisions with no states exceeding the national productivity level.

Miller (1980b) also calculates these indexes for two-digit manufacturing industries in the metropolitan sector and compares them to the national average for these industries. Overall, manufacturing productivity is only 2.5 percent greater in SMSAs, which as Miller observes is not surprising, since much manufacturing activity occurs in metropolitan areas.

[1] The index is the ratio of the value added in manufacturing per production worker in the region or state in 1972 to a hypothetical productivity level for the region or state. The hypothetical level is calculated by assuming that each industry in the state or region has the corresponding national level of productivity. Local employment weights are then used to calculate the hypothetical regional average. If this index is greater than 100, it can be loosely interpreted to indicate that the region's industries have a productivity level higher than the national average.

In addition, Miller (1980a) examined manufacturing productivity for 52 individual metropolitan areas, again standardizing for industry mix. The degree of interurban variation found is significant. San Jose and New York City have the greatest above-average performance, 25 and 22 percent above the national average, respectively. The Allentown-Bethlehem-Easton metropolitan complex has the lowest, almost 20 percent below the national average.

Thus, available evidence indicates that regional disparities in labor productivity exist and that they cannot be attributed entirely to industry structure. In the next section potential sources of these differentials are reviewed. A concise summary of several econometric studies of cross-sectional productivity variation is presented in Section III. Section IV considers some of the issues raised by these studies and points to future avenues of research.

II. SOURCES OF SPATIAL PRODUCTIVITY DIFFERENTIALS

Assuming that industrial mix effects have been controlled for, one region is apt to have more productive industries than another if it has: (a) a higher capital-labor ratio; (b) the newest technology; (c) a younger capital stock, one of the advantages of which is that the new capital stock can incorporate newer technology; (d) a more highly skilled labor force; and (e) greater localization and urbanization economies. Although this list is not inclusive, significant spatial variation in any of these five factors may result in spatial productivity differentials.

CAPITAL-LABOR RATIO

Large differences in the capital-labor ratio among regions would have large effects on labor productivity and its variation among regions. One of the few bits of evidence on the existence of such variation is due to Browne, Mieszkowski, and Syron (1980). They have developed a capital stock series for the manufacturing sector and selected industries for states and regions which shows that "the average capital-labor ratio in the Northeast is substantially below that in the country as a whole; it is relatively high in the North Central region and the South" (p. 10). They further conclude that this somewhat surprising finding is not due to industry structure.

TECHNOLOGY ADOPTION AND DIFFUSION

According to Carlino (1978, p. 27), "there is evidence which indicates that the spatial diffusion of innovation begins in the largest urban places and then tends to be transmitted down along the hierarchy of cities." It follows that industries in different cities may employ different technologies.

A related notion is based on the idea of the regional product cycle as discussed by Norton (1979). In the first stages of a product cycle an industry engages in significant experimentation and development; then it proceeds in the second stage to an era of rapid growth and rapid technical change. The industrial core or seedbed area of an economy likely will have a relative advantage in these two stages. Industries are expected to be attracted to peripheral regions in the third stage, which "is characterized by stable technology, long production runs, and a reliance less on technical or managerial talent than on unskilled and semiskilled labor" (Norton 1979, p. 126).

The implications of these two related concepts for spatial productivity variations are not clear. If firms in the largest cities are more likely to have the latest technology, then they may have greater productivity. Based on product cycle ideas, however, firms in the periphery may have a higher or lower level of productivity than their counterparts in the core, depending upon the stage of the product cycle. If the industry is in the second stage, with rapid growth of technology and output, and is concentrated in the core, then the productivity of peripheral firms is likely to lag behind firms in the core because firms that disperse early may not have kept up with the improving technology. Alternatively, if the product cycle has reached its third mature stage before significant dispersal to the periphery, then the peripheral firms are likely to have the latest technology and hence be more productive.

THE AGE OF THE CAPITAL STOCK

The age of a region's capital stock can affect productivity in the region relative to other regions. It is possible that the public capital stock, the infrastructure, is not compatible with the most up-to-date private capital stock (Varaiya and Wiseman 1979). The classic example of this is a center-oriented city in an age where manufacturing plants tend to use land extensively and to locate in the peripheral areas of cities.

Varaiya and Wiseman (p. 118) also suggest that older cities (and presumably regions) have a large fraction of private production capacity that is economically marginal "due to deterioration and technological obsolescence." As a result, the latest technologies may not have been embodied in the area's capital stock. This hypothesis contradicts the hypothesis discussed earlier that firms in larger, and usually older, cities adopt new technologies first.

Although it is obvious that the capital stock of rapidly growing cities and areas is younger than the capital stock of slowly growing cities and areas, precise measurements of these age differences require a long time series of capital stock estimates for each area. Although Fogarty and Garofalo (1981) have begun the construction of such data for SMSAs, the data for states and regions from Browne et al. (1980) are the only comprehensive data available. They indicate that capital formation in the manufacturing sector was more rapid in the South and West than in the Northeast and North Central regions from 1960-1976. Hence the former have a younger capital stock.

THE QUALITY OF THE LABOR FORCE

Differentials in labor force composition — education, experience, age, sex — over space can also be expected to result in productivity variation. To the extent that the workers of one region have lower levels of education and less industrial experience, that region will tend to have lower productivity. Griliches (1967), for instance, finds that interstate variations in labor quality have significant effects in manufacturing production functions.

LOCALIZATION AND URBANIZATION ECONOMIES

Localization and urbanization economies are spatial sources of spatial productivity differentials. Localization economies arise as the size of an industry, measured by output or establishments, increases in a given area. With a greater derived demand for specialized maintenance and repair services, for instance, individual firms can spin off their in-house maintenance and repair activities. Although underutilized by a single firm, specialized maintenance and repair firms will be able to operate at full capacity as the demand for their services gets sufficiently large. Firms in the original industry can now hire repair services cheaper than they can provide them for themselves (Carlino 1978; Evans 1972; Stigler 1951).

Similarly, urbanization economies result as the scale of economic activity in the city expands. The sources of urbanization economies include access to large pools of skilled labor, entrepreneurial talent, wholesalers of specialized items, and specialized business services (Carlino 1978).

The definition of urbanization economies or localization economies used to organize this review can be developed by multiplying a firm's production function $f(\cdot)$ by an efficiency function $g(\cdot)$ to get $g(\cdot)f(\cdot)$ (Yezer and Goldfarb 1978).[2] Although the arguments of $f(\cdot)$ are under the firm's control, the arguments of $g(\cdot)$ are taken to be internal to the region in question but external to the firm and thus outside its control. Thus, $g(\cdot)$ is a way of representing external effects as shifters of the efficiency parameter of a firm's production function; this formulation suggests, as is implied in the immediately preceding discussion, that localization and urbanization effects are similar phenomena and that both are external economies or diseconomies. If the relevant argument in $g(\cdot)$ is some measure of industry scale within the region, the

[2] Other definitions are possible. The approach used by Carlino (1978) is discussed in Section IV, along with the reasons for not using it here. See also footnote 4.

effect is termed localization. If the relevant argument is some measure of overall economic activity or scale in the region, it is termed urbanization. Whether the effect is an economy or diseconomy depends upon the sign of the effect.

III. ECONOMETRIC STUDIES OF PRODUCTIVITY VARIATION

Studies that have examined the variation of productivity over geographical regions are summarized in this section as a prelude to a critical evaluation. The summary is limited to cross-sectional studies that have estimated production functions as a first step toward the examination of productivity variation in manufacturing. This review stresses studies that are innovative in technique or that have an aspect particularly relevant to the questions reviewed in the next section.

Rocca (1970) uses production function analysis to examine variations among the 21 Brazilian states in output per worker in the manufacturing sector. He estimates a Cobb-Douglas (CD) production function with value added per establishment in the industry as a function of the average number of employees per establishment, installed horsepower per establishment as a proxy for capital, and total manufacturing output for the state. This latter variable is included to capture external economies, such as the greater availability of intermediate goods and business services, a larger and more experienced pool of labor, and a generally higher level of economic development associated with greater manufacturing output. For twenty industries, using 1960 data, the capital variable is significant in 14 industries, labor in 20, and total manufacturing activity in 15. The coefficients of capital and labor average 0.171 for capital and 0.844 for labor. Mildly increasing returns to internal scale are suggested; 11 industries display increasing returns at the 90 percent significance level, but nine industries do not. The coefficient measuring productivity variation as a function of total manufacturing in the state ranges from −0.021 to 0.322; its average is 0.152. This implies that for every doubling of manufacturing output in a state, productivity increases by 15.2 percent. Rocca attributes the causes of labor productivity differences over states to capital per worker, economies of scale, and differences in total factor productivity.

In a closely related study of states in the United States, Nicholson (1978) assumes that external economies are related to the proportion of a state's work force residing in SMSAs. Specifically, he tests the hypothesis that efficiency is greater in urban states. By experimenting, he determines that classifying a state as rural if 25 percent or less of its employed workers lives in SMSAs, and urban otherwise, gives the best results.

Using data which includes gross capital stock from the 1957 *Annual Survey of Manufacturers,* Nicholson estimates CD production functions for two digit industries for both the urban and rural sample of states. He presents the following average production function for each sample (p. 93):

$$\text{urban: } \ln Q = 0.430 + 0.564 \ln L + 0.435 \ln K \text{ and}$$
$$\text{rural: } \ln Q = 0.314 + 0.718 \ln L + 0.297 \ln K.$$

The average production functions suggest constant returns to scale, a suggestion confirmed by the industry equations. Of 34 estimated equations (18 in the urban sample and 16 in the rural) only four show increasing returns to scale and only one decreasing returns to scale (at the 90 percent confidence level).

The antilogs of the constant term in the equations above are 1.54 and 1.37, giving a 12 percent productivity advantage for states in the urban sample. For individual industries the results are not as clearcut. Nicholson finds no efficiency difference in over two-thirds of the industries considered, which weakens the overall conclusion of a 12 percent efficiency advantage for urban states.

Unlike the studies by Rocca and Nicholson, the remaining three Cobb-Douglas studies reviewed did not have capital stock data or a direct proxy for such data. Aaberg's (1973) approach, followed by Moomaw (1981a), is based on the CD production function, $Q = g(\cdot)K^cL^d$, where Q is physical output, K is capital services, L is labor services, $g(\cdot) = aN^b$ is Hicks-neutral productivity or efficiency, and N is urban population. Since Q and K are unobserved, multiply by P, divide by L, and multiply and divide the right hand side by L^c and R^c, where P is output price and R is the price of capital services, yielding

$$PQ/L = PR^{-c}\, g(\cdot)\ (RK/L)^c L^{c+d-1}. \qquad (1)$$

In this formulation, labor productivity depends inter alia on capital intensity, which is measured as capital income (value added minus payroll) per unit of labor, and average firm size.

Aaberg argues that the income from capital can be used as a proxy for capital if the rate of return to capital is constant among regions. The rate of return is:

> equivalent to the yield from capital when this has been corrected for the degree of utilization and the technical quality. Therefore, in order for the income from capital . . . to be used as a measure . . . the rate of return [must be] constant between the regions . . . differences in the degree of utilization and technical quality of the capital will be recorded in the measure of capital (p. 134).

Thus, he states that this measure of capital adjusts for degree of utilization and the differing efficiencies of different vintages of capital. Taking logarithms of (1) gives the equation estimated by Aaberg, namely

$$\ln PQ/L = \ln(aPR^{-c}) + b \ln N + c \ln(RK/L) + (c + d - 1) \ln L. \qquad (2)$$

This equation estimated for the Swedish manufacturing sector explains about 90 percent of the regional variation in labor productivity. The elasticities of labor productivity with respect to the three explanatory variables are: capital intensity 0.420; firm size 0.042; and population 0. 017. All coefficients are highly significant. The estimation of the equation at the industry level yields similar results. The capital intensity elasticity ranged from 0.247 to 0.473 with an average value of 0.351; the firm size elasticity ranged from 0.016 to 0.055 with an average value of 0.032; and the population elasticity ranged from 0.009 to 0.039 with an average value of 0.020. For the 15 coefficients estimated, all t-statistics but one are two or greater (the renegade is 1.8). The R^2s for these equations range from 0.73 to 0.88, with a mean of 0.81.

Aaberg uses his results for the manufacturing sector to demonstrate that about 43 percent of the difference between labor productivity in the most and least productive regions is accounted for by differences in capital intensity. Population accounts for about 32 percent of the difference, with firm size (16 percent) and other unexplained factors (9 percent) accounting for the remainder.

Moomaw (1981a) adapts this model to U.S. SMSA data by assuming constant returns to scale and including regional dummy variables and SMSA population, which is intended to measure the net effect of agglomeration economics. He also includes the median education level of the adult population, Ed, as a measure of the quality of the labor force. Thus, Moomaw's estimating equation is

$$\ln PQ/L = \ln(aPR^{-c}) + b \ln N + c \ln(RK/L) + eNE + fNC + gWE + h \ln Ed, \qquad (3)$$

where NE, NC, and WE are dummy variables taking the value of one for the Northeast, North Central, and West Census Regions, respectively, and zero otherwise. The overall results of estimating this equation for 14 two-digit industries are: 31 of the 42 regional coefficients are significant (at least 90 percent level), and generally positive; 7 of 14 city-size coefficients are significant and positive; 4 of the 14 education coefficients are significant and positive; and all of the capital intensity coefficients are significant and positive. As in Aaberg's estimates, R^2s are high, ranging from 0.75 to 0.96, but not too much should be made of this because the variable measuring capital intensity (PQ − WL)/L is a component of the dependent variable PQ/L. The coefficient of ln RK/L, the proxy for capital intensity, averages 0.47, which might appear high. It does, however, correspond to the average value of 0.435 that Nicholson found for his urban sample and to the average of 0.42 found by Aaberg for all manufacturing.

The final CD study to be summarized is an estimate of an aggregate production function for urban areas (Segal 1976). Segal estimates a CD production function using capital stock data that he calculated from investment data using the perpetual inventory method and an assumed rate of embodied technical change. The investments for each year (vintage), depreciated and appreciated on the basis of assumed rates of depreciation and technical change, are summed to get total effective capital stock. The production function is estimated using capital stock, labor, measures of labor quality such as education and percent female, and certain regional characteristics. A dummy variable taking the value of one for the larger cities in the sample is used to pick up the effect of city size on productivity. Preferred estimates were obtained when the dummy represented the eleven cities with populations of two million and more. Its coefficient of approximately 0.08 suggests that total factor productivity is approximately 8 percent greater in SMSAs with a population of two million than in smaller SMSAs.

Other studies have relied on the general framework of the Constant Elasticity of Substitution (CES) production function to estimate the importance of localization and/or urbanization economies. The CES production function with constant returns to scale can be written as

$$Q = aN^{b}\,[tK^{-p} + (1 - t)L^{-p}]^{-1/p} \qquad (4)$$

where p and t are parameters. As before, aN^b represents Hicks-neutral productivity as a function of population or some other variable. Equating the marginal product of labor and the wage rate implies that

$$\ln PQ/L = \text{constant} + (1 - s)\,b \ln N + s \ln W \qquad (5)$$

where s is the elasticity of substitution and W is the wage rate (Sveikauskas 1974, p. 552). In the absence of direct data on capital, (5) can be used to estimate the increase in Hicks-neutral productivity with N. Comparing (5) with (3) shows that (5) uses wages to control for capital intensity. In the process, however, the coefficient of population becomes complex and is no longer a direct measure of the effect of population on productivity.

Shefer's (1973) estimate of (5) is an example of the use of this method to measure localization economies for two-digit manufacturing industries and all manufacturing in SMSAs in the United States. The variable N in the equation estimated by Shefer is total industry output in the SMSA; therefore, b is the increase in productivity with industry size in the SMSA. The adjusted R^2s range from 0.22 to 0.94; overall, they indicate that the equation fits the data fairly well. For 1958, productivity increases by about 7 percent with each doubling of industry output in the SMSA. The effect on productivity of local industry size, b, however, varies from −0.24 to 0.82. For 1963 the results are that b averages almost 0.17, indicating a 17 percent increase in productivity with each doubling of the size of the local industry; the estimates of b again have a wide range, −0.41 to 0.87.

Shefer's estimates of b are unstable over time. The industry with the largest value for 1958, Food and Kindred Products (0.81), has the smallest value in 1963 (−0.41). An examination of his results for other industries confirms the suggestion of instability given by the food industry. The mean estimate of b more than doubles over this short period. In addition to this large change, the sign of b changes for 9 of of the 19 industries considered.

Anticipating difficulties in estimating s and b, Sveikauskas (1975) assumes that the efficiency part of (1) can be estimated separately from f(K,L). He estimates

$$\ln g = a + b \ln N + eNE + fNE + gWE + h \ln Ed \qquad (6)$$

where the included independent variables are the same as those of (3). However, g is not observable; consequently, Sveikauskas substitutes labor productivity, PQ/L, for g. As a result, he estimates (3) without a capital intensity variable.

Moomaw's (1981a) estimates provide a comparison of productivity differentials derived from (3) and (6). Based on (6), the average advantage of the Northeast, North Central, and West regions relative to the South for 14 industries is 11, 13, and 26 percent, respectively.

A similar result obtains for the elasticity of productivity with city size as measured by the coefficient of N. With (6) the elasticity averages 0.057, and with (3) it averages 0.015. In short, the regional differentials are lower by 38 to 69 percent, and the city-size elasticity is lower by 75 percent in the equation with a proxy for capital intensity.

In Section IV the studies summarized here and other studies are used as a basis for examining the state of the art of cross-sectional productivity analysis.

IV. A SURVEY OF UNRESOLVED ISSUES AND AVENUES FOR FUTURE RESEARCH

The treatment of urbanization and localization economics and the resolution of the capital stock data problem are two important issues in this literature. A related issue pertains to the role of capital intensity, vintage, labor quality, and localization and urbanization economics in explaining spatial productivity differences. Another issue to be considered is the reconciliation of the findings of industrial productivity advantages for large cities and for the industrial states with their industrial stagnation.

EXTERNAL ECONOMIES AND OTHER VARIABLES

The production function approach to the examination of productivity differences across SMSAs requires some general assumptions. Let the production function be

$$Q = g(Z_i)\ f(K,L) \qquad (7)$$

with Q = output; $g(\cdot)$ = Hicks-neutral productivity; Z_i = a vector of variables that affect productivity; K = capital services; and L = labor services. For purposes of discussion, assume that SMSA population, N, is the only element in the vector Z and that f(K,L) or f(·) takes a multiplicative form. Equation (7) can then be written in the Cobb-Douglas form,

$$Q = aN^bK^cL^d. \quad (8)$$

One approach to the development of systematic comparisons is to assume that the parameters of this production function are the same in every city. This approach, used in the studies discussed previously, implies two powerful restrictions on the analysis. One restriction is that agglomeration economies or other influences cause Hicks-neutral variations in productivity or efficiency. This implies that these economies reduce capital and labor requirements per unit of output equally. An alternative assumption, used for instance by Kelley (1977), results in agglomeration economies augmenting labor.[8]

The second restriction is that the production function for an industry be the same in every city or group of cities. Cross-section estimates are limited in the degree to which f(·) can differ by spatial unit. Obviously, if cities are the spatial units considered, then a cross-section estimate cannot allow f(·) to be different for every city; if allowed, only one observation would be available to fit the equation. Regional groupings of cities do allow the estimation of production functions that differ by spatial units. Specifically, regional groupings permit the use of dummy variables to shift g(·), Hicks-neutral efficiency, or to shift the parameters of f(·), allowing them to vary by region. Neither device avoids the criticism that both parts of the production function, g(·) and f(·), are unique to each city.

Carlino (1978) and Norton (1979), among others, suggest that technology diffusion and regional product-cycle notions imply that production functions of industrial firms are (potentially) different in each city. Another argument along similar lines is that industry mix differs, resulting in production function differences. Although Alperovich (1980) finds little evidence that the elasticity of substitution for two-digit industries differs among Census Divisions, and Lovell (1973) suggests that industry mix variations within two-digit industries among states should have neutral effects on technology, cross-section analyses are always subject to the criticism that production functions differ over space.

Carlino's (1978) response, using a technique of Shefer (1973) and Dhrymes (1965), is to estimate the return to scale (RTS) parameter of the production function for each industry for each SMSA for

[8] Kawashima (1975) assumes a Cobb-Douglas production function with an additional additive labor term. It is af(·) + vL. The coefficient v is then taken to be a function of population. Consequently, population affects the marginal product of labor in a non-neutral way. Kawashima finds, in general, that larger cities have greater labor productivity. Evidence is also found that at some relatively large population (SMSA population of from 4.5 to 7 million) the relationship reverses.

which the necessary time series data exist. RTS, that is (c + d) in (8), rather than g(·), is taken by Carlino as a measure of external economics or productivity. In effect, Carlino argues that allowing the parameters of the production function to vary for each SMSA can capture external economies of localization and urbanization. Under these conditions, however, the RTS parameter may not index productivity. Consider a firm using a given vector of inputs in different SMSAs; output increases unambiguously with RTS only if g, the efficiency parameter in the production function, is invariant over SMSAs. If this is assumed, a larger RTS implies a greater output from the given input vector, allowing the inference that external economies have led to greater productivity. On the other hand, if g varies among SMSAs, then increases in RTS with the same input vector do not imply increases in output.[4] Thus, Carlino must assume that g is constant while RTS varies over space. The analyses described previously assume that RTS is constant and g varies. On a priori grounds little, if any, reason exists to choose one assumption over the other.

Carlino (1978, p. 75) also argues that population, the most popular argument in g(·),

> is a worthless surrogate for business agglomeration economies. The latter tends to be related to industry size (localization economies) and/or inter-industry size (urbanization economies). Therefore, proxies which capture these influences are more appropriate.

Elsewhere, Carlino (1979, p. 365) suggests that population scale operates as a diseconomy, offsetting somewhat the business agglomeration economies available to many urban industries. Those studies that use population as a surrogate for business agglomeration economies have recognized that diseconomies of population scale exist by assuming either explicitly or implicitly that population scale leads to net rather than gross agglomeration economies. Nevertheless, Carlino's critique should stimulate future research activity.

One avenue is to follow Carlino's lead and attempt to identify the arguments of g(·) more precisely. He regressed his estimates of RTS on measures of internal scale economies (average establishment size), localization economies (the location quotient), urbanization economies (the number of manufacturing establishments in the SMSA), and urbanization diseconomies (SMSA population). Although his results are hard to interpret because his procedure does not hold g constant across SMSAs, the attempt to develop better proxies for these various influences on productivity is important. Other variables that might be tried are population density, the availability of business services, age of city, and age of capital stock. Furthermore,

[4] It follows that Carlino's use of RTS to measure localization and/or urbanization economies is inappropriate in a cross section because g is not held constant. His time-series estimates, for which it may be appropriate, are not reviewed here because they are not directly relevant.

following Segal (1976) and others, labor quality variables can be included in g(·).

Two econometric problems arise in studies that fail to specify the additional variables in g(·). The omission of relevant variables that are correlated with population would result in their effect being captured by the coefficient of population. Thus, the coefficient of population could attribute productivity differentials to population rather than to such factors as labor quality, localization economies, or omitted variables. If we are to isolate the effect, if any, of population scale on productivity, additional variables need to be included in g(·). By virtually ignoring the numerous sources of productivity differentials discussed in Section II, many of the existing studies have failed to yield a comprehensive understanding of factors influencing these differentials. Perhaps more importantly, they may also have yielded biased estimates of the importance of population scale, especially if the population coefficients are interpreted as measuring urbanization economies. In short, it may be necessary to have variables that reflect urbanization economies, urbanization diseconomies, and localization economies if clean estimates of external effects are to be obtained. Almost all of the studies surveyed, however, have been limited to just one variable as a measure of external effects.

Another econometric problem is that population and other variables suggested to account for such influences as urbanization economies and localization economies are really just proxies or indicators for unobserved or latent variables. The use of these indicators as independent variables implies the use of stochastic regressors and results in the biases associated with errors-in-variables.[5] There is, therefore, a potential for the use of the latent variable approach to isolate the various determinants of productivity differentials (Aaker and Bagozzi 1979).

Another alternative that might be explored is to use a production function, such as $Q = gK^cL^d$, to calculate a frontier production function using linear programming techniques (Forsund and Hjalmarsson 1974; Timmer 1971). The frontier production function for a two-digit industry would be defined by the ability of firms in the three most "efficient" cities to transform capital and labor inputs into value added. (To prevent an anomaly from defining the frontier, a 95 or 90 rather than 100 percent efficient frontier might be used.) Deviations from this frontier can then be measured for each city-industry observation in the sample. Deviations could occur because of different production function parameters (g and/or RTS) in the deviant cities or because of

[5] One referee raised this point. He suggested that the use of population to proxy the factors that make a city more productive probably results in an upward bias on the population coefficient since the same factors that make a city more productive also tend to make its population larger.

differences in labor quality, external economics, or inefficiency. The deviations could be regressed on the various proxies for urbanization economics, localization economics, labor quality, and other variables to attempt to capture their relative importance. This frontier approach may assist in resolving some of the previously mentioned problems. Its data requirements, however, are severe, and the reliability of the frontier is not subject to statistical testing.

Any of the approaches described above requires some resolution of the problem of measuring capital, which in turn is related to the choice of a production function to estimate. Moreover, these approaches require consideration of a more extensive list of variables that might affect productivity.

SPECIFICATION QUESTIONS

The absence of usable, current, capital-stock data for metropolitan areas and states has been the factor that has most influenced the direction of almost all of the studies surveyed. Three routes have emerged: (1) analysts have developed or used methods that do not require capital data; (2) they have used proxies for capital data; and (3) they have developed their own capital data.

Each route has shortcomings. To estimate parameters of a production function without capital data requires restrictive assumptions about the production function. To use proxies for capital data involves the danger of not knowing how closely the chosen variable proxies the capital data. To develop one's own capital-stock estimates entails an expensive research project.

Sveikauskas (1975) assumes that $g(\cdot)$ can be estimated independently of $f(\cdot)$, obviating the need for capital data. To estimate (6) and expect b to measure the effect of population on productivity, one must assume that capital intensity or the wage rate (see (3) or (5)) is uncorrelated with population. Since wages and presumably capital intensity are positively correlated with city size, this assumption may be false. Two reasons for suspecting that estimates of (6) result in biased estimates of b have been advanced by Moomaw (1981a, 1981b).

First, one can calculate a value for a population elasticity from the equilibrium condition that the increase in a firm's revenue due to the increased productivity of location in a larger city just equals the increase in labor cost because of the higher wage. This strategy can be interpreted as requiring that the percentage increase in productivity be equal to the percentage increase in wages multiplied by labor's share of total cost. Based on this relationship and using the same 14 industries as Sveikauskas, the population elasticity in equilibrium would range from 0.006 to 0.047, with a mean of 0.027. These calculated estimates are about 50 percent lower than those obtained from a least squares regression of (6).

Second, a comparison of estimates of b from (6) with those from (3) shows that the (3) estimates are substantially lower, averaging 0.015. Moomaw (1981a) demonstrates that the lower estimates are closer to the differentials consistent with profit maximization by firms. To the extent that the estimates differ from the calculated equilibrium ones, the estimates of (3) indicate that the South and smaller cities are more profitable locations. This indication of greater profitability is consistent with the increasing attraction that the South and smaller cities have had for manufacturing. The estimates from (6) imply the opposite.

Another approach that obviates the need for capital data is to estimate (5), which is derived from the CES production function by assuming profit maximization. Capital intensity is controlled for indirectly in this equation by the wage rate. To identify b, however, it is necessary to have an estimate of s; but as Sveikauskas (1974) has argued, the coefficient of ln W may be a biased estimate of the elasticity of substitution if Hicks-neutral productivity and the wage rate are interrelated. If so, the calculation of b requires that s be adjusted by an unknown amount. In addition, as Shefer (1973) points out, the calculation of b is impossible if s equals one and becomes problematic as s approaches one from either side. Finally, even if the first two problems can be overcome, the calculation of b from estimates of $(1 - s)$ b and s results in a biased, although consistent, estimate. The instability of b in Shefer's estimates may result from these problems. For instance, the Food and Kindred Products industry, with the largest value of b for 1958 (0.81), had the smallest value (0.41) in 1967. In addition, the mean value of b more than doubles over this short period, and it changes sign for 9 of the 19 industries considered.

In short, neither omitting any type of control for capital intensity nor relying on the profit-maximization conditions from a CES production function appears to provide a method of estimating the importance of agglomeration economies. Aaberg's solution is to estimate a CD production function using nonlabor costs per unit of labor as a proxy for capital intensity. This approach has the advantage that the coefficients of the variables in $g(\cdot)$ are direct estimates of the effects of the variables on labor productivity. As Aaberg specifies the equation, internal economies of scale are also estimated. Furthermore, (2) could be expanded to include other variables that influence productivity, thus dealing with some of the problems raised above.

The use of this residual from value added as a measure of capital services, however, is subject to serious qualifications. First, nonlabor costs include payments to land as well as capital. As a result, the capital intensity variable includes some of the effects of agglomeration economies, if the latter are capitalized into land rents. Second, the U.S. Census payroll data that are used to create the residual do not include some fringe benefits. Consequently, capital intensity is overestimated;

moreover, and more importantly, this overestimate is not necessarily constant or uncorrelated with other independent variables. The coefficient of capital intensity, as a result, is overestimated; furthermore, it may pick up some of the effects of other variables. Third, the use of the proxy requires that the price of capital services and the rate of return to capital be constant over space. Differentials in state and local taxes on capital can lead to differential prices of capital services. Fourth, if the rate of return differs, then firms in highly productive locations may have large capital (nonlabor) income per unit of labor. The existence of these location rents may result in the incorrect identification of these firms as high capital intensity firms relative to firms in a less productive location. It would follow that the productivity advantages associated with location would be incorrectly attributed to capital intensity.[6] On the other hand, if the rate of return were constant because location rents were driven to zero by entry, the problem would disappear because the residual measure then would correspond directly to capital intensity. Since the residual approach provides the easiest solution to the capital data lacunae, additional empirical analyses of the usefulness of this proxy could provide helpful information.

The final alternative to be considered is the development of capital-stock or capital-services data to be used in the estimation of production functions. For states, the *Annual Survey of Manufacturers* intermittently reports book-value of capital assets for two-digit industries, which has been used in production function estimation by Griliches (1967) and Brown and Medoff (1978), among others. As Brown and Medoff recognize, this book-value data is subject to a number of reservations; the most important in a period of rapid inflation is that it does not correct for price level changes.

Segal's (1976) development of capital-stock data for SMSAs illustrates some of the problems associated with using constructed data in cross-section analysis. Fogarty and Garofalo (1978) and Moomaw (1981b) suggest that Segal underestimated the capital stock of older cities. To the extent that older cities (in his sample) tend to be larger cities, even if no agglomeration economies existed they would be indicated in such cities because of the underestimate of the capital stock. Although the point arises in Segal's study because initial capital stock was assumed to be zero, it is more general. It can also arise if the assumed depreciation rate is too high. Furthermore, in developing a cross section of capital-stock estimates using the perpetual inventory approach, the same depreciation rate would presumably be used over the entire time span and for all cities. If depreciation rates vary over time, a systematic bias could develop between older and newer cities. Or, such a bias could develop if newer cities have systematically different industry mixes and hence depreciation rates. In short, in addition

[6] Professor Edward Miller, Rice University, and an anonymous referee brought a number of these points to my attention.

to the cost of developing capital-stock estimates at, say, the two-digit level for a large cross section of SMSAs, there is a danger that unrecognized biases could arise in cross-sectional comparisons of productivity levels and their determinants.

On the other hand, as Fogarty and Garofalo (1981, 1982) have shown, a capital-stock series for the manufacturing sector of individual cities allows the exploration of a number of questions that are more difficult if not impossible to address in a cross-sectional analysis. For a limited number of cities, they have estimated time-series production functions that allow them to estimate the rate of growth of labor productivity and of total factor productivity. They allow the production function to differ for different cities, testing hypotheses about RTS. The existence of a productivity slowdown has been addressed. They have also examined the life cycle notion suggested by Norton. Indeed, the whole question of technology adoption and diffusion can be addressed most profitably in the time-series context.

Moving beyond the question of capital data, another specification issue relates to simultaneous equation bias. Hoch (1958), Nerlove (1965), Walters (1963), and others have raised this issue in production-function estimation. A priori, bias due to simultaneity may exist; Griliches (1967), however, presents empirical evidence in support of single equation estimates.

Fogarty and Garofalo (1978) and Kelley (1977) incorporate simultaneity by estimating labor demand and supply models. The labor demand function includes an external economy variable. Fogarty and Garofalo extend Segal's model; they find no evidence of simultaneous equation bias in the ordinary least square estimates of the labor demand equation. With a somewhat different specification of the production function, they find a 10 percent size effect associated with SMSAs of more than two million population rather than Segal's 8 percent. This difference, however, is not due to simultaneous equation bias.

Kelley derives a labor demand equation, which incorporates labor augmenting agglomeration effects, from a CES production function. He finds large agglomeration effects, particularly when the sample is restricted to SMSAs with population greater than one million. Although the calculation of the agglomeration effect in Kelley's model may break down as the elasticity of substitution approaches one, just as in the previously mentioned CES studies, this model is one that might be applied usefully to other spatial productivity issues.

The final specification issues to be considered relate to the appropriate industry detail and the appropriate geographic detail. The feasible extent of industrial disaggregation is limited because of data availability and because the more that industry is disaggregated the fewer will be the state-industry or city-industry observations. Moreover, if capital data are to be constructed, industrial disaggregation complicates the task. An important factor that has received little attention is the sensitivity of the estimates of productivity differentials to industrial disaggregation. A study based on greater disaggregation might reveal whether the differentials observed at the two-digit industrial level are simply a matter of industry mix variations.

The level of geographic detail chosen is conditioned by the questions broached and by available data. In general, current data about state characteristics are more readily available than current data about metropolitan areas. Consequently, the underlying determinants of productivity differentials may be analyzed best with state data. Using state data, however, makes the measurement of localization or urbanization economics problematic. For instance, an urbanization (localization) variable based on either the state's total population (industry employment) or its population density (employment density) is unlikely to proxy the desired effects well. The problem arises because the state is not a compact regional economy. If total population is used, a simple redrawing of state boundaries that increased population would result in a prediction of a change in productivity. Such a result is unacceptable. The use of an average density variable is also a problem because state density is not necessarily correlated with the appropriate urbanization concept. Based on Nicholson's study, it remains an open question whether the percent of a state's population in metropolitan areas, or some similar variable, will serve the purpose.

To capture these external economies appropriately, it may be necessary to go to the metropolitan level, in which case some of the richness of the data on other variables is sacrificed.

A RECAPITULATION OF THE STUDIES SURVEYED

To conclude this survey, a summary of the results of eight spatial productivity analyses is presented in Table 1. Of the seven population coefficients reported, the first four range from 0.014 to 0.039, implying that the productivity advantage of the largest SMSA relative to the smallest ranges from 11 to 31 percent. The two estimates of a population coefficient for manufacturing of about 0.06 (or a 48 percent advantage) are from equations that exclude capital intensity. The Segal estimate of an 8 percent advantage of very large SMSAs relative to large (not the smallest) SMSAs applied to manufacturing and other sectors of the economy. This 8 percent advantage of very large SMSAs over large ones, when all sectors of the economy are considered, can be compared to a 1 to 6 percent advantage found by other studies for the manufacturing sector. This comparison suggests that the significant productivity advantages of large cities are in sectors other than manufacturing.

The two estimates of the elasticity of productivity with respect to total manufacturing output of a state and an SMSA are 0.15 and 0.27. Both estimates, which imply large productivity advantages for large

TABLE 1

A SUMMARY OF SPATIAL PRODUCTIVITY ANALYSES

			ELASTICITY OF PRODUCTIVITY WITH RESPECT TO:							
Study	Country	Industry Detail	Geographic Region	Popu-lation	Total Manu-facturing Output	Capital Intensity	Firm Size	Regions (Percent Differences)	Other	Data For Year
Aaberg (1973)	Sweden	Two Digit	M	0.020	XX	0.351	0.032	XX	No	1965-68
Kawashima (1975)	United States	All Manufacturing	M	0.014	XX	NC	XX	XX	No	1963
			M	0.039	XX	NC	XX	XX	No	1963
Moomaw (1981a)	United States	Two Digit	M,R	0.015	XX	0.47	XX	6,8,8	Yes	1967
			M,R	0.057	XX	XX	XX	11,13,26	Yes	1967
Nicholson (1978)	United States	Two Digit	U	XX	XX	0.435	0.0	XX	No	1958
			R	XX	XX	0.297	0.01	XX	No	1958
Rocca (1970)	Brazil	Two Digit	S	XX	0.15	0.171	0.02	XX	No	1960
Segal (1976)	United States	Total Economy	M	0.08[a]	XX	0.12	0.00	XX	Yes	1967
Shefer (1973)	United States	All Manufacturing	M	XX	0.27	NC	XX	XX	No	1963
Sveikauskas (1975)	United States	Two Digit	M,R	0.060	XX	XX	XX	11,15,26	Yes	1967

Legend: M = Metropolitan Area, R = Census Regions, U = Urban States, R = Rural States, S = States, XX = Not Included, NC = Not Comparable.

[a] This is the productivity advantage of SMSAs of population 2 million or more. Using Segal's data and a different model, Fogarty and Garofalo (1978) find this effect to be 0.10; Moomaw (1981b), on the other hand, calculates it to be 0.06.

agglomerations of economic activity (large states or SMSAs), control for capital intensity. A comparison of the results for population and for total manufacturing shows that the productivity advantage of large areas is greater when manufacturing output measures external economics. Since the differences are so large, the question of the appropriate variable to measure agglomeration, which Carlino (1978) emphasizes, becomes more important.

With respect to other elasticities, the coefficient of capital intensity is large (0.35 to 0.47) in the Aaberg-type studies that measure capital intensity as the return to capital per unit labor. Economies of scale (the coefficient of firm sizes) are small where estimated. Although not summarized in the table, labor quality variables are found to influence productivity in some studies.

Finally, regional differences in productivity in the United States appear to exist. For other regions relative to the South, they range from 6 to 8 percent higher or 11 to 26 percent higher for 1967, depending upon whether capital intensity is controlled for in the estimate.

Since the most recent data used in these studies is for 1967, their relevance today can be questioned. In particular, if large cities and the non-South regions currently have industrial productivity advantages, why are their industrial sectors experiencing such difficulty? Moomaw (1981a) addresses this issue by pointing out that the productivity advantage estimated may not be sufficiently large to outweigh the wage rate disadvantages. If this were true in 1967, one would anticipate the changes in the location of manufacturing employment that actually occurred in the 1970s.

Others, including Hawley and Fogarty (1981), have argued that: (a) these productivity differentials may have shrunk; (b) environmental or preference changes may have made large cities less attractive, resulting in unfavorable wage changes; and (c) these estimated productivity advantages may be inaccurate.

The existence or nonexistence of urban and regional productivity differentials is directly relevant to current regional and urban problems. New studies of productivity differentials using current data and improved techniques are needed. Issues to be examined include the existence of the differentials, means of estimating the differentials, the development of capital data and proxies, causes of the differentials, and whether the differentials are shrinking.

References

Aaberg, Y. 1973. Regional productivity differences in Swedish manufacturing. *Regional and Urban Economics* 3, 2: 131-56.

Aaker, D. A. and Bagozzi, R. P. 1979. Unobservable variables in structural equation models with an application in industrial selling. *Journal of Marketing Research* 16: 147-58.

Alperovich, G. 1980. Regional elasticities of substitution. *Journal of Regional Science* 20, 4: 503-12.

Browne, L. with Mieszkowski, P. and Syron, R. 1980. Regional investment patterns. *New England Economic Review* July-August: 5-23.

Carlino, G. A. 1980. Contrast in agglomeration: New York and Pittsburgh reconsidered. *Urban Studies* 17: 343-51.

Carlino, G. A. 1979. Increasing returns to scale in metropolitan manufacturing. *Journal of Regional Science* 19: 363-74.

Carlino, G. A. 1978. *Economies of scale in manufacturing location: theory and measurement.* Leiden: Martinus Nijhoff.

Dhrymes, P. J. 1965. Some extensions and tests for the CES class of production functions. *The Review of Economics and Statistics* 48: 357-66.

Evans, A. W. 1972. The pure theory of city size in an industrial economy. *Urban Studies* 9, 1: 49-78.

Fogarty, M. S. and Garofalo, G. 1982. Estimates of returns to scale in the manufacturing sector of older cities: how important are capital stock estimates? Unpublished.

Fogarty, M. S. and Garofalo, G. 1981. The life cycle of cities and the urban capital stock. Working Paper WP-3. Morgantown, W.Va.: Regional Research Institute, West Virginia University.

Fogarty, M. S. and Garofalo, G. 1980. Urban size and amenity structure of cities. *Journal of Urban Economics* 8, 3: 350-61.

Fogarty, M. S. and Garofalo, G. 1978. An exploration of the real productivity effects of cities. *The Review of Regional Studies* 8, 1: 65-82.

Forsund, F. and Hjalmarsson, L. 1974. On the measurement of productive efficiency. *Swedish Journal of Economics* 76: 131-53.

Griliches, Z. 1967. Production functions in manufacturing: some preliminary results. In *The theory and empirical analysis of production,* ed. M. Brown, pp. 275-332. National Bureau of Economic Research, New York: Columbia University Press.

Hawley, C. B. and Fogarty, M. S. 1981. Can agglomeration economies explain why people are leaving large cities? *Environment and Planning A* 13: 225-30.

Hoch, I. 1958. Simultaneous equation bias in the context of the Cobb-Douglas production function. *Econometrica* 26: 34-53.

Kawashima, T. 1975. Urban agglomeration economies in manufacturing industries. *Papers of the Regional Science Association* 34: 157-75.

Kelley, K. C. 1977. Urban disamenities and the measure of economic welfare. *Journal of Urban Economics* 4: 379-88.

Lovell, C. A. K. 1973. CES and VES production functions in a cross-section context. *Journal of Political Economy* 81: 705-20.

Miller, E. 1980a. Your location can affect your productivity. *Executive Magazine,* forthcoming.

Miller, E. 1980b. Variation in productivity, wages and profitability with location. Paper delivered at the Southern Economic Association Meetings, Washington.

Moomaw, R. L. 1981a. Productive efficiency and region. *Southern Economic Journal* 48, 2: 344-57.

Moomaw, R. L. 1981b. Productivity and city size: a critique of the evidence. *Quarterly Journal of Economics* 94: 675-88.

Moomaw, R. L. 1980. Optimal firm location and city size: productivity vs. wages. Paper delivered at the Southern Economic Association Meetings, Washington.
Nerlove, M. 1965. *Estimation and identification of Cobb-Douglas production functions.* Chicago: Rand McNally.
Nicholson, N. 1978. Differences in industrial production efficiency between urban and rural markets. *Urban Studies* 15, 1: 91-95.
Norton, R. D. 1979. *City life-cycles and American urban policy.* New York: Academic Press.
Peterson, G. E. and Muller, T. 1980. The economic and fiscal accompaniments of population change. In *Population redistribution and public policy,* eds. B. J. L. Berry and L. P. Silverman, pp. 70-113. Washington, D.C.: National Academy of Sciences.
Rocca, C. A. 1970. Productivity in Brazillian manufacturing. In J. Bergsman, *Brazil: Industrialization and trade policies,* Appendix 2, pp. 222-41. Cambridge: Oxford University Press.
Segal, D. 1976. Are there returns to scale in city size? *Review of Economics and Statistics* 53, 3: 339-50.
Shefer, D. 1973. Localization economies in SMSAs: a production function analysis. *Journal of Regional Science* 13: 55-64.
Stigler, G. J. 1951. The division of labor is limited by the extent of the market. *Journal of Political Economy* 59: 185-93.
Sveikauskas, L. A. 1975. The productivity of cities. *Quarterly Journal of Economics* 89, 3: 392-413.
Sveikauskas, L. A. 1974. Bias in cross-section estimates of the elasticity of substitution. *International Economic Review* 15, 2: 522-28.
Timmer, C. 1971. Using a probabilistic frontier production function to measure technical efficiency. *Journal of Political Economy* 79: 776-94.
Varaiya, P. and Wiseman, M. 1979. The age of cities and the movement of manufacturing employment, 1947-77. *Regional Science Association Papers and Proceedings* 41: 127-40.
Walters, A. A. 1963. Production and cost function: an econometric survey. *Econometrica* 31: 1-66.
Yezer, A. M. J. and Goldfarb, R. S. 1978. An indirect test of efficient city sizes, *Journal of Urban Economics* 5: 46-65.

[4]

THE PURE THEORY OF CITY SIZE IN AN INDUSTRIAL ECONOMY

ALAN W. EVANS

One of the most well-known empirical regularities in urban studies is the existence within almost every national economy of a size distribution of cities and towns which is statistically fairly regular. Yet 'no scientific explanation worthy of the name has been advanced so far' (Tinbergen, 1968). In this paper we develop a theory of city size which provides an economic explanation for the existence of a regular size distribution of cities in an industrial economy. We also show that the assumptions and the predictions of the theory are in accord with the empirical evidence.

The structure of the paper is as follows. We first review the two alternative approaches to the theory of city size which generate predictions of an urban hierarchy. Next we state, and attempt to justify, the assumptions we intend to make. In the third and fourth sections we show that both wage rates and rents increase with city size and in the fifth section we show that the cost of certain services can be expected to decrease with city size (the so-called 'external economies', or 'localisation economies' or 'agglomeration economies'). In the sixth section we consider the single firm and show how it selects its optimal location among the set of cities of varying sizes, whilst in the seventh section we show that in general equilibrium the location decisions of all the individual firms acting separately will cause the existence of an urban hierarchy.[1] Some of the welfare implications of the theory are discussed in the eighth section and in the ninth section we discuss the effects of a reduction in the cost or an increase in the speed of commuting on the structure of the urban hierarchy. Finally we discuss the relationship between the theory presented in this paper and other theories of location and suggest ways in which the theory might usefully be extended.

Alternative theories of the urban hierarchy

The main attempts to explain the empirical regularities in the size distribution of cities and towns fall into two main categories, systems theory and central place theory.

(1) *Systems theory* (see, for example, Simon, 1955; Berry, 1964; Berry and Woldenberg, 1967). A systems theory approach explains the empirical regularity as being the most probable statistical distribution under certain conditions. In

[1] In this paper I 'assume hierarchy to mean simply the order of size-rank', since I am concerned with the rank-size problem. This usage contrasts with that in 'articles concerned with the functional level of cities which assume hierarchy to mean that restricted functions are higher in level (i.e. the-higher-the-fewer)' (Lukermann, 1966). So Parr (1970) would take the view that the theory advanced in this paper is nonhierarchical.

The author is at the Centre for Environmental Studies and was until recently a Lecturer in Urban Studies in the Department of Social and Economic Research, University of Glasgow.

particular it is assumed that the rate of growth or decline in the size of any city is uncorrelated with its size. Although if viewed purely as applied mathematics these theories are intellectually stimulating, in most respects they are not very useful since the only thing they can 'explain' is the existence of an urban hierarchy. Furthermore, the theories rest on insecure foundations since the assumption mentioned above would seem to be wrong, at least in the short run, for recent work has shown that rates of growth are correlated with city size (Stanback and Knight, 1970; von Böventer, 1969; Muth, 1968). See also Mills (1972).

(2) *Central place theory* (see, for example, Berry, 1967; Berry and Pred, 1961; Parr, 1970). Central place theory explains the existence of the urban hierarchy in terms of a hierarchy of market areas. The larger the city the wider the range of goods and services which it provides and the larger its market area.

Central place theory provides an explanation of the urban hierarchy which is more satisfactory than systems theory since it yields predictions which can be tested and, indeed, have been, extensively (see for example Berry, 1967). Thus its explanation of the urban hierarchy is buttressed by empirical research relating to other aspects of the spatial economy whilst the explanation provided by systems theory must needs stand on its own. Nevertheless the empirical regularity in the size distribution of cities in an industrial economy cannot be completely explained by central place theory since it can only account for the spatial distribution of retail trades, services, etc. Whilst central place theory may be adequate to explain the urban hierarchy in areas such as S.W. Iowa where there is little manufacturing, it is inadequate to explain the size distribution of cities and towns in manufacturing areas such as the N.E. United States or the United Kingdom.[2] 'The existence of urban hierarchies in the heavily industrialised regions remains a fact in search of a theory' (Higgs, 1970).

The Assumptions of the Theory

In this paper we develop a pure theory of city size. We call it a 'pure' theory not because we intend the theory to be taken as an abstraction having little to do with the real world but because we have tried to abstract a theory which disregards all aspects of the economy which we judge to be irrelevant. This has been done for two connected reasons. In the first place it is easier to carry out the analysis and in the second place it is easier to understand.

The assumptions we wish to make are these.

(1) There are two sorts of industry in the economy. We call these 'manufacturing' industry and 'business services', or, sometimes, 'services'. These names are meant to have only a slight descriptive content.

(2) All the output of the firms providing business services is sold to firms in manufacturing industry.

(3) All the output of the firms in manufacturing industry is sold to consumers or to other firms in manufacturing industry.

(4) The cost of transport of the output of manufacturing industry is zero so that the sales of any manufacturing firm do not vary with its spatial location.

(5) The cost of transport of the output of the firms providing services is infinitely high but the whole range of business services is provided in every urban place. Since business services are an input to manufacturing firms, both business services and manufacturing firms locate in the centre of each city (the Central Business District or CBD). It might possibly be more realistic to assume that the cost of transport of business services is very high and that all business services are not provided in every city. This would necessitate the introduction of some type of central place theory to explain the location of the services which are not available everywhere. I do not think the small gain in the explanatory capacity of the theory would be enough to

[2] But it should be noted that Tinbergen (1968) has sketched out a type of central place theory which deals with manufacturing industry.

compensate for the increase in complexity. We thus ignore what von Böventer (1970) calls the common agglomeration economies and positive overspill effects which arise when a town is located close to another (bigger) centre.

(6) The plants which provide business services are indivisible. There are therefore economies of scale in the provision of business services.

(7) All firms attempt to maximise profits and households attempt to maximise utility. We assume perfect competition between firms except that where this is not possible, in the case of some business services, we assume that the services are sold at average cost (including 'normal' profits).

(8) The cost of commuting within the city is neither zero nor infinite but is at some intermediate level. Since employment in any city is at a single workplace, namely the CBD, the analyses of residential location by Alonso (1964), Wingo (1961), or Muth (1969) are applicable. Furthermore we take over unchanged the simplifying assumptions which are made by Alonso in order to develop a workable theory of residential location, e.g. each city is situated on a flat plain with no topographical features, the cost and speed of commuting is uniform in all directions, etc.

(9) All commuters' fares are equal to marginal social cost. There is no unpriced congestion. In particular there is an efficient road pricing system. We thus avoid having to consider a problem which has tended to dominate at least one earlier discussion of the economics of city size (Neutze, 1965). See also Reynolds (1966).

(10) Households can remove themselves from one permanent location to another at negligible cost.

It can no doubt be argued that the above assumptions are unrealistic, and it must be admitted that to some extent they are. But they are no more unrealistic than the assumptions which are made in many other branches of economic theory. The closest case conceptually is the theory of international trade where assumptions such as 'perfectly competitive markets, the absence of transport costs, the complete mobility of factors within countries and immobility between countries are still made in the basic formulations of the modern theory' (Findlay, 1970, p. 17). The theory of international trade explains international trade in a non-spatial world economy. We explain the size distribution of cities in a (virtually) non-spatial national economy. In both theories it is hoped that the assumptions are realistic enough to derive useful explanations and predictions whilst being unrealistic enough to handle conceptually!

Input Prices as a Function of City Size—Rents

We can classify the inputs of firms in manufacturing industry as labour, land (or floor space), capital, and business services. In this section and the two following sections we shall show that, with one exception, the prices of these inputs can be expected to vary with city size. Hence manufacturing firms must take these price variations into account in selecting the city in which to locate. The exception is capital. There is no reason to suppose that the cost of capital will vary with city size nor is there any evidence that it does so.

We shall show in this section that rent, the price of floor space, will tend to increase with city size but at a diminishing rate.

Fig. 1 shows a cross-section through the rent surface of a city of a given size. The rent per unit of floor area is indicated on the vertical axis and distance from the city centre on the horizontal axis. The city centre is denoted by the point O, the radius of the built up area of the city is OR, and the rent at the city centre is OP. We assume that the market for space in the city is in long-run equilibrium. The density of floor space (and persons per acre) is thus a monotonic function of the rent per unit of floor space, the characteristics of the function being determined by the state of building technology. Both rent and density are highest at the city centre and decline at a decreasing rate as distance from the city centre increases. On this see particularly Muth (1969) Chapter 3.

Now compare the long-run equilibrium in a city which is substantially larger. Since the population of the large city is, by definition, larger,

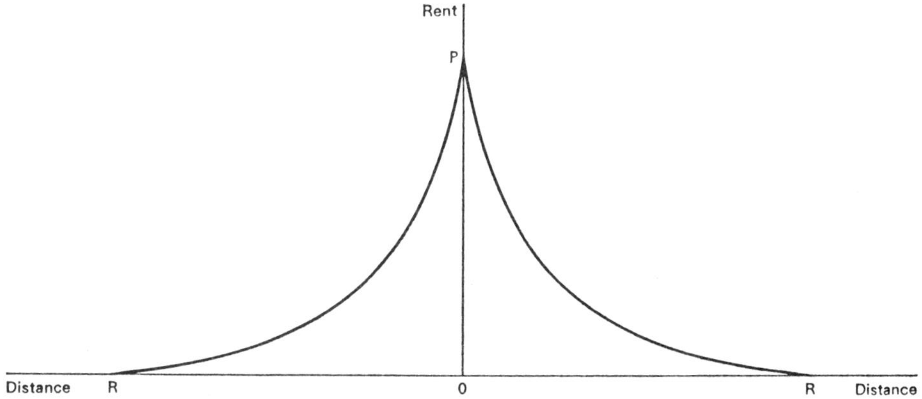

FIG. 1

either the population density must be greater in some parts of the city, or its built-up area must be greater, or both. But the density will be greater at some distance only if the rent is higher at that distance since, by assumption, in both cities the housing markets are in long-run equilibrium. Provided that the characteristics of the populations of the two cities are similar there is no reason to suppose that the shape of the rent surface of the larger city will differ substantially from the shape of the rent surface of the smaller city. Hence if the rent at some given distance from the centre in the larger city is higher than it is at the same distance from the centre in the smaller city, it will be higher at all distances from the centre; if it is higher at all distances from the centre then the radius of the larger city will be greater than that of the smaller, and rents at the centre of the larger city will be higher than in the centre of the smaller. In Fig. 2 the cross section through the rent surface of the larger city is shown by the curve $R'P'R'$ which lies above the curve RPR at all distances from the centre. In particular $OP' > OP$; we would expect city centre rents to increase with city size.

Little direct evidence is available to support

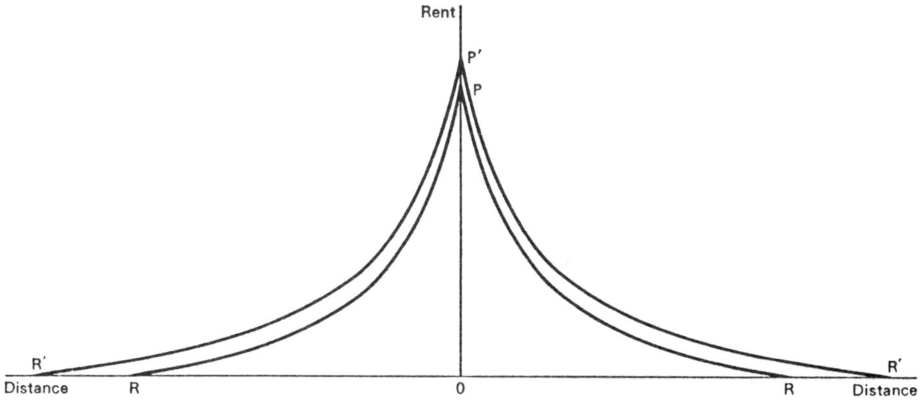

FIG. 2

this assertion though casual empiricism would suggest that two corollaries of the argument are correct. The density of floor space at the city centre (indicated by the height of buildings) tends to increase with city size, and the radius of the built-up area of the city tends to increase with city size. So far as I am aware more direct evidence is only available for Switzerland where Widmer (1953) found that the rent of housing was positively correlated with city size.

We can only go on to assert that the rent of floor space at the city centre will not only increase with city size but will tend to increase *at a diminishing rate*. Fig. 3 indicates the expected relationship. The rent per unit of floor area is shown on

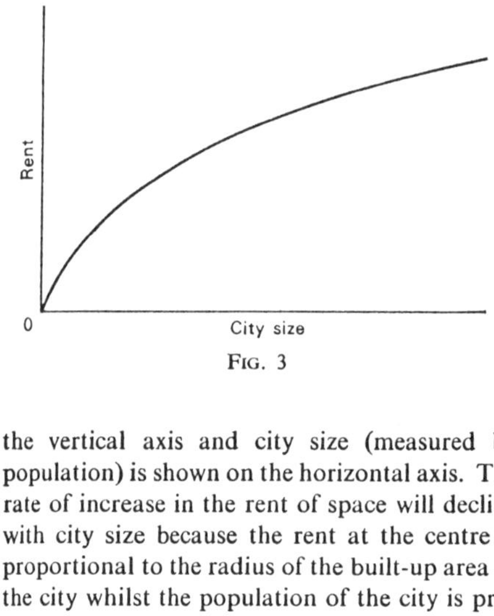

FIG. 3

the vertical axis and city size (measured by population) is shown on the horizontal axis. The rate of increase in the rent of space will decline with city size because the rent at the centre is proportional to the radius of the built-up area of the city whilst the population of the city is proportional to the area and, hence, to the square of the radius. As the area of the city increases, a given increase in the population can be accommodated by smaller and smaller increases in the radius of the city and will therefore result in smaller and smaller increases in central city rent. As evidence in support of the assertion it may be noted that Widmer (1953) fits a semi-logarithmic linear regression to his data for Swiss cities and whilst he gives no statistical evidence to suggest that this form of regression fits the data better than a linear form, he does publish the scatter diagram which shows that the semi-logarithmic transformation fits the data well.

Input prices as a function of city size—wages

In this section we shall show that wage rates will tend to increase with city size at a decreasing rate. The argument is a continuation of that in the preceding section.

We use as a tool of analysis the concept of the set of bid price curves introduced by Alonso (1964). A bid price curve connects the set of points indicating rents and locations between which a household is indifferent. A household's preferences are described by an infinite set of bid price curves just as in the usual analysis of consumer behaviour a household's preferences are described by an infinite set of indifference curves. However, whilst the household prefers to consume the bundles of goods represented by points on higher indifference curves to those represented by points on lower indifference curves, it prefers locations and rents represented by points on lower bid price curves to those represented by points on higher curves, since the household obviously prefers to pay a lower rent to a higher rent at any given distance from the centre. At its optimal location therefore the rent gradient will be tangential from above to the lowest attainable bid price curve. In Fig. 4 we reproduce one-half of Fig. 1 but show in addition one of the bid price curves of a representative household. The curve

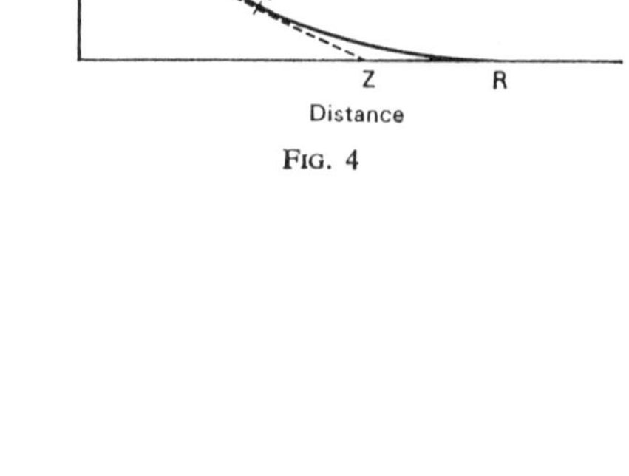

FIG. 4

XYZ is the lowest bid price curve attainable by the household; the point Y indicates the optimal location and rent. Suppose now that the household, with an unchanged schedule of preferences, is transferred to a larger city where the rent surface is that indicated by the curve $R'P'R'$ in Fig. 2. The bid price curve XYZ is no longer attainable since $R'P'R'$ lies everywhere above RPR and therefore lies everywhere above XYZ. The lowest bid price curve which is now attainable by the household is one which is tangential to $P'R'$ and this must be a higher bid price curve than XYZ. The household is made worse off by an increase in city size because of the increase in its rent and/or travel costs. If migration between cities is possible at a negligible cost, some benefit must accrue to residents of the larger city which compensates them for the higher rent and/or travel costs payable in the larger city and prevents them migrating to the smaller city. In the real world these compensatory benefits might accrue through cheaper food or other goods, or through the availability of certain services (e.g. theatres, art galleries, etc.) or merely through the *ambiance* of the larger city. There is however a significant amount of evidence to suggest that higher money wage rates provide at least a significant part of the compensatory benefit in the real world, and this is the only form of compensation which does not conflict with the assumptions of the theory.

Widmer (1953) found, using simple regression, that the average hourly rate of pay in Switzerland was positively correlated with city size. Fuchs (1967) concluded from his analysis of U.S. data using multiple regression that 'the relation between earnings and city size is large, persistent, and cannot be explained by correlation between city size and other variables'. The author found a generally significant positive correlation between British clerical salaries and city size (Evans, 1970a, Chapter XII).

In the same way that we showed that rents can be expected to increase at a decreasing rate, we can show that wage rates should not only increase with city size but should also increase at a decreasing rate. The population of the city is proportional to the area of the city and hence to the square of the radius, whilst the rent and travel costs are proportional to the radius of the city and hence to the square root of the area. Thus the increase in wage rates necessary to compensate for the increase in rent and travel costs consequent upon a given increase in the population of the city will get less and less as the city increases in size. As evidence in support of the assertion we may note that Widmer fits a semi-logarithmic linear regression to the data for Switzerland of the form $Y = a+b \log X$. The scatter diagram shows that this fits the data well. Studies of U.S. data provide conflicting evidence. Fuchs fits a regression of the form $\log Y = a+bX$. If this form of regression were correct it would indicate that wage rates increase with city size at an increasing rate. On the other hand Mattila and Thompson (1968) fit a regression of the form $Y = a+b \log X$ which would indicate that wage rates increase at a decreasing rate.

In the preceding section we could treat land or floor space as a homogeneous good but it would not be correct to do this with labour. Different types of labour are paid at different wage rates, and it may be that the different wage rates will have different rates of increase with city size. There are some grounds for expecting that although the *absolute* rate of increase of high wage rates will be greater than the *absolute* rate of increase of low wage rates, the *proportional* rate of increase will be lower.

We assume that we can use the theory of residential location to show that households of any given income group will always locate in the same relative position in any size city in which the characteristics of the households are the same, i.e. if these households locate half-way between the centre and the edge in one city they will in all cities. The compensation these households will require for living in a larger city will be equal to the increase in rent costs plus the increase in travel costs. For those living at the centre only the increase in rent costs is relevant and for those living at the edge only the increase in travel costs is relevant, and we would expect that the further the household lived from the centre the less would be the importance of the increase in rents relative to the increase in travel costs.

There is evidence to justify the assumptions that, firstly, the value of time spent travelling is a constant fraction of the wage rate and this fraction does not vary with income, and, secondly, the average income elasticity of demand for housing is equal to one so that the amount spent on housing is a constant fraction of total income.[3] Therefore the amount necessary to compensate households in each income group for increased rents and increased time spent travelling will increase proportionately with income. On the other hand the amount necessary to compensate households for the increased direct financial costs of travel will not increase with income. Hence we would expect that the increase in wages necessary to compensate households for living in a larger city would be proportionately smaller but absolutely larger, the higher the household's income. Furthermore, because, as a rough approximation, the average income of resident households increases with distance from the centre in Anglo-American cities, the costs of increases in city size are mainly rent costs for poor households and mainly travel costs for rich households. Hence the total increase in costs with city size for poor households will tend to be nearly proportional to their income whilst the total increase in costs for rich households will be much less than proportional. Thus this argument tends to reinforce the previous argument.

It is also possible to argue that the absolute rate of increase of high wage rates with city size may be less than the rate of increase of low wage rates. Suppose that tastes of the population tend to vary with income and that those with high incomes are a considerably smaller proportion of the population than those with low incomes. We also assume that there are economies of scale in the provision of the services demanded by the members of each income group. It follows that the possible economies of scale in the provision of the services demanded by members of low income groups will be achieved in much smaller cities than the possible economies of scale in the provision of the services demanded by the members of the high income groups. As a result the members of high income groups will not have to be fully compensated for the higher rent and travelling costs associated with residence in large cities since they will be partially compensated for these costs by the availability of the services they require (e.g. theatres, concerts, art, cinemas, department stores, specialist shops). In passing we may note that some members of the high income groups may have no particular desire for these services and will therefore be unwilling to live in large cities because of the high rent and travel costs; others will be unwilling to live elsewhere because of the absence of the sort of services they want.

There is little concrete evidence in support of the assertion that the rate of increase of high wage rates will be proportionately smaller than the rate of increase of lower rates. A casual study of the various 'London Living Allowances' which are incorporated in many British salary scales suggests that whilst they increase with income they certainly do not increase proportionately. Some evidence appears to conflict with the hypothesis. Farbman (1971) using data for S.M.S.A.'s in the United States found that family income inequality tends to increase with the size of the S.M.S.A. (in terms of population). This is rather less direct evidence however and its apparent contradiction of the hypothesis might be due to the fact that Farbman uses the Gini coefficient as a measure of inequality. Our hypothesis might be stated in statistical terms as a prediction that both the mean wage level and the standard deviation of wage rates about the mean will increase with city size, but the coefficient of variation will decrease. Since the Gini coefficient

[3] Thus British evidence suggests that the value of travelling time is equal to approximately 25% of the wage rate (Ministry of Transport, 1969). American evidence suggests that the income elasticity of demand for housing space must be approximately equal to one since it must be greater than 0·5, the income elasticity of demand for rooms, and less than 1·5 to 2·0, the income elasticity of demand for value of housing (Reid, 1962).

is not necessarily measuring inequality in the same way as the coefficient of variation, Farbman's findings do not refute the assertion.[4]

Input prices as a function of city size—business services

If the cost of labour and of floor space increases with city size whilst the cost of capital does not vary, there must be some compensatory reduction in costs with city size which allows the firms located in larger cities to remain profitable. In other economic discussions of the role of the large city authors have described various ways in which costs might be reduced in large cities. These economies of city size have been called 'external economies' (Lichtenberg, 1960; Hoover and Vernon, 1959; Vernon, 1960) or 'urbanisation economies' and 'localisation economies' (Isard, 1956).

The most extensive empirical study of the nature of these 'external economies' was a product of the study of the economy of the New York Metropolitan Region under the direction of Raymond Vernon. From this study it would appear that these external economies are basically of two kinds.

In the first place there is the reduction in uncertainty which comes from location in a large city in close proximity to many possible sources of information. Vernon stresses that the manufacturing industries which cluster in the centre of the New York region are those which are characterised by extreme uncertainty.

> The shops and plants of these industries ... are plagued by the fact that their output is unstable in one way or another. It may be unstable because of seasonality. But more important, as a rule, are the instability and uncertainty which come with a swiftly changing product or a highly variable demand (Vernon, 1960, p. 101).

Despite the possible economic importance of the reduction in uncertainty which may be possible in a large city we shall ignore this type of external economy here. In our analysis we shall concentrate on the second type of external economy. This economy results from the availability of a variety of specialised facilities and services in the large city.

> For example there are commercial laboratories which provide technical and research services on a contract basis; firms that design patterns for apparel manufacturers; agencies that maintain comprehensive files of pictures for magazines; and free-lance specialists in art work (Lichtenberg, 1960, p. 67).

Hence 'certain operations and services that a firm in a small place would have to do for itself can, in the city, be farmed out to separate enterprises specialising in those functions and operating on a large enough scale to do them more cheaply'. (Hoover, 1948).

Now, as Isard (1956, p. 182) remarks, the theory of urbanisation and localisation economies is in an unsatisfactory state. But we require a theory to explain the fall in the costs of certain services with city size (i.e. the external economies or urbanisation economies of city size). The approach we shall adopt is to regard urbanisation economies as a result of the greater division of labour possible in the large city. We can then bring to bear the theoretical analysis of the division of labour. This approach seems to be justified in that the descriptions of these economies by Lichtenberg or Hoover quoted above are exactly descriptions of the process of the division of labour. Moreover other students of the city have also equated the division of labour with the external economies of city size. Lampard (1968), for example, has commented on its importance as a cause of the growth of cities.

As Lampard observes, however, 'division of labor ... has not excited much theoretical interest

[4] Other explanations of Farbman's result are also possible. It might be due to systematic variations in the pattern of residential location of income groups as cities increase in size coupled with a tendency for the area defined as the S.M.S.A. to exclude the fringe areas, or 'exurbs' of the central city (Farbman, 1971). Alternatively it might be due to the substitution of higher paid workers for lower paid workers in larger cities as suggested in a later section of this paper.

or sustained observation. Division of labor, to be sure, was central to Adam Smith's scheme for enlarging the wealth of nations and he devoted all of three or four pages to the topic. Since Smith there have been no more than half-a-dozen noteworthy discussions of the topic'. One of them is a paper by Stigler (1951) in which he clarifies Smith's theorem that 'the division of labour is limited by the extent of the market'. We shall use his method of analysis. We first present an outline (and extension) of Stigler's analysis, then use it to understand the nature of the 'external economies' of city size and to explain the way in which the cost of business services will vary with city size.

In Stigler's view the firm can be conceived as engaging in a series of distinct operations or activities or as being composed of a number of functions. Those familiar with the literature of urban economics will recognise this idea as being identical to that proposed by R. M. Haig in his classic 1926 paper, namely that the firm is viewed as consisting of a bundle of functions. The costs per unit of production of these activities may either be related or independent. Here we assume (as Stigler does) that the costs are independent, and therefore that the cost per unit of output of each activity depends only on the rate of output of that activity. It is also necessary to assume that the output of each activity is a constant proportion of the output of the final product by the firm. The purpose of making these assumptions is that they allow the cost curves of all the functions to be drawn on the one diagram and the conventional long-run average cost curve of the firm to be drawn by summing vertically the cost curves of the various activities.

We should expect to find that the (long-run) average cost curve of each of the functions of a firm would have a different shape. The three variations are shown in Fig. 5, where the output of the firm's final product is indicated on the horizontal axis, and the average cost of the output of each activity or of the final product of the firm is indicated on the vertical axis. The cost curves of some functions (Y_1) fall throughout the

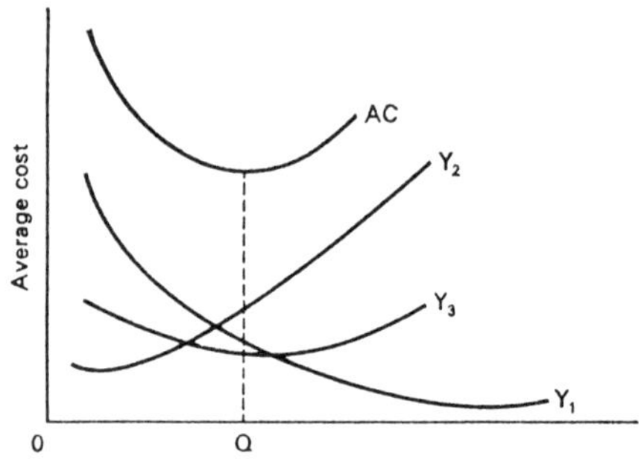

FIG. 5

probable range of the firm's output; some rise continuously (Y_2); some have the conventional U-shape over that range, indeed determine that range (Y_3). The average cost of production of the final product of a firm which used these three activities is shown in Fig. 5 as AC. The lowest point on this average cost curve occurs when the firm's output is Q. If all three activities have to be carried on by the same firm Q would be the firm's optimal output.

If all three activities don't have to be carried on together some readjustment is possible in order to reduce the cost of production. We assume that the long-run average cost curves of the functions shown in Fig. 5 will be the same whether these functions are carried on by this firm or any other and whether they are carried on singly or in multiples.[5]

The first thing that the firm can do is to produce the output of activity Y_2 from several processes and not from one single process which is subject to decreasing returns to scale.[6] If the activity or process Y_2 has a mimimum cost at an output of Q_2 where $Q_2 < Q$, the firm may be able to use the activity in multiples in order to minimise its

[5] I am indebted to L. C. Hunter for pointing out that this assumption is necessary to the analysis.

[6] It may be noted that Stigler does not deal with this case though it would appear to be implied by his analysis.

average costs of production. If the activity Y_2 can be carried out in multiples at constant (or nearly constant) cost, the average cost to the firm of the output of Y_2 and the average cost of the final output can be reduced.

The new situation is shown in Fig. 6. The

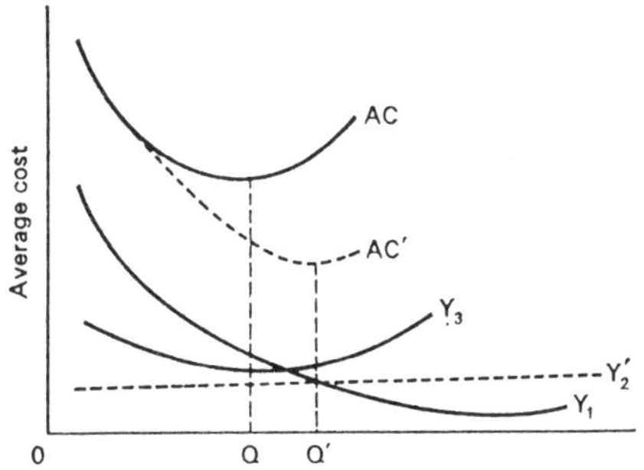

FIG. 6

curves marked AC, Y_1, and Y_3 are reproduced from Fig. 5. The new constant cost curve for the activity Y_2 if it is carried out in multiples is marked Y_2'. The new average cost curve for the firm is marked AC' It lies an increasing amount below the old average cost curve AC because the amount by which the average cost of the final product is reduced by using multiples of Y_2 is an amount which increases as the output of the firm increases. Thus the minimum average cost of the final product will be reduced and the optimal output Q' will be greater than Q since the lowest point of AC' will lie to the right of the lowest point of AC.[7]

The second way in which the firm could reduce its costs is by varying the output of activity Y_1. It is obvious that it would be to the firm's advantage to allow processes like Y_1 to be run to produce an output greater than that necessary for the firm's production of its final product whether this output is Q or Q'. This can only be done if the market for the production of the activity is greater than Q (or Q'): that is to say, it can only be done if the excess production from the process can be sold to other manufacturers.

If this is possible there is no necessary reason for the process Y_1 to be controlled by any one of the firms using the output. Indeed since the firms buying the output of the process will usually be rival manufacturers, they will certainly prefer purchasing from an independent firm to purchasing from a plant owned by one of their own number. Therefore a new firm (firm B) will be set up using only the process Y_1 and this firm will sell the production from the process both to the firm represented here (firm A) and to other firms. Firm A could then purchase what it required of the output of process Y_1 from firm B at a price lower than the cost to firm A of running the process Y_1 itself. Hence the final product of Firm A can be produced at a lower average cost. This result is illustrated in Fig. 7. By buying in what the firm requires of the output of the process Y_1 the cost of the input from Y_1 is reduced to a constant level Y_1. The process Y_2 is still assumed to be run in multiples and the product of that process is therefore available at a constant cost Y_2'. The process Y_3 still has the same (long-run) average cost curve. The average cost curve for the final product of the firm is lowered by the firm's ability to buy out but is lowered by an amount which decreases as the output of the firm increases. The average cost curve falls from AC' to AC''; furthermore the new opcimal output Q'' will be smaller than Q' since the lowest point of AC'' will lie to the left of the lowest point of AC'. This follows necessarily from the fact that the amount by which the average cost is reduced by purchasing from outside is an amount which decreases as the firm's output increases.

It is clear that Stigler's analysis yields an explanation of the nature of certain of the external economies or urbanisation economies of cities. Those functions which have an optimal output greater than is required as an input by a single firm will operate as separate firms. This will be particularly true of services which are required

[7] The implication of this result is that mass production leads to an increase in the scale of operation of the firm.

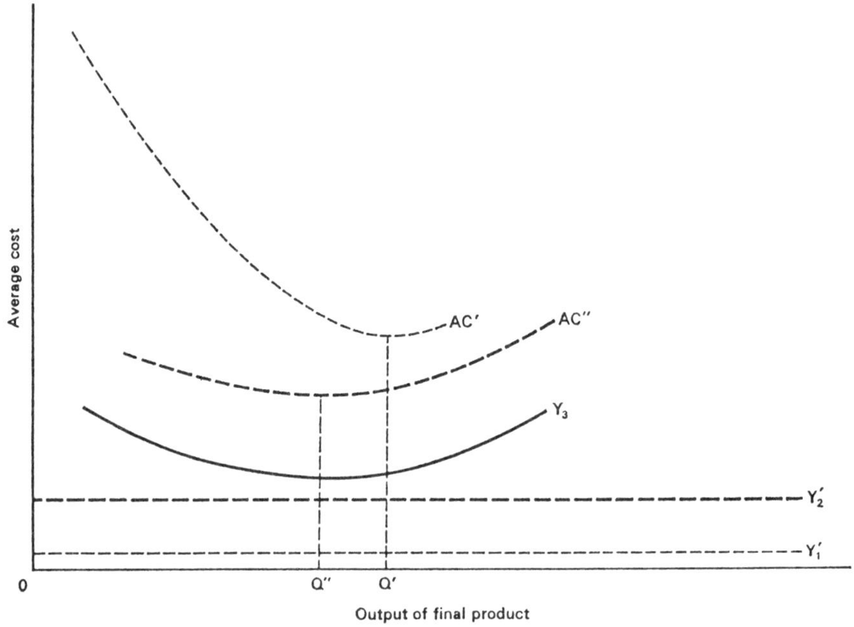

FIG. 7

relatively infrequently by most firms, e.g. the advice of accountants and lawyers. These firms will tend to locate where they can be sure that the demand will be great enough for them to achieve maximum economies of scale, i.e. in the centre of the city. Thus we would expect the range of business services to be greatest in the largest city in the economy. Partial confirmation of this result is provided by Clemente and Sturgis' finding that there is statistically significant correlation between industrial diversification and city size (Clemente and Sturgis, 1971).

The theory of intra-urban location lies outside the scope of this paper but we may note that since firms providing specialised services will tend to locate at or near the centre of the city, the smaller firms which rely on these services will tend also to locate at or near the centre since they will be willing to pay the high rent costs associated with location near the centre in order to gain proximity to these services.

As the scale of a firm expands and more and more activities are incorporated within the firm's production system, so its ties with the firms providing business services at the centre become weaker and the transport costs of the firm to and from these firms also fall. As they fall the profit maximising location of the firm becomes more distant from the centre. Hence if the theoretical analysis is correct we would expect to find that the average size of firms would tend to increase with the distance they are located from the city centre. This of course is what Martin (1969) found in Greater London and Hoover and Vernon (1959) found in the New York Region:

> If we look at the 101 industry groups in the Region for which comparisons can be made in 1956, we find that in 83 of them the average plant in New York City was considerably smaller than the average plant outside the city.

Returning to the main theme of the argument, for the purpose of construction of the theory we wish to assume that the whole range of business services is available in all cities, but that the cost of any service will tend to decline with city size as the demand for the product increases and economies of scale become possible. What is assumed to be absent from the system is the possibility that firms in a small town can use the business services of a nearby city which is larger. This 'hinterland' effect may be important in practice but is obviously difficult to allow for in a general theory of city size since the spatial system of cities will vary from country to country and region to region.[8]

We shall show that for a representative business service the average cost of production will be decreasing if the total production demanded is less than the optimal output of a single plant, that at rates of output greater than this it will sometimes be increasing but will usually be decreasing and at high rates of output it will tend towards a constant cost of production equal to the minimum cost of production in a single plant.

We assume that a firm operates a process or activity which can provide a particular service at a minimum average cost per unit of output equal to C when the output of the firm is equal to Q. For simplicity we also assume that costs increase and decrease linearly with output and that the average cost per unit of output of the service is equal to $1{\cdot}5C$ if the output is equal to $0{\cdot}5Q$ or $1{\cdot}5Q$. Hence the average cost of the service will be $2C$ if $2Q$ is produced and will approach $2C$ as the output of the service approaches zero. The shape of the average cost curve of the firm is shown in Fig. 8 below.

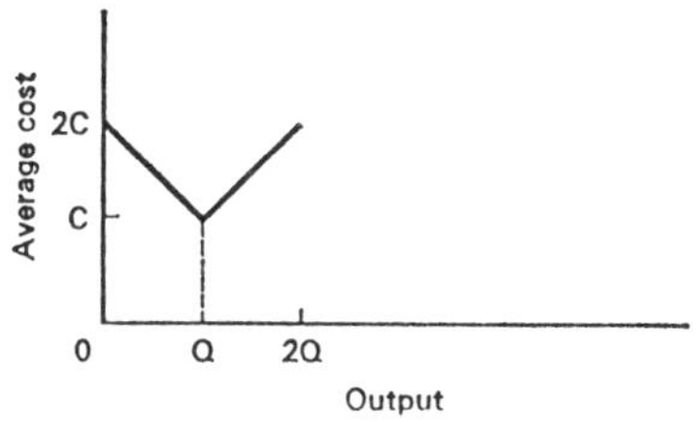

FIG. 8

It is obvious that the output of $2Q$ can be produced more cheaply if two processes are used instead of one. When production is equal to NQ, and N is an integer, the average cost of the service will be C. It might be assumed from this that the average cost curve of the industry could be found by simply repeating the average cost curves of the firm as shown in Fig. 9 where an

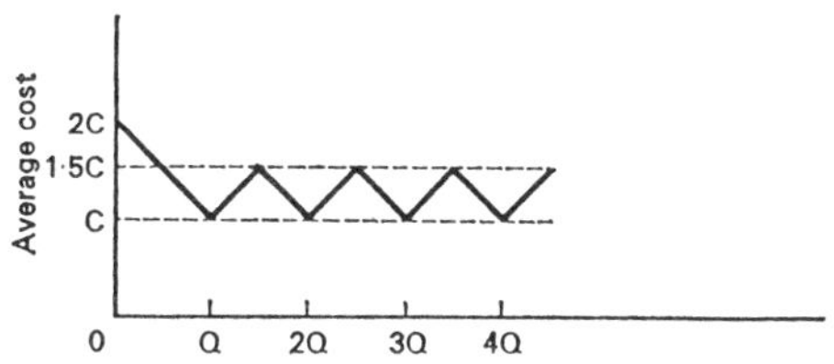

FIG. 9

output of $(N+0{\cdot}5)Q$ is always produced at an average cost of $1{\cdot}5C$.

The average cost curve of the industry does not look like this, however. It is true that $1{\cdot}5Q$ can be produced by one process operated on its own but it can be produced more cheaply if two processes are used, both producing $0{\cdot}75Q$. The average cost of production of $1{\cdot}5Q$ is therefore $1{\cdot}25C$ instead of $1{\cdot}5C$. Similarly the average cost of producing $4{\cdot}5Q$ will not be $1{\cdot}5C$ but $1{\cdot}1C$, whilst the average cost of producing $24{\cdot}5Q$ will be $1{\cdot}02C$. The actual shape of the average cost

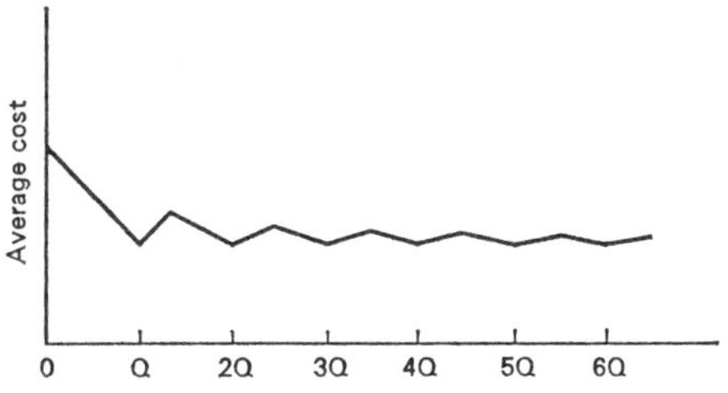

FIG. 10

curve of the industry is shown in Fig. 10. As the number of processes or plants being used to

[8] For a theoretical analysis of the effect of proximity to a large city on a smaller town's growth prospects see von Böventer (1970) and for an empirical study see von Böventer (1969).

provide the service increases, the average cost curve of the industry tends toward a straight line and constant returns to scale, even though considerable economies of scale are available for the individual firm. When the average cost curve of the firm is of the conventional U-shape the average cost curve of the industry will tend towards linearity even more quickly, as shown in Fig. 11,

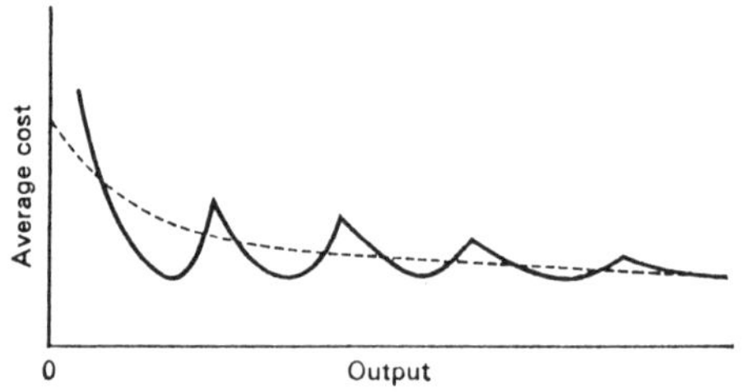

FIG. 11

since only the flattened bottoms of the cost curves are relevant once the demand is great enough.[9]

A curve of the shape shown in Fig. 11 is difficult to handle analytically, but it seems reasonable to approximate the irregular curve by a smooth curve of the type shown as a dotted line in Fig. 11. The trend curve has the property that it passes 'through the average ordinate of each section of the [irregular] curve half-way between its consecutive minima. . . . The trend curve decreases continually at a decreasing rate and is asymptotic to the horizontal line of constant minimum cost' (Joseph, 1933, p. 394).

Since the demand for a business service will be positively correlated with city size, it follows that the trend curve shown in Fig. 11 might also be taken to show the cost of the service as a function of city size. There is one qualification which must be made, however. Since land and labour will be used in the production of the service, the cost of the service as a function of city size will not decrease continually but will start to increase at some point, first at an increasing rate and then at a decreasing rate, as shown by the curve AA' in Fig. 12. The curve AA shows the cost of supplying the service if the cost of land and labour did not vary with city size. When the curve AA is

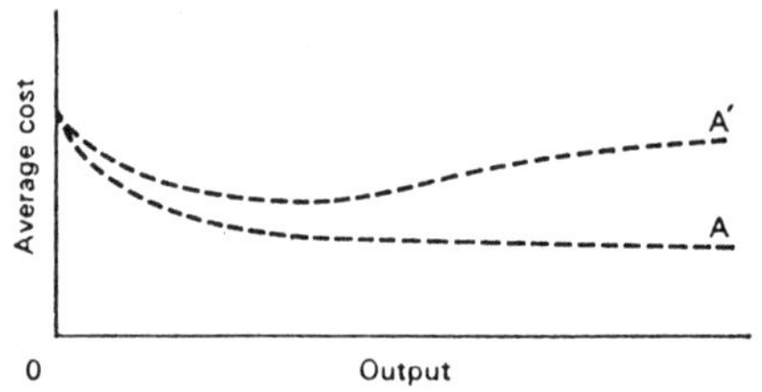

FIG. 12

nearly horizontal the shape of the curve AA' is determined by the variation in the cost of land and labour with city size, and the curve slopes upward at a decreasing rate.

The cost of supplying each of the various business services as a function of city size will be different and can be represented by a different supply curve. Services which can achieve all the attainable economies of scale with a small output will be supplied at minimum cost in a small town or city, particularly if the production process uses little capital and a lot of land and labour. On the other hand services which require a large output to achieve all the economies of scale and which use a lot of capital and little land and labour will be supplied most cheaply in the largest city in the

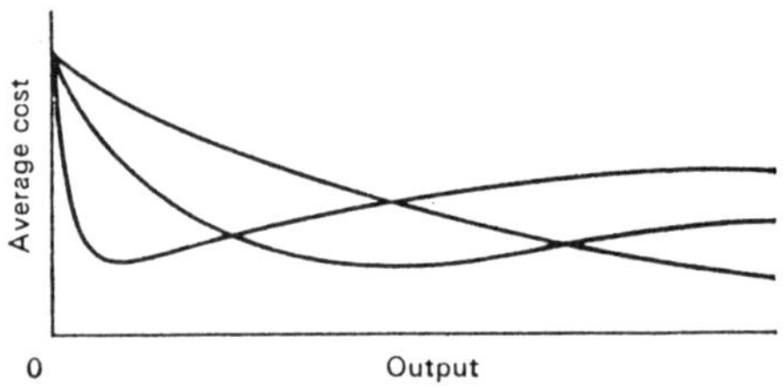

FIG. 13

economy and even there all the economies of scale may not be achieved. Three possible cost of supply curves are shown in Fig. 13.

[9] The Figure is a reproduction of Figure IV in an article by M. F. W. Joseph (1933). See also Patinkin (1947), Figure 3.

The locational choice of the manufacturing firm—partial equilibrium

For the purpose of construction of the theory we have divided the firms in the economy into two types; 'manufacturing' firms which operate at constant returns to scale, and for which the cost of transporting the final product is zero; and firms providing 'business services' whose plants are indivisible and which therefore operate at increasing returns to scale, the service being transportable only at an infinitely high cost.[10]

By assumption, all business services are available in all cities, though, as the analysis in the preceding section shows, the cost of business services will vary with size, being highest in the smallest towns and cities and tending to decrease with city size. On the other hand we assume that each manufacturing firm can choose in which of the cities in the economy to locate. Since the cost of transport of the products of the manufacturing firms is zero and the sales of the firms do not vary with their location, it follows that the most profitable location will be the one at which their manufacturing costs are least.

Consider the locational choice of the individual firm. From its point of view the size distribution of cities in the economy is given, and the relative costs of location in each size of city can be ascertained. The firm will tend to locate in the size of city in which its costs are minimised and profits maximised. It will do this either because it deliberately chooses to locate there or because, if it does not, it will be driven out of business by firms which are located there. In the latter case the process of natural selection ensures that the location of the firm is the same as if it had deliberately set out to maximise profits. For the sake of brevity therefore we assume that the location of the firm is the result of a deliberate choice.

We also assume initially that the firm's inputs are used in fixed proportions. Thus a manufacturing firm uses specified quantities of floor space, labour, business services and capital to produce its output. The prices of these inputs vary with city size as shown in the two previous sections. By calculating the cost of each input as a function of city size and adding the various costs together the firm will be able to find the city size which minimises its costs.

The calculation is illustrated diagrammatically in Fig. 14. The cost of the firm's floor space as a function of city size is shown in part (a), the cost of labour costs is shown in part (b), the cost of the business services it uses is shown in part (c), and the cost of capital is shown in part (d). The curve showing its total costs as a function of city size is shown in part (e), and is found by summing vertically the curves in parts (a), (b), (c), and (d).

When cities are small, the total costs of the firm fall as city size increases because the decreasing cost of business services outweighs the increasing cost of labour and floor space. At some city size total costs are constant for small changes in city size and this is the firm's optimal location; the rate of decrease of the cost of business services exactly equals the rate of increase of the cost of labour and floor space. When cities are larger in size the increasing cost of land and labour outweighs the decreasing cost of business services and the firm's total costs increase as cities increase in size.

It may be noted that a stable equilibrium location at some intermediate city size is only possible if the cost of at least one of the three inputs, land, labour, or business services, either decrease at a decreasing rate or increase at an increasing rate. In previous sections we showed that the price of land and labour are expected to increase at a decreasing rate so that it was essential to the analysis to show in the preceding section

[10] The locational behaviour of the two other possible types of firms is relatively uninteresting and it would add nothing to the analysis to consider them. Firstly, there are firms for which there are economies of scale but which can transport their product at zero cost. The analysis of their locational pattern would not differ from that of the 'manufacturing' firm. Secondly, there are firms which operate at constant returns to scale but for which the cost of transporting the product is 'infinitely' high. These firms could be considered as providing business services.

cost of business services should decrease at a decreasing rate. If, for example, the cost of business services decreased at an increasing rate, there would only be two possible city sizes, very small and very large, since all firms would find it unprofitable to locate in a city of any intermediate size.

For each manufacturing firm there is, however, an optimal city size, and location in a city of this size reduces the firm's costs to a minimum and maximises its profits. Obviously since in any national economy there are not cities of every possible size but only a limited number, most firms will not be able to locate in a city which is optimal in size for them. A firm which cannot locate in the optimal size city will have to locate either in the largest city which is smaller than the optimal size or in the smallest city which is larger than the optimal size. In one of these cities (and, possibly, but not necessarily, in both) its costs will be minimised and profits maximised. This city size we call 'nearly optimal'.

The optimal, or nearly optimal, city size will not be the same for all types of manufacturing firm but will depend upon the proportions in which they use the various kinds of input. At one extreme, firms or plants which use large quantities of land and low wage labour relative to their use of high wage labour, capital and business services will locate in the smallest cities. An example of this type of firm would seem to be firms in the textile industry which require cheap labour and tend to locate in small towns. Morse, Mathur, and Swamy (1968) show that the textile industry in the U.S.A. tends to be concentrated in small towns.[11] British Census data shows that this is also true in Great Britain.

Table 1 shows that the proportion of the working population employed in the textile industry is greatest in urban areas with populations less than 50,000. It also shows that it is second greatest in the conurbations but this is misleading since the cotton towns of Lancashire and the woollen towns of the West Riding of Yorkshire are included in the South-East Lancashire and West Yorkshire conurbations though for the

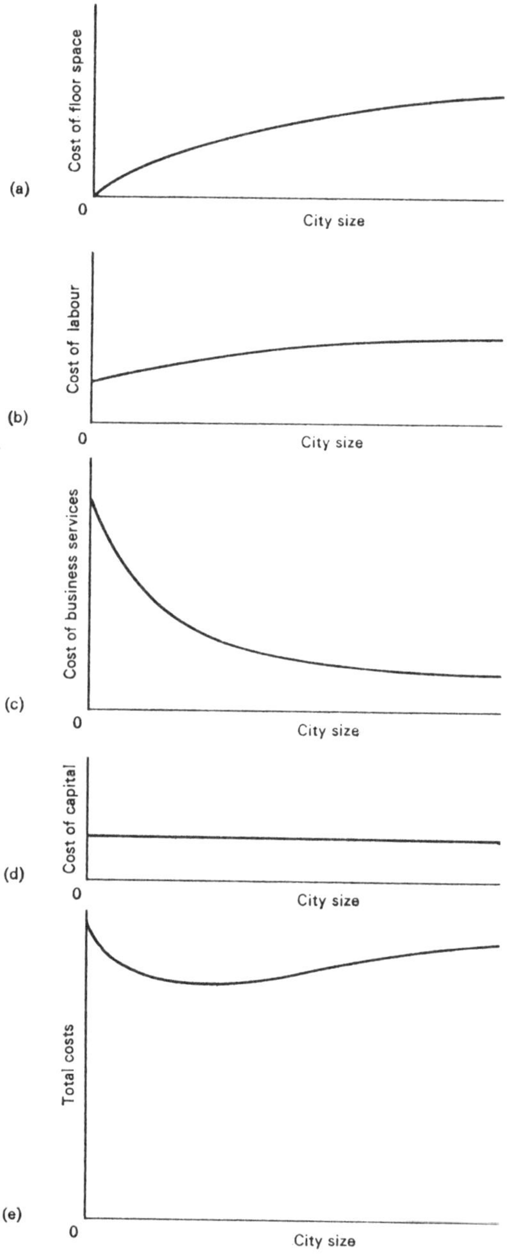

FIG. 14

[11] But they note that this is 'not evident in India except perhaps in incipient form'.

Table 1

PROPORTIONS PER 100,000 PERSONS IN EMPLOYMENT BY INDUSTRY, ENGLAND AND WALES, 1961

Industry Order or Minimum List Heading	*Six Conurbations*	*Areas outside conurbations — Urban areas with population of 100,000 or more*	*50,000 and less than 100,000*	*less than 50,000*	*Rural Districts*
Order X Textiles	377	304	212	448	138
M.L.H.411 Production of man-made fibres	5	42	18	36	16
412 Spinning and doubling of cotton, flax, and man-made fibres	9	81	15	28	58
413 Weaving of cotton, linen, and man-made fibres	30	35	47	113	30
414 Woollen and worsted	151	9	29	35	17
423 Textile finishing	39	26	8	42	12

Source: Census 1961, England and Wales, Industry Tables part I (London: H.M.S.O. 1966) Table A.

the purposes of the theory they should probably be considered as individual towns.

At the opposite extreme, firms or plants which use large quantities of business services, capital, and high-wage labour relative to their use of low-wage labour and floor space will locate in the largest cities. Example of this type of firm might be found in the insurance, banking, and finance complexes which dominate the centres of the largest cities although it is difficult to know whether firms in the complex constitute 'business services' subject to indivisibilities or are the firms using the business services. A better example of plants of this type are the head offices of manufacturing companies which tend to concentrate in the largest cities of any national economy. Thus 52% of the 500 largest British industrial companies had their headquarters in London in 1969 (Evans, 1970b) whilst 33% of 500 largest U.S. industrial companies had their headquarters in New York City in 1963 (Goodwin, 1965).

If we relax our initial assumption that the firm's inputs are used in fixed proportions, and allow the proportions to be varied, then we cannot use the diagrammatic analysis. A mathematical solution to the problem is possible, however, though little is added to the analysis. At the cost minimising or profit maximising location, once the firm has adjusted its inputs to take account of the price structure ruling in that city, any move to a slightly smaller or slightly larger city will result in no increase in costs. The increase in rent and wages and, possibly, in the cost of some business services will be just equal to the decrease in the cost of other business services. Any move to a distinctly larger or distinctly smaller city will result in an increase in costs, however.

One point of interest which does arise when firms can vary the proportions in which they use inputs to take account of differences in relative prices is that, as prices vary, firms will tend to substitute cheaper inputs for dearer. In the large city business services, capital, and high-wage labour will tend to be substituted for floor space and low-wage labour. Thus we would expect to find, for example, that the proportion of the working population in the higher paid occupations increases with city size. Mathur (1970) demonstrates that this is true for S.M.S.A.'s in the United States. Possibly this is the explanation for the fact that, as mentioned earlier, income inequality in U.S. cities increases with city size.

The urban hierarchy—general equilibrium

In the previous section we dealt with the locational choice of the individual firm in partial equilibrium. In this section we attempt to show how the locational choices of all the manufacturing firms in the economy will interact to determine the size distribution of cities in the economy in general equilibrium.

The distribution of city sizes has been studied extensively by geographers and others starting with the pioneering work of Singer (1936) and Zipf (1949). These two authors suggested that the size distribution of cities generally corresponds to a rank-size distribution or the similar Pareto distribution. Later researchers (e.g. Berry, 1961; Stewart, 1958; Rosing, 1966) have questioned the general applicability of the rank-size rule. In particular Berry (1961) analysed the city-size distributions in 38 countries and showed that whilst 13 of the countries had rank-size distributions the remainder had either primate distributions or distributions intermediate between primacy and rank-size. Primacy exists 'when a stratum of small towns and cities is dominated by one or more very large cities and there are fewer cities of intermediate sizes than would be expected from the rank-size rule' (Berry, 1961).

One characteristic which is general to every city-size distribution is that the number of cities in any size-class tends to increase as the average size of cities in any size-class is reduced; e.g. there tend to be more cities with populations between 300,000 and 400,000 in any economy than there are cities with populations between 400,000 and 500,000. If we use the term 'dense' to denote the number of cities in any size class, then we can say that empirical evidence shows that the distribution of city sizes decreases in density as average city size increases. It is this pattern which we intend to try to explain.

What we shall do here is to develop an intuitive approach to a solution of the problem. We are not yet able to give a rigorous mathematical proof although it is clear in what way the problem should be approached. Each city can be viewed as a 'club' or 'coalition' of which manufacturing firms are members. The firms in the economy can be viewed as players in an n-person game in which each firm acting independently can join coalitions of other firms and usually cannot be barred. The 'pay-off' to each firm is a function of the size of coalition of which he is a member and the 'pay-off functions' of the firms are not all the same. Research on the theory of economic clubs may, in due course, help to provide a rigorous solution of the city size distribution in general equilibrium but to date it has usually been assumed that all the participants have identical tastes. See Buchanan (1965), Pauly (1968, 1970). Other research which may be relevant is being carried out into the economic importance of the 'core', the allocation of resources in the economy which cannot be blocked by any coalition, but here the concern is usually with the situation as the number of participants tends to infinity.[12] See Aumann (1964), Vind (1965), Hildenbrand (1968). It is, however, obvious that there is a finite number of cities and a rigorous solution of the problem of the equilibrium urban hierarchy can only result from considering an economy in which there is a finite number of firms, so that most of the work on the core of an economy is not relevant.[13]

We shall demonstrate with two simple models that the city size distribution is likely under most circumstances to have the property mentioned earlier. We assume that each firm uses its inputs in fixed proportions and that labour costs, land costs, and the cost of business services are each a function of city size. Then each firm's costs and profits are a function of city size and a graph of its costs can be drawn as in Fig. 14d. We also assume that the size of a city is a linear function of the number of manufacturing firms in the city. Furthermore we regard each city as a coalition formed by a group of manufacturing firms. Each firm will tend to join the coalition of the size which minimises its production costs; either it joins it deliberately or, by a process of natural selection, only those firms which are members of the optimal size coalition or of the nearly optimal size coalition survive.

Imagine that the economy starts without any cities but that each firm knows the costs of

[12] As the number of participants increases the core shrinks to a single point which is both a competitive allocation and Pareto optimal.

[13] But see Pauly's 1970 paper on 'Clubs and Cores'. It is worth noting that Pauly remarks that cities, among other things, could be profitably treated as clubs for the purposes of economic theory.

location in each possible coalition size (but not the costs for other firms). The firms would tend to form coalitions, initially on a random basis, later more purposefully. At the first stage those firms which wished to be single-member coalitions would stay apart but those which wished to join larger coalitions would immediately join with others. Any coalition which was larger than the rest at the end of the first stage would become the optimal location of those firms desiring to locate in coalitions of that size or larger who would then move to it. Other firms would move out of it on the third stage as it became too large for them and would join smaller coalitions. The process of movement and adjustment would continue until a size distribution of coalitions was reached. In most circumstances this would approximate to the sort of size distribution of cities which is usually observed, in that the density of the distribution would decrease as with increases in average city size. We illustrate with two simple models.

(1) Suppose that each of the firms in an economy would minimise its costs by location in a coalition of a different size, and that there are as many firms as there are possible sizes of coalitions, i.e. if there are M firms in the economy the possible sizes of coalition are 1, 2, 3, ..., M. Thus there is one firm whose costs are at a minimum if it is on its own, one firm whose costs are minimised in a coalition of two, one whose costs are minimised in a coalition of three, etc. With each integer there is associated a firm which finds its lowest costs in a coalition of firms equal to that integer in number. For simplicity we can use these integers to name or number the firms.

We also suppose that if each firm is not in its optimal size coalition but in a coalition which is one firm larger or smaller then its costs are increased by $x\%$, and that, more generally, if it is in a coalition which is n firms larger or smaller than the optimum then its costs are increased by $nx\%$. A reasonably stable hierarchy of coalitions under these conditions is shown in Table 2 where the coalitions are shown in inverse order of magnitude.

The reason why the hierarchy of coalitions is reasonably stable can be seen in Fig. 15. The firms are numbered along the horizontal axis; the numbers also indicate the optimal size coalition of each firm. The vertical axis indicates the costs of each member of each coalition as a proportion of its costs in its optimal coalition. The graphs show the costs of each member of the smaller coalitions shown in Table 2. The relative stability of the hierarchy will be realised if the straight lines of the graph are extended upwards. It can easily be checked that given the existing size distribution of coalitions every firm's costs would be increased by a move to any other coalition. The marginal firms in each coalition are listed in the second row of Table 2; these are the firms that would lose least by a move to the next smallest or next largest coalition.

It may be noted that if firms are not short-sighted and realise that if they move to another coalition the size of that coalition will be changed

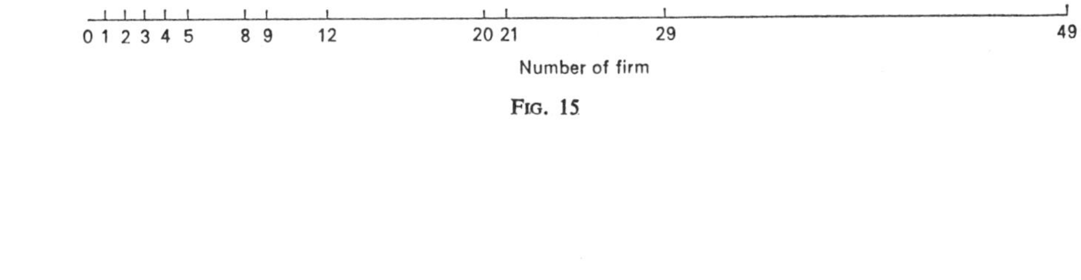

FIG. 15

Table 2

THE HIERARCHY OF COALITIONS (MODEL 1)

	Characteristics of coalitions												
Coalition size	1	2		5		12		29		70		169	
Marginal firms in each coalition by the numbers of the firms' optimal coalition sizes	1	2	3	4	8	9	20	21	49	50	119	120	288
Costs of the marginal firms in each coalition as a proportion of their optimal costs	1·0	1·0	1·1	1·1	1·3	1·3	1·8	1·8	3·0	3·0	5·9	5·9	12·9

then the hierarchy becomes rather less stable. Marginal firms whose optimal coalition size is smaller than the one they are in will not be made worse off by a move to a smaller city and the system may move away from equilibrium but should return to it.[14]

Note that the hierarchy of coalitions is such that the size of each one (above the third smallest) is equal to approximately 0·414 the size of the next highest,[15] so that the main feature of the usual city size distribution is reproduced, i.e. the density of the distribution decreases as the coalitions increase in size. In this model, however, the costs of the marginal firms diverge further and further from the optimum as the size of the coalitions increases. In the case of real world cities this is unlikely to be true, since, if it were true, variations in city size would be considered much more important by firms and the lack of cities which are intermediate in size between the larger cities in the economy would have been thought a serious problem. In the second model presented below this feature is absent.

(2) In the second model we again suppose that there is associated with each positive integer a single firm and that this firm would minimise its production costs in a coalition of firms equal in number to that integer. We now assume, however, that the costs of firms vary in a different way. We assume that if the firm's optimal coalition is N firms in size and it is in a coalition of $N+n$ firms or $N-n$ firms, then its costs will be $(N+n)/N$ times its minimum costs.

This pattern of cost variation seems more realistic than that in the first model. It states that equal proportional changes in coalition size result in equal proportional changes in costs, whereas in the first model equal *absolute* changes in coalition size result in equal proportional changes in costs. The new assumption is more in keeping with the earlier theoretical analysis of the rate of variation of input costs. The rate of increase of land and labour costs as city size increases is much greater when cities are small than when they are large. Similarly the rate of decrease in the cost of business services as city size increases is much greater when cities are small. It follows that if a firm's optimal coalition size were small the proportional increase in a firm's costs resulting from its having to locate in a coalition a certain number larger or smaller than its optimum will be much greater when this optimum is small than when it is large. One can see intuitively that if a firm would minimise its costs by location in a city of 100,000, but it has to locate in a city of 1,100,000, its costs are likely to be proportionately greater than the minimum than if it wished to locate in a city of 10,000,000 and had to locate in one of 11,000,000.

Details of the hierarchy of coalitions which

[14] Thus suppose Firm 9 accidentally or deliberately moves to Coalition 5 making it 6. F(irm) 4 then gains by a move to C(oalition) 2 making it 3. F2 moves to C1 making it C2. Then F9 gains by returning to C11 making it C12, F4 returns to C4 making it C5, F1 leaves C2 and F2 rejoins F3.

[15] If X_n is the number of firms in the nth smallest coalition,

$$X_{n+1} = 2X_n + X_{n-1} \text{ and } X_{n+1} = (\sqrt{2}-1)X_n.$$

Table 3

A Hierarchy of Coalitions (Model 2)

	Characteristics of Coalitions										
Coalition Size	1	3		9		27		81		243	
Marginal firms in each coalition by the numbers of the firms' optimal coalition sizes	1	2	4	5	13	14	40	41	121	122	364
Costs of the marginal firms in each coalition as a proportion of their optimal costs	1·0	1·3	1·3	1·4	1·4	1·5	1·5	1·5	1·5	1·5	1·5

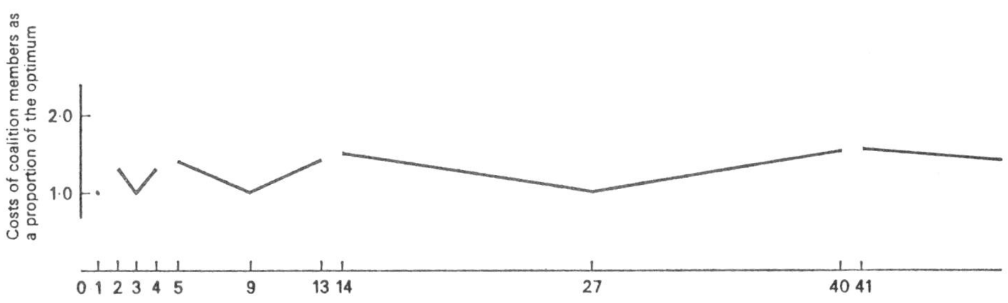

Fig. 16

might be the result of firms attempting to minimise their costs under these conditions are shown in Table 3 and Fig. 16.

The most interesting feature of the second model as compared with the first is that the costs of the marginal firms do not diverge by increasing amounts from the optimum as the size of their coalition increases. Despite the existence of a hierarchy of coalitions in which each coalition is three times the size of the next largest, no firm's costs are greater than 50% above the minimum.

It may be noted that if firms are not short-sighted and realise that if they move to another coalition the size of that coalition will be changed the hierarchy becomes rather unstable. It is always worthwhile for Firm 2 to join Firm 1 and then for Firm 1 to move again. A similar hierarchy could be formed of coalitions of 1, 2, 7, 21, 63, 189, etc. This has much the same characteristics as the hierarchy detailed in Table 3 but Firm 2 can no longer reduce its costs by moving. On the other hand Firm 4 can then reduce its costs by joining Firms 2 and 3 which puts Firm 2 back in its previous situation.

These stability problems are relatively unimportant, however. What we have shown with these two models is that an 'urban hierarchy' can result from the locational choices of individual firms each acting to maximise its own profits. Obviously a final conceptual leap is required to get from the notion of a hierarchy of coalitions to the idea of a hierarchy of cities, but, after allowing for variations in the size of firms and the existence of firms in business services and consumer services, the above analysis does provide an explanation for the existence of urban hierarchies in industrial economies. Furthermore this explanation appears to be relatively robust for, despite the differences in the assumptions made in the construction of the two models, a recognisable hierarchy is obtained in both.

There would appear to be only two cases in which we would not obtain a hierarchy of coalitions recognisably similar to the usual urban hierarchy. In the first place, if all the manufacturing firms required all the inputs in identical proportions, their cost functions would be identical and the result would be a number of coalitions (or cities) identical in size. In the second place if the number of firms for whom N was the optimal size coalition was directly proportional to N the hierarchy of coalitions would not decrease in density as the coalitions increase in size. In that case the hierarchy would be uniformly dense. Both these conditions are highly unlikely so that a hierarchy of coalitions with the sort of characteristics usually observed in the urban hierarchy is the most likely form of hierarchy.

The actual hierarchy in any economy will depend upon the size of the economy (i.e. the number of firms in the economy) and the state of technology (i.e. the proportion of the firms in the economy for which each coalition size is optimal and the variation in their costs with city size). As an example of the effect of an increase in the size of the economy a simple doubling of the number of firms in the economy represented in the second model, so that there are two firms associated with each positive integer instead of one results in a change in the hierarchy of coalitions from 1, 3, 9, 27, 81, etc. or 1, 2, 7, 21, 63, etc., to 1, 1, 2, 4, 6, 10, 16, 28, 46, etc., which is a considerably denser hierarchy than the others. Thus the number of coalitions with less than 30 members increases from four to eight if the number of firms in the economy is doubled. Other results of the increase in the size of the economy are that the largest coalition (or city) increases in size and the maximum divergence of any firm's costs from the minimum is reduced; in the example this maximum divergence is reduced from 50% above the minimum to 25% above the minimum.

By manipulating the number of firms in the economy and the proportions finding their optimal location in each coalition size it would no doubt be possible to generate a hierarchy of coalitions which obeyed the rank-size rule. Possibly this could be done using simulation techniques. Another line of research might be to attempt to find the size-distribution which is maximally non-committal with respect to the missing information on the number and cost characteristics of firms, and this might be done using the methods of entropy maximisation. See Wilson (1970).

One way in which the discussion in this section might be modified and improved would be to relax the assumption that the inputs of each firm are fixed in proportion. We should then allow cheaper inputs to be substituted for dearer as the price structure changes with city size. It is probable that a hierarchy of the expected type would still result, however, whilst the complexity of the problem would be increased enormously and an analytical solution of this sort of n-person game would be extremely difficult.

Normative aspects of the city size distribution

Even when we can show that an urban hierarchy will come about if each firm in the economy attempts to maximise profits, we still would like to know whether this hierarchy is in some sense socially optimal. It can be shown that in a world-of-equals economy in which each firm wishes to locate in the same size of coalition then the economy will be Pareto optimal provided that the number of firms in the economy is divisible without remainder by the number of firms in the optimal size coalition (Pauly, 1970). This is a highly artificial and unrealistic model, however, and whilst Pauly conjectures that the 'tendencies' described by the world of equals model may also hold for non-homogeneous cases, considerably more work is required before we can completely understand the welfare economics of the urban hierarchy.

If we allow firms to adjust their inputs to minimise the effect of variations in relative prices as city size increases then it can be shown that the competitive allocation of resources will definitely not be Pareto optimal, since business services will be under-utilised and land and labour will be over-utilised in any city.

We consider business services first. Any expansion in the demand for business services will allow the firms providing the services to reduce the average cost of the services as they take advantage of the possible economies of scale. If a firm in any city expands its output then its demand for business services will increase and this will result in a reduction in the cost of business services. This reduction in the cost of business services will benefit both the firm expanding its output and all the other manufacturing firms in the city. Thus an expansion in the firm's demand for business services causes external economies, but these external economies are not taken into account by the firm when it decides its optimal output and its use of business services. Because of this the use of business services in any city will be less than would be socially optimal.

Contrast this with the use of labour. Any expansion in the use of labour will lead to an increase in wage rates since the increase in the population will lead to an increase in the area of the city and hence to an increase in rents and transport costs. Wage rates will therefore increase to compensate for increased living costs. The increase in wage rates and rents will raise the costs of both the expanding firm and all the other manufacturing firms in the city.

The same argument applies to increases in the use of floor space. Any expansion in the use of floor space by firms takes it away from residential use and causes a compensating increase in the area of the city. As a result rent, travel costs and wage rates increase.

To the extent that these increases in rents and wage rates reflect increases in the value of land (land, itself, not floorspace) they only result in a transfer of capital value and not in a diversion of resources. These capital transfers are merely pecuniary external diseconomies and do not cause the economy to diverge from Pareto optimality. On the other hand, to the extent that they reflect increases in travel costs and building costs they are technological external diseconomies causing a diversion of resources which results in the economy diverging from optimality.[16] Because of this the use of labour and floor space in any city will be greater than would be socially optimal.

Two points of interest arise out of this discussion. In the first place there is no suggestion that there is some single optimal size of city. Instead the analysis implies that there is some optimal city size distribution which may or may not differ from the existing hierarchy. In the second place it is argued above that business services are underused and labour and floor space is overused in all cities both large and small. Indeed, since the cost of business services declines with output *at a decreasing rate* and wages and rents increase with city size *at a decreasing rate*, it may be that the divergence from optimality is greater in small cities than in large cities. This conclusion runs counter to much theorising on city size in which it is usually argued that very large cities should be reduced in size implying that the deviation from optimality increases with city size (above a certain size). The difference in conclusions may of course result from the fact that previous researches have usually been concerned about congestion costs whilst we assume that the pricing problems of the transport system are solved and that there is no unpriced congestion. See Neutze (1965), Reynolds (1966).

There is, however, one way in which, using the theory of city size, we may show both that large cities may become too large and that new towns ought to be built. Suppose that in the course of an economy's development new firms come into existence which would minimise their location costs in very small towns. These firms could move into existing small towns but if they did it is probable that, initially, they would have to pay very high wages because the supply of labour would be inelastic in the short run. They would have to draw workers from surrounding towns and cities by high wages and also encourage workers to move to the small town. It may be that it would take a very long time for equilibrium to be reached during which time the cost of location in the town would be high. The firm could avoid these costs by location on the periphery of an existing large city. The firm would have to pay a wage which would draw workers

[16] In a recent paper Lave (1970) correctly describes increases in travel costs as technological diseconomies but incorrectly describes *all* increases in rent costs as pecuniary diseconomies. Increases in the rent of floor space result in the diversion of resources into the construction of more floor space on each site.

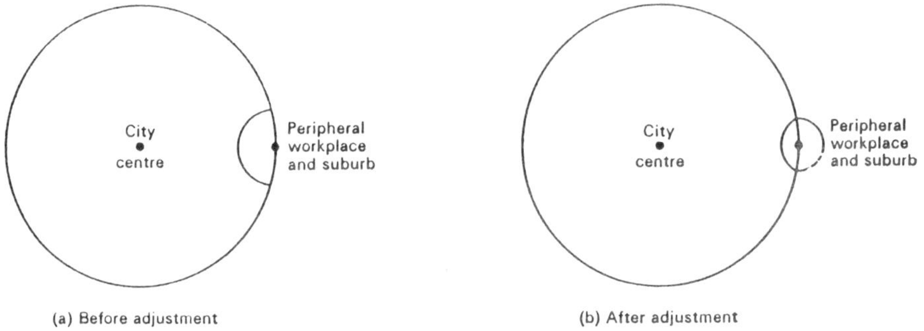

FIG. 17

away from the city centre, but the wage rate would not have to be as high as it would be in the short run in the small town whilst rents would be cheaper. Furthermore some adaptation to the changed situation would take place within the city. Workers would change their residences to live nearer their work and would move to new housing built on the periphery beyond the new industrial firms. The pattern of location before and after the process of relocation is shown in Fig. 17. In equilibrium the firm's rent would have increased and its wage rates would have decreased until they were both slightly above the equilibrium rate in a small town. If other firms locate in the same area the cost of business services will tend to fall until it too is slightly above the cost in the small town in equilibrium.

The increase in the cost to the firms at the centre of the large city will not be too great unless the number of firms at the periphery is large and the city becomes ringed with industrial suburbs as in Fig. 18. Because the drain on the labour supply is now very great, firms at the centre will have to pay considerably higher wages. Furthermore any increase in their demand for labour will result in a higher increase in wages and rents at the centre than would otherwise be necessary since the increased demand can only be met by the new workers living beyond, and travelling to work across, the new industrial suburbs.

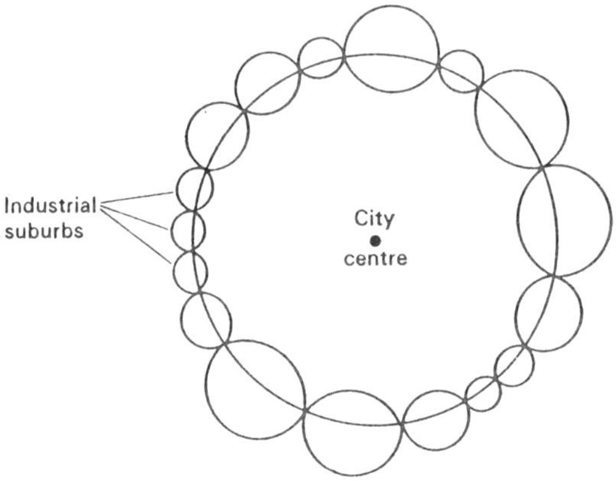

FIG. 18

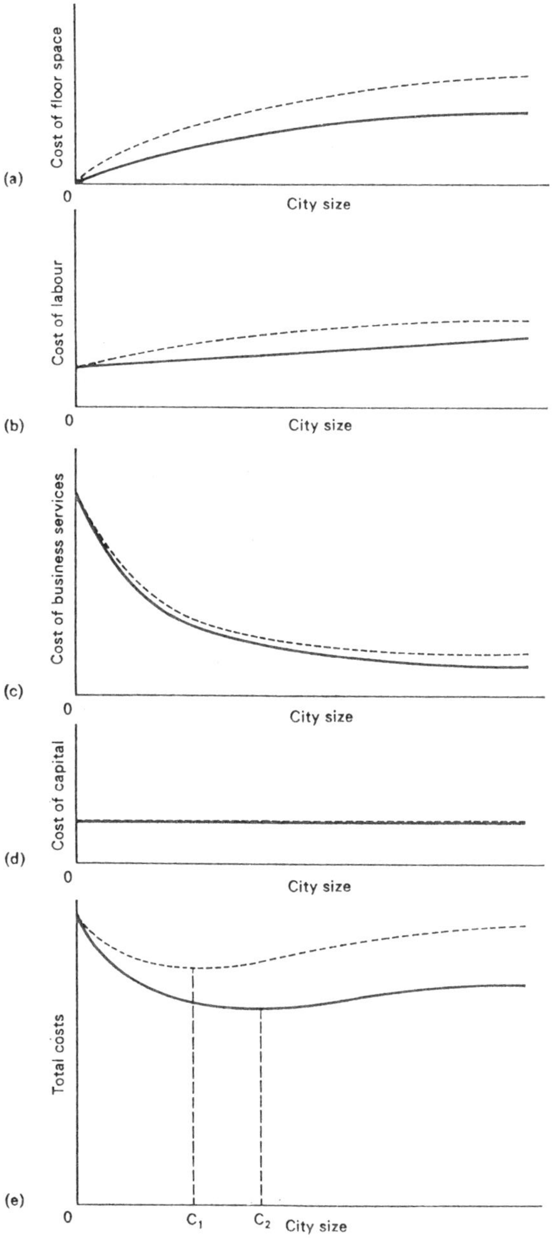
Cost of floor space
(a)
0
City size
Cost of labour
(b)
0
City size
Cost of business services
(c)
0
City size
Cost of capital
(d)
0
City size
Total costs
(e)
0
C1
C2
City size

FIG. 19

Obviously one way of solving this problem would be to construct new small towns and encourage or direct both the suburban firms and their labour force to locate in these new towns. The analysis therefore provides some justification for a 'new towns' policy and gives a possible answer to Alonso's question 'What are new towns for?' (Alonso, 1970). It must be borne in mind, however, that we have no theory of the intra-urban location of firms and we therefore have not taken into account the benefits of location near to or within a large city but not at its centre. These benefits are not negligible. Therefore the above analysis does not provide an unqualified justification for a policy of 'overspilling' firms and people to new or expanded towns.

The effect of changing transport technology

What will be the effect of changes in transport speeds on the city size distribution? We shall show that if the speed of transport of commuters increases or the relative cost of commuting falls, then small towns will, on average, lose population whilst large towns will gain population.

An increase in the speed of transport of commuters or of a reduction in the relative cost of commuting will result in a fall in the slope of the rent gradient (Evans, 1970a, Chapter XI). Furthermore if the population of the city stays the same, the rent at the city centre and the wage premium required by workers to live in that size city will both fall. If the transport improvements occur in all cities simultaneously, these cost reductions will occur in all cities, though, obviously, the larger the city, the larger the reduction. Furthermore, because of the fall in rents and wage rates the cost of business services will also fall in the cities of every size, though, again, the fall will be larger in larger cities. The resulting change in the production costs of a representative firm is shown in Fig. 19. The cost of the firm's floor space as a function of city size is shown in part (a), the cost of labour is shown in part (b), and the cost of the business services it uses is shown in part (c). The curves indicating the functional relationships before and after the change in transport technology are shown by dotted and solid lines respectively. The unchanged cost of capital is shown in part (d). The curves indicating the firm's total costs as a function of city size before and after the change are shown in part (e) and are found by summing vertically the curves in parts (a), (b), (c) and (d).

The total production costs of the firm fall at each possible city size but they tend to fall by an amount which increases with city size. Therefore the optimal size city for this firm will be greater after the change in transport technology than it was before it. In Fig. 19(c) this is shown by the fact that the minimum point of the solid line, C_2, lies further to the right than the minimum point of the dotted line, C_1. This will be true for every manufacturing firm; each one will find its minimum cost location in a larger city. How much larger will depend on the characteristic inputs of each firm, but it is clear that the smaller towns will generally lose firms (and population) whilst the largest will generally gain firms (and population). The proportionate increase or decrease in the size of cities as a function of city size predicted by this analysis is shown by a line *AA* in Fig. 20.

If the total population and the total number of firms is increasing over the period of adjustment of the economy to the change in transport technology, small towns are less likely to decrease in size and large cities are likely to increase still more in size. The changed relationship between growth and city size is shown in Fig. 20 by the line *BB*.

It is interesting to compare this prediction with the rates of growth of U.S. S.M.S.A.'s in the decade 1950-60. Stanback and Knight (1970) found that the rate of growth was greatest for medium-size S.M.S.A.'s rather than large size S.M.S.A.'s as shown in the graph in Fig. 21. Furthermore the pattern of growth was the same in all the regions of the United States. It is probable that this result is due to the fact that the major transport improvements of the period did not affect all cities equally. The major change would be the increased use of automobiles and the beginnings of the construction of urban freeways. This type of transport improvement would

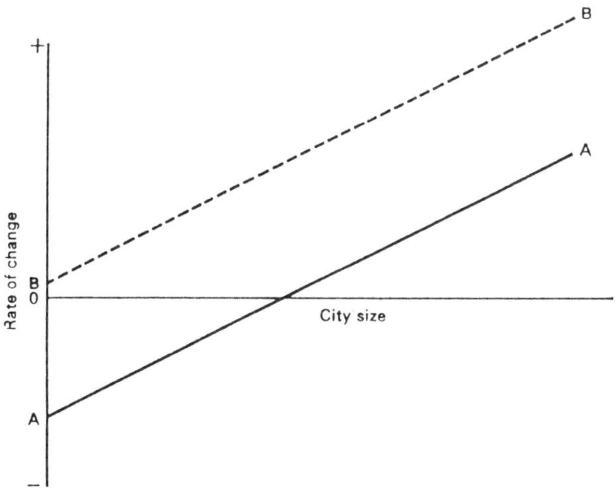

FIG. 20

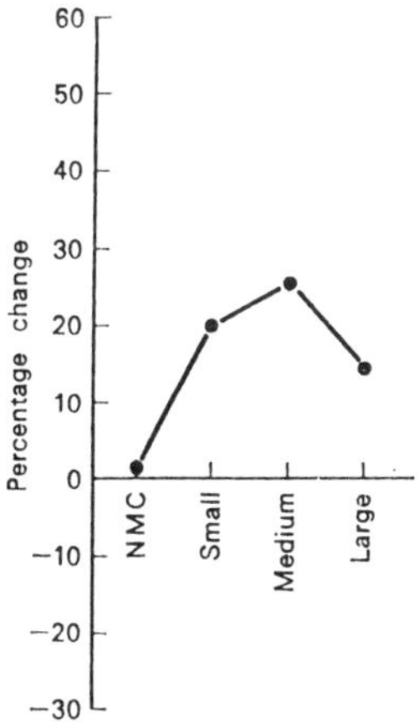

FIG. 21

Source: Stanback and Knight (1970) p. 97

Notes: NMC = Non-metropolitan counties
Small = S.M.S.A.'s with 50,001-200,000 population non-S.M.S.A. counties with a city of 25,000 or more
Medium = S.M.S.A.'s with 200,001-1,600,000 population
Large = S.M.S.A.'s with 1,600,001 or more population

affect large cities least since they usually have efficient public transport systems, congestion restricts the use of the automobile, and land costs restrict the construction of freeways. As a result we would not expect the rate of growth of large cities to be as great as the rate of growth of medium-size cities, since in medium-size cities the transport improvements would have their greatest effect.

In conclusion

In this paper we have constructed a theory which explains the existence of urban hierarchies in industrial economies. In so doing we deliberately excluded the spatial aspects of the economy from consideration. We did this to simplify the construction of the theory and also to reveal the articulation of the theory more clearly. What we did not wish to imply is that city size is the only factor which enters into the choice of location of the manufacturing firm.

Other theories of location emphasise other factors, however; Weberian location theory tends to emphasise proximity to markets or to sources of supply; central place theory emphasises the importance of choosing the most profitable location to serve the market area or the supply area.

In the understanding of patterns of location in the real world all types of theoretical explanation must be taken into account. Thus a manufacturing firm will be located either near its raw materials or at its market; if it is located at its market, it will tend to locate near the centre of its market area in order to maximise its profits, but in choosing its location it must also weigh up the relative costs of location in each of the cities in the area in order to decide whether it is worth trading centrality for location in a larger or smaller city. Yet since each type of theory explains location in a different way and stresses some economic forces at the expense of others, each will be able to explain the location patterns of different types of plant, firm or industry.

In two major respects the theory presented in this paper is inadequate. In the first place it fails to take uncertainty into account. This may be an important omission. Lichtenberg (1960) and Vernon (1960) both stress the importance of location in New York City as a means of reducing uncertainty both through the great speed with which information can be obtained and through the fact that almost any business service is available on demand when it is needed. Uncertainty is a difficult concept to handle, however; developing a theory of city size which allowed for risk and uncertainty might be a difficult task. A possible line of approach might be to use the methods of portfolio analysis and to regard each city as a 'portfolio' of firms.[17]

In the second place the theory fails to incorporate a theory of the intra-urban location of firms. The assumption that all employment is located at the centre of the city is a considerable simplification but it obviously conflicts with the facts. On the other hand it is true that the density of employment is highest at the city centre and declines steeply with distance from the centre so that the conflict is hopefully not too important.

REFERENCES

ALONSO, W. (1970). What are new towns for? *Urban Studies*, Vol. 7, No. 1, pp. 37-55.

—— (1964). *Location and Land Use*. Cambridge, Mass: Harvard U.P.

AUMANN, R. J. (1964). Markets with a continuum of traders. *Econometrica*, Vol. 32, No. 1-2, pp. 39-50.

BERRY, B. J. L. (1961). City Size Distributions and Economic Development. *Economic Development and Cultural Change*, Vol. 9, No. 4, pp. 573-588. Partially reprinted in Berry and Horton (1970).

—— (1964), Cities as Systems within Systems of Cities. *Papers and Proceedings of the Regional Science Association*, Vol. 13, pp. 147-163.

—— (1967). *Geography of Market Areas and Retail Distribution*. Englewood Cliffs, N.J.: Prentice-Hall, Inc.

—— and HORTON, F. E. (1970). *Geographical Perspectives on Urban Systems*. Englewood Cliffs, N.J.: Prentice-Hall, Inc.

—— and PRED, A. (1961). *Central Place Studies: A*

[17] The clearest exposition of portfolio analysis is given by Sharpe (1970).

Bibliography of Theory and Applications. Philadelphia: Regional Science Research Institute.

—— and WOLDENBERG, M. J. (1967). Rivers and Central Places: Analogous Systems? *Journal of Regional Science*, Vol. 7, No. 2, pp. 129-139.

VON BÖVENTER, E. (1969). Determinants of Migration into West German Cities, 1956-61, 1961-66. *Papers and Proceedings of the Regional Science Association*, Vol. 23, pp. 53-62.

—— (1970). Optimal Spatial Structure and Regional Development. *Kyklos*, Vol. 23, No. 4, pp. 903-926.

BREIT, W. and HOCHMAN, H. M. (1968). *Readings in Microeconomics.* New York: Holt, Rinehart, and Winston, Inc.

BUCHANAN, J. M. (1965). An Economic Theory of Clubs. *Economica*, Vol. 32, No. 1, pp. 1-14.

CLEMENTE, F. and STURGIS, R. B. (1971). Population Size and Industrial Diversification. *Urban Studies*, Vol. 8, No. 1, pp. 65-68.

EVANS, A. W. (1970a). Residential Location in Cities. Unpublished manuscript.

—— (1970b). The Location of the Headquarters of Industrial Companies. Unpublished manuscript.

FARBMAN, M. (1971). Family Income Concentration in Urban Areas in the United States. Unpublished manuscript. The University of Glasgow.

FINDLAY, R. (1970). *Trade and Specialization.* London: Penguin Education.

FUCHS, V. R. (1967). *Differentials in Hourly Earnings by Region and City Size, 1959.* N.B.E.R. Occasional Paper 101. New York: National Bureau of Economic Research.

GOODWIN, W. (1965). The Management Center in the United States. *The Geographical Review*, Vol. 55, No. 1, pp. 1-16.

HAIG, R. M. (1926). Toward an Understanding of the Metropolis: Part II. *Quarterly Journal of Economics*, Vol. 40, No. 3, pp. 402-434.

HIGGS, R. (1970). Central Place Theory and Regional Urban Hierarchies: an empirical note. *Journal of Regional Science*, Vol. 10, No. 2, pp. 253-255.

HILDENBRAND, W. (1968). The Core of an Economy with a Measure Space of Economic Agents. *Review of Economic Studies*, Vol. 35, No. 4, pp. 443-452.

HOOVER, E. M. (1948). *The Location of Economic Activity.* New York: McGraw-Hill.

—— and VERNON, R. (1959). *Anatomy of a Metropolis.* Cambridge, Mass.: Harvard University Press.

ISARD, W. (1956). *Location and Space Economy.* Cambridge, Mass.: The M.I.T. Press.

JOSEPH, M. F. W. (1933). A Discontinuous Cost Curve and Increasing Returns. *The Economic Journal*, Vol. 43, No. 3, pp. 390-393.

LAMPARD, E. E. (1968). The Evolving System of Cities in the United States. *Issues in Urban Economics*, edited by Harvey S. Perloff and Lowdon Wingo Jr., Baltimore: The Johns Hopkins Press for Resources for the Future, Inc.

LAVE, L. B. (1970). Congestion and Urban Location. *Papers and Proceedings of the Regional Science Association*, Vol. 25, pp. 133-150.

LICHTENBERG, R. M. (1960). *One-tenth of a Nation* Cambridge, Mass.: Harvard University Press.

LUKERMANN, F. (1966). Empirical Expressions of Nodality and Hierarchy in a Circulation Manifold. *East Lakes Geographer*, Vol. 2, No. 3, pp. 17-44. Partially reprinted in Berry and Horton (1970).

MARTIN, J. E. (1969). Size of Plant and Location of Industry in Greater London. *Tijdschrift voor Economische en Sociale Geografie*, Vol. 60, No. 6, pp. 369-374.

MATHUR, V. K. (1970). Occupation Composition and its Determinants: an intercity size class analysis. *Journal of Regional Science*, Vol. 10, No. 1, pp. 81-91.

MATTILA, J. M. and THOMPSON, W. R. (1968). Appendix: Toward an Econometric Model of Urban Economic Development. *Issues in Urban Economics*, ed. Harvey S. Perloff and Lowdon Wingo Jr., Baltimore: The Johns Hopkins Press for Resources for the Future, Inc.

MILLS, E. S. (1972). Welfare Aspects of National Policy Toward City Sizes. *Urban Studies*, Vol. 9, No. 1.

MINISTRY OF TRANSPORT (1969). The Value of Time Savings in Transport Investment Appraisal. A paper prepared by the Economic Planning Directorate.

MORSE, R. M., MATHUR, O. P. and SWAMY, M. C. K. (1968). *Costs of Urban Infrastructure as Related to City Size in Developing Countries.* Palo Alto, Calif.: Stanford Research Institute. Partially reprinted in Berry and Horton (1970).

MUTH, R. F. (1968). Differential Growth among Large U.S. Cities. *Papers in Quantitative Economics*, ed. James P. Quirk and Avid M. Zarley. Laurence, Kansas: The University Press of Kansas.

MUTH, R. F. (1969). *Cities and Housing.* Chicago: Chicago University Press.

NEUTZE, G. M. (1965). *Economic Policy and the Size of Cities.* Canberra: The Australian National University.

PARR, J. B. (1970). Models of City Size in an Urban System. *Papers and Proceedings of the Regional Science Association*, Vol. 25, pp. 221-253.

PATINKIN, D. (1947). Multiple-Plant Firms, Cartels and Imperfect Competition. *The Quarterly Journal of Economics*, Vol. 61, No. 2, pp. 173-205.

PAULY, M. V. (1968). Clubs, Commonality, and the Core. *Economica*, Vol. 35, No. 3, pp. 314-324.

—— (1970). Cores and Clubs. *Public Choice*, Vol. 9, pp. 53-65.

REID, M. G. (1962). *Housing and Income.* Chicago: University of Chicago Press.

REYNOLDS, D. J. (1966). *Economics, Town Planning, and Traffic.* London: The Institute of Economic Affairs.

ROSING, K. E. (1966). A Rejection of the Zipf Model (Rank-Size Rule) in Relation to City Size. *The Professional Geographer*, Vol. 18, No. 2, pp. 75-82.

SHARPE, W. F. (1970). *Portfolio Theory and Capital Markets.* New York: McGraw Hill.

SIMON, H. A. (1955). On a Class of Skew Distribution Functions. *Biometrika*, Vol. 42, Nos. 3, 4, pp. 425-440.

SINGER, H. W. (1936). The 'Courbe des Populations'. A Parallel to Pareto's Law. *The Economic Journal*, Vol. 46, No. 2, pp. 254-263.

STANBACK, T. M. and KNIGHT, R. V. (1970). *The Metropolitan Economy*. New York: Columbia University Press.

STEWART, C. T., Jr. (1958). The Size and Spacing of Cities. *Geographical Review*, Vol. 48, No. 2, pp. 222-245. Reprinted in *Readings in Urban Geography*, ed. Harold M. Mayer and Clyde F. Kohn. Chicago: Chicago University Press.

STIGLER, G. J. (1951). The Division of Labor is limited by the Extent of the Market. *Journal of Political Economy*, Vol. 59, No. 3, pp. 185-193.

TINBERGEN, J. (1968). The Hierarchy Model of the Size Distribution of Centers. *Papers and Proceedings of the Regional Science Association*, Vol. 20, pp. 65-68.

VERNON, R. (1960). *Metropolis 1985*. Cambridge, Mass.: Harvard University Press.

VIND, K. (1965). A Theorem on the Core of an Economy. *Review of Economic Studies*, Vol. 32, No. 1, pp. 47-48.

WIDMER, G. (1953). L'Inegalité dans la Grandeur des Villes et ses Correlations Economiques. *Revue Economique*, Vol. 4, No. 3, pp. 305-338.

WILSON, A. G. (1970). *Entropy in Urban and Regional Modelling*. London: Pion.

WINGO, L., Jr. (1961). *Transportation and Urban Land*. Washington D.C.: Resources for the Future, Inc.

ZIPF, G. K. (1949). *Human behavior and the principle of least effort*. Cambridge, Mass.: Harvard University Press.

Acknowledgements. I am indebted to Resources for the Future Inc. for financial support and to G. C. Cameron, L. C. Hunter, W. F. Lever, and Lowdon Wingo Jr. for their helpful discussion. In no case is any measure of agreement implied.

[5]

A THEORY OF THE URBAN LAND MARKET

By William Alonso

The author is Assistant Professor of City Planning in Harvard University.

THE EARLY THEORY of rent and location concerned itself primarily with agricultural land. This was quite natural, for Ricardo and Malthus lived in an agricultural society. The foundations of the formal spatial analysis of agricultural rent and location are found in the work of J. von Thunen, who said, without going into detail, that the urban land market operated under the same principles.[1] As cities grew in importance, relatively little attention was paid to the theory of urban rents. Even the great Marshall provided interesting but only random insights, and no explicit theory of the urban land market and urban locations was developed.

Since the beginning of the twentieth century there has been considerable interest in the urban land market in America. R.M. Hurd[2] in 1903 and R. Haig[3] in the twenties tried to create a theory of urban land by following von Thunen. However, their approach copied the form rather than the logic of agricultural theory, and the resulting theory can be shown to be insufficient on its own premises. In particular, the theory failed to consider residences, which constitute the preponderant land use in urban areas.

Yet there are interesting problems that a theory of urban land must consider. There is, for instance, a paradox in American cities: the poor live near the center, on expensive land, and the rich on the periphery, on cheap land. On the logical side, there are also aspects of great interest, but which increase the difficulty of the analysis. When a purchaser acquires land, he acquires two goods (land and location) in only one transaction, and only one payment is made for the combination. He could buy the same quantity of land at another location, or he could buy more, or less land at the same location. In the

[1] *Johan von Thunen*, DER ISOLIERTE STAAT IN BEZIEHUNG AUF LANDWIRTSCHAFT UND NATIONALEKONOMIE, *1st. vol., 1826, 3d. vol. and new edition, 1863.*

[2] *Richard M. Hurd*, PRINCIPLES OF CITY LAND VALUES, *N.Y.: The Record and Guide, 1903.*

[3] *Robert M. Haig. "Toward an Understanding of the Metropolis"*, QUARTERLY JOURNAL OF ECONOMICS, *XL: 3, May 1926; and* REGIONAL SURVEY OF NEW YORK AND ITS ENVIRONS, *N.Y.: New York City Plan Commission, 1927.*

analysis, one encounters, as well, a negative good (distance) with positive costs (commuting costs); or, conversely, a positive good (accessibility) with negative costs (savings in commuting). In comparison with agriculture, the urban case presents another difficulty. In agriculture, the location is extensive: many square miles may be devoted to one crop. In the urban case the site tends to be much smaller, and the location may be regarded as a dimensionless point rather than an area. Yet the thousands or millions of dimensionless points which constitute the city, when taken together, cover extensive areas. How can these dimensionless points be aggregated into two-dimensional space?

Here I will present a non-mathematical over-view, without trying to give it full precision, of the long and rather complex mathematical analysis which constitures a formal theory of the urban land market.[4] It is a static model in which change is introduced by comparative statics. And it is an economic model: it speaks of economic men, and it goes without saying that real men and social groups have needs, emotions, and desires which are not considered here. This analysis uses concepts which fit with agricultural rent theory in such a way that urban and rural land uses may be considered at the same time, in terms of a single theory. Therefore, we must examine first a very simplified model of the agricultural land market.

AGRICULTURAL MODEL

In this model, the farmers are grouped around a single market, where they sell their products. If the product is wheat, and the produce of one acre of wheat sells for $100 at the market while the costs of production are $50 per acre, a farmer growing wheat at the market would make a profit of $50 per acre. But if he is producing at some distance- say, 5 miles - and it costs him $5 per mile to ship an acre's product, his transport costs will be $25 per acre. His profits will be equal to value minus production costs minus shipping charges: 100-50-25 = $25. This relation may be shown diagrammatically (see Figure 1). At the market, the farmer's profits are $50, and 5 miles out, $25; at intermediate distance, he will receive intermediate profits. Finally, at a distance of 10 miles from the market, his production costs plus shipping charges will just equal the value of his produce at the market. At distances greater than 10 miles, the farmer would operate at a loss.

In this model, the profits derived by the farmers are tied directly to their location. If the functions of farmer and landowner are viewed as separate, farmers will bid rents for land according to the profitability of the location The profits of the farmer will therefore be shared with the landowner through rent payments. As farmers bid against each other for the more profitable locations, until farmers' profits are

---

[4] *A full development of the theory is presented in my doctoral dissertation*, A MODEL OF THE URBAN LAND MARKET: LOCATIONS AND DENSITIES OF DWELLINGS AND BUSINESSES, *University of Pennsylvania, 1960.*

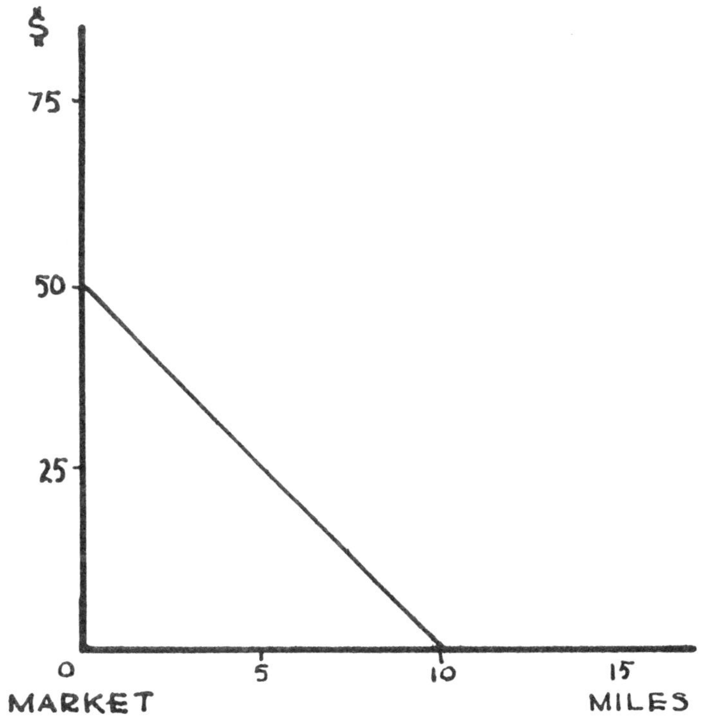

FIGURE 1

everywhere the same ("normal" profits), what we have called profits becomes rent. Thus, the curve in Figure 1, which we derived as a farmers' profit curve, once we distinguish between the roles of the farmer and the landowner, becomes a bid rent function, representing the price or rent per acre that farmers will be willing to pay for land at the different locations.

We have shown that the slope of the rent curve will be fixed by the transport costs on the produce. The level of the curve will be set by the price of the produce at the market. Examine Figure 2. The lower curve is that of Figure 1, where the price of wheat is $100 at the market, and production costs are $50. If demand increases, and the price of wheat at the market rises to $125 (while production and transport costs remain constant), profits or bid rent at the market will be $75; at 5 miles, $50; $25 at 10 miles, and zero at 15 miles. Thus, each bid rent curve is a function of rent vs. distance, but there is a family of such curves, the level of any one determined by the price of the produce at the market, higher prices setting higher curves.

Consider now the production of peas. Assume that the price at the market of one acre's production of peas is $150, the costs of production

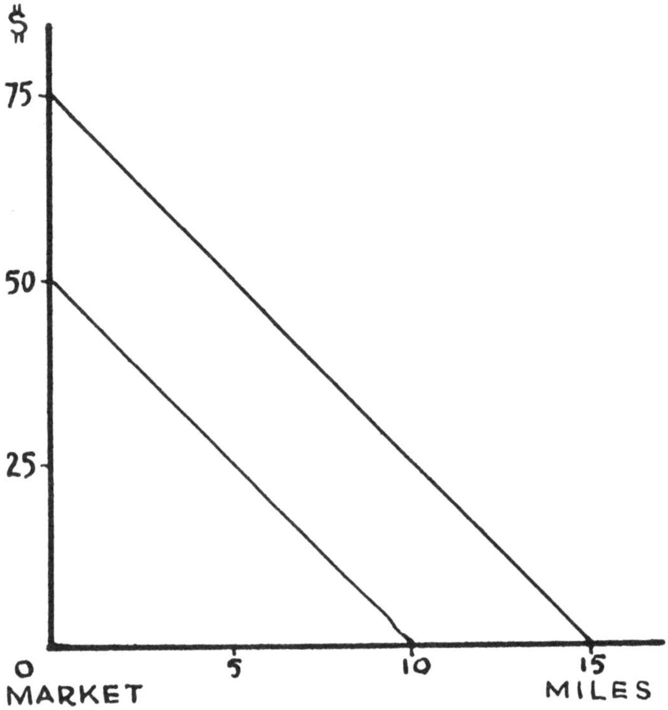

FIGURE 2

are \$75, and the transport costs per mile are \$10. These conditions will yield curve MN in Figure 3, where bid rent by pea farmers at the market is \$75 per acre, 5 miles from the market \$25, and zero at 7.5 miles. Curve RS represents bid rents by wheat farmers, at a price of \$100 for wheat. If will be seen that pea farmers can bid higher rents in the range of 0 to 5 miles from the market; farther out, wheat farmers can bid higher rents. Therefore, pea farming will take place in the ring from 0 to 5 miles from the market, and wheat farming in the ring from 5 to 10 miles. Segments MT of the bid rent curve of pea farming and TS of wheat farming will be the effective rents, while segments RT and TN represent unsuccessful bids.

The price of the product is determined by the supply-demand relations at the market. If the region between zero and 5 miles produces too many peas, the price of the product will drop, and a lower bid rent curve for pea farming will come into effect, so that pea farming will be practiced to some distance less than 5 miles.

Abstracting this view of the agricultural land market, we have that:

(1) land uses determine land values, through competitive bidding among farmers;

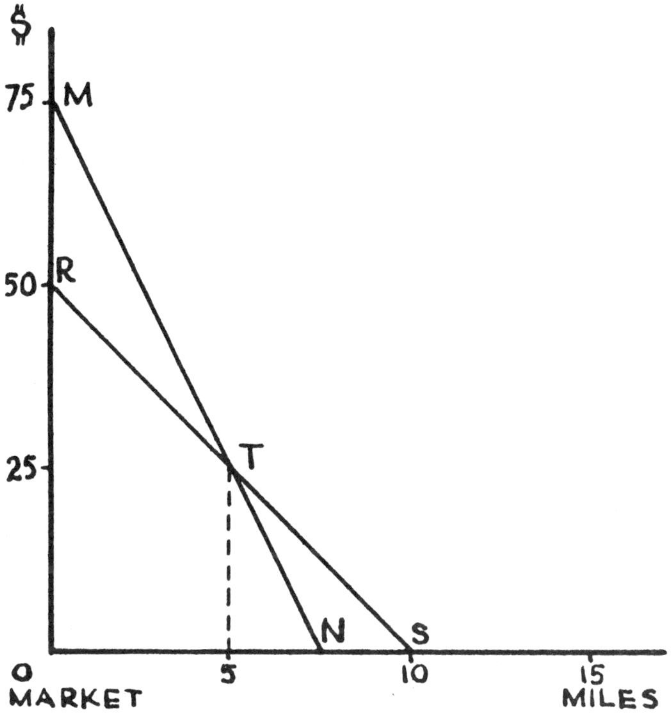

FIGURE 3

(2) land values distribute land uses, according to their ability to pay;
(3) the steeper curves capture the central locations. (This point is a simplified one for simple, well-behaved curves.

Abstracting the process now *from* agriculture, we have:

(1) for each user of land (e.g., wheat farmer) a family of bid rent functions is derived, such that the user is indifferent as to his location along any *one* of these functions (because the farmer, who is the decision-maker in this case, finds that profits are everywhere the same, i.e., normal, as long as he remains on one curve);
(2) the equilibrium rent at any location is found by comparing the bids of the various potential users and choosing the highest;
(3) equilibrium quantities of land are found by selecting the proper bid rent curve for each user (in the agricultural case, the curve which equates supply and demand for the produce).

BUSINESS

We shall now consider the urban businessman, who, we shall assume, makes his decisions so as to maximize profits. A bid rent curve for the businessman, then, will be one along which profits are everywhere the same: the decision-maker will be indifferent as to his location along such a curve.

Profit may be defined as the remainder from the volume of business after operating costs and land costs have been deducted. Since in most cases the volume of business of a firm as well as its operating costs will vary with its location, the rate of change of the bid rent curve will bear no simple relation to transport costs (as it did in agriculture). The rate of change of the total bid rent for a firm, where profits are constant by definition, will be equal to the rate of change in the volume of business minus the rate of change in operating costs. Therefore the slope of the bid rent curve, the values of which are in terms of dollars per unit of land, will be equal to the rate of change in the volume of business minus the rate of change in operating costs, divided by the area occupied by the establishment.

A different level of profits would yield a different bid rent curve. The higher the bid rent curve, the lower the profits, since land is more expensive. There will be a highest curve, where profits will be zero. At higher land rents the firm could only operate at a loss.

Thus we have, as in the case of the farmer, a family of bid rent curves, along the path of any one of which the decision-maker - in this case, the businessman - is indifferent. Whereas in the case of the farmer the level of the curve is determined by the price of the produce, while profits are in all cases "normal", i.e., the same, in the case of the urban firm, the level of the curve is determined by the level of the profits, and the price of its products may be regarded for our purposes as constant.

RESIDENTIAL

The household differs from the farmer and the urban firm in that satisfaction rather than profits is the relevant criterion of optional location. A consumer, given his income and his pattern of tastes, will seek to balance the costs and bother of commuting against the advantages of cheaper land with increasing distance from the center of the city and the satisfaction of more space for living. When the individual consumer faces a given pattern of land costs, his equilibrium location and the size of his site will be in terms of the marginal changes of these variables.

The bid rent curves of the individual will be such that, for any given curve, the individual will be equally satisfied at every location at the price set by the curve. Along any bid rent curve, the price the individual will bid for land will decrease with distance from the center at a rate just sufficient to produce an income effect which will balance to his satisfaction the increased costs of commuting and the bother of a long trip. This slope may be expressed quite precisely in mathematical terms, but it is a complex expression, the exact interpretation of which is beyond the scope of this paper.

Just as different prices of the produce set different levels for the bid rent curves of the farmer, and different levels of profit for the urban firm, different levels of satisfaction correspond to the various levels of the family of bid rent curves of the individual household. The higher curves obviously yield less satisfaction because a higher price is implied, so that, at any given location, the individual will be able to afford less land and other goods.

INDIVIDUAL EQUILIBRIUM

It is obvious that families of bid rent curves are in many respects similar to indifference curve mappings. However, they differ in some important ways. Indifference curves map a path of indifference (equal satisfaction) between combinations of quantities of two goods. Bid rent functions map an indifference path between the price of one good (land) and quantities of another and strange type of good, distance from the center of the city. Whereas indifference curves refer only to tastes and not to budget, in the case of households, bid rent functions are derived both from budget and taste considerations. In the case of the urban firm, they might be termed isoprofit curves. A more superficial difference is that, whereas the higher indifference curves are the preferred ones, it is the lower bid rent curves that yield greater profits or satisfaction. However, bid rent curves may be used in a manner analogous to that of indifference curves to find the equilibrium location and land price for the resident or the urban firm.

Assume you have been given a bid rent mapping of a land use, whether business or residential (curves $brc_{1,2,3}$, etc., in Figure 4). Superimpose on the same diagram the actual structure of land prices in the city (curve SS). The decision-maker will wish to reach the lowest possible bid rent curve. Therefore, he will choose that point at which the curve of actual prices (SS) will be tangent to the lowest of the bid rent curves with which it comes in contact (brc_2). At this point will be the equilibrium location (L) and the equilibrium land rent (R) for this user of land. If he is a businessman, he will have maximized profits; if he is a resident, he will have maximized satisfaction.

Note that to the left of this point of equilibrium (toward the center of the city) the curve of actual prices is steeper than the bid rent curve; to the right of this point (away from the center) it is less steep. This is another aspect of the rule we noted in the agricultural model: the land uses with steeper bid rent curves capture the central locations.

MARKET EQUILIBRIUM

We now have, conceptually, families of bid rent curves for all three types of land uses. We also know that the steeper curves will occupy the more central locations. Therefore, if the curves of the various users are ranked by steepness, they will also be ranked in terms of their accessibility from the center of the city in the final solution.

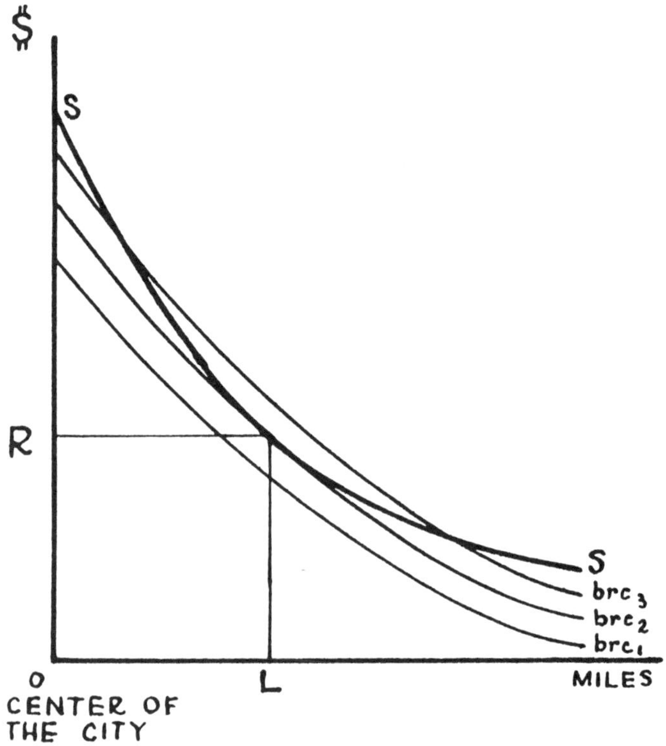

FIGURE 4

Thus, if the curves of the business firm are steeper than those of residences, and the residential curves steeper than the agricultural, there will be business at the center of the city, surrounded by residences, and these will be surrounded by agriculture.

This reasoning applies as well within land use groupings. For instance, it can be shown that, given two individuals of similar tastes, both of whom prefer living at low densities, if their incomes differ, the bid rent curves of the wealthier will be flatter than those of the man of lower income. Therefore, the poor will tend to central locations on expensive land and the rich to cheaper land on the periphery. The reason for this is not that the poor have greater purchasing power, but rather that they have steeper bid rent curves. This stems from the fact that, at any given location, the poor can buy less land than the rich, and since only a small quantity of land is involved, changes in its price are not as important for the poor as the costs and inconvenience of commuting. The rich, on the other hand, buy greater quantities of land, and are consequently affected by changes in its price to a greater degree. In other words, because of variations in density among different levels of income, accessibility behaves as an inferior good.

Thus far, through ranking the bid rent curves by steepness, we have found the relative rankings of prices and locations, but not the actual prices, locations, or densities. It will be remembered that in the agricultural case equilibrium levels were brought about by changes in the price of the products, until the amount of land devoted to each crop was in agreement with the demand for that crop.

For urban land this process is more complex. The determination of densities (or their inverse, lot size) and locations must be found simultaneously with the resulting price structure. Very briefly, the method consists of assuming a price of land at the center of the city, and determining the prices at all other locations by the competitive bidding of the potential users of land in relation to this price. The highest bid captures each location, and each bid is related to a most preferred alternative through the use of bid rent curves. This most preferred alternative is the marginal combination of price and location for that particular land use. The quantities of land occupied by the land users are determined by these prices. The locations are determined by assigning to each successive user of land the location available nearest the center of the city after the assignment of land quantities to the higher and more central bidders.

Since initially the price at the center of the city was assumed, the resulting set of prices, locations, and densities may be in error. A series of iterations will yield the correct solution. In some cases, the solution may be found by a set of simultaneous equations rather than by the chain of steps which has just been outlined.

The model presented in this paper corresponds to the simplest case: a single-center city, on a featureless plain, with transportation in all directions. However, the reasoning can be extended to cities with several centers (shopping, office, manufacturing, etc.), with structured road patterns, and other realistic complications. The theory can also be made to shed light on the effects of economic development, changes in income structure, zoning regulations, taxation policies, and other. At this stage, the model is purely theoretical; however, it is hoped that it may provide a logical structure for econometric models which may be useful for prediction.

[6]

Migration, Unemployment and Development: A Two-Sector Analysis

By JOHN R. HARRIS AND MICHAEL P. TODARO*

Throughout many less developed economies of the world, especially those of tropical Africa, a curious economic phenomenon is presently taking place. Despite the existence of positive marginal products in agriculture and significant levels of urban unemployment, rural-urban labor migration not only continues to exist, but indeed, appears to be accelerating. Conventional economic models with their singular dependence on the achievement of a full employment equilibrium through appropriate wage and price adjustments are hard put to provide rational behavioral explanations for these sizable and growing levels of urban unemployment in the absence of absolute labor redundancy in the economy as a whole. Moreover, this lack of an adequate analytical model to account for the unemployment phenomenon often leads to rather amorphous explanations such as the "bright lights" of the city acting as a magnet to lure peasants into urban areas.

In this paper we shall diverge from the usual full employment, flexible wage-price models of economic analysis by formulating a two-sector model of rural-urban migration which, among other things, recognizes the existence of a politically determined minimum urban wage at levels substantially higher than agricultural earnings.[1] We shall then consider the effect of this parametric urban wage on the rural individual's economic behavior when the assumption of no agricultural labor surplus is made, i.e., that the agricultural marginal product is always positive and inversely related to the size of the rural labor force.[2] The distinguishing feature of this model is that migration proceeds in response to urban-rural differences in *expected earnings* (defined below) with the urban employment rate acting as an equilibrating force on such migration.[3] We shall then use the overall model for the following purposes:

1) to demonstrate that given this po-

* The authors are assistant professor of economics, Massachusetts Institute of Technology and research fellow, Institute for Development Studies, University College, Nairobi, respectively. They would like to thank the Rockefeller Foundation for making possible their research on economic problems of East Africa. Peter Diamond, Richard Eckaus, Joseph Stiglitz, two anonymous referees, and the managing editor made valuable comments on a previous draft. The authors, of course, are responsible for remaining errors.

[1] For some empirical evidence on the magnitude of these real earnings differentials in less developed economies, see Reynolds, Berg, Henderson, and Ghai.

[2] We do not make the special assumption of an agricultural labor surplus for the following reasons: Most available empirical evidence to date tends to cast doubt on the labor surplus argument in the context of those economies of Southeast Asia and Latin America where such a surplus would be most likely to exist (see Kao, Anschel, and Eicher). Moreover, few if any economists would seriously argue that general labor surplus exists in tropical Africa, the area to which this paper is most directly related.

[3] For a dynamic model of labor migration in which urban unemployment rates and expected incomes play a pivotal role in the migration process, see Todaro. However, unlike the present model which attempts to view the migration process in context of aggregate and intersectoral welfare considerations, Todaro's model was strictly concerned with the formulation of a positive theory of urban unemployment in developing nations. As such, it did not specifically consider the welfare of the rural sector, nor was it concerned with the broader issues of economic policy considered in the present paper.

litically determined high minimum wage, the continued existence of rural-urban migration in spite of substantial overt urban unemployment represents an economically rational choice on the part of the individual migrant;

2) to show that economists' standard policy prescription of generating urban employment opportunities through the use of "shadow prices" implemented by means of wage subsidies or direct government hiring will *not* necessarily lead to a welfare improvement and may, in fact, exacerbate the problem of urban unemployment;

3) to evaluate the welfare implications of alternative policies associated with various back-to-the-land programs when it is recognized that the standard remedy suggested by economic theory—namely, full wage flexibility—is for all practical purposes politically infeasible. Special attention will be given here to the impact of migration cum unemployment on the welfare of the rural sector as a whole which gives rise to intersectoral compensation requirements; and, finally,

4) to argue that in the absence of wage flexibility, an optimal policy is, in fact, a "policy package" including *both* partial wage subsidies (or direct government employment) and measures to restrict free migration.

I. *The Basic Model*

The basic model which we shall employ can be described as a two-sector internal trade model with unemployment. The two sectors are the permanent urban and the rural. For analytical purposes we shall distinguish between sectors from the point of view of production and income. The urban sector specializes in the production of a manufactured good, part of which is exported to the rural sector in exchange for agricultural goods. The rural sector has a choice of either using all available labor to produce a single agricultural good, some of which is exported to the urban sector, *or* using only part of its labor to produce this good while *exporting* the remaining labor to the urban sector in return for wages paid in the form of the manufactured good. We are thus assuming that the typical migrant retains his ties to the rural sector and, therefore, the income that he earns as an urban worker will be considered, from the standpoint of sectoral welfare, as accruing to the rural sector.[4] However, this assumption is not at all necessary for our demonstration of the rationality of migration in the face of significant urban unemployment.

The crucial assumption to be made in our model is that rural-urban migration will continue so long as the *expected* urban real income at the margin exceeds real agricultural product—i.e., prospective rural migrants behave as maximizers of *expected* utility. For analytical purposes, we shall assume that the total urban labor force consists of a permanent urban proletariat without ties to the rural sector plus the available supply of rural migrants. From this combined pool or urban labor, we assume that a periodic *random job selection process* exists whenever the number of available jobs is exceeded by the number of job seekers.[5] Consequently, the expected

[4] In tropical Africa especially, this notion that migrants retain their ties to the rural sector is quite common and manifested by the phenomenon of the extended family system and the flow of remittances to rural relatives of large proportions of urban earnings. However, the reverse flow, i.e., rural-urban monetary transfers is also quite common in cases where the migrant is temporarily unemployed and, therefore, must be supported by rural relatives. For an excellent discussion of this phenomenon from a sociological point of view, see Gugler (pp. 475–78).

[5] The qualitative conclusions of the model do not depend on the precise nature of the selection process. We have assumed random selection not merely for analytic convenience but also because it directly corresponds to an appropriate dynamic construct developed in Todaro's 1969 article. There it is shown that over time expected and actual earnings will converge to a positive number even though the rate of job creation is less than the rate of migration so that unemployment is increasing.

urban wage will be defined as equal to the fixed minimum wage (expressed in terms of manufactured goods) times the proportion of the urban labor force actually employed (see equation (6)). Finally, we assume perfectly competitive behavior on the part of producers in both sectors with the further simplifying assumption that the price of the agricultural good (defined in terms of manufactured goods) is determined directly by the relative quantities of the two goods produced.

Consider now the following formulation of the model.

Agricultural Production Function:

$$(1) \quad X_A = q(N_A, \bar{L}, \bar{K}_A), \qquad q' > 0, \quad q'' < 0$$

where,

- X_A is output of the agricultural good,
- N_A is the rural labor used to produce this output,
- $\bar{L}$ is the fixed availability of land,
- $\bar{K}_A$ is the fixed capital stock,
- q' is the derivative of q with respect of N_A, its only variable factor.

Manufacturing Production Function:

$$(2) \quad X_M = f(N_M, \bar{K}_M), \qquad f' > 0, \quad f'' < 0$$

where

- X_M is the output of the manufactured good,
- N_M is the total labor (urban and rural migrant) required to produce this output.
- $\bar{K}_M$ is fixed capital stock, and
- f' is the derivative of f with respect to N_M, its only variable factor.

It is interesting to note in this context that sociologist Gugler who has spent considerable time studying labor migration in Africa has recently concluded that rural-urban migration is essentially an economic phenomenon that can be portrayed as a "game of lottery" in which rural migrants come to the city fully aware that their chances of finding a job are low. However, the great disparity between urban and rural wages makes the successful location of an urban salaried job so attractive that unskilled migrants are willing to take a chance (pp. 472–73). See also Hutton.

Price Determination:

$$(3) \quad P = \rho\left(\frac{X_M}{X_A}\right), \qquad \rho' > 0$$

where

P, the price of the agricultural good in terms of the manufactured good, (i.e., the terms of trade) is a function of the relative outputs of agricultural and manufactured good when the latter serves as numeraire.[6]

Agricultural Real Wage Determination:

$$(4) \quad W_A = P \cdot q'$$

where

W_A, the agricultural real wage, is equal to the value of labor's marginal product in agriculture expressed in terms of the manufactured good.

Manufacturing Real Wage:

$$(5) \quad W_M = f' \geqq \bar{W}_M.$$

The real wage in manufacturing, expressed in terms of manufactured goods, is equated with the marginal product of labor in manufacturing because of profit maximization on the part of perfectly competitive producers. However, this wage is constrained to be greater than or equal to the fixed minimum urban wage. In our analysis, we shall be dealing only with cases in which $f' = \bar{W}_M$ (i.e., there is never an excess demand for labor at the minimum wage).

Urban Expected Wage:

$$(6) \quad W_u^e = \frac{\bar{W}_M N_M}{N_u}, \qquad \frac{N_M}{N_u} \leq 1,$$

[6] A sufficient, but not necessary, condition for this assumption is that all individuals in the economy have the same homothetic preference map. Again, the assumption is made for analytical convenience. The qualitative conclusions of our analysis will remain unaffected under several plausible assumptions about distribution of income and tastes.

where the ***expected*** real wage in the urban sector, W_u^e, is equal to the real minimum wage $\overline{W}_M$ adjusted for the proportion of the total urban labor force (permanent urban plus migrants, denoted as N_u) actually employed, N_M/N_u.[7] Only in the case of full employment in the urban sector ($N_M = N_u$) is the expected wage equal to the minimum wage (i.e., $W_u^e = \overline{W}_M$).

Labor Endowment:

$$(7) \qquad N_A + N_u = \overline{N}_R + \overline{N}_u = \overline{N}$$

There is a *labor constraint* which states that the sum of workers actually employed in the agricultural sector (N_A) plus the total urban labor force (N_u) must equal the sum of initial endowments of rural ($\overline{N}_R$) and permanent urban ($\overline{N}_u$) labor which in turn equals the total labor endowment ($\overline{N}$).

Equilibrium Condition:

$$(8) \qquad W_A = W_u^e$$

Equation (8), an equilibrium condition, is derived from the hypothesis that migration to the urban area is a positive function of the urban-rural *expected* wage differential. This can be written formally as

$$(9) \qquad \dot{N}_u = \psi\left(\frac{\overline{W}_M N_M}{N_u} - P \cdot q'\right), \qquad \psi' > 0, \quad \psi(0) = 0$$

where $\dot{N}_u$ is a time derivative. Clearly then, migration will cease only when the expected income differential is zero, the condition posited in (8).[8] It is important to note that this assumes that a migrant gives up only his marginal product.[9]

We thus have 8 equations in 8 unknowns X_A, X_M, N_A, N_M, W_A, W_u^e, N_u and P. Given the production functions and fixed minimum wage $\overline{W}_M$, it is possible to solve for sectoral employment, the equilibrium unemployment rate and, consequently, the equilibrium expected wage, relative output levels and terms of trade. Let us analyze how such an unemployment equilibrium can come about.

The essence of our argument is that in many developing nations the existence of an institutionally determined urban minimum wage at levels substantially higher than that which the free market would allow can, and usually does, lead to an equilibrium with considerable urban unemployment. In our model migration is a disequilibrium phenomenon. In equilibrium $\overline{W}_M N_M/N_u = Pq'$ and migration ceases. (See Appendix I for proof that this equilibrium is stable.) Now we know from equation (5) that in the competitive urban manufacturing sector, $\overline{W}_M = f'$. We also know from equation (7) that $\overline{N} - N_A = N_u$ and from equation (3) that $P = \rho(X_M/$

[7] This assumes a very particular form of wage expectation, namely that the expected wage is equal to the average urban wage. Although this is a convenient expression to work with, we could be more general and make the expected wage some function of the average urban wage. Indeed, the only restrictions on such a function that are necessary for our results are that, *ceteris paribus*, the expected wage varies directly with the minimum wage and inversely with the unemployment rate.

[8] $\psi(0) = 0$ is purely arbitrary. If, instead, we assume $\psi(\alpha) = 0$ where α can take on any value, migration will cease when the urban-rural expected wage differential is equal to α. None of the subsequent analysis is affected qualitatively by specifying $\alpha = 0$. Equation (8) would merely be written as $W_A + \alpha = W_u^e$.

[9] Other assumptions could be made. Much of the literature has stressed that in peasant economies producers receive their average product which is higher than their marginal product. Indeed, this is at the heart of the well-known Lewis and Fei-Ranis models. However, these models ignore the migration decision and seem to assume that migrants continue to receive their share of peasant production yet migrate only if jobs are actually available. In much of Africa it appears that migrants continue to receive income from land after migration and commonly hire labor to work on their farms in their absence. There is also a considerable group of landless individuals who work on farms for wages. Thus it would appear that our assumption is not unreasonable. The analysis could easily be modified to make earnings foregone equal to average product, however.

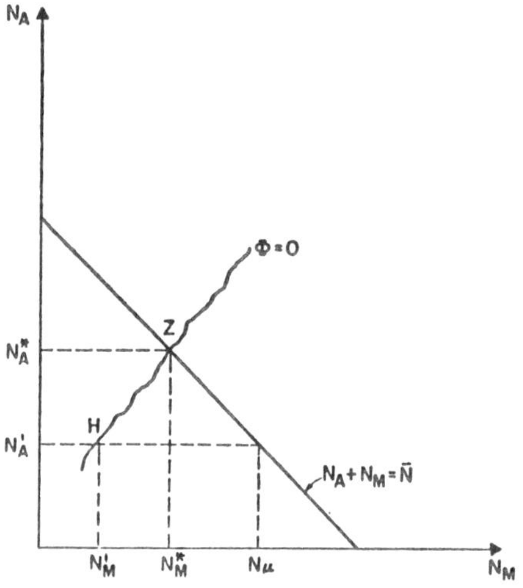

FIG 1.

X_A). Therefore, we can rewrite our equilibrium condition (8) as

$$(8')\quad \Phi = \rho(X_M/X_A)q' - \frac{f'N_M}{\bar{N} - N_A} = 0.$$

Since X_M and X_A are functions of N_M and N_A respectively, Φ is an implicit function in N_A and N_M which, for any stated minimum wage, can be solved for the equilibrium combination of agricultural and manufacturing employment. From this solution the levels of urban unemployment and commodity outputs can also be determined. There will be a unique equilibrium associated with each possible value of the minimum wage, and the locus of these equilibria is plotted in Figure 1 as the line $\Phi=0$ in N_A, N_M space.[10] The line N_A $+N_M=\bar{N}$ in Figure 1 is the locus of full-employment points.

Point Z is the only equilibrium full-employment point in Figure 1 at which N_M^* workers would be employed in manufacturing and N_A^* in agriculture. Points on the locus $\Phi=0$ east of Z are infeasible and will not be considered further, while points to the west of Z are associated with min-

[10] In Figure 1 we have assumed that

$$\frac{dN_A}{dN_M} = -\left[\Phi_{N_M}/\Phi_{N_A}\right] > 0$$

although this need not necessarily hold true. Differentiating (8') partially with respect to N_A we find that

$$\Phi_{N_A} = \frac{-\rho' f q'^2}{q^2} + \rho q'' - \frac{\rho q'}{\bar{N} - N_A}$$

which is unambiguously negative since $q''<0$ and $\rho'>0$. Differentiating (8') partially with respect to N_M we find that

$$\Phi_{N_M} = \frac{1}{\eta_{LW}} - \eta_P \frac{f'N_M}{X_M} + 1$$

which is less than, equal to, or greater than zero as

$$-\frac{1}{\eta_{LW}} + \eta_P \frac{f'N_M}{X_M} \gtreqless 1,$$

where

$$\eta_{LW} = -\frac{dN_M}{d\bar{W}_u}\cdot\frac{\bar{W}_u}{N_M}$$

is the wage elasticity of demand for labor and

$$\eta_P = \frac{dP}{d\left(\frac{X_M}{X_A}\right)}\cdot\frac{X_M/X_A}{P}$$

is the elasticity of the terms of trade with respect to a change in relative outputs. It follows, therefore that the slope of the locus of equilibria, dN_A/dN_M depends on the respective employment and price elasticities.

A sufficient condition for Φ_{N_M} to be negative (making dN_A/dN_M positive) is for the wage elasticity of employment to be less than one, a situation which recent empirical studies suggest is likely to exist (see Erickson, Harris and Todaro (1969), and Katz). However, even if η_{LW} exceeds unity, dN_A/dN_M can still be positive providing price elasticity is sufficiently high. The logic of these conditions is clear. If η_{LW} is less than one, a decline in the minimum wage will lower the urban wage bill even though employment and output increase. This causes the expected urban wage to decline thereby reducing the expected rural-urban earnings differential which gives rise to reverse migration and increased rural employment and output. If η_{LW} exceeds unity, a fall in the minimum wage is accompanied by an increased urban wage bill and, hence, a higher expected urban wage. However, the expected rural-urban earnings differential can either increase or decrease in this case depending on the movement in terms of trade which raises the value of the marginal product in agriculture. For example, if η_{LW} were 1.5 and the wage share of manufacturing output ($f'N_M/X_M$) were .50, then an agricultural price elasticity greater than 0.67 would be sufficient to make dN_A/dN_M positive.

imum wages higher than the full-employment wage. There is a monotonic mapping such that higher minimum wages are associated with points on $\Phi=0$ lying farther to the west. Thus we can demonstrate that the setting of a minimum wage above the market-clearing level causes an economy to settle at a point such as H in Figure 1. At H, N'_A workers are employed in agriculture, N'_M in manufacturing, and $N_u - N'_M$ workers are unemployed. It is evident that the minimum wage causes a loss of employment and hence output in both sectors.[11]

It is important to note that even though an equilibrium at point H represents a suboptimum situation for the economy as a whole, it does represent a rational, utility maximizing choice for individual rural migrants given the level of the minimum wage.

One final point might be raised at this juncture. So far we have assumed that the urban minimum wage is fixed in terms of the manufactured good. What if, instead, the minimum wage were fixed in terms of the agricultural good? We would then substitute for equation (5):

$$(5') \qquad W_M = \frac{f'}{P} \geqq \overline{W}_M.$$

Substituting (4), (5'), and (6) into (8) we get the equilibrium relationship

$$(11) \qquad Pq' = \frac{\left(\frac{f'}{P}\right)\cdot N_M}{N_u}.$$

[11] If $dN_A/dN_M<0$, which we believe to be empirically unlikely, this statement would have to be modified. In such a case, increasing the minimum wage will decrease manufacturing employment but will increase agricultural employment and output. Unemployment will result from the imposition of a minimum wage but we can no longer assert that the level of unemployment will increase concomitantly with the level of the minimum wage.

We can then imagine an economy starting initially at the point on the production possibilities frontier at which X_M is that for which equation (5') is satisfied and assume that

$$Pq' < \frac{\left(\frac{f'}{P}\right)\cdot N_M}{N_u}$$

at that point. The equilibrium point will again be reached through a simultaneous raising of Pq' and lowering of W_u^e in response to migration. As relative agricultural output falls, P will rise. This in turn will cause output of the manufactured good to fall as well, since producers will produce up to the point that $f' = \overline{W}_M P$ which rises in terms of the manufactured good. Note that f' can be raised only through output restriction (since $f''<0$). Therefore, in general, we would find that imposition of a minimum wage gives rise to an equilibrium characterized by unemployment and loss of potential output of both goods. A new locus $\Phi'=0$ will be defined in Figure 1 such that the point on Φ' corresponding to any given minimum wage will be west of the corresponding point on Φ.

Although our initial assumption is a bit easier to handle, the principal conclusion remains unaffected if we make the minimum wage fixed in terms of the agricultural good. Equilibrium is only achievable with unemployment. Actual minimum wage setting is usually done with reference to some general cost of living index, and food is the largest single item in the budget of most urban workers. (See Massell and Heyer, and the Nigeria report.) Hence, the second case may be somewhat more realistic. Note that in the first case the "true" real wage was reduced somewhat by the rising agricultural price, while in the latter case it is increased by the falling relative price of the manufactured good.

III. *Implications for Development Policy*

A. *Planning in Terms of Shadow Prices*

The standard solution to the problem of an institutionally determined wage that is higher than the equilibrium level is to employ labor in the public sector according to a shadow wage and/or to grant a payroll subsidy to private employers that equates private costs with this shadow wage.[12] Two main problems arise with this prescription: first, how can one determine the appropriate shadow wage? and, secondly, what are the implications of executing such a scheme when the institutional wage will continue to be paid to the employed? Our model can shed light on both of these issues.

In a static framework the appropriate shadow wage is the opportunity cost of labor hired by the industrial sector. Hence, if labor is hired to the point that its marginal product in industry is equated with the shadow wage which in turn is equated with the marginal product in agriculture, marginal productivity of labor will be equal in both sectors, a necessary condition for an optimal allocation of resources. Naturally, this assumes a positive marginal product in agriculture and sufficient factor mobility to ensure full employment of labor. The existence of urban unemployment, however, suggests that there may be a pool of labor that can be tapped without sacrificing output. Consequently, it might be suggested that even though agricultural labor is fully employed at peak seasons, the appropriate shadow wage for urban labor is likely to be one that is lower than the marginal product in agriculture. This would be correct if the two labor forces, urban and rural, were separate noncompeting groups. In linear programming terms, there are two labor constraints and each may well have a different associated shadow wage.

Now, the essence of our model is that the two sectors *are* intimately connected through labor migration. If one additional job is created in the industrial sector at the minimum wage, the expected wage will rise and rural-urban migration will be induced. In Appendix II it is shown that more than one agricultural worker will likely migrate in response to the creation of one additional industrial job. Hence, the opportunity cost of an industrial worker will exceed the marginal product of an agricultural worker. On the other hand, an increase in agricultural income will induce reverse migration with no diminution of industrial output. Thus, the opportunity cost of labor is lower to the agricultural than to the industrial sector!

The literature has been strangely silent for the most part about the full implications of using shadow-wage criteria. In a static context, Stolper has pointed out that financing subsidies or losses of public enterprises gives rise to fiscal problems, but unfortunately this issue has not yet been pursued in sufficient detail.[13] If the problem is considered at all, the analyst usually assumes that a system of nondistorting lump-sum taxes is available. Little, Lefeber, and

[12] Hagen (p. 498) states, "a subsidy per unit of labor equal to the wage differential [between agriculture and industry] will increase real income further [than a tariff] and if combined with free trade will permit attaining an *optimum optimorum*." Bardhan (p. 379) similarly adds. "The best remedy for the misallocation caused by a wage differential is . . . an appropriate subsidy to the use of labor in the manufacturing industry." It is important to recall that this argument is dependent on variable proportions production functions. If production coefficients are fixed, a wage subsidy will have no effect in the short run. The classic statement of this case is by Eckaus. Bardhan explores its implications for subsidy in a dynamic context. Both of these papers, however, posit surplus labor in agriculture, an assumption we do not wish to make in an African context.

[13] Lefeber assumes that a wage subsidy can be financed by a profits tax, while other writers, e.g. Hagen, Bardhan, and Chakravarty never even consider the problem. Even Little and Mirrlees who present an excellent discussion of how to calculate a shadow wage never mention the fiscal problems of implementation.

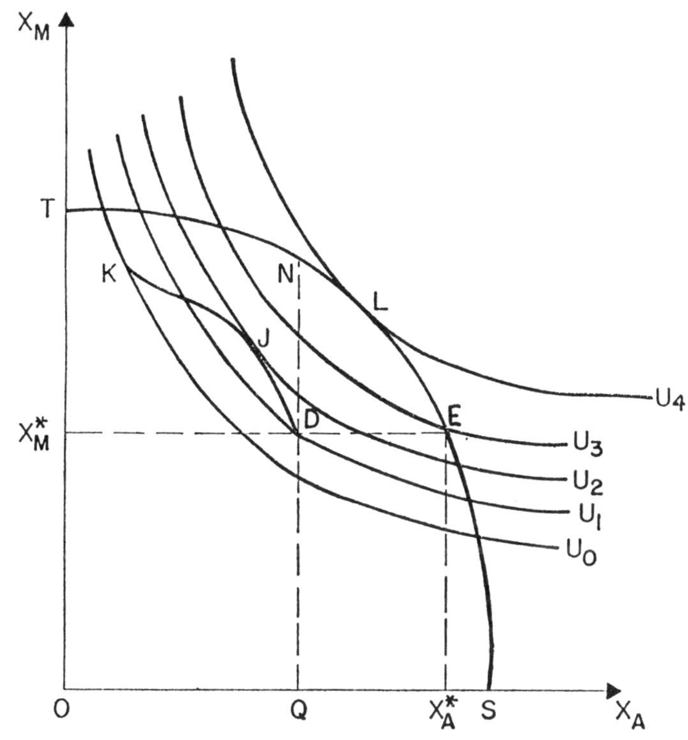

FIGURE 2

Little and Mirrlees have pointed out that in a dynamic setting, the extra consumption arising from payment of the institutional wage diverts resources from investment to consumption; thus some of the foregone future consumption should be considered in calculating the shadow wage. In our model, payment of the minimum wage to additional industrial workers will induce more rural-urban migration. Therefore, implementation of a shadow-wage employment criterion will have important effects on the level of agricultural output and on urban unemployment. The argument can be clarified with reference to Figure 2.

The initial equilibrium, given the minimum wage, is at point D with output of the manufactured good restricted to OX_M^*. If individuals did not migrate in response to expected wage differentials, the economy could product at point E, but migration reduces agricultural output to the level OQ. The theory of shadow pricing suggests that with an appropriate wage subsidy (or public-sector-hiring rule) the economy could move to point L on the production possibilities frontier which, with the posited social indifference map, is the optimum position. Welfare would be increased from a level U_1 to a higher level U_4.

In the context of our model, such a point is unattainable. The effect of implementing a shadow wage will be to increase production of the manufactured good. But creation of an additional job at the minimum wage will induce some additional migration (see Appendix II) from the rural sector and therefore agricultural output will fall. Hence, movement from D can only be in a northwest direction. The line DK in Figure 2 is the locus of all such attainable points and it is evident that there is only one point, K, at which there can be full employment of the economy's labor resources. At that point the expected wage will be equal to the minimum wage since there is no urban unemployment. Therefore, the marginal product in agriculture will have to be equal to the minimum wage. But, with the subsidy, the marginal product of labor in manufacturing will be lower than in agriculture, hence K lies inside the production possibilities frontier. (In the extreme case in which marginal productivity in agriculture can never be as high as the minimum wage, K will coincide with T, the point of complete specialization in manufactures.) This situation will certainly not meet the conditions for a general optimum which can be met only at L. Thus, implementing a shadow wage criterion to the point that urban unemployment is eliminated will not generally be a desirable policy.[14]

However, some level of wage subsidy will usually lead to an improvement. In Figure 2 it is clear that point J, with a welfare level U_2, will be preferable to D. The criterion for welfare maximization, derived in Appendix III, is the following:

$$f' = Pq'\left(\frac{dN_u}{dN_M}\right). \tag{12}$$

Note what this means. Creating one additional job in the industrial sector increases output by f' but, since increased employment will raise the expected urban wage, migration will be induced in an amount dN_u/dN_M. The right-hand side of equation (12) states the amount of agricultural output sacrificed because of migration. Thus the shadow wage will be equal to this opportunity cost of an urban job and the amount of subsidy will be $\overline{W}_M - f'$. So long as $f' > Pq'\ (dN_u/dN_M)$, aggregate welfare can be increased by expanding industrial employment through subsidy or public sector hiring. Clearly the more responsive is migration to industrial employment, the higher is the social cost of industrialization and the smaller is the optimal amount of subsidy. In many African economies it is likely that dN_u/dN_M exceeds unity. If so, it will be optimal for the marginal product of labor in industry to be higher than in agriculture and urban unemployment will be a persistent phenomenon so long as minimum wages are set above a market-clearing level.

The discussion so far has ignored two other adverse effects of using a shadow wage. As mentioned earlier, several writers have noted that payment of a subsidized minimum wage to additional workers will increase total consumption, thereby reducing the level of resources available for investment. If foregone future consumption is positively valued, the opportunity cost of industrial labor will be higher than indicated in equation (12) and the shadow wage will be raised correspondingly. Furtermore, wage subsidies or public enterprise losses must be financed and if revenue cannot be raised through costless lump-sum taxes, the opportunity cost of raising taxes must be considered. Both of these effects will reduce the desirable amount of subsidized job creation in the industrial sector.

It is interesting to note that this model implies different opportunity costs of labor to the two sectors. While the creation of an additional job in the urban area reduces

[14] As shown in Appendix III, DK is not uniformly convex. Therefore, K may be the best attainable point in some cases and the first-order conditions may not ensure optimality. As drawn in Figure 2, moving from D to K represents a worsening of welfare, but this clearly is not a necessary conclusion.

agricultural output through induced migration, additional employment can be generated in the agricultural sector without reducing manufacturing output. If this phenomenon is not taken into account, standard application of investment criteria is likely to be biassed in favor of urban projects.

B. *Migration Restriction*

An alternative approach to the problem of urban unemployment is to physically control migration from the rural areas. Such controls have recently been introduced in Tanzania and have been used for some time in South Africa.[15] Other countries, such as Kenya, are giving serious consideration to instituting such a policy. Although we personally have grave reservations about the ethical issues involved in such a restriction of individual choice and the complexity and arbitrariness of administration, it seems desirable to investigate the economic implications of such a policy.

Looking at Figure 2 it is obvious that with the minimum wage such that industrial output is OX_M^*, prohibition of migration in excess of the labor required to produce that output will allow the economy to produce at point E. The movement from D to E arising from restriction of migration leads to an unambiguous aggregate welfare improvement providing appropriate lump-sum redistribution is effected. Since such compensation is notoriously difficult to carry out in practice, it will be useful to examine the welfare implications of such a move on each of the two sectors in the absence of compensation.

Recall that the two sectors were defined to be a permanent urban group and a rural sector that produces both agricultural goods and exports labor to the urban area in exchange for wages in the form of manufactured goods.[16] In Figure 3 the line $T'S'$ represents production possibilities for the agricultural sector when labor export is allowed. If its entire labor endowment is devoted to agricultural production, it can produce a quantity OS'. However, by exporting its labor, the agricultural sector can "produce" the manufactured good (wages are paid in the form of this good). Hence this production possibilities frontier depends on market forces (wage levels and unemployment) as well as on purely technological factors. The amount of agricultural output foregone if a unit of labor is to be "exported" is its marginal product; the amount of manufactured goods obtained by the exported labor unit depends on the wage, the amount of employment obtained by the exported unit, and its effect on employment of previously exported units.

In addition to these production possibilities, the rural sector also has the opportunity to trade some of its agricultural output with the permanent urban sector in exchange for manufactured goods. Corresponding to each point on the production possibilities frontier $T'S'$, there is a determinate price of the agricultural good. The manner in which alternative constellations of production and trade affect the

[15] See Harris and Todaro (1969) for an analysis of the Tanzanian program.

[16] In considering the welfare of the rural sector as a whole we are making the tacit assumption that there is redistribution of goods between individuals in this sector. This is a very strong assumption. Yet there is considerable evidence from tropical Africa that employed urban migrants repatriate substantial portions of their earnings to their kinsmen remaining in the rural areas and conversely that income both in cash and kind is received by unemployed migrants from kinsmen remaining on the farm. To the extent that the extended family system does redistribute goods between members, this assumption may be tenable as a first approximation. As Gugler (p. 480) has pointed out, it is appropriate to view the extended family as maximizing its income by allocating its members between agriculture and urban wage employment. Although there is some evidence that growing numbers of urban workers are settling permanently and gradually eliminating rural ties, it will be many years before such ties are completely severed.

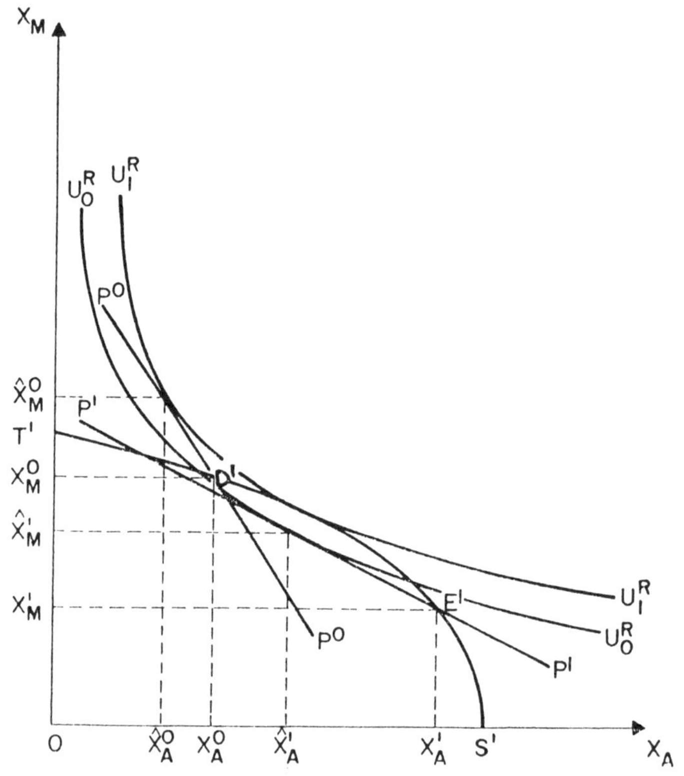

FIGURE 3

sector's welfare can be illustrated by Figure 3.

D' corresponds to the initial unemployment equilibrium D (Figure 2). At that point the rural sector as a whole "produces" $X_A{}^0$ and $X_M{}^0$ of the two goods. It also has the opportunity to trade at the price P^0. By trading some of its agricultural output to the permanent urban sector for additional manufactured goods, it consumes $\hat{X}_A{}^0$, $\hat{X}_M{}^0$ and achieves a welfare level of U_1^R. Restriction of migration results in the sector's producing X_A' X_M'. If it could still trade at price P^0, the agricultural sector would clearly be better off. But this is impossible. At E' (which corresponds to E in Figure 2), the price of agricultural good will fall to P' and with trade the best consumption bundle attainable by the sector is $\hat{X}_A$, $\hat{X}_M$ which corresponds to a lower level of welfare U_0^R. (Note that if P' did not cut $T'S'$ there could be no incentive to migrate at E'.)

It can be shown that $Pq'(1-1/\eta)$ (where η is the price elasticity of demand for the agricultural good) is the amount of the manufactured good sacrificed by the rural sector as a result of removing one worker from producing the agricultural good which could have been exchanged for the manufactured good at the market price $1/P$. This quantity is less than the value of labor's marginal product in agriculture (Pq') since the reduction in output has a favorable terms-of-trade effect. If the demand for the agriculture good is inelastic ($\eta<1$) we reach the startling conclusion that the sacrifice becomes negative! This is, of course, the familiar proposition that aggregate farm income may be increased by reducing output. The *direct* gain in manufactured goods achieved by the rural sector through exporting an additional unit of labor is $\overline{W}_M N_M/N_u$, the expected urban wage. But additional migration, by increasing unemployment, reduces the earnings of *all* migrants already in the urban labor force by a factor $(1-R)$, where R is the fraction of the total urban labor force supplied by the rural sector.[17]

As long as $Pq'(1-\eta)<\overline{W}_M N_M/N_u(1-R)$ the welfare of the rural sector will be increased by allowing migration even though unemployment ensues and the economy as a whole sacrifices output. Since Pq' and $\overline{W}_M N_M/N_u$ are always positive and $R\leq 1$, additional migration will always benefit the rural sector when $\eta<1$. In general, the lower is Pq', η, or R and the higher is $\overline{W}_M N_M/N_u$, the more will the rural sector benefit from the opportunity to migrate.

From the foregoing, one can conclude that although migration restriction will improve aggregate welfare of the economy, given plausible values of η and R, substantial compensation to the rural sector will be required if it is not to be made worse off by removing the opportunity for free migration. The permanent urban labor force clearly will be made better off by becoming fully employed at the high minimum wage while also being able to buy food at a lower price. Each unit of labor exported by the rural sector will similarly earn more but this gain will be offset by reduced total labor exports and lower agricultural prices. Whether or not this will be true depends, of course, on the values of the specific parameters of the economy. If η is sufficiently high, the rural sector could be made better off by restricting migration in the absence of compensation, but this seems very unlikely.

C. *A Combination of Policies*

It has been shown that either a limited wage-subsidy or a migration-restriction policy will lead to a welfare improvement. Which of the two policies will lead to the better position cannot be determined without knowing all the relevant parameters for a particular economy. It is clear, however, that neither policy alone is capable of moving the economy to the optimum that could be achieved with competitive wage determination (point L in Figure 2).

At first sight it may seem strange that with a single market failure, the wage level, a single policy instrument is unable to fully correct the situation.[18] The reason is that the wage performs two functions in this model. It determines *both* the level of employment in the industrial sector *and* the allocation of labor between rural and urban areas. While a subsidy changes the effective wage for determination of industrial employment, so long as the wage actually received by workers exceeds agricultural earnings there will be migration and urban unemployment. Restriction of migration prevents the minimum wage having its effect on unemployment but does nothing to increase the level of industrial employment. Therefore, if the optimum position is to be achieved, a combination of both instruments will have to

[17] If the urban unemployment were experienced only by migrants, this term would equal zero since the total amount of earnings through labor export would be constant. It can be positive only because the permanent urban labor force shares in unemployment, thereby reducing its share of the constant wage bill in the manufactured good industry. An interesting extension of the model would be to incorporate different employment probabilities for the permanent urban and migrant rural labor forces and then to check the sensitivity of results with our more simplified assumption of equal probabilities.

[18] We wish to thank a referee of this *Review* for drawing this to our attention.

be used. In order to reach point L a wage subsidy must be instituted such that industrial employment will increase to the extent that with full employment the marginal product of labor will be equal in manufacturing and agriculture. The subsidy will be positive and equal to the difference between the minimum wage and marginal productivity. At that point $W_u^* = \overline{W}_M$ and $\overline{W}_M > Pq'$. Therefore, individuals would still find it in their interest to migrate and the point will not be attainable unless migration is restricted.

The agricultural sector has to be better off at L than at E since each additional unit of labor exported earns the full minimum wage, marginal productivity in agriculture is less than the minimum wage, and the price of the agricultural good rises. Whether the agricultural sector is better off at L than at D, however, depends again on the parametric values of the model.[19] It can be stated with certainty that the amount of compensation needed to make the rural sector *no worse off* than at D will be less at L than at E, and, furthermore it should be easier to finance since total income is greater.

Even so the fiscal requirements of subsidy (or public enterprise losses) and compensation cannot be taken lightly.[20] A government may find it difficult to find nondistorting taxes capable of raising sufficient revenue. Perhaps a head-tax on all urban residents would be feasible although this too raises the question of how minimum wages are set (unions in tropical Africa have, in some cases, successfully fought to maintain the real after-tax wage). A tax on rural land is ruled out if there must be *net* compensation to the rural sector which, in the absence of pure profits in manufacturing, leaves an urban land tax as the remaining potential ideal tax.

All of the above suggests that altering the minimum wage may avoid the problems of taxation, administration, and interference with individual mobility attendant to the policy package just discussed. Income and wages policies designed to narrow the rural-urban wage gap have been suggested by D. P. Ghai, and Tanzania has formally adopted such a policy along with migration restriction. In the final analysis, however, the basic issue at stake is really one of political feasibility and it is not at all clear that an incomes policy is any more feasible than the alternatives.

[19] As drawn in Figure 2, L must represent a higher welfare level than D for the rural sector since P rises and the sector produces more of both goods. In fact if L lies along TS north of the ray going through D there will be an unambiguous sectoral welfare improvement. However, if L lies south of the ray on TS, the rural sector could be worse off than at D since P falls.

[20] This argument coincides with the statement by Stolper (p. 195), "It should be noted, however, that even at best the application of shadow prices leads to the substitution of one problem, the budget, for another one, an imperfect market."

We would not go as far as Stolper in rejecting out of hand any use of shadow pricing because of the fiscal implications. The general point is valid that one cannot disregard the consequences of implementation of shadow-price criteria if actual prices or wages continue to diverge from the shadow prices or wages.

Appendix I

Proof of Stability of Unemployment Equilibrium

In order to prove that our urban unemployment equilibrium is stable, we can differentiate ψ (equation (9)) with respect to N_u remembering that $dN_u = -dN_A$ according to (7). We therefore obtain

$$\frac{d\dot{N}_u}{dN_u} = \psi'(\cdot)\left[-\frac{\overline{W}_M N_M}{(N_u)^2} + Pq'' + \frac{\partial P}{\partial X_A}(q')^2\right]. \tag{1.1}$$

Stability requires $d\dot{N}_u/dN_u < 0$ which is satisfied if

$$\frac{\partial P}{\partial X_A} < \frac{\dfrac{\overline{W}_M N_M}{(N_u)^2} - Pq''}{(q')^2}.$$

The right side of this inequality is unambiguously positive since $q''<0$. Hence our assumption that $\partial P/\partial X_A<0$ will ensure stability and, indeed, is stronger than necessary. The adjustment mechanism may be made clear by the following phase diagram in which the function ψ is plotted. Its positive slope reflects the hypothesis that migration flows will increase with the magnitude of the urban-rural expected wage differential. In Figure 4, ψ is plotted under the assumption that $\psi(0)=0$, hence the horizontal intercept is at the origin (in general the intercept would be α). Furthermore, we have arbitrarily assumed that ψ is a linear function. The arrows show the direction of adjustment in accordance with (1.1). If $\overline{W}_M N_M/N_u - Pq'>0$, then $\dot{N}_u>0$ but we know that if $\dot{N}_u>0$, the expected wage differential will decrease since $d\dot{N}_u/dN_u<0$. Additional migration by increasing N_u without affecting N_M will reduce the expected urban real wage through increased unemployment. Concomitantly, the transfer of labor out of agriculture raises q' and reduced agricultural output also causes P to rise. Thus migration reduces the expected wage differential to zero and equilibrium is achieved when there is no further incentive for migration. See Todaro for a more detailed analysis of this process in a dynamic setting.

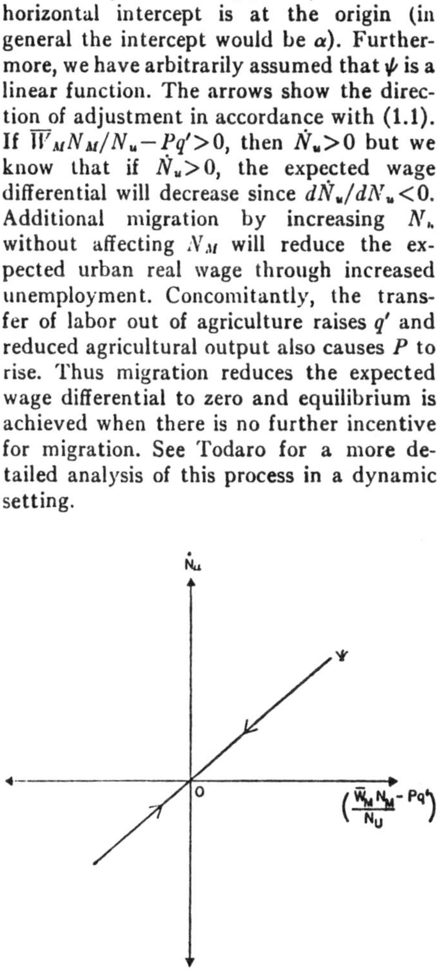

FIGURE 4.

APPENDIX II

Differentiating the equilibrium condition (8) with respect to N_M, recalling that $dN_u = -dN_A$, we obtain the expression

$$\text{(II.1)}\quad \frac{dN_u}{dN_M} = \frac{\dfrac{\overline{W}_M}{N_u} - q'p'\dfrac{f'}{X_A}}{\dfrac{\overline{W}_M N_M}{N_u^2} - pq'' + q'p'\dfrac{q'X_M}{X_A^2}}.$$

Defining the elasticity of demand for the agricultural good as

$$\text{(II.2)}\quad \eta_A = -\frac{\partial X_A}{\partial P}\cdot\frac{P}{X_A} = \frac{pX_A}{p'X_M},$$

(II.1) can be rewritten as

$$\text{(II.3)}\quad \frac{dN_u}{dN_M} = \frac{\dfrac{\overline{W}_M}{N_u} - \dfrac{pq'f'}{\eta_A X_M}}{\dfrac{\overline{W}_M N_M}{N_u^2} - pq'' + \dfrac{p(q')^2}{\eta_A X_A}}.$$

Differentiating the expression partially with respect to its various arguments it can be shown that dN_u/dN_M will vary directly with $\overline{W}_M$, N_M, η_A and inversely with p, q', f', N_u, and q''. In general, the greater is the urban-rural wage differential, and the less sensitive are prices and marginal products in agriculture, the greater will be the migration induced by creation of an additional job. If the minimum wage exceeds agricultural earnings, (II.3) will generally be positive and, with parameter values relevant for many African economies, will exceed unity.

When $dN_u/dN_M>1$, creation of an additional job at the minimum wage will increase the absolute level of unemployment although the *rate* of urban unemployment will have to fall. This can be seen by converting (II.3) to an elasticity measure.

$$\text{(II.4)}\quad \frac{dN_u}{dN_M}\cdot\frac{N_M}{N_u} =$$

$$\frac{\dfrac{\overline{W}_M N_M}{N_u^2} - \dfrac{N_M \rho q' f'}{N_u \eta_A X_M}}{\dfrac{\overline{W}_M N_M}{N_u^2} - \rho q'' + \dfrac{\rho (q')^2}{\eta_A X_A}} < 1$$

since $q'' < 0$.[21] To give an example of what this means, suppose that an economy initially has an urban unemployment rate of 25 percent. If in response to the creation of 100 additional industrial jobs, 125 additional individuals migrate to the urban area, the absolute number unemployed increases by 25 although the unemployment rate will drop, since the marginal unemployment rate is only 20 percent.

Appendix III

If minimum wages are maintained and migration takes place in accordance with equation (8), aggregate welfare will be maximized if the following Lagrangean expression is maximized:

$$\begin{aligned} \Omega = {} & U(X_A, X_M) \\ & + \lambda_1[q(\overline{N} - N_u) - X_A] \\ & + \lambda_2[f(N_M) - X_M] \\ & + \lambda_3 \left\{ \rho \left(\frac{f(N_M)}{q(\overline{N} - N_u)} \right) \right. \\ & \left. \cdot q'(N - N_u) - \frac{\overline{W}_M N_M}{N_u} \right\} \end{aligned} \tag{III.1}$$

where U is the social welfare function and the succeeding terms are the constraints imposed by equations (1), (2), and (8) (recall that $N_A = \overline{N} - N_u$ from equation (7)).

Maximizing (III.1) we get the following first-order conditions:

$$\frac{\partial \Omega}{\partial X_A} = \frac{\partial U}{\partial X_A} - \lambda_1 = 0 \tag{III.2}$$

$$\frac{\partial \Omega}{\partial X_M} = \frac{\partial U}{\partial X_M} - \lambda_2 = 0 \tag{III.3}$$

$$\frac{\partial \Omega}{\partial N_u} = -\lambda_1 q' + \lambda_3 \left[\rho' \frac{f q'}{q^2} - \rho q'' + \frac{\overline{W}_M N_M}{N_u^2} \right] = 0 \tag{III.4}$$

$$\frac{\partial \Omega}{\partial N_M} = \lambda_2 f' + \lambda_3 \left[\rho' \frac{f' q'}{q} - \frac{\overline{W}_M}{N_u} \right] = 0 \tag{III.5}$$

and the $\partial \Omega / \partial \lambda_i = 0$ $(i = 1, 2, 3)$ which ensures that the constraints hold.

Substituting (III.2) and (III.3) into (III.4) and (III.5) we get

$$\frac{\dfrac{\partial U}{\partial X_M} f'}{\dfrac{\partial U}{\partial X_A} q'} = \frac{\dfrac{\overline{W}_M}{N_u} - q' \rho' \dfrac{f'}{q}}{\dfrac{\overline{W}_M N_M}{N_u^2} - \rho q'' + q' \rho' \dfrac{f q'}{q^2}} . \tag{III.6}$$

We know that in equilibrium $(\partial U / \partial X_M)/(\partial U / \partial X_A) = 1/P$ and it has been shown in Appendix II that the right-hand side of (III.6) is equal to dN_u/dN_M. Therefore (III.6) can be rewritten as

$$f' = P q' \frac{dN_u}{dN_M}, \tag{III.7}$$

which is the condition used in the text to determine the optimal wage subsidy.

Condition (III.7) can also be written as

$$-P = \frac{-f'}{q' \dfrac{dN_u}{dN_M}} = \frac{dX_M}{dX_A} . \tag{III.8}$$

We know that $-P$ is equal to the marginal rate of substitution between the two commodities and dX_M/dX_A is the marginal rate of transformation. Hence (III.8) states the familiar condition for optimality: equate marginal rates of substitution and transformation. dX_M/dX_A is the slope of the line DK in Figure 2 and it clearly will be negative. However, its derivative with respect to N_M,

$$\text{(III.9)} \quad \frac{d\left(\frac{dX_M}{dX_A}\right)}{dN_M} = \frac{-q'\frac{dN_u}{dN_M}f'' - f'\left(\frac{dN_u}{dN_M}\right)^2 q'' + f'q'\frac{d^2N_u}{dN_M^2}}{\left(q'\frac{dN_u}{dN_M}\right)^2}$$

is of indeterminate sign since f'', $q''<0$ and d^2N_u/dN_M^2 will generally be negative as well. (III.9) must be positive if the effective production possibilities frontier (*DK*) is to be convex, a condition that is likely to hold but the possibility of concavity as full employment is approached must be considered. The slope of *DK* in Figure 2 seems plausible on a priori grounds.

REFERENCES

P. K. Bardham, "Factor Market Disequilibrium and the Theory of Protection," *Oxford Econ. Pap.* (New Series), Oct. 1964, *16*, 375–88.

E. J. Berg, "Wage Structure in Less Developed Countries," in A. D. Smith, ed., *Wage Policy Issues in Economic Development*, London 1969.

A. Callaway, "From Traditional Crafts to Modern Industries," *ODU: University of Ife Journal of African Studies*, July 1965, *2*.

S. Chakravarty, "The Use of Shadow Prices in Programme Evaluation," in Rosenstein-Rodan, ed., *Capital Formation and Economic Development*, London 1964.

Y. S. Cho, *Disguised Unemployment in Developing Areas, with Special Reference to South Korean Agriculture*, Berkeley 1960.

R. S. Eckaus, "The Factor-Proportions Problem in Underdeveloped Areas," *Amer Econ. Rev.*, Sept. 1955, *45*, 539–65.

J. Erickson, "Wage Employment Relationships in Latin American Industry: A Pilot Study of Argentina, Brazil, and Mexico," International Labour Office, 1969, typescript.

J. Fei and G. Ranis, *Development of the Labor Surplus Economy*, Illinois 1964.

D. P. Ghai, "Incomes Policy in Kenya: Need, Criteria and Machinery," *East Afr. Econ. Rev.*, June 1968, *4*, 19–35.

J. Gugler, "The Impact of Labour Migration on Society and Economy in Sub-Saharan Africa. Empirical Findings and Theoretical Considerations," *African Social Research*, Dec. 1968, *6*, 463–86.

E. E. Hagen, "An Economic Justification of Protectionism," *Quart. J. Econ.*, Nov. 1958, *72*, 496–514.

J. R. Harris and M. P. Todaro, "Urban Unemployment in East Africa: An Economic Analysis of Policy Alternatives," *East Afr. Econ. Rev.*, Dec. 1968, *4*, 17–36.

——— and ———, "Wages, Industrial Employment, and Labour Productivity: The Kenyan Experience," *East Afr. Econ. Rev.* (New Series), June 1969, *1*, 29–46.

J. P. Henderson, "Wage Policy in Africa," Paper prepared for delivery at the African Conference on Economics, Temple University, mimeo, April 1968.

C. R. Hutton, "The Causes of Labour Migration," in Gugler, ed., *Urbanization in Sub-Saharan Africa*, Kampala 1969.

C. H. C. Kao, K. R. Anschel, and C. K. Eicher, "Disguised Unemployment in Agriculture: A Survey," in C. K. Eicher and L. W. Witt, eds., *Agriculture in Economic Development*, New York 1964, 129–44.

J. M. Katz, "Verdoorn Effects; Returns to Scale, and the Elasticity of Factor Substitution," *Oxford Econ. Pap.*, Nov. 1968, *20*, 342–52.

L. Lefeber, "Planning in a Surplus Labor Economy," *Amer. Econ. Rev.*, June 1968, *58*, 343–73.

W. A. Lewis, "Economic Development with Unlimited Supplies of Labour," *Manchester Sch. Econ. Soc. Stud.*, May 1954, *22*, 139–91.

I. M. D. Little, "The Real Cost of Labour, and the Choice Between Consumption and

Investment," in P. N. Rosenstein-Rodan, ed., *Pricing and Fiscal Policies: A Study in Method*, Cambridge 1964, 77–91.

——— and J. A. Mirrlees, *Manual of Industrial Project Analysis*, Vol. II, "Social Cost Benefit Analysis," Paris 1969.

B. F. Massell and J. Heyer, "Household Expenditure in Nairobi: A Statistical Analysis of Consumer Behaviour," *Econ. Develop. Cult. Change*, Jan. 1969, *17*, 212–34.

L. G. Reynolds, "Wages and Employment in a Labor-Surplus Economy," *Amer. Econ. Rev.*, Mar. 1965, *55*, 19–39.

W. F. Stolper, *Planning Without Facts: Lesson's in Resource Allocation from Nigeria's Development*. Cambridge 1966.

M. P. Todaro, "A Model of Labor Migration and Urban Unemployment in Less Developed Countries," *Amer. Econ. Rev.*, Mar. 1969, *59*, 138–48.

Nigeria, *Report of the Commission on the Review of Wages, Salary and Conditions of Service of the Junior Employees of the Governments of the Federation and in Private Establishments 1963–64*.

[7]

JOURNAL OF REGIONAL SCIENCE, VOL. 24, NO. 4, 1984

A HEDONIC APPROACH TO THE DECENTRALIZATION OF MANUFACTURING ACTIVITY*

Paul R. Blackley†

1. INTRODUCTION

The decentralization of manufacturing activity within metropolitan areas in the United States has been well documented.[1] There have been many attempts to explain this phenomenon in terms of the land requirements and locational needs of urban manufacturing and the changing distributions of repelling and attracting location factors over the metropolitan area. By placing the location decision within a hedonic framework, this paper examines at the level of individual sites a substantial number of physical and locational attributes which may operate as important factors in the site selection process.

Previous work has identified some of the factors which should be considered. For example, Kain (1968) argued that many modern technologies require single-story facilities on spacious sites, thereby leading to the selection of a suburban site where larger tracts of relatively inexpensive land are more readily available. Similarly, the attraction of a growing suburban labor force [Steinnes (1982)] and a desire to avoid higher central city taxes [Hamer (1973) and Wasylenko (1980)] have been offered as important factors in the decentralization process.[2]

Past models of the manufacturing location process have often divided the metropolitan area into geographical or jurisdictional zones [Moomaw (1980), Erickson and Wasylenko (1980), and Stone (1974)].[3] Characteristics such as

---

*Helpful comments on an earlier draft which was presented at the Northeast Regional Science Association meetings in New York City, May 1983, were made by David Greytak, James Follain, Larry Schroeder, Jan Ondrich, and two anonymous referees. The author thanks Roger Schmenner of Duke University for making the Cinncinati data set available.

†Assistant Professor of Economics, Le Moyne College.

[1]Kain (1968) documented that the central cities' share of manufacturing employment in the 40 largest SMSA's declined from 67 percent in 1948 to 48 percent in 1963. Findings by Leone and Struyk (1976) for manufacturing employment shifts in four major metropolitan areas between 1965 and 1968 and by Solomon (1980) between 1963 and 1972 for Kain's set of cities indicate that the process continued into the 1970's.

[2]See Scott (1982) for a comprehensive review of the literature assessing the determinants of location behavior on the part of urban manufacturing firms. Scott concludes that urban location patterns are the result of a Heckscher-Ohlin effect by which capital-accumulating firms with standardized production processes develop internal economies of scale which allow them to decentralize to larger sites. In contrast, firms producing nonstandardized products remain dependent upon external economies as well as interfirm linkages and, consequently, select central locations in order to minimize their joint distance from the entire metropolitan area's labor force.

[3]The author will provide a detailed review of this literature upon request.

Date received: April, 1983; revised, July and November, 1983.

quantity of vacant land, population density, skill level of nearby labor force, access to transportation inputs, availability of agglomeration economies, and effective property tax rates are among the variables used to explain the level and composition of manufacturing activity contained in each zone. A firm then selects that zone which provides the minimum cost location within the metropolitan area, with decentralization resulting from the existence of lower cost sites in the suburbs.

However, there are several serious shortcomings associated with these previous studies which this paper attempts to overcome. After demonstrating the sensitivity of a simulation model of urban industrial location to the level of aggregation used to form geographical zones, Schmenner (1977) warns that "there is simply not a proper level of zone data aggregation [and] studies using zone level data should be abandoned" [Schmenner (1977, p. 188)]. A related problem is that average zonal characteristics often are not representative of specific sites within respective zones. As a result, unincluded intrazonal variations in locational variables may well be as significant as interzonal variations in determining manufacturing locations.[4] In contrast, this paper takes into account the heterogeneity of industrial sites by viewing the site as a bundle of attributes similar to hedonic studies of housing markets.[5]

Additionally, Alonso (1967) has demonstrated that urban rent theory is the appropriate allocative mechanism for industrial location analysis when competition for space is involved. Thus, a firm's ability to bid upon alternative sites determines its ultimate location, with the desire to minimize costs being a precursor to the rent maximization objective. The latter objective is, of course, constrained by the attainment of a satisfactory level of profits. Using survey data detailing the characteristics of individual firms and the attributes of their sites, this paper estimates a bid rent model of manufacturing location which incorporates the hedonic nature of the manufacturing site. In this manner the zonal aggregation problem is avoided and a role is provided for the allocative mechanism underlying urban location patterns.

The bid rent-cum-hedonic theory of manufacturing location is presented in Section 2. The model is empirically tested in Section 3 using survey data for individual firms from the Cincinnati metropolitan area. The results indicate that several site attributes are important factors in the location decision and that the geographical distributions of these attributes contribute to the decentralization on the part of many types of manufacturing firms. A brief summary concludes the paper.

2. A THEORY OF MANUFACTURING LOCATION

The following model of manufacturing location uses as its starting point Alonso's (1964) theory of bid price determination for the urban firm. The

---

[4]See Carlton (1977) for elaboration upon this point.

[5]Alonso (1967) argued that a firm bids upon a location as well as a production site when evaluating prospective sites, and Linneman (1982) has suggested that such a hedonic approach be taken in examining urban industrial location decisions. Recent work by Blackley (forthcoming) and Cooke (1983) has made use of site attributes in modeling manufacturing site selection, but neither is directly concerned with identifying attributes which are important determinants of location as is done in the hedonic analyses which follow.

fundamental outcome of the bid price model is the derivation of a negative relationship between distance from city center and land price. For any given level of profit, lower land prices at more distant locations reflect higher transportation costs to a centrally-located market, while lower transportation costs to the same market are capitalized in the form of higher land prices at more central locations. In locational equilibrium, firms producing at different locations within the urban area should earn equal profits.

However, in reality, a firm actually bids upon a bundle of attributes contained in a site rather than only distance from city center. In particular, the size of a site and the structural characteristics of any buildings on it, the package of local public services and taxes, proximity to various nonsite factors of production, and accessibility to product markets are all attributes that can vary considerably among urban locations. Thus, replacing distance from the city center as the sole locational determinant of a firm's bid price function is a set of site attributes. Together with a set of firm-specific characteristics (e.g., the firm's production technology, size, and product market orientation), these attributes jointly determine a firm's bid for any given site.[6]

Accordingly, the representative manufacturing firm is assumed to have a general production function of the form

$$Q = Q[X,L(Z)] \tag{1}$$

where Q is the level of output, X is a vector of nonsite factors of production which measure firm characteristics, and L is the site factor of production which depends upon a vector of site attributes, Z, such as those mentioned above.[7] The firm's profit equation can be expressed as

$$\pi = pQ[X,L(Z)] - nX - RL(Z) \tag{2}$$

where π is profit, p is the product price at the market (so product transportation costs are treated as a component of total cost), n is a vector of average nonsite factor prices, and R is the unit price of the firm's site. By using market average prices in n, all differentials in factor availability over the metropolitan area are capitalized into the site price. Thus, the expenditure on the site input, $RL(Z)$, is a function of site attributes, a formulation consistent with the hedonic theory of housing price determination.

Solving Equation (2) for R and introducing a specific level of satisfactory profits, π_0, the bid price function to be maximized can be written as

$$R = \frac{pQ[X,L(Z)] - nX - \pi_0}{L(Z)} \tag{3}$$

[6]It is important to note that Schmenner (1981), utilizing a subset of firms employed in this study and controlling for physical site attributes, found distance from city center to be an insignificant factor in explaining site prices. The hedonic models estimated below consider the underlying site attributes for which distance from city center proxies in most other studies.

[7]The production function is a variant of those employed by Lee (1982) and Blackley (forthcoming). In this case the term $L(Z)$ is formulated so as to capture the hedonic nature of the site factor. The derivation below of the logit specification from the bid price model is based upon Blackley's modification of a model of manufacturing employment location developed by Lee for Bogota, Colombia.

If p is used as a numeraire and n is suppressed as a constant, a general form of Equation (3) becomes

$$\tilde{R} = f(X, L(Z), \tilde{\pi}_0) \tag{4}$$

where $\tilde{R}$ and $\tilde{\pi}_0$ indicate that the dollar amounts of site price and profit have been standardized by the product price. As a result, a firm's bid for a prospective site is determined by its specific production characteristics, the attributes contained in the site, and its level of acceptable profits.

Lee (1982) has demonstrated that the logit specification can be easily derived from Equation (4) in order to test this type of model. First, recall that in locational equilibrium $\tilde{\pi}_0$ can be treated as a constant, since any variation in profit levels among firms would imply further adjustments in production and location behavior. Additionally, assume there are S site types and N_s sites of type s in the metropolitan area. Equation (4) can then be written as

$$\tilde{R}_{sn} = g_{sn}(X) \qquad (n \in N_s) \tag{5}$$

where the firm's bid for the nth site of type s is a function of its characteristics in X. Introducing a random error term for unexplained variations in bids upon sites of type s and realizing that a site is occupied by the maximum bid offered enables the use of the logit specification[8]

$$p(s \mid X) = \frac{\exp\,[g_s(X)]}{\sum_{s' \in S} \exp\,[g_{s'}(X)]} \tag{6}$$

Equation (6) expresses the probability of a site of type s being occupied by a firm with characteristics X, i.e., the likelihood that a firm defined by X can make a winning bid upon a site of type s. By using attributes positively associated with suburban (central) sites, the estimation of Equation (6) can provide information on the types of firms which are (not) decentralizing and therefore provide insight into the determinants of the decentralization process.

The model is tested in a three-step manner. First, hedonic regression models are estimated for both renter and owner firms in order to identify attributes considered to be important in site price determination. Evidence of significant attributes will provide support for the capitalization into site prices of attracting and repelling factors in the manufacturing site market. Second, the attributes are identified as being associated primarily with central, suburban, or no specific geographical location by means of a chi-square analysis. Third, a set of attribute demand equations are estimated with the logit specification in order to identify the types of firms demonstrating an ability to make winning bids for sites with attributes associated with suburban versus central locations. Several specific

[8]By assuming that the error terms associated with maximum bids offered are distributed with independent and identical Weibull distributions, Ellickson (1981) and Lee (1982) have shown that the logit specification follows. See Domencich and McFadden (1975) for the appropriateness of using the Weibull distribution to obtain their logit specification when estimating the behavior of maximizing agents.

hypotheses advanced in urban manufacturing location theory are addressed as well.

3. DATA AND ESTIMATION RESULTS

The manufacturing location model derived above is estimated for a set of firms drawn from the Cincinnati metropolitan area. The data are taken from a 1975–1976 survey conducted by Schmenner (1978), who asked individual firms to provide detailed information in the areas of production, marketing, and adminstration as well as on site attributes such as land area, number of stories in production facilities, and access to various product and input markets.[9] The Cincinnati area has experienced a good deal of manufacturing decentralization, with the central city's share of manufacturing employment having fallen from 50.7 percent in 1967 to 40.2 percent in 1977 [U.S. Department of Commerce (1976, 1981)]. Coupled with its history as a major center of diversified manufacturing activity (the leading industries being transportation equipment, machinery, fabricated metals, and food), this decentralization makes the Cincinnati area well suited for a test of the location model.

Hedonic Regressions

The hedonic regression analysis is conducted separately for renters and owners. The data do not include annual profit levels for individual firms nor the rates of depreciation used for tax purposes. Thus, it is not possible to estimate the user cost of capital for individual firms in order to transform owner site values into annual rental prices. Additionally, the variation in the estimation results below indicates that there are substantial differences in the effects of structural and locational attributes upon site prices between the two sectors.

The variables used to measure the prices and attributes of individual sites are listed in Table 1. For the subset of firms in the survey on which site price information is available, the average annual rental is just over $28,000 while the average site value is nearly $1,400,000. As is customary, the hedonic model attempts to explain site prices as a function of site attributes in order to obtain implicit market prices for each attribute. Therefore, the estimated equation is a reduced form model in which both demand and supply factors work simultaneously to determine each implicit price. With a cross-sectional sample, it can be assumed that the supply of manufacturing sites is relatively fixed, so that demand considerations dominate the price determination process.

Attributes considered to be of value to manufacturing firms should be positively capitalized into site prices, while undesirable features should work to lower site prices. Accordingly, positive signs are anticipated for all the attributes in Table 1 except *HGWY* (greater distance from an expressway is associated with a greater value for *HGWY*), *PROPTAX*, *YTAX*, and *YEARS* (the effects of inflation being more accurately accounted for in recent transactions in the manufacturing site market). *UTILTAX* is expected to have a positive sign, with

[9]Schmenner (1978) provides a description of the survey methodology employed and an extensive location analysis of all manufacturing activity in the Cincinnati SMSA and the sample of firms responding to the survey.

TABLE 1: Definition of Site Attributes

Variable Name	Description
RENTAL	Annual rental rate for site in thousands of dollars, including structures
VALUE	Value of site in thousands of dollars, including structures
LANDAREA	Site area in acres
BLDGAREA	Building floorspace in thousands of square feet
STORY	= {1 if all structures are single-story; 0 if not
SPACE	= {1 if there is room for expansion; 0 if not
VACANT	= {1 if site not previously used; 0 if site previously used
MFGUSE	= {1 if site previously used by a manufacturer; 0 if not
GAS	= {1 if site is served by local natural gas company; 0 if not
SEWER	= {1 if site is served by local sewer authority; 0 if not
RAIL	= {1 if site is located on railroad siding; 0 if not
HGWY	= {4 if more than 5 miles from expressway; 3 if within 5 miles, but not 2 miles, of expressway; 2 if within 2 miles, but not 1/2 mile, of expressway; 1 if within 1/2 mile of expressway
LABOR	= {1 if proximity to labor is close and important; 0 if not close or not important
PRODUCTMKT	= {1 if proximity to customers is close and important; 0 if not close or not important
SERVICE	= {1 if proximity to repair, legal, accounting, advertising, or other special services is close and important; 0 if not close or not important
PROPTAX	Effective local property tax rate
YTAX	Effective local income tax rate
UTILTAX	= {1 if utilities and taxes are included in rent; 0 if not
STATE	= {1 if located in Ohio; 0 if not
YEARS	number of years firm has occupied site

Source: Survey data set used in Schmenner (1978). The proximity and importance of labor, customers, and services are assessed by individual firms.

companies paying their own taxes and utilities being compensated in the form of lower rentals.

A Box-Cox procedure is used to estimate maximum likelihood parameters for both the renter and owner equations. Due to the prevalence of categorical explanatory variables, only the dependent variable is transformed in each case.[10]

[10]See Goodman (1981) for an identical transformation used in a hedonic analysis of housing submarkets.

TABLE 2: Hedonic Price Equations—Maximum Likelihood Estimates

Dependent Variable / Explanatory Variables	*RENTAL*$^{(-0.002)}$ Coefficient	*RENTAL*$^{(-0.002)}$ t-Statistic	*VALUE*$^{(0.122)}$ Coefficient	*VALUE*$^{(0.122)}$ t-Statistic
INTERCEPT	0.554	0.60	4.154*	2.16
LANDAREA	0.013*	1.28	0.037*	2.36
BLDGAREA	0.015*	3.58	0.003*	2.03
STORY	0.090	0.39	0.671*	1.28
SPACE	0.062	0.31	1.247*	2.08
VACANT	0.612*	2.04	0.711*	1.46
GAS	0.308	1.12	1.991*	2.41
SEWER	0.414	1.12	1.385*	1.62
RAIL	0.481	1.15	1.515*	2.35
HGWY	−0.034	−0.23	0.351	1.06
LABOR	0.354*	1.58	−0.538	−1.12
PRODUCTMKT	0.483*	2.27	0.102	0.22
SERVICE	−0.077	−0.37	0.376	0.77
PROPTAX	−0.666*	−1.45	−0.980	−1.04
YTAX	−0.108	−0.76	−0.011	−0.03
UTILTAX	0.383*	1.28	—	—
STATE	1.573*	2.97	0.110	0.11
YEARS	−0.008	−0.90	0.015	1.21
R^2	0.49		0.53	
N	90		139	

*Significant at 0.10 level for one-tail test.

Note: Both equations are estimated by nonlinear least squares with a Box-Cox transformation of the dependent variable. The transformation parameter, θ, for the maximum likelihood estimates of the coefficients is −0.002 for the renter equation and 0.122 for the owner equation.

Thus, the hedonic model can be expressed as

$$[RL(Z)]_i^{(\theta)} = \sum_{j=1}^{K} \beta_j Z_{ij} + \epsilon_i \tag{7}$$

where $[R\,L(Z)]^{(\theta)} = [R \cdot L(Z)]^{\theta} - 1/\theta$; K is the number of explanatory variables, Z, as defined in Table 1, plus a constant term; θ and the β_j are unknown parameters; and ϵ_i is an error term which for the true functional form is assumed to be independently and identically distributed with a normal distribution of mean zero. Dividing each observation on the dependent variable by its geometric mean, the maximum likelihood estimates of θ and the β_j are found by nonlinear least squares.[11] The results for the renter and owner equations are shown in Table 2. The maximum likelihood estimates of θ converged to −0.002 and 0.122 for the renter and owner equations, respectively. With roughly half the variation in site prices being explained in each model, the application of the hedonic method to manufacturing sites is similar in explanatory power to previous applications to urban housing markets. As such, the logical extension of the hedonic technique to industrial location analysis would appear to be upheld in this case.

[11]See Spitzer (1982) for details on the Box-Cox estimation procedure, especially for the proper estimation of the maximum likelihood covariance matrix.

We turn now to the results for specific site attributes. Although there are only a few, similarities do exist between the renter and owner equations. It is no surprise that larger sites with more floor space have higher rentals and values. Moreover, the finding that previously vacant sites are associated with higher prices lends support to the incubating potential of preexisting structures. Specifically, the availability of previously occupied sites at lower prices is one of the chief tenets of the incubator hypothesis of new manufacturing location. However, Leone and Struyk (1976) offer only mixed evidence concerning the extent to which affordable production space directly leads to the birth of new manufacturing activity. As a result, it may be that the higher price for previously vacant sites captures the cost savings associated with not having to demolish outdated structures and the efficiencies of a layout built specifically for the current occupant's production technology.[12] Additionally, the lack of significance of access to business services in both equations suggests that improvements in metropolitan transportation systems have effectively diffused agglomeration economies to locations throughout most urban areas [Schmenner (1981) and Hamer (1973)].

As indicated above, there is greater variation than similarity between the results for the renter and owner equations. Besides those mentioned above, structural site attributes do not figure significantly in the determination of prices in the rental market, while in every case they are significant attributes in the owner market. On the other hand, it is only in the rental market that locational attributes prove to be significant determinants of site price. In particular, attributes such as access to local labor and product markets and location in the state of Ohio are significant positive factors in determining site rents. Given that average time at site for renters is 9.5 years as compared to 24.4 years for owners, it appears that less-established firms are willing to pay more for sites which allow them to develop close ties with the local population in terms of both their labor forces and customers. In addition to having located more recently, renters are more likely than owners to be considering a plant relocation by a margin of 34 percent to 21 percent. This greater tendency towards footlooseness on the part of renters allows locational factors to play an important role in their site selection process. Similarly, the positive impact of location in the state of Ohio for renters is apt to reflect the benefits of access to well-established and more extensive input and product markets. For example, in 1977 over 90 percent of the metropolitan area's manufacturing labor force worked in the Ohio portion of the SMSA [U.S. Department of Commerce (1981)].

The local effective property tax rate has a significant but negative effect upon site rents. The most plausible explanation for this result is that landlords facing higher property tax rates have less incentive to maintain or improve their properties and as a result must accept lower bids than otherwise. Despite the fact that there is substantial variation in income tax rates levied by local governments throughout the metropolitan area, these differentials are not significantly capital-

---

[12]Hamer's (1973) calculations for the Boston SMSA show that the costs of renovating existing structures or demolishing and rebuilding are very high, so that less incubating activity occurs than might be expected with these cheaper structures.

ized by either renters or owners in the form of lower site prices. The fact that local taxes are such a small percentage of total costs has often been cited as a reason for their insignificance in most manufacturing location decisions [see Due (1961) and Schmenner (1982)]. As expected, inclusion of utilities and property taxes in a lease has a positive influence on site rent.

The dominance of structural over locational attributes in the owner market is demonstrated by the fact that all of the structural attributes contribute significantly to site value while access to various markets and local taxes are in every case insignificant factors. Because firms which own their sites are more likely to be well established in their product and input markets, there is less of a role for access in determining overall site value. Rather, the nature of a site's production space, to which the firm has contributed substantial resources, is of primary concern in the owner market.

In addition to the areal attributes discussed above, owners appear to be willing to pay a premium for extra space for future expansion. Relatedly, the existence of single-story structures serves to increase the value of a manufacturing site. Together these results lend support to Kain's (1968) contention that technologies such as assembly-line operations are best suited to single-story layouts on more spacious sites. Cramped facilities and multistory structures are likely to be outdated and, therefore, negative attributes in the site bundle.

Finally, sites equipped with essential elements of the local infrastructure are valued more highly than otherwise. In each case the on-site provision of gas, sewer, or rail service adds to site value.[13] Their significance in the owner equation as opposed to their insignificance in the renter equation is reflective of the long-term commitment to a site which ownership implies. Although substitutes can be found for each of these attributes, it is reasonable that their historical role as the cheapest alternatives for energy, waste disposal, and bulk transportation contributes to their importance in the owner market. The locational inertia associated with site ownership may also be indicated by the positive impact of number of years at site. Greater time for growth and expansion are most likely responsible for this result.

Overall, the hedonic approach to the manufacturing site market appears to be a useful method of analysis. Not only have individual attributes proven to be significant in the determination of site prices, but the results also suggest important differences between renters and owners in evaluating sites. The primary finding is that firms in the rental market are shopping for locational as well as structural attributes, while owners are interested in only the structural attributes of individual sites. Additionally, measures such as access to labor force and customers appear to perform better than a single distance from city center variable more commonly used in such studies. However, the relative importance of structural attributes and insignificance of the *SERVICE* and *HGWY* variables may indicate that locational aspects of the manufacturing site are less important

[13]The availability of local water service is omitted from the hedonic models due to its high correlation with *SEWER*. *MFGUSE* is omitted because of its high correlation with *VACANT*. Simple correlations among the included variables are generally below 0.2 in absolute value.

TABLE 3: Geographical Distribution of Site Attributes

Attribute	Percentage of Sites With Attribute		N
	Core[a]	Noncore	
LANDAREA[b]*	26.5	44.9	348
*STORY**	37.7	81.6	425
*SPACE**	58.6	73.8	444
*VACANT**	14.4	44.8	421
*MFGUSE**	50.6	26.1	421
LABOR	54.7	55.7	425
*PRODUCTMKT**	45.0	36.9	403
SERVICE	35.2	31.8	390

Notes:

*Asterisk indicates chi-square statistic for rejecting independence of geographical and attribute distributions is significant at the 0.10 level.

[a]Core defined as locations in Cincinnati CBD and in two rings of ZIP codes surrounding CBD, including sites in Kentucky.

[b]For discrete analysis, *LANDAREA* = 1 if lot size is greater than or equal to four acres; *LANDAREA* = 0 if lot size is less than four acres.

than in earlier eras when a central location near other elements of economic activity was vital to the existence of many firms.

Chi-Square Analysis

Having documented the usefulness of the hedonic approach to the analysis of manufacturing sites, insight into the process of manufacturing decentralization can be gained by observing the distributions of individual attributes over the urban area. In Table 3, for both the core and noncore areas of the Cincinnati SMSA, the percentage of sites possessing eight dichotomously defined attributes are listed.[14] In six of eight cases there is a significant difference between the percentage of sites possessing each attribute at core versus noncore locations. Several points are noteworthy in demonstrating the sample's representativeness of the typical declining industrial city.

First, for each of four structural attributes (*LANDAREA, STORY, SPACE,* and *VACANT*) determined to be important components of the site bundle, a significantly greater percentage of noncore rather than core locations possess the desired attribute. As such, the growing preference on the part of manufacturing firms for single-story structures on large, previously vacant sites appears to be a reasonable explanation for manufacturing decentralization. As the capital and land intensities of manufacturing operations continue to increase with technological advances, the inability of central areas to accommodate larger firms indicates that the decentralization process is unlikely to abate in the near future. Second, a

[14]For the chi-square analysis and logit models discussed below, the estimations include observations on firms which did not report a site price. The number varies among the attributes considered due to the incompleteness of individual survey responses.

greater potential for incubating activity exists at central locations in the Cincinnati area, as evidenced by the much greater percentage of core as opposed to noncore sites which were previously occupied by another manufacturer (*MFGUSE*). However, despite this potential, Schmenner (1982) has shown that the core area of Cincinnati did not perform well relative to the rest of the SMSA in terms of plant openings between 1971 and 1975.

Perhaps contributing to this finding is that the Cincinnati core appears to have lost the traditional advantage of a central location, access to other elements of economic activity. In particular, the extensiveness of highway coverage over the metropolitan area may be breaking the historical link between manufacturing and the core. The nearly identical percentages for *LABOR* between core and noncore areas is indicative of the suburbanization of the residential labor force, while the suspected diffusion of external economies throughout the metropolitan area is seen in the similar percentage of sites with access to business services at core and noncore locations. In addition, the low percentage of firms reporting that access to such services is important and close by may reflect the growing self-sufficiency of manufacturing activity which accompanies the development of economies of scale in production [Scott (1982)].

Although access to product markets is still more likely to be associated with sites in the core, the difference between core and noncore percentages is smaller than for the structural attributes. In addition, the importance of regional and

TABLE 4: Definition of Firm Characteristics

Variable Name		Description
*CLASS**	=	1 if durable good output 0 if nondurable good output
EMPLOY		Average plant employment during past year
SKILL	=	1 if employ little or no unskilled labor 0 if employ some unskilled labor
LOCOUT		Percentage output value sold within Cincinnati metropolitan area
LOCIN		Percentage input value purchased within Cincinnati metropolitan area
INDPROD		Percentage output value sold to other industrial firms
TRAN-COST	=	1 if transport costs considered a locational constraint 0 if not
BRANCH	=	1 if branch of multiplant firm 0 if single plant firm
ACQUIRE	=	2 if built structures 1 if purchased structures 0 if rent structures
RELO-CATE	=	1 if considering plant relocation or branch 0 if not

Source: Survey data set used in Schmenner (1978).

*Durable goods include lumber; furniture; stone, clay, and glass; primary and fabricated metals; machinery; electrical and transportation equipment; and instruments. Nondurable goods include food and tobacco, textiles and apparel, paper and printing, chemicals, petroleum, rubber and plastics, leather, and miscellaneous goods.

national markets as opposed to local markets in manufacturing is evident, given that less than 50 percent of all firms report proximity to customers as important and close by. Thus, for the most part, the locational pull of the core as a primary manufacturing location appears to be gone in the Cincinnati area. Coupled with the attractiveness of noncore locations in terms of structural attributes, the general decentralization of manufacturing activity documented above for Cincinnati is a logical consequence.

Logit Models of Attribute Demand

Despite the fact that most of the important site attributes are associated with noncentral sites in the Cincinnati area, the model of manufacturing location developed in Section 2 suggests that there should be substantial variation in the types of firms attracted to each specific attribute. Because of the number of site attributes considered, the logit analysis is confined to a set of binary choice models. Thus, the probability of a firm making a winning bid upon a site of type s reduces to

$$p(s \mid X) = \frac{1}{1 + \exp[-g(X)]} \tag{8}$$

where $g(X)$ is a linear function of firm characteristics.

The attribute demand approach is demonstrated by estimating the demands for two structural attributes (*LANDAREA* and *STORY*) and two locational attributes (*PRODUCTMKT* and *SERVICE*).[15] It should be remembered that larger lots and single-story structures tend to be located in noncore areas, while access to product markets and business services is only slightly more likely to be associated with sites in core areas. The firm characteristics used to differentiate the abilities of individual firms to make winning bids upon sites are listed in Table 4. (*YEARS* is defined in Table 1.) Variables related to a firm's production technology (*CLASS, EMPLOY, SKILL*), market orientation (*LOCOUT, LOCIN, INDPROD, TRANCOST*), and administrative organization (*BRANCH, ACQUIRE, RELOCATE, YEARS*) are included in the analysis.

CLASS provides a measure of product standardization which Stone (1974) found to be an important factor for manufacturing location in the Boston metropolitan area. Durable goods production is assumed to be more standardized than nondurable goods production and, therefore, requires larger sites with single-story facilities in order to utilize modern technologies. On the other hand, the manufacturing of nondurable goods in industries such as food, rubber and plastic, printing, and apparel is often subject to production changes in response to

[15] Models for other attributes were also estimated but for the sake of brevity are not shown here. They are available from the author upon request. In Blackley (forthcoming) I estimate a multinomial logit model to test whether differences in firm capabilities for utilizing technological innovations influence variations in site selection behavior with respect to access to business services and land area. In order to explore more fully the hedonic nature of the manufacturing site, here I consider the demands for these attributes separately in addition to the two others, *PRODUCTMKT* and *STORY*. Because the joint nature of the demand for a bundle of attributes suggests a multinomial approach, the results should be taken as being suggestive of actual attribute demand relationships.

changing demand conditions. Consequently, firms in these industries may need more flexible production processes and are expected to locate on sites with ready access to interfirm linkages and business services as well as the local Cincinnati product market [Scott (1982)].

Firm size is measured by *EMPLOY*, which should be directly related to *LANDAREA*. Because larger firms are likely to serve regional and national markets and to develop their own advertising, legal, and maintenance services, they are not expected to require access to local markets and services to the same degree as smaller and less self-sufficient firms. Also, firms able to utilize unskilled labor (*SKILL* = 0) are likely to use production methods of the assembly-line variety. As a result they should favor single-story structures on larger sites. Firms employing labor of greater skill may engage in more specialized production on a smaller scale. They would, therefore, prefer smaller sites with better access to customers and services as demand and cost considerations vary over time.

Firms selling larger percentages of their output locally are likely to be highly dependent upon access to customers. Given their location in a relatively declining metropolitan area, these firms are in less need of larger sites for expansion purposes. Firms receiving most of their inputs from local suppliers are likely to be dependent upon other local services and therefore require less land for warehousing and other on site activities than firms dealing with nonlocal suppliers. Similarly, those constrained by transportation costs (*TRANCOST* = 1) are likely to locate in close proximity to their product and service markets. Although firms selling primarily to other firms should value access to such customers, the production of intermediate goods need not require the support of specialized outside services. Since such production frequently involves heavy manufacturing with substantial negative externalities, these firms are likely to be noncentrally located and, therefore, in single-story facilities on larger sites.

Firms often establish a branch plant to develop new markets or implement more modern production methods [Schmenner (1982)]. Thus, it is expected that relative to single-plant firms they will tend to occupy single-story facilities on larger sites, while at the same time maintaining access to local customers. Because branch plants also operate within larger organizations, they are less likely to require nearby firms to provide services in areas such as maintenance and marketing. *ACQUIRE* serves as a proxy for the suitability of a firm's plant to its production process and as an indication of a firm's commitment to the local area. In order to be able to adjust their plants as technological changes occur, firms which own their plants are expected to select larger sites with single-story structures. As demonstrated above, renters are more mobile than owners and therefore can more readily move to a different site when constrained by a lack of space. This should allow them to base their location decisions more on the need for access to customers and business services than on modern structural attributes.

Firms with fewer years at their present site may occupy single-story facilities on larger sites in order to accommodate newer production layouts, yet their shorter time at site may be indicative of smaller operations. Likewise, there is evidence from recent location behavior in and around London that younger firms with fewer years at their site often select sites with easy access to nearby product markets

TABLE 5: Logit Estimation of Selected Attribute Demand Equations

Explanatory Variables[b]	Dependent Variable (Number of Observations)[a]			
	LANDAREA (348)	*STORY* (425)	*PRODUCTMKT* (403)	*SERVICE* (390)
INTERCEPT	1.108 (2.42)*	0.898 (2.48)*	−1.572 (−4.55)*	−0.823 (−2.06)*
CLASS	0.357 (1.18)	0.678 (2.96)*	−0.280 (−1.17)	−0.139 (−0.58)
EMPLOY	0.007 (4.62)*	−0.001 (−1.10)	0.000 (0.00)	0.001 (1.01)
SKILL	1.001 (2.89)*	−0.450 (−1.47)*	—	0.432 (1.42)*
LOCOUT	0.013 (−2.51)*	−0.005 (−1.28)*	0.028 (7.06)*	0.003 (0.87)
LOCIN	0.007 (1.46)*	−0.002 (−0.45)	−0.002 (−0.62)	0.002 (0.62)
INDPROD	0.003 (1.00)	0.005 (2.00)*	0.003 (1.15)	−0.005 (−2.00)*
TRANCOST	—	—	0.820 (3.24)*	0.383 (1.56)*
BRANCH	1.043 (3.11)*	−0.244 (−0.86)	0.464 (1.64)*	−1.426 (−4.03)*
ACQUIRE	0.661 (3.59)*	0.546 (3.76)*	0.287 (1.96)*	−0.052 (−0.37)
RELOCATE	−0.770 (−2.12)*	−0.339 (−1.31)*	−0.371 (−1.34)*	−0.593 (−2.14)*
YEARS	−0.007 (−0.77)	−0.038 (−5.32)*	−0.011 (−1.61)*	0.004 (0.61)
Model Chi-Square	145.6*	78.5*	87.2*	34.5*
Percentage Observations Predicted Correctly	80.2	72.2	69.7	67.7

[a]The number of observations varies among models because some survey responses by individual firms were incomplete with respect to attributes used in this study.

[b]t-statistics are in parentheses. An asterisk indicates a coefficient is significant at the 0.10 level for a one-tail test.

[Nicholson, Brinkley, and Evans (1981)]. However, the locational inertia associated with many years at a site may also leave a long-term occupant in close proximity to other elements of economic activity. Thus, although time at site is certain to reflect a firm's demand for specific attributes, there is no a priori expected sign for *YEARS* due to these conflicting effects. Finally, because each of the attributes is defined as a positive location factor, *RELOCATE* should be negatively related to each.

The results for the attribute demand equations are shown in Table 5. They serve to illustrate the pattern of manufacturing location decisions with respect to specific site attributes, which is consistent with the outcome of the competitive bid rent process. The model chi-square statistics and significance of most of the firm characteristics in each equation suggest that the bid rent approach is the appropriate model for analyzing the manufacturing location process. Additionally, the models appear useful for predictive purposes, with more than two-thirds of the observations in each case being correctly predicted.[16]

For the most part, the results conform to the hypotheses advanced above and indicate that the hedonic nature of manufacturing sites plays an important role in

[16]An observation is considered to be correctly predicted if its estimated probability is less than 50 percent away from the actual 0 or 1 decision regarding a specific attribute.

the location behavior of manufacturing firms. The similar results for *LANDAREA* and *STORY* are reflective of the complementary relationship between these attributes in the site bundle. Firms utilizing the standardization involved with durable goods production tend to make winning bids for single-story structures on larger sites. Also, the use of unskilled labor is associated with these kinds of sites. Taken together with the fact that recent locators strongly favor single-story facilities, these results support the hypothesis that newer technologies are better suited to spacious suburban locations. Further evidence along this line, which is consistent with hypotheses advanced above, is provided by the finding that branch plants as well as intermediate goods producers prefer larger sites.

Although not exclusively located in the core, there appears to be indirect support for the incubating potential of older sites characterized by the presence of multistory structures on smaller lots. Renters, as opposed to those who purchase or build their own facilities, tend to occupy such sites as do firms which sell their products and purchase their inputs primarily in local markets. Similarly, the likelihood of a relocation of operations is associated with these less modern sites, a predictable pattern of behavior once the incubating period is completed.

Production characteristics explain little of the location behavior with respect to access to product markets and business services on the part of manufacturing firms in the Cincinnati area. The only significant finding is that the use of unskilled labor tends to occur away from other elements of economic activity, indicating that there is little need for support services by these firms. The coefficients for *CLASS* are of the anticipated sign, but insignificant in both cases.

Those firms citing transportation costs as a locational constraint also report that access to customers and services is important and close by. Thus, there is evidence that distance still plays a role in the intrametropolitan location decision; however, given the distributions of these attributes over the metropolitan area, distance from the CBD no longer appears to be the relevant variable in the decision. Those selling their output locally also tend to select sites which are near to their customers, while those selling in retail rather than industrial markets appear to select sites with close proximity to advertising and other related business services.[17] The preference of firms selling to regional and national markets for larger sites away from local markets is explained by their need to produce greater levels of output and a desire for easier access to interurban highways at the periphery.

As hypothesized above, branch plants in the Cincinnati area have been located so as to be near a product market of the parent firm. Still, the importance of company ties is suggested by the strong negative relation between status as a branch plant and access to business services. Although it was expected that renters rather than owners would seek customer access in order to establish a market identity, the positive coefficient for *ACQUIRE* in the *PRODUCTMKT* equation indicates just the opposite result. This may be reflective of the fact that access to product markets acts as a prerequisite for long-term commitment to a local area as

[17]The substitution of product market access in place of larger sites by firms serving local markets is an example of Isard's (1956) substitution principle of location behavior.

it is often cited as the most important factor in many industrial location surveys. Even so, the association of fewer years at site with access to customers is consistent with the recent experience for London mentioned above. Finally, firms satisfied with their access to customers and services are unlikely to consider a relocation within the metropolitan area. This is similar to a finding by Leone and Struyk (1976) that firms demonstrating an initial dependence upon external economies in the core often maintain a core location even after the early period of firm development has been completed.

4. SUMMARY REMARKS

The empirical results for the sample of firms from the Cincinnati metropolitan area support the bid rent-cum-hedonic theory of manufacturing location. The hedonic models have identified a set of site attributes, both structural and locational, which are significant determinants of manufacturing site prices. The chi-square analysis reveals that the important structural attributes tend to be located on noncore sites, while access to various input and product markets is fairly uniform throughout the metropolitan area. Together, these analyses indicate that central locations in Cincinnati may have had their locational advantage eroded by improvements in transportation while at the same time suburban sites have become attractive in terms of available space for modern technologies.

Furthermore, the attribute demand results have provided support for the location model derived in Section 2. By utilizing individual attributes in the analysis, Kain's production technology-location hypothesis, aspects of Scott's urban Heckscher-Ohlin effect, and the importance of intrametropolitan access have all proven useful in explaining firm location decisions. Given the trend within many industries towards more standardized production in larger scale plants as documented by Scott (1982), the results here indicate that the decentralization of manufacturing activity should continue in Cincinnati and similar urban areas throughout the United States. Nevertheless, it has been shown that firms serving local markets with less standardized products (e.g., firms in the printing and apparel industries) are able to utilize less modern facilities in order to maintain a central location for marketing and distribution purposes.

Further investigation into the location behavior of both manufacturing and nonmanufacturing businesses is needed, especially in the area of the firm-specific nature of the process. It is decisions within individual firms in response to new technologies and changing geographical distributions of key location factors which are in large part determining the evolving spatial structures of our metropolitan areas.

REFERENCES

Alonso, William. *Location and Land Use*. Cambridge: Harvard University Press, 1964.

———. "A Reformulation of Classical Location Theory and its Relation to Rent Theory," *Papers, Regional Science Association*, 19 (1967), 23–44.

Blackley, Paul R. "The Demand for Industrial Sites in a Metropolitan Area: Theory, Empirical Evidence, and Policy Implications," *Journal of Urban Economics*, forthcoming.

Carlton, Dennis W. *Locational Decisions of Manufacturing Firms*, Report 7728, Center for Mathematical Studies in Business and Economics, University of Chicago, 1977.

Cooke, Timothy W. "Testing a Model of Intraurban Firm Relocation," *Journal of Urban Economics*, 13 (1983), 257–282.

Domencich, Thomas A. and Daniel McFadden. *Urban Travel Demand.* New York: Elsevier-North Holland, 1975.

Due, John F. "Studies of State-Local Tax Influences on Location," *National Tax Journal*, 14 (1961), 163–173.

Ellickson, Bryan. "An Alternative Test of the Hedonic Theory of Housing Markets," *Journal of Urban Economics*, 9 (1981), 56–79.

Erickson, Rodney A. and Michael J. Wasylenko. "Firm Relocation and Site Selection in Suburban Municipalities," *Journal of Urban Economics*, 8 (1980), 69–85.

Goodman, Allan C. "Housing Submarkets Within Urban Areas: Definitions and Evidence," *Journal of Regional Science*, 21 (1981), 175–185.

Hamer, Andrew M. *Industrial Exodus From Central City.* Lexington: D.C. Heath, 1973.

Isard, Walter. *Location and Space Economy.* New York: Wiley, 1956.

Kain, John F. "The Distribution and Movement of Jobs and Industry," in J.Q. Wilson (ed.), *The Metropolitan Enigma.* Cambridge: Harvard University Press, 1968.

Lee, Kyu S. "A Model of Intraurban Employment Location: An Application to Bogota, Colombia," *Journal of Urban Economics*, 12 (1982), 263–279.

Leone, Robert A. and Raymond Struyk. "The Incubator Hypothesis: Evidence from Five SMSAs," *Urban Studies*, 13 (1976), 325–331.

Linneman, Peter. "Hedonic Prices and Residential Location," in D.B. Diamond and G.S. Tolley (eds.), *The Economics of Urban Amenities.* New York: Academic Press, 1982.

Moomaw, Ronald L. "Urban Firm Location: Comparative Statics and Empirical Evidence," *Southern Economic Journal*, 46 (1980), 404–418.

Nicholson, B.M., Ian Brinkley, and Alan Evans. "The Role of the Inner City in the Development of Manufacturing Industry," *Urban Studies*, 18 (1981), 57–71.

Schmenner, Roger W. "Urban Industrial Location: An Evolutionary Model," *Journal of Regional Science*, 17 (1977), 179–194.

———. *The Manufacturing Location Decision: Evidence form Cincinnati and New England*, Report of the Office of Economic Research, Economic Development Administration, U.S. Department of Commerce, 1978.

———. "The Rent Gradient for Manufacturing," *Journal of Urban Economics*, 9 (1981), 09–96.

———. *Making Business Location Decisions.* Englewood Cliffs, N.J.: Prentice-Hall, Inc., 1982.

Scott, Allen J. "Locational Patterns and Dynamics of Industrial Activity in the Modern Metropolis," *Urban Studies*, 19 (1982), 111–141.

Solomon, Arthur P. "The Emerging Metropolis," in A.P. Solomon (ed.), *The Prospective City.* Cambridge: MIT Press, 1980.

Spitzer, John J. "A Primer on Box-Cox Estimation," *Review of Economics and Statistics*, 64 (1982), 307–313.

Steinnes, Donald N. "Do 'People Follow Jobs' or do 'Jobs Follow People'? A Causality Issue in Urban Economics," *Urban Studies*, 19 (1982), 187–192.

Stone, Donald N. *Industrial Location in Metropolitan Areas: A General Model for Boston.* New York: Praeger, 1974.

U.S. Department of Commerce, Bureau of the Census. *1972 Census of Manufacturers, Area Statistics, 3.* Washington, D.C.: U.S. Government Printing Office, 1976.

———. *1977 Census of Manufacturers, Geographic Area Statistics, 3.* Washington, D.C.: U.S. Government Printing Office, 1981.

Wasylenko, Michael J. "Evidence of Fiscal Differentials and Intrametropolitan Firm Relocation," *Land Economics*, 56 (1980), 339–349.

[8]

Urban Studies (1979), 16, 29–43 ©

Inner Areas as Spatial Labour Markets: a Critique of the Inner Area Studies

Paul C. Cheshire

[*First received January* 1978; *in final form May* 1978]

Summary. After briefly sketching a suitable analytical framework for local labour markets the paper applies the analysis to the problems identified as peculiar to the inner city. It concludes that inner city labour market problems are not peculiar to such areas but result from the economics of urban structure compounded by general labour market deterioration.

There has recently been a flow of studies of spatial labour markets. The work of Brechling (1967), Davies (1967) and Thirlwall (1966) in the 1960s was not in general infused by any coherent labour market analysis but rather examined differences in industrial structure and general regional characteristics. More recent work by Cheshire (1973), Metcalf (1975), Metcalf and Richardson (1976) has had, though implicitly, a more developed labour market analysis as a background reference. There have also been valuable contributions from specifically urban rather than labour economists, such as Vipond (1974) and Evans (1976). To this flow of literature has recently been added the reports and working papers of the Inner Area Studies (1977a and b).

It is not intended here to present substantial new research findings. There are three aims. First, to develop a general view of the working of labour markets and the way in which spatially differentiated labour markets can be defined and interact; then, within this framework, to synthesise and to an extent re-interpret existing work. Finally, in the light of the review of this existing body of theory and evidence it is intended to provide a critique of the labour market findings of the Inner Area Studies and consequent upon this critique, to evaluate the inner area policies that have been developed.

It is thought that this slightly tangental approach to assessing the particular question of inner area labour market problems and the more general one of spatial differences in unemployment is worth while since neither question can be adequately analysed without reference both to general labour market and urban theory. The highly critical assessment of the Inner Area Studies' labour market analysis finally reached in this paper stems from this fundamental point that in the author's view at least, the Studies conspicuously failed to offer either a labour market analytical basis for their diagnosis or even, perhaps more surprisingly, an adequate basis in urban theory.

In order to make my central argument quite unambiguous it is worth stating it at the outset. It will be argued that the most important single source of differences between spatial labour markets, such markets being spatial sub-divisions of a national market, is differences in the level of excess demand for labour. An important contributory factor, when the spatial labour markets are contiguous sub-divisions of a metropolitan area, is supply side differences arising from the logic of urban structure.

Perhaps the most helpful analytical model of the labour market for present purposes is provided by Holt (1970a and b). This incorporates the actual mechanisms – the basic stocks and flows – that are peculiar to labour markets; an explicit supply and demand side and a plausible set of market related behavioural characteristics. From it a basic Phillips curve relationship and unemployment (U) and vacancy (V) relationship can be deduced. The model is not set out here but will provide a background

Paul C. Cheshire is in the Department of Economics, University of Reading.

reference to what follows. A useful simple statement of the Holt model can be found in Trevithick and Mulvey (1975) and the derivation of the log linear UV relationship in Cheshire (1977).

Inner areas, however, are only a particular case of spatial labour markets. Thus to analyse their labour market problems one needs not only a basic labour market analytical framework but also a definition of a 'spatial labour market'. Once labour is allowed to be heterogeneous rather than homogeneous space can be incorporated as just one dimension of its heterogeneity. For labour is most usefully viewed as a continuum but a continuum in many dimensions. We may draw boundaries in labour markets with respect to a particular dimension, between occupations or skills, on industrial lines or between classes, or primary and secondary segments, but I wish to emphasise the extent to which such lines are crossed, and more importantly the fact that both the volume and direction of net flow are not exogenous but endogenous and a function of excess demand.

We can envisage a skill dimension taking the form of a continuum from the most highly skilled manual or white collar worker to the completely unskilled; substitution is possible at all levels on this continuum and the exact qualifications demanded of a potential employee, and therefore the volume and direction of net flow across what might be thought of as skill-boundaries, will vary with the level of excess demand. There will similarly be industrial mobility – Hunter and Reid (1968) have shown only a third of job changes remain in the same industry – and the total amount of job changing taking place, as work on turnover data by for example Bowers, Cheshire and Webb (1970) has shown, is, like other forms of mobility, a function of the level of excess demand; it increases as demand rises.

The spatial dimension of labour markets is simply one more dimension in terms of which mobility occurs. This implies a dynamic view of labour markets and suggests a problem with respect to the definition of a particular spatial labour market. Attempts have been made for example to define local labour markets or labour catchment areas. These, however, have been defined (see, for example, Goodman, 1970) in a static equilibrium context where boundaries have been identified as contours of equal commuting in either direction. In a dynamic context where space is only an additional labour market dimension and mobility occurs, such lines must be arbitrary or impossible to distinguish, except as they occur at points in time.

It is useful to define two sorts of mobility in the spatial dimension; continuous mobility may be defined as job mobility without residential relocation; discontinuous mobility involves both job mobility (or a move from unemployment or inactivity to employment) and residential relocation. We are thus defining mobility in terms of spatial labour market analysis rather than in terms of, say, urban structure.

Evidence suggests that the volume of both continuous spatial mobility and discontinuous spatial mobility is a function of the level of excess demand for labour. Although not identical, turnover data may be taken as a proxy for continuous mobility and the volume of turnover, as was noted above, has been shown to be a positive function of excess demand. The volume of inter-regional migration, which may be taken as a proxy for discontinuous mobility, has likewise been shown to be a function of the level of excess demand. This was demonstrated in Vanderkamp's (1971) interesting study of inter-regional migration in Canada. As numerous studies have shown the direction of net flow of inter-regional migration is a function of relative levels of excess demand as measured for example by relative earnings or job opportunities. It would be virtually inconceivable that the direction of net flow of continuous spatial mobility was not similarly a function of relative excess demand levels.

Given that continuous mobility imposes only small costs on those who undertake it but that discontinuous mobility involves a substantial cost and probably represents the most significant labour market friction, we may expect a short-run and a long-run effect on local labour markets as a result of changes in the spatial pattern of excess demand. If we consider just two markets, then in the short run if the relative level of excess demand rises in one relative to the other there will be induced continuous mobility and its labour catchment area will expand. In the longer run there will be induced discontinuous mobility which in a naïve neo-classical model would tend to reduce the physical size of the labour catchment area but which, if it reinforced the differences in levels of excess demand, might further expand the labour catchment area. It is in this sense that local labour market boundaries defined by equal commuting in either direction are arbitrary or exist only at a point in time.

We can apply these ideas to the particular case of inner areas. Changes in the pattern of excess demand occur as localised 'events'; an example might be a factory closure in an inner area. Any event such as this will have a particular structure of characteristics in terms of the dimensions of the labour market. A factory will employ a particular structure of skills and occupations; it will be in a particular industry and place. The effects of its closure will be diffused along the various labour market dimensions; the less costly is mobility on a particular dimension, the more quickly will the effects ripple out. Thus, if industrial and continuous spatial mobility are the least costly, the general level of unemployment in other local industries and contiguous local labour markets will be most immediately affected. By both a process of chain interdependence and discontinuous mobility more distant local labour markets will be influenced over time. Similarly, unemployment in the whole range of skills and occupations in the local labour market will be influenced as mobility occurs with respect to those dimensions. By the same mechanisms, however, unemployment will be affected in the inner area if a factory closes (or opens) in the suburbs. Although urbanists may tend to think of suburbs as prosperous places it is as well in this context to remind oneself that gross changes in factory openings/closures are brought about by changes in the level of excess demand rather than location. In the depressed 1970s factory closures in suburban locations have been commonplace.

The dimensions of the labour market, however, which we have been discussing in generalised terms, can be grouped into two sets. Some dimensions, such as those of skill or class, are ordered in hierarchies; others, such as the spatial or industrial, are not. In the hierarchically ordered dimensions the unpleasant effects of localised events work their way differentially downwards. A skilled worker can always do a less skilled job and the skill standard demanded of workers in apparently similar jobs will vary across spatial markets or over time as the level of excess demand varies. For illustration of this phenomenon, at least over time, we need look no further than the standards required of new academic recruits in 1978 compared to those demanded at the height of the 1960's expansion of higher education. This argument has been extensively discussed in the literature, for example by Reder (1955). In the non-hierarchically organised labour market dimension there will be no such tendency for events to work their way differentially 'downwards'.

Spatial Differences in Excess Demand and the Role of Industrial Structure

The concern with labour market problems of inner areas, specifically unemployment, is based apparently on two considerations. That inner area unemployment is high in absolute terms and that it is high relative to non-inner areas. The first and most obvious possible cause for both these symptoms must be variations in the pressure of excess demand. High unemployment in absolute terms is consistent with a lower level of excess demand in recent years than in the past; high relative unemployment with systematic spatial differences in excess demand.

To take the last first, and incidentally illuminate the workings of inner area labour markets, we may examine research findings on spatial – whether regional, subregional, urban or borough – labour market unemployment differences. Conventional wisdom on regional unemployment differences is that their most significant cause is differences in industrial structure leading to systematic differences in the level of excess demand for labour in regional labour markets. Thus, the concentrated presence of industries such as shipbuilding in the north, subject to long-run secular decline, leads to a long-run deficiency of demand for labour in the north compared to regions favoured by a concentration of expanding industries. As has been shown by a number of writers, however, including one of the first to investigate the problem, Beveridge (1944), there is only the slightest relationship between the change in employment in an industry over a period and its measured unemployment rate at the end of the period.

Whilst a plausible explanation for the failure to find the expected consistent negative relationship between industrial employment growth and unemployment rate is the degree of industrial mobility that occurs, as Metcalf and Richardson (1976) point out, the observed low association could result not from this, but from the effects on the employability of a region's labour force of long-term industrial decline, depressed demand and differential migration.

The important role of industrial mobility is perhaps

indirectly confirmed, however, by their own findings which are consistent with a high degree of spatial mobility between contiguous local markets but not between spatially separated markets. In their study of unemployment differences between London boroughs in 1971 they included a borough's percentage employed in manufacturing in 1966 as an explanatory variable on the grounds that that sector had been the main source of employment loss in London. Thus, it should have proxied for the susceptibility of a borough's industrial structure to employment loss and so in turn have been a proxy for changes on the demand side of the labour market. On testing, the coefficient[1] emerged as insignificant and negative! This is in sharp contrast to Metcalf's work (1975) on urban unemployment differences where, given that nationally manufacturing employment relatively increased between 1966 and 1971, analogous arguments would lead one to expect that an urban area concentrating on manufacturing in 1966 would have had less unemployment in 1971. Testing confirmed this hypothesis; the coefficient was significant though the explanatory power of the variable was not high. This finding is consistent with a far greater degree of interdependence – 'chain' interdependence – between contiguous local labour markets than between spatially separated markets. In this latter case, where adjustment requires workers to move house, very substantial frictions exist. This implies that there will be a much stronger tendency for spatial differences in excess demand within an urban area to disappear than there will be for similar differences between urban areas.

Metcalf and Richardson's findings on the effects of redundancies on a borough's unemployment rate supply even more striking evidence on this point. Two measures were included; total redundancies in the borough, 1966–69, and those in 1970. Both redundancy coefficients were significant but the sign on redundancies, 1966–69, was the 'wrong' way. The more redundancies there were in that period the lower the unemployment rate was in 1971. It is uncertain why the coefficient should have been significant but its sign is certainly consistent with the view that localised events very quickly dissipate themselves over surrounding labour markets and thus only redundancies in the most recent past are associated with higher unemployment in the current time period.

Despite the difficulty of finding a strong and direct link between an area's industrial structure and its level of unemployment, all work has shown that spatial unemployment differences, whether interregional, inter-urban or intra-urban, have been relatively stable over time. Investigations of regional unemployment differences show the relative pattern to have been stable since the First World War, though almost the inverse of that which existed before 1914. Metcalf (1975) notes the stability of inter-urban unemployment differences and Metcalf and Richardson (1976) show a stability of relative London borough rates over the post World War II period investigated by them.

Reasons for the stability of relative intra-urban area unemployment rates are almost certainly different from those for the stability of regional and inter-urban unemployment differences. Despite failure to find evidence providing direct confirmation, the most plausible explanation of the latter remains differences in industrial structure between areas. This, coupled with the stability of long-run trends in industrial growth and decline and the small friction of continuous mobility relative to discontinuous mobility, leads to persistent long-run differences in aggregate excess demand for labour between areas. The relative stability of intra-urban unemployment differences, as is argued below, probably results mainly from the logic of urban structure and patterns of residential location.

Spatial Unemployment Differences and the Role of Excess Demand

The foregoing review suggests that though demand differences may be crucial in explaining unemployment variations over time and hence the high absolute level of inner area unemployment in the 1970s, they can have only a minor role in explaining high unemployment in inner areas relative to say a suburban area within the same metropolitan area at a point of time. The labour market implications of demand differences must be examined, nevertheless, if we are to have an adequate theoretical framework within which to interpret the role of different explanatory variables.

[1] The equations with the highest R^2s in Metcalf and Richardson (1976) and Metcalf (1975) to which this and subsequent discussion refers are reproduced as Appendix A.

One reason for this is that conventional distinctions between 'demand deficiency' and 'non-demand deficiency' unemployment are ultimately blurred. This is because the level of excess demand itself interacts with the factors causing 'non-demand deficiency' unemployment. In terms of the Holt model already mentioned these factors can be summarised under three elements: first, the rate of flow of new hires and recalls, itself a function of the rate of lay-offs; second, the average time it takes for employers with vacancies and workers looking for jobs to find each other and evaluate respective offers, i.e. search and evaluation time; and thirdly, the probability that a particular UV contact will result in an accepted job offer.

As has been argued at greater length elsewhere (see Cheshire, 1977) all these elements must be expected to interact with the levels of excess demand. As Knight and Wilson (1974) have persuasively argued in the context of the national UV shift post 1966, lay-off and therefore recall rates may be affected by differences in expected 'normal' levels of excess demand for labour. In areas of low demand employers would anticipate less difficulty in expanding employment as demand rose and so labour hoarding would be less attractive.

The average search and evaluation time, although partly determined by factors such as the spatial characteristics of the labour market which may be regarded as exogenous, has other determinants which vary with demand. Most obviously, information availability will vary with demand as employers' expenditures on recruiting vary; in addition, private sector employment agencies may have a greater incentive to operate in markets with a positive level of excess demand for labour, since placements will be easier and employed persons and or employers will be able to pay fees more readily than the unemployed.

The probability that a UV contact will result in an accepted job offer will vary with, amongst other factors, the selectivity of employers and employees – the selectivity of employers may be expected to vary with the characteristics of those offering themselves for employment and these characteristics will be unfavourably affected by the differential effects of migration. Thus an area persistently losing population net by migration as a result of a relatively unfavourable level of excess demand must be expected to have a labour force with relatively unfavourable employment characteristics and hence may have a lower probability of any UV contact resulting in an accepted job offer.

With these considerations in mind, let us now attempt to interpret research findings on the role played by different factors in the variation of unemployment between spatially defined markets.

Spatial Characteristics

These deserve more attention than perhaps they have had. Cheshire (1973) found that the absolute size of a labour exchange area's labour force was negatively and significantly associated with its unemployment rate. This, though the R^2 was low, was taken to be consistent with Davies (1967) who had argued that new plants were interested not just in rates of unemployment but in the number available for employment in their assessment of an area. It could also be consistent with the influence of population/job density on search time. Work by Vipond (1974) and Sirmans (1977) using Census rather than Department of Employment data suggested that the size of a town had a significant effect on its unemployment rate though the relationship appeared to be non-linear and not easy to interpret. Using population as a measure of size, for men the function was an inverted U and for females U-shaped. As Vipond acknowledged there is a data problem with analyses such as these, however, since the unemployment coverage of the Department of Employment's figures is not entirely satisfactory and the spatial divisions of the Census are not entirely satisfactory, corresponding as they do to neither truly urban nor local labour markets.

Personal Characteristics of the Unemployed

In studies of spatial unemployment considerable attention has been paid to the personal characteristics of either the unemployed by, for example, Paish (1968), Wood (1972), and the Inner Area Studies (1977a, 1977b), or to those of the labour force, e.g. by Metcalf (1975), Metcalf and Richardson (1976), and again in the Inner Area Studies. As was shown by Cheshire (1973) the implications of even *differences* in the observed personal characteristics of the unemployed are impossible to identify and the personal characteristics of the unemployed in one single spatial labour market can tell one nothing about the causes of unemployment. The Inner Area Studies which discuss the personal characteristics of both the unemployed and the labour forces in their chosen areas seem not to have been fully aware of the difficulties of interpretation.

These difficulties arise because of the effects of the level of excess demand on the unemployment of different sections of the labour force. Viewing employability as a continuum, not all of even the least employable will be continuously out of work. The proportion who will be out of work will be a function of the level of excess demand. Thus, where or when demand is low one must expect to observe large numbers of 'less employables' out of work. Taking the registered disabled as representative of the less employable we find across regions at a point of time, April 1964, that an increment of 1 percentage point in the regional unemployment rate was associated with an increase of 3.4 percentage points in the unemployment rate of the registered disabled in the region. Over time, from 1965 to 1976, an increase of 1 percentage point in national unemployment was associated with an increase of some 2 points in the registered disabled unemployment rate; during this period, however, there were a number of changes in official policy towards the employment of the disabled, which may have influenced this relationship.

If we look at the unemployment rate of the unskilled, another group in which the less employable may be concentrated, we find that over the same period it changed by about 2.5 points for every 1 per cent change in aggregate unemployment; in contrast that of administrative, professional and technical workers only changed by 0.5 points for every 1 point change in aggregate unemployment. A similar pattern is observed for age groups, with the unemployment rate of older workers generally rising more rapidly as demand falls than that of workers of prime working age. Relatively disadvantaged and less employable groups experience (not surprisingly) a disproportionate share of unemployment. From this it follows that more of such workers will be found to be out of work when unemployment is high; but the fact that more, say, unskilled workers, are out of work at a particular time or in a particular place does not mean that their lack of skill has in any direct and simple sense caused either their unemployment or the higher unemployment generally; nor does it mean that they would become employed if they could be 'converted' into skilled workers. The facts would be perfectly consistent with a general deficiency in the demand for labour and a shortage of jobs.

Although most of the evidence and argument has related to changes over time there is no reason for supposing that the conclusion does not apply to spatial unemployment differences. Indeed, since the assumed possibility of a deficiency of demand for labour in a spatial submarket should not cause concern to even believers in the 'natural' rate of unemployment, the arguments should be even more generally acceptable. Thus the observation that there are more unskilled workers (or any other category of relatively disadvantaged workers) unemployed in one spatial labour market compared to another is perfectly consistent with spatial differences in excess demand for labour; it does not imply any causal link from the number of unskilled unemployed to the amount of unemployment.

An analogous argument applies to observed differences in 'mismatch' between worker skills and job opportunities if that is defined as differences in the absolute excess of unemployment over vacancies between different groups. Given the relationship between aggregate unemployment and vacancies (for further discussion of this see Cheshire (1977)) and the fact that there are particular groups who disproportionately experience unemployment, we should expect 'mismatch' to be greater where (or when) unemployment was higher. Since vacancies may be expected to behave like the mirror image of unemployment for individual groups we must expect increased 'mismatch' where aggregate unemployment is high. Evidence on the behaviour of vacancies for subgroups of the labour force is more difficult to discover than is comparable unemployment data. There are no published data on age specific vacancies or vacancies for the registered disabled and such would be unlikely to exist. As previously mentioned, perhaps the most significant response to variation in excess demand is variation in hiring standards, but in addition there is some data on vacancies by skill. Between 1965 and 1972, whilst the total vacancy rate fell by just over half a percentage point the vacancy rate for administrative, managerial, professional and technical workers fell by about 0.2 percentage points; that for unskilled workers fell by the same amount as the overall vacancy rate fell, but from a lower base. Thus increased 'mismatch' over time is consistent with a fall in the level of excess demand for labour just as demand differences between areas may cause differences in perceived 'mismatch'. This suggests that an observed degree of 'mismatch' in a particular labour market at a point of time tells us, by itself, virtually nothing.

Yet it is this sort of evidence that the Inner Area Studies appear to place reliance on: 'In the local labour market, which includes Central London where half Stockwell's residents work, job opportunities and the skills of people needing work, have increasingly become out of balance', Inner Area Studies (1977a), Inner London, para. 19. The relevant period is not specified, but since the level of excess demand for labour had been falling rapidly since 1966, and in Inner London had been falling, relative to other areas, such increased 'mismatch' should almost certainly be regarded as a symptom rather than a cause of unemployment in Lambeth.

The Characteristics of their Labour Forces

The characteristics of the unemployed, therefore, can reveal little or nothing about the causes of unemployment in an area. The characteristics of local labour forces have been used more persuasively, however, in attempts to explain spatial differences in unemployment rates. In their cross-sectional study of variations in unemployment rates between London boroughs, Metcalf and Richardson (1976) found that considerably the most significant independent variable was the percentage of a borough's labour force that was unskilled; in his study of inter-urban unemployment differences, using a very similar methodology, Metcalf (1975) found the percentage of a town's labour force that was unskilled was one of the more significant variables. The rationale for the inclusion of this variable appears to be a supply side view of the determination of unemployment. Since groups such as the unskilled experience higher unemployment rates, where there are proportionately more of them there will be proportionately more unemployed.

Whilst this in the short run may be accepted, however, what Metcalf (1975) calls the 'simultaneity problem' must be emphasised if we are trying to understand the underlying causes of long-run differences in unemployment between areas. We know that the current geographical pattern of unemployment differences has persisted over nearly two generations and that high unemployment areas have been consistent net losers of population via migration for much of that time. Further, we know that migrants tend to be younger, better educated and more skilled than non-migrants. Hence, it seems more reasonable to view the characteristics of a region or town's labour force as primarily the outcome of long-term unemployment differences which are themselves the outcome of long-term differences in the spatial pattern of the excess demand for labour.

Supply Side Factors: Intra-urban Unemployment Differences and the Role of Urban Structure

A feature of urban structure common to Western industrialised cities is the concentration of the poor living at high densities on expensive central land and the rich living at low densities on cheaper suburban land. Numerous urban economists, including Alonso (1964), Muth (1969) and Evans (1973), have documented this pattern of residential location and provided models of urban land use consistent with it. We can reasonably expect income therefore to be associated with family location within a city, and income will be closely correlated with skill level and employment status and if it is defined as income per dependent family member, family size. When Metcalf and Richardson (1976) find that a borough's percentage unskilled and the ratio of dependents to male population of working age are both significantly and positively associated with its unemployment rate, it is plausible to see this as confirming urban economists' work on spatial structure. As they suggest, the quality and nature of the housing stock in a borough may be an underlying variable.[2] Cheap housing at high densities attracts low-income families who experience disproportionate unemployment. In the long run this may, via the political process, be reinforced by the provision of low-income local authority housing, although the evidence on this is not clear cut.

If the central argument of this paper is correct these supply side factors (i.e. factors which determine the quality of an area's labour supply) should be far less important in determining inter-urban differences. This is indeed observed. In Metcalf's

[2] In this context it is perhaps unfortunate that the intra-London study did not find a suitable housing stock variable, though such a variable was included in the inter-urban study.

(1975) study of inter-urban differences the size of family variable is not significant and the percentage unskilled appears to be relatively less significant. Furthermore, as was argued above, inter-urban or regional differences in the skill and age structure of the labour force may be viewed as reflecting long-run differences in demand.

The insignificance or perverse sign of all identifiably demand side variables, except redundancies in the most recent period, in the intra-urban study, is consistent with either demand not varying over London, or London existing as one local labour market, or, as was suggested above, a high degree of local labour market interactions, where such markets are contiguous, which renders their spatial definition ultimately arbitrary. In contrast, in Metcalf's inter-urban study, demand side variables were highly significant. Estimated regional demand deficiency unemployment appeared to be the single most important variable in explaining unemployment differences between urban areas; this despite the measure relating to regional and not urban demand-deficient unemployment. The percentage of a town's labour force in manufacturing was also highly significant.

A final difference between the two studies was in the role of immigrants, defined as New Commonwealth immigrants in the intra-urban study (Metcalf and Richardson, 1976) and as *all* immigrants from outside the UK in the inter-urban study (Metcalf, 1975). The sign of this variable in both studies was negative, but it was quite insignificant in the intra-urban study. Again, this may be interpreted as supporting a strong interconnection between neighbouring local labour markets within a metropolitan area and the role of demand differences in explaining unemployment differences between urban areas. Whilst it is true that migration studies have demonstrated the importance of the 'friends and neighbours' effect (see Greenwood (1970) for example) still most studies have shown variables such as job opportunities, or mean wages associated with expected life-time earnings differences, to be significant. Thus with other factors held constant and so abstracting from sudden inflows of migrants from a single source such as the inflow of Ugandan Asians, we must expect more migrants to be observed in towns with better job opportunities; if job opportunities are associated with demand differences we may conclude that the differences in unemployment between towns and their proportion of immigrants ultimately result from differences in the level of excess demand for labour.

Intra-urban Unemployment Differences and the 'Trapped' Argument

Against these findings and their interpretation we may consider the arguments of the Inner Area Studies. All three study teams espouse variants of what Evans (1976) calls the 'trapped' hypothesis, i.e. that large numbers of unskilled workers have, as a result of their inferior mobility, become 'trapped' in the inner cities as industry has moved to the suburbs and have thus become ensnared in a vicious circle of unemployment and immobility. The Liverpool study, for example, claims (para. 10): 'Regional policy . . . has brought 100,000 new manufacturing iobs to Merseyside. . . . However, all of these have been located on the periphery of the conurbation. . . . Between 1961 and 1971 the City of Liverpool lost 28,000 jobs in the port, railways, construction and utilities; 21,000 in retail and wholesale distribution; and 31,000 jobs in manufacturing industry. . . . The impact has been felt mainly in the inner area where jobs have disappeared even more rapidly than people, especially for unskilled workers. . . . Many unskilled workers walk to work and for those who live in the dock-side areas, the time and cost of travel by public transport, and their lack of cars, effectively put the growing centres of new employment beyond reach', Inner Area Studies (1977a).

The study goes on to quote a 1971 unemployment rate for men of 11 per cent in Inner Liverpool and over 20 per cent in the inner council estates. Yet since these were areas with high concentrations of unskilled workers in a metropolitan area with a relatively low level of demand, this is perhaps not surprising. The study contrasts the 11 per cent unemployment rate in Liverpool with the national unemployment rate of 4 per cent. Yet at the same date the national unemployment rate for the unskilled was, according to Evans (1976), 9.4 per cent and of British regions, the North West suffered from a level of demand deficiency unemployment more than 20 per cent higher than the weighted mean of all regions.

The Inner Area Studies did not give evidence to support their assertion that the unskilled had become trapped in the central area by the changing pattern of industrial employment. Nor did they take account of the findings of either Metcalf and Richardson (1976) or Evans (1976) who appeared to reject the hypothesis. The former rejected the trapped hypothesis on the grounds that there was no association between a borough's employment in manufacturing (the main declining sector) in 1966 and its unemployment rate in 1971. Evans rejected the hypothesis on the grounds that over all constituencies in the south-east there was practically no more variation in unemployment rates of the unskilled than there was of other groups of workers. Both findings would appear to be consistent with the view of the labour market taken in this paper.

Evans also rejected the trapped argument on the basis of his findings about the spatial incidence of unemployment within London. After allowing for skill differences in area (in this case parliamentary constituency) populations, systematic differences were observed in unemployment rates; some areas, especially in outer Inner London, had higher than national unemployment rates at all skill levels (apparently defined by social class); as an example Evans cites Hampstead and suggests that the trapped hypothesis 'is implausible . . . to say the least [as an explanation] of high unemployment rates of professionals and managers in Hampstead'. Instead Evans suggests the cause may be a high rate of in-migration of young people.

Changes in the Spatial Pattern of Unemployment in the London Metropolitan Region and Changes in the Spatial Pattern of Demand

Whilst this might be a factor in explaining high unemployment rates in particular areas of London, where there are concentrations of short-stay geographically mobile people, however, it is not immediately obvious how, as a general explanation, it is compatible with Metcalf and Richardson's (1976) finding that the proportion of a borough's population between 15 and 24 was not significantly associated with its unemployment rate.

It may again be that if we are looking for an explanation we should look at changes in the spatial pattern of demand for labour. From Evan's work the general pattern appears to be that whilst unemployment in both the GLC and the south-east was below the national level, with respect to the GLC area, this was less true the higher the social class.

The figures in Table 1 suggest that if one defines suburbanisation in terms of changes in the spatial distribution of population rather than direct urban–suburban migration, the GLC area has lost more economically active males relative to Great Britain the higher the skill level; thus in the GLC area economically active male professional and other workers, i.e. SC I, fell by 4.3 per cent between 1966 and 1971 whilst in Great Britain this group increased by 4.4 per cent. The percentage fall in Great Britain

Table 1

Social class	% of GLC constituencies where male unemployment rate > national	Difference between % change in economically active males in GB, 1966–71, and local area	
		GB–GLC	GB–OMA[1]
I	51	8.7	−11.6
II	47	1.7	−12.8
III	36	7.6	−3.5
IV	18	−3.4	−9.0
V	6	4.8	−1.5

[1] OMA = Outer Metropolitan Area.
Source: Evans (1976) and Census.

amongst the least-skilled groups however – the semi-skilled and unskilled taken together – exceeded that in the GLC area by 0.9 per cent. The converse was true in the outer metropolitan area where the numbers of economically active males rose faster compared to Great Britain the higher the social class. So far this simply provides factual confirmation of conventional wisdom; suburbanisation, defined rather crudely as changes in the distribution of economically active males between the GLC and OMA areas *vis-à-vis* Great Britain as a whole, was occurring most rapidly amongst the higher social classes/skill levels. Such an observation could even be taken as being consistent with the trapped argument.

Taken together with the figures in the first column, however, which are derived from Evans,[3] such a conclusion is no longer plausible. It was not the lower socio-economic groups who might have been trapped that suffered relatively the most unemployment in the GLC area, but the higher groups. If

[3] The definition of SC II and III used by Evans did not exactly conform to the Census definition; any resulting discrepancy would be most unlikely to be large enough to alter the figures in a way which would nullify the conclusion in the text above.

demand for labour is defined as employment plus vacancies, since both vacancies and unemployment are very small relative to employment, there is some basis for taking the economically active as a proxy for demand – at least if we are looking at changes over a 5-year period. This suggests that the overall pattern observed in Table I is best explained by a changing pattern of spatial demand for labour; the higher relative levels of unemployment amongst the higher socio-economic groups in the GLC area being explained by the more rapid rate of suburbanisation of demand for such workers. The most highly skilled suffered relatively worst because the demand for their services in the GLC area was falling relative to the demand for them nationally.

Although the process of continuous and discontinuous mobility described above may have been taking place, the whole London metropolitan area is a very large labour market, so continuous mobility has relatively less effect and spatial mobility defined in terms of residential re-location (that is, 'discontinuous' mobility) represents a substantial friction. Thus, the pattern of unemployment rates in the GLC area is quite consistent with a process of dynamic adjustment to changing spatial patterns of demand. It is not consistent with the trapped argument.

There is a further explanation of the observed patterns of skill-specific unemployment rates in the GLC area relative to national rates. A part of the difference will be accounted for by a composition effect. The higher the skill level the larger the proportion of the nationally economically active who live in the London area, and therefore the higher, will be the London weight in the national rate. The numerical importance of this effect is likely to be only minor, however, since in 1971 the percentage of nationally economically active males living in the GLC area ranged only from 17.4 of SC I to 13.3 of SC IV.

The Inner Area Studies; Background and Methodology

With this background behind us let us now consider the contributions of the Inner Area Studies. The first observation is that as case studies of particular areas at particular times, they were not able to make a serious comparative evaluation of the local labour market problems they identified. Evans, for example, found that the area chosen for study in London, Lambeth, was not, after allowing for skill levels of its population, amongst the very worst areas of London nor one where deterioration was most apparent. Nor can the problem identified be described as in any sense a new one. Its essential features have been amply documented from the nineteenth century in such studies as Engels's (1958), Booth's (1903)[4] or the Royal Commission on the Poor Laws and Relief of Distress (1909). A casual reading of any one of several novels by Dickens would vividly reveal it. Urban economists, such as Muth (1969) and Alonso (1964) amongst others, have devoted considerable energy to providing analytical models of urban land use consistent with observed patterns.

As long as society is organised on inegalitarian lines there will be poor and the poor will tend to be spatially concentrated. In the developed countries of the West the historical pattern clearly documented in Engels's (1958) description of Manchester in the 1840s has tended to be for the poor to be concentrated in inner urban areas. This suggests that the first question any new study of inner urban areas should have addressed itself to was the comparative one; in what ways and to what extent do current problems of such areas differ from problems of the past? In addition, a central question was, how far, if inner urban area problems have worsened, does this represent some new factor? How far is it explicable simply in terms of a period of generally depressed demand in post-war terms? The nature of the surveys and their methodology, effectively ensured from the start that none of these fundamental questions could be answered.

In terms of their contribution to our understanding of how urban labour markets work and what their problems are, our conclusions must be even more negative. Not only did the form of the studies preclude consideration of many of the relevant questions, but the studies conspicuously failed to take account of any of the corpus of relevant labour market research surveyed in this paper.

The studies were by different teams of investigators and, although they shared a common methodological strait-jacket, in other respects they varied. Let us consider here the study in which the labour market

[4] It is interesting to note that on Booth's measure of 'social conditions', a composite quantitive measure, Lambeth ranked eighth worst out of 49 districts of London; a position not dissimilar to that suggested by Evans's work (1976) 80 years later.

analysis appears to the present author to be most open to criticism – the Lambeth study.

The Lambeth Study

'Mismatch' and the Definition of a Local Labour Market

The conclusions on the local labour market are presented in paragraphs 18 to 27 of the Summary Report. The problem is stated in these terms: 'Stockwell residents face serious job problems; high unemployment, low earnings and many young mothers working to supplement inadequate incomes. Difficulties are greater for men than for women; for manual workers, particularly the less skilled than for other workers; for black than for white workers; for school leavers and young adults than for people at other stages in life.' In view of the evidence discussed at length in the earlier part of this paper any other discovery would of course have been wholly inexplicable.

Reference has already been made to the study team's diagnosis of these problems' causes; the main cause discussed is that of 'mismatch': 'In the local labour market, which includes Central London where half Stockwell's residents work, job opportunities and skills of people needing work have increasingly become out of balance. On the one hand there are people out of work or earning very little; on the other hand certain kinds of skilled job cannot be filled'.

Neither in the summary nor final reports was evidence to support these conclusions presented. It is implausible that adequate evidence could be produced since the implicit labour market model appears hardly to have a demand side and the symptoms noted are exactly those one would expect to find in a market with a concentration of poor unskilled residents and relatively depressed demand such as the inner part of Greater London in the 1970s. Given the observed concentration of the less skilled and poor in areas such as Stockwell, 'mismatch' is a permanent feature of such places, especially if the labour market is defined in the way suggested above which includes Central London – with probably the largest concentration of high-skill jobs anywhere in Britain – but does not include equally accessible areas with a higher proportion of unskilled jobs. The fact that half Stockwell's residents work in Central London tells us as much about where the demand for the kind of skills the residents have is located as it does about the necessary boundaries of the local labour market in terms of job search. If the jobs of those residents currently working in Central London were relocated in Croydon probably about the same proportion of Stockwell's residents would work in Croydon as previously worked in Central London.

The diagnosis also fails to take account of the crucial effects of changing levels of excess demand for labour on the observed degree of 'mismatch'. In the period from 1966 to 1971 the unemployment rate was rising continuously in Great Britain and by any reasonable measure the level of excess demand for labour in 1971 was far below that of say, 1966, though above that of say, 1977; the ratio of total vacancies to total unemployed averaged 0.85 in 1965 but only 0.17 in 1971. As was shown above such a change in the level of demand inevitably creates the appearance of increased 'mismatch'. Thus the question as to how far 'mismatch' was a cause of the problem in Stockwell's labour market and how far it was an effect of low demand nationally, and especially in Stockwell, remains entirely unanswered. It is the present writer's view that increased 'mismatch' was almost entirely determined by lower demand nationally though supply side factors associated with normal patterns of urban residential location were important in determining the degree of 'mismatch' in Stockwell's labour market compared to that which would have been observed in other local labour markets within the London metropolitan region in a cross-sectional study.

It is true that the Report mentions other factors in the 'mismatch'; it cites the decline in manufacturing in London though it is not clear whether this is viewed as a structural factor in changing the skill structure of demand relative to supply or as an indicator of the changing spatial pattern of labour demand. The national shift towards professional, technical and administrative employment is mentioned as a cause of 'mismatch' in Stockwell; this appears to ignore the debate that has been going on in Britain since 1970 or earlier and started in the US in the late 1950s about the possible increase in 'structural', sometimes called 'technological', unemployment and in the British context the outward shift of the UV curve. The British evidence was briefly summarised in the Department of Employment Gazette in 1976. Neither here nor elsewhere has much evidence been produced to suggest that 'technological' unemployment was an important factor either in the increased level of unemployment generally or in 'mismatch'. Finally, although paragraph 20 mentions that inner areas suffer disproportionately in periods of national economic recession, the insuperable identification problem which this creates, given the study team's methodology, is inadequately recognised.

A Critique of the Recommendations

In the light of the above criticisms of the study's diagnosis of Lambeth/Stockwell's labour market problems, it follows that the Report's recommendations in paragraphs 22–27 are inadequately founded. The Report's main emphasis is given to training schemes and to a lesser extent subsidised mobility for the unskilled. Rather less emphasis is given to proposals aimed at increasing the demand for labour in Inner London.

Given the argument above that perceived 'mismatch' in a local labour market is primarily a function of that market's prevailing level of excess demand (as, too, is employers' willingness to provide training), government provision of training is likely to be no more than a palliative. Put at its simplest, if there is an overall excess supply of labour in a local labour market (abstracting from the problem of appropriate definition of labour market boundaries), providing training for the unskilled, even if such training could place them in the skill continuum at the identical point occupied by workers with established skills, will have only a minimal effect on their probability of employment. Since no additional jobs will be created the most favourable possible outcome would be a shift along the appropriate skill UV function; given that the supply of skilled workers will have risen relative to demand whilst employment of the originally unskilled workers will increase, this will be partly at the expense of previously skilled workers who will now have an increased duration of unemployment when they become unemployed. In practice, even this outcome is unlikely since it is improbable that the previously unskilled workers will be regarded as the equivalent of the previously skilled group and will therefore remain further down the skill hierarchy. Those retrained workers who experience unemployment after training will suffer skill erosion and rapidly move further down the skill hierarchy and become less acceptable to potential employers of skilled labour. There is thus a *prima facie* case for regarding expenditure on retraining as extremely cost ineffective in terms of unemployment reduction. Little evidence has been produced from experience elsewhere to demonstrate its efficacy though more research on the cost effectiveness of government training schemes, in the light of actual experience, is still needed.

Objections can also be raised against the recommendation of subsidised migration for the unskilled. This policy would appear analogous to the long-standing 'work to the workers' or 'workers to the work' controversy in regional economic policy. Although not finally resolved, considerations of local multiplier/accelerator effects have usually weighed against subsidised migration. In this case two further factors should be considered; unskilled workers, whether employed or unemployed, tend to have relatively low incomes and hence need cheap housing. The geographical availability of cheap housing has therefore to be considered. Such housing is almost certainly disproportionately concentrated in inner urban areas. The second factor is the employability of the unskilled in any location. To the present writer this would seem to be primarily a function of the level of excess demand in the local labour market concerned.

This may initially suggest that policies aimed at changing the spatial distribution of demand would be more appropriate. Apart from policies such as those mentioned in paragraphs 23 and 24 of the Lambeth team's Report one might consider more general policies such as those that have been employed to influence the inter-regional distribution of demand. The comparative success of these policies has been recently documented by studies such as those of A. J. Brown (1972), Moore and Rhodes (1973, 1976) and Buck and Atkins (1976). Apart from some costless modifications of certain current policies, such as Industrial Development Certificate and Office Development Permit control, that put inner London at a relative disadvantage, there would seem to be a case for considering the introduction of location subsidies.

Even here, however, labour market analysis suggests hidden pitfalls. The qualified success of policies to manipulate the inter-regional distribution of demand has been achieved against the background of the substantial friction of discontinuous mobility. Policies aimed at managing the spatial pattern of demand in inner city areas relative to the whole metropolitan area will have to contend with virtually costless continuous mobility. If, by the use of location subsidies, IDCs or ODPs, development is diverted from suburbs or satellite centres to inner areas, employment in the suburbs will be less than otherwise and there will be induced changes in commuting patterns. Again, by a process of 'chain interdependence' the expectation must be that the beneficial effects on the inner area local labour market will disappear within quite a short space of time in the same way as the damaging effects of local redundancies are observed to diffuse. Thus the conditions which give rise to regional unemployment differences via differences in levels of excess demand themselves enable policy to manipulate patterns of regional demand. Such conditions do not obtain with respect to the distribution of demand within a metropolitan area. As was seen with the patterns of relative unemployment by skill in London the best such policies might hope to achieve is to tip the balance of dynamic adjustment in favour of, as opposed to against, the inner areas.

There are other reasons why such a policy of intra-urban demand manipulation would need to be carefully evaluated. Compared to locations in less prosperous regions industrial location in inner cities might impose higher relative cost penalties. In addition, the methodology of the Inner Area Studies, whereby each area was examined in virtual isolation, precluded an examination of the regional implications. Thus the Lambeth study team might favour incentives for firms to locate in central London because unemployment in their view might have been high relative to an area such as Croydon or Basingstoke; but the elimination of IDC and ODP control would not affect inner London *vis-à-vis* Basingstoke but rather inner London *vis-à-vis* inner Liverpool or Newcastle. The facts as they currently appear at best favour treating inner cities on an equal or more favoured basis compared to other urban areas in the regions in which they are located rather than putting inner London on an equal basis with inner Glasgow or Liverpool.

Conclusions

As the Liverpool inner area study team point out (1977a), 'poverty stems from the persistence of divisions of status and income in society at large'. There is a further and inevitable feature of this social fact, however, and that is that as long as society is unequal and divided, residential segregation will tend to reflect these divisions. Primarily for economic reasons the areas in which the poor have been concentrated have been the inner cities. Spatial inequality may thus be just another and rather unimportant dimension of social inequality. It may consequently be best relieved by policies aimed at greater social equality and of these one of the most powerful and currently least favoured is managing the economy at the highest level of overall demand for labour compatible with other goals. In this context it is interesting that given the observed range of the variables identified by Moore and Rhodes (1976), changes in the pressure of demand as measured by the male unemployment rate had as much effect on industrial moves to development areas as any of the specifically designed policy instruments.

Although poverty and unemployment are associated problems they are not identical. The unemployed constitute a large group amongst the officially designated poor and, taking account of accumulated stocks of wealth and life cycle needs, probably a far larger proportion of the truly poor. But in the words of Beveridge (1944), 'Idleness is not the same as want; it is a positive separate evil from which men do not escape by having an income. . . . A person who cannot sell his labour is in effect told he is of no use . . . idleness even on an income corrupts; the feeling of not being wanted demoralises'. There is a further possibility and that is that spatially concentrated unemployment may have more than proportionately demoralising effects. If a few people in an area are out of work they will be socially isolated and suffer in a number of ways. But it is possible that if unemployment is bad enough in one area there may be some threshold level where a separate subculture of unemployment develops, to an extent self-sustaining and hostile to official work-orientated society. For certain groups such as young blacks in inner areas this threshold may have been already reached and if this is so it would further reinforce Beveridge's conclusion. Although the most ruinous effects of unemployment are relieved by welfare payments it remains a 'separate evil' and it may be an evil which increases more than proportionately with local concentrations.

Thus while the surest way of relieving inner area

unemployment is a higher level of demand for labour nationally there is a case for considering specific policy instruments to influence the spatial pattern of demand in inner areas relative to non-inner areas. But there does not seem to be any immediately obvious reason why such policies should negate attempts to influence the inter-regional pattern of demand and the arguments in this paper suggest a pessimistic view of the effectiveness of such policies.

REFERENCES

ALONSO, W. (1964). *Location and Land Use: Towards a General Theory of Land Rent.* Cambridge, Mass.: Harvard University Press.

BEVERIDGE, SIR W. H. (1944). *Full Employment in a Free Society.* London: Allen and Unwin.

BOWERS, J. K., CHESHIRE, P. C., and WEBB, A. E. (1970). The change in the relationship between unemployment and earnings increases: a review. *National Institute Economic Review*, No. 54.

BOOTH, C. (1903). *Life and Labour of the People in London*, Final Volume. London: Macmillan.

BRECHLING, F. (1967). Trends and cycles in British regional unemployment. *Oxford Economic Papers*, Vol. 19: 1–21.

BROWN, A. J. (1972). *The Framework of Regional Economics in the U.K.* London: Cambridge University Press.

BUCK, T. W., and ATKINS, M. H. (1976). The impact of British regional policies on employment growth. *Oxford Economic Papers*, Vol. 28: 118–132.

CHESHIRE, P. C. (1973). *Regional Unemployment Differences in Great Britain.* Regional Papers II. London: Cambridge University Press/NIESR.

CHESHIRE, P. C. (1977). A framework for analysing spatial labour markets: a review of progress and a critique of the inner area studies. *University of Reading Discussion Papers in Economics*, Series A, No. 95.

DAVIES, G. (1967). Regional unemployment, labour availability, and redeployment. *Oxford Economic Papers*, Vol. 19: 59–74.

DEPARTMENT OF EMPLOYMENT GAZETTE, October 1976.

ENGELS, F. (1958). *The Condition of the Working Class in England.* First published in German in 1845. English edition translated and edited by W. O. Henderson and W. H. Chaloner. Oxford: Basil Blackwell.

EVANS, A. W. (1973). *The Economics of Residential Location.* London: Macmillan.

EVANS, A. W., with RUSSELL, LYNNE (1976). A portrait of the London labour market. Paper read at Inner City Employment Conference, York, September, 1976.

GOODMAN, J. F. B. (1970). The definition of local labour markets; some empirical problems. *British Journal of Industrial Relations*, Vol. 8: 179–196.

GREENWOOD, M. J. (1970). Lagged response in the decision to migrate. *Journal of Regional Science*, Vol. 10: 375–384.

HOLT, C. C. (1970a). Job search, Phillips's wage relation, and union influence; theory and evidence. In E. S. PHELPS (ed.), *Microeconomic Foundations of Employment and Inflation Theory.* W. W. Norton.

HOLT, C. C. (1970b). How can the Phillips curve be moved to reduce both inflation and unemployment? In E. S. PHELPS (ed.), *Microeconomic Foundation of Employment and Inflation Theory.* W. W. Norton.

HUNTER, L. C., and REID, G. L. (1968). *Urban Worker Mobility.* OECD.

INNER AREA STUDIES (1977a). Liverpool, Birmingham and Lambeth. *Summaries of Consultants' Final Report*, Department of the Environment. London: HMSO.

INNER AREA STUDIES FINAL REPORTS (1977b). *Change or Decay?*, Hugh Wilson and Lewis Womersely; *Unequal City*, Llewelyn-Davies, Weeks, Forestier-Walker and Bor; and *Inner London*, Shankland Cox Partnership, Department of the Environment (passive author). London: HMSO.

KNIGHT, K. G., and WILSON, R. A. (1974). Labour hoarding, employment and unemployment in British manufacturing industry. *Applied Economics*, Vol. 6: 303–310.

METCALF, D. (1975). Urban unemployment in England. *Economic Journal*, Vol. 85: 578–589.

METCALF, D. and RICHARDSON, R. (1976). Unemployment in London. In G. D. N. Worswick (ed.), *Measurement of Unemployment.* London: Allen and Unwin.

MOORE, B., and RHODES, J. (1973). Evaluating the effects of British regional economic policy. *Economic Journal*, Vol. 83: 87–110.

MOORE, B., and RHODES, J. (1976). Regional economic policy and the movement of manufacturing firms to development areas. *Economica*, Vol. 43: 17–31.

MUTH, R. F. (1969). *Cities and Housing.* Chicago: University of Chicago Press.

PAISH, F. W. (1968). How the economy works. *Lloyds Bank Review*, Vol. 88: 1–30.

Poor Laws and Relief of Distress, Report of the Royal Commission (1909). Cd. 4499. London: HMSO.

REDER, M. (1955). The theory of occupational wage differentials. *American Economic Review*, Vol. 44: 833–852.

SIRMANS, C. F. (1977). City size and unemployment: some new estimates. *Urban Studies*, Vol. 14: 91–101.

THIRLWALL, A. P. (1966). Regional unemployment as a cyclical phenomenon. *Scottish Journal of Political Economy*, Vol. 13: 205–219.

TREVITHICK, J. A., and MULVEY, C. (1975). *The Economics of Inflation.* Glasgow Social and Economic Research Studies 3. London: Martin Robertson.

VANDERKAMP, J. (1971). Migration flows, their determinants and the effects of return migration. *Journal of Political Economy*, Vol. 79: 1012–1031.

VIPOND, J. (1974). City size and unemployment. *Urban Studies*, Vol. 11: 39–46.

WOOD, J. B. (1972). *How Much Unemployment?* The Institute of Economic Affairs Research Monograph 28.

Appendix A

Inter- and intra-urban unemployment differences: Highest R^2 equations, t statistics in parenthesis

	(1) County borough	(2) London borough
Dependent variable:		
Male unemployment rate 1971		
Independent variables:		
Percentage of male labout force:		
Aged 15–24	0.159	0.035
	(1.27)	(0.31)
Aged 54+	0.347	0.054
	(4.34)	(1.25)
Married	−0.205	−0.217
	(−2.14)	(−3.48)
All persons aged 0.14 as a percentage of males 15–64	—	0.057
		(2.97)
Percentage of male labour force:		
New Commonwealth immigrants	—	−0.016
		(−0.69)
Inmigrants from outside UK	−0.164	
	(−2.73)	
Unskilled	0.116	0.257
	(2.30)	(10.27)
Employed in manufacturing, 1966	−0.039	−0.018
	(−3.22)	(−1.07)
Independent variables:		
Number of male redundancies:		
1966–69	—	−0.011
		(−2.47)
1970	—	0.045
		(2.28)
Percentage of population in large families	0.025	
	(0.27)	
Number of people per room	5.253	
	(0.88)	
Regional deficient demand unemployment	1.073	
	(5.10)	
Constant	−1.156	12.006
	(−0.15)	(2.50)
R^2	0.692	0.98
n	78	32

Source: (1) Metcalf (1975), Table 1.
(2) Metcalf and Richardson (1976), Table 11.2.

[9]

Urban Studies (1987), 24, 379–388

The Supply of Land for a Particular Use

Max Neutze

[*First received June 1986; in final form, December 1986*]

A number of features of land markets in and around cities are not well explained by existing theories of the allocation of land. Although there has been a good deal of work on the demand for urban land, in particular how the demand varies with distance from major centres of activity, relatively little attention has been given to the supply of land for urban uses, or for particular urban activities within cities. Recent articles by Evans (1983) and Wiltshaw (1985) have put more emphasis on factors affecting supply. Using a quite different approach Titman (1985) has also added to our understanding of the supply process.

The supply of land is generally assumed to be fixed in the aggregate so that the aggregate supply curve is vertical. Supply of land to a particular activity, however, is very elastic as land will be used for that purpose which yields the highest rent; in principle the supply is perfectly elastic. Ricardo qualified this by recognising that land varies in fertility and von Thunen by recognising that land varies in location. Alonso's model applies the method of von Thunen to an urban context. Both the von Thunen and Alonso models assume that land will be used for the activity that can pay the highest rent so that land in a given location will have a horizontal supply curve for any given use, its level being its rental value for its next most profitable use.

Among the puzzling features of urban property markets is the fact that vacant and under-utilised land can be found in close proximity to highly developed land. Around the fringe of cities this produces scattered development, which is difficult and expensive to service and makes the areas unattractive as well as taking land out of rural production a good deal earlier than is necessary to provide for urban requirements. Something similar occurs within cities when individual sites in and close to commercial centres are used for low density housing or for surface car parking. Both kinds of mixtures of land uses of very different densities often continue for long periods of time.

Another feature that requires explanation is the considerable margin that exists at the urban fringe between the price of land used for urban purposes and its price (value) for non-urban purposes. The models of Alonso (1964) and others that focus on demand implicitly assumed that at the margin of a city land for urban use could be purchased at a price only slightly above its rural value: just enough to bid it away from farmers. In reality, even at the urban fringe, urban values are frequently many times rural values. Again the same phenomenon occurs within cities where land used for commercial or office development generally changes hands at much higher prices than residential and industrial land even where they abut one another.

Together these two puzzling features produce situations where land at margins between different uses has a much higher market value than its current use value over a long time period and yet no development or redevelopment occurs.

Max Neutze is at the Urban Research Unit, in the Research School of Social Sciences, the Australian National University, Canberra.
A number of people have made valuable comments on earlier drafts of this paper, including Alan Evans who was working along similar lines to Part 2 when the first draft was being prepared. I have benefited from discussions with Barry Pearce, Desmond Wiltshaw and Gavin Wood. Referees comments were also very helpful.

One possible explanation of the large price differences is that artificial shortages are created by land use controls. This is a specially popular explanation for the rural/urban land price difference. Although such controls may well contribute to the size of the margin they are certainly not a sufficient explanation. Large margins occur in places where there are few if any land use controls, and where such controls are far from binding in that there is a large enough supply of developable land with no regulatory limits to development to last for many years. Again, commercial developments are seldom highly constrained by land use controls. The controls cannot even help to explain scattered development and redevelopment. Indeed they are often used as a means of trying to make development more compact.

A similar, and perhaps more persuasive explanation is that accessibility to public and private urban services quite sharply distinguishes land with urban from land with non-urban value. In the case of utility services the boundary can be quite distinct and access to such services can add greatly to land values. Like land use controls access to services can explain major price differences but it cannot even help to explain scattered development or redevelopment. Services seldom constrain the conversion of land to high density commercial use. Yet another possibility is that much of the land available for development is owned by one or a few owners who can profit from releasing it only very slowly for development (Markusen and Scheffman, 1978). There is, however, not much evidence of very concentrated ownership and it would not normally lead to scattered development.

What seems to be needed is an explanation of why property owners and developers defer development and redevelopment even in circumstances where the returns from development appear to be high, and why some land owners and developers defer, while others in apparently very similar circumstances develop. The latter part of the explanation is needed to understand why the supply curve of land for a particular use in a particular location slopes upward. Deferral of development under these circumstances reduces the supply and creates the price margin. Differences in decisions about the timing of development by owners of adjacent land create scattered development. One explanation puts a good deal of emphasis on dynamic aspects of urban development including speculation in property markets: owners defer development because they expect future development to be more profitable than current development by enough of a margin to more than offset the returns forgone by maintaining the lower level of use in the interim. Evans and Wiltshaw, however, advance an alternative, somewhat different explanation, relying on static rather than dynamic factors.

This paper examines the Evans and Wiltshaw explanations in turn to see to what extent they are alternatives to the dynamic-speculative explanation or whether both static and dynamic approaches can be used to explain the characteristics mentioned.

1. A Static Theory Including Non-Financial Returns

Evans (1983) focussed on the supply of land for urban uses by assuming an Alonso type city and examining the market in a particular ring within which accessibility, the relevant aspect of location in such a model, can be assumed uniform. He argued that in such circumstances the supply schedule for land for urban uses, rather than being a horizontal line, is upward sloping because the occupants of the land derive varying amounts of economic surplus from its occupation. Each owner will be willing to sell his or her land for urban use at a margin above the current use value which varies with the size of the surplus the owner gets from the current use. Since, at any time, the remaining rural users presumably derive a substantial surplus from rural use, a margin between rural and urban values can be expected. Since there is no reason why those occupants who derive the lowest surplus from occupation of their land should be adjacent to the fringe of development, the result is likely to be that scattered properties are developed first for urban use.

Wiltshaw (1985) elaborated on this analysis by adapting to the supply of land the standard model used to analyse the supply of labour. In the analysis of labour supply it is generally assumed that work involves a loss of utility so that people have to be compensated by wages for forgoing leisure. Figure 1 is the standard diagram in which OH represents the total number of hours in a week or a year, HW' the non-wage income of the person concerned, II' one of a family of indifference curves showing the rate at which a worker is prepared to work for more or

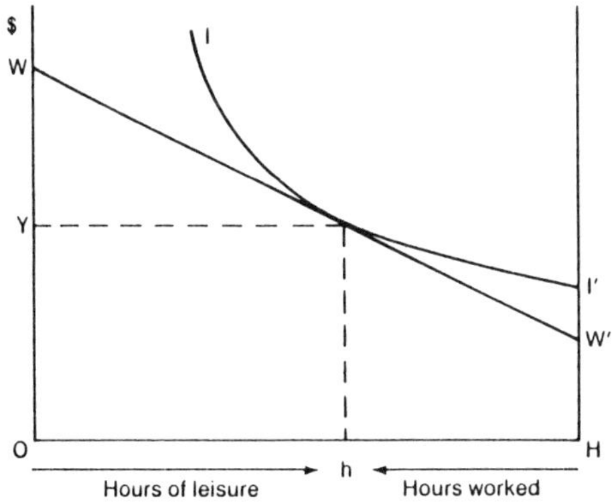

Fig. 1. Leisure and work.

fewer hours for greater or less income and the slope of WW' the wage rate. In this case the person will work Hh hours, have a total income of OY and Oh hours of leisure.

Wiltshaw believes that the supply behaviour of the owners of land can usefully be analysed in the same way as the supply behaviour of the owners of labour. Just as workers are assumed to prefer leisure, land owners are assumed to get the greatest satisfaction from using their land for some non-commercial use such as landscaped parks, and have to be compensated through rent for the loss of direct utility if they are to commit it to a commercial use. A non-commercial use is defined as one that produces direct utility but no rent. Commercial and non-commercial use are regarded as the equivalent of work and leisure.

A choice between different commercial uses is portrayed by Wiltshaw in the same way as Mishan (1981, p. 211) portrays a choice between jobs. He uses a diagram similar to Figure 1 but with another quadrant to the right of the vertical axis through H which is a mirror image of Figure 1 and which applies to a different commercial land use. Such a diagram can be used to make such a comparison by lining up indifference curves so that they intersect the common vertical axis at the same points. In effect a conversion from one commercial use to another is assessed by comparing both with the utility obtainable from the non-commercial alternative.

This approach seems unnecessarily laboured and artificial even for heuristic purposes. While the zero point on the horizontal axis of the labour supply diagram is easily understood as a position at which all of the person's time is available for leisure, it is not nearly as obvious what it means in the case of land. Few owners use any of their land for non-commercial purposes but we all have some leisure. Furthermore the comparison between a non-commercial use and some particular commercial use is seldom the important one: it is much more likely that owners will want to compare salient alternative commercial uses for their land.

A more fundamental difficulty with adapting the labour supply analysis to land is that its primary objective is to throw light on the aggregate supply of labour through analysing the decision of an individual about how many hours to work. By contrast if we want to understand the supply of land for urban development we are examining its supply to a particular industry or use. Given its fixed aggregate supply, supply of land for one use involves its withdrawal from another and any analysis should be concerned with both aspects. It seems both simpler and more correct, then, to analyse the supply of land to a particular use by making comparisons between alternative "commercial" uses. The alternatives may, of course, return different levels of income and yield different levels of direct utility. In some cases one alternative may even yield direct utility and no rent but we should not limit ourselves to such comparisons. For example, either a landlord or an owner occupant could get greater satisfaction, but a lower level of rent, from farming than from urban use. Similarly, an owner occupant of a house could derive a good deal of direct satisfaction from the house, in addition to its imputed rent (market rental value), but little, if any, if it is used for offices. A landlord may prefer to deal with residential rather than commercial tenants, or the reverse.

Figure 2 is drawn in a way that assumes that the present (preferred) use is the one that provides greater direct utility. It, in some respects, takes the place of Wiltshaw's non-commercial use and is shown with its vertical axis on the right hand side of the diagram. It can be used to analyse the allocation of a specific site between alternative uses. The greater direct utility provided by the use with its vertical axis on the right is reflected in the downward slope of the indifference curve II': the owner is willing to give up income in order to use more of the site for its present and less for the alternative use. A

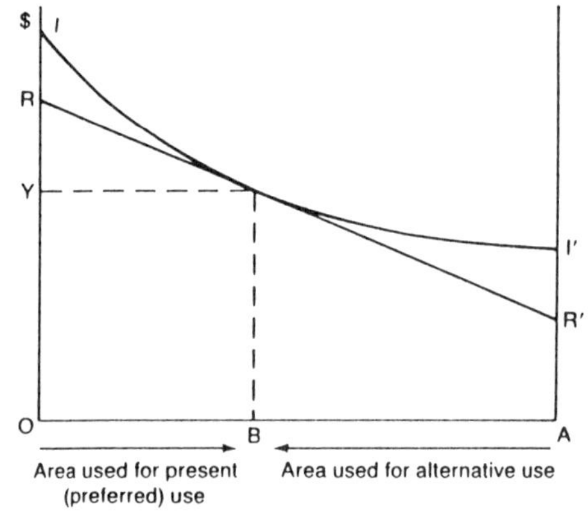

Fig. 2. Trade-off between two land uses.

move along the horizontal axis means that more land is in one use *and* less in the other. Whereas the slope of the indifference curve in Figure 1 represents the rate at which a person is willing to reduce hours of leisure if compensated by increasing income the slope of the corresponding curve in Figure 2 shows the rate at which he or she is willing to *switch* from a preferred to a less preferred use if compensated by an increse in rental income. In Figure 1 the slope shows the marginal utility of leisure; in Figure 2 it shows the *difference between* the marginal utilities derived from the two land uses: MU_a-MU_p (p = preferred, a = alternative).

Income from all sources apart from property, plus the rental income from having all of the land in the preferred use, is shown by AR'. If the whole site was converted to the alternative use the total income would be OR. The slope of the line RR' is the difference in the rental yield of land in the two uses and RR' shows an income possibility frontier. Given the relative rents shown in the diagram and the indifference curve the owner will use OB of the land for the preferred use and BA for the alternative use and total income will be OY.

One implication of the difference between the two figures can be seen in the shape of the indifference curves. In the case of labour diminishing marginal utility of income and leisure will generally result in the indifference curves being convex downwards.[1] There can be no such presumption if we are studying the supply of land, or indeed labour, to a particular industry. A neutral assumption would be for them to be straight lines, and they could be concave downwards if an owner preferred to have all of his land in one use or the other rather than some in each. (In the most simple situation they would be horizontal straight lines if the owner was solely concerned to maximise rents and did not otherwise care about the use of his land). To see how this analysis can produce an upward sloping supply curve for land to an industry, we will assume straight line indifference curves and that five owners, each owns one hectare of farm land near an expanding urban area. Their indifference curves are shown in Figure 3a as I_1, I_2 ... I_5. We assume no income from other sources and that each of them can earn AR rent from farming. As urban rents rise above AR to OR_1, OR_2 ... OR_5 successive owners convert their land to urban use so that the supply curve will look like SS' in Figure 3b. With a larger number of owners it would be smoothed. This result is very similar to that of Evans (1983).

2. A Dynamic Theory

The important difference between dynamic and static theories of supply is that the former emphasise that the anticipation of future changes in conditions can have an important influence on both the current price and the current supply of land for a particular use. The models of this kind focus on the timing of a change in land use since the earlier a change occurs in response to an increase in price, the greater the supply response to the price increase. The following diagramatic exposition of this model is derived very largely from the author's 1973 paper for OECD. Basically the same approach was used in an algebraic model by several writers who were interested in the impact of a tax on development gains on the supply and price of land for urban development (Rose, 1973; Foster and Glaister, 1975; Evans, 1982). The value of land for a particular purpose is the present value of the expected flow of net returns if it is used for that purpose. If there is to be a change in use the value of the site is the present value of the flow from the first use up to the time of the

[1] Another difference, argued by the classical economists but not central to this analysis, is that while a subsistence wage sets a minimum price at which labour will be supplied to an industry there is no such floor on the price of land.

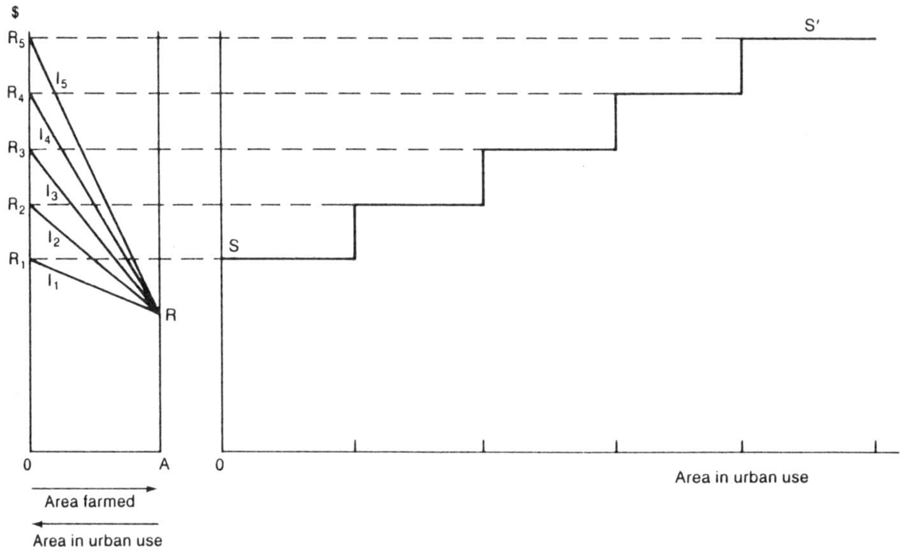

Fig. 3. Indifference curves and the land supply curve.

change and thereafter from the new use. The net returns from any particular use can also change over time. The value of land can, then, be defined as follows (Rose, 1973):

$$V_0 = \int_0^D f(t)e^{-rt}dt + \int_D^\infty h(t,D)e^{-r(t-D)}dt.e^{-rD} \quad (1)$$

where V_0 = value of the site at time O;

f(t) = net returns per period from the first use, a function of time;

r = the discount rate;

D = date of conversion from the first to the second use;

h(t,D) = net returns from the second use.

The first part of the equation is the value at time 0 of the flow of returns from the predevelopment use up to the time of development (D). The second part is the value at time 0 of the returns after development. The level of those returns, h(t,D), depend not only on the actual year when the returns occur (t) but also on when the development itself takes place (D).

Figure 4 represents a simplified version of the equation. It is assumed that the flow of returns from the predevelopment use, which might be farming, is expected to be constant. Figure 4 does not permit any choice about the type or density of development so that h is a function of t but not of D. In this case rent from the developed use exceeds farm rent from t_d onwards.

The current value of the land for the particular post-development use, when development is assumed to occur at t_d, is shown in the V_u curve. The sum of the value of the interim and expected final use is shown as V_t. Expected returns after development increase the market value of land (V_t) above its value for farming (V_f) well before the time of actual development and before the higher post-development rents, R_u, can be obtained. Well before development (from t_u) the prospective urban value of the land (V_u) exceeds its value for its current farm use. Even in the absence of any land use controls the value of fringe land for urban purposes will commonly be well in excess of its farm value. The current value of the returns from the interim use for farming (V_t-V_u), starts off as OV_f when V_u is zero at a time when urban development is expected in the very remote future, and becomes smaller as the date of development approaches. That t_d is the optimum time for development, can be seen by differentiating V_0 with respect to D. Intuitively, the cost of

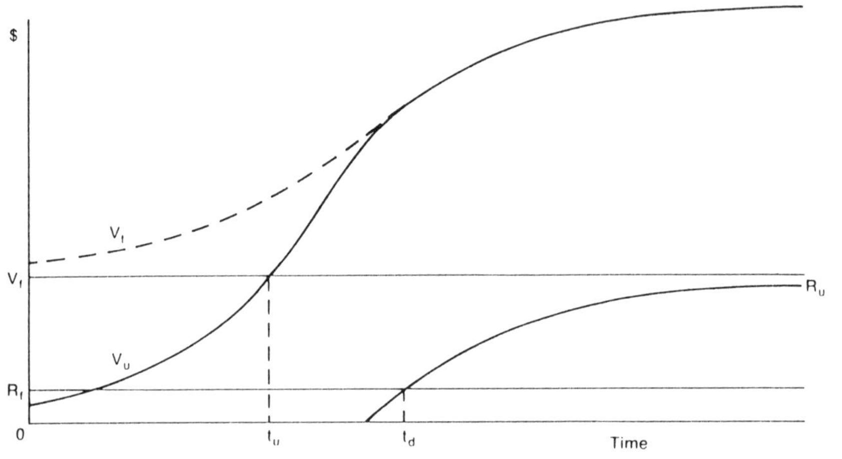

Fig. 4. Flow of returns.

deferring development is foregone post-development rent, R_u, and the returns from deferring development are continued farm rents, R_f. Development when R_u rises to equal R_f will maximise V_0. Note that the margin between urban and rural values occurs not only without any land use controls but also, in an important sense, without speculative withholding of land from development since it is assumed that the land is developed as soon as the net return from urban use exceeds the net return from farming.

Figure 4 abstracted from speculative land holding by assuming that there is only a single profitable urban use. The opportunity for speculative activity can be illustrated when we make the model a little more complex by recognising that different kinds of development of a site may be profitable at different stages in the urban development of a locality. One of the main reasons why the flow of returns from the post-development use varies with the time of development is that the most profitable kind or density of development will, itself, vary with the time of development. For example semi-rural subdivisions could be the most profitable kind or density of development when the particular site is beyond the fringe of an urban area, ordinary single family housing some years later and flats at an even later stage. In some circumstances these uses can follow one another but in other circumstances (discussed below) the expected life of lower density urban uses will be so short that the different urban uses have to be seen as alternatives rather than members of a sequence. Speculative withholding of land under these latter circumstances occurs when continuing to farm is more profitable, even when low density development would return greater rents, because it keeps open the option for an even more profitable use in the future. This can be illustrated in Figure 5 which is derived from Figure 4. To simplify we limit our consideration to two possible levels or types of development, though the analysis would be essentially the same with more than two alternatives.

The rents from the two alternative urban uses are shown as R_u and R_u' respectively. The variation over time in the discounted values of the flow of returns from the interim use followed by each of the alternative urban developments at times t and t' would be V_t and V_t' respectively. In Figure 5 V_t and V_t' are both drawn on the assumption that the land is farmed up to time t and t' respectively and then developed. Considered at time 0 the value of the flow of returns from the earlier and less intense development is higher and the same is true at the time (t), which might be seen as a time of decision, when that development first becomes profitable. A landowner in these circumstances would be expected to choose the earlier development, notwithstanding the fact that at a later date his site would become

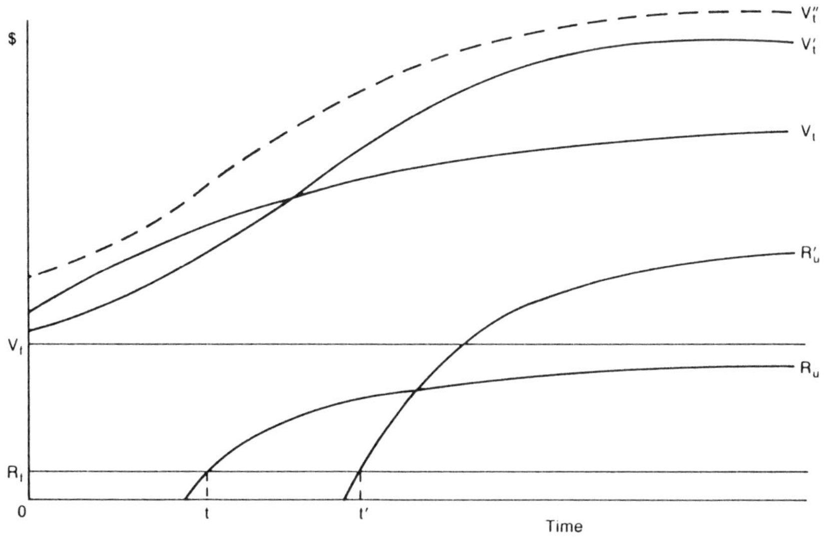

Fig. 5. Alternative land uses.

more valuable if it was still vacant and available for use for the more intensive development represented by R_u'.

If, of course, the total discounted value of the expected flow of returns from the more intensive form of development were to be as shown by V_t'' instead of V_t' it would be more profitable for the owner to keep the land vacant until the higher density use became profitable: the present value at time 0 and time t of the loss of revenue from continuing farming between t and t' would be more than offset by the present value of higher revenue after t'. In this case, between t and t' the owner would be deferring development even though there was an urban use which would return more in rent than farming.

Under what circumstances are land uses alternatives rather than potential members of a sequence? Figures 4 and 5 are not suitable for examination of this question because they assume that net rents from a land use change fairly smoothly over time if they change at all. The typical time pattern of net rents from urban development, however, is for net rents to be large and negative in the first year or two when the site is being prepared and construction costs are incurred, and much smaller and positive in following years when returns are being received. Such sequences come in bundles: the positive returns come only after the costs. The present value of such a flow of returns will depend crucially on how long the flow of positive returns is expected to continue. When considering whether or not an interim low-density urban use is a worthwhile part of a sequence, a land owner will compare the discounted value of the flow of returns from continuing the current use. The shorter the expected duration of the interim use, *ceteris paribus*, the less likely it is to form part of an optimal sequence.

Once land has been committed to a use by the construction of durable structures a change in use is desirable if, after paying the cost of demolition, the site is worth more in the new use than the site and buildings are worth in the current use. One could argue that the value of a vacant site is greater than the value of a site with buildings because a vacant site can be committed to its most profitable use with less sacrifice of returns from alternative production. It is more correct, though, to define site value as its value if it was vacant and to regard the value of buildings as the residual. The buildings on a site which could be much more profitably used for another purpose have little economic value.

It is easy to distinguish, then, between existing

uses, whether farming or housing, which require little or no new investment, and new uses which require a lot. In Figure 5 V_t and V_t' can be regarded as valuations of alternative sequences of land use. The fact that they cross does not reduce the superiority of V_t at time 0 and up to time t when the first decision must be made. It shows that, even though the flow of returns from R_u' is worth more from the time V_t and V_t' cross, that gain is worth less at time 0 than the sacrifice from the loss of R_u between t and t'. The greater value of V_t' at later dates reflects the financial advantage of keeping options open by deferring development. The V_ts are not site values but the value at different times of alternative flows of net returns. The true site value is the highest V_t at any one time, reflecting the most profitable sequence of uses if the site was vacant at that time.

The analysis of urban land when there are alternative sequences of development shows that it is sometimes worth holding land vacant, in an existing use, even when it could bring higher net returns in another use. This occurs because committing it to the second use may be less valuable than holding it vacant in order to be able to commit it later to an even more profitable use. It follows that urban and rural values will diverge even further than would be expected from the analysis in Figure 4.

Does the model help explain scattered development? It does so in two ways. First, some land is more suitable for future higher density use and will be more likely to be held out of development. Second, property owners have varying discount rates. Those with higher discount rates will choose to develop earlier, and owners' discount rates are not likely to be closely related to the closeness of a property to the established urban (or commercial) area.

3. Uncertainty

Analysing alternative sequences of future returns as though they were known with certainty omits a major determinant of land use. Uncertainty influences the results of the analyses in Section 2 in two ways.

First, owners' assessments of likely future prices, costs and other conditions vary. Owners who are optimistic about the value of future development opportunities will tend to keep their land vacant in order to be able to take full advantage of them. Owners of adjacent sites may make very different predictions. As with discount rates, there is no reason why owners who are more or less optimistic should be clustered together so scattered development is likely.

Second, individual owners are likely to be uncertain about the future. This could be illustrated by introducing different R_u' curves, each of which may occur. In this context, as Titman (1985) shows, vacant land can be likened to an option to develop in the way which emerges in the course of time as being most profitable. His example is land in commercial areas which is held for many years in a low intensity use such as surface car parking:

> "... a vacant lot can be viewed as an option to purchase one of a number of different possible buildings at exercise prices that are equal to their respective construction costs. This approach provides a valuation formula that is a function of observable variables and is independent of the investor's preferences." (pp. 505–6)

The value of the vacant site is then the value of the option to choose the future level of development in the light of those future conditions. Using the valuation of options from the theory of finance, Titman shows how this can be expressed as a function of the alternative levels of profitability of building condominiums at the future date, annual rentals, the risk free interest rate and the value of the site for current construction.[2] If its option value for future construction exceeds its value for current construction it will pay the owner to keep it vacant.

An important result of this analysis is that it can formally demonstrate that the greater the level of uncertainty about future market conditions the greater the value of the option to decide the level and type of development in the light of those conditions as they emerge rather than determine them immediately in order to build forthwith. With a high level of uncertainty a decision to develop immediately is relatively unattractive. It follows that the higher the level of uncertainty the higher the

[2] Brown and Achour (1984) have shown in a more conventional analysis how the value of options can be adapted to the property market.

value of vacant land relative to developed land and the smaller the supply of such land to (for) development. The level of uncertainty about future opportunities itself then contributes to the margin between value of property in its existing use and its value for a new expanding use.

An important policy implication follows. Planning of land use, and land use controls that are adopted to implement plans, to the extent that they reduce the level of uncertainty about the form and level of development that will be appropriate and permissible, can actually hasten development. The result would be to *increase* the supply and *reduce* the price of land for development and redevelopment. This implication is directly contrary to the general conclusion about the impact of land use planning on prices of land for urban use: namely that it restricts the supply and therefore causes prices to be higher (Hall *et al* 1973; Neutze, 1973).

Land use controls are often seen as a source of uncertainty about future returns rather than as a means of reducing uncertainty since the authority administering the controls has discretion about whether or not certain kinds of developments will be permitted (Wiltshaw, 1986). Such uncertainty would not, however, increase the option value of vacant land. Nor does it counter the major increase in certainty about future patterns of land use provided by land use planning. In general, planning makes the whole context within which development takes place less uncertain, though it is possible for plans to be changed so frequently that they, themselves, cause increased uncertainty about the future pattern of development. It may be, of course, that the effect of uncertainty is small relative to the direct effect of supply restrictions on prices.

4. Discussion

This paper has analysed three explanations for the features of the urban land market that seem inconsistent with a straightforward static theory. They are: (1) the non-financial direct utility which is obtained from occupation and ownership of land varies with its use and between owners, (2) land use decisions and land values depend on expectations about the future as well as on present conditions in the market, and (3) uncertainty about future conditions results in owners' expectations varying and the greater the uncertainty the greater the gains from deferring development. These explanations are additive rather than alternatives. An owner who enjoys his land being farmed will be even more likely to refrain from development if he believes that it will continue to appreciate with expanding urban development opportunities. Furthermore, his decision will be reinforced if it seems possible that even more profitable development possibilities could emerge in the future. For many land owners the relevant aspect of future expectations is their impact on the future market value. The second and third explanations are specially closely related since future expectations are always uncertain. The degree of uncertainty, however, varies greatly.

In particular circumstances one or other of the explanations is likely to be of greater importance. Titman was correct in focussing on the high degree of uncertainty attached to the profitability of high density redevelopment. Direct utility is an important factor inhibiting the sale of attractive rural properties for urban use but it is unimportant in areas where rural land is unused and gathers rubbish and weeds or in the case of derelict land in old industrial areas. The relative importance could be investigated in two ways. The first is to ask property owners about the reason for their decisions about the timing of development. Such questions would need to be very carefully framed and to recognise that decisions by owners to develop may be taken in very different contexts (Goodchild and Munton, 1985). The second is to formulate hypotheses about observable features of the market that would occur if one or other of the explanations was the most important.

REFERENCES

ALONSO, W. (1964). *Location and Land Use*. Cambridge, Massachusetts: Harvard University Press.

BROWN, R. L. and ACHOUR, D. (1984). 'The pricing of land options', *Urban Studies*, Vol. 21, 317–23.

EVANS, A. W. (1982). 'The neutrality of a development gains tax', *National Tax Journal*, Vol. 37, 59–65.

EVANS, A. W. (1983). 'The determination of the price of land', *Urban Studies*, Vol. 20, 119–29.

FOSTER, C. D. and GLAISTER, S. (1975). 'The anatomy of the development value tax', *Urban Studies*, Vol. 12, 213–8.

GOODCHILD, R. and MUNTON, R. (1985). *Development and the Landowner: An analysis of the British experience*. London: George Allen and Unwin.

HALL, P. G., GRACEY, H., DREWETT, R. and THOMAS, R. (1973). *The containment of Urban England*. London: George Allen and Unwin.

MARKUSEN, J. R. and SCHEFFMAN, D. T. (1978). 'Ownership concentration and market power in urban land markets', *Review of Economic Studies*, Vol. 45, 519–26.

MISHAN, E. J. (1981). *Introduction to Normative Economics*. New York: Oxford University Press.

NEUTZE, M. (1973). 'The price of land and land use planning', *OECD*, Paris (mimeographed) also in Bendixson, T., (ed.), *The Management of Urban Growth*, Environment Directorate, OECD, Paris, 1977. The relevant part is reprinted in McMaster, J. C. and Webb, G. R., (eds.), *Australian Urban Economics: A Reader*, Australia and New Zealand Book Co., Brookvale NSW, 1976.

ROSE, L. A. (1973). 'The development value tax', *Urban Studies*, Vol. 10, 271–85.

TITMAN, S. (1985). 'Urban land price under uncertainty', *American Economic Review*, Vol. 75, 505–14.

WILTSHAW, D. G. (1985). 'The supply of land', *Urban Studies*, Vol. 22, 49–56.

WILTSHAW, D. G. (1986). 'Land investment, planning permission, and uncertainty: a state-preference analysis', *Environment and Planning A*, Vol. 18, 207–15.

[10]

THE ECONOMICS OF URBAN RENEWAL*

Otto A. Davis† and Andrew B. Whinston‡

Introduction

In light of two implications of urban renewal, it is not at all surprising that this phenomenon provides an excellent area for the application of welfare economics. These implications are: First, that the market mechanism has not functioned "properly" in urban property; and second, that positive action can "improve" the situation. The propositions of welfare economics provide some tools for judging public policy measures such as urban renewal. But since these propositions themselves are based upon ethical postulates, it seems desirable that we begin our discussion of urban renewal by stating explicitly what we consider the role of the economist to be in this situation.

I

Welfare Economics and Urban Renewal

Welfare economics itself provides one criterion, the Pareto condition, for judging public policy measures. The Pareto condition states that a social policy measure can be judged "desirable" if it results in either (1) everyone being made better off, or (2) someone being made better off without anyone being made worse off. This rule is, of course, an ethical proposition, but it requires a minimum of premises and should command wide assent.

On the other hand, the economist need not be limited solely to the Pareto condition in giving policy advice. This becomes especially true when the objective ambiguity of the terms "better off" and "worse off" is considered. Indeed, the role of the economist in the formation of social policy may be compared to that of the consultant to an industrial firm. The consultant to a firm serves two functions. First, given the goals of the firm, he tries to find the best or most efficient means of achieving these goals. The second function of the consultant is equally important; he must try to clarify vague goals by pointing out possible inconsistencies and determining implications in order that re-evaluations and explicit statements can be made.

We conceive of the role of the economist as quite similar to that outlined for the consultant. First, the economist may try to clarify social goals by pointing out

* The authors would like to express their appreciation to Professors Donald A. Fink and Merton Miller, both of Carnegie Institute of Technology, and to Edgar M. Hoover and Melvin K. Bers, both of the Pittsburgh Regional Planning Association, for reading and criticizing the manuscript. Conversations with Professor W. W. Cooper, of the Carnegie Institute of Technology, were also beneficial.

† A.B. 1956, Wofford College; M.A. 1957, Ph.D. 1960, University of Virginia. Assistant Professor of Economics, Graduate School of Industrial Administration, Carnegie Institute of Technology; Staff Economist, Pittsburgh Regional Planning Association.

‡ B.A. 1957, University of Michigan; M.S. (Industrial Economics) 1960, Graduate School of Industrial Administration, Carnegie Institute of Technology.

inconsistencies and determining implications of possible social rules. Second, if a goal happens to be given and agreed upon—*i.e.*, if a social welfare function is defined—then the economist might try to advise the body politic by proposing policies for the attainment of the defined goals.

It is in the above spirit that we consider the problem of urban renewal. Granted the individualistic basis of western civilization, it seems reasonable to assume that any action which satisfies the Pareto condition would improve social welfare and, therefore, should be desired by society. On the other hand, society might desire, granted the institutional form of political decision-making, certain actions which violate the narrowly conceived Pareto condition.[1] Certainly income redistribution would fit this category. And so may urban renewal.

Specifically, the social welfare function which we use has the following properties: If the sum of the benefits, measured by changes in capital values, exceeds the sum of the costs, then the action is termed desirable. While this welfare criterion may not seem clear at this point, it is appropriate to note here that a major portion of the remainder of the paper will be devoted to determining how benefits and costs are to be measured. What is important here is to make clear the basis upon which our judgments will be made.

Several characteristics of this welfare criterion should be noted here. First, any action which satisfies the narrowly conceived Pareto condition will satisfy this criterion. On the other hand, any action which satisfies the welfare criterion need not meet the Pareto condition unless compensation is required. Second, our criterion is concerned with the efficient allocation of resources. The question of the ethically desirable distribution of income will not be considered here, although some might hold that urban renewal is concerned with income redistribution. We merely point out that income redistribution can be more efficiently achieved through other means than urban renewal.

II

THE PRICE MECHANISM AND URBAN BLIGHT

Having stated the position from which we shall make policy judgments, we now must examine the question of why urban renewal is necessary. In other words, why do "blighted" areas develop and persist? Why do individuals fail to keep their properties in "acceptable" states of repair?

Several arguments may be advanced as answers to the above questions. For example, it has been asserted that property owners have exaggerated notions of the extent and timing of municipal expansion. Hence they may neglect possible improvements of existing structures in anticipation of the arrival of more intensive uses which might bring capital gains.[2] Note that even if this argument is accepted

[1] It is worthy of note that it can be argued very convincingly, if the individualistic ethic is adopted, that any social welfare function must satisfy a broadly conceived Pareto condition—that is, a Pareto condition defined by political consensus. See, *e.g.*, Buchanan, *Positive Economics, Welfare Economics, and Political Economy*, 2 J. LAW & ECONOMICS 124 (1959).

[2] Fisher, *Economic Aspects of Zoning, Blighted Areas, and Rehabilitation Laws*, 3 AM. ECON. REV. 334 (1942).

as plausible—and the reason why property owners might have exaggerated notions about municipal expansion is by no means evident—it does not constitute an argument for urban renewal. Instead, one might infer that, given sufficient time, a transition to intensive and profitable uses would take place.[3] Then too, it can be argued that there is no reason to expect governmental authorities to have better judgment than individual entrepreneurs.

Aside from the previous "mistaken judgments" argument, it might seem plausible at first glance to believe on the basis of price theory and the profit maximization assumption that urban blight could not occur. After all, would not profit-maximizing individuals find it to their advantage to keep their property in a state of repair? Certainly it seems reasonable to suppose that if individual benefits from repair or redevelopment exceed individual costs, then individual action could be expected and no social action would be necessary. We shall now attempt to demonstrate why rational individual action might allow property to deteriorate and blight to occur.

First of all, the fact that the value of any one property depends in part upon the neighborhood in which it is located seems so obvious as hardly to merit discussion. Yet, since this simple fact is the villain of the piece, further elaboration is warranted. Pure introspective evidence seems sufficient to indicate that persons consider the neighborhood when deciding to buy or rent some piece of urban property.[4] If this is the case, then it means that externalities are present in utility functions; that is to say, the subjective utility or enjoyment derived from a property depends not only upon the design, state of repairs, and so on of that property, but also upon the characteristics of nearby properties. This fact will, of course, be reflected in both capital and rental values. This is the same as saying that it is also reflected in the return on investment.

In order to explain how interdependence can cause urban blight, it seems appropriate to introduce a simple example from the theory of games. This example, which has been developed in an entirely different context and is commonly known as "The Prisoner's Dilemma," appears to contain the important points at issue here.[5]

[3] Indeed, it can even be argued that this line of reasoning considered alone leads to the conclusion that urban renewal expenditures are wasteful. See, *e.g.*, Davis, *A Pure Theory of Urban Renewal*, 36 LAND ECONOMICS 221 (1960).

[4] This interdependence of urban property values has, of course, long been recognized. See, for example, the discussion in ALFRED MARSHALL, PRINCIPLES OF ECONOMICS bk. 5, ch. 11 (8th ed. 1920). The following quote is especially interesting in this regard. "But the general rule holds that the amount and character of the building put upon each plot of land is, in the main (subject to the local building bylaws), that from which the most profitable results are anticipated, with little or no reference to its reaction on the situation value of the neighborhood. In other words, the site value of the plot is governed by causes which are mostly beyond the control of him who determines what buildings shall be put on it." *Id.* at 445.

[5] For an explanation of the "game theoretic" points of interest in the Prisoner's Dilemma example, see R. DUNCAN LUCE & HOWARD RAIFFA, GAMES AND DECISIONS 94-102 (1957). The reason for the intriguing title of this type of game theory analysis is interesting in itself. The name is derived from a popular interpretation. The district attorney takes two suspects into custody and keeps them separated. He is sure they are guilty of a specific crime but does not have adequate evidence for a conviction. He talks to each separately and tells them that they can confess or not confess. If neither confesses, then

For the sake of simplicity, let us consider only two adjacent properties. More general situations do not alter the result but do complicate the reasoning. Let us use the labels Owner I and Owner II. Suppose that each owner has made an initial investment in his property from which he is reaping a return, and is now trying to determine whether to make the additional investment for redevelopment. The additional investment will, of course, alter the return which he receives, and so will the decision of the other owner.

The situation which they might face can be summarized in the following game matrix:

		Owner II	
		Invest	Not Invest
Owner I	Invest	(.07, .07)	(.03, .10)
	Not Invest	(.10, .03)	(.04, .04)

The matrix game is given the following interpretation: Each property owner has made an initial investment and has an additional sum which is invested in, say, corporate bonds. At present, the average return on both these investments, the property and the corporate bonds considered together, is four per cent. Thus if neither owner makes the decision to sell his corporate bonds and make a new investment in the redevelopment of his property, each will continue to get the four per cent average return. This situation is represented by the entries within brackets in the lower right of the matrix where each individual has made the decision "Not Invest." The left hand figure in the brackets always refers to the average return which Owner I receives, and the right hand figure reflects the return of Owner II. Thus for the "Not Invest, Not Invest" decisions, the matrix entry reflects the fact that both owners continue to get a four per cent return.

On the other hand, if both individuals made the decision to sell their bonds and invest the proceeds in redevelopment of their property, it is assumed that each would obtain an average return of seven per cent on his total investment. Therefore, the entry in the upper left of the matrix, the entry for the "Invest, Invest" decisions, has a seven per cent return for each owner.

The other two entries in the matrix, which represent the situation when one owner invests and the other does not, are a little more complicated. We assumed, as was mentioned earlier, that externalities, both external economies and diseconomies, are present. These interdependencies are reflected in the returns from investment. For example, consider the entries in the brackets in the lower left corner of the matrix. In this situation, Owner I would have decided to "Not Invest" and Owner II would have decided to "Invest."

he will book them on some minor charge and both will receive minor punishment. If both confess, then they will be prosecuted but he will recommend less than the most severe sentence. If either one confesses and the other does not, then the confessor will receive lenient treatment for turning state's evidence, whereas the latter will get "the book" slapped at him. The Prisoner's Dilemma is that without collusion between them, the individually rational action for each is to confess.

Owner I is assumed to obtain some of the benefits from Owner II's investment, the redevelopment contributing something to a "better neighborhood." For example, if the two properties under consideration happened to be apartment buildings, the decision of Owner II to invest might mean that he would demolish his "out-dated" apartment building and construct a new one complete with off-street parking and other amenities. But this would mean that the tenants of Owner I would now have an easier time finding parking spaces on the streets, their children might have the opportunity of associating with the children of the "higher class" people who might be attracted to the modern apartment building, and so forth. All this means that (as soon as leases allow) Owner I can edge up his rents. Thus his return is increased without having to make an additional investment. We assume that his return becomes ten per cent in this case, and this figure is appropriately entered in the matrix. Owner II, on the other hand, would find that, since his renters also consider the "neighborhood" (which includes the ill effects of Owner I's "out-dated" structure), his level of rents would have to be less than would be the case if his apartment building were in an alternative location. Thus we assume that the return on his total investment (the investment in the now-demolished structure plus the investment in the new structure) falls to three per cent. This figure is also appropriately entered in the matrix. For simplicity, the reverse situation, where Owner I decided to invest and Owner II decides not to invest, is taken to be similar. Thus the reverse entries are made in the upper right corner of the matrix.[6]

Having described the possible situations which the two owners face, consider now the decision-making process. Both owners are assumed to be aware of the returns which are available to themselves in the hypothesized situations. Owner I will be considered first. Owner I must decide whether to invest or not invest. Remember that the left hand entries in the brackets represent the possible returns for Owner I. Two possible actions of Owner II are relevant for Owner I in his effort to make his own decision. Therefore, Owner I might use the following decision process: Assume, first, that Owner II decides to invest. Then what decision would be the most advantageous? A decision to invest means only a seven per cent return on Owner I's capital, whereas the decision not to invest would yield an average return of ten per cent of the total relevant amount of capital. Therefore, if Owner II were to decide to invest, it would certainly be individually advantageous to Owner I not to invest. But suppose that Owner II decided not to invest. Then what would be the most advantageous decision for Owner I? Once again the results can be seen from the matrix. For Owner I the decision to invest now means that he will

[6] Economists might think that we have used inappropriate and sleight-of-hand methods by lumping together old and new investments, and also by considering the average rate of return instead of marginal rates. Actually these methods are completely appropriate here due to the way we have simplified the problem to make the exposition of the game theory easier. The old investment does not represent a sunk cost, since it is yielding a return and thus has economic value. Both owners are assumed to have precisely the amount of money in bonds that is required for the redevelopment of their property. The rate of return on the bonds can be assumed to be the "social rate of return" and the best alternative available to the two individuals. Since the owners are interested in maximizing the total income from their capital, the above assumptions allow us to lump together and to use average rates.

receive only a three per cent return on his capital, whereas the decision not to invest means that he can continue to receive the four per cent average return. Therefore, if Owner II were to decide not to invest, it would still be individually advantageous to Owner I not to invest.

The situation for Owner II is similar. If Owner I is assumed to invest, then Owner II can gain a ten per cent average return on his capital by not investing and only a seven per cent return by investing. If Owner I is assumed not to invest, then Owner II can gain only a three per cent return by investing, but a four per cent average return by not investing. Therefore, the individually rational action for Owner II is also not to invest.

The situation described above means, of course, that neither Owner I nor Owner II will decide to invest in redevelopment. Therefore, we might conclude that the interdependencies summarized in the Prisoner's Dilemma example can explain why blighted areas can develop[7] and persist. Before concluding the analysis, however, we might try to answer some questions which may at this point be forthcoming.

First of all, it might be suggested that we have imposed an unrealistic condition by not allowing the two owners to coordinate their decisions.[8] After all, does it not seem likely that the two owners would get together and mutually agree to invest in the redevelopment of their properties? Not only would such action be socially desirable, but it would seem to be individually advantageous. Note that while it might be easy for the two property owners in our simple example to communicate and coordinate their decisions,[9] this would not appear to be the case as the number of individuals increased. If any single owner were to decide not to invest while all other owners decided to redevelop, then the former would stand to gain by such action. The mere presence of many owners would seem to make coordination more difficult and thus make our assumption more realistic. Yet, this is precisely the point; it is the objective of social policy to encourage individuals in such situations to co-ordinate their decisions so that interdependencies will not prevent the achievement of a Pareto welfare point. In this regard, it is worthwhile to note that, if coordination and redevelopment do take place voluntarily, then no problem exists, and urban renewal is not needed.

Second, it might be observed that, if coordinated action does not take place, incentive exists for either Owner I, Owner II, or some third party to purchase the properties and develop both of them in order that the seven per cent return can be

[7] It is to be emphasized that these results depend upon the interdependencies or neighborhood effects being "sufficiently strong" to get a combination of returns similar to those which we used in the example. It is unlikely that this condition would be satisfied for all urban property. Our point is that similar combinations seem possible, and if they do occur, then they can explain one peculiar phenomenon of urban property. The explanation is presented later in the paper.

[8] It is worthy of note that experimental data concerning the prisoner's dilemma in other contexts tend to indicate that, if communication does not take place, players continually choose individually rational strategies. For the results of these laboratory experiments, see Scodel, Minas, Ratoosh & Lipetz, *Some Descriptive Aspects of Two-Person Non-Zero-Sum Games*, 3 J. CONFLICT RESOLUTION 114 (1959).

[9] It will be recalled that we made the example overly simple only for the purpose of exposition. While the consideration of many individuals would make the example more realistic, it would only make the game theory more complicated and not alter the result as far as this case is concerned.

obtained. And certainly, it cannot be denied that this often occurs in reality. However, it is necessary to point out here that, because of the institutional pecularities of urban property, there is no assurance that such a result will always take place. Consider, for example, an area composed of many holdings. Suppose that renewal or redevelopment would be feasible if coordination could be achieved, but that individual action alone will not result in such investment due to the interdependencies. In other words, the situation is assumed to be similar to the previous example except that many owners are present. Incentive exists for some entrepreneur to attempt to purchase the entire area and invest in redevelopment or renewal.

Now suppose that one or more of the owners of the small plots in the area became aware of the entrepreneur's intentions. If the small plots were so located as to be important for a successful project, then the small holders might realize that it would be possible to gain by either (1) using their position to expropriate part of the entrepreneur's expected profits by demanding a very high price for their properties, or (2) refusing to sell in order to enjoy the external economies generated by the redevelopment. If several of the small holders become aware of the entrepreneur's intentions, then it is entirely possible, with no communication or collusion between these small holders, for a situation to result where each tries to expropriate as much of the entrepreneur's profit as possible by either of the above methods. This competition can result in a Prisoner's Dilemma type of situation for the small holders. Individually rational action on their part may result in the cancellation of the project by the entrepreneur. Indeed, anyone familiar with the functioning of the urban property market must be aware of such difficulties and of the care that must be taken to prevent price-gouging when an effort is made to assemble some tract of land.[10]

If the above analysis is correct, then it is clear that situations may exist where individually rational action may not allow for socially desirable investment in the redevelopment of urban properties. Now such situations need not—indeed, in general will not—exist in all urban properties. The results of the analysis not only required special assumptions about the nature of investment returns caused by interdependencies, but it was also shown that, due to the special institutional character of tract assembly, the presence of numerous small holdings can block entrepreneurial action for redevelopment. These two conditions may or may not be filled for any given tract of land. However, we now may use the above results to *define* urban blight.[11] Blight is said to exist whenever (1) strictly individual action does not result in redevelopment, (2) the coordination of decision-making via some means would result in redevelopment, and (3) the sum of benefits from renewal

[10] For example, Raymond Vernon states, "As the city developed, most of its land was cut up in small parcels and covered with durable structures of one kind or another. The problem of assembling these sites, in the absence of some type of condemnation power, required a planning horizon of many years and a willingness to risk the possibility of price gouging by the last holdout." RAYMOND VERNON, THE CHANGING ECONOMIC FUNCTION OF THE CENTRAL CITY 53 (1959).

[11] It is to be pointed out and emphasized that our definition of the term "blight" does not seem to be what is meant by the term in common usage where it has a connotation of absolute obsolescence. Our definition refers to the misuse of land in general and carries no such connotation. The difference in meanings is unfortunate, but we could not find a more appropriate term.

could exceed the sum of costs. These conditions must be filled. We shall devote a major portion of the latter part of the paper to making this definition operational; but, for the moment, let it suffice for us to point out two factors. First, it is a problem of social policy to develop methods whereby blighted areas can be recognized and positive action can be taken to facilitate either redevelopment or renewal. Second, and this point may be controversial, blight is not necessarily associated with the outward appearance of properties in any area.

Since this second point may be subtle and seem contrary to intuitive ideas about blight, further discussion may be warranted. Note that we have defined blight strictly in relation to the allocation of resources. The fact that the properties in an area have a "poor" appearance may or may not be an indication of blight and the malallocation of resources. For several factors, aside from tastes, help to determine the appearance of properties. The situation which we have described, where individually rational action may lead to no investment and deterioration, is only one type of case. Another may be based on the distribution of incomes. Poor classes can hardly be expected to afford the spacious and comfortable quarters of the well-to-do. Indeed, given the existence of low income households, a slum area *may* represent an efficient use of resources. If the existence of slums per se violates one's ethical standards, then, as economists, we can only point out that for elimination of slums the main economic concern must be with the distribution of income, and urban renewal is not sufficient to solve that problem. Indeed, unless some action is taken to alter the distribution of income, the renewal of slum areas is likely to lead to the creation of slum areas elsewhere.[12] It is to be emphasized that slums may or may not satisfy the definition of a blighted area. On the other hand, the mere fact that the properties in some given area appear "nice" to the eye is not sufficient evidence to indicate that blight (by our definition) is absent.

One additional remark of clarification seems warranted. It is obvious that not all individuals are free to purchase or rent property in all areas of the metropolis. Discrimination—*e.g.*, by race—may create two or more "separate" markets, and there seems to be no reason to suspect short-run equilibrium in the sense of investment return *between* markets. We simply note here that, granted the discrimination, this fact does not affect our definition of blight, nor does it alter the proposals which we shall present.

[12] It is a curious fact that renewal seems to be regarded as a "cure" for slum areas. For, granted the distribution of income and the fact that the poor classes simply cannot afford to pay high enough rents to warrant the more spacious and confortable quarters, the renewal of all slum areas, unless accompanied by an income-subsidy program, would only be self-defeating and lead to social waste. Renewal of all slum areas could cause rents for the "nicer" quarters to fall temporarily within the possible range of the poor classes, but the rents would not be sufficiently high to warrant expenditures by the landlord to maintain the structure. New slums would appear, calling for more renewal activity. This process would simply continue. On the other hand, efficient slum-removal programs are possible, and one will be presented at a later point in this paper.

III

A BRIEF CRITIQUE OF PRESENT PRACTICES

Having seen that, due to externalities or interdependencies and the difficulty of tract assembly, individually rational action may allow blight to develop, we now turn our attention to questions of public policy. It bears repeating that wherever our definition of blight is satisfied, then resources are misallocated in the sense that some institutional arrangement—some means—exists under which redevelopment or renewal could profitably be carried out. The problem is to discover that institutional arrangement. We begin our search by examining briefly the relevant aspects of the present practices.

Title I of the Housing Act of 1949[13] seems to have set the general pattern for urban renewal practices. While the Act of 1954[14] broadened the concept, the general formula for urban redevelopment remains essentially unchanged. Both federal loans and capital grants are provided for the projects. Loans are generally for the purpose of providing working capital. The capital grants may cover up to two-thirds of the net cost of the project, with the remainder of the funds being provided by either state or local sources.[15]

The striking fact about the present program, and also about many of the proposals for extending that program, is the utter lack of a relevant criterion for expenditures. How much should be invested in urban renewal? How does one determine whether projects are really worthwhile? Does the present program attempt to "correct" the allocation of resources or does it simply result in further misallocation? There seems to have been little or no serious effort to find answers to these questions. In fact, it is widely admitted that there is a lack of adequate criteria even to determine what projects should be undertaken.[16]

It seems evident from the statements of mayors and others who propose expansions of the present program that the need approach to governmental expenditures underlies their suggestions. That is to say, a certain project "needs" to be carried out; and, granted this requirement, money is sought for the project. It should be evident that this approach to governmental expenditures may not result in the correct allocation of resources. The need approach obscures budgetary considerations and makes comparison of alternatives difficult, since a need is simply assumed without reference to other possible areas of expenditure. The need approach is arbitrary and overlooks

[13] 63 Stat. 413, 42 U.S.C. §§ 1441-60 (1958).

[14] 68 Stat. 622, as amended, 42 U.S.C. §§ 1450-62 (1958); 68 Stat. 596, as amended, 12 U.S.C. §§ 1715*k*, 1715*l* (1958).

[15] There are, of course, conditions which must be satisfied before a community can be eligible for federal funds. See, *e.g.*, COMM'N ON INTERGOVERNMENTAL RELATIONS, TWENTY-FIVE FEDERAL GRANT-IN-AID PROGRAMS (1955).

[16] A remark by Morton J. Schussheim, Deputy Director of the Area Development Division of the Committee for Economic Development, is interesting in this respect. Mr. Schussheim writes, "It is true . . . that local officials responsible for urban renewal programs do not have adequate criteria for determining what projects to undertake and on what scale." *A Pure Theory of Urban Renewal: A Comment*, 34 LAND ECONOMICS 395 (1960).

the return on investment, an extremely important consideration for the problem of a rational allocation of resources.[17]

IV

REDISTRIBUTION, THE COST-BENEFIT CRITERION, AND URBAN RENEWAL

Having pointed out that the existing institutional arrangements concerning urban renewal contain no explicit criterion for determining either the amount of such expenditure or when a project is desirable, we now propose the previously introduced benefits-cost criterion and will discuss later the institutional arrangements under which it could be applied. First, however, let us detail more fully our use of this criterion and the reasons for its selection.

We assume that income and utility are positively correlated. This means that if potential benefits, appropriately-defined, exceed costs, then the conditions for Pareto optimality, in the absence of corrective measures, are not filled. It is possible for some action to be taken which will make one or more persons better off without making anyone worse off.[18] In this context, the action will take the form of investment in urban renewal.

It is to be emphasized again that the benefits-cost criterion refers only to the problem of efficiency—*i.e.*, to the allocation of resources on the basis of a given distribution of income. However, it is possible to design programs which do redistribute income but which still are completely compatible with the benefit-cost criterion. The point is that the two problems—distribution and allocation—must be kept conceptually separate.

Given the fact that interdependencies are a cause of blight, two kinds of actions are possible—preventive and reconstructive. We consider first preventive action.

As was pointed out earlier, the problem in preventing the development of blight consists essentially in finding methods of coordinating the decisions about investment in repair and upkeep so that the socially and individually desirable choices are equated. One step in this direction can be made through the development and use of a special type of building code which bears a superficial resemblance to municipal zoning.[19] It can be seen from the Prisoner's Dilemma example discussed earlier that it is individually desirable to invest *if there is assurance that all individuals*

[17] It may be commonplace to point out that there exists for any given social action a social welfare function which is maximal for that action, and by definition this resource allocation is optimal. Our point is simply that it seems dubious that a type of need approach to forming criteria is reasonable, given that urban problems are not unique as a social problem.

[18] It is easy to see the exact relation between benefits-costs and the Pareto condition. If the sum of benefits exceeds the sum of costs for some particular action, then although some individual might be made worse off by the action, it is theoretically possible to pay compensation to that individual so that the Pareto condition will be satisfied.

[19] It is to be emphasized that the building code envisioned here bears only a superficial resemblance to zoning. The two tools are aimed at different problems. Municipal zoning tries to prevent the establishment of "undesirable" properties in specified neighborhoods. These special building codes would be aimed at the elimination of interdependencies affecting repair and upkeep decisions. For an elaboration on the complexities involved in municipal zoning, see Davis & Whinston, *The Economics of Complex Systems: The Case of Municipal Zoning* (O.N.R. Research Memorandum, Graduate School of Industrial Administration, Carnegie Institute of Technology, 1961).

will be constrained to make a similar decision. The special building code specifying minimum levels of repair and upkeep can provide a rough approximation toward optimal levels of coordination.

A brief outline of the scheme follows: Since it is intuitively obvious that different types of property require different kinds of repair and types of upkeep, it would seem desirable that these building codes differ according to the type property under consideration. The role of the planner would be to try to determine the proper restrictions for each type of property. He could try to gather information on interaction effects through the use of statistical sampling techniques and questionnaires. He then could draw up districts and try to estimate the proper level of the building code for each district. A crude approximation to the benefit-cost criterion is easily supplied. It is advantageous to property owners mutually to constain themselves to make "appropriate" repair expenditures, for this coordinates decisions. Therefore, the planner can simply submit the proposed code for each district to the property owners of that district; if the planner has proposed an appropriate code, then mutual consent should be forthcoming. If mutual consent is not obtained, then it would seem suitable to assume that the proper code for the district has not been proposed and that a new proposal would be necessary.[20]

While codes adopted via the above scheme should be helpful in preventing blight, it must be noted that implementation of this plan would require the selection of an appropriate institutional and legal framework. As economists, we do not pretend to know the legal difficulties which might be involved; but a joint effort by the two professions to set up the framework for such a scheme seems to us to be desirable.

Let us now turn our attention to the policy problem when blight is already in existence. Present practices provide something of a framework here; what is missing is a relevant criterion. Of course, it should be noted that it may sometimes be possible to obtain redevelopment through individual effort via the previously-stated special-building-code method. In other instances, the optimal property uses may have changed from what they formerly were. The area may be composed of lots too small to obtain an orderly transition of property uses by means of the building code. It may be desirable to replan streets, or other reasons may be advanced for the usual type of urban renewal effort. Therefore, let us try to determine the appropriate comparison of costs and benefits when the usual type renewal activity takes place.

Let us assume that the city government has marked some blighted area for redevelopment. Taking the property tax rate as given, suppose that the city has raised funds for the project by selling bonds. With the money thus raised, the city has purchased the blighted area, using the right of eminent domain wherever needed.

[20] Our use of the term "mutual consent" may represent something of a subterfuge. In actuality, it may not be desirable to insist on unanimity nor would it seem desirable to use a simple majority. Something on the order of eighty to ninety per cent may be reasonable. For a discussion of the problems involved in voting and the difficulties associated with the selection of political decision rules, see the unpublished manuscript by JAMES M. BUCHANAN & GORDON TULLOCK, THE CALCULUS OF CONSENT (mimeo.) (Department of Economics, University of Virginia, 1959).

Suppose that the city has demolished the outdated structures, made adequate provision for public services, and then, having finished its part of the operation, sold lots to entrepreneurs who have agreed in advance to build, say, modern apartment buildings.

Note what city action has accomplished. It has removed the obstacles to private renewal. The right of eminent domain has removed the possibility of price-gouging and stubborn property owners acting so as to prevent the assembly of a large enough tract. Each entrepreneur who buys the lots from the city is assured that adjoining lots will also be suitably developed, so that interaction difficulties are eliminated.

One fact needs great emphasis here. *The elimination of externalities or interaction effects causes social and private products to be equated.* Therefore, if possible redistribution is left aside; and if for the moment problems are waived which arise from public projects where the market mechanism does not serve as an adequate guide, then it can be stated that revenues and expenditures can be made identical to costs and benefits. Therefore, renewal projects are warranted if, and only if, revenues exceed expenditures. And, even where problems associated with redistribution and public projects are not waived, it is still possible to make the revenue-expenditure criterion approximate the benefit-cost criterion, although some administrative difficulties are involved.

What are the appropriate comparisons of costs and benefits? Consider first the case without the complications. The costs of the local government include the acquisition of land, demolition and improvements, aiding the relocation of displaced families, and interest expenses.[21] The measurement of revenues is slightly more complicated. The primary item, of course, would be receipts from the sale of lots. Since we are dealing with local government, however, a tax on real property will exist. Since the discounted value of the tax is likely to be shifted onto the immobile resource—land—it is necessary to account for this factor. If the project is successful, the new structures should have a higher value than the old; so there should be a net addition to tax revenues. This net addition should be discounted to a present value and counted as a receipt from the project. Thus, a comparison of revenues and expenses is possible, and the project is warranted only if revenues exceed expenses.

We now consider the second case with the additional complications. Note that the previous discussion still applies here, with the following qualifications upon the administrative rules involved. If public projects such as parks, playgrounds, public buildings, and so forth, are planned in conjunction with the renewal effort, then estimates of the social benefit to be derived from these projects must be made by the

[21] Peculiarly enough, the present-day requirement that individuals be paid for their property and the administrative rule of aiding individuals who may be dislocated to find new quarters affords a method of approximate compensation so that the Pareto condition can be satisfied.

governmental unit or units which ordinarily pay for them.[22] These estimated benefits are to be considered as revenues from the renewal effort, and the appropriate governmental units are to be required to contribute these amounts to the authority which administers the renewal activity. Thus the revenue-expenditure criterion should very closely approximate the benefits-cost criterion, depending, of course, upon how well the governmental units estimate the social benefits derived from the special public projects.

If there happens to exist some agreed-upon ethical distribution of income, then we point out first that urban renewal is not an efficient method of achieving redistribution. Possible benefits might accrue to special groups instead of the low-income classes. Other methods for simple redistribution exist which should be preferred to urban renewal. However, if the ethical distribution is connected with some arbitrary housing standard below which conditions are viewed as inadequate for "decent living," the cost-benefit criterion need not be rendered useless. Conditional subsidies could be granted to the low income households living in substandard housing. Thse subsidies would make it possible for the cost-benefit criterion to work effectively for renewal purposes.

Several corollaries to the cost-benefit criterion should be pointed out. If problems of ethical income distribution are waived, then from the standpoint of a rational allocation of resources, no federal or state subsidies are needed for urban renewal purposes per se. Of course, the adjustments made for the second case may have to be accomplished, but note that in reality these are based upon considerations not directly dependent upon urban renewal. Renewal projects should not lose money. Indeed, they should result in a profit. On the other hand, granted the fact that constitutional and/or statutory debt limits have often been imposed upon local governments, these should be waived for borrowing for urban renewal purposes. Finally, the local governments should be granted the power of eminent domain for urban renewal purposes.

CONCLUSION

In arriving at these indications for the use of the cost-benefit criterion in urban renewal, we started with the Pareto condition. However, it was suggested that other social welfare functions, which allow for income redistribution or even minimum condition housing, need not affect the usefulness of this criterion as long as the rational allocation of resources is viewed as a *conceptually separate* problem. It is to be emphasized that for the purpose of urban renewal, conceptual separation of the two problems can be achieved through the methods outlined above.

[22] We assume that the units which ordinarily pay for this type of public projects are identical to the units which derive the benefits from these projects. If this is not the case, then further administrative adjustments have to be made, but these adjustments should be made anyway and should not be dependent upon possible urban renewal projects.

[11]

A PURE THEORY OF LOCAL EXPENDITURES[1]

CHARLES M. TIEBOUT
Northwestern University

ONE of the most important recent developments in the area of "applied economic theory" has been the work of Musgrave and Samuelson in public finance theory.[2] The two writers agree on what is probably the major point under investigation, namely, that no "market type" solution exists to determine the level of expenditures on public goods. Seemingly, we are faced with the problem of having a rather large portion of our national income allocated in a "non-optimal" way when compared with the private sector.

This discussion will show that the Musgrave-Samuelson analysis, which is valid for federal expenditures, need not apply to local expenditures. The plan of the discussion is first to restate the assumptions made by Musgrave and Samuelson and the central problems with which they deal. After looking at a key difference between the federal versus local cases, I shall present a simple model. This model yields a solution for the level of expenditures for local public goods which reflects the preferences of the population more adequately than they can be reflected at the national level. The assumptions of the model will then be relaxed to see what implications are involved. Finally, policy considerations will be discussed.

THE THEORETICAL ISSUE

Samuelson has defined public goods as "*collective consumption goods* ($X_n + 1, \ldots, X_n + n$) which all enjoy in common in the sense that each individual's consumption of such a good leads to no subtraction from any other individual's consumption of that good, so that $X_n + j = X_n^i + j$ simultaneously for each and every *i*th individual and each collective good."[3] While definitions are a matter of choice, it is worth noting that "consumption" has a much broader meaning here than in the usual sense of the term. Not only does it imply that the act of consumption by one person does not diminish the opportunities for consumption by another but it also allows this consumption to be in another form. For example, while the residents of a new government housing project are made better off, benefits also accrue to other residents of the community in the form of the external economies of slum clearance.[4] Thus many goods that appear to lack the attributes of public goods may

[1] I am grateful for the comments of my colleagues Karl de Schweinitz, Robert Eisner, and Robert Strotz, and those of Martin Bailey, of the University of Chicago.

[2] Richard A. Musgrave, "The Voluntary Exchange Theory of Public Economy," *Quarterly Journal of Economics*, LII (February, 1939), 213–17; "A Multiple Theory of the Budget," paper read at the Econometric Society annual meeting (December, 1955); and his forthcoming book, *The Theory of Public Economy;* Paul A. Samuelson, "The Pure Theory of Public Expenditures," *Review of Economics and Statistics*, XXXVI, No. 4 (November, 1954), 387–89, and "Diagrammatic Exposition of a Pure Theory of Public Expenditures," *ibid.*, XXXVII, No. 4 (November, 1955), 350–56.

[3] "The Pure Theory . . . ," *op. cit.*, p. 387.

[4] Samuelson allows for this when he states that "one man's circus may be another man's poison," referring, of course, to public goods ("Diagrammatic Exposition . . . ," *op. cit.*, p. 351).

properly be considered public if consumption is defined to include these external economies.[5]

A definition alternative to Samuelson's might be simply that a public good is one which should be produced, but for which there is no feasible method of charging the consumers. This is less elegant, but has the advantage that it allows for the objections of Enke and Margolis.[6] This definition, unfortunately, does not remove any of the problems faced by Musgrave and Samuelson.

The core problem with which both Musgrave and Samuelson deal concerns the mechanism by which consumer-voters register their preferences for public goods. The consumer is, in a sense, surrounded by a government whose objective it is to ascertain his wants for public goods and tax him accordingly. To use Alchian's term, the government's revenue-expenditure pattern for goods and services is expected to "adapt to" consumers' preferences.[7] Both Musgrave and Samuelson have shown that, in the vertically additive nature of voluntary demand curves, this problem has only a conceptual solution. If all consumer-voters could somehow be forced to reveal their true preferences for public goods, then the amount of such goods to be produced and the appropriate benefits tax could be determined.[8] As things now stand, there is no mechanism to force the consumer-voter to state his true preferences; in fact, the "rational" consumer will understate his preferences and hope to enjoy the goods while avoiding the tax.

The current method of solving this problem operates, unsatisfactorily, through the political mechanism. The expenditure wants of a "typical voter" are somehow pictured. This objective on the expenditure side is then combined with an ability-to-pay principle on the revenue side, giving us our current budget. Yet in terms of a satisfactory theory of public finance, it would be desirable (1) to force the voter to reveal his preferences; (2) to be able to satisfy them in

[5] There seems to be a problem connected with the external-economies aspect of public goods. Surely a radio broadcast, like national defense, has the attribute that A's enjoyment leaves B no worse off; yet this does not imply that broadcasting should, in a normative sense, be a public good (the arbitrary manner in which the level of radio programs is determined aside). The difference between defense and broadcasting is subtle but important. In both cases there is a problem of determining the optimal level of outputs and the corresponding level of benefits taxes. In the broadcasting case, however, A may be quite willing to pay more taxes than B, even if both have the same "ability to pay" (assuming that the benefits are determinate). Defense is another question. Here A is not content that B should pay less. A makes the *social judgment* that B's preference *should* be the same. A's preference, expressed as an annual defense expenditure such as $42.7 billion and representing the majority view, thus determines the level of defense. Here the A's may feel that the B's *should pay* the same amount of benefits tax.

If it is argued that this case is typical of public goods, then, once the level is somehow set, the voluntary exchange approach and the benefit theory associated with it do not make sense. If the preceding analysis is correct, we are now back in the area of equity in terms of ability to pay.

[6] They argue that, for most of the goods supplied by governments, increased use by some consumer-voters leaves less available for other consumer-voters. Crowded highways and schools, as contrasted with national defense, may be cited as examples (see Stephen Enke, "More on the Misuse of Mathematics in Economics: A Rejoinder," *Review of Economics and Statistics*, XXXVII [May, 1955], 131–33; and Julius Margolis, "A Comment on the Pure Theory of Public Expenditure," *Review of Economics and Statistics*, XXXVII [November, 1955], 247–49).

[7] Armen A. Alchian, "Uncertainty, Evolution, and Economic Theory," *Journal of Political Economy*, LVIII (June, 1950), 211–21.

[8] The term "benefits tax" is used in contrast to the concept of taxation based on the "ability to pay," which really reduces to a notion that there is some "proper" distribution of income. Conceptually, this issue is separate from the problem of providing public goods and services (see Musgrave, "A Multiple Theory . . . ," *op. cit.*).

the same sense that a private goods market does; and (3) to tax him accordingly. The question arises whether there is any set of social institutions by which this goal can be approximated.

LOCAL EXPENDITURES

Musgrave and Samuelson implicitly assume that expenditures are handled at the central government level. However, the provision of such governmental services as police and fire protection, education, hospitals, and courts does not necessarily involve federal activity.[9] Many of these goods are provided by local governments. It is worthwhile to look briefly at the magnitude of these expenditures.[10]

Historically, local expenditures have exceeded those of the federal government. The thirties were the first peacetime years in which federal expenditures began to pull away from local expenditures. Even during the fiscal year 1954, federal expenditures on *goods and services exclusive of defense* amounted only to some 15 billions of dollars, while local expenditures during this same period amounted to some 17 billions of dollars. There is no need to quibble over which comparisons are relevant. The important point is that the often-neglected local expenditures are significant and, when viewed in terms of expenditures on goods and services only, take on even more significance. Hence an important question arises whether at this level of government any mechanism operates to insure that expenditures on these public goods approximate the proper level.

Consider for a moment the case of the city resident about to move to the suburbs. What variables will influence his choice of a municipality? If he has children, a high level of expenditures on schools may be important. Another person may prefer a community with a municipal golf course. The availability and quality of such facilities and services as beaches, parks, police protection, roads, and parking facilities will enter into the decision-making process. Of course, non-economic variables will also be considered, but this is of no concern at this point.

The consumer-voter may be viewed as picking that community which best satisfies his preference pattern for public goods. This is a major difference between central and local provision of public goods. At the central level the preferences of the consumer-voter are given, and the government tries to adjust to the pattern of these preferences, whereas at the local level various governments have their revenue and expenditure patterns more or less set.[11] Given these revenue and expenditure patterns, the consumer-voter moves to that community whose local government best satisfies his set of preferences. The greater the number of communities and the greater the variance among them, the closer the consumer will come to fully realizing his preference position.[12]

[9] The discussion that follows applies to local governments. It will be apparent as the argument proceeds that it also applies, with less force, to state governments.

[10] A question does arise as to just what are the proper expenditures to consider. Following Musgrave, I shall consider only expenditures on goods or services (his Branch I expenditures). Thus interest on the federal debt is not included. At the local level interest payments might be included, since they are considered payments for services currently used, such as those provided by roads and schools.

[11] This is an assumption about reality. In the extreme model that follows the patterns are assumed to be absolutely fixed.

[12] This is also true of many non-economic variables. Not only is the consumer-voter concerned with economic patterns, but he desires, for example, to associate with "nice" people. Again, the greater the number of communities, the closer he will come to satisfying his total preference function, which includes non-economic variables.

A LOCAL GOVERNMENT MODEL

The implications of the preceding argument may be shown by postulating an extreme model. Here the following assumptions are made:

1. Consumer-voters are fully mobile and will move to that community where their preference patterns, which are set, are best satisfied.

2. Consumer-voters are assumed to have full knowledge of differences among revenue and expenditure patterns and to react to these differences.

3. There are a large number of communities in which the consumer-voters may choose to live.

4. Restrictions due to employment opportunities are not considered. It may be assumed that all persons are living on dividend income.

5. The public services supplied exhibit no external economies or diseconomies between communities.

Assumptions 6 and 7 to follow are less familiar and require brief explanations:

6. For every pattern of community services set by, say, a city manager who follows the preferences of the older residents of the community, there is an optimal community size. This optimum is defined in terms of the number of residents for which this bundle of services can be produced at the lowest average cost. This, of course, is closely analogous to the low point of a firm's average cost curve. Such a cost function implies that some factor or resource is fixed. If this were not so, there would be no logical reason to limit community size, given the preference patterns. In the same sense that the average cost curve has a minimum for one firm but can be reproduced by another there is seemingly no reason why a duplicate community cannot exist. The assumption that some factor is fixed explains why it is not possible for the community in question to double its size by growth. The factor may be the limited land area of a suburban community, combined with a set of zoning laws against apartment buildings. It may be the local beach, whose capacity is limited. Anything of this nature will provide a restraint.

In order to see how this restraint works, let us consider the beach problem. Suppose the preference patterns of the community are such that the optimum size population is 13,000. Within this set of preferences there is a certain demand per family for beach space. This demand is such that at 13,000 population a 500-yard beach is required. If the actual length of the beach is, say, 600 yards, then it is not possible to realize this preference pattern with twice the optimum population, since there would be too little beach space by 400 yards.

The assumption of a fixed factor is necessary, as will be shown later, in order to get a determinate number of communities. It also has the advantage of introducing a realistic restraint into the model.

7. The last assumption is that communities below the optimum size seek to attract new residents to lower average costs. Those above optimum size do just the opposite. Those at an optimum try to keep their populations constant.

This assumption needs to be amplified. Clearly, communities below the optimum size, through chambers of commerce or other agencies, seek to attract new residents. This is best exemplified by the housing developments in some suburban areas, such as Park Forest in the Chicago area and Levittown in the New York area, which need to reach an optimum size. The same is true of communities that try to attract manufacturing industries by setting up certain facilities and getting an optimum number of firms to move into the industrially zoned area.

The case of the city that is too large and tries to get rid of residents is more difficult to imagine. No alderman in his right political mind would ever admit that the city is too big. Nevertheless, economic forces are at work to push people out of it. Every resident who moves to the suburbs to find better schools, more parks, and so forth, is reacting, in part, against the pattern the city has to offer.

The case of the community which is at the optimum size and tries to remain so is not hard to visualize. Again proper zoning laws, implicit agreements among realtors, and the like are sufficient to keep the population stable.

Except when this system is in equilibrium, there will be a subset of consumer-voters who are discontented with the patterns of their community. Another set will be satisfied. Given the assumption about mobility and the other assumptions listed previously, movement will take place out of the communities of greater than optimal size into the communities of less than optimal size. The consumer-voter moves to the community that satisfies his preference pattern.

The act of moving or failing to move is crucial. Moving or failing to move replaces the usual market test of willingness to buy a good and reveals the consumer-voter's demand for public goods. Thus each locality has a revenue and expenditure pattern that reflects the desires of its residents. The next step is to see what this implies for the allocation of public goods at the local level.

Each city manager now has a certain demand for n local public goods. In supplying these goods, he and $m - 1$ other city managers may be considered as going to a national market and bidding for the appropriate units of service of each kind: so many units of police for the ith community; twice that number for the jth community; and so on. The demand on the public goods market for each of the n commodities will be the sum of the demands of the m communities. In the limit, as shown in a less realistic model to be developed later, this total demand will approximate the demand that represents the true preferences of the consumer-voters—that is, the demand they would reveal, if they were forced, somehow, to state their true preferences.[13] In this model there is no attempt on the part of local governments to "adapt to" the preferences of consumer-voters. Instead, those local governments that attract the optimum number of residents may be viewed as being "adopted by" the economic system.[14]

A COMPARISON MODEL

It is interesting to contrast the results of the preceding model with those of an even more severe model in order to see how these results differ from the normal market result. It is convenient to look at this severe model by developing its private-market counterpart. First assume that there are no public goods, only private ones. The preferences for these goods can be expressed as one of n patterns. Let a law be passed that all persons living in any one of the communities shall spend their money in the particular pattern described for that community by law. Given our earlier assumptions 1 through 5, it follows that, if the consum-

[13] The word "approximate" is used in recognition of the limitations of this model, and of the more severe model to be developed shortly, with respect to the cost of mobility. This issue will be discussed later.

[14] See Alchian, *op. cit.*

ers move to the community whose law happens to fit their preference pattern, they will be at their optimum. The n communities, in turn, will then send their buyers to market to purchase the goods for the consumer-voters in their community. Since this is simply a lumping together of all similar tastes for the purpose of making joint purchases, the allocation of resources will be the same as it would be if normal market forces operated. This conceptual experiment is the equivalent of substituting the city manager for the broker or middleman.

Now turn the argument around and consider only public goods. Assume with Musgrave that the costs of additional services are constant.[15] Further, assume that a doubling of the population means doubling the amount of services required. Let the number of communities be infinite and let each announce a different pattern of expenditures on public goods. Define an empty community as one that fails to satisfy anybody's preference pattern. Given these assumptions, including the earlier assumptions 1 through 5, the consumer-voters will move to that community which *exactly* satisfies their preferences. This must be true, since a one-person community is allowed. The sum of the demands of the n communities reflects the demand for local public services. In this model the demand is exactly the same as it would be if it were determined by normal market forces.

However, this severe model does not make much sense. The number of communities is indeterminate. There is no reason why the number of communities will not be equal to the population, since each voter can find the one that exactly fits his preferences. Unless some sociological variable is introduced, this may reduce the solution of the problem of allocating public goods to the trite one of making each person his own municipal government. Hence this model is not even a first approximation of reality. It is presented to show the assumptions needed in a model of local government expenditures, which yields the same optimal allocation that a private market would.

THE LOCAL GOVERNMENT MODEL RE-EXAMINED

The first model, described by the first five assumptions together with assumptions 6 and 7, falls short of this optimum. An example will serve to show why this is the case.

Let us return to the community with the 500-yard beach. By assumption, its optimum population was set at 13,000, given its preference patterns. Suppose that some people in addition to the optimal 13,000 would choose this community if it were available. Since they cannot move into this area, they must accept the next best substitute.[16] If a perfect substitute is found, no problem exists. If one is not found, then the failure to reach the optimal preference position and the substitution of a lower position becomes a matter of degree. In so far as there are a number of communities with similar revenue and expenditure patterns, the solution will approximate the ideal "market" solution.

Two related points need to be mentioned to show the allocative results of this model: (1) changes in the costs of one of the public services will cause changes in the quantity produced; (2) the

[15] Musgrave, "Voluntary Exchange . . . ," *op. cit.*

[16] In the constant cost model with an infinite number of communities this problem does not arise, since the number of beaches can be doubled or a person can find another community that is a duplicate of his now filled first choice.

costs of moving from community to community should be recognized. Both points can be illustrated in one example.

Suppose lifeguards throughout the country organize and succeed in raising their wages. Total taxes in communities with beaches will rise. Now residents who are largely indifferent to beaches will be forced to make a decision. Is the saving of this added tax worth the cost of moving to a community with little or no beach? Obviously, this decision depends on many factors, among which the availability of and proximity to a suitable substitute community is important. If enough people leave communities with beaches and move to communities without beaches, the total amount of lifeguard services used will fall. These models then, unlike their private-market counterpart, have mobility as a cost of registering demand. The higher this cost, *ceteris paribus*, the less optimal the allocation of resources.

This distinction should not be blown out of proportion. Actually, the cost of registering demand comes through the introduction of space into the economy. Yet space affects the allocation not only of resources supplied by local governments but of those supplied by the private market as well. Every time available resources or production techniques change, a new location becomes optimal for the firm. Indeed, the very concept of the shopping trip shows that the consumer does pay a cost to register his demand for private goods. In fact, Koopmans has stated that the nature of the assignment problem is such that in a space economy with transport costs there is *no* general equilibrium solution as set by market forces.[17]

Thus the problems stated by this model are not unique; they have their counterpart in the private market. We are maximizing within the framework of the resources available. If production functions show constant returns to scale with generally diminishing factor returns, and if indifference curves are regularly convex, an optimal solution is possible. On the production side it is assumed that communities are forced to keep production costs at a minimum either through the efficiency of city managers or through competition from other communities.[18] Given this, on the demand side we may note with Samuelson that "each individual, in seeking as a competitive buyer to get to the highest level of indifference subject to given prices and *tax*, would be led as if by an Invisible Hand to the grand solution of the social maximum position."[19] Just as the consumer may be visualized as walking to a private market place to buy his goods, the prices of which are set, we place him in the position of walking to a community where the prices (taxes) of community services are set. Both trips take the consumer to market. There is no way in which the consumer can avoid revealing his preferences in a spatial economy. Spatial mobility provides the local public-goods counterpart to the private market's shopping trip.

[17] Tjalling Koopmans, "Mathematical Groundwork of Economic Optimization Theories," paper read at the annual meeting of the Econometric Society (December, 1954).

[18] In this model and in reality, the city manager or elected official who is not able to keep his costs (taxes) low compared with those of similar communities will find himself out of a job. As an institutional observation, it may well be that city managers are under greater pressure to minimize costs than their private-market counterparts—firm managers. This follows from (1) the reluctance of the public to pay taxes and, what may be more important, (2) the fact that the costs of competitors—other communities—are a matter of public record and may easily be compared.

[19] "The Pure Theory . . . ," *op. cit.*, p. 388. (Italics mine.)

EXTERNAL ECONOMIES AND MOBILITY

Relaxing assumption 5 has some interesting implications. There are obvious external economies and diseconomies between communities. My community is better off if its neighbor sprays trees to prevent Dutch elm disease. On the other hand, my community is worse off if the neighboring community has inadequate law enforcement.

In cases in which the external economies and diseconomies are of sufficient importance, some form of integration may be indicated.[20] Not all aspects of law enforcement are adequately handled at the local level. The function of the sheriff, state police, and the FBI—as contrasted with the local police—may be cited as resulting from a need for integration. In real life the diseconomies are minimized in so far as communities reflecting the same socioeconomic preferences are contiguous. Suburban agglomerations such as Westchester, the North Shore, and the Main Line are, in part, evidence of these external economies and diseconomies.

Assumptions 1 and 2 should be checked against reality. Consumer-voters do not have perfect knowledge and set preferences, nor are they perfectly mobile. The question is how do people actually react in choosing a community. There has been very little empirical study of the motivations of people in choosing a community. Such studies as have been undertaken seem to indicate a surprising awareness of differing revenue and expenditure patterns.[21] The general disdain with which proposals to integrate municipalities are met seems to reflect, in part, the fear that local revenue-expenditure patterns will be lost as communities are merged into a metropolitan area.

[20] I am grateful to Stanley Long and Donald Markwalder for suggesting this point.

[21] See Wendell Bell, "Familism and Suburbanization: One Test of the Choice Hypothesis," a paper read at the annual meeting of the American Sociological Society, Washington, D.C., August, 1955. Forthcoming in *Rural Sociology*, December, 1956.

POLICY IMPLICATIONS

The preceding analysis has policy implications for municipal integration, provision for mobility, and set local revenue and expenditure patterns. These implications are worth brief consideration.

On the usual economic welfare grounds, municipal integration is justified only if more of any service is forthcoming at the same total cost and without reduction of any other service. A general reduction of costs along with a reduction in one or more of the services provided cannot be justified on economic grounds unless the social welfare function is known. For example, those who argue for a metropolitan police force instead of local police cannot prove their case on purely economic grounds.[22] If one of the communities were to receive less police protection after integration than it received before, integration could be objected to as a violation of consumers' choise.

Policies that promote residential mobility and increase the knowledge of the consumer-voter will improve the allocation of government expenditures in the same sense that mobility among jobs and knowledge relevant to the location of industry and labor improve the allocation of private resources.

Finally, we may raise the normative question whether local governments *should*, to the extent possible, have a fixed revenue-expenditure pattern. In a large, dynamic metropolis this may be

[22] For example, in Cook County—the Chicago area—Sheriff Joseph Lohman argues for such a metropolitan police force.

impossible. Perhaps it could more appropriately be considered by rural and suburban communities.

CONCLUSION

It is useful in closing to restate the problem as Samuelson sees it:

> *However, no decentralized pricing system can serve to determine optimally these levels of collective consumption.* Other kinds of "voting" or "signaling" would have to be tried. . . . Of course utopian voting and signaling schemes can be imagined. . . . The failure of market catallactics in no way denies the following truth: given sufficient knowledge the optimal decisions can always be found by scanning over all the attainable states of the world and selecting the one which according to the postulated ethical welfare function is best. The solution "exists"; the problem is how to "find" it.[23]

It is the contention of this article that, for a substantial portion of collective or public goods, this problem *does have* a conceptual solution. If consumer-voters are fully mobile, the appropriate local governments, whose revenue-expenditure patterns are set, are adopted by the consumer-voters. While the solution may not be perfect because of institutional rigidities, this does not invalidate its importance. The solution, like a general equilibrium solution for a private spatial economy, is the best that can be obtained given preferences and resource endowments.

Those who are tempted to compare this model with the competitive private model may be disappointed. Those who compare the reality described by this model with the reality of the competitive model—given the degree of monopoly, friction, and so forth—*may* find that local government represents a sector where the allocation of public goods (as a reflection of the preferences of the population) need not take a back seat to the private sector.

[23] "The Pure Theory . . . ," *op. cit.*, pp. 388–89.

[12]

JOURNAL OF URBAN ECONOMICS 25, 325–345 (1989)

Urban Land Supply: Natural and Contrived Restrictions[1]

LOUIS A. ROSE

Department of Economics and Social Science Research Institute, University of Hawaii, Porteus Hall 542, Honolulu, Hawaii 96822

Received August 21, 1986; revised October 22, 1986

Both large bodies of water and local governments restrict the supply of urban land. In this paper we measure water's restriction on supply and test its effect on land price. We then extend Hamilton's and Fischel's pioneering work on governmental restriction, providing an improved test of the monopoly zoning hypothesis that such restriction further affects land price. Regression analysis of data from 45 urban areas suggests that the two restrictions combine to explain 40% of typical interurban price differentials. © 1989 Academic Press, Inc.

Empirical studies of price and related behavior in most markets are based on models that specify both demand and supply variables. Interurban studies of land price are an exception to this rule. While they specify exogenous determinants of land demand such as population and income, they are notable for their omission of land supply variables.[2]

There are two types of restrictions on the availability of land for urban use. One is natural, the other contrived. There is considerable interurban variation in both types. The primary natural restrictions are water bodies, although mountains and flood plains pose obstacles to development in a few areas. While half of the 40 most populous urban areas in the United States are landlocked, the other half are near oceans or lakes that substantially reduce their supply of land. The primary artificial restrictions are those imposed by local governments in the form of zoning ordinances and related land-use regulations. Williams [23] and Fischel [1, 3] describe considerable variation in the degree of zoning restrictiveness across cities and states.

[1]I am thankful to William Fischel for his helpful advice on many points, to Moheb Ghali and Sumner LaCroix for additional comments, to Ev Wingert for cartography assistance, and to Claire Golveo for general research assistance.

[2]Maisel [11] and Witte [24] employ an endogenous variable reflecting demand as well as supply influences when they include the price of agricultural land as an explanatory variable in their estimating equations. Gottlieb [5] does the same in his use of the quantity of vacant lots as an explanatory variable.

0094-1190/89 $3.00

The relevant theoretical literature on natural restrictions begins with the intraurban monocentric model of Muth [16] and Mills [13]. Their basic model assumes an urban center situated on an unbounded featureless plane, so there is initially no topographical restriction. Then Mills incorporates well-behaved bodies of water in his allowance for less than 2π radians of land about the center. The relevant empirical literature on natural restrictions, which ought to quantitatively account for bodies of water that are not so well-behaved, is composed of two studies. In his study of population density gradients, Muth [16] employs a dummy explanatory variable to indicate whether or not the city is bounded by an ocean or lake. Ozanne and Thibodeau [18] do the same in their interurban study of housing prices.

The relevant literature on contrived restrictions is composed entirely of interurban studies of the price of housing rather than land. In this context, White [22] first advanced the so-called monopoly zoning hypothesis: homeowners' desire to increase the value of their homes through restrictive zoning can be achieved to a greater extent the larger the fraction of urban area land controlled by the local government. Hamilton [7] more fully developed the theory and provided evidence that monopoly power increases the price of housing. Fischel [1] qualified the hypothesis and presented additional evidence that cast some doubt on its ability to explain interurban housing price variation. The monopoly zoning hypothesis has not heretofore been tested in urban land markets, even though the zoning restrictions impinge more directly on the supply of land than they do on the price of housing.

The purpose of this paper is to analyze the supply side of urban land markets by identifying and measuring two determinants of land supply, and by testing their ability to explain interurban land price variation. More specifically, we will (i) test the natural hypothesis that water's restriction of land supply increases land price, and (ii) test the monopoly hypothesis that local governments with monopoly zoning power restrict land supply and thereby increase land price.[3]

Section I specifies a simple model of urban land price that incorporates a water-restricted land supply variable. We measure the amount of land naturally supplied around 45 major U.S. urban areas, and use these figures to estimate the price model and test the natural hypothesis. Section II adds a monopoly power variable to the land price model and employs alternative measures of the variable to test the monopoly hypothesis. Section III briefly concludes.

[3]Monopoly zoning and bodies of water may be complementary in their functions. In some urban areas (e.g., San Francisco and Chicago) it is land-use restrictions rather than the cost of fill that restrains the conversion of bays and lakes into useable land. I owe this point to Fischel.

I. A TEST OF THE NATURAL HYPOTHESIS

In the simplest model for explaining interurban land price, the quantity of land demanded is

$$D = D(P, N, Y), \tag{1}$$

where P is the price of land, N is population, and Y is per capita income in the urban area. We assume the relation has a logarithmic functional form,[4]

$$\ln D = \ln \alpha_0 + \alpha_1 \ln P + \alpha_2 \ln N + \alpha_3 \ln Y, \tag{2}$$

where $\alpha_1 < 0$, $\alpha_2 > 0$, and $\alpha_3 > 0$.

In equilibrium, the price is determined by equating this quantity demanded with the quantity supplied, L, and solving for the reduced form,

$$\ln P = -\frac{\ln \alpha_0}{\alpha_1} - \frac{\alpha_2}{\alpha_1}\ln N - \frac{\alpha_3}{\alpha_1}\ln Y + \frac{1}{\alpha_1}\ln L. \tag{3}$$

We add an additional explanatory variable, the expected rate of change in population, $\dot{N}$, to account for the possibility that current observed prices differ from equilibrium values corresponding to current population. Because higher future population implies higher future land price, the amount by which current observed price exceeds equilibrium price should be a positive function of $\dot{N}$.

Our purpose is to fit the equation

$$\ln P = a_0 + a_1 \ln N + a_2 \ln Y + a_3 \ln \dot{N} + a_4 L + \varepsilon \tag{4}$$

to cross section data so as to test the null hypothesis that land supply, as restricted by water, has no influence on price. A statistically significant coefficient on this land supply variable, and improved goodness of fit from its inclusion in the equation, will provide evidence of the effect of interurban differences in natural restrictions on interurban differences in price.

The selection of data for performing these tests is restricted to the available estimates of prices. There exist only three published sets of prices for recent years. The Federal Housing Administration (FHA [20]) has

[4] The logarithmic form is used for expositional ease. Later in the paper we report that our empirical results are all robust with respect to functional form.

published estimates of the average price of sites under existing FHA-insured homes in 226 U.S. cities for 1980 and other years. The nature and limitations of these data are discussed in Muth [17] and Greenlees [6]. The Urban Land Institute (ULI [19]) has published estimates of the average prices of both improved lots and raw acreages near the so-called urban fringe of 30 cities for 1980 and other years. The ULI prices are based on surveys of real estate experts in each of the areas. Unfortunately, neither the FHA nor the ULI report the distances at which their prices are estimated. Our inability to control the distance at which the dependent variable is measured increases the error term ε, and our omission of distance as an explanatory variable leads to a specification bias noted later in the paper.

All three prices—those for FHA home sites, ULI improved lots, and ULI acreages—are equally appropriate for testing the natural hypothesis. They are all prices of land zoned for residential use. As this is the primary urban use, we employ them as measures of the price of urban land generally. If, in analyzing all three measures of the 1980 price, we obtain empirical results supporting the same conclusions, then we shall have more confidence in these conclusions.[5]

To measure the supply of urban land, we ought to sum weighted land units (square miles) around the urban center, with each unit weighted to reflect its relative contribution to the supply. The most reasonable weights are rents, for they indicate the relative importance of each unit. Empirical studies show that rents decline exponentially with distance from the center.[6] This plausibly suggests that a body of water close to the center decreases the urban land supply, and increases the price, more than does more distant water, and water at a sufficient distance decreases the supply, and increases the price, negligibly. We can accordingly measure urban land supply as

$$L = \sum_{u=0}^{\bar{u}} s(u) \cdot e^{-\delta u}, \tag{5}$$

where $s(u)$ is a vector of land units, net of water, at various distances from

[5]We use not only FHA and ULI 1980 prices, but also an average of FHA prices in 1975, 1980, and 1983, and an average of ULI prices in 1975, 1980, and 1985 to suppress any short-term local influences on price. Our regression results are essentially unaffected by this substitution. The correlation coefficients for the 21 urban areas common to FHA and ULI data sets are .81 between home site and lot prices, .61 between home site and acreage prices, and .61 between lot and acreage prices.

[6]Strong empirical support for the exponential form is provided by Mills [12] and Kau and Sirmans [8].

the center; $e^{-\delta u}$ is the weights vector, with δ as the percentage rate of decline in rent per square foot per mile; and $\bar{u}$ is a practical bound for the summation, great enough to ensure that L is a close approximation of the true sum.

There are no published estimates of rent gradients, δ, appropriate for interurban analysis, so we shall use population density gradients. The legitimacy of this substitution follows from Mills' [13] theoretical result that under plausible assumptions, intraurban population density is proportional to rent, so that population and rent gradients are the same. The most recently published and carefully estimated population density gradients are Macauley's [10] estimates in 18 SMSAs for 1980. We shall use these as the basis for our tests.[7]

Macauley's gradients vary between .11 and .47. One reason for gradient variation is that per mile costs of transportation differ from one monocentric urban area to another. An area with a more efficient transportation system tends to have an (absolutely) smaller gradient and a larger supply of urban land. Another reason for gradient variation is that urban areas are not strictly monocentric; indeed, they differ in the size and spatial distribution of secondary employment and shopping centers. In one with more and larger secondary centers, trips are shorter and trip costs are smaller, so that the gradient is smaller and the supply of urban land is larger.

Notwithstanding the variation in gradients, we shall calculate a conditional land supply using a constant gradient common to all urban areas. There are two reasons for this. First, we have neither a theory of gradient determination, nor sufficient estimated gradients to employ such a theory.[8] Second, the constant gradient is quite suitable for our purpose of estimating the partial effect of natural restrictions on price, so long as bodies of water have no effect on the per mile cost of transportation, and thence on the gradient. The strength of any such effect depends on the geographical configuration of the water. In some urban areas, the effects are likely to be substantial, but in most quite negligible.

[7]Macauley fits the relation $\ln D(u) = \ln D(0) - \delta u$. Some other published gradients are for larger samples of cities. However, they are either for an earlier period for which observations of key variables are unavailable, or they are for another country. Muth [16] reports gradients for 46 U.S. cities in 1950. Mills and Ohta [15] report gradients for 22 Japanese cities in 1965 and 1970.

[8]If the gradient is in fact a function of income or population, the least-squares estimate of the coefficient on L calculated with each city's own gradient (though not with a common gradient) will be biased and inconsistent. Mills [13] provides a theoretical link between income and the gradient. Moreover, Muth [16] and Mills and Ohta [15], provide evidence of a relationship between both income and especially population and the gradient. Thus, (4) is apparently not an appropriate basis for estimating the full unconditional effect of urban land supply on price.

We calculate the urban land supply for each of 45 urban areas. These include the 40 most populous MSAs, for which FHA prices are available, and 26 of the 30 cities surveyed by ULI.[9] To obtain the land vector $s(u)$ in each urban area, we center a transparency with 10 concentric rings 3 miles apart on the urban center on a recent U.S. Geological Survey 250,000:1 scale topographical map. Then with a digitizer we measure 10 annular areas net of water. We calculate the weights vector by using Macauley's median gradient of .22 and distances to the 10 annular areas. Finally, we multiply the weights times the annular areas and then sum.[10] When the resulting supply figures are divided by a hypothetical supply around a point on a waterless plane, they yield indexes that are as low as .520, .547, and .561 for San Francisco, Norfolk, and Chicago, respectively, and almost as high as unity for several landlocked areas.

Measures of the remaining explanatory variables in (4) are standard. Y is the 1980 Census MSA per capita income. N is the 1980 Census MSA population, and $\dot{N}$ is the percentage change between 1970 and 1980.[11]

Table 1 summarizes the units of measurement and means of variables for the data sets used in this paper (for now, ignore the last three columns). The first row displays means for the 40 most populous urban areas in the United States. The second and third rows display means for 26 of the 30 ULI urban areas; they include both ULI measures of price.

We fit two equations to explain each of the three price variables: the price of FHA home sites in the 40 most populous urban areas, the price of ULI improved lots in 26 urban areas, and the price of unimproved acreage in these 26 areas. The first equation is (4) excluding the conditional land supply variable; the second full equation includes this variable.

The results, displayed in Table 2, provide persuasive evidence that natural restrictions on the supply of land affect its price. A comparison of the adjusted R^2 values, standard errors, and F statistics in the bottom row of full equation columns (2), (4), and (6) with those in columns (1), (3), and

[9]The method of land supply measurement based on the monocentric model is inappropriate in the case of 4 of the 30 ULI cities surveyed, Ft. Lauderdale, Boulder, San Jose, and Tacoma, because they are included in the CSAs of dominant PSAs, Miami, Denver, San Francisco, and Seattle, respectively.

[10]With the summation bound of 30 miles and gradient of .22, the sum includes 99% of the true land supply if there is no water. We add to this sum a fraction of the excluded 1%. This fraction is the ratio of net (of water) weighted area to gross weighted area within the bound. We employ the same imputation procedure to adjust the sum obtained later with a gradient of .15. Then the adjustment is more important, since the sum includes only 94% of the true land supply.

[11]The incomes and populations are for CSAs where reported. Some rates of population change are negative, the lowest being -8.9%. To avoid taking logarithms of negative numbers, we initialized $\dot{N}$ at zero by defining it as $((N_{1980} - N_{1970})/N_{1970}) + 8.9$.

TABLE 1

Variable Means in Data Sets[a]

Source of dependent variable	Land type	No. of observations	P (\$ per sq. foot^2)	N (1000s of persons)	Y (\$ per year per person)	$\dot{N}$ (% change 1970–1980)	L (weighted sq. miles^2)	Concentration ratios C_u	C_s	G (No. of governments)
FHA	Home site	40	1.60	2811	10,256	13.5	109.99	.352	.509	72
ULI	Improved lot	26	1.70	1584	9957	18.4	117.06	.277	.503	47
ULI	Raw acreage	26	0.33	1584	9957	18.4	117.06	.277	.503	47

[a] The last three columns pertain to variables used exclusively to test the monopoly zoning hypothesis. For this test, the FHA sample is composed of only 39 observations . . . the most populous 40 areas, less Houston. The ULI sample when G is specified is composed of the 30 areas surveyed, less the 4 dominated PSAs, less Houston. The ULI sample when C_u or C_s is specified is composed of the same 25 areas less Lexington.

(5) reveals that inclusion of the land supply variable substantially improves the model's explanatory power. The three land supply coefficients have the expected negative sign, and their t statistics lead us to reject the null hypothesis that natural restrictions are ineffective.[12, 13] These findings are all robust with respect to functional form: by fitting linear–linear, log–linear, and linear–log equations, we obtained essentially the same results.[14]

The size of the land supply coefficients, in conjunction with the wide range of land supply variation between .520 and .999, suggests the extent to which water's preemption of land can affect land price. To illustrate the typical size of this effect, we divide the 40 most populous areas into 24 essentially landlocked areas with indexes greater than .900, and 16 water-bounded areas with indexes less than .900. The 40, 24, and 16 areas have mean indexes of .873, .974, and .721, respectively. The coefficient −1.01 in column (2) is convenient for our calculation. It indicates that an 11.6% increase in the index from .873 to .974 will decrease price by the same percentage, and a 17.4% decrease in the index from .873 to .721 will increase price by the same percentage. The full 29% spread in price is attributable to a land supply differential that is typical of our major urban areas. Of course, the absolutely larger supply coefficient point estimates of −1.30 and −2.18 in columns (4) and (6) indicate even greater sensitivity.

[12] The omission of u, the distance at which price is observed, in the estimating equations can bias the estimate of a coefficient on an explanatory variable that is related to distance. The only explanatory variable that is likely to be strongly related to distance is population; the clearly positive relation imparts a downward bias to our estimated population coefficient. There is conceivably a bias to our estimated land supply coefficients. In general, the sign of the relation between L and distance and therefore the direction of bias depend on the geographical distribution of water in the samples of urban areas. Map inspection suggests a negative relation and therefore some upward bias to the coefficient.

[13] Table 2 coefficients on N and Y provide empirical support for the monocentric model. The monocentric model incorporates two land uses, with rents in farm use at the boundary of housing use. Of course, rents at locations within this boundary depend on N and Y. Prices both within and on an advancing bound depend on $\dot{N}$ as well. In contrast, our model allows for urban use alone, with rents that depend on N and Y at all locations within the urban area as defined in the text above. Corresponding prices depend on $\dot{N}$ as well.

The FHA prices of existing home sites are generally observed well within the so-called urban fringe, whereas the ULI prices are reportedly estimated near the fringe. In view of this, the coefficients and t values for N, $\dot{N}$, and Y in FHA price equations in Table 2 are consistent with both models, whereas the insignificance of some coefficients in the ULI price equations is consistent with the monocentric model alone. We refer to the first two coefficients in column (4) and the second coefficient in column (6).

[14] In all regressions the coefficients on all explanatory variables have the expected sign when they are statistically significant at the 0.05 level. The land supply coefficients are all significant at this level.

TABLE 2
Effects of Natural Restriction on Price

Dependent variables:	Price of FHA home site		Price of ULI improved lot		Price of ULI acreage	
Independent variables	(1)	(2)	(3)	(4)	(5)	(6)
Population	0.270**	0.184*	0.160	0.0435	0.504**	0.354*
	(2.25)	(1.61)	(1.24)	(0.36)	(2.17)	(1.57)
Income	1.71**	1.76**	0.550	0.807	−0.339	−0.196
	(1.96)	(2.20)	(0.56)	(0.94)	(−0.19)	(−0.12)
Population change	0.196**	0.231**	0.0848	0.0279	0.600***	0.541***
	(2.42)	(3.08)	(0.91)	(0.33)	(3.60)	(3.47)
Conditional land supply		−1.01***		−1.30***		−2.18**
		(−2.80)		(−2.82)		(−2.22)
Constant	−18.1**	−13.3**	−6.00	−0.177	−3.71	6.61
	(−2.39)	(−1.86)	(−0.71)	(−0.02)	(−0.25)	(0.45)
$\bar{R}^2$	.36	.46	.08	.30	.36	.46
SE	.43	.39	.31	.27	.56	.52
F	8.16***	9.24***	1.74	3.69**	5.71***	6.28***
	(3,36)	(4,35)	(3,22)	(4,21)	(3,22)	(4,21)

Note. All variables are in logarithms. The numbers in parentheses below the coefficients are *t* statistics. One, two, and three asterisks indicate one-tail significance levels of .10, .05, and .01, respectively. The numbers in parentheses below the *F* statistic are degrees of freedom for the *F* tests.

In sum, the three coefficients suggest that interurban price variations of 30 to 60% may be due to natural restrictions on the supply of land.[15]

This interpretation of the land supply coefficient—that it indicates the extent to which water's preemption of land can affect its price—neglects the possibility that water-related amenities are also likely to affect the price. The price model does not separate out any water-related amenity effects from those attributable to the water-related paucity of useable land. All we can say with certainty is that the coefficient indicates the effect of water on price.

[15]Although the estimation of elasticities is not central to our inquiry, it is interesting to note the point estimates of price and income elasticities of demand implied by the equations in Table 2. The FHA equation price elasticity is $\alpha_1 = 1/\hat{a}_4 = 1/(-1.01) = -.99$, and the income elasticity is $\alpha_3 = -\alpha_1 \cdot \hat{a}_2 = -(-.99)(1.76) = 1.74$. The ULI equation price elasticities are −.77 and −.46 for improved lots and acreage, respectively. Our estimates conform with the finding of Kau and Sirmans [9] that the demand for residential sites is inelastic. The absolutely lower price elasticity of demand for acreage is what one should expect, since acreage comprises a smaller fraction of housing than do improved lots or home sites.

TABLE 3
Insensitivity of Results to Gradient

Dependent variables:	Price of FHA home site			Price of ULI improved lot			Price of ULI acreage		
Independent variables	(1)	(2)	(3)	(4)	(5)	(6)	(7)	(8)	(9)
Population	0.177**	0.184*	0.193*	0.0435	0.0435	0.101	0.320*	0.354*	0.405**
	(1.58)	(1.61)	(1.64)	(0.36)	(0.36)	(0.81)	(1.42)	(1.57)	(1.78)
Income	1.75**	1.76**	1.83**	0.807	0.807	0.507	0.0645	−0.196	−0.411
	(2.23)	(2.20)	(2.22)	(0.94)	(0.94)	(0.55)	(0.04)	(−0.12)	(−0.25)
Population change	0.226***	0.231***	0.239***	0.0279	0.0279	0.0776	0.511***	0.541***	0.589***
	(3.09)	(3.08)	(3.06)	(0.33)	(0.33)	(0.89)	(3.27)	(3.47)	(3.71)
Conditional land supply ($\delta_0 = .15$)	−1.06***			−1.30***			−2.04**		
	(−3.07)			(−2.82)			(−2.37)		
Conditional land supply ($\delta_0 = .22$)		−1.01***			−1.30***			−2.18**	
		(−2.80)			(−2.82)			(−2.22)	
Conditional land supply ($\delta_0 = .35$)			−0.914**			−1.27**			−2.11**
			(−2.39)			(−2.00)			(−1.83)
Constant	−12.0**	−13.3**	−15.3**	−0.177	−0.177	−0.345	5.45	6.61	5.70
	(−1.70)	(−1.86)	(−2.12)	(−0.02)	(−0.02)	(−0.04)	(0.38)	(0.45)	(0.37)
$\overline{R}^2$	.48	.46	.43	.30	.30	.19	.47	.46	.42
SE	.39	.39	.40	.27	.27	.29	.51	.52	.53
F	9.92***	9.24***	8.34***	3.69**	3.69**	2.48	6.59***	6.28***	5.59***
	(4,35)	(4,35)	(4,35)	(4,21)	(4,21)	(4,21)	(4,21)	(4,21)	(4,21)

Note. Same note as in Table 2.

The above findings are based on the use of a conditional land supply variable that captures the partial effect of natural restrictions at Macauley's median gradient of $\delta = .22$. One can question whether these findings will hold at alternative gradients. To test the sensitivity of our results to gradient selection, we fit the equations again using L values calculated at $\delta = .15$ and $.35$ in the tails of Macauley's distribution. The resulting coefficients and statistics presented in Table 3 show that our findings are robust with respect to gradient selection. The supply variable coefficients remain highly significant, and there are only minor changes in the equation statistics.

II. A TEST OF THE MONOPOLY HYPOTHESIS

The monopoly zoning argument which appears in detail in the pathbreaking papers of Hamilton [7] and Fischel [1], begins with homeowners who seek to maximize property value. They achieve this goal by persuading their local governments to zone restrictively. The resulting artificial scarcity of land for additional homes raises the prices of existing ones. This scheme works best if a single zoning authority has jurisdiction over the entire urban area housing market. It can also work if separate jurisdictions act as a monopoly by colluding to restrict land's availability for housing. However, because the probability of effective collusion is inversely related to jurisdictional fragmentation, if there is a large number of small local governments, the strategy is not likely to work. Thus, the extent to which the zoning strategy raises home prices ought to be positively related to the monopoly power possessed by the zoning jurisdictions.

Hamilton tests the hypothesis with two regressions of house price on monopoly power and other (mostly housing quality) variables. The dependent variable is median house price from five tracts in each of 13 SMSAs. In one equation the measure of monopoly power is the number of municipalities in the SMSA.[16] In the other equation, it is a dummy variable that takes the value of one if there are more than four governments and zero otherwise. According to the theory, these coefficients ought to be negative. Although both coefficient estimates are the correct sign, neither are statistically significant at standard confidence levels. Nonetheless, the coefficients are sufficiently large to suggest that interurban housing price variation of as much as 50% may be due to governmental restriction of land supply.

In a test of the same hypothesis, Fischel employs two alternative counts of local governments with zoning authority that measure monopoly power

[16] Hamilton also employs municipalities per capita. However, the explanatory variables are entered in log form, and population is one of the explanatory variables. As he points out, with log population included, the denominator in log (municipalities/population) is redundant.

more accurately than do Hamilton's. These two variables count governments within Urbanized Areas (UAs) rather than SMSAs, and they count local governments of all types including townships as well as municipalities, provided they have zoning authority. Using these measures with Hamilton's sample, Fischel replicates Hamilton's two price regressions only to find that the monopoly power coefficients remain insignificant and even have the wrong sign.

Following this, Fischel employs a different and arguably better-suited sample to test the hypothesis. Whereas Hamilton's data are predominantly from small urban areas, Fischel's are from larger ones where, he persuasively argues, monopoly zoning should be more easily detectable. His data are from 19 to 40 tracts in each of 10 urban areas, only two of which (Baltimore and Washington) have few surburban governments; the other eight have many governments. His single regression equation is similar to Hamilton's. The main difference is that Fischel employs, as explanatory variables, two dummies that assume the value of unity if the house price is from a tract in the two monopolistic areas, and zero otherwise. Theory predicts the two dummy variable coefficients, which are the dollar premiums for houses in these two areas, will be positive. However, Fischel finds that neither coefficient estimate differs significantly from zero by standard criteria; indeed, one of the two estimates is negative. Fischel then uses the same regression specification for separate pairwise comparisons of each of the two monopolistic areas with the other eight areas. This analysis is composed of 17 regressions. While 14 of the 17 dummy variable estimated coefficients are statistically significant, only six have the expected sign. Moreover, the largest correctly signed price differential between a monopolistic area and a fragmented one is 25%—half of the 50% that Hamilton's results suggest. Of course, even 25% is quite substantial. Thus, Fischel concludes, "The potential impact of metropolitan government land monopolies seems too great to dismiss the monopoly zoning hypothesis." Further study is warranted.

Our approach differs in several ways from Hamilton's and Fischel's, and most of these differences strengthen the test. On the one hand, it enhances the prospect of detecting any effect of monopoly zoning. On the other hand, if our approach turns up no such effect, we should be more thoroughly persuaded that the hypothesized relationship does not exist. In the first place, we test for the effect of monopoly zoning on the price of home sites rather than homes. This approach affords a more direct test of the hypothesis, since zoning and other land-use controls have their primary impact in land markets. Also, we test three different measures of land price. Although all three were equally appropriate for testing the natural hypothesis, there are two reasons to believe that the ULI prices of raw acreages and improved lots are less appropriate than the FHA house site prices for testing the monopoly hypothesis. First, acreage and lot prices in the more restrictive markets are likely to be lower than our model predicts, due to a greater likelihood of acreage downzoning and greater risks and costs attendant to the permitting of development and construction.[17] Second, the ULI sample is composed of smaller urban areas in which monopoly zoning should be less easily detectable. We, nevertheless, test the hypothesis using all three prices.

Second, there are several model specification differences. Because our model is an extension of that tested in Section I, it includes population, per capita income, rate of change of population, and partial effect of water on the natural supply of land as explanatory variables in our land price estimating equation. As Fischel's equations include none of these variables and Hamilton's includes only population, our specification should perform better. An additional improvement should result from our elimination of another specification error, viz., Hamilton's and Fischel's omission of additional housing quality explanatory variables. Although they include some housing attributes, they note that others are missing. By explaining land price instead of house price, we need not include any such attributes in our equation. Unfortunately, our specification is weaker than Hamilton's and Fischel's in one important respect, viz., the absence of a distance variable; we cannot observe the distances at which prices are observed.

Third, most of our measures of zoning power differ from those used in the prior studies. Hamilton employs a count of governments in his first equation, and a dummy variable based on that count in his second. We use a modification of his count that conforms with Fischel's more careful definition described above.[18] Fischel relies exclusively on dummy variables to indicate zoning power. While dummy variables are often used in studies of this type, Fischel's interpretation of their coefficients in this case is particularly tenuous for two reasons. First, as noted above, his model of interurban price is incompletely specified; the only explanatory variable other than housing quality is distance. Second, Fischel's sample includes only two observations of urban areas with much zoning power, Baltimore and Washington. In view of this, it should not be surprising that his results are mixed: the dollar premium for houses in Washington and the dollar discount for houses in Baltimore can be due to a number of omitted

[17]The routine massive downzoning of acreages in many suburban counties during the 1970s, as reported in Frieden [4], underscores the weakness of acreage prices for the purpose of testing the monopoly hypothesis. I owe this point to Fischel.

[18]We do not employ Hamilton's dummy variable as a measure of monopoly power. In 1980, only 4 out of 44 urban areas with zoning governments (Houston is excluded) in the FHA and ULI samples had four or fewer jurisdictions.

explanatory variables.[19] We avoid this problem by employing a continuous measure of the number of governments along with a larger number of observations.

Finally we employ two additional heretofore unused measures of monopoly zoning power that Fischel carefully defines in another paper [2]. They are two concentration ratios analogous to the four-firm ratio used in studies of industry concentration in industrial organization. Each ratio is the fraction of an appropriately defined urban area land market that is in the four largest (in area) suburbs. Thus, each ratio's numerator is the area of the four largest suburbs. The first ratio's denominator is the entire UA. The second ratio's denominator is the UA net of the central city area. Fischel prefers the second ratio because the appropriate place to look for monopoly zoning is among the suburban jurisdictions rather than in presumably prodevelopment central cities. The advantage of the concentration ratios over the count of governments is that they incorporate more information on the size distribution of local governments.

Fourth, our samples differ in two respects from those in prior studies: government count sample size and the year of observation. Our FHA and ULI samples of urban areas are larger. Whereas Hamilton's sample includes 13 observations of the number of governments, and Fischel's sample includes 10, we employ FHA and ULI samples of 39 and 24–25 urban areas, respectively.[20]

Finally, our sample observations are for 1980, whereas data used in the prior studies were necessarily for 1970. As Fischel notes, in 1970 few suburban areas appeared to have monopoly power over land use, but since then there has been a trend toward the creation of monopoly zoning boards at state, regional, and metropolitan levels of government. If officials at these levels have been responsive to homeowner interests, they have tended to adopt monopoly restrictions. Fischel also notes that during the 1970's, the range of the rights assigned to local governments was broadened by such innovations as environmental impact statements. For these reasons, our use of the 1980 data not available for the earlier studies provides a stronger test.

To incorporate the effect of zoning restrictions in the price model of Section I, we specify that the quantity of land supplied for urban use is no

[19] It would be interesting to replicate Fischel's work on 1970 housing price with estimating equations that include our interurban variables. The 1970 values of N_i, Y_i, $\dot{N}_i$, and L_i are all higher for Washington than for Baltimore. The first three of these four differentials help to explain Fischel's results; the fourth does not.

[20] The need to delete one or two areas from the FHA sample of 40 and the ULI sample of 26 employed in Section I will be explained below after the model is specified.

longer L, but

$$Q = zL, \tag{6}$$

where L is the quantity that is naturally available, given δ and $s(u)$, and where the fraction of L that is zoned for urban use is

$$z = \gamma_0 C^{-\gamma_1}, \qquad \gamma_0 > 0, \gamma_1 > 0. \tag{7}$$

C is a concentration ratio. This functional form is plausible in that the fraction zoned for urban use decreases at a decreasing rate as the concentration ratio increases. This form, and others that follow, will also make for easy interpretation of the estimating equation coefficients. To obtain the reduced form, we first substitute (7) into (6), and take logarithms to obtain the logarithm of supply. We equate this to the logarithm of demand (2), add the population growth variable $\dot{N}$, and solve the resulting expression to obtain the reduced form and corresponding estimating equation,

$$\ln P = b_0 + b_1 \ln N + b_2 \ln Y + b_3 \ln \dot{N} + b_4 \ln L + b_5 \ln C + \varepsilon. \tag{8}$$

This equation is identical with (4) except there is now an additional monopoly power term $b_5 \ln C$. The expected sign of b_5 is positive because $b_5 = -\gamma_1/\alpha_1$ where $\gamma_1 > 0$ and $\alpha_1 < 0$.

As an alternative indicator of monopoly power, we also employ the number of local governments, G, and in the place of (7), we specify

$$z = \sigma_0 G^{\sigma_1}, \qquad \sigma_0 > 0, \sigma_1 > 0. \tag{9}$$

This functional form is sensible in that the fraction of land zoned for urban use increases at a decreasing rate as the number of governments increases. It leads to an estimating equation identical with (8) except that G displaces C, and the expected sign of b_5 is negative:

$$\ln P = b_0 + b_1 \ln N + b_2 \ln Y + b_3 \ln \dot{N} + b_4 \ln L + b_5' \ln G + \varepsilon. \tag{8$'$}$$

We estimate nine regressions to explain three prices, each with three alternative measures of monopoly power. First we fit (8) and (8′) to data from 39 of the 40 most populous urban areas to explain variation in FHA home site prices.[21] We estimate (8) twice using alternative measures of zoning concentration: C_u is the four largest suburbs as a fraction of the UA, and C_s is the four largest suburbs as a fraction of the UA net of the central city. We also regress ULI lot and acreage prices on these explanatory variables, using data from 24 urban areas to estimate (8) and 25 urban areas to estimate (8′).[22] Table 1 (last three columns) displays the means of the three measures of monopoly power in the data sets used for estimating the nine regressions.

The distribution of each measure of monopoly power is quite wide. Consider the range of measures observed in our combined FHA–ULI sample of 45 urban areas. The highest concentration ratios, C_u, are observed in Richmond (.825), Norfolk (.801), and Baltimore (.780). The highest ratios, C_s, are 1.0 in Charlotte, Norfolk, and Tampa. The lowest counts of zoning governments, G, are in Lexington (1), Charlotte (2), and Raleigh (2). At the other extreme, Houston has no zoning, and numerous other urban areas have essentially no concentration of zoning power. The lowest C_u values are observed in Minneapolis (.035), Columbus (.052), and Los Angeles (.074). The lowest C_s values are in Minneapolis (.040), St. Louis (.083), and Chicago (.090). The highest government counts are in New York City (360), Chicago (347), and Philadelphia (239).

Table 4 displays the regression results, which (taken as a whole) provide moderate support for the monopoly zoning hypothesis. Although all nine coefficients on the monopoly power measures have the expected sign, only four are significant at the 10% level, and only one at the 5% level. The addition of the monopoly power variable to the equations with conditional land supply either increases the $\bar{R}^2$ values or leaves them approximately unchanged in all cases. One can verify this by comparing the $\bar{R}^2$ values in Table 4 with the corresponding values in Table 2, columns (2), (4), and (6). The strongest support for the monopoly zoning argument is from the FHA home site regressions. The weakest support is from the ULI acreage and lot price regressions. Coefficients estimated from the FHA sample of 39 areas are roughly twice the size of those estimated from the ULI samples of 24 or 25 areas. This result is expected from our prior arguments that (i) FHA sites are free of the risks and costs that depress ULI acreage and lot prices

[21] We must remove Houston because it has no zoning jurisdictions.

[22] We must remove not only Houston from all three data sets, but also Lexington from two data sets used in fitting (8), because the Lexington UA has no suburban jurisdictions.

TABLE 4
Effects of Natural and Monopoly Restrictions

Dependent variables:	Price of FHA home site			Price of ULI improved lot			Price of ULI acreage		
Independent variables	(1)	(2)	(3)	(4)	(5)	(6)	(7)	(8)	(9)
Population	0.264**	0.259**	0.301**	0.193*	0.194	0.177	0.567**	0.540**	0.531*
	(2.37)	(2.20)	(2.15)	(1.42)	(1.26)	(1.05)	(2.21)	(1.90)	(1.72)
Income	2.01***	2.16***	2.18***	0.940	0.885	0.976	0.367	0.170	0.515
	(2.64)	(2.71)	(2.67)	(1.02)	(0.89)	(1.07)	(0.21)	(0.09)	(0.31)
Population change	0.255***	0.238***	0.191**	0.0983	0.0960	0.0601	0.646***	0.646***	0.589***
	(3.55)	(3.20)	(2.16)	(1.11)	(1.03)	(0.57)	(3.87)	(3.77)	(3.06)
Conditional land supply	−0.754**	−0.845**	−0.741**	−0.809*	−0.955*	−0.993*	−1.28	−1.59*	−1.50*
	(−2.15)	(−2.36)	(−1.89)	(−1.41)	(−1.51)	(−1.69)	(−1.18)	(−1.37)	(−1.39)
Concentration ratio, C_u	0.182**			0.124*			0.159		
	(2.30)			(1.44)			(0.98)		
Concentration ratio, C_s		0.146*			0.0508			0.0201	
		(1.67)			(0.51)			(0.11)	
Number of governments			−0.111*			−0.0535			−0.0784
			(−1.32)			(−0.72)			(−0.58)
Constant	−17.20***	−18.14***	−18.77***	−5.84	−4.77	−5.04	−4.49	−1.19	−4.31
	(−2.49)	(−2.49)	(−2.46)	(−0.66)	(−0.48)	(−0.58)	(−0.27)	(−0.07)	(−0.27)
$\overline{R}^2$	.54	.51	.49	.37	.31	.29	.52	.50	.49
SE	.37	.38	.38	.27	.28	.28	.50	.52	.51
F	9.92***	8.85***	8.39***	3.76**	3.09**	2.97**	6.08***	5.59***	5.63***
	(5,33)	(5,33)	(5,33)	(5,18)	(5,18)	(5,19)	(5,18)	(5,18)	(5,19)

Note. Same note as in Table 2.

in restricted markets, and (ii) FHA observations are from larger urban areas.[23] The results in Table 4 are all robust with respect to functional form.[24]

To indicate the typical effects of monopoly zoning power on price, one must take account of the size of the estimated coefficients on the monopoly power variables in relation to the observed range of monopoly power measures in U.S. urban areas. Table 4 shows substantial variation in coefficient size. We shall provide an example calculation, based on a selected coefficient, to convey the sense of our argument. Following this, we suggest a range of typical effects, based on calculations employing a range of coefficients.

The largest coefficient on concentration ratio C_u is 0.182 in column (1) of Table 4. It implies that a 50% decrease from the sample mean ratio of .352 to .176 will decrease price by 9.1%; likewise, a 50% increase to .528 will increase price by 9.1%. The 18.2% price difference is explained by the C_u

[23]A portion of the variation in estimated coefficients could be due to our specification of a model that excludes some difficult-to-quantify political variables. Fischel [1] states that an ideal sample for testing the monopoly zoning hypothesis is composed of urban areas with suburbs that are "independent" of the central city, with "stable" boundaries of both suburbs and central city. He also argues that in the ideal sample the posture of state courts toward local government zoning ought to be "permissive." Differences in these characteristics between FHA and ULI urban areas may be responsible for some of the variation in coefficient size.

[24]We conducted the same tests on an alternative specification. In place of the original demand equation (2), the alternative model has

$$D = \ln \alpha_0 + \alpha_1 \ln P + \alpha_2 \ln N + \alpha_3 \ln Y.$$

In place of the original monopoly power equation (7), we assume

$$z = \gamma_0 - \gamma_1 C.$$

These two changes lead, via the manipulations previously employed, to the estimating equation

$$\ln P = a_0 + a_1 \ln N + a_2 \ln Y + a_3 \ln \dot{N} + a_4 L + a_5 LC + \varepsilon.$$

We first estimated this equation using the three different prices and our apparently best-performing measure of zoning power, the concentration ratio, C_u. The coefficient on the interactive variable LC is statistically significant in all three equations, and the $\bar{R}^2$ values are even higher than for the corresponding log–log equations in columns (1), (4), and (7) of Table 4. We then estimated three additional regressions with C_s instead of C_u, and three more with LG in place of LC. The results roughly follow the pattern of Table 4, viz., the coefficients on these alternative measures of monopoly power are insignificant and the $\bar{R}^2$ values are lower than when C_u is employed.

difference between .176 and .528. This particular calculation demonstrates that since 10 of the 39 observed C_u ratios are below .176, and 9 are above .528, the 18% price spread due to monopoly zoning should not be uncommon.[25] To indicate a common range of effects, we eliminated the two outlying coefficients and performed similar calculations using the remaining seven. The results suggest that variation in price due to monopoly zoning power is commonly between 5 and 16% of the mean price. The strength of this monopoly zoning effect is somewhat weaker than that found by Hamilton, but in our judgment stronger than that obtained by Fischel. Of course, both were testing for the effect of monopoly zoning in housing rather than land markets.

Our interpretation of the monopoly zoning coefficients—that they indicate the extent to which governments' preemption of urban land usage can affect its price—neglects the possibility that zoning creates amenities that also affect the price. The price model does not separate out any zoning-related amenity effects from those attributable to the contrived scarcity of useable land. All we can say with certainty is that the coefficients indicate the effect of zoning on price.

The combined effect of natural and contrived restrictions can now be summarized. First, note the results of an F test of joint significance of these two variables; it tests the null hypotheses that $b_4 = b_5 = 0$ in (8), and $b_4 = b_5' = 0$ in (8′). When we use the FHA sample and C_u as the measure of monopoly power, the null hypothesis is rejected at the .01 level; when C_s and G are used as measures of monopoly power, it is rejected at the .05 level. However, when we employ the ULI samples, the same test does not permit rejection even at the .10 level.

Second, note the extent to which the combined restrictions typically explain interurban price variation. The coefficients on the land supply variable range between .74 and 1.59 and have a mean of 1.05.[26] By the argument of Section II, this suggests that interurban price variation of 20–40% will commonly be due to natural restriction. And by the argument immediately above, price variation of an additional 5–16% will typically be due to contrived restriction. It is reasonable to conclude that combined supply restrictions can typically explain interurban variations in price of about 40% of the mean.

[25] As an alternative example, consider the coefficient −0.111 on G in column (3). An 11.1% difference in price is due to the G difference between 36 and 108. Twenty of the 39 areas have fewer than 36 governments and seven have more than 108. This suggests that observed variation in monopoly power is commonly responsible for a price differential that is 11% of the mean price.

[26] Note that addition of the monopoly zoning variable reduces the size of the coefficient on land supply. Compare Table 4 with Table 2.

III. CONCLUSION

In this paper we measured natural and contrived restrictions on the supply of urban land. Our conditional land supply measures the amount of land available for urban use, net of natural restrictions, viz., bodies of water. We have supplemented this measure to account for the tendency of urban governments with greater monopoly zoning power to permit use of a smaller fraction of the naturally available land.

Using the limited data available from 45 U.S. urban areas, we have employed regression analysis to test the ability of conditional land supply and monopoly zoning power to explain interurban variation in three prices of land. The land supply coefficients have the expected sign and are significant; the monopoly zoning power coefficients also have the expected sign, although most of them are not significant. The coefficients are large enough to explain typical interurban price differentials of 40% of the mean. About three-fourths of this explanatory power is commonly due to natural restriction and one-fourth to contrived restriction.

REFERENCES

1. W. A. Fischel, Zoning and the exercise of monopoly power: A reevaluation, *J. Urban Econom.*, **8**, 283–293 (1980).
2. W. A. Fischel, Is local government structure in large urbanized areas monopolistic or competitive?, *Nat. Tax J.*, **34**, 95–104 (1981).
3. W. A. Fischel, "The Economics of Zoning Laws," Johns Hopkins, Baltimore, MD (1985).
4. B. J. Frieden, "The Environmental Protection Hustle," MIT Press, Cambridge, MA (1979).
5. M. Gottlieb, Influences on values in urban land markets, USA, 1956–1961, *J. Reg. Sci.*, **6**, 1–16 (1965).
6. J. S. Greenlees, Sample truncation in FHA data: Implications for home purchase indexes, *South Econom. J.*, **48**, 917–931 (1982).
7. B. W. Hamilton, Zoning and the exercise of monopoly power, *J. Urban Econom.*, **5**, 116–130 (1978).
8. J. B. Kau and C. F. Sirmans, Urban land value functions and the price elasticity of demand for housing, *J. Urban Econom.*, **6**, 112–121 (1979).
9. J. B. Kau and C. F. Sirmans, The demand for urban residential land, *J. Reg. Sci.*, **21**, 519–528 (1981).
10. M. K. Macauley, Estimation and recent behavior of urban population and employment density gradients, *J. Urban Econom.*, **18**, 251–260 (1985).
11. S. J. Maisel, Price movements of building sites in the United States—A comparison among metropolitan areas, *Pap. Reg. Sci. Assoc.*, **10**, 47–60 (1964).
12. E. S. Mills, The value of urban land, *in* "The Quality of the Urban Environment" (Perloff, Ed.), Resources for the Future, Washington, DC (1969).
13. E. S. Mills, "Urban Economics," Scott, Foresman, Glenview, IL (1972).
14. E. S. Mills, "Studies in the Structure of the Urban Economy," Johns Hopkins Press, Baltimore, MD (1972).
15. E. S. Mills and K. Ohta, Urbanization and urban problems, *in* "Asia's New Giant" (Patrick and Rosvosky, Eds.), The Brookings Institution, Washington, DC (1976).
16. R. Muth, "Cities and Housing," Univ. of Chicago Press, Chicago (1969).

17. R. Muth, The derived demand for urban residential land, *Urban Stud.*, **8**, 243–254 (1971).
18. L. Ozanne and T. Thibodeau, Explaining metropolitan housing price differences, *J. Urban Econom.*, **13**, 51–66 (1983).
19. Urban Land Institute, "Residential Land Price Inflation Survey," ULI, Washington (1985).
20. U.S. Department of Housing and Urban Development, "FHA Homes: Data for States and Selected Areas on Characteristics of FHA Operations under Section 203," USGPO, Washington (1975, 1980, 1983).
21. K. J. White and H. G. Horsman, "Shazam: The Econometrics Computer Program, Version 5," University of British Columbia, Vancouver (1985).
22. M. J. White, Fiscal zoning in fragmented metropolitan areas, *in* "Fiscal Zoning and Land Use Controls" (E. S. Mills and W. E. Oates, Eds.), Heath-Lexington, Lexington, MA (1975).
23. N. Williams, Jr., "American Land Planning Law," Callaghan & Co., Chicago (1975).
24. A. D. Witte, The determination of interurban residential site price differentials: A derived demand model with empirical testing, *J. Reg. Sci.*, **15**, 351–364 (1975).

[13]

REGIONAL AND INTERREGIONAL INPUT-OUTPUT MODELS: AN APPRAISAL

CHARLES M. TIEBOUT*

Northwestern University

It is not too much of an overstatement to say that post World War II regional research has been almost completely dominated by regional applications of input-output models. Whatever the form of the variations, the basic input-output theme is present. While users of, and writers on, input-output techniques are quite honest in admitting its limitations, one does sense a feeling that this approach is clearly preferable to other frameworks in attacking regional problems. Indeed, one leading writer in the field of regional analysis notes that, "too many of (the economists) tools represent transfers of concepts and methods traditionally used by the national-international type of economist."[1] It is not the function of this paper to put forth the case for the Keynesian-style "national-international" framework in regional analysis as an alternative form of or supplement to input-output. This has been done elsewhere.[2] Rather it is the purpose of this paper to review the various operational uses of regional input-output analysis. Such a review will not only give the reader some idea of the current uses of input-output in regional analysis, but will also enable him to more adequately judge its possibilities and limitations.

NATIONAL AND REGIONAL INPUT-OUTPUT MODELS: SUMMARY VIEW

The conceptual framework of an open, static input-output model is given by Leontief.[3] The accounting balance equation is given as:

$$X_i - \sum_{k=1}^{m} x_{ik} = Y_i. \tag{1.1}$$

Here X_i represents the total output of industry i. x_{ik} gives the amount of i products absorbed by industry k. Given the number of industries $1, 2 \cdots, m$;

* In am indebted to my former colleagues, Stefan Valavanis and Alfred Conrad, now of Harvard University, and to Robert Strotz of Northwestern University, for their criticisms and suggestions. By tradition and as a point of fact, I alone am responsible for the errors.

[1] Walter Isard, "The Value of the Regional Approach to Some Basic Economic Problems," *Regional Income, Studies in Income and Wealth*, XXI, (Princeton: Princeton University Press, 1957), p. 78.

[2] See M. C. Daly, "An Approximation to a Geographic Multiplier," *Economic Journal*, June-September 1940, L, pp. 248-58. George Hildebrand and Arthur Mace, "The Employment Multiplier in an Expanding Industrial Market: Los Angeles County, 1940–47," *Review of Economics and Statistics*, August 1950, XXXII, pp. 241–49. Charles M. Tiebout, "Exports and Regional Economic Growth," *Journal of Political Economy*, April 1956, LXIV, pp. 160-65.

[3] Wassily Leontief, "Structural Change," in Wassily Leontief, *et al.*, *Studies in the Structure of the American Economy* (New York: Oxford University Press, 1953), p. 18.

equation (1.1) yields the amount of i products going to final demand, that is to Y_i.

The structural equations are given by the production coefficients for each industry,

$$x_{ik} = a_{ik}X_k \qquad i = 1, 2, \cdots, m. \qquad k = 1, 2, \cdots, m. \tag{1.2}$$

where, a_{ik} is the production coefficient indicating the amount of i needed to produce a unit of k. Substituting (1.2) in (1.1) yields:

$$X_i - \sum_{k=1}^{m} a_{ik}X_k = Y_i. \tag{1.3}$$

This system of linear equations may be solved for X_i if a bill of final demands, $Y_1, Y_2, \cdots, Y_m$, is known.

Regional models have the effect of adding another dimension to national models, namely the regions are identified. X_i become ${}_rX_i$, which represents the total output X, of industry i, in *region r*. Here ${}_{rs}x_{ij}$ represents the flow from industry i in region r to industry j in region s. If the number of regions $r, s = 1, 2 \cdots, n$ is known, the interregional model takes the form,

$$ {}_rX_i - \sum_{s=1}^{n} \sum_{j=1}^{m} {}_{rs}x_{ij} = {}_rY_i \qquad j = 1, 2, \cdots, m. \tag{2.1}$$

In this equation ${}_rY_i$ represents the final demand for the products of industry i in region r.

Production coefficients are given as,

$$\frac{{}_{rs}x_{ij}}{{}_rX_i} = {}_{rs}a_{ij}. \tag{2.2}$$

(2.2) states that the inputs from industry i in region r to industry j in region s are some proportion of the total production, X, of good j in region s. (Note that the production coefficient now has a spatial as well as technical component.)

Total output for the whole system of regions and industries may be determined by substituting (2.2) in (2.1) and solving for ${}_rX_i$. This is the same process as used in equations (1.1), (1.2), and (1.3). Four further considerations apply to regional models.

(1) Not all of the sub-boxes come into interregional trade, i.e., possibly, ${}_{rs}x_{ik} = 0$. Such industries as barber shops do not enter interregional trade.

(2) Regional models, like their national counterpart, may be open or closed. Here, however, a greater variety of alternatives exist. Models may be open regionally; for example, households within the region may be part of final demand. Models may also be closed regionally, e.g., households are endogenous. Either of these two possibilities may be combined within a national model which, in turn, may be either open or closed.

(3) Another characteristic of regional models is that they may or may not assume technological equivalence. That is to say, the production coefficients, equation (2.2), may be assumed the same throughout the nation or they may vary from region to region.

(4) The final point concerning regional models is that the balance of regional payments equilibrium, may be considered. Not all models are concerned with this condition.

Yet the major item to note is that equations (2.1) and (2.2) merely add a spatial component to national models. This is important. National models have limitations of their own which have been discussed elsewhere.[4] Any limitations placed on national models also apply with equal force to regional models. Above and beyond these limitations, regional models have limitations of their own.

INPUT-OUTPUT MODELS IN REGIONAL ANALYSIS

In general there are three frameworks in which the input-output techniques may be used in regional analysis: (1) *local impact studies*; (2) *regional balance of payments studies*; and (3) *interregional flows studies.* Other uses may exist, but they will not be discussed here.

Regional impact analysis poses the following question: if a new industry were to be located in an area, what would be the *total* change in the level of economic activity?[5] One method of studying the total impact is through the interrelations of an input-output matrix. Using steel as an example, not only is the expansion due to a new steel plant taken into account, but secondary effects are considered as well. Other industries will expand in response to the increase in steel output. Some of these industries will agglomerate at the site of the new steel plant whiel other inputs will come from outside the region under consideration. Those which do agglomerate, however, are part of the increased activity of the region. Just which industries will agglomerate around the new steel plant can only be decided on the basis of location theory. Of course, the industries which do agglomerate will have input requirements of their own which may be analyzed.

Regional balance of payments studies have been carried out using input-output techniques.[6] Essentially, these studies seek to show, in a quantified way, the relation of a region to the rest of the nation. Thus, for example, an autonomous change in the level of exports can be shown to have certain implications for the regional economy.

One of the more interesting applications of this technique is the work of Moore and Petersen.[7] Strictly speaking, their study is not merely a balance of payments

[4] Robert Dorfman, "The Nature and Significance of Input-Output," *Review of Economics and Statistics*, May 1954, XXXVI, pp. 121–33. Carl Christ, "A Review of Input-Output Analysis," *Input-Output Analysis: An Appraisal, Studies in Income and Wealth* (Princeton: Princeton University Press 1955), pp. 137–69. Wassily Leontief, "Some Basic Problems of Empirical Input-Output Analysis," *ibid.*, pp. 9–22.

[5] Walter Isard and Robert Kuenne, "The Impact of Steel Upon the Greater New York-Philadelphia Urban-Industrial Region," *Review of Economics and Statistics*, November 1953, XXXV, pp. 289–301. Walter Isard and Vincent Whitney, "Atomic Power and Regional Development," *Bulletin of Atomic Scientists*, April 1952, III, pp. 119–24. Walter Isard, Robert Kavesh, and Robert Kuenne, "The Economic Base and Structure of the Urban Metropolitan Region," *American Sociological Review*, June 1953, XVII, pp. 317–21.

[6] Walter Isard, "Regional Commodity Balances and Interregional Commodity Flows," *American Economic Review, Supplement*, May 1953, XLIII, pp. 167–80. Fredrick Moore and James Petersen, "Regional Analysis: An Interindustry Model of Utah," *Review of Economics and Statistics*, November 1955, XXXVII, pp. 368–80.

study, since it contains elements of intraregional analysis. The Moore-Petersen model used regional production coefficients wherever possible. Also, they close the model somewhat at the regional level by placing households within the bill of goods. National figures, however, were used to estimate the consumption aspects of the multiplier.

Their technique in estimating the balance of trade is similar to that used by Isard.[8] Total production of the *i*th commodity in the region was measured against total consumption in both the industrial and household sectors. The difference, by assumption, represents the net imports or exports.

Interregional flows studies attempt to show, again in a quantifiable manner, the structural relationships between regions. The effects of an autonomous shock may be traced to, and through, the *n* regions under consideration.

The only empirical study of interegional flows is the splendid work of Leon Moses.[9] Moses uses the conceptual framework discussed earlier for a three region eleven matrix. Solving this system he shows, for the first time, the interregional flows within the United States. The assumptions of the Moses model, as well as greater details concerning the assumptions of the other models, will be discussed next when we turn to the limitations of regional input-output techniques.

LIMITATIONS OF REGIONAL INPUT-OUTPUT MODELS

Two choices are open to us in reviewing these regional uses of input-output techniques. (1) We may take up each type of study in turn; or (2) we may take up the assumptions common to all or most of the studies, and then see what implications this has for the various areas under review. While neither method is completely satisfactory, the second method seems to provide the simplest exposition.

Regional Production Coefficients

The criticism of regional input-output analysis may well start with the whole issue of production coefficients. If their use at the national level is at all dubious, even more is left to be desired at the regional level. This will be apparent in the discussion of three aspects of regional production coefficients: (1) the use of national coefficients at the regional level; (2) the use of "average" coefficients; and (3) the implications of the spatial component of the production coefficient.

As an operational necessity, all models discussed (Moore and Petersen excepted) have used national coefficients as regional coefficients. That is to say the production functions for various industries are assumed to be uniform throughout the whole country. Yet a mere examination of Northern versus Southern fuel bills is enough to indicate that this is not the case. Obviously, other instances could be cited.

Production coefficients may be divided into three categories: (1) average coefficients as determined, operationally, by the last Census of Manufacturers;

[7] *Op. cit.*

[8] "Regional Commodity . . . ," *op. cit.*

[9] "Interregional Input-Output Analysis," *American Economic Review*, December 1955, XLV, pp. 803–32.

(2) best coefficients which represent the coefficients of the newest of "planning board" plants in the industry; and (3) the worst coefficients which represent the coefficients of the marginal firm. Which coefficient one chooses depends on the assumed capacity of the industry and which firms bear the impact of demand changes. If demand is assumed to increase, best coefficients will apply if the industry was previously operating at capacity; added production will have to come from new plants. If the industry is assumed to be operating at less than capacity, worst coefficients could be the ones to use. Further, with a decrease in demand, worst coefficients will come into play, it is the older marginal firm which is assumed to drop out.

In regional studies, it is important to use the correct coefficients. In regional impact studies, for example, best coefficients are the ones to use. They are not used, however, since they are not known or can only be ascertained at great expense. In balance of payments and in interregional flows studies the difference between best, worst, and average coefficients is important. The best coefficients are associated with newer or more efficient producers in the industry. Insofar as newer producers are more efficient than older firms, a drop in demand may have relatively less effect on the producers using best coefficients. For example, a general drop in textile demand may have a greater impact on older New England mills than mills in the South. If average production coefficients are used throughout, this result will not be shown in the model.

Regional coefficients have still another serious pitfall. They not only specify the amount of needed inputs per unit of output, but they also specify the regional source. This source is assumed to be a constant proportion of total output, i.e., trading patterns are assumed to be stable. Thus if region *h* imports half of its coal from region *i* and the other half from region *j*, this trade pattern is assumed to told for *all* levels of output.

Now there is no logical reason to expect trading patterns to exhibit stability. Moses, aware of this, attempts to investigate the stability of trade coefficients for the years 1947, 1948, and 1949, using I.C.C. Waybill data.[10] His hesitant conclusion is that "the author believes that they have exhibited sufficient stability to warrant their being subjected to further statistical evaluation on various levels of regional and commodity aggregation."[11] Such instabilty as exists in the data given by Moses *may* be correlated with changes in the demand of the sectors under consideration.[12] The real test which trade coefficients must withstand is stability in the face of changes in final demand.

[10] *Op. cit.*

[11] *Op. cit.*, p. 826.

[12] Variations in total shipments were checked against the stability of Moses' coefficients. A weighted average of per cent changes in trade coefficient (Moses, *op. cit.*, p. 824) with per cent changes in I.C.C. waybill total tonnage for each of the five commodity classes. [Interstate Commerce Commission, *Statistics of Railways in the United States:* 1947, (Washington: U. S. Government Printing Office, 1949), p. 43., and the 1948 and 1949 editions.] Changes in the coefficients and total tonnage were compared for the years 1947–48 and 1948–49. The coefficient of linear correlation = .61. With a standard error of 1.83, this correlation could happen by chance about 6.5 per cent of the time. This is certainly not conclusive evidence, but may offer a clue for further testing.

The case for stable trading coefficients presents an interesting paradox. Moses is quite explicit that "the assumption of stable trade coefficients is the crucial issue."[13] Even for short run predictions, "the following conditions should be satisfied: (1) There is excess capacity in the transport network between every pair of regions. (2) Each industry in each region has excess capacity. (3) There is a pool of unemployed labor for each region."[14] These assumptions are necessary to justify constant costs. Constant costs, Moses feels, are needed to justify stable trade patterns.

Now let us go back to the operational method, not that of Moses, by which net imports or exports were determined. In every case it is the residual of regional production measured against regional consumption. Thus it is possible for a region to produce a commodity and import it as well. Indeed, the Moses model contains many examples of such flows. But this is inconsistent, (except when spatial extent is considered—a region may import a commodity at one border and export it at another border.) Surely, if local producers have excess capacity and constant costs, the region cannot import that commodity. Local producers with lower transport costs would be able to undersell their more distant rivals. Neither the assumption of stable trade patterns nor that of importing and exporting the same commodity makes too much sense alone—granting a case can be made for the latter. Together they clash head on.

Product Mix

The residuals method of determining export balances is not only inconsistent with the assumptions of constant cost and excess capacity, but may not measure imports and exports in any meaningful manner at all. This is an extreme statement; but if excess capacity is assumed for industry i in region r, any imports of i into r may be more indicative of product mix, the degree of heterogeneity of products in an industrial classification, than of an import balance.[15]

The failure to handle product mix adequately can lead to some ridiculous results in determining net exports and imports. In Wisconsin, for example, where the internal production of automobiles just about equals consumption, there would be no imports of automobiles. This implies, in turn, that Wisconsin residents drive only the local product, a Nash or Hudson. Clearly, this is one area where no further research is needed to see if Wisconsinites do actually

[13] *Op. cit.*, p. 810.

[14] *Op. cit.*, p. 812. While it will not alter the analysis that follows, Moses may be too severe on this point. If various costs *rise proportionately*, trade patterns will be stable.

[15] This point raises an interesting side issue. The usual method by which the various industrial sectors are classified runs in terms of similarity of input requirements. A supplementary method might be to divide the economy into m regions. For any arbitrary interindustry classification, the degree of product mix is indicated to the extent to which regions import and export the same commodity. That classification which minimizes this simultaneous flow may be considered as containing the least product mix. In some cases the export-import flows are not known. Where excess capacity exists and is known, product mix may be assumed if the same commodity is imported—for reasons shown above. Again, to the extent that this inconsistency is minimized, the product mix is cut. The possibility of simultaneous imports and exports due to spatial extent, as discussed above, is no problem since all we are seeking is a minimum, not a zero.

drive only Nash or Hudson cars. Yet, even a more homogeneous product such as premium beer, a major Wisconsin industry, does not eliminate imports. Budweiser from St. Louis and Hamms from St. Paul are large sellers in Wisconsin.

A moments reflection will point out the general inadequacy of the residuals method of determining the volume of net exports and imports. In an economy where the degree of product variation is as high and the ratio of transport cost to total cost is as low, one might expect a great deal of product mix, even in a 200 industry matrix. The residuals assumption is not a very safe one. Those concerned with export-import balances might do well to try alternative approaches.[16]

The final problem relating to product mix and net exports and imports, comes in determining the regional multipliers. Moore and Petersen have calculated a series of Utah income multipliers which average, unweighted, 3.9. This multiplier should not be confused with the simple Keynesian consumption function multiplier. The Utah multiplier has two components: (1) the intraregional interindustry effect of a change in export demand, and (2) the consumption function multiplier effect via changes in household income. Moore and Petersen note that, "the multiplier would be different if gross figures (for exports and imports) had been used."[17] In other words, in measuring the imports and exports as net figures instead of gross flows, the sum of the import leakages is understated. It is impossible with the data now available to estimate this error, but it may be substantial.

Regional Impact Studies and Agglomeration

The final operational criticism of input-output models deals with agglomeration considerations in regional impact studies. It is argued that once the new industry is established in a region other industries will agglomerate and they, in turn, will need inputs. Just which industries will agglomerate, it is argued, can be decided on the basis of location theory. This is a bit too glib. It may be stated, without trepidation, that, except for a limited number of industries, location theory is not in a condition to predict at the fine margin this analysis requires.[18] At best, all that can be hoped for is a rough approximation. Moreover, any failure in predicting the production coefficients of the impact industry (steel in our example) will appear in the estimates of agglomeration. Beyond this, nonap-

[16] Alternative approaches includes: the use of I.C.C. waybill data, unfortunately given in weights and not values; direct estimates from local producers; and money flow analysis from the Federal Reserve Districts.

[17] *Op. cit.*, p. 379.

[18] The shortcomings in location predictions stems in part from the shortcomings in location theory. At present, partial equilibrium analysis in location theory can do no more than specify the conditions for spatial equilibrium. This is not the same as specifying the conditions and showing the operational well behaved conditions of calculus by which this optimum may be reached. This is what Lösch had in mind when he stated, quite bluntly, that, "there is no scientific solution for the location of the individual firm, but only the practical one: the test of trial and error." [August Lösch, *The Economics of Location*, trans. William Woglom with the assistance of Wolfgang Stolper (New Haven: Yale University Press, 1954), p. 29.]

pearance of an industry which is expected to agglomerate will break the link in the interindustry effect. Alternatively, any industry which unexpectedly does agglomerate will have just the opposite effect.[19]

Regional and Interregional Input-Output Models: Summary

The past discussion of input-output techniques as applied to regional analysis has been wholly one-sided. Only the operational limitations have been discussed.[20] No doubt this may appear to be unfair, but for purposes of review and appraisal it was necessary. The empirical results of regional input-output analysis present us with a set of data which is supposed to describe reality. Unfortunately, there is no alternative set of data with which the researchers' results may be compared. Hence, it is vital to scrutinize the method and assumptions to see such limitations as may exist.

It seems fair to state that most operational regional studies have produced only the most tentative results. Basically this stems from two considerations: (1) the lack of adequate data; and (2) the necessity to make certain operational assumptions which depart, in varying degrees, from what we usually assume about reality. It may be that further work in this area will eliminate some of the problems raised above. Note, however, that this is not necessarily a call for further research in this area. Such a call for further research, certainly a common expression in academic circles, implies a judgment as to the allocation of scarce research resources. Before such a call is put forth in behalf of regional input-output research, alternative methods of attacking similar issues should be appraised.

[19] Isard, Kavesh and Kuenne feel that input-output techniques are useful in describing the "economic base" of a city. (Isard, Kavesh, and Kuenne, *op. cit.*) Again using the steel plant as an example, they construct a city around such a plant. Evidently they assume a closed regional model, since "households which receive wages, salaries, and other income in the first round . . . also behave like industries" (*op. cit.*, p. 318). Adding to the total of steel and agglomerating export industries the total of local activities, "yields a meaningful net of economic interrelations which may be viewed as the economic base of the city" (*op. cit.*, p. 319).

Ordinarily the "economic base" of a community consists of the exogenous activities which, when known, determine the level of income for the whole city. Yet this use of the term implies that the economic base of the city is all of the economic activities within the community. If this is what the authors mean, it isn't very useful. If it is not what they mean, they would do well to create an exogenous and endogenous sector. Under their current usage, all activity is export or export linked which, in terms of the usual base analysis, means the whole economy is exogenous.

[20] At the *conceptual* level input-output analysis offers many advantages. The reader is reminded that this is not the issue at hand.

[14]

Excerpt from *National Institute Economic Review*, **40**, 33

APPENDIX: REGIONAL MULTIPLIERS

If Y_a is change in GNP (factor cost) in a region A,
C_a is change in consumers expenditure (market prices)
T_{da} „ direct tax payments
T_{ia} „ indirect tax payments (net)
G_a „ government expenditure on *value added* in A
M_a „ imports for consumption (from outside region)
R_a „ net transfers to households in the region,
then, in the absence of changes in exports from the region or in capital formation within it:

$$Y_a = C_a + G_a - M_a - T_{ia}$$

and if $C_a = c(Y_a - T_{da} + R_a)$,
$T_{da} = t_d Y_a$,
$T_{ia} = t_i C_a$ (all indirect taxation being assumed to fall on consumption)
$R_a = -uY_a$ (i.e., variable transfers consist of unemployment relief and other assistance which vary inversely with income)

and $M_a = m_a C_a$
then:

$$Y_a = cY_a(1 - t_d - u)(1 - m_a - t_i) + G_a$$

$$= \frac{G_a}{1 - c(1 - t_d - u)(1 - m_a - t_i)}$$

Substituting 1 for the numerator gives the 'regional multiplier' in the usual sense of the multiplier applicable to an autonomous change in *net* output in the region.

Suppose $c = 0.8$
$t_d = 0.18$ (Prest's[1] marginal estimate for personal taxation)
$u = 0.2$ (half the ratio of unemployment benefit to earnings as given by Archibald)
$t_i = 0.16$ (average value from Bluebook)

The value of m_a is the problem. Archibald regresses the minimum expenditures that he regards as certainly local (local value added) on disposable personal income, and gets a coefficient of 0.23. Correcting for saving, so as to relate this spending to consumption, would raise the coefficient to about 0.28. The marginal *foreign* import content is probably 0.2 or more, so that about half of consumption expenditure is on United Kingdom goods and services ('mobile United Kingdom content') that might have been produced either inside or outside Region A, giving a *possible* range for m_a from about 0.2 to 0.7. If the 'mobile United Kingdom content' came from outside and inside A in proportion to the total outputs of those two zones of the British economy, then, where A stood for the development areas (1/5 of the U.K.), m_a would be 0.6. Where A stood for (say) the South West development area alone, it would be very little short of 0.7. There is likely, in practice, to be some bias towards local production of this 'mobile United Kingdom content'; a fairly generous allowance for it would be to place m_a halfway between the values just mentioned and the *minimum* value of 0.2. This gives a value of 0.4 for the development areas collectively, and one of 0.45 for a small area, like the Cornwall and North Devon one.

Inserting these values gives a multiplier for the development areas a whole of:—

$$\frac{1}{1 - 0.8(0.62)(0.44)} = 1.28$$
(assuming perfect mobility of 'mobile United Kingdom content' the value would be 1.14)

On the same assumptions the *national* multiplier would be:—

$$\frac{1}{1 - 0.8(0.62)(0.64)} = 1.46$$

and that for a very small area:—

$$\frac{1}{1 - 0.8(0.62)(0.39)} = 1.24$$

The repercussions on (and from) the rest of the country should, however, be considered as well. If the rest of the country is referred to as 'B', then we have:—

M_b = B's extra imports for consumption from outside itself
$= M_{bf}$, foreign imports, $= m_f C_b$
$+ M_{br}$, imports from rest of country (i.e. from A) $= m_{br} C_b$
$= m_{br} Y_b (1 - t_a - u)$

To the stimulus provided by G_a, we have an addition provided by the extra imports of B from A consequent upon A's extra imports from B.

Hence,

$$Y_a = \frac{G_a + m_{br} Y_b (1 - t_a - u)}{1 - c(1 - t_d - u)(1 - m_a - t_i)}$$

while similarly,

$$Y_b = \frac{m_{ar} Y_a (1 - t_d - u)}{1 - c(1 - t_d - a)(1 - m_b - t_i)}$$

whence:

$$Y_a = \frac{G_a[1 - c(1 - t_d - u)(1 - m_b - t_i)]}{[1 - c(1 - t_d - u)(1 - m_a - t_i)][1 - c(1 - t_d - u)(1 - m_b - t_i)] - [m_{ar}(1 - t_d - u)][m_{br}(1 - t_d - u)]}$$

The value of m_{bf} may be taken as 0.2 (like m_{af}), and m_{br}, where B is 4/5 of the United Kingdom, would be 0.1 on the 'perfect mobility' hypothesis, but 0.05 on the compromise adopted earlier, so that $m_b = 0.25$. Then $(1 - m_b - t_i) = 0.59$, $m_{br}(1 - t_d - u) = 0.031$, and $m_{ar}(1 - t_d - u) = 0.124$

and

$$Y_a = \frac{G_a(1 - .29)}{(.78)(.71) - (.03)(.12)} = G_a \frac{.71}{.554 - .004} = 1.29\ G_a$$

The multiplier is thus only marginally increased by putting in the effects of repercussions.

---

[1] See *Economic Journal*, Vol. 72, 1962.

[15]

Excerpt from '*The Community Economic Base Study*', Supplementary Paper 16

Chapter 6

Structural Interrelations in the Local Economy

The two previous chapters have shown how the local economy can be looked at in terms of industries serving sectors and how these can be measured. Implicit in that discussion was a theoretical framework of analysis. This chapter makes the theoretical foundation of base analysis explicit by considering the structural interrelations in the local economy. After a discusson of the long-run versus short-run time element in base analysis, a simple economic base "model" is developed. Finally, a fuller model is considered along with some of the conceptual issues of base studies.

The Time Factor in Community Studies

The discussion of community income and how the local economy can be divided up and measured has proceeded, so far, without a time dimension. Just as the local economy has been divided up at a point in time, it can be analyzed over time. Time enters in a twofold sense: the effect of the level of activity in one year on succeeding years, and the time span over which the study is to provide information.

The level of the economy in one time period in many instances influences the level of the economy in the following time period. By way of an example, note that the level of output in one year may affect the decision to invest in plant and equipment the following year. Today's consumption by families will depend, in part, on past income levels. When elements of this type are introduced, the analysis becomes *dynamic*. The advantage of dynamic analysis is that it permits built-in adjustments. Instead of long leaps into the future, more of a step-by-step process occurs. But there are difficulties. Dynamic frameworks, technically, are quite hard to handle. Further, they are chiefly useful in larger regions. This volume does not go into the details of such a framework.

The time horizon of a study is another matter. Here the division between short-run and long-run time spans is under consideration. Short-run time spans, as a rule of thumb, refer to periods from a few months up to around two years. Long-run analysis is usually concerned with five, ten and/or twenty-five year time periods. Sometimes, the distinction is made with reference to cyclical and secular changes. Cyclical represents the year-to-year variations as in business cycle analysis. The analysis of growth deals more with secular changes. In this context, the community which is concerned with the level of employment next year is asking a short-run question. If the community asks about employment ten years hence, its concern is long-run.

The Simple Base Relations

The first chapter illustrated the simple concept of the basic and non-basic dichotomy. Now, more explicitly, a "model" of the economic base can be developed which extends this simple concept.

The introduction of models in community research serves a useful purpose; major relationships are explicitly stated. Models involve groupings and statements about the relationship between these groupings. Naturally, models, like road maps, are abstractions. It is simply impossible to describe everything. The mere identification of basic and non-basic industries and the relations between them constitutes a model. By casting the analysis in the form of a model, the reader knows precisely what is assumed.

For exposition it is easier to consider first a short-run model and then a long-run model.

Assumptions: A Short-Run Analysis

Imagine that a community's economy has been divided into three sectors: exports, local investment, and local consumption. The unit of measurement is income accruing to residents. Thus, income accrues to local families from the three sectors mentioned.

Examples of such income would include: (export) wages and salaries paid by a toy manufacturer whose market is nationwide, wages and salaries paid by a local box manufacturer who sells to the toy firm, income received from the rent of a summer home to non-residents; (local investment) profit income of a local contractor, wages and salaries paid by a local cement plant; and (local consumption) income to a local barber, wages and salaries of the local ice cream manufacturer, the income of a dentist. The ties to these sectors, as the examples indicate, may be direct or only indirect. Finally, the interest, at this time, is in the year-to-year (short-run) variations in income levels.

In the short run, the level of income created not only in the export but also in the local investment sector depends largely on forces other than the level of local income. Exports depend on external market demands. The community is such a small part of this total market that it does not affect this market but is affected by it. Year-to-year variations in local investment are also assumed to depend on outside forces; interest rates, general credit conditions, and other such non-local factors. All of this means that, for short-run analysis, export and local investment income are taken as given, that is, they are measured but not explained by a base study. This leaves the local consumption sector which is "explained." What is meant by this?

The income derived from the local consumption sector depends upon local spending out of the income originating in the other sectors, just as non-basic employment was said to depend upon basic employment. In this sense it is explained. The nature of this explanatory dependency is important and needs examination.

The Local Consumption Sector

Income from local consumption is derived via a two-step process: (1) residents spend some of their income on local goods and services creating the sales dollars for local consumption goods and services; and (2) part of these sales dollars remain within the local economy and become local income.

Residents Spending on Local Consumption

What determines how much the typical family will spend locally on consumer goods? One of the most important factors is the level of current income. For present purposes other factors can be disregarded. The relationship between income and consumer spending is: the higher the income, the higher the spending.

Suppose that residents spend 50 per cent of their income locally on goods and services. Some of these goods and services may be produced locally like haircuts, while others are produced outside of town such as most items on a retailer's shelf. This can be called a propensity to consume locally with a value of .5. What do they do with the other 50 per cent of their income? Some is saved, some spent outside the community, and some is paid out for taxes. To keep things really simple, imagine a community where people always spend half (.5) of their income locally. Suppose dividend income (a type of export income) goes up one dollar. Does this mean that from this extra dollar of local income an additional 50 cents of income will be created through local spending? The answer is no, for there is a second component in the dollar flow stream which must be recognized.

Income Earned by the Local Sales Dollar

Not all of the 50 cents out of every income dollar that is spent locally is local income. Part of this 50 cents is paid out to bring in merchandise from outside the community (pay for imports), some may go as wages to non-residents, and to other such non-local sources. Yet, part will accrue as local income in the form of wages and salaries, profits, rents, and other such sources of local income. Suppose that 40 per cent remains as local income. If it is assumed that 40 per cent is a stable figure, .4 can be called the "income propensity of the local sales dollar."

This added propensity, when combined with the first, shows the relation between income, local consumption spending, and the local income derived therefrom. Out of every dollar of local income 50 cents will be spent locally on consumer goods and services and 40 per cent of this 50 cents, or 20 cents, *remains as local income.*

The Multiplier Process: Local Consumption

The added 20 cents of income through local consumption spending is not the total expansion of income. The "multiplier" process has not been completed. What does this mean?

So far, local incomes have risen—over and above the assumed one dollar increase—by an additional 20 cents. Part of this will be spent locally by consumers; in fact, one-half or 10 cents will be spent. Again, .4 of these sales dollars will remain as local income, 4 cents. But now local income is up by 4 cents and some of this will be spent—and on and on.

Fortunately, it is not necessary to trace out each round of spending and the local income created. A multiplier formula can give the answer more simply. The formula is:

$$1.\ \text{Total Income Increase} = \text{Increase in (Export plus Local Investment Income)} \times \frac{1}{1 - (\text{propensity to consume locally} \times \text{income created per dollar of local consumption sales})}$$

Equation (1) is much simpler than it looks. Use the above numbers and suppose again income from the export and local investment industries goes up one dollar. What is the total income increase? Since we assumed no change in investment income, the first term on the right hand side is the $1.00 from increased exports. That plus the two propensities yields:

$$2.\ \text{Total Income Increase} = \$1.00 \quad \times \quad \frac{1}{1 - (.5 \times .4)} = \$1.00 \quad \times \quad \frac{1}{1 - .2} = \$1.25$$

The multiplier value is 1.25. The original income change of $1.00 has been increased to $1.25 through the effect of the local consumption sector.

The more traditional base approach will yield the same result. Suppose that before any changes took place local income amounted to $125 million of which $100 million was basic and $25 million was non-basic. Now the base analyst is asked to measure the total income impact of just a $1.00 increase in basic income. Since the basic/non-basic ratio is 4 to 1, he would say that for every dollar of basic income another $.25 of non-basic income will be created.

If the base analyst wanted to be quite sophisticated he could use a multiplier formula as follows:

$$3.\ \text{Total Income Increase} = \text{Increase in Basic Income} \quad \times \quad \frac{1}{1 - \dfrac{\text{Non-basic Income}}{\text{Total Income}}}$$

Substituting the assumed values:

$$4.\ \text{Total Income Increase} = \$1.00 \quad \times \frac{1}{1 - \dfrac{\$25\ \text{million}}{\$125\ \text{million}}} = \$1.00 \quad \times \quad \frac{1}{1 - .2} = \$1.25$$

This is also the same answer as derived through the multiplier process in equation (2). Since either method produces the same result as the multiplier in equation (2), why use the more complicated approach?

The advantage of the first formulation is that it points up the two propensities involved, the propensity to consume locally (.5), and the propensity of a sales dollar to become local income (.4). In discussing below such concepts as the stability of the basic/non-basic ratio this is important.

[16]

Urban Studies (1988), 25, 267–281

A Synoptic View of Regional Growth and Unemployment: I — The Neoclassical Theory

J. S. L. McCombie

[*First received, August 1986; in final form, June 1987*]

Summary. This paper is the first part of a consideration of the implications of the current controversies in macroeconomics for regional growth theory. It is concerned with the neoclassical explanation of disparities in regional growth and unemployment rates. The one-sector and two-sector neoclassical models are surveyed and it is shown how this approach explains differences in productivity growth in terms of the progressive eradication of an initial misallocation of resources (both interregionally and intraregionally). Involuntary unemployment is ascribed to the classical view that real wages are too high. The effect of the spatial diffusion of innovations on productivity growth is also examined.

Introduction

It is perhaps somewhat ironical that in the United Kingdom there has been a recent diminution of concern with the 'regional problem' as the national unemployment rates have risen dramatically since 1973 (and especially since 1979). Of course, this is for the simple reason that the regional problem has become subsumed in the larger 'national problem' of how to reduce the overall rate of unemployment. An indication of the size of the current unemployment problem is the fact that the national unemployment rate now (1987) stands at a value that was rarely reached in even the most depressed regions in the postwar years prior to 1973.

The difficulty in finding a solution to the regional problem has been compounded by the breakdown in the last decade of the consensus that seemed to have emerged in macroeconomics with the neoclassical synthesis of the 1960s, leading to what Nordhaus (1983) has aptly called the 'macroconfusion'. This has also been mirrored in the disagreements over the causes of regional growth and stagnation since, of course, the region may be viewed as a nation within a common currency area, although largely devoid of internal demand management policy weapons. At present and at the inevitable risk of oversimplification, we may identify two competing paradigms, namely, the neoclassical and the post-Keynesian frameworks.[1] Nevertheless, this shift in emphasis concerning the regional problem has occurred irrespective of the precise views held about the causes of the current recession.

The neoclassical paradigm assumes that an unfettered working of the market mechanism will be equilibrating and any disparities in regional wages will tend to disappear over time. Any differences in regional productivity growth are seen as being fundamentally the result of the gains accruing from a progressive reduction in an initial interregional or intraregional misallocation of resources, or in both. Consequently, any disparities in productivity growth will eventually vanish as the misallocation is progressively corrected and regional growth rates approach the steady state.

Although neoclassical regional growth theory has

J. S. L. McCombie is in the Department of Economics, University of Melbourne, Victoria, Australia.
I am grateful to Robert Dixon for helpful discussions.

[1] The term post-Keynesian is used here to distinguish the approach discussed in this paper and in McCombie (1988) from the Keynesian-neoclassical synthesis.

not generally analysed the reasons for the existence of regional unemployment, within such a framework the cause must be classical in nature. In other words, unemployment is seen as the result of real wages being too high. The implication is that to reduce unemployment labour must accept a fall in the real wage rate sufficient to price itself back into the regional labour market.

The 'Treasury View' of the 1930s has thus re-emerged as the view of the Treasury in the 1980s. Any expenditure on regional policy is seen as being ultimately ineffective since it will merely lead to 'crowding out' with an offsetting decrease in private investment. While there may be some increase in employment in the region where the expenditure is undertaken, this will simply be at the expense of jobs in other areas.

On the other hand, the post-Keynesian approach stresses the crucial role that the growth of autonomous demand (most notably that generated by the growth of exports) plays in determining regional growth. The present high regional unemployment rates, apart from the small proportion due to structural or frictional factors, are seen as the result of insufficient effective demand and can only be alleviated by a substantial expansion of monetary and fiscal policy at the national level (Moore and Rhodes, 1982). An increase in government expenditure in the regions would lead to a net gain in both regional and national employment; but even a return to the levels of expenditure that were incurred when regional policy was at its height pales into insignificance when confronted with the size of the present problem in the United Kingdom. Another implication of the post-Keynesian theory is that a reduction in real wages, *ceteris paribus*, may only serve to exacerbate the situation by reducing effective demand.

A related, though logically independent, aspect of this approach is that manufacturing industry is subject to substantial economies of scale of both the static and dynamic variety (as demonstrated by the 'Verdoorn Law' — Verdoorn, 1949). This means that there are strong endogenous forces that lead to faster growing regions (countries) experiencing a greater growth of productivity than the more slowly growing areas. Thus, rapidly growing regions benefit from an increasing competitiveness and growth proceeds in the manner of cumulative causation. (However, it is not difficult to construct formalisations of such models that lead to (differing) equilibrium growth rates, or, indeed, to a convergence in the various regional growth rates if supply constraints become binding).

The purpose of this and a complementary paper (McCombie, 1988) is to contrast these two major paradigms with their markedly different policy implications. (We shall be mainly concerned with the broad theoretical issues rather than a detailed consideration of regional policy, *per se*. See Armstrong and Taylor, 1985, for a comprehensive discussion of the latter).

In this paper, the focus of attention is on the neoclassical approach while in McCombie (1988) the post-Keynesian explanation is considered. In particular, it will become apparent that these approaches are not just alternative models of the regional economy whose validity is capable of empirical resolution but rather that they represent distinctive and mutually exclusive views of the way the economic system functions.

The paper proceeds as follows. The one-sector neoclassical regional growth model, which is based on the aggregate production function, is outlined first. Next, we discuss the explanation that one of the causes of disparities in regional productivity growth is the eradication of an initial interregional misallocation of resources. It is also shown why, in the neoclassical approach, the cause of both regional and national involuntary unemployment is ascribed to real wages being too high. Following this, the impact of a progressive reduction in the degree of intraregional misallocation of resources on productivity growth is considered. Finally, we examine the role of the spatial diffusion of innovations in regional productivity growth, although the potential importance of this factor is not restricted to the neoclassical approach.

Neoclassical Theories of Regional Growth

The great attraction of the neoclassical paradigm is that a wide range of economic phenomena can be analysed deductively, often with determinate outcomes on the basis of a small number of axioms. Neoclassical regional growth theory rests firmly within this tradition, relying particularly on the assumptions underlying the concept of perfect competition. The appropriateness of this approach has not, however, been without its critics.

In particular, Richardson (1973, p. 22) argues that:

> 'The background assumptions of neoclassical growth theory are inapplicable to the regional economy. For instance, the full employment assumption is not usually relevant to regional economics since to a marked extent regional problems emerge because of substantial interregional differences in the degree of resource (and particularly labour) utilisation. Similarly, perfect competition cannot be assumed in regional economic analysis since space itself and the existence of transport costs limits competition; oligopoly, pure monopoly or monopolistic competition are much more appropriate market structures. Indeed, if we were to adopt neoclassical models in their pure unadulterated form there would be no such field as regional economics.'

Nevertheless, these strictures are analogous to those that are often levelled at aspatial neoclassical economic theory and adherents to the latter approach maintain that, notwithstanding the heroic assumptions, useful insights are still gained into the workings of the market economy from this method of analysis.[2]

It is, perhaps, not very surprising that neoclassical regional growth theory draws heavily on the one-sector neoclassical aggregate growth model, together with the allocation models of the (neoclassical) pure theory of international trade.

It would be unfair, though, to give the impression that regional models have been totally derivative. Although written over twenty years ago, Borts and Stein's (1964) book entitled *Economic Growth in a Free Market* still has claims to being the definitive statement of the neoclassical explanation of regional economic growth. This analysis anticipated a number of developments which were to occur in both growth theory and international trade theory.[3]

The One-Sector Regional Growth Model

The simplest neoclassical growth model uses a one-sector aggregate production function together with the aggregate marginal productivity theory of distribution. It is useful to begin the exposition with the assumption that each region is subject to the same Cobb-Douglas production function which exhibits constant returns to scale.[4]

$$Y_i = A_i e^{\phi t} K_i^{\alpha} L_i^{(1-\alpha)}, \qquad (1)$$

where Y, K and L are the levels of output, capital and labour, respectively; A is a constant; ϕ is the rate of exogenously given technical progress, which is assumed to be spatially invariant; α and $(1-\alpha)$ are the output elasticities of capital and labour which are assumed to be the same for each region and under perfect competition equal the relevant factor shares; and i denotes the region under consideration.

If initially it is assumed that there is no misallocation of resources, the growth of regional productivity ($\mathring{P}_i$) is determined by the rate of technical progress and the growth of the capital-labour ratio,

$$\mathring{P}_i = \phi + \alpha(\mathring{K}_i - \mathring{L}_i). \qquad (2)$$

[1] It has long been accepted by even the most ardent of neoclassical economists that even in an aspatial context their approach represents a drastic simplification of modern capitalist economies. But it is argued that the methodological basis of neoclassical economics rests firmly on instrumentalism as popularised and simplified by Friedman's (1953) famous essay on 'The Methodology of Positive Economics'. This has been interpreted as implying that the realism or otherwise of a model's assumptions is irrelevant. What is important is the predictive ability of the model and prediction is treated as synonymous with explanation. If this argument is accepted, it presents a very powerful methodological defence of the unrealistic assumptions of neoclassical economics. But see Katouzian (1980, Chapter 3) for a critique of instrumentalism.

It is only necessary to consider the superior predictive ability that 'naive' economic forecasting models (i.e., those based on extrapolating past trends) have sometimes had over those constructed from estimated economic relationships to realise that prediction and explanation are not identical and the former does not necessarily imply the latter.

[3] The intention of Borts and Stein was to develop a dynamic neoclassical theory of resource allocation rather than a regional growth model, *per se*. Their use of United States state data to test their models was, to a certain extent, incidental, being the most suitable for their purpose in that such data minimise the differences in socio-economic factors and trade barriers are absent.

[4] More general specifications such as the CES and translog production functions represent further refinements of the neoclassical production function. However, we shall confine our discussion to the Cobb-Douglas production function since this does not affect the substance of the argument.

In equilibrium, the regional rates of growth of real wages and of the rate of return are equal to the national average and are given by

$$\mathring{w}_i = \phi + \alpha(\mathring{K}_i - \mathring{L}_i) = \mathring{w}_n, \qquad (3a)$$

and

$$\mathring{r}_i = \phi + (\alpha - 1)(\mathring{K}_i - \mathring{L}_i) = \mathring{r}_n, \qquad (3b)$$

where $\mathring{w}$ and $\mathring{r}$ are the rates of growth of real wages and of the rate of return, respectively, and the subscript n denotes the national average.

The following relationships also hold in steady state growth with a given rate of interest:

$$\mathring{Y}_i = \frac{\phi}{(1-\alpha)} + \mathring{L}_i = \mathring{K}_i. \qquad (4)$$

The growth rates of factor payments are given by

$$\mathring{w}_i = \frac{\phi}{(1-\alpha)}. \qquad (5a)$$

and

$$\mathring{r}_i = 0. \qquad (5b)$$

Hence, the growth of wages is determined by the rate of exogenous technical progress. The rate of return is constant and is equal to the rate of interest.

There is no independent investment function and all savings are automatically invested. There is full utilization of all resources. Regional savings are assumed to be a constant proportion of regional output, $S_i = sY_i$, and the propensity to save is the same for all regions. However, regional savings may diverge from the regional level of investment. Following Borts and Stein (1964), let us assume that output growth varies between regions. The rate of growth of capital that can be financed from a region's own savings is given by $\mathring{K}_i' = sY_i/K_i$. Since, from the marginal productivity condition, $r = \alpha Y_i/K_i$, the internally financed growth of the capital stock may also be expressed as $\mathring{K}_i' = rs/\alpha$.

Since the requirement of steady state growth is a constant capital-output ratio, it follows that a region will import capital if its rate of growth of output exceeds rs/α. Furthermore, in a closed economy, the rate of interest will act in the (national) capital market to equilibrate the aggregate demand for, and supply of, the total of the regions' savings. While interregional capital flows will be observed, all regions will have the same growth of productivity and an identical growth rate of real wages. Capital will earn the same rate of return wherever it is invested. Differences in the growth of output are due ultimately to variations between regions in the growth of their labour force.

If regional productivity growth disparities are to be explained in terms of this framework then it is necessary to assume some initial violation of the Pareto optimality conditions. Taking this into account, the growth of productivity may be expressed as

$$\mathring{P}_i = \mu_i + \pi_i + \phi_i' + \phi + \alpha(\mathring{K}_i - \mathring{L}_i). \qquad (6)$$

In addition to the rate of exogenous technical progress, ϕ, and the steady state growth of capital deepening, $(\mathring{K}_i - \mathring{L}_i)$, which, from equation (4), is the same for all regions, productivity growth is determined by:

(i) μ_i, which is the growth of productivity due to the improved interregional allocation of resources;

(ii) π_i, which is the growth of productivity due to the improved allocation of resources between industries within a given region (i.e., the improved intraregional allocation of resources);

(iii) ϕ_i', which is the rate of technical progress in addition to ϕ and is due to the diffusion of innovations caused by differences in the level of technology to which the regions have access. In other words, the rate of technical progress will temporarily accelerate in a region as it acquires knowledge of more sophisticated techniques and adopts them. ϕ_i' is, by definition, equal to zero for the most technologically advanced region.

These three disequilibrium factors include any effects on productivity growth of a temporary divergence of the growth of the regional capital-labour ratio from its steady state value.

It is useful to examine these factors in greater

detail, commencing with the gains from the improved interregional allocation of resources.

Improvements in the Interregional Allocation of Resources

If factors of production are, for whatever reason, initially being used sub-optimally between regions (so that there are differences in the regional profit rates and real wages), any improvements in the efficiency with which these resources are used will register as an increase in productivity. Over time, with the gradual spatial integration of labour and financial markets and the reduction in impediments to the functioning of the market mechanism, the gains in productivity growth from this source will diminish as the national economy approaches a Pareto optimal allocation of resources between regions. This temporary acceleration in productivity growth is the result of non-optimal growth in the past.

In many countries, the interregional transfer of resources is inextricably bound up with the intersectoral movement of labour, especially from agriculture to industry. The latter has a spatial counterpart because the importance of these two sectors varies considerably between regions. McCombie (1980) found, for example, that, under certain assumptions, well over one-third of the postwar productivity growth of those advanced countries with a large agricultural sector (most notably Japan, West Germany, France and Italy) could be attributed to this movement from the low productivity (agricultural) to the high productivity (industrial) sector. On the other hand, this has proved to be insignificant in the case of the United States and the United Kingdom, since both countries have a highly commercialised agricultural sector exhibiting a high level of productivity. Moreover, in the case of the United Kingdom, agriculture only employs 3 per cent of the total labour force so the relative size of any transfer would be small. Thus, it is likely that any gains from the improved interregional allocation of resources are likely to be minimal in the United Kingdom and it will be argued below that this is indeed true. However, possible gains may be considerably bigger in Japan and Continental Europe.

A simple case of the spatial misallocation of resources may be demonstrated by considering an economy which comprises of two regions designated A and B. It is assumed that the regions produce an identical commodity using the same technology. (There are, of course, other assumptions that could be made such as the regions produce different products and have different production functions. Our intention, however, is merely to outline the main elements of this approach rather than to discuss the various specific results. See, for example, Carlberg, 1981). It is also assumed that the size of the total labour force and the capital stock is fixed and there is no technical progress. Fig. 1a represents the familiar Edgeworth-Bowley box diagram which shows the distribution of the factors of production between the two regions together with the isoquants and the contract curve. Because we have assumed that both regions have the same production function, the contract 'curve' is, in fact, the diagonal between O_A and O_B. Initially, for some reason, there is a misallocation of resources with production occurring at the point a which is off the contract

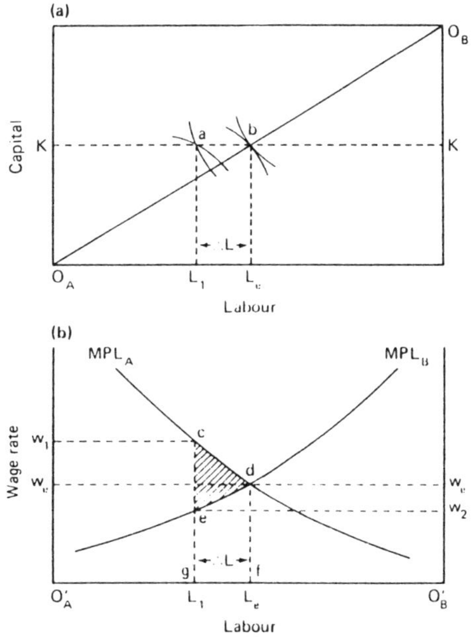

Fig. 1. The interregional misallocation of labour.

curve. Region A has O_AL_1 of the labour force while the rest is employed in Region B. Similarly, O_AK of the capital stock is allocated to Region A with the remainder being in Region B. All factors of production are fully employed.

Fig. 1b is a cross-section of Fig. 1a taken along the dotted line KK. It depicts the marginal product curves of labour of Region A and Region B (namely, MPL_A and MPL_B) given the fixed allocation of total capital stock between the two regions. Because of the fixity of the capital stock, the regional marginal product of labour curves decline as more labour is employed in Region A and Region B, measured from O_A' and O_B'. Under profit maximising conditions, entrepreneurs will employ the amount of labour where the marginal product of labour equals the real wage rate. Initially, the wage in Region A is given by w_1 and this exceeds that of Region B which is w_2. Conversely, the profit rate in Region A is lower than that of Region B. The misallocation of resources is eradicated over time as the wage differential is reduced. It is assumed that the capital stock is immobile so that ΔL of the labour force migrates from Region B to Region A as, in terms of Fig. 1a, production moves from point a to b. Point b is efficient, being on the contract curve. (See Neary, 1978, especially pp. 496–499, for a discussion of the more general case where there are two industries whose production functions have different factor intensities and both capital and labour adjust as the wage differential changes).

In Fig. 1b, the area under the marginal product curve of labour of Region A from O_A' to L_1 is equal to the region's output. The area under the MPL_B curve from L_1 to O_B' likewise measures the output of Region B. In equilibrium, $O_A'L_e$ of the labour force is employed in Region A, L_eO_B' is employed in Region B and the wage rate is w_e. Hence, it may be seen that the net gain in output due to the spatial reallocation of labour from Region B to Region A is the area cde. An interesting question is what is likely to be the order of magnitude of this gain? Some approximate calculations have been made by Brown (1972, pp. 245–249) who suggests that in the case of the United Kingdom the maximum potential gain is likely to be relatively small, a result that is in accord with the so-called 'law of small triangles'. (This 'law' comes from the fact that the losses due to other static misallocations of resources — most notably due to monopoly or tariffs — are also generally an insignificant proportion of GDP.) To estimate the loss, Brown assumes that, in the area of interest, the marginal product of labour schedules are linear and the area of the triangle cde is equal to $1/2\,(w_1 - w_2)\Delta L$.

While data are available directly for the values of w_1 and w_2, ΔL has to be inferred from the elasticity of the wage rate with respect to employment (which is assumed to take the same numerical value in both regions and which is calculated from a Cobb-Douglas production function). If it is assumed that the two regions have a labour force of ten million employees each and wages are 5 per cent higher in region A, the necessary transfer of labour from B to A is three quarters of a million workers and the gain in output is insignificant, being less than 0.1 per cent of GDP.

It may be that the regional wage differential is not due to labour being misallocated relative to capital but occurs because both labour and capital are misallocated with respect to natural resources, broadly defined. This would necessitate both labour and capital being reallocated and the interregional transfer of labour would be larger than in the previous example, perhaps by a factor of three or four according to Brown (1972). This would mean that the gains from the improved allocation of resources would be commensurably higher and may be as much as five times as large as the original estimate. Nevertheless, the gain in ouput would still be small being less than 0.5 per cent of GDP.

However, the gain in output may be much larger in those countries where regional productivity disparities are significantly greater than in the United Kingdom. This is likely to occur especially where some of the regions are dominated by a large inefficient agricultural sector. Moreover, the use of regional wage differences to estimate the gain in output will lead to an underestimate if rural wages are equal to the average rather than the marginal product of labour. (The former often is found to be the case where the production unit is the family farm.)

This situation is depicted in Fig. 2 where it is assumed that Region B is predominantly rural and the wage is determined with reference to the average product of labour curve (APL_B). In Region A, the wage equals the marginal product of labour.

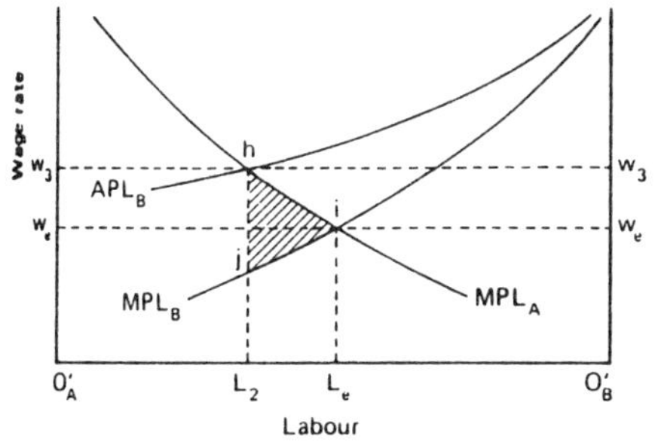

Fig. 2. The interregional misallocation of labour when the wage in Region B equals the average product of labour.

Let us assume that initially the wages in the two regions are identical being equal to w_3. Nevertheless, this does not mean that the gains from the improved allocation of resources have been exhausted.

The initial value of regional output in Fig. 2 is the area under the relevant marginal product of labour curves from O_A' to L_2 in the case of Region A and L_2 to O_B' in the case of Region B. However, in the case of Region B, the total wage bill comprises the whole of the regional output (although the distinction between wages and profits becomes blurred in the case of family farm income).

With the development of a commercialised agricultural sector with labour now being paid its marginal product, it can be seen from Fig. 2 that the equilibrium outcome will be that wages fall in *both* regions to w_e as labour migrates from Region B to Region A. The increase in total output is given by the area hij.

Since 1973, unemployment rates in all regions of the United Kingdom have risen dramatically and it may be legitimately argued that regional unemployment rates are now a more serious problem than regional disparities in wage rates. Within the neoclassical paradigm the explanation for this phenomenon is to assume that the value of the real wage is too high in all regions. (A substantial proportion of the increase in unemployment may also be attributed to an increase in the regional 'natural rate of unemployment'.) This position is shown diagramatically in Fig. 3. The initial loss of output due to the regional wage differential when labour is fully employed is again given by the triangle cde and is associated with regional wage rates of w_1 and w_2. If, for some reason due, for example, to the increased bargaining power of organised labour, the wage rate rises in both regions simultaneously so that the new wage rates are w_4 and w_5, the total reduction in output below the maximum potential is given by the area ndklm. $O_a'L_3$ and L_4O_B' of the total labour force are employed in Region A and Region B, respectively, with the remainder unemployed. (It is assumed that the capital stock is malleable and hence is still fully utilized). If we assume that, as at present in the United Kingdom, the level of output is some fifteen per cent below its potential level then it is clear that these losses are substantially larger than any gains that could be achieved by the improved spatial allocation of resources. (See Brecher, 1974, for a discussion of the impact of a minimum real wage in the context of the pure theory of international trade.)

This brings us to the paradox mentioned in the introduction to the paper that although in absolute (but not in relative) terms regional unemployment disparities have never been greater in the postwar period, the regional problem has become synonymous with the national unemployment problem. The most effective way to reduce regional disparities is to increase national output, which, since we are dealing with 'classical unemployment', must be accomplished through a fall in the real wage. It is implicitly assumed in Fig. 3 that the supply of labour is inelastic with respect to the wage rate, although this does not affect the substance of the argument. The more general case is discussed in McCombie (1988). (In that paper, the neoclassical argument is outline in greater detail and is contrasted with the post-Keynesian explanation of the cause of regional unemployment. The latter holds that such unemployment is due to the level of effective demand being too low.)

Testing the predictions of the single-sector model has suffered, until recently, from the dearth of data on regional profit rates and indices for the capital stock and most tests have been of an indirect nature. However, the early work of Borts and Stein (1964) showed that the single-sector model performed badly. An implication of the neoclassical model is that the low-wage regions should experience the fastest growth rates of both capital and the capital-labour ratio. Furthermore, the low-wage regions should also achieve the fastest growth of wages as a result of the increasing capital-labour ratio. However, statistical tests showed that the theory was refuted in two of the three time periods considered

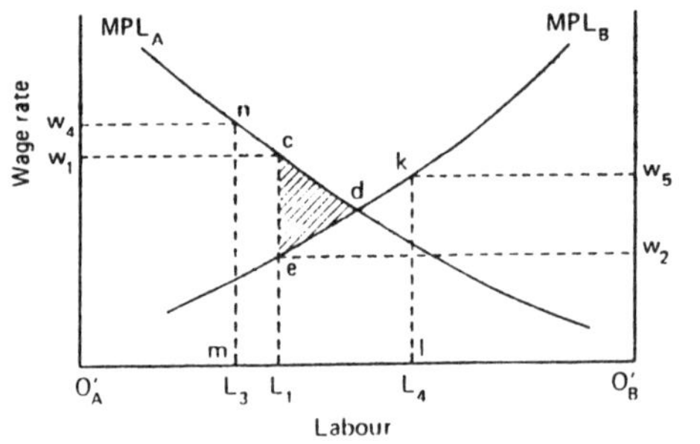

Fig. 3. Neoclassical regional unemployment.

by Borts and Stein, namely, 1919–29 and 1948–53. It was only compatible with the data for the period 1929–48. Given the tendency of both advocates and critics of the neoclassical approach to concentrate on the single-sector model, it is worth quoting Borts and Stein on the implications. 'The conclusion of this statistical section is that the popular aggregative theory has very little predictive accuracy and that one should place little confidence in it as an explanation of regional growth and maturity' (1964, p. 55).[5] Borts and Stein argue that the differential economic performance of the United States states can only be understood primarily in terms of the intraregional improvement of resources within any particular region.

Improvements in the Intraregional Allocation of Resources

The analysis of the gains achieved from the improved intraregional allocation of resources is very similar to that outlined above except attention is now confined to the allocation of labour and capital between two industries or sectors within the region that are assumed to produce the total regional output. The framework of discussion is again analogous to the neoclassical pure theory of trade except mobility of the factors of production is permitted between regions. It is convenient to use the model of Borts and Stein (1964, Chapter 7) to demonstrate this approach, although once again a modification of the assumptions will alter the exact results derived from the analysis. However, Borts and Stein argue that their model is a plausible explanation of the historical economic performance of the regions of the United States.

We begin by considering an individual region which produces two commodities, X, an export good and Z, a domestic good. There is also an imported good, M, which is not produced in the region. (Capital goods are also imported at a constant price.) Sector X is assumed to be capital-intensive while sector Z is labour-intensive. This assumption is crucial for the results that follow but it is argued by Borts and Stein that it is not unrealistic, since most exports are manufactured commodities which are produced with a higher capital-labour ratio than domestic goods which tend to be predominantly services. The region is small compared with the size of the remainder of the national economy and so the price of X is taken as a constant and is determined outside the region. (Hence, the demand for X is perfectly elastic.) All resources are fully employed. There is, however, a misallocation of resources between the sectors caused by an initial money wage differential, $W_X = \rho W_Z$, where W is the money wage and ρ is greater than unity. In other words, it is assumed that initially the wage in the tradable goods sector exceeds that paid in the domestic sector. (In the United States the value of ρ empirically has often been between 1.2 and 2.0.) 'The differential has been generated by labor market immobilities and by lagged adjustment of labor supply to new job opportunities. The lags are due perhaps to tastes, ignorance, and the lack of training' (Borts and Stein, 1964, p. 130). It is further assumed that there is a perfectly competitive interregional market for capital and there is no technical change. All these assumptions ensure that for sector X, the capital-labour ratio, the wage and the profit rate are constant.

If all prices, the rate of interest and the intersectoral wage differential do not alter, then the region will grow at an equilibrium rate determined by the growth of the labour supply. Growth will be balanced in that the two sectors will retain a constant share of both the labour force and regional output.

[5] A more recent test of the single-sector neoclassical aggregate model by regression analysis undertaken by Smith (1975) finds the model performs better.

However, in order to analyse the consequences of a decline in the wage differential it is convenient to assume that the labour force is constant.

The consequences of an initial wage differential for the allocation of resources may again be seen in terms of the Edgeworth-Bowley box shown in Fig. 4 where the corners of the initial box are given by O_X and O_Z. Production is originally given by the point p which lies on the 'inefficient contract curve' given by the dotted line between O_X and O_Z. On this curve there is the constant intersectoral wage differential, $W_X = \rho W_Z$, while the rate of return is the same in the two industries. The solid curve between O_X and O_Z is the Pareto efficient contract curve.

It is assumed that over time the value of ρ decreases exogenously until it takes a value of unity at which point the regional economy is efficient. It is useful to trace the consequences of this in two parts. First, the economy moves along the rigid capital-labour ray of sector X (namely, the line $(K/L)_X'$) from p to q. At point q the economy is on the efficient contract curve. This reallocation of resources (which Borts and Stein term a substitution effect) has the effect of contracting the output of the export sector while giving rise to an expansion of the domestic sector.

The value of regional output has increased since the region is now on its Pareto optimal production possibility curve. Since the size of the labour force is fixed, regional productivity will have increased as a result of the adjustment process.

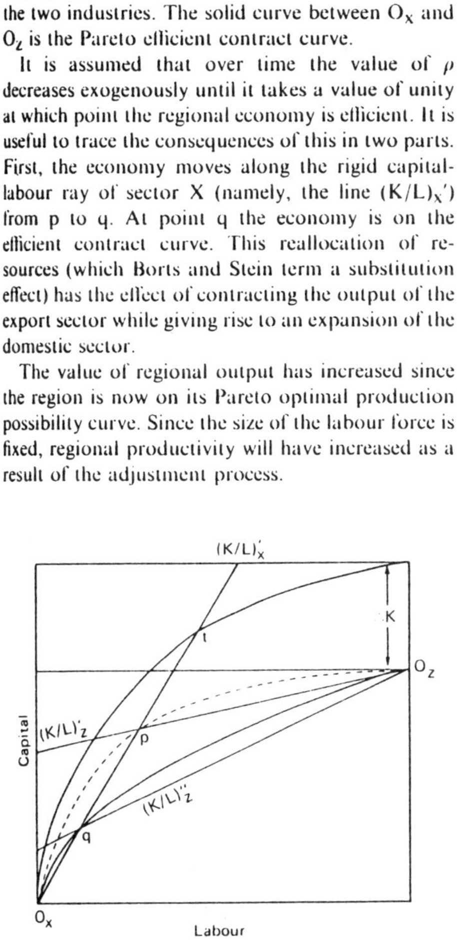

Fig. 4. The intraregional misallocation of resources.

However, this is not the end of the story and we come to the second part, *viz.*, the expansion effect. As the output of Z increases so its price rises and it will be higher relative to the price of the imported capital good. This leads to an increase in the total capital stock of the region (denoted by ΔK in Fig. 4) and an expansion of the dimensions of the Edgeworth-Bowley box. The final equilibrium allocation of resources is given by the point t which is on the contract curve of the expanded Edgeworth-Bowley box. Borts and Stein prove that the share of labour employed in sector Z has decreased while the output of sector X has increased. It will be remembered that there has been no change in the money wage rate of sector X since both the capital-labour ratio of the sector and the price of X are constant. What has occurred is that the wage rate of sector Z has increased until the wages in the two sectors are equal.

An increase in the demand for exports may also be analysed within this framework (Borts and Stein, 1964, Chapter 7, and Armstrong and Taylor, 1985, pp. 59–63). We shall not discuss this in detail but, briefly, the rise in demand is reflected in a rise in the price of the export good. This results in an increase in the value marginal product of both capital and labour. The former leads to an increase in capital accumulation which raises the capital-labour ratio of the export sector. This reduces the rate of return until it again equals the cost of borrowing. The increase in the capital-labour ratio causes a further rise in the value marginal product of labour. If we assume perfect mobility of labour between regions and sectors and no misallocation of resources there will be an increase in the employment of labour until both the intersectoral and interregional equality of wages is re-established.

Finally, there is an important difference between the predictions of the single-sector regional model, where it is assumed that there is one product produced for the national market, and the two-sector regional economy. In the former, an increase in the regional capital-labour ratio will be accompanied by a fall in the rate of return and a rise in the real wage.

However, this does not necessarily follow in the two-sector case. Even when all resources are efficiently allocated, it is possible that an increase in the overall capital-labour ratio of the region may not lead to a rise in the capital-labour ratio of the two sectors, and, hence, to a rise in the wage rate. For example, an increase in the stock of capital may be accompanied by an increase in the share of regional output produced by the capital-intensive sector such that there is, in fact, a decline in the capital-labour ratios of both sectors. In this case, an increase in the aggregate regional capital-labour ratio would be accompanied by a fall in the regional wage rate.

In the two-sector regional model, it is no longer the case that capital and labour will necessarily flow in opposite directions, as in the single-sector model, with capital moving to regions with a low capital-labour ratio and labour migrating to where the capital-labour ratio is high. For example, it is possible that, under certain circumstances, both capital and labour will move to the same region.

As in the case of the interregional misallocation of resources, the two-sector model may be extended to incorporate regional unemployment by introducing a wage rate that is above the competitive value in both sectors, although this argument will not be pursued here.

Regional Productivity Growth and the Spatial Diffusion of Innovations

Once an allowance has been made for the contribution to regional productivity growth of improvements in the allocation of resources and the impact of the growth of the capital-labour ratio, a 'residual' remains. In the 'Growth Accounting' exercises this is usually interpreted as 'exogenous technical progress' although it also captures the effect of measurement errors. (See, for example, Denison, 1967.)

If at any moment, however, there are regional differences in the level of technology, part of technical progress may be the result of the diffusion of new techniques from the relatively advanced to the more backward areas. The explanation for this is as follows. In the early stages of the development of a particular country when the space economy is not fully integrated, the friction of distance prevents equal access to the same 'blue-print' of techniques. If there are economies of scale in invention, then the prosperous regions which are able to devote a large volume of investment to research and development may have been able to develop a progressively more advanced technology than the poorer, often peripheral, regions. This advantage, however, tends to disappear with the development of a single national market. The increasingly oligopolistic nature of industry results in the relatively backward regions gaining increasing access to this advanced technology. This leads to the backward regions experiencing a temporary increase in their rate of productivity growth with a resulting convergence in regional productivity levels.

This argument assumes that there exist techniques of production which, if known in the peripheral regions, would immediately be adopted and raise the level of productivity. In other words, the effect (in a simple malleable capital model) would be to shift the production function upwards and act as an increase in technical progress. In a vintage model, this new process would be embodied in investment and so the increased rate of technical progress would be a function of the level of gross investment.

While the hypothesis of the importance of the spatial diffusion of innovations in explaining regional growth disparities is by no means confined to the neoclassical paradigm, it will be noticed that the cause is similar to market failure. In this case, the failure is due to the supposed fact that information is not instantaneously available everywhere but takes time to diffuse. As this is corrected over time to the extent that the rate of diffusion increases, there will be equilibrating effects similar to those generated by the improved allocation of the more tangible inputs. Hence, it is convenient to discuss the diffusion of innovations at this juncture.

At the moment, there seems to be little agreement as to just how important empirically the diffusion process is in regional growth, at least so far as the advanced countries are concerned. For example, Dixon and Thirlwall (1975, Chapter 6) find no evidence of regional differences in exogenous technical progress for the United Kingdom. Borts and Stein (1964, p. 8) consider that a 'new manufacturing process or a new machine is, under competition, available to all'. Brown (1972) in his detailed study of the United Kingdom regional economy did not consider that the topic was of sufficient importance to warrant discussion. Richardson (1973, p. 113), on the other hand, thinks this neglect is misplaced. 'The assumption that new technical knowledge is freely available to all except for the barriers imposed by imperfectly competitive markets runs contrary to empirical observation. Instead, the diffusion of innovation over space occurs according to predictable patterns which fail, at least so far as entrepreneurial as opposed to household innovations are concerned, to penetrate all conceivable locations.'[6]

Certainly, ever since Hägerstrand's (1952) influential study of agricultural innovations, substantial evidence has accumulated to show that many innovations do not appear randomly over the space economy. Rather, they both take a contiguous pattern with diffusion from a centre into the surrounding area and also flow down the urban hierarchy with the time to adoption inversely related to city size. One problem, though, with many of the earlier studies is that the phenomena for which it was possible to obtain data on both the time of appearance and the spatial co-ordinates have very little relevance for the process of economic growth. In other words, they tended to be product rather than process innovations. Typical examples included television stations, shopping plazas, and Rotary Clubs. More recent studies have, however, concentrated on the diffusion of innovations that are of greater relevance for economic growth. See, for example, Gibbs and Edwards (1983), Thwaites (1983) and Thwaites and Oakey (1985).

At the aspatial level, there are numerous studies of industrial processes that also show that new inventions are not immediately adopted by every firm. Often the percentage of firms which have innovated follows a logistic curve over time, a path that is replicated in many spatial studies.

At this point, it is worth emphasising a matter that does not always seem to have been fully appreciated in the literature on the spatial diffusion of innovations. This is that the existence of differences between regions, countries or firms in the speed of adoption of best-practice techniques or the fact that there are regional disparities in the age-structure of machinery does not necessarily imply differences in the knowledge of best-practice technology.

It is possible (indeed, likely) that innovations will diffuse over time as a result of profit maximisation even if there is perfect information concerning the availability of all possible techniques.

The pioneering study that modelled the economic forces affecting the adoption of new techniques is the vintage capital approach of Salter (1966). The rationale of his analysis may be summed up in Jevons' dictum that 'in commerce, bygones are forever bygones and we are always starting with a view to future utility.' Thus, once a piece of equipment has been purchased, the only costs related to this machinery relevant to the decision of the entrepreneur as to whether or not it should be scrapped are, after installation, the variable costs of running the equipment (i.e., the cost of labour and materials, etc.). On the other hand, *ex ante*, the decision whether or not to buy the machine is a function of the total costs of production with the equipment (i.e., including amortisation and interest payments). A new technique will be only introduced if the total costs involved in its use are less than the variable costs of producing with the machine it is to replace; and an important element of such costs is the real wage rate. At any moment, there will be a difference between the average productivity of an industry and the productivity of the best-practice technique. The lower the regional wage relative to the price of investment, *ceteris paribus*, the greater this difference will be; the average age of the capital equipment will also be older. Even substantial differences between the average productivity of an industry in different regions do not imply that one area has access to a superior technology if there are exogenous differences in the regional wage rates. Likewise, if it is found that a region has a larger proportion of firms adopting a particular innovation, it does not necessarily mean that it is in any sense more aware of the existence of this particular technique.

It should be noted that if there are, indeed, regional differences in the level of technology, this is likely to be reflected in differences in the level of productivity and in real wages. The Salter argument, however, shows that the existence of such differences in productivity or real wages does not necessarily imply that some regions (or nations) have access to a more advanced technology compared with other areas.

Generally speaking studies by economists have tended, perhaps not surprisingly, to emphasize the economic reasons for diffusion, while others, such as geographers, have placed greater emphasis on the informational causes of diffusion. Griliches (1957), for example, in his classic study of the diffusion of hybrid corn in the United States attributed the date

[6] Richardson (1973) provides a useful if now somewhat inevitably dated survey of the literature.

of the introduction of hybrid varieties of corn in a particular state and the speed of adoption to the degree of profitability and economic forces.

Berry (1972), on the other hand, provides a good example of a non-economic model (there is no role for profitability or relative prices in his approach) that seeks to explain differential growth rates in terms of the filtering of information down the urban hierarchy.

Berry's analysis is interesting, perhaps not so much for its specific results as for the method it typifies.

After generating a rank-size hierarchy of city sizes through a maximum entropy procedure, Berry proceeds to consider a probabilistic model whereby innovations diffuse down this hierarchy until a threshold level is reached. The adoption lag at a particular city is postulated to be a function of the information flows between it and other cities in the hierarchy which have already received (adopted) the innovation. The mechanism draws heavily on diffusion models borrowed from the physical sciences including the gravity model. A city's (or a region's) growth is a function of the length of time before it receives the innovation because the impact of an innovation in increasing income, and productivity, is assumed to decline with time. (If this were not the case, a constant lag with a steady stream of innovations would not cause differences in growth rates.) The benefits of the innovation are also assumed to spread out contiguously from the adopting centre. The implication to be drawn from this approach is that in order to raise a region's growth rate the length of the innovation lag should be reduced and spread forces encouraged.

An indirect empirical test of the model is undertaken by examining the diffusion of television stations (and TV sets) through the United States over the period 1940 to 1965. The proportion of cities adopting a television station follows the familiar logistic pattern over time. The model is tested by the use of regression analysis to determine how successfully the date of adoption is explained by a number of variables proxying information flows. These include the population size of a city (to capture hierarchical diffusion) and the population potential (to capture contiguous diffusion). A number of other explanatory variables representing demand factors are also included. The model is successful in that there is a significant statistical relationship with the smaller cities opening TV stations at later dates than larger cities as predicted by the theory.

This analysis, however, clearly demonstrates the problem outlined above in distinguishing between the effects of non-economic and economic forces. A similar pattern could equally be explained by economic factors even though information about the availability and costs involved of operating a TV station were not spatially restricted. A logistic adoption curve could also be generated by assuming that over time the cost of operating a TV station falls because of technical progress. Consequently, immediately after the initial development of TV stations with their high costs, only those cities with a large population (and, hence, a sufficiently large advertising revenue) were able to support a station. However, with both costs falling and *per capita* income rising over time, TV stations became progressively economically viable in smaller and smaller cities leading to the observed diffusion pattern.

This example clearly shows that it is not sufficient to assume that the observed existence of the diffusion of innovations necessarily means that they are a significant factor in explaining differences in regional growth.

McCombie (1982) attempted to test the importance of the diffusion of innovations on regional productivity growth by developing an approach suggested by Gomulka (1971). Gomulka argued that, in an international context, the part of a country's productivity growth that is due to the diffusion of advanced technology will be a function of what he terms the 'technological gap'. This is defined as $(P^* - P_i)/P_i$ where P^* and P_i are the levels of productivity in the most advanced country (which, in the postwar period, is the United States) and the country under consideration. The hypothesis is that, for the advanced countries, the larger the technological gap, the greater the potential for the diffusion of innovations. Hence, if diffusion is an important factor then productivity growth should be positively related to the technological gap.[7] However, the

[7] In an earlier stage of development (or in the case of the present less developed countries) diffusion lags may well increase and lead to greater regional disparities in productivity levels. In the case of the less developed countries, the dual nature of the economy may encourage this since the small modern industrial sector may be based on highly sophisticated techniques of production imported from the advanced countries. The traditional sector will not have the capacity to learn of and adopt these methods of production, with the result that differences in regional productivity levels will increase over time.

reservations expressed above about the use of such a proxy for the level of technology should be borne in mind.

McCombie (1982) used growth rate data for total manufacturing industry drawn from the United States states for the period 1963–1973. Various specifications of a production function, expressed in terms of growth rates, were estimated using these cross-regional data, and a proxy for the differences in the level of technology was included as a regressor to test the diffusion hypothesis. (The proxy was an index of the ratio of the level of total factor productivity of a particular state to that of the technologically most advanced state. The ratio of the relevant levels of labour productivity was also used but this made little difference to the interpretation of the results.) The coefficient of the 'technological ratio' proved to be statistically insignificant in all the estimated specifications. Thus, within the limitations of the model, it appears that the diffusion of innovations is not an important determinant of productivity growth in an advanced country.

A related weakness of this type of empirical approach is that it is within a malleable capital rather than the vintage (Salter) framework mentioned above. The former suffers from the disadvantage that any new technique will, in practice, be embodied in investment and may have little, if any, impact on the efficiency of machines already installed.

Gomulka and Sylwestrowicz (1976) have developed a vintage approach which attempts to quantify the gains in productivity growth, in an international context, resulting from the use of technologically more advanced imported capital equipment. The model is used to estimate the benefits of the 'direct effect of embodied diffusion' which is the additional productivity obtained by using an imported capital good over and above what the productivity would have been if domestic machinery of the same vintage had been used. They also calculated the extent to which the use of imported machinery in the domestic capital goods industry leads to domestically manufactured machinery of better design. This is termed the 'indirect effect of embodied diffusion'. If the estimates of Gomulka and Sylwestrowicz are largely correct, diffusion would seem to explain much of the international disparities in the growth of productivity.

In principle, a vintage approach to diffusion may be applied to the regional case. As a simple example, consider the case of a peripheral region that has a stock of capital of various vintages which is comprised of domestically produced equipment and more efficient imported machinery.

Two crucial assumptions of this approach are (i) the existence of constant returns to scale and (ii) any differences in the productivity obtained by using machines of a given vintage requiring the same labour input are due solely to differences in the level of technology embodied in the equipment. These are not innocuous assumptions since they rule out, *ab initio*, all other major explanations of disparities in productivity. These include differences in the degree of overmanning and restrictive practices, in the efficiency of management and in the effect of dynamic and static increasing returns to scale.

Regional output from capital equipment of vintage t is assumed to be given by

$$Y_t = (\theta_t K_t)^{\alpha} L_t^{(1-\alpha)}, \tag{7}$$

and the level of productivity is

$$P_t = (\theta_t K_t / L_t)^{\alpha}, \tag{8}$$

where θ_t is a measure of the technical efficiency of the capital stock of vintage t. (It is assumed that there is no disembodied technical progress.)

The capital stock of vintage t consists of domestically produced and imported capital goods, namely K_{Dt} and K_{Mt}, respectively.

Thus,

$$\theta_t K_t = \theta_{Dt} K_{Dt} + \theta_{Mt} K_{Mt} \tag{9}$$

and, by assumption, $\theta_{Mt} > \theta_{Dt}$.

Equation (9) may be written alternatively as

$$\theta_t K_t = \theta_{Dt}(K_{Dt} + K_{Mt}) + (\theta_{Mt} - \theta_{Dt})K_{Mt}, \tag{10}$$

where $(\theta_{Mt} - \theta_{Dt}) > 0$.

Consequently, the productivity obtained using machinery of vintage t may be expressed as

$$P_t = \left\{ \left[\frac{\theta_{Dt}(K_{Dt} + K_{Mt})}{L_t} \right] + \left[\frac{(\theta_{Mt} - \theta_{Dt})K_{Mt}}{L_t} \right] \right\}^{\alpha}. \tag{11}$$

If there was no difference in the level of technology of the imported and the domestically produced capital goods, the level of productivity would be a function of only the expression in the first square brackets in equation (11). The additional productivity resulting from the diffusion effect due to the more advanced level of technology of the imported machinery is thus a function of the expression in the second square brackets. It is possible to use this framework, with suitable aggregation of the various vintages, to calculate the contribution that embodied diffusion makes to regional productivity growth. It is necessary to have data on the size of the imported capital stock and proxies for the technological indices of the domestically produced and imported capital goods so that the relevant growth rates may be calculated. One measure of the level of technology of the imported machinery is, for example, the observed level of labour efficiency obtained by using this equipment in the advanced region. It must be assumed that, for this to be the case, the same level of labour efficiency would be achieved with the use of this machinery in the less advanced region.

The difficulty, in practice, is, of course, that there are no data sources comparable to international trade statistics from which estimates of the value of capital goods imported from other regions could be made. Nevertheless, equation (11) is useful in not only theoretically incorporating the diffusion process but also enabling us to clarify further the implications of a crucial assumption underlying the diffusion explanation of productivity growth.

It is implicitly assumed that the superior efficiency of the capital goods imported into the region is not captured in their value. In a competitive situation, however, this greater efficiency would be capitalized into the price of the imported capital equipment. Under these circumstances, there would be no difference between θ_{Mt} and θ_{Dt} and the component in the second square brackets of equation (11) would be equal to zero. The difference in technology would be reflected in the value of K_{Mt} in the first square brackets of equation (11). Any increase in the amount of capital imported from the advanced region would only increase productivity to the extent that it augmented the value of the regional capital stock and would not represent a costless increase in efficiency. This, of course, merely substantiates the earlier argument that the existence of the diffusion of new techniques does not necessarily mean a costless increase in regional productivity growth. Any observed differences in the regional level of productivity obtained using the same value per worker of capital of a given vintage would thus be due to the efficiency with which this capital equipment was used in the various regions rather than differences in the level of technology, *per se*. Given the highly oligopolistic nature of modern economies with the hundred largest industrial firms typically producing about half of the output, it would be surprising if imperfect information with regard to production techniques could account for anything but a small part of regional differences in productivity growth. However, this surmise must, to a certain extent, await the results of future research.

Evidence from the work of Schmookler (1966) suggests that much of the pattern of invention (at least in so far as it is reflected in patents) is demand-led. A faster rate of growth and a greater confidence in expected growth rates leads to both a greater willingness to undertake research and development and to an increase in risk-taking. A faster rate of growth of output will, through the impact of learning by doing and dynamic economies of scale, cause a greater growth of productivity. The latter is thus to a large extent endogenous to the growth process being determined by the growth of output. Such models that stress the process of cumulative causation are considered in the complementary paper (McCombie, 1988).

Concluding comments

In this paper, it has been shown how the neoclassical approach explains disparities in regional productivity growth as the result of the progressive eradication of both interregional and intraregional misallocation of resources. These are caused by market imperfections that resulted in differences between regions (and also between industries within any one region) in wage rates and/or profit rates. The implication is that the free play of market forces should lead to a general convergence in the level of regional productivity. Likewise, substantial differences in regional wage rates should not persist indefinitely.

The existence of regional unemployment may be incorporated into this approach by assuming that the real wage is too high and this is again the result of market imperfections such as the excessive bargaining power of organised labour. The policy prescription that may be derived from this approach is that a necessary and sufficient condition for a reduction in the regional level of unemployment is for the real wage to fall towards its market clearing level.

It was also suggested that, for the advanced countries at least, it is not clear that the diffusion of innovations has necessarily been a major cause of differences in regional productivity growth.

The most effective way of assessing the explanatory power of a particular paradigm is to compare it with an alternative. In a subsequent paper (McCombie, 1988) we discuss one such competing paradigm, namely, the post-Keynesian theory of regional growth and unemployment, which provides a marked contrast to the approach discussed here.

REFERENCES

ARMSTRONG, H. and TAYLOR, J. (1985). *Regional Economics and Policy*. Oxford: Philip Allan.

BORTS, G. H. and STEIN, J. L. (1964). *Economic Growth in a Free Market*. New York: Columbia University Press.

BERRY, B. J. L. (1972). 'Hierarchical diffusion: the basis of developmental filtering and spread in a system of growth centers'. In Hansen, N. M. (ed.), *Growth Centers in Regional Economic Development*. New York: The Free Press.

BRECHER, R. A. (1974). 'Minimum wage rates and the pure theory of international trade'. *Quarterly Journal of Economics*, Vol. 88, pp. 98–116.

BROWN, A. J. (1972). *The Framework of Regional Economics in the United Kingdom*. Cambridge: Cambridge University Press.

CARLBERG, M. (1981). 'A neoclassical model of interregional economic growth', *Regional Science and Urban Economics*, Vol. 11, pp. 191–203.

DENISON, E. (1967). *Why Growth Rates Differ: Postwar Experience in Nine Countries*. Washington, D.C.: The Brookings Institution.

DIXON, R. J. and THIRLWALL, A. P. (1975). *Regional Growth and Unemployment in the United Kingdom*. London: Macmillan.

FRIEDMAN, M. (1953). 'The methodology of positive economics'. In *Essays in Positive Economics*. Chicago: Chicago University Press.

GIBBS, D. C. and EDWARDS, A. (1983). 'Some preliminary evidence for the interregional diffusion of selected process innovations'. In Gillespie, A. (ed.), *Technological Change and Regional Development*. London: Pion.

GOMULKA, S. (1971). *Inventive Activity, Diffusion, and the Stages of Economic Growth*. Aarhus: Aarhus University, Institute of Economics.

GOMULKA, S. and SYLWESTROWICZ, J. D. (1976). 'Import-led growth, theory and estimation'. In Altmann, F. L., Kyn, O. and Wagener, H. J. (eds.), *On the Measurement of Factor Productivities*. Gottingen: Vandenhoeck and Ruprecht.

GRILICHES, Z. (1957). 'Hybrid corn: an exploration in the economics of technical change', *Econometrica*, Vol. 25, pp. 501–522.

HÄGERSTRAND, T. (1952). *'The Propagation of Innovation Waves'*. Lund Studies in Geography, B, Human Geography, Vol. 4.

KATOUZIAN, M. A. H. (1980). *Ideology and Method in Economics*. London: Macmillan.

MOORE, B. and RHODES, J. (1982). 'A second great depression in the U.K. regions: can anything be done?' *Regional Studies*, Vol. 16, pp. 323–333.

MCCOMBIE, J. S. L. (1980). 'On the quantitative importance of Kaldor's laws', *Bulletin of Economic Research*, Vol. 32, pp. 102–112.

MCCOMBIE, J. S. L. (1982). 'How important is the spatial diffusion of innovations in explaining regional growth disparities?' *Urban Studies*, Vol. 19, pp. 377–382.

MCCOMBIE, J. S. L. (1988). 'A synoptic view of regional growth and unemployment: II — the post-Keynesian theory', *Urban Studies*, forthcoming.

NEARY, J. P. (1978). 'Short-run capital specificity and the pure theory of international trade', *Economic Journal*, Vol. 88, pp. 488–510.

NORDHAUS, W. D. (1983). 'Macroconfusion: the dilemmas of economic policy'. In Tobin, J. (ed.), *Macroeconomics, Prices and Quantities. Essays in Memory of Arthur M. Okun*. Oxford: Basil Blackwell.

RICHARDSON, H. W. (1973). *Regional Growth Theory*. London: Macmillan.

SALTER, W. E. G. (1966). *Productivity and Technical Change*, 2nd ed. Cambridge: Cambridge University Press.

SCHMOOKLER, J. (1966). *Invention and Economic Growth*. Cambridge, Mass.: Harvard University Press.

SMITH, D. M. (1975). 'Neoclassical growth models and regional growth in the U.S.', *Journal of Regional Science*, Vol. 15, pp. 165–181.

THWAITES, A. T. (1983). 'The employment implications of technical change in a regional context'. In Gillespie, A. (ed.), *Technological Change and Regional Development*. London: Pion.

THWAITES, A. T. and OAKEY, R. P. (ed.) (1985). *The Regional Economic Impact of Technical Change*. London: Frances Pinter.

VERDOORN, P. J. (1949). 'Fattori che regolano lo sviluppo della produttività del lavoro', *L'Industria*, Vol. 1, pp. 3–10.

[17]

SCOTTISH JOURNAL
OF
POLITICAL ECONOMY
November 1970

THE CASE FOR REGIONAL POLICIES*

NICHOLAS KALDOR

In Britain, as in other countries, we have become acutely aware in recent years of the existence of a 'regional' problem—the problem, that is, of different regions growing at uneven rates; with some regions developing relatively fast and others tending to be left behind. In some ways this problem of fast and slow growing regions has not led to the same kind of inequalities in regional standards of living, in culture or in social structure, in the case of Britain as in some other countries—such as Italy, the United States or France. And in general, the problem of regional inequalities within countries is not nearly so acute as that between the rich and poor countries of the world—with differences in living standards in the ratio of 20:1, or even 50:1, as between the so-called 'advanced' countries and the 'developing' countries. Yet, as investigations by Kuznets and others have shown, the tremendous differences that now divide the rich and poor nations are comparatively recent in origin. They are the cumulative result of persistent differences in growth rates that went on over periods that may appear long in terms of a life-span, but which are relatively short in terms of recorded human history—not more than a few centuries, in fact. Two hundred, or two-hundred-and-fifty years ago, the differences in living standards, or in the 'stage' of both economic and cultural development of different countries, or parts of the globe, were very much smaller than they are today.

The primary question that needs to be considered is what *causes* these differences in 'regional' growth rates—whether the term 'regional' is applied to different countries (or even groups of countries) or different areas within the same country. The two questions are not, of course, identical; but up to a point, I am sure that it would be illuminating to consider them as if they were, and apply the same analytical technique to both.

In some ways an analysis of the strictly 'regional' problem (within a common political area) is more difficult. There is first of all the question of

* The fifth annual Scottish Economic Society Lecture delivered in the University of Aberdeen on February 18th, 1970.

how to define a ' region ' within a political area—a problem that does not arise when political boundaries, however arbitrary they may be from an economic or social point of view, are treated as a given fact one need not enquire about. There is in fact, no unique way of defining what constitutes a ' region '—there are innumerable ways; the most that one can say is that some ways of drawing such boundary lines are more sensible than others; and given the fact that this is so, the exact demarcation of a ' region ' may not make too much difference to the subsequent analysis.

Another aspect in which the analysis of ' region ' within a country is more difficult is in terms of the identification of the fate of an area with the fate of its inhabitants. The mobility of both labour and capital within countries tends to be considerably greater than between countries—even though economists, in their desire for clear-cut assumptions on which to build, tended to over-estimate the one and to under-estimate the other. (There is only an imperfect mobility within countries, and there is also some mobility between them.)

Finally, a region which is part of a ' nation ' or a ' country ' tends to have common political institutions, a common taxing and spending authority and a common currency—all of which have important implications on the manner in which its external economic relations are conducted.

THE ROLE OF ' RESOURCE ENDOWMENT '

But subject to these differences, what can we say about the causes of divergent regional growth rates—whether inter-nationally or intra-nationally? If one refers to classical or neo-classical economic theory, the common explanation is in terms of various factors—summed up under the term ' resource endowment '—which are themselves unexplained. Some areas are favoured by climate or geology; by the ability, vitality, ingenuity of their inhabitants, and by their thriftiness, and these innate advantages may be enhanced by good political and social institutions. Beyond suggesting that the right kind of human material is fostered by a temperate climate—in zones which are neither too hot nor too cold—and all of this owes a great deal to historical accidents and to luck, the theories which explain riches or poverty in terms of ' resource endowment ' do not really have anything much to offer by way of explanation.

Nevertheless one must agree that they go as far as it is possible to go in explaining that part of economic growth—and until fairly recently this was much the most important part—which consisted of ' land based ' economic activities, such as agriculture or mineral exploitation. These are clearly conditioned by climatic and geologic factors—the suitability of soil, rainfall, the availability of minerals, and so on. These provide the natural explanation why some areas are more densely settled than others; and why the comparative advantage in procuring different products (and which settles the nature of their external trading relations) should differ as between one area and another. No sophisticated explanation is needed why it is better for some areas to grow wheat and for others bananas; or why some areas which are lucky in possessing things with a fast-growing demand (such as oil or uranium) are fortunate, from the point of view of their growth-potential, in relation to others which possess minerals with a slow-growing or declining demand—coal, for example. We would all agree that some part of the interregional specialisation and the division of labour can be adequately accounted for by such factors.

It is when we come to comparative advantages in relation to processing activities (as distinct from land-based activities) that this kind of approach is likely to yield question-begging results. The prevailing distribution of real income in the world—the comparative riches or poverty of nations, or regions—is largely to be explained, not by ' natural ' factors, but by the unequal incidence of development in industrial activities. The ' advanced ', high-income areas are invariably those which possess a highly developed modern industry. In relation to differences in industrial development, explanations in terms of ' resource endowment ' do not get us very far. One can, and does say, that industrial production requires a great deal of capital—both in terms of plant and machinery, and of human skills, resulting from education—but in explaining such differences in ' capital endowment ' it is difficult to separate cause from effect. It is as sensible—or perhaps more sensible—to say that capital accumulation results from economic development as that it is a cause of development. Anyhow, the two proceed side by side. Accumulation is largely financed out of business profits; the growth of demand in turn is largely responsible for providing both the inducements to invest capital in industry and also the means of financing it.

We cannot therefore say that industries will be located in regions which are ' well endowed ' with capital resources for reasons other than industrial development itself. It was not the result of the peculiar thriftiness of the inhabitants of a region, or of a particularly high degree of initial inequality in the distribution of income which ' induced " a high savings-ratio, that some regions became rich while others remained poor. The capital needed for industrialisation was largely provided by the very same individuals who acquired wealth as a result of the process of development, and not prior to it. The great captains of industry, like Henry Ford or Nuffield were not recruited from the wealthy classes—they started as ' small men '.

Nor is there a satisfactory ' location theory ' which is capable of explaining the geographic distribution of industrial activities. The only relevant factor which is considered in this connection is that of transport costs. But transport cost advantages can only help to explain location in those particular activities which convert bulky goods—where transport costs are an important element, and where processing itself greatly reduces the weight of the materials processed. If say, two tons of coal and four tons of iron are needed to make a ton of steel, it is better to locate steel plants near the coal mines and the iron ore deposits; and if these are themselves situated at some distance from each other, it is best to locate the steel plants near both places, in proportions determined by the relative weight of the two materials per unit of finished product—i.e., in this example, two-thirds of the plants near the iron ore, and one-third near the coal mines—since this arrangement would alone ensure full utilization of transport capacity in both directions.

But where the effect of processing in reducing bulk is not so important, the location of the processing activity may be a matter of indifference—whether it is near the source of the materials, near the market for the products, or anywhere in between. It is often suggested that such 'foot-loose' industries tend naturally to develop near the market for their products. But this again is a question-begging proposition. Great urban conurbations are normally large centres of industrial activity—the 'markets' are there where the 'industry' is. The engineering industry in this country is highly concentrated in and around Birmingham—it is also a great 'market' for engineering goods of various kinds. But it does not explain why either of these should be located there, rather than in some other place, say Leeds or Sheffield.

The Principle of 'Cumulative Causation'

To explain why certain regions have become highly industrialised, while others have not we must introduce quite different kinds of considerations—what Mydral (1957) called the principle of 'circular and cumulative causation'. This is nothing else but the existence of increasing returns to scale—using that term in the broadest sense—in processing activities. These are not just the economies of large-scale production, commonly considered, but the cumulative advantages accruing from the growth of industry itself—the development of skill and know-how; the opportunities for easy communication of ideas and experience; the opportunity of ever-increasing differentiation of processes and of specialisation in human activities. As Allyn Young (1928) pointed out in a famous paper, Adam Smith's principle of the 'division of labour' operates through the constant sub-division of industries, the emergence of new kinds of specialized firms, of steadily increasing differentiation —more than through the expansion in the size of the individual plant or the individual firm.

Thus the fact that in all known historical cases the development of manufacturing industries was closely associated with urbanisation must have deep-seated causes which are unlikely to be rendered inoperative by the invention of some new technology or new source of power. Their broad effect is a strong positive association between the growth of productivity and efficiency and the rate of growth in the scale of activities—the so-called Verdoorn Law. One aspect of this is that as communication between different regions becomes more intensified (with improvements in transport and in marketing organisation), the region that is initially more developed industrially may gain from the progressive opening of trade at the expense of the less developed region whose development will be inhibited by it. Whereas in the classical case—which abstracts from increasing returns—the opening of trade between two regions will necessarily be beneficial to both (even though the gains may not be equally divided between them) and specialisation through trade will necessarily serve to reduce the differences in comparative costs in the two areas, in the case of the 'opening of trade' in industrial products the differences in comparative costs may be enlarged, and not reduced, as a result of trade; and the trade may injure one region to the greater benefit of the other. This will be so if one assumes two regions, initially isolated from one another, with each having both an agricultural area and an industrial and market centre; with the size of agricultural production being mainly determined by soil and climate, and the state of technology; and the size of industrial production mainly depending on the demand for industrial products derived from the agricultural sector. When trade is opened up between them, the region with the more developed industry will be able to supply the needs of the agricultural area of the other region on more favourable terms: with the result that the industrial centre of the second region will lose its market, and will tend to be eliminated—without any compensating advantage to the inhabitants of that region in terms of increased agricultural output.

Another aspect of assymetry between 'land-based' and 'processing' activities (which is basically due to economies of large-scale production) is that in industrial production, contractual costs form an important independent element in price-formation; competition is necessarily imperfect; the sellers are price-makers, rather than price-takers. Whereas in agricultural production it is prices that are derived from, or dependent on, contractual incomes (i.e. on the level of wages).

As a result, the 'exchange process'—the nature of the adjustment mechanism in inter-regional trade flows and money flows—operates differently in the two cases. In the case of trade between agricultural regions, the classical theory of the adjustment process is more nearly applicable. The price of agricultural commodities rises or falls automatically with changes in the balance of supply and demand; these price changes in individual markets will automatically tend to maintain the balance in trade flows between areas, both through the income effects and the substitution effects of price changes. Where the goods produced by the different regions are fairly close substitutes to one another, a relatively modest change in price—in the 'terms of trade' —will be sufficient to offset the effects of changes in either supply or demand schedules as may result from crop failures, the uneven incidence of technological improvements, or any other 'exogenous' cause. If the goods produced by the different regions are complements rather than substitutes to each other, the adjustment process may involve far greater changes in the terms of trade of the two areas, and would thus operate mainly through the 'income effects'. But in either case, the very process which secures an equilibrium between the supply and demand in each individual market through the medium of price changes will also ensure balance between sales and purchases of each region.

In the case of industrial activities ('manufactures') the impact effect of exogenous changes in demand will be on production rather than on prices. 'Supply', at any rate long-run supply, is normally in excess of demand —in the sense that producers would be willing to produce more, and to sell more, at the prevailing price (or even at a lower price) in response to an increased flow of orders. In this situation the adjustment process operates in a different manner—through the so-called 'foreign trade multiplier'. Any exogenous change in the demand for the products of a region from outside will set up multiplier effects in terms of local production and employment which in turn will adjust imports to the change in exports; on certain assumptions, this adjustment will alone suffice to keep the trade flows in balance.[1]

Some time ago Hicks (1950, p. 62) coined the phrase 'super-multiplier' to cover the effects of changes of demand on investment, as well as on consumption; and he showed that on certain assumptions, both the rate of growth of induced investment, and the rate of growth of consumption, become attuned to the rate of growth of the autonomous component of demand, so that the growth in an autonomous demand-factor will govern the rate of growth of the economy as a whole.

From the point of view of any particular region, the 'autonomous component of demand' is the demand emanating from *outside* the region; and Hicks's notion of the 'super-multiplier' can be applied so as to express the doctrine of the foreign trade multiplier in a dynamic setting. So expressed, the doctrine asserts that the rate of economic development of a region is fundamentally governed by the rate of growth of its exports. For the growth of exports, via the 'accelerator', will govern the rate of growth of industrial capacity, as well as the rate of growth of consumption; it will also serve to adjust (again under rather severe simplifying assumptions) both the level, and the rate of growth, of imports to that of exports.

The behaviour of exports on the other hand will depend both on an exogenous factor—the rate of growth of world demand for the products of the region; and on an 'endogenous' or quasi-endogenous factor—on the movement of the 'efficiency wages' in the region relative to other producing regions, which will determine whether the region's share in the total (overall) market is increasing or diminishing. The movement of 'efficiency wages' (a phrase coined by Keynes) is the resultant of two elements—the relative movement of money wages and that of productivity. If this relationship (the index of money wages divided by the index of productivity) moves in favour of an area it will gain in 'competitiveness' and *vice versa.*

As regards the movement of money wages the one uncontroversial proposition that one can advance is that given *some* mobility of labour, there is a limit to the differences in the levels of wages prevailing between industrial regions, or between different industries of a region. Indeed, it is a well

[1] The necessary assumptions are that all other sources of demand except exports are endogenous, rather than exogenous—i.e., that both Government expenditure and business investment play a passive role, the former being confined by revenue from taxation, and the latter by savings out of business profits.

known fact that whilst the general level of money wages may rise at highly variable rates at different times, the pay differentials between different types of workers, or between workers doing the same job in different areas, are remarkably constant. This may be the result partly of the mobility of labour but also of the strong pressures associated with collective bargaining for the maintenance of traditional comparabilities.[2] But this means that the rates of growth of money wages in different regions will tend to be much the same, even when the rates of growth in employment differ markedly. On the other hand, under the Verdoorn Law, the rates of growth of productivity will be the higher, the higher the rates of growth of output, and differences in the rates of productivity growth will tend to exceed the associated differences in the rates of growth of employment.[3] Hence differences in the rates of productivity growth are not likely to be compensated by equivalent differences in the rates of increase in money wages.

In other words, 'efficiency wages' will tend to fall in regions (and in the particular industries of regions) where productivity rises faster than the average. It is for this reason that relatively fast growing areas tend to acquire a cumulative competitive advantage over a relatively slow growing area; 'efficiency wages' will, in the natural course of events, tend to fall in the former, relatively to the latter—even when they tend to rise in both areas in absolute terms.

It is through this mechanism that the process of 'cumulative causation' works; and both comparative success and comparative failure have self-reinforcing effects in terms of industrial development. Just because the induced changes in wages increases are not sufficient to offset the differences in productivity increases, the comparative costs of production in fast growing areas tend to fall in time relatively to those in slow growing areas; and thereby enhance the competitive advantage of the former at the expense of the latter.

I am sure that this principle of cumulative causation—which explains the unequal regional incidence of industrial development by endogenous factors resulting from the process of historical development itself rather than by exogenous differences in 'resource endowment'—is an essential one for the understanding of the diverse trends of development as between different regions. In reality, the influences and cross-currents resulting from processes of development are far more complex. The intensification of trade resulting from technological improvements in transport or the reduction of artificial barriers (such as tariffs between regions) has important diffusion

[2] It has also been true in an international context that the comparative differences in the rates of growth of money wages in the different industrial countries had been smaller (in the post-war period at any rate) than the differences in the rates of productivity growth in the manufacturing industries of those countries, though the reasons why this has been so are not as yet well understood (cf. e.g. Kaldor (1960), paras. 22-23 and Table I).

[3] Recent empirical analyses of productivity growth in manufacturing industry suggest that a 1 per cent. increase in the growth of output is associated with a 0·6 per cent. increase in productivity and a 0·4 per cent. increase in employment (cf. e.g.: United Nations, 1970).

effects as well as important concentration effects. The increase in production and income in one region will, as such, stimulate the demand for 'complementary' products of other regions; and just as, in terms of microeconomics, falling costs generally lead to oligopoly rather than monopoly, so the principle of cumulative causation leads to the concentration of industrial development in a number of successful regions and not of a single region. These 'successful' regions in turn may hold each other in balance through increasing specialisation between them—some area becomes more prominent in some industries and another area in some other industries.

Actually, in terms of national areas, Kuznets found that different industrialised countries are remarkably similar in industrial structure, at similar stages of industrial development. The tremendous increase in international trade in industrial products between highly industrialised countries since the Second World War was more the reflection of specialisation within industries than that between industries: it was mainly in parts and components and machinery for industrial use. For example, in the case of the motor car industry, whilst most developed countries have a developed and highly competitive motor car industry (and are large net exporters) there has been a huge increase in international trade in motor car components—with some countries supplying some part of a carburetter to everybody, and some other country doing the same for some other part of the engine, or the carburetter.

There are also important dis-economies resulting from excessive rates of growth in industrial activities in particular areas: the growing areas will tend to have fast rates of population growth (mainly as a result of immigration) with the associated environmental problems in housing, public services, congestion, and so on, and these at some stage should serve to offset the technological economies resulting from faster growth. But as is well known, many of these dis-economies are external to the individual producer and may not therefore be adequately reflected in the movement of money costs and prices. A counterpart to this are external economies in the slow growing or declining regions—in terms of unemployment of labour, or an underutilised social infrastructure, which again tend to be external to the firm and hence inadequately reflected in selling costs or prices. There is some presumption therefore for supposing that, if left to market processes alone, tendencies to regional concentration of industrial activities will proceed farther than they would have done if 'private costs' were equal to 'social cost' (in the Pigovian sense) and all economies and dis-economies of production were adequately reflected in the movement of money costs and prices.

Regions and Countries

It is time now that we consider some of the basic differences in the mode of operation of this principle—i.e. of 'cumulative causation' as between different regions of a single country and as between different political areas.

There is, first of all, the fact that the inter-regional mobility of labour is very much greater than the international mobility of labour. As a result differences in regional growth rates cannot cause differences in living standards of the same order as have emerged in the last few centuries between more distant regions, separated by political and cultural barriers. Real earnings no doubt improve faster in the areas of immigration rather than in areas of emigration, but the very fact of easy migration limits the extent to which differences in regional growth rates will be associated with divergent movements in earnings per head. The fact that trade unions are nation-wide and collective bargains in most countries are on a national basis, is a further reason why the movement of real earnings in various regions broadly tends to keep in step.

A second, and even more important fact is that a region which forms part of a political community, with a common scale of public services and a common basis of taxation, automatically gets 'aid' whenever its trading relations with the rest of the country deteriorate. There is an important built-in fiscal stabilizer which arrests the operation of the export-multiplier: since taxes paid to the Central Government vary with the level of local incomes and expenditure, whilst public expenditures do not (indeed they may vary in an offsetting direction through public works, unemployment benefit, etc.), any deterioration in the export-import balance tends to be retarded (and ultimately arrested) by the change in the region's fiscal balance —in the relation between what it contributes to the central Exchequer and what it receives from it.

This 'built-in' fiscal stabiliser—i.e. that a fall in exogenous demand leads to an increase in the public sector deficit, and thereby moderates the effect of the former on employment and incomes—operates of course on the national level as much as on the regional level; and it is one of the main reasons why a fall in exports does not generate a sufficient fall in the level of incomes to maintain equilibrium in the balance of payments through the adjustment in imports. But the important difference is that in the case of the region the change in the local fiscal balance is externally financed; in the case of the nation the balance of payments deficit causes a fall in reserves, or requires 'compensatory finance' from abroad, which is by no means 'automatic'.

This seems to me the main reason why there appears to be no counterpart to the 'balance-of-payments problem' on the regional level. It is often suggested, by the 'monetary school' that the reason why a country with a separate currency gets into balance of payments difficulties, whilst a region never does, is because in the one case the 'local money supply' is reduced in consequence of an excess of imports over exports; in the other case the monetary authorities offset the effects of the adverse balance on current account by 'domestic credit expansion'—by replacing the outflow of money (resulting from the excess of imports) with 'new' money. In my view this way of looking at the problem is putting the cart before the horse. The 'replacement of the money' is simply a facet of the fact that the foreign trade multiplier is arrested in its operation through the induced fiscal deficit —possibly aggravated also by the fall in private saving in relation to private domestic investment (though in practice the latter factor may be quantitatively of less importance, since the foreign-trade multiplier will tend to induce a reduction in local investment, and not only in local savings). But exactly the same thing happens at the regional level—with the outflowing money being (at least partially) replaced by a larger net inflow from the Exchequer, which is a direct consequence of the 'outflow'; but since it happens automatically as part of the natural order of things nobody kicks up a fuss, or even takes notice of it.

In these ways 'regions' are in a more favourable position than 'countries'. On the other hand sovereign political areas can take various measures to offset the effect of an unfavourable trend in their 'efficiency wages' which is not open to a 'region'—i.e. by diverting demand from foreign goods to home goods, through varying forms of protection (tariffs and non-tariff barriers, such as preferences given in public contracts) and occasionally also—though usually only very belatedly, in extremities—through adjustment of the exchange rate.

Of these two instruments for counteracting adverse trends in 'efficiency wages'—protection and devaluation—the latter is undoubtedly greatly superior to the former. Devaluation, as has often been pointed out, is nothing else but a combination of a uniform *ad-valorem* duty on all imports and uniform *ad-valorem* subsidy on exports. The combination of the two allows the adjustment in 'competitiveness' to take place under conditions which give the maximum scope for obtaining the advantages of economies of scale through international specialisation. Protection on the other hand tends to reduce international specialisation, and forces each region to spread its industrial activities over a wider range of activities on a smaller scale, instead of a narrower range on a larger scale. The effects of protection in inhibiting the growth of industrial efficiency is likely to be the greater the smaller the G.N.P. (or rather the gross industrial product) of the protected area. It is no accident that all the prosperous small countries of the world—such as the Scandinavian countries or Switzerland—are (comparatively speaking) 'free traders'. They have modest tariffs, and a very high ratio of trade in manufactures (both exports and imports) to their total output or consumption.

It has sometimes been suggested—not perhaps very seriously—that some of the development areas of the U.K.—such as Scotland or Northern Ireland—would be better off with a separate currency with an adjustable exchange rate vis-à-vis the rest of the U.K. For the reason mentioned earlier, I do not think this would be a suitable remedy. However, we have now introduced a new instrument in the U.K.—R.E.P.—which potentially could give the same advantages as devaluation for counteracting any adverse trend in 'efficiency wages', but with the added advantage that the cost of the consequent deterioration in the terms of trade (the cost of selling exports at lower prices in terms of imports) is not borne by the region, but by the U.K. taxpaying community as a whole.

For this same reason, perhaps, the drawback of R.E.P. as an instrument is that it would be politically very difficult to introduce it on a scale that could make it really effective. The present R.E.P. is equivalent to a 5-6 per cent. reduction in the 'efficiency wages' in the manufacturing sector of the development areas. Since 'value added by regional manufacturing' is no more than a quarter, or perhaps a third, of the total cost of regional export-commodities (the rest consist of goods and services embodied that are mainly produced outside the region) the effect of a 6 per cent. R.E.P. is no more than that of a 2 per cent. devaluation (for the U.K. as a whole). It thus could have only one-fifth of the effect on 'regional competitiveness' which the recent U.K. devaluation had on the U.K.'s competitiveness in relation to the rest of the world.

Development Area policy comprises a host of other measures as well, of which the differential investment grant is the most costly and the most prominent. In my view investment grants as an instrument are less effective for the purpose of countering adverse trends in competitiveness than subsidies on wages (and not only because they stimulate the wrong kind of industries—those that are specially capital intensive) but I would agree that this is an issue that requires closer investigation than it has yet received.

I should like to end by mentioning one other possibility. Given the limitation on the scope of development expenditures by the natural disinclination of the Central Government (or the Parliament at Westminster) to spend huge sums in subsidising particular regions, isn't there a case for supplementing Central Government sources from local sources—through more local fiscal autonomy? For example, if it was found (and agreed) that R.E.P. is an efficacious way of subsidising regional exports (I suppose this is far from agreed at the moment) and that this may have dramatic effects in terms of enhanced regional development in the long run, would it not be in the interest of the regions to supplement the centrally financed R.E.P. by the proceeds, say, of a local sales tax? Perhaps this is a dangerous suggestion since in practice the growth of locally financed subsidies might simply be offset by lesser subsidies from the Centre. It would be less 'dangerous' however, if it was the Central Government which offered to raise the level of such subsidies—R.E.P. or even investment grants—on condition that a proportion of the cost should be raised by local taxation. Clearly, far more could be spent for the benefit of particular areas, if the areas themselves would make a greater, or a more distinct, contribution to the cost of such benefits. But these are thoughts for the distant future; long before they become practical politics we shall be deeply involved in the same kind of issues in connection with our negotiations to enter the Common Market.

Cambridge

REFERENCES

HICKS, J. R. (1950). *A Contribution to the Theory of the Trade Cycle*. Oxford.

KALDOR, N. Monetary Policy, Economic Stability and Growth, a memorandum submitted to the *Committee on the Working of the Monetary Systems*. Principal Memoranda of Evidence, Vol. 3, pp. 146-153, London, H.M.S.O.

MYRDAL, GUNNAR (1957). *Economic Theory and Underdeveloped Regions*. London.

UNITED NATIONS (1970). *Econômic Survey for Europe for 1969*. Geneva.

YOUNG, ALLYN (1928). Increasing Returns and Economic Progress. *Economic Journal*, December 1928.

[18]

Urban Studies (1975), 12, 1-29 ©

Regional Growth Theory[1]

Edwin von Böventer

[*Received May 1974*]

The following paper consists of two parts: a review of H. W. Richardson's book *Regional Growth Theory* (Part A) and, partly based on Richardson's analysis and partly on my own experiences and analyses, the presentation of an extended two-level model of regional growth as the basis for further empirical investigations (Part B).

PART A. RICHARDSON'S REGIONAL GROWTH THEORY

Regional economics has a long and continuous history which is impressive indeed: what is less impressive is the guidance that it has been able to offer to the many policy makers in all parts of the world who have to deal with regional growth problems—problems how to foster national growth by an appropriate regional allocation of private and public investment outlays, how to help lagging regions in catching up with the development of the national economy, and how to attain certain objectives in all parts of the country that range from income distribution goals to ecological ends, to name only a few. There has been a lot of policy making or planning without explicit theory, in many cases even 'planning without facts', or on the basis of incomplete theory and even of more or less overt ideology. The general feeling is that there is not enough operational theory available for the task. In this situation one can only welcome the publication of an easily accessible account of the problems of regional growth and of the answers that regional economic theory can give, or rather not give—as yet, it is to be hoped.

Richardson's *Regional Growth Theory* is comprehensive in a relatively small volume, it is well written, and it is based on good judgment. Precisely because in most respects it is so balanced in its views and cautious in its judgments, it is not a *bold* book, but all the more an important one: it is indeed the best statement on the present situation of regional growth theory that in my view is available at this time. The book does not contain a new theory that significantly differs from the main body of our knowledge about regional growth processes, but it describes and evaluates the elements of these processes as they have been incorporated in various theories in an extremely lucid way. Whereas Richardson's *Regional Economics* had been 'only mildly critical of neoclassical models', the new publication 'places emphasis on spatial agglomeration economies and locational preferences' and recognises 'that a satisfactory theory must explain unbalanced growth in

The author is at Institut für empirische Wirtschaftsforschung, University of Munich

1 For many helpful suggestions, the author is much indebted to J. Hampe, G. Lippert and K.-P. Lotze.

the inter-regional system and the spatial unevenness of development within each region' (Preface, p. vii). It tries to integrate interregional and intra-regional growth theory, and to formulate an operational model for one region *vis-a-vis* the rest of the economy, a model in which historical data loom large as initial conditions, and among these, certain *locational constants* are factors of great importance—theoretical and empirical. An important thesis of Richardson's that pervades the whole book is that 'after a phase of initial concentration associated with the beginnings of the industrialisation process itself, sustained national economic growth is associated with dispersion into different areas of the economy', and that 'at a later stage of development associated with transportation improvements and higher income levels metropolitan growth is accompanied by decentralisation', (p. 8).

The book has two chapters on existing models of regional growth or development (chs. 2 and 3), two chapters on resource mobility and investment decisions (chs. 4 and 6), two chapters dealing with the elements of a general theory of economic growth and development in space (chs. 5 and 7), and a chapter (9) on policy implications. Chapter 8 represents a description of the author's Operational Model and as such contains a summary of the main ideas and positions of the author.

In the following, I shall first give a brief introduction into the first seven chapters and chapter 9 (section II) and then describe in more detail Richardson's Model (section III).

I. Theories of Regional Growth

The following outline of Richardson's statement on existing models of regional development can be short because these models are known from the literature and because Richardson's exposition is on the whole very clear as well as very fair to the authors. After chapter 1 an introduction has been given into the problems of regional growth, the definition of regions and the differences between regions and nations, in the following chapter (2) the author discusses and evaluates Export Base, Neo-classical and Cumulative Causation Models, Econometric and Input-Output Models as well as Multisector Development Planning Models. In chapter 3, the author deals with theories that relate the transport sector and regional growth; with potential and gravity models; with models that focus on agglomeration factors—growth pole theory, industrial complex analysis, locational attraction models, development axes; and finally, with the problem of 'competitive' versus 'generative' growth. These two chapters 2 and 3, about a third of the book, are carefully written, and though they are very critical of current regional growth theory, the author always tries to isolate what useful elements for further analysis even the most unsatisfactory theories may contain. In view of all this, there is no need to go into more detail—important elements of the analysis will be taken up again later on anyway, in connection with the discussion of Richardson's Operational Model.

(*a*) *Neo-classics* v. *Cumulative Growth*

At this point, I should like to comment only on the main thesis of the book with regard to the literature—that the significance of neo-classical adjustment mechanisms has, on the whole, been overrated and that cumulative processes and agglomeration factors should be given much more attention than has been the case in the past, and that so far, the theory of economic growth has been of little help in explaining *intra*-regional growth. My comments on these theses are closely interrelated.

1 Richardson is fully correct in this: there has indeed existed a noticeable gap between regional growth theory as well as regional equilibrium theory on the one hand and the approaches taken in empirical investigations on regional growth and in regional planning models in the other. The first set of theories, which might be called 'pure theory', has largely been developed in line with foreign trade theory, which traditionally has focused on factor endowments and relative scarcities but has widely neglected agglomeration factors: this followed directly from the neglect of space and intra-regional transport costs and the assumption of homogeneous regions.[2] By contrast, all the theories dealing with spatial structures do take agglomeration factors into account, in one way or another, no matter what their

[2] The *classical* statement of this approach is Ohlin's great opus *Interregional and International Trade*, Cambridge 1933. The same approach is to be found in Isard's general equilibrium models, as well as in Lefeber's important *Allocation in Space*, Amsterdam 1959; also in my *Theorie des räumlichen Gleichgewichts*, Tübingen 1962 (tran. Théorie de L'Equilibre en Economie Spatiale, Techniques Economiques Modernes, Sèrie Espace Economique 7, Paris 1966).

specific approaches and terminologies. This holds for all theories of spatial structures from Christaller and Lösch on, as for Isard's models of this type. It is only in *exact* formulations that agglomeration economies are missing: their introduction appeared to lead into difficulties of such a magnitude that they were excluded by the authors. This is the important wide gap which is even more apparent if one compares 'general' growth theory with regional growth problems and which Richardson tries to bridge in his analyses. One might thus distinguish between *'pure and exact'* regional theory *without agglomeration economies*, on the one hand, and *applied regional theory* which is *inexact but takes agglomeration factors* into account, on the other hand.[3] Thus neo-classical theory has been the dominating one, but only on one of the two parts of the arena.

2 Even with these qualifications, Richardson writes as though he took his main adversary, Neo-classical Theory, either more seriously or more literally than it deserves in the context of spatial development. For the neo-classical price adjustment mechanism to work, it is *not* necessary that there exists perfect competition and that production functions are identical[4]: Students of spatial economic relationships have in general not worked with narrow neo-classical models in Richardson's sense, in particular if they were interested in *spatial economic structures*, even if on the whole they followed a neo-classical tradition; scale and agglomeration economies have always loomed large in such models.

Nor have these effects been ignored in empirical analyses of growth and migration. Richardson is perfectly correct, however, in questioning the importance of factor return differentials as compared with the role of agglomeration factors. In this context, neo-classical analysis stresses adjustment processes *along given* (say) supply or demand functions, whereas agglomeration or cumulative causation theories are, in effect, concerned with *shifts* of these functions. The two effects always arise simultaneously, and in very many cases the latter effects have certainly been the more important ones. And the point is indeed that in regional planning, one can not, and should not, rely on *marginal* analyses, much the same as in deciding about large investment projects one could not do this, even in a spaceless world.

3 (*Please see Addendum on page 29.*)

4 Neo-classical and cumulative growth models differ not only in their assumptions about production functions, but are significantly different with regard to the level of *information* or *certainty* about factor income possibilities, or *chances*. Neo-classical theory has never really come to grips with the problem that large agglomerations offer *more chances*: to find the right job or the precise quality of economic commodities that one is looking for and this, of course, raises the *expected* returns for particular factors. This is what adds to making large agglomerations so attractive, beyond the higher *average* level of factor remuneration. With very *broad groups* of homogeneous factors and goods, this would be less of a problem and there would be much *less factor migration on this account.*

5 Return differentials, information levels and agglomeration sizes are to be seen as closely interrelated factors determining movements in space and the development of spatial structures. For these reasons, it is impossible, in the real world, to separate return adjustment effects from agglomeration effects in an exact way, say in econometric models. One might even express this through the question: 'What else are agglomeration economies than improved profitabilities or factor return differentials?' Thus there is in general a high degree of multicollinearity between (relative) agglomeration sizes and factor return differentials. In this context, the most important sets of variables are (i) the spatial outlay (agglomeration) of economic activities, (ii) the sectoral (output) structure and (iii) the price structures. Even if one specifies an operational model of a 'purely neo-classical' kind one necessarily also catches *some* agglomeration effects when one tries to measure price adjustment effects, simply because the spatial *price system* is defined for a *particular*

[3] This gap is also seen in my own work: The Walrasian-type *Theorie des räumlichen Gleichgewichts* deals with market imperfections but leaves out agglomeration economies while a study undertaken alongside with this book (as an *application* which was originally a part of the same manuscript), 'Die Struktur der Landschaft. Versuch einer Synthese und Weiterentwicklung der Modelle von J. H. von Thünen, W. Christaller und A. Lösch,' stresses agglomeration factors and their role in the development of spatial structures in a setting in which effects of scarcities and price adjustments come into play—but in an *inexact* way.

[4] Furthermore, it is not necessary that production functions be homogeneous of degree *one*. There is a *wide range* around unity (though with a certain upper bound, certainly) within which this value may vary or fluctuate.

spatial distribution of all the economic activities and for particular levels of information. Conversely, systems of agglomerations have particular *price structures*. Therefore agglomeration effects can never be exactly separated from price effects and from sectoral structural effects, because the three sets (i), (ii), and (iii) above are always interrelated. It may indeed be worth the effort to scrutinise the results of various economometric analyses from this angle: to what extent have price effects entered the empirical results of agglomeration effects studies, and vice versa?

6 The fact remains, open to no doubt, that in this world one can find instances for both balanced and unbalanced growth—for a preponderance of either the neo-classical or the agglomeration effects. In *very broad* terms, the conditions are known under which the one or the other occur. But *when exactly, under what conditions* planning should stop relying mostly on the one type of effects and turn to the other effects and use them: this has not been answered satisfactorily by any theory or analysis as yet, even for limited applications—even though this is such an important regional policy question, for densely populated areas in industrial countries no less than in developing countries. Thus though the role of the agglomeration factor has been an impressive one in many development processes, its *limits* are much less wellknown. Summarising at this point, I have the impression that Richardson's shift of emphasis—away from neo-classics—has led to an *over*emphasis of the size of agglomerations as a *general* precondition of regional growth. This is more true of Richardson's Model than of his verbal statements in the preceeding chapters.

Chapter 4 contains a very comprehensive discussion of the factors determining inter-regional factor movements: here Richardson does again correctly point out that the neo-classical model and the other models (gravitational etc.) are not mutually exclusive but should be thought of as supplementing each other. Here one should stress that it is often not enough that certain other factors are 'theoretically' not excluded or that they *might* also be included in the model—the *focus* of the analysis often makes all the difference: there Richardson is certainly also right. There follows a thorough statement of the approaches that describe the spatial diffusion and hierarchical diffusion processes of knowledge and information. Agglomeration factors are again at the centre of the author's interest, and it is here that factors which take sizes and agglomerations into account certainly have *much* more to offer than neo-classical analysis alone if one tries to explain regional growth. But nevertheless it remains true that the spatial and hierarchical diffusion process is just as difficult to *derive* on the basis of agglomeration sizes as on the basis of neo-classical factors. Indeed, if one had exact detailed data, *expected rates of return* in various agglomerations (whose necessary minima decline during the diffusion process) might even be a better gauge than absolute agglomeration sizes. But surely, it is again the *two* aspects: differential *returns* in different *agglomeration sizes*, that come into play.

In chapter 6, Investment, similar considerations are taken up again, and the interdependence between private and public investment decisions is briefly discussed. The Markov Chain model of savings and investment in space may have a certain heuristic value, but I do not see the operational side of the matter yet; to me, the model does not seem to go beyond the illustration of certain interrelationships that have been clarified beforehand anyway. One would certainly not expect that the transitional probabilities for different regions remain constant over time—else there would be no room for either the neo-classical adjustment processes or the particular agglomeration processes that are discussed in other parts of the book.

(*b*) *Regional Growth: General Statements in the Book*

Richardson works towards a general statement on growth in space along two avenues: first, he concentrates on 'the essential features of development in the space economy that a satisfactory theory of spatial (regional and urban) growth must explain' (p. 134 ch. 5), and later on he focuses on the various *elements* of the growth process that bring about these features (ch. 7). This is a good division of labour, because the various elements of growth may be put together with variable or flexible weights (and may be at work for variable lengths of time)—in line with the specific situations in various countries. To determine such weights would be the task of econometric models—this topic is discussed in chapter 8.

In chapter 5, the regional growth process, with its interrelationships between national or regional and urban development processes, is aptly described as a system of particular sequences: (i) *national growth* is associated with a *dispersion of economic expansion* from leading regions into other regions; (ii) regional *growth* means *spatial concentration and urbanisation*, and (iii) *metropolitan growth* is accompanied by *decentralisation*—yielding, in toto, a process of '*decentralised concentrated dispersion*' (pp. 134-135). I think that, as a general statement, the discussion in chapter 5 is an excellent integration of regional and urban growth processes. The only drawback of such a general discussion is that one necessarily has to be either very broad or has to cover very long periods of time. The relative speeds of the various decentralisation-concentration-dispersion processes are naturally dependent on a host of different factors which in general work differently in different countries and this, also naturally, reduces the analytical value of the model in terms of *particular* applications, even more so if one is interested in predictions or in deriving the best policy measures. But then this is true of all general statements about economic life.

To keep the discussion open for flexible applications of the general statement on spatial growth, the important *elements* of growth are analysed in detail in the second 'general' chapter, in particular the various kinds of agglomeration economies that make for concentration or decentralised concentration of economic activities in space. It is important that any *operational* theory of spatial economic development starts with the *historical* distribution of all economically relevant factors rather than with any ideal situation. This is done by Richardson under the heading 'Locational Constants' in chapter 7: sites of resources, cities, and transportation routes in particular. The following discussion on agglomeration economies and their measurement is indeed a very good summary of the formal and empirical approaches to these problems, and encompasses economic as well as social influences in a broad way: in this chapter, there is little that one could quarrel about. Household agglomeration economies as well as business agglomeration economies are treated as intensively as is possible on such a general level—at that, a very clear account.

(c) The Agglomeration Factor: Concept and Measurement

With regard to the possibilities of measuring agglomeration economies one has to agree with the author: 'Perhaps the search for a single measure is a chimera, and real progress in measurement may have to be based on breaking down agglomeration economies into many components' (p. 182). But I would go a definite step further. The agglomeration economies that a *particular* city offers are indeed different for each industry, for each firm, and for each level of activities within a firm. It is not only that they have to be broken down into many components, but that it is impossible to give *unique weights* to these components.

1 Exact measurements that are meaningful are possible, even theoretically, only for a *given activity* or a *given economic unit* in alternative cities of different sizes (leaving all other factors out of the picture at this moment—economic and social structures of the cities, and so on). Thus one may determine the *unit cost* differentials for a certain *productive process* that are to be attributed to *city size differentials*; on the one hand, for a particular firm, this could lead to calculating profit differentials, while on the other hand for a particular *urban service*, this would involve the measurement of unit costs and supply prices as a function of (variable) activity levels and of (variable) input prices—all these variables as functions of the sizes of the cities. For households, exact measurements of *overall* agglomeration economies and diseconomies are certainly impossible because nonmonetary factors play a very significant part in the well-being of urban dwellers as well as commuters. One could only try to determine individual states of indifference for combinations of income levels, city sizes, and amenity levels, to name only the most important factors.

2 All this cannot mean that cost analyses (for urban services, say) are useless: they are meaningful as *one* important piece of information for planners. If *all other factors* are similar, then an efficient transportation network or an efficient structure of the whole landscape—from the point of view of public services and transportation cost—is certainly preferable to one that is less efficient. And in the absence of all other information, one can not blame planners if they rely heavily on cost differentials as important guides.

3 Total agglomeration economies are thus always a weighted sum of the partial agglomeration economies (partly non-measurable) for all the firms, households

and public enterprises. If non-monetary elements are neglected, then

> *income level differentials* (per factor unit) as between *agglomerations of different sizes* would indeed measure *differentials in agglomeration economies—provided* the *compositions* of the sets of production factors and the *structures* of the industries are allowed for and the *intercity* agglomeration effects are also taken into account.

All these effects, obviously, are extremely difficult to determine. Nevertheless, there exists a high degree of unanimity that *incomes* are indeed a rising function of agglomeration sizes. But how do we measure and evaluate the vast sum of intangibles that an increasingly ecology-conscious academic community has only recently turned to systematically? And how far can *this* help us? There are upper *limits* to city sizes that should (reasonably) be encouraged else there would not be so much discussion about optimal urban policies and there would be *more* migration into the largest centres of all economies. The difficulties in giving definite (numerical) answers are related to two further points: first, one has to distinguish between *marginal* and *average* agglomeration economies, and second, non-monetary household agglomeration economies are obviously a function of people's preferences, and these preferences have always been shaped by where people have grown up, and can therefore also be influenced by regional and urban policy measures.

All this is indeed much more defeatist, as far as measurements and quantitative answers are concerned, than it sounds hopeful, and it is certainly less optimistic (or rather much more pessimistic) than Richardson's position as formulated in the book.

4 What remains? Economists cannot shy away from the problems of big agglomerations and the difficulties that all kinds of agglomeration economies and diseconomies present. I submit that one should continue looking for indicators of the positive and negative effects that are generated by large agglomerations, measure them, weigh them and try to arrive at conclusions, however partial or incomplete they may be. But one should not think that one can ever derive *one* satisfactory or unambiguous measure of the agglomeration economies of a city.

Nevertheless, there are agglomeration effects, in particular effects *on growth*—specifically with regard to the ability of agglomerations to attract factors of production and to obtain information from elsewhere (such as technical knowledge). Looking at the *effects* of agglomerations with regard to growth, one is indeed on much safer ground than if one tries to measure agglomeration economies *per se*, how ever difficult this much more limited task of measuring the *effects of agglomeration* sizes on such magnitudes as *structural changes* and *the migration of factors* still is. From the point of view of all the economies, or all the problems, that agglomerations generate, this is a *partial* aspect; it is less ambiguous than the study of *agglomeration economies in general* and it is highly relevant in the context of regional growth analyses.

The agglomeration factor[5] plays necessarily a dominant part in Richardson's Model in chapter 8 and in chapter 9 'Policy Implications of the Theory'. In this last chapter, Richardson naturally puts more weight on *cumulative causation factors* than on the working of the price mechanism (though certainly not neglecting the latter one-sidedly) and in this, he stresses what might be called another type of *locational constants* of the region: 'the institutional environment of the economy, its traditional public-private sector mix and its spatial structure' (p. 227). In particular, he considers also the geographic mobility, the values and traditions of the society, entrepreneurial qualities and corporate structures as well as the 'normal' degree of government intervention in economic affairs (ibid.). Within this framework, agglomeration economies should be built up in leading centres, and for lagging regions 'infrastructure subsidies may need to be supplemented by a direct subsidy to private firms', but not in the form of capital subsidies but of wage subsidies for a number of years (pp. 235-236). These are general statements, the concrete steps that are best for a given country depending very much on the specific parameters of the region, including the actual and potential industry structure.

II. Richardson's Model of Regional Growth

Richardson's *Model* of Regional Growth has two closely related functions: first, it is a summary

[5] Richardson's suggestions in chapter 7 as to how to measure agglomeration economies will be taken up in Section III.

statement of the theories advanced in the book, and second, it is to serve as the basis of empirical tests. As a summary statement, the Model is in certain ways more exact or more narrowly specified, while in other ways it is less specified than the verbal formulations in the previous chapters are. The verbal statements refer to a complicated decentralised-concentration-dispersion process — which might depend on the particular phase of economic development that the countries and different regions within countries may have reached—while the Model's emphasis seems to lie on simpler concentration processes as a result of agglomeration economies. At the same time, the Model is *open* in the sense that it would not exclude the possibility that econometric analyses show all kinds of diverging results, even a preponderance of neo-classical effects over agglomeration effects. But, as will be further discussed below, the Model may be *too general* to test the working of *two* factors that are so closely interrelated and partially counteract each other.

As to the empirical tests of the Model, it is true that for much of the testing adequate data are not available yet, which Richardson regrets because, quite correctly in my view, 'the crucial test for any theory is not its elegance and logical consistency but its explanatory and predictive power' (p. 216). Many readers will nevertheless regret that not even some preliminary testing has been attempted by the author. Against this he argues that it would be unfortunate if the theory had to be 'rejected prematurely because it failed to pass incomplete, flimsy and poorly designed tests' (p. 217). Not knowing of any tests that might be relevant in this context other the many studies quoted in the book, I respect this attitude though I do not fully agree with it. Some readers of the book might have wanted to learn more about what exactly is missing, in terms of data, in order to design a good test, and how statisticians might help the economists in procuring the data that are needed.

In the following I shall make some remarks on the way the operational model has been formulated and furthermore I shall discuss the points at which I think the model may run into difficulties if tested empirically. Partly on the basis of this, I shall try to extend the model where I think this may be useful (in Part B of this article).

With his Model of Regional Growth, Richardson sets out to explain (in the sense this word is normally used in econometric studies) the rate of growth of a *particular region* within a national economy. As the basis for the definition of a region, Richardson favours nodality criteria (p. 8), to obtain areas that are a kind of functional economic area but larger than metropolitan areas. But Richardson's definition remains vague. 'The "region" as opposed to the "metropolitan area" may then define itself in the sense that regional boundaries are found, even if they cannot be precisely drawn, in the no-man's land at the spatial limits of the geographical spread of agglomerating forces internal to contiguous regions' (p. 8-9). Agglomerating forces are to be examined: hence one cannot assume beforehand that one knows where their spatial limits are. The relevant economic variables of the *national economy* are taken as data: in this sense the model is a partial model. The growth of the Region that is studied depends on:

(i) particular *regional variables*—macroeconomic variables of the Region as well as certain spatial characteristics of the Region;

(ii) certain variables pertaining to the aggregative *rest of the economy* (such as the rate of return on capital, the wage rate) or to the total economy (its rate of technical progress); and

(iii) certain *spatial relationships* between the Region and particular other regions.

(a) The Equations of the Model

The Model contains five equations (pp. 212-14), (1) a 'definitional growth equation', (2) a capital stock equation, (3) a labour supply function, (4) a locational preference function and (5) a technical progress function. These functions are formulated with much cautioning—as kinds of tentative suggestions ('. . . a possible formulation . . . might be . . .') which are to be revised in the light of new insights; but they nevertheless contain a definite summary statement of the author's ideas: with qualifications to be discussed later, an operational statement.

1 The regional growth rate y is described by the definitional equation

$$y = (ak + (1-a)l)^{\alpha} + t$$

in which k and l are the growth rates of capital and labour, and a and $(1-a)$ their respective income shares. The exponent α reflects returns to scale, and t is the rate of technical progress. With regard to the returns to scale, Richardson is thinking above all of agglomeration economies that appear both as a generator and as a consequence of growth.[6]

2 The growth rate of the capital stock depends on
a measure of regional agglomeration economies (A);
the growth rate of the Region's income and the absolute level of the Region's capital stock;
the coefficient of variation of the capital stock per unit of area in the urban centres of the Region; and
the capital return differential between the Region and the rest of the economy.

The agglomeration factor A (pp. 179, 213) is a weighted sum of (i) the *number* of urban centres (above an—as yet unspecified—threshold size), (ii) the average agglomeration economies of the z urban centres of the Region (with the economies for each centre i calculated as its population N_i to the β_ith power[7], where β_i is an unspecified function of N_i), and (iii) the average distance between all pairs of urban centres in the Region (the latter with a negative parameter). Apart from β and its dependence on N, the weights for the three components of A have to be determined before this variable A becomes operational. Besides, $\beta(N)$ could be expected to depend on the Region's industry structure.

3 The growth rate of the Region's labour supply is a function of the Region's natural population growth, its agglomeration factor A (as above), a measure of its locational preferences (see below) and of the wage rate differential between the Region and the rest of the system.

4 The locational preferences, in turn, are themselves dependent on the Region's agglomeration economies A, on the population potential of the Region's leading city, on the average length of residence in the Region, on the wage rate differential (as above), and on the mobility costs between the Region and the closest higher income Region.

5 Technical progress in the Region is determined by the agglomeration factor A, by the growth rate of the capital stock, the rank of the leading city in the national urban hierarchy, and the national rate of technical progress $\bar{t}$, with the impact of $\bar{t}$ on the Region depending on the (as yet unspecified) degree of the Region's connectivity with the rest of the economy.

It is seen that the model incorporates both unbalanced growth tendencies and tendencies towards factor price equalisation through inter-regional factor movements; and furthermore the import of the distance factor, both intra-regional and inter-regional, is taken into account.

(i) Agglomeration economies A appear in all equations—save the definitional growth equation (1): their levels influence the movements of labour and capital as well as the flow of technical progress, and they appear once more, in a different form, in the population potential (in 4) as well as in the rank in the national urban hierarchy (in 5) of the Region's leading city. All these factors (with appropriate signs) make for *unbalanced* inter-regional—as well as intra-regional growth.[8]

(ii) Factors that may either reinforce or counterbalance these tendencies are the inter-regional differentials in wage rates (in (3) and (4)) and in capital return rates (in (2)), both of which figure so important in neo-classical analyses, together with the absolute size of the capital stock (in (2), whose influence is supposed to be inversely related—*partially*—to its size).

(iii) Initial conditions are put into the system, first, via the locational preferences of labour: the longer people have (on the average) lived in the region, and the greater the distance to the closest higher income region, the smaller is the chance that labour moves out—*ceteris paribus*, of course, cf. (4). Secondly, the effect of distance is to slow down the diffusion of technical progress over space: the smaller the distances (and the better the traffic connections) between the Region and the rest of the system, the greater is the Region's connectivity with the national economy and the greater consequently is its technical progress *rate*—this is Richardson's hypothesis (which is not related to the level of technical know-

[6] Rather than criticising this equation in detail, I should just like to remark that it would have been useful to explain more carefully why this particular form has been chosen (also, ρ should have been used instead of t).

[7] The exponent β of N should obey the same function for all cities, hence its subscript i should have been dropped.

[8] The one factor that is—even theoretically—least convincing is the inter-urban variation in the capital stock per area unit: great density differentials as between cities are supposed to reduce the inflow of capital. I do not see this, much less how this variable should convincingly be tested (see below).

ledge). These arguments lead naturally back to the agglomeration factor since a good connectivity in this context is, of course, the same thing as a high level of (inter-urban or inter-regional) *common agglomeration economies* that are conducive to the diffusion of innovation.

On the basis of the arguments advanced in connection with the five equations and the variables appearing in them, the following determinants of the regional income growth rate are obtained in Richardson's reduced form equation (p. 214) there is no need to reproduce the formula here:

Regional agglomeration economies: the size and distance structure of the regional urban system; the Regional centre's population potential and national importance; the size and the spatial density variation of the Regional capital stock—condensed into five variables;
the connectivity of the Region with the rest of the system and the transport costs to the closest higher income region (two variables);
the regional population growth rate and the average length of residence in the region (two variables);
the regional-national wage rate and capital earnings differentials (two variables); and
the national technical progress rate. There is in total a set of 12 explanatory variables for the regional growth rate.

(*b*) *Evaluation of the Model*

As a general remark, notice that there is a difficulty in testing Richardson's fundamental thesis about regional growth (as quoted on page 2 above) which differentiates between *stages* of development —a phase of initial *concentration* and the stage of sustained economic growth associated with *dispersion*, apart from a later stage of decentralised *metropolitan* growth which is not relevant here: a test would necessarily have to take this into account. By contrast, in Richardson's Model, there exists only *one stage* and there is *no reversal*: there obtains either a concentration process or a dispersion process (or a straight regional deconcentration process if the agglomeration factor would turn out to have a negative influence). The apparent formulation of the Model is one that only refers to a concentration process through agglomerating factors. Thus there is a discrepancy between the verbal formulations and the specification of the Model, which should be kept in mind from the outset. This is not just a *mistake* that might be corrected easily; it poses a severe problem which is not easily solved at all, and which leads back to the question whether it is not too much of a burden for *one* Model to be applicable to two stages of economic development that differ in an extremely important spatial aspect.

The questions that should be answered in the following are:

(i) Do these hypotheses appear to be fruitful, in particular in the light of the underlying theory?
(ii) Does the operational form of these hypotheses satisfy certain criteria so one can expect that econometric analyses—in the ideal case that sufficient data are available—yield good results?
(iii) Can the operational model be improved upon —in order to minimise the danger that the theory is rejected prematurely?

My position should be clear: I have so much sympathy with Richardson's basic position on the effects of agglomeration economies *vis-a-vis* the 'pure' neo-classical adjustment process that I support Richardson wholeheartedly in these endeavours. Furthermore, I think that questions (i) and (ii) cannot be treated separately if, as is Richardson's objective, one wants to go beyond very general hypotheses. What shall not be discussed in the following is the set of more narrowly *econometric* questions that arise in the course of testing the model. Richardson has, quite deliberately, not formulated all parts of the model in an operational way: many questions have been left open—to be settled only after one knows what data are to be used, and there would be no sense in going into this again. Also I shall not remark on the general and extremely important question of where and how *leads and lags* should be introduced if such a model is to be tested—leads and lags whose introduction might help solve some of the identification problems of the model.

1 The model might be used either for a cross-section analysis of many regions within a national system, or a combined cross-section time-series analysis. A pure time-series analysis for *one* region would run into the danger that—even if enough annual data were available—the variations in many of the independent variables would not be great enough

to make meaningful tests possible; thus it might turn out that in such an analysis only the regional population growth rate and the national technical progress rate obtain significant coefficients, while *all other effects* enter only the *constant factor* of the equation. This kind of a simple analysis is certainly not what Richardson intends to suggest. But such reflections do bring into mind that beside the national technical progress rate, at least *one* other *national* growth variable should be included in all such analyses—growth of total demand, growth of the national capital stock, or possibly the growth rate of GNP—even if one is not interested in cyclical changes. There are longer term or secular variations which are not sufficiently covered by Richardson's variables.

2 Among the variables included in the model, there are two which I would criticise. The first is the area density variation of the regional capital stock: I just don't know what to make out of this variable—in an operational context. The second variable is the length of residence in the region. The average length $\bar{L}$ may be great because (i) people do *not* move *in and out* very easily (which would indicate that locational preferences of people *born in the Region* are indeed great), but also because (ii) most of the young people emigrate (so only old people with long residences stay). In any case, there are many combinations of facts possible that yield either high or low values for $\bar{L}$, and therefore I doubt very much whether there is a unique relationship between the locational preferences for a region and the average length of residence; hence I would not include such a variable in the model. I would rather look for particular features of the region (such as natural resorts and climatic characteristics) and possibly also consider past migration rates as indicators of locational preferences.

3 The other variables included in the model make sense to me: these variables do have a bearing on growth: I think I interpret Richardson correctly if I take their list not as a number that should by all means be included (if the data were available) but rather as a set from which to choose, depending on how the variables are defined for operational purposes.

But I suspect that there is not enough *independent variation* in the intra-regional spatial variables—size and distance structure of the urban system, the Regional centre's population potential and national importance, as well as the size of the capital stock, considering in particular that the agglomeration variable has four coefficients itself and a functional relationship, all of which have to be determined in the course of the econometric analysis. In answer to this, the correct reply would be: so let's *see* which ones do exhibit enough independent variation and in addition do have an influence on growth—and get rid of the others. (There is a certain flaw in this argument, but that is—not yet—Richardson's problem, at least on this more theoretical, rather than econometric, level of the discussion).

The more important question is whether—with the relatively great number of variables—enough variables are included to cover the *most relevant* theoretical interdependencies in connection with economic growth in space: whether these are the best variables, from the point of view of Richardson's own objectives.

4 Turning to the *implications* of the Model, in terms of the concentration-dispersion process mentioned above, the implications of the model may be studied by comparing the results obtained in a hypothetical empirical analysis for a small region (A) and, alternatively, in (roughly) the same geographical area, a larger region (B). Assume that the small region has a given spatial structure and industry structure, a given income level and growth rate, and a given location within the whole system of the (given) national economy, so all the explanatory variables of the regional growth rate assume particular values, and on the basis of these, a certain *estimated* regional growth rate is derived within an econometric study for the whole system (Case A). Now compare this with the *estimated* growth rate that is obtained if this region is *larger* than considered first, but apart from this fact all other changes are as small as can reasonably be assumed: the rest of the economy is (almost) the same, and so are the region's relationships (or differentials) with it; within the region, the average population density is the same as before and again the same as the national average; but the total population and hence also the urban populations are greater, hence there are more large urban centres than in the smaller region; assume that accordingly the region's largest city is also greater than before (Case B). The variables that are necessarily greater in Case B than in Case A

are all the agglomeration-economies variables[9] and the regional capital stock. Thus unless the level of the capital stock has a significant dampening effect, which neutralises the effect of the increased agglomeration variable, i.e., unless in the reduced form the coefficient of the capital stock has the same order of magnitude as that of the agglomeration variables,[10] the *estimated growth rate* for B is greater than for A. This obtains because against the effects of his variable *A*, the only countervailing influence is that of *K*. Now it is true that a larger *private* capital stock may discourage (to some extent) further investment, *ceteris paribus* of course. This is not true of *infrastructure capital*, however, whose level should have a positive effect on capital movements and on regional growth. Furthermore, even the *private* capital stock would have a negative impact on growth only if the *per capita* values (or the values per employee) were higher than before. At the same time there is the encouraging influence of the agglomeration factor on investment: so a large *K* can only be thought of as a partially neutralising factor—I think this is also Richardson's position, with which I would fully agree. A large private capital stock might have a negative impact on the *inflow of capital*, but at the same time it may make it easier to attract additional labour. For these reasons, it is questionable whether a larger capital stock has indeed a net negative effect on the overall regional growth rate. Richardson is justified in leaving this question open—to be settled by empirical analyses. But for the reasons just given, I am doubtful whether definite results are obtained with regard to *K*. It might even be that there is a high degree of multicollinearity between *A* and *K* and that their two influences cannot be identified or isolated: thus *K* might receive a (statistically significant) *positive* coefficient in empirical analyses while A might drop out. Such results must always be interpreted with great care.

5 The model is indeed formulated in such a way that it can better describe the *initial concentration* processes than the *concentrated dispersion* that takes place in many countries and that Richardson analyses in the text. In the light of the arguments of the last paragraph, I do suspect that in an empirical test of Richardson's model for most industrialised countries,

either all larger and more urbanised regions (as Region B), would obtain a larger growth rate than smaller regions (Case A), as a result of Richardson's assumptions about the working of the agglomeration factor;

or more likely, that the bias introduced by the treatment of the agglomeration economies leads to the result that variable *A* is not statistically significant at all.

It might indeed be that in the example with the two regions A and B, an *overstatement* of the larger, and more urbanised, region's growth chances is introduced through the agglomeration variable. In any case, it would at least be possible that in reality, depending on the particular spatial structure of the larger region as compared with the smaller region the growth chances of the larger region are *no* greater. It might be that some measure of *per capita* agglomeration economies is a better variable (though not necessarily): such a procedure would also leave the *capital stock per head* unchanged. In investigations of growth rates one might expect to obtain more consistent results if only explanatory variables are taken that may all be read as *per capita variables*, or else if all variables are *aggregative* ones. This argument applies mostly to the agglomeration variable; other illustrations of the significance of this argument could be construed but would not add anything not covered by the above mentioned arguments.

6 Thus the main argument against Richardson's formulation of the model is that the *levels* of income of different regions are not identical with the determinants of the rates of growth of income. A similar argument applies to the way the diffusion of technical knowledge is treated in connection with growth. It is correct that a low degree of connectivity of a region with the rest of the economy may be expected to result in particularly long delays in the absorption of new ideas or new techniques. Income may be low in that region because it has not absorbed yet many of the innovations that were introduced in more centrally located regions in the past. If the backward region experiences lags of say ten years behind all other regions, is it not conceivable that the *rate* of innovation is nevertheless the same? Indeed,

[9] Unless one has the extremely implausible situation of slight changes in the average distance between all pairs of urban centres are much more important than the rise in the *number* and *sizes* of centres.

[10] *Order of magnitude*, because not *all* other variables can remain exactly constant in Case B as compared with Case A.

if it were not, the development lag and the income differential compared with the rest of the system would *necessarily* become *ever greater*:[11] this is certainly not Richardson's hypothesis in the verbally formulated parts of the book. Richardson can only mean that this holds for certain *phases* of economic development (with this, I would agree), but not that it is generally true for *all stages* of economic development.

7 The conclusion to be drawn from this discussion is this: the model applies much more to a take-off period, or a period of *accelerated growth*, than to more normal (or more frequent) phases of economic development. This view is substantiated if the agglomeration variable is considered again from a different point of view—if the implications of the model are compared with reality, and if the intentions of the model are being kept in mind—to explain *rates* of growth. Only compare regions that have high degrees of urbanisation and of concentration of economic activities with regions that are less urbanised or even have smaller average population densities: the general result that the application of Richardson's model would yield is that the former always have higher growth rates than the latter. This again is not true of reality: this again holds more for take-off periods than other phases of development, as mentioned above.

III. The Model: Summary

The evaluation of Richardson's Model may be summarised from a more narrow specification, or testing, point of view and from a broader economic point of view.

1 Starting with the first point of view, the Model is in many ways not operational yet. The author leaves it open how it is to be used either as a time series and/or a cross section model. The formulations are more in the spirit of an explanatory model, but the question is how it could or should also be used as a predictive model and what kinds of changes this would necessitate. Many formulations are only provisional—and Richardson himself would insist that the exact specification of the model could only be completed in the course of testing the model, when one knows what data are available for what kind of regions. In particular, the time structure of the equation system is left open: lead and lag relationships are not discussed at all. The reduced form of the model implies however, that all variables refer to the same time period. So one has yet to explore how the relationships of the Model could be improved upon by the introduction of dynamic relationships (other than just growth rates for the same period of time). The consideration of dynamic relationships would also be relevant in the context of the problem of identifying particular influences.

2 As to the five equations, I am most sceptical about the regional technical progress function, not only on statistical, but even more on theoretical grounds, as mentioned in paragraph (6) of the last section: one should distinguish more clearly between the *level* of technical knowledge of say, lagging regions and their *rates* of progress. I have doubts about the locational preference equation and hence indirectly also about important variables in the labour supply function: For reasons of multicollinearity I suspect that in the latter, only the natural rate of population increase and a kind of potential-variable will turn out to be statistically significant; this does not mean that in specific studies particular other variables will not also be useful. Similar arguments apply to the capital return differential in the capital stock equation: in addition to the problems of multicollinearity, there it is the data problem. I mentioned that I do not believe in the capital stock density variable (paragraph (2), last section) and that the *absolute level* of the existing capital stock might not be a useful variable to take (paragraph (5))—unless the populations are the same for different regions, and that one should take into account the amount of capital invested in *infrastructure*. From all this follows that one has to doubt whether more than a very few of the variables will turn out to be statistically significant in the reduced form equation of the regional growth rate.

3 As to the broader theoretical arguments, I would conclude in this way. While it was correct to put more stress on the importance of agglomeration economies and the diffusion of technical and organisational knowledge over space than had been the case in most systematic statements of regional

[11] Since I see no offsetting forces in the *other* variables.

growth theory, Richardson has overstated his case a bit in so far as he is talking of *growth rates*. Nothing has to be taken away from what he says about the preconditions of growth; but the application to differential growth rates has to be limited to periode of accelerated growth. A *minimum* of total (intra-metropolitan plus inter-metropolitan) agglomeration economies is always required for a satisfactory rate of economic growth, and this minimum varies as between different phases of economic development. Also, different regions within a national economy may experience accelerated growth at different times. The question is how such observations can be incorporated into one model. In an attempt to deal with these problems, one has to try and go beyond Richardson's operational model.

4 In extending Richardson's model, a particular problem to be tackled is the *definition* of regions (apart from the data problem): there are model economic areas on different levels—from metropolitan areas up to the whole national economy. No matter how such areas are chosen, there will always be one nodal region that contains the national capital and there will be a lot of others with a much smaller economic significance. What holds for small economic areas may not hold for larger ones, even if the national importance of the regional centre is taken into account. The conclusion should be that (below the national level) *one* regional level is not enough: one should distinguish between larger regions and subregions within the larger regions and consider their interdependencies—but this goes beyond a criticism of Richardson's book.

Concluding, one should not lose sight of the fact that by formulating an operational model, Richardson has inspired his readers much more than by a formulation that would have been less suceptible to criticism: his readers have advanced one step further than if he had confined himself to an unassailable presentation. There has been more occasion for the readers to continue thinking along these lines than would have been the case otherwise.

PART B. AN EXTENDED MODEL

In this second part of the paper, an attempt is made to present, in outline form, an extended model of regional growth, in which growth is defined as the *growth rate of income*. This is a more complex variable than either the rate of population growth or the rate of *per capita* income growth. In a more complex system the latter two variables should be distinguished: here this will not be done. The purpose of the model is to enable us to learn more about growth processes in reality by testing certain hypotheses about historical developments. This clearly separates the following discussions from all studies that focus on theoretical implications of certain (theoretical) assumptions. The discussion of all kinds of implications (for regional policy etc.) of the model is of great importance, but is secondary here: this could in any case only be done after the model, in one or the other form, has been tested.

I. Basic Considerations: The Growth Process

A satisfactory model of regional growth has to take account of

the factors on which locational decisions of the economic agents are based; and of

fundamental economic relationships between aggregative variables on the regional, subregional and metropolitan levels; and it has to

describe characteristic features of the regional growth processes as observed in reality, which—in turn—are important arguments in the decision functions for further actions of the economic agents.

Since spatial systems and their development processes can not realistically be derived on the basis of the technological and behaviour functions of individual economic households and firms, the best procedure in formulating a regional growth model seems to be to use the *historical developments* of economies as the basis for formulating *broad hypotheses* that are to describe these developments, and only subsequently to reformulate the hypotheses in such a way that they become part of an *operational model*—in the light of the available investigation methods and data.

In the following statement, both the historical description and the theoretical analysis will be short. I shall rely heavily on the body of knowledge that exists on these matters, in particular on Richardson's verbal statements and on my remarks in the first half of this article and I shall focus on those relationships that can be quantified and tested.

The basic facts that I take as given in the following are:

the process of industrialisation as observed both in older and in newly industrialised countries entailed, during phases of *accelerated growth*, an increased concentration of activities in and around the most important raw material sites as well as trading centres and administrative centres, the process of concentration being most marked if these different types of centres coincided in the national capital;

the industrialisation process spreads to other—regional and subregional—centres as it continues, and leads to relative concentration processes in different parts of the spatial economy as well; and

the larger the agglomerations become, the more sub-nuclei within them develop and become sub-centres in a kind of hierarchical, partly specialised system of centres within metropolitan areas.

Thus one has (i) *concentration*, (ii) concentrated *decentralisation*, and (iii) at least partly, *decentralised concentrations* (Bövener, 1973, 162) or, as Richardson has described this kind of development, a process of 'concentrated decentralised dispersion' (p. 135). From a much simplified theoretical point of view, the concentrated dispersion process may be viewed in the following way. Economic development needs among many other things a minimal division of labour, i.e. large enough markets: this implies a certain degree of *integration* of the economic units, and this, in turn, means a minimal degree of

agglomeration: this yields *intra-urban agglomeration effects*; also one has improved *traffic connections* between *different agglomerations*; these rise to graving inter-urban agglomeration effects.

Total agglomeration effects as the sum of intra-urban and inter-urban agglomeration effects depend on the

number of economic activities in the various agglomerations; and on

the *levels* of these activities (their net values added).

If for satisfactory self-sustained economic growth a minimum of total agglomeration economies is necessary and if the rate of growth is a positive function of these economies, then a cumulative *process is initiated* as soon as this minimum is reached at any location C, say the Centre, in particular if with growing population numbers, rising incomes and improved traffic networks the *economic distances* from the Centre also decline. Ever smaller centres will attain the minimum value of agglomeration economies that is necessary for growth, because they benefit from common (inter-urban agglomeration economies with other centres; hence incomes in such secondary centres also rise and with the ensuing immigration from its own hinterlands, their own (intra-urban) agglomeration effects also continue growing.

In an advanced stage of economic development with high productivity and income levels, the development and diffusion of *further new* techniques require ever larger markets and still more *integration*: this has a certain dampening effect on the growth and diffusion processes but can not alter them in a qualitative way. Much more often it happens that the growth processes in the largest centres, rather than in smaller ones above the minimal agglomeration values, run into difficulties because certain *bottlenecks* arise.

(i) If a centre grows larger and larger absolutely, additional immigrants have to overcome greater and greater distances if the same rate of growth of the labour force is to be maintained;

(ii) intra-metropolitan distances grow with the expansion of the city, and commuting distances also rise on the average—furthermore, people have to spend more and more time travelling if they want to spend weekends in the country; and

(iii) with rising incomes and rising population numbers, wages and land values assume values which make large centres less attractive for many firms and even employees though they may be more attractive than ever before for certain other lines of business (those that push the former ones out) and also certain other households; and the fact that there is also

(iv) in many parts of the centre, sites may not be available any more in the desired quantities.

These factors strengthen

the *inter-regional dispersion* processes which lead to *additional regional concentration* processes, as well as

the processes of *suburbanisation* and *decentralisation* within large agglomerations, and

processes of concentration *around* the largest centres, in satellite developments or even somewhat more 'independent' developments within the largest centres' umlands or regions.

It is impossible to generalise about the relative rates of growth of various centres as a (partial) function of their relative sizes. At first, due to a predominance of the agglomeration factor, the biggest centres have the highest growth rates, while later on, in the process of *concentrated dispersion*, smaller centres grow faster than before and (in relative terms) possibly faster than their bigger predecessors; during all this time thinly settled areas and the smallest communities lose population—unless they are attractive for touristic activities or as favourite residential sites not too far from agglomeration centres. Thus in general—as mentioned above—there is a minimum value of total population that a town or city must have reached in order to be able to participate in this dispersion process of economic growth.

This minimum depends not only on the overall economic structure and technology of the economy and of the particular centres, but also on the population densities and the mobility of the population. In particular, this minimum value is determined by the sum of *intra*-community plus *inter*-community agglomeration economies; thus minimum values in the neighbourhood of urbanised areas may be smaller than for more isolated locations in lagging regions. This would not be true if at least one of two conditions is fulfilled: either the mobility of the population is very small so business has to move out into the (lagging) regions instead of labour moving into economically more attractive areas, or regional policy measures strongly induce firms to expand their business in these areas. In such cases, successful take-off processes are more readily started in the less developed regions than otherwise.

As to the relative growth rates of various centres above this minimum size, there are two important possibilities that must be considered:

(*a*) The biggest centre manages to *keep growing* faster than smaller centres (i.e. with the highest growth *rate*), though this must not apply to the city centre, but rather to the whole metropolitan area.

(*b*) Once the diffusion process has reached smaller centres and a take-off has been initiated in them, these centres attain *higher* growth rates than bigger centres because in the latter, bottlenecks have made themselves felt.

Whenever case (*b*) holds true—and if, in addition, *size* were the only determinant of growth, which is certainly not true—the sequence of growth rates of centres of different sizes may be pictured as a wave-like movement— a movement that starts at the Economic Capital and other big centres and moves down to ever smaller centres above the minimum of intra-urban and inter-urban agglomeration economies.[12] Fig. 1 shows these relationships between *sizes* and *growth rates* in a very schematic way.

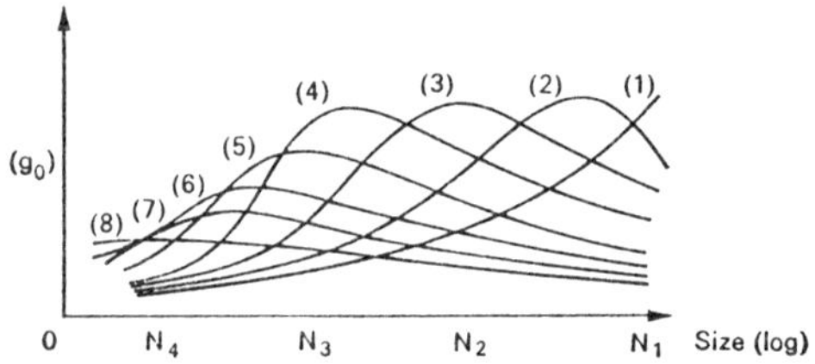

Fig. 1. Growth Waves

Note again that *own size* and *integration with other centres* are partial substitutes for each other and that this is completely neglected in the diagram. Thus the functional relationships should be thought of as applying, not to *particular* cities in an however (in-)exact way, but to the *average* centre of a given size, since the growth of a particular city always depends on much more than its size alone; above all, the spatial aspect is neglected in this diagram. And it is to be interpreted as a *description*, one that is neither rigid nor has anything to do with notions of equilibrium. The numbers in the diagram refer to eight successive time periods. In order that all centres can keep their places on the abscissa for all periods, the *sizes* of the centres refer to the values reached at the beginning of the take-off period. The graph shows—and this certainly is an *arbitrary* assumption at this point—that *peak* growth rates for all centres above size N^3 are the same and that, *in the end, marked differences* in the growth rates have disappeared. This may or may not be true but is in any case not at all interesting because no country has reached such *final stage*—or may ever reach such a state of proportional growth *at all locations*, or of zero growth *everywhere*, for that matter. Whether at the left tail—for smaller centres, say below N_4—growth rates of total income are positive in the face of out-migration—i.e. *where exactly* the point g_0 of a zero growth rate is located—

12 It should be noted that similar growth waves, first defined with regard to diffusion processes over space, have been discussed by Morrill (1968, 1973) and by Kariel and Vaselenak (1973).

depends strongly on the mobility and on the rates of natural population growth in the various regions. In a particular country, or during a certain phase of economic development, the consequences of the spatial dispersion process may be such that for (regional) *centres* (with a population above N_2) growth rates and sizes are *inversely* related while for smaller centres (below N_2), the concentration process is still in full swing: growth is still an increasing function of size t (in phase 3).

Note that the growth processes illustrated by the diagram, in particular by the changes in the slopes of the growth functions down to that for periods (4) and (5), may be interpreted in two ways. Looking at the matter from the point of view of the largest centres and considering the rest of the system, one has a dispersion process which might be described in neo-classical terms. By contrast, from the point of view of the less industrialised, rural areas whose largest centres grow into industrial and tertiary centres in the growth process, the whole development is one of cumulative growth that goes on at the expense of the least developed parts (anyway those that are losing population through migration to the regional and subregional centres). And the whole development process may be considered as one of balanced growth or unbalanced growth depending on whether the growth function for a particular period, say (6), (7) or (8), has a predominantly negative or a positive slope. An extreme case of unbalanced growth would obtain if a growth function like line (1) in Fig. 1 were to remain valid *throughout*.

II. Scope of the Model

An operational model of regional growth may be conceived so it either (i) captures essential features of more than one phase of economic development and is also able to account for *changes* in important parameters (and thus describes all of the various typical cases or alternatives that were illustrated by the diagram in the last section) or (ii) it applies to only one particular phase of development and aims at embodying the typical growth function that holds for this phase. Or (iii) the model could be deviced so as to test, for various *types* of centres, particular relationships: between growth on the one hand, and size, location and economic structure, on the other.

In all these cases, size plays an important role, but other elements, such as locations and locational advantages as well as economic structure, also have to come in.[13]

By contrast, prices play a secondary role only. My basic position with regard to sizes and prices is the following. It is the aggregate of the interdependencies and hence increasing returns to scale for the whole urban economic structure—rather than industry scale economies alone, even less so pure price effects—that are at the bottom of the rapid metropolitan growth processes. High prices are paid because of high productivities, and not because factors are scarce from the beginning: rather they *become scarce* because they are in great demand by industries that take advantage of large markets. *Prices are the effects of growth and therefore should not be used to explain this growth.*[14]

The size and location aspects have to do with the *redistribution of economic agents*
as between *centres of different* sizes and at *different locations* within the national economy. Other aspects have to do with the redistribution of economic agents
as between *metropolitan areas* and (more rural) *hinterlands* and as between the *cores* of metropolitan areas and their *suburbs*, and, in addition to these which had already been mentioned before, there is in many cases also a redistribution;
as *between large regions* of the economy,
though it is obvious that the latter are in most cases also related to the sizes of the centres in alternative regions.

Before one can start formulating a growth model, it has to be clear what kinds of spatial growth and redistribution processes are to be studied, what the basic hypotheses are, and what consequences these aims have for the delimitation of regions: the latter are important for the way individual behaviour functions and economic restrictions are to be aggregated.

Of the four spatial redistribution processes listed above, the first—relating to *sizes* and *locations*; the second—relating to differential growth rates of *various regions* have important places in a regional model. The basic problem that is to be studied in

[13] If this were not the case, simple studies of rank-size curves and their movements over time would suffice.
[14] In this connection, the studies by Muth should be mentioned.

quantitative terms is the combined roles of *sizes* and *distances* and, in addition, of sectoral *structures* in shaping growth in space, apart from the role of other *locational advantages* or *locational preferences*. The notion that has particular implications is that the (partial) relationship between sizes and growth rates may not be monotonic (as would be the case in phase 1—or in phase 8—in Fig. 1). The function may in a qualitative way be different for different size ranges of the centres and the question is, to what extent it is possible to explain the different functional types by other variables. Therefore the spatial units must be such that the identification of both arms of a growth function like the ones mentioned in Fig. 1 (say phase 3) is not made impossible from the outset. Furthermore, interactions between industrial regions and less developed agrarian areas should not be aggregated away. All this means that not only *large regions* can be considered. One needs to study the development of functional economic areas around smaller centres as well. But most of such *lower order* functional economic areas are also part of the (higher order) functional economic area of a *large* regional centre.

In this situation, the best solution seems to be to consider, below (1) the national level, two further levels of aggregation; (2) large *regions* and (3) *sub-regions* within the regions. The large *regions* would necessarily be nodal regions of the highest order; in another terminology: here one looks for the highest order growth poles of the economy, and one defines borders on the basis of dominance within the whole area of the national economy. Apart from the National Economic Capital, the centres of the *regions* may at least roughly all belong into the *same* category (as far as the orders of their influences, or the orders of centrality, are concerned). This is not in general true of the *subregions*. If one thinks of about *10 to 15 regions* and *10 subregions* in *each* region, certainly regions with different economic structures will be obtained even if all of them should turn out to be nodal regions. Some will be less industrialised, or more agrarian, with significantly lower average incomes and of a lower order of centrality than others. This is in any case true if the *sub*region that is formed around a regional capital is compared with the other subregions within the same region.

A quantitative model of economic growth has to analyse, for each of the regions and subregions, aggregate input changes and to determine how these translate into output growth while at the same time, it has to consider how input and output quantities are affected by demand variations.

This means that special attention has to be given to

factor quantity changes and *technological changes* which result in economic growth, and in particular to

intra-regional agglomeration processes; as well as *inter-regional factor movements*

and in the study of the above-mentioned spatial redistribution processes;

locational advantages or preferences will play an important role.

The specification must be such that the characteristics of the regional growth process as outlined above can be captured—that they may be described by the model and are tested in the econometric application of the model. In the model that is to be outlined below, the focus will be on the third aspect mentioned at the beginning of this section. The primary goal is to capture the characteristic growth processes during one particular phase first, and then work towards the first-mentioned aspect by (*a*) expanding the application of the basic model and (*b*) by combining the results for various phases in a systematic way. While in case (*a*), one carries out a combined cross-section time-series analysis from the start, case (*b*) is easier and should be attempted first: a systematic comparison of the parameters obtained for cross-section analyses (for different phases), and possibly an explanation of the parameter variations as between different phases by other variables.

III. Structural Relationships

(a) *General Description*

In the following, the basic structural relationships of the model will first be described in *very broad terms*. The general notion is that

growth depends on *factor augmentations* as well as technological and organisational and other *structural change*, and that all these changes cannot be separated from changes in *demand*; and that

factor input changes at a particular location (or region) have to be explained (or described) in terms of (both economic and non-economic) *characteristics of the location*.

This means that a combination of *capacity variables* and *capacity utilisation determinants* is considered. Again, only in a more complex approach could these two facets of the matter be distinguished. The simplifying approach taken here has, among others, the advantage that certain identification problems are avoided.

Since growth rates of locations are of principal interest in the following, I shall focus on them first—though still remaining on a very general level but trying to indicate where problems of specification and of measurement may arise later on—and then turn to the individual decisions taken for the factors of production: here a central question—to be discussed later—will be at what levels of spatial aggregation what kinds of arguments might be relevant. The discussion on determinants of growth and on decision processes is very general because it can only serve as an introduction to the question which factors in the decision processes can be made operational and in particular, what kinds of inter-relationships between these factors exist. It is only after these points have been clarified that a more exact specification of the fundamental hypotheses is possible. Obviously the possible restrictions on the parameters of the model, as suggested by the characteristics of the spatial growth processes, and econometric specification problems of the variables and the hypotheses can only be discussed much later.

1 *The growth rate of income.* For a given location i, the rate of growth of aggregate income may be considered (as is standard practice in macroeconomic growth models) as being a function of the growth rates of labour (l) and of capital (k) and of technological change (if purely qualitative variations in the factor inputs are neglected here, which need not concern us as a separate element). In analysing actual growth, one should also bring in the development of *demand*, furthermore *structural elements* should be considered explicitly, and technological change should be broken up into

technological innovation (in a narrow sense of the word) and

organisational improvements: intrafirm reorganisation as well as *interfirm spatial reorganisation*—relocation and spatial *concentration* or *dispersion*.

This means that the rate of growth y_i of output of a location i should be related on the one hand; to the

rates of growth of all *inputs* available in i: in particular, of *labour* (l) and of *capital* (k)

the location's *industry structure* (S_i);

the location's *spatial structure* (and its changes), in particular the extent to which it gives rise to internal or *intra-locational agglomeration economies* (A_i^I); and

the rate of *technological innovation* (ρ_i).

On the other hand, an important element should be the growth rate of demand for the location's products. In the determination of total demand for the location, one can expect that—beyond the factors already mentioned—three factors are of particular importance:

the *growth rate of national demand* or the national rate of growth of production (y); and

the *geographical location* of the spatial unit within the whole economy, its connectivity with the rest of the economy or, to use *one* expression that may for the time being summarise this complex, the total of the *inter-locational agglomeration economies* (A_i^{II}), which is based on the proximity to existing.[15]

Furthermore, if the spatial unit is a *region*, the pull exerted by the region's centre may be important, as measured by—

the growth rate y_i^C *of the Central Subregion* of the region.

The growth of *demand* also depends, of course, heavily on the industry structure (S_i), which is to be taken as a datum, apart from the rate y that was mentioned explicitly. y is determined by factors which—at that level—are partly analogous to those effective at the level of a particular spatial unit and they include special demand factors that cause *cyclical* changes. It is not for this regional model to analyse these. Instead, one should as we do rely on the results of (national) macroeconomic analyses and thus take the national growth rate as given: regional models cannot neglect such macroeconomic inter-relationships and they should not be overburdened with such macroeconomic studies of their own. Similar arguments hold for the national technical progress rate. Presumably the regional

[15] Markets both for factors and for commodities.

technical progress rate is a function of the national rate ρ. Thus unless *specific information* is available on particular technical diffusion processes, the national rate ρ should be taken for the region, too—but since the effect of ρ makes itself felt though variations in y, this variable will be dropped altogether. However, if special information on technical progress in i is available a *specific* value ρ_i should be taken.

In the light of these arguments, one can simplify in the following way and write in general terms

$$y_i = y_i(l_i, k_i, S_i, A_i^I, A_i^{II}, y, y_i^c) \qquad (1)$$

Of the seven determinants of y_i that are now left, five are considered as data for this spatial unit. For a *region i* these would be S_i, A_i^I, A_i^{II} on the regional level, y on the national level, and y_i^c on the subregional level (to be discussed later). Turning to the two regional variables l_i and k_i, it should be clear that they ought to influence y_i *beyond* the impact of y and ρ only in so far as the regional factor growth rates are higher than the corresponding national rates.

2 The variables that determine the *growth of the labour force*[16] may—in even broader terms—be summarised as the following:

- the natural rate of growth of the labour force, and, as the variables that have a bearing on *migration rates*;[17]
- labour market characteristics (structure, size and wage levels);
- costs (cost of living, in particular of housing);
- variety of goods offered (consumer goods as well as cultural and recreational and entertainment facilities;
- infrastructure (quality and rates charged, in particular concerning the transportation system);
- distances to other centres as well as to tourist resorts;
- climatic and landscape features of the spatial unit; and
- characteristics which are not covered by this enumeration and which may be termed locational preferences.

It should be noted that, first, at least some of the variables listed here are influenced by new *investment outlays*: the 'labour market characteristics' include job openings which are thus also a function of the rate of *growth of capital*: This list also includes supply and demand elements. Secondly, the factors mentioned in this list have not been defined in any exact way; but this is not necessary at this point anyway because the *inter-relationships* between the various factors have to be discussed before the model can be formulated in an operational way. Therefore there is no need even to try to give a symbolic summary in the form of an equation.

3 The *rate of investment*, as k_i, is a function of local (or regional) savings and of capital movements, and in particular depends on

- market characteristics (size and incomes);
- industry structure;
- cost levels (in particular wages, tax rates);
- infrastructure (quality and cost);
- distances to (the markets of) other centres,

all of which determine together, in one way or another, the growth chances or the profit chances of a firm. In all this, expected rates of inmigration of labour also play a role. To a certain extent again, the residential qualities of the location come in, i.e. in so far as they enter the entrepreneurs' locational preferences and decision processes. If the spatial unit i is again interpreted as a region, then the whole procedure could be repeated for the subregions. The arguments presented under (1), (2) and (3) form an interdependent system. If the relationships were formulated as an equation system and numerical parameters were introduced, the theoretical implications of all sorts of exogenous changes might be studied. Since our aim is to capture certain characteristic features of actual growth processes and since *at this stage* the model should be kept within limits, the focus of the analysis is on the interregional *results* of growth processes, which may again be considered as the vehicles of further economic growth.

The main purpose is to study how *combinations of influences*, or even *conglomerate* variables have affected the growth process, *not* to isolate as *many individual influences* as possible—that should be done in further steps only. If four or five influences could be identified, among them say the *partial*

[16] I just mention Muth (1968) in place of a large literature on the subject.
[17] Some of these are normally included in the agglomeration variable.

influences of sizes, structures and distances, one should be satisfied for the moment. For all these reasons the main purpose of the discussion in the following is to *simplify* the hypotheses in a direction that makes them more operational. In doing this, special attention should be given to the question which influences may be expected to become effective at which levels—national, regional, or subregional. A further consideration—to be discussed in the next section—will be the purpose of the model and the implications to be derived from whether the model is to be used mainly for predictive or for explanatory purposes.

(b) *Interrelationships between the Variables*

The crucial role of the agglomeration factor has been stressed throughout in this paper, together with the difficulties in defining and measuring agglomeration economies. Obviously the agglomeration factor must in many contexts be considered as a proxy variable for a host of influences that are related to sizes of agglomerations:

commodity market as well as *labour market* sizes; and the
variety of goods and services offered; as well as
incomes, *wages*, unit *cost* levels; and
characteristics of the *infrastructure*.

To a large extent this is also true of the

sectoral structures; and
spatial structures of various centres.

This means that any one of these variables can only be expected to exhibit definite influences on factor (labour) migration and growth rates in a quantitative study if its magnitudes are significantly different from the values that are 'normally' associated with the particular sizes of the centres.

For these reasons one must doubt whether for the rates of *migration* more variables than

sizes, *structures*, *distances* from other centres on the one hand; and
particular locational factors, on the other, will turn out to be either necessary or important—if at all they have indeed had a significant impact and if they have been specified the right way.

For inter-regional capital movements and for the diffusion of technical progress similar arguments hold: unless a peculiar situation prevails in a particular region, many of the variables listed above may not be able to contribute anything to an explanation.[18]

This may especially be true of the *expected returns* and of the size of the *private capital stock*. What is important, however, in this context is the *availability* of *labour*.

Thus apart from the

locational qualities, however defined,
there may again only remain the variables connected with:
sizes, *structures*, and *distances*, and in addition;
the *availability of labour*;
the quality of the *infrastructure* as well as the expected public investment outlays in infrastructure; and
special incentives offered by public authorities.

In the case of capital movements, there is an additional difficulty, however: data on capital stocks of (small) regions and on interspatial capital movements are in many countries either not available or they are not very reliable and meaningful aggregates. In any case, the explanation of capital movements and of investment in smaller spatial units would require a much more sophisticated model than is possible in this approach and it might well be much more useful to start such an investigation within a study of its own and on the basis of small spatial units, rather than (larger) regions.

For these reasons, the capital growth equation will be dropped in the following. In its stead, the influences that should enter such an equation and that are not captured by other variables, should directly be taken over into the income growth

[11] However, there may be lags, between the time an innovation is introduced in the national centre and in more backward regions or subregions, though the overall *rate* of progress need not be smaller in the latter areas. It is only if there exist lags *and* if the national technical progress rate varies significantly over time, that such lags should be considered. The appropriate way to do this would be to work with distributed lags with variable lengths of time: the average lag for a particular region should be an increasing function of the distance between this region and the most advanced regions. Thus for the central region, there would have to be no lag at all (it would have to be identically zero). In computing distances between a region and more advanced regions, one might need to compute a special potential-measure. All this may yield extremely complex relationships, and I am doubtful whether the introduction of any technical progress function for subnational units will—in this context—yield any satisfactory results.

equations. The *national* rate of growth of capital, in any case, comes in as a determinant of the national growth rate, so the growth of capital is *not* altogether excluded. The same holds for the technical progress rate which enters indirectly through the national growth rate.

Thus only two structural equations are left, an income growth equation and a labour force growth equation. Because of the interdependencies, these two equations contain the same variables. Moreover, the number of the overall, though as yet unspecified, variables has been reduced; but this is more true of large regions than of the subregions. For small regions (as in smaller countries) and for subregions, additional *specific* variables should be introduced, while for (large) regions particular influences may either average out or not be significant if they are related to the whole region.

From a structural point of view my theses can now be summarised as follows. The determination of regional income growth rates and factor growth rates requires the specification of three interdependent equations. But due to the peculiar difficulties connected with the specification and estimation of the capital growth equation, I would, at the start, only work with two structural equations: for the growth rates of income and of the labour force, which due to the interdependencies mentioned above have to contain the same variables. Of these two equations, the income growth equation is of the greatest direct interest. Taking the regional level and thus abstracting from special factors that are effective only on lower levels of aggregation, one has

$$y_i = y_i(A_i, S_i, Q_i, n_i, y, y_i^c) \qquad (1)$$

i.e. the regional growth rate is determined by the combined influences of agglomeration factors (A_i—sizes and distances), the industry structure (S_i), locational qualities (Q_i) (including an index of infrastructure services), as well as the natural rate n_i of growth of the labour force and the income growth rates of the whole economy (y) and—as yet also predetermined—of the Central Subregion (y_i^c) of the region i.

It should be noted that in this formulation the industry structure assumes an additional significance. The rate of growth of employment in fast growing modern industries and hence the rate of income growth in a region depends, among other things, on the rate at which employees are released by declining industries, in particular the rate at which young people leave agriculture. This becomes important under conditions of full employment and for regions with a sizeable share of agriculture. The *infrastructure* variable is included in the locational qualities variable Q, and is also no longer mentioned here for the regional level, though it may turn out that this variable can more usefully be defined for smaller spatial units where their levels may have more meaning. Similar arguments may apply to the labour market bottlenecks, as far as the regional level is concerned.

Thus after the doubtful variables for regions are omitted, only the six variables: A_i, S_i, Q_i, n_i, y, y_i^c are left. Now note in particular that *wage rate differentials* and *capital return differentials are not listed any more*. From a technical point of view, there is the multicollinearity between these differentials and differences in A and S. But more fundamentally, the chain of causation runs from innovations and market sizes and high productivities to price and return differentials. Above all during take-off periods and during periods characterised by increasing concentration of economic activities, the agglomeration factor is a much more significant variable than factor return differentials are.

If during other phases of development, by contrast, the *scarcity* of production factors, say labour, is the most important single element that limits growth, then the *availability of factors* should be used as an additional explanatory variable, again *not* the return differential. Also the industry structure is an important determinant of the average wage level (as compared with other regions): this give one more reason for leaving the wage rate differential out of the picture—apart from the difficulties one encounters when one tries to measure comparative regional wage levels in a meaningful way. All this means that in actual practice, one should be even *less* neo-classical in a narrow sense, than Richardson is—though only as to the use of *prices* in econometric studies of regional growth, not necessarily with regard to *scarcities*.

IV. Specification of Variables: Sizes and Distances

The specification of the broadly formulated hypotheses is to be guided by the principle—which has been underlying most of the previous discussions anyway—that instead of enumerating factors that *may* have influenced growth, one should only take those determinants of growth that fulfill three conditions: it is to be suspected that such influences have actually existed; data must be available (or it must be possible to collect or construct relevant series); and there must be reason to expect that it will be possible to identify the expected effects in a quantitative study—i.e. these effects have not already been captured by another variable.

Furthermore it should be mentioned that some more simplifications are possible if the purpose of the model is (short-run) prediction rather than explanation (in the sense the econometricians use this term). For predictions one is above all interested in *stable* relationships of the variable in question with other variables about whose future changes one has some information. Such simplifications are above all possible with regard to the locational qualities variable, as will be discussed in detail in section V below. Before that is done, I shall turn to the agglomeration factors—all those influences which more or less directly have to do with *sizes and distances*. All the other variables—those related to the industry structure and to economic qualities of a spatial unit—do not present any specification problems of a *general* nature. An important variable that also need not be discussed any more is the natural rate of growth of the *region's labour force* (in the form of the *differential* as compared with the national rate. In the specification of a regional growth model, the treatment of the agglomeration factors and the decentralisation process is the single most difficult problem; it is also at the heart of the cumulative growth *v.* neo-classical growth controversy. The difficulties arise partly because the structural parameters may vary from one stage of development to the next—these difficulties would not arise only if from the start, the model is only specified for just one particular phase of development. But even then, there is the problem of allowing for different parameters of the agglomeration factors for different types or sizes of cities (cf. section VI). The agglomeration factor variables of regions should not be influenced heavily by changes in the boundaries between them (which to some extent may have to be drawn arbitrarily, from an economic point of view, if only the existing administrative units can be taken for data problems); furthermore, the agglomeration variable should be defined on a *per capita* basis. Agglomeration sizes and distances shall be brought in through four variables—which are to some extent correlated with each other: in addition to the intra-urban and inter-urban agglomeration factors, the traffic connections with other parts of the economy as well as will be considered the size of the hinterland of a centre—the area for which the spatial unit is, or has, the largest centre and from which it may most likely be expected to draw immigrants.

1 *The Agglomeration Factor*

The definition of the agglomeration factor A is based on the following notion, which, in a grossly simplifying manner, is to summarise all that has been discussed on agglomeration economies so far: If all structural differences between various agglomerations are neglected, then for a given economic unit h at location i the potential benefits ${}^hA_{ij}$ that h can reap from the economic activities at any location j may—*as a very rough approximation*—be thought of as a (multiplicative) function of

its own activity level ${}^hY_i$;
the number of participants in economic processes in j—as the number of employees, or more simply, of inhabitants N_j;
their average incomes Y_j; and
the (economic) distance d_{ij} between i and j (inverse value).

Thus

$${}^hA_{ij} = {}^hYi\,Y_jN_jd_{ij}^{-1}.$$

Summing overall inhabitants (N_i) in i and also taking the average income Yi, one obtains the following sum of the *intercity agglomeration economies as*

$$A_{ij} = YiN_iY_jN_jd_{ij}^{-1}.$$

Now writing $-\gamma^j$ instead of -1 and taking exponents β_1 and β_2 for Ni and N_j leaves the contents of this equation unchanged so long as

$$\gamma = \beta_1 = \beta_2 = 1.$$

$$A_{ij} = Y_iN_i^{\beta_1}y_jN_j^{\beta_2}d_{ij}^{-\gamma},$$

a formula well known from gravity models: to allow for more generality, and to harmonise the approach with the one that underlies the probablity approach of the gravity models, the exponents β_1 and β_2 have been introduced. Setting $i=j$, one obtains as $Y_i^2N_i^{\beta_1+\beta_2}$ the sum (A_i^I) of the *intra-city agglomeration effects* (if $d_{ii}\equiv 1$). Then aggregating over all *other* centres j yields the *sum* of all *inter-city agglomeration effects* A_i^{II} for city i. Assuming that income differences between all the locations or centres may be neglected (and setting $Y = 1$), one may write for sums ${}^SA_i^I$ and ${}^SA_i^{II}$ of the two kinds of agglomeration factors:

$$^SA_i^I = N_i^{\beta_1+\beta_2} \qquad \text{(intra-city) } (i = j) \qquad (2^I)$$

$$^SA_i^{II} = N_i^{\beta_1} \sum_j N_j^{\beta_2} d_{ij}^{-\gamma} \qquad \text{(inter-city) } (i \neq j). \qquad (2^{II})$$

It is useful to keep these two factors separate because for the *intra-city* level, *dis*economies may make themselves felt, while the effect of higher values for the *inter-city* agglomeration variable and hence of a higher degree of integration with other centres is clearly positive—in any case, their marginal effects may be different, and if so, this should be captured by the model. To place the two formulae on a *per capita* basis, they should be divided by N_i which yields *per capita agglomeration factors* A_i

$$A_i^I = N_i^{\beta_1+\beta_2-1} \qquad \text{(intra-city) } (i = j) \qquad (3^I)$$

$$A_i^{II} = N_i^{\beta_1-1} \sum_j N_j^{\beta_2} d_{ij}^{-\gamma} \qquad \text{(inter-city) } (i \neq j). \qquad (3^{II})$$

For the application of the formulae, only those centres should be included among the i and j which at least in some sense may be called 'agglomerations'. For our purposes—for a regional model—the minimum should be 50,000 inhabitants, and for purely practical reasons, in order to avoid discontinuities if this number is *just* surpassed, a value of N_0 = 50,000 should be subtracted from the population numbers of all centres. For subregions, the magnitude of N_0 should be lowered to a value between 15,000 and 20,000 inhabitants (for large countries, higher values might suggest themselves).

Thus the inter-city agglomeration variable (*per capita*) is

$$A_i^{II} = (N_i - N_0)^{\beta_1-1} \sum_j (N_j - N_0)^{\beta_2} d_{ij}^{-\gamma} \qquad (\text{all } N_j > N_0) \qquad (4^{II})$$

Note that due to the reduction of the N-values, the exponents can not be considered as being the same as in (3). Furthermore, the first exponent β_1 has a value of *one* subtracted from it: this way the expression is reduced to a *per capita* basis of centre i. Now to make the formula an operational one, values for the exponents β_1, β_2 and γ have to be determined. The *sum* of $\beta = \beta_1 + \beta_2$ may be taken as unity, and I would experiment with basic values $\beta_1 = 0{\cdot}75$ and $\beta_2 = 0{\cdot}25$: thus the weight of the own population is relatively much greater than that of other centres, apart from the fact that their weights are fast reduced with greater distances. It should be noted that $\beta_1 < 1$ implies that the positive growth effects of centre j on centre i are, for a given size of j, relatively larger for smaller cities than for bigger ones: The growth *rate* of a smaller centre is more strongly effected by neighbouring agglomerations than that of a larger centre. For the *intra*city agglomeration variable A_i^I one may choose sums $\beta_1 + \beta_2 = \beta \neq 1$, and then make β a function of N_i. But note that if $\beta < 1$ and constant, this implies that *bigger centres* have *worse growth chances* than smaller centres *on account of their sizes alone*, which may not at all be unrealistic because this negative factor may be made up for by *more favourable structural factors* of the larger centres and by *other* variables.

The agglomeration variable for a *region* k would be obtained by aggregating over all centres i_k in this region ($N' = N - N_0$)

$$A_k = \sum_{i_k} \sum_j (N'_{i_k})^{\beta_1-1} (N'_j)^{\beta_2} d_{i_k j}^{-\gamma} \qquad (5)$$

Here one should differentiate betweeen the calculation of the intercity agglomeration factor as based on other cities in k and interregional agglomeration factor A_k^{II} as based on cities outside the region. For the calculation of the agglomeration factor^I, a useful simplification would be to define the spatial *units outside the region* k as *other regions* l rather than the individual centres.

2 *Diffusion down the City Hierarchy*

If the model is to be specified so as to apply to *all phases* of development (as illustrated by Fig. 1) and to capture all the complex diffusion processes in a quantitative way, things become more involved. Short of any specific information about the particular country, one could only work with a lagged size-distance function (with distributed lags), which translates the acceleration of growth that has started at the National Economic Centre into stepped up growth rates in non-central regions (k).

Since I cannot offer any general prescription on how to proceed along these lines in an operational model, this approach will not be followed up any more. Since in any case the diffusion processes are based, among other things, on *market sizes* (as introduced with the agglomeration variable) and on certain *structural features*, it seems to be more promising to consider these directly—the latter in connection with the *structures* of the spatial units.

3 *Traffic Connections and Hinterlands*

In the definition of the inter-regional agglomeration factor (A^{II}), the traffic connections of the region or subregion have not been mentioned, though it was stressed from the outset that this influence becomes effective *via the connections* with other centres and that one should consider *economic distances*. An *additional traffic connections* variable can therefore only have the function to introduce exceptionally good or bad connections with other parts of the economy *in so far as they are not represented by the size of* A^{II}.

The definition suggested here is the following: take the *direct traffic connections* V_i between all *pairs of subregions* or regions that run through the subregion i—railroads and highways, with weights (v_{kl}) depending on the relative importance of the various connections—and weigh each connection with the two population numbers (N_k, N_1) that are connected, divided by the respective distances from i and by N_i in order to obtain a *per capita* value. Thus the connectivity variable V_i for i is:[19]

$$V_i = \sum_{k<1} v_{kl} N_k d_{ik}^{-\gamma} N_l d_{il}^{-\gamma} N_i^{-1}$$

Note that the multiplication of the N_k and N_l values makes this variable qualitatively different from a potential-variable.

The second additional variable is related to the population in the area that is dominated by the regional or subregional centre and therefore may be considered as a natural destination for outmigrants of that area. This is the hinterland variable H which considers especially the existing markets in *lower-order* centres that are dominated by the centre and in particular it brings in the potential for attracting additional labour: the greater this hinterland in terms of population numbers, the greater the rate of immigration into the subregion whose centre dominates this area. This is the basis of the typical *concentrated* dispersion process. The hinterland variable H_i may be defined—again on a *per capita* basis—as:

$$H_i = {}^{H}N_i^{\beta_H}/N_i,$$

in which distances are only implicitly considered; the exponent β_H should be smaller than unity, may be one-half: this thesis of a less than proportional impact is based on the general rule that the area and hence the average distances that have to be overcome by the migrants, are an increasing function of the number ${}^{H}N_i$. Only if densities vary much as between regions, this fact might have to be introduced in the form of corrective factors. The two variables V and H are supplementary to the agglomeration factors. Presumably there is a high degree of correlation between these two pairs of variables, which is probably much higher for (large) regions than for smaller centres. Therefore I expect that V and H will be more useful for *subregions* than for *regions*: for the latter, I would omit V and H.

V. Structural Factors and Locational Qualities in Explanatory and Predictive Models

(a) *General Remarks*

The determinants of regional growth have been summarised under the broad headings sizes and distances, structure, and locational qualities. If among the determinants of growth of a location, structural factors as well as the influences of sizes and distances could be isolated correctly, then the residuum would constitute the effects of all the *locational qualities*. Indeed the best way of specifying regional variables, above all the locational preference or locational qualities variable, depends very much on the purpose of the model. The question is: does one want to explain locational preferences on the basis of *characteristic features* of the regions, or is one mainly interested in the *effects* through which locational preferences have become manifest in the past? Note in passing that a difficulty lies in the fact that these *effects* contain elements of *structural* adjustments. There is no clear-cut difference, more a change of focus, between the two methods; this is because short of using personal interviews (which are of doubtful value in this context anyway) one can discover personal preferences only by studying how people have actually *behaved* in the past. Locational choices may have been influenced or shaped by income differentials (or wage or price or profit differentials), agglomeration sizes, mobility costs, length of resi-

[19] For small centres (below the subregional level), I would suggest to take a simple weighted sum of the roads running through the centre, but then also allow for closeness to other roads (this can not be discussed in detail here).

dence as well as by such factors as climate and landscape features. In a very *narrow* interpretation of locational preferences, one could approach them in the following way: If there are *systematic (constant) differences* between various regional growth rates—or the (inter-regional) migration flows—that *cannot* be explained by all these factors, the particular *non-explained systematic differences* between the regions are defined as the *locational preference factors* (for income growth, for migration) for the various regions. As long as such differences remain constant over time for each region (and the structural parameters of the model do not change), each of these constants can fully serve its purpose in any *forecasting* model: due to the same (though unspecified) influences, migration rates and hence income growth rates may be expected to be higher (or lower) than otherwise—in the future just as well as in the past.[20]

For forecasting purposes, the best definition of the term would be one that is much less narrow, however: it would be preferable to have included in this locational preferences variable the influences of such typical constants as climate, topography etc. because in this way the number of the explanatory variables can be reduced. This would yield a *composite locational preferences variable*, whose usefulness hinges exclusively on the *stability* of underlying relationships. All this holds for forecasting models—but an analysis aimed specifically at the *explanation* of past events would preferably work with *all* the important factors that can be quantified and whose particular influences in particular regions may hopefully be identified. This indeed is what location theory has always attempted to do. In *predictive models*, one may even go an important step further and introduce *past growth rates, or past migration rates* as explanatory variables for future growth rates or future migration flows. Indeed—apart from the national growth rate—past migration rates might well turn out to be the most significant of all the predetermined variables, as far as its predictive power is concerned—possibly in conjunction with the overall (total national) migration rate; the latter might be a function of the cyclical position of the economy, i.e. of the national rate of growth, y. This means that the simplest forecasting equation for the growth of a region i, based on a time series analysis, might be

$$\hat{y}_i(t) = \alpha_0 + \alpha_1 \frac{m_i}{m}(t-1) + \alpha_2 \hat{y}(t),$$

in which $\hat{y}$ and $\hat{y}_i$ are predicted growth rates for the economy (a predetermined variable) and for region i, respectively, and m_i/m is the share of total inter-regional migrants who moved into region i (as the *net* gain). Here the magnitudes of both α_0 and α_2 as well as the second term reflect, all taken together, the region's locational qualities—in an extremely broad interpretation of the term. Interpreted more narrowly, it would reflect locational qualities as well as the effect of the spatial and industrial structures of the region.[21]

Such a procedure might work well not only for a constant level of (conglomerate) preferences or qualities of the region but also for *constant rates of change*[22] of the *attractiveness* and *connectivity* of the region relative to other regions (both within the economy and with foreign economies).

(*b*) *Structural Factors*: *Definitions*

Structural factors will be considered in three variants: (i) the growth effects of the industry structure (as mentioned above), (ii) the employment shares of particular industries, and (iii) employment shifts from low-productivity to higher-productivity industries. The variables are the following: (i) the *industry-structure factor* s_i: the ratio between the growth rate obtained for the region if *each* of the *industries* of the region would grow exactly as fast as its national average, on the one hand, and the national growth rate, on the other. The computation of a structural factor poses severe problems because the usual industry classification cannot be used as its base: above all, the *production processes* have to exhibit a minimum of homogeneity in each class. (This can not be discussed here any further, however). The appropriate variable is thus $s_i \cdot \hat{y}$—i.e. s_i multiplied

20 This holds for combined cross-section time-series analyses; the same would be true, though with a smaller degree of reliability, of the residuals obtained for specific migration rates in pure cross-section analyses.

21 Alternatively, one might just as well single out the structural-factor and the location-factor, as mentioned above, and then forecast on the basis of these two plus the predicted national rate of growth.

22 Only second derivatives with regard to the time matter here since we are concerned with growth rates as dependent variables.

by the predicted national growth rate. (ii) An alternative that should only be introduced as a second choice is the use of the employment shares of characteristic fast growing or slowly growing industries or sectors. In this connection it should be mentioned that a large share of employment in agriculture might mean either (*a*) backwardness and slow growth *or* (*b*) rapid growth if people move out of agriculture and into newly established industrial plants. (iii) To take this latter point into account, the *reduction in employment* (ΔB_k^h) in a typical low-productivity industry h (which often is indeed agriculture), *per time period*, divided by total employment of the region (B_k) should be introduced as the following structural variable: $b_k = \Delta B_k^h / B_k$, which indicates how growth chances of other industries are enhanced by the possibility to employ more labour than otherwise.

(*c*) *Locational Qualities*

This variable should capture influences that are not included in the variables listed so far though often—because of multicollinearity—it may capture either more influences or fewer ones. However there is still a price variable that will be presented below. Locational qualities may be considered under three headings

the quality of the (sub)region's *infrastructure* beyond what is covered through the traffic connections variable (V), as measured through some index, and *per capita investment in infrastructure* during the preceeding year (or years);
the quality of residential areas: Variable R_i as measured through some index; and
cultural and climatic features of the region: Variable C_i.

For *cities* (say in narrow valleys), the former variables might be supplemented by an index of open space available for new construction. The latter qualitative features (C_i) may be quantified in a very rough way by taking a weighted sum of such things as

theatre and concert hall seats;
university study places; and
art galleries and exhibitions on the one hand; and
average number of sunny days per year;
average degrees of temperature above zero during the holiday seasons;
number of resorts in the neighbourhood (weighted by lake or seashore mileage) and
other special attractions of the regions (sports and other indoor or outdoor activities), on the other.

It is difficult to generalise about the special features that should be taken into account and to make any general statement about relative weights: in this respect the formulation must indeed remain non-operational. Note again that the above-mentioned features may be important not only for potential migrants as employees, but that the preferences of executives may have an important impact on the locational choices of industrial enterprises and hence also on capital movements.

(*d*) *Price Variables*

Income and price variables have not been introduced at all so far since (i) they are closely related to size variables and structural variables and (ii) there is often an identification problem: factor incomes may be high *because* conditions for growth are favourable and industries thus are interested in attracting additional factors of production. In the model, an exception should be made, however: housing rents (for standard apartments) will be introduced, which may reflect the scarcity of land. (To avoid identification problems, it might help to use lagged values for these two variables.)

VI. Specifications and Applications of the Model

The hypotheses presented so far may be tested in different ways in time-series analyses, in cross-section analyses, or in combinations of these two. Accordingly, the focus varies and with this, the specification of the model, in particular the predetermined variables to be used in each case. The proper use should be the third type, but simpler approaches are also suggested as first steps. Consider them briefly in turn.

(*a*) *Pure Time Series Analyses*

Time-series analyses may be made for one region each to estimate
(i) regional *production functions* on the basis of labour and capital (or their augmentations, if data allow this), with technical progress as a residual;
(ii) the association of the *regional and national growth rates* (y_k and y), in which equation the

constant term (α_0^k) would be an indicator of (industry) structural, space-structural and of other qualitative features of the region;

(iii) the influence on *regional growth* rates of the *national growth* rates and the region's *sectoral structure* (y_k as a function of $s_k y$), which yield, a residuum that includes location-factors. In all these applications, the introduction of more regional variables would promise only limited chances of success because most of these variables do not change fast over time. An additional step might consist, however, in comparing different α_0 values for different regions. Various applications to changes in migration rates over time might similarly be attempted;

(iv) an application that might be of some interest should be mentioned: the correlation between (*a*) y_k and A_k and (*b*) y_k and $\dot{A}_k$: growth rates and the (two) agglomerations factors or their changes over time. The first kind of association varies much as between countries or regions; the second may only be described as a correlation because (spatial) structural change is both a *precondition* and a *result* of growth. A further and more complete, enumeration of such possibilities is neither possible nor useful.

(*b*) *Cross-section Analyses*

Cross-section analyses on the basis of the discussions in this paper may be carried out on the following levels:

1 regions in their relationships to the national level
2 all subregions considered simultaneously in their relationships to:
 (*a*) the national level only or
 (*b*) the respective regional levels
3 the subregions of only one region in their relationships with that region.

The two approaches (1) and (3) are similar approaches at different levels, approach (2*b*) is a combination of approaches of type (3), and approach (2*a*) is different in that the regional level is left out. A more complicated later step would be the combination of approaches (1) and (2). The following description will be limited to the approaches (1) and (3): the formulations for the other two approaches are only more or less direct extensions: anyhow, whether subregions are to be linked to their respective regions or to the national level may be a matter of expediency, to be decided in the course of the actual testing.

Subregions

Starting with the subregional level, the growth equation for the subregions k of a region r may be written in the following way, if the simple approach (3) is taken:

$$y_k = \alpha_0 + \alpha_1 A_k^I + \alpha_2 A_k^{II} + \alpha_3 V_k + \alpha_4 H_k + \alpha_5 s_k y_r + \alpha_6 b_k + \alpha_7 I_k + \alpha_8 n_k + \alpha_9 R_k + \alpha_{10} C_k + \alpha_{11} P_k \quad (6)$$

in which one has

(i) the size and distance factors A^I, A^{II}, V, H;
(ii) the industry structure ($s_k y_r$), the role of low-productivity industries (b_k), infrastructure-stock or t investment in infrastructure (I_k), and the natural rate of growth of the labour force (*nk*);
(iii) qualitative features (R and C); and
(iv) the housing market (P).

Note that for A^I, and possibly also for A^{II}, several ranges should be separated through the introduction of appropriate dummy variables (a technical matter not to be discussed any further).

For the subregions, the variable V (traffic connections) has one special function: to capture the growth processes of *development axes* or industrial zones along certain traffic arteries. This reduced form equation may be applied to income growth rates and to migration rates. It contains all the four types of variables that have been listed in the last section.

It should be mentioned that *lags* should be introduced for the traffic connections and the infrastructure variables as well as the price variables, because it takes time until such influences have made themselves felt. (Otherwise it might also happen that these prices are high because the growth rate is high). One should keep in mind that equation (6) contains 11 variables, rather than the *one* variable (size) that is considered in Fig. 1 which must be interpreted as describing a *gross* relationship between sizes and growth rates. By contrast, with the approach in equation (6) one tries to establish *net* influences. Thus it might be that the coefficient of the size variable A^I turns out to be negative—

meaning that larger sizes *require* structural changes (represented by s_k) if growth is to continue. On the other hand, positive influences of agglomeration sizes may partly be neutralised by certain bottlenecks (as represented by the housing rent variable).

No matter whether approaches (3) or (2*b*) are chosen, one has to observe that the weighted sum of the growth rates y_k for the subregions must be the same as the growth rate for the respective region, y_r. If the weights are w_k, this means

$$\sum_k w_k y_k = y_r \quad \text{(all } k \text{ in } r \text{ only)} \qquad (7)$$

A similar restriction would have to be introduced if migration rates are considered.

For (large) regions *r* as contrasted with subregions *k*, one may expect that the variables *V* and *H*—considered side by side with the agglomeration variables—are less significant because the degree of correlation between these two pairs of variables is greater (subregional differences may disappear in the regional totals). Furthermore, infrastructure variables and housing market price variables are certainly less meaningful statistics for large regions than they may turn out to be for subregions (or cities). It is for these reasons that I suggested to introduce the growth rate y_r^C of the respective central subregion into the analyses of each region, as a kind of growth pole element for the region. Certainly one might experiment with more variables, but in accordance with my objective to keep the number of variables down I would formulate a growth equation for region *r* as:

$$\begin{aligned} y_r = \alpha_0 + \alpha_1 A_r^I + \alpha_2 A_r^{II} + \alpha_3 y_r^C \qquad (8) \\ + \alpha_4 s_r y + \alpha_5 b_r + \alpha_6 n_r \\ + \alpha_7 R_r + \alpha_8 C_r \end{aligned}$$

Again, since the coefficients α_1 may be significantly different for large and small values of A^I, one should introduce (at least) two dummy variables which would make it possible that the two coefficients α_0 and α_1 assume (at least) two different values for different ranges A^I—and a similar procedure for A^{II} may be appropriate.

Also a restriction corresponding to (7) is necessary

$$\sum_r w_r y_r = y \qquad (9)$$

Furthermore, it should be observed that the regional equation takes a subregional rate (i.e. y^c) as given, and vice versa: for the subregions the regional rates are predetermined variables. Therefore an iterative procedure should be applied which moves back and forth between the two levels. (Technical questions related to this cannot be discussed here.)

In any case, a cross section analysis of this kind refers to a particular time period (say one the phases described in Fig. 1). In analogy to what was said about the combination of various time-series analyses, here one may make cross-section analyses for various time periods (or phases of development) and then compute quantitative relationships between particular coefficients and other variables such as the absolute level of *per capita* income (*y*) or simply the time factor (*t*) itself. Indeed, such an approach might be a first step towards the combination of cross-section and time-series analyses.

(*c*) *Combinations of Cross-section and Time-series Analyses*

The two methods may be combined, and in doing this, the relationship discussed in the last paragraph should be allowed for. The phase of development must appear as an additional variable, preferably as measured by the national *per capita* income. One may either consider the regions and the subregions separately and apply again a kind of iterative procedure in moving back and forth between them, or one combines the levels into *one* somewhat more complicated approach—whose details do not have to be discussed here any more.

Summarising, it was suggested that the analysis should be simple, that the ambitions should be modest at the beginning, but that nevertheless different types of analyses be applied to different kinds of regions. As to simplicity, it is important to repeat that the consideration of *growth rates* has the great advantage that the *bases* of further growth —as initial conditions which are taken as data—do not have to be explained or even analysed. This point is relevant for all centres which have developed in the past on account of, say, political decisions or which depend on foreign trade and owe their past developments to the trade connections with other countries: such international determinants of growth are part of the locational qualities that need to be introduced as an additional explanatory factor only if there are drastic changes in the foreign trade situation.[23]

For all applications, in all cases, the focus was on the interplay of sizes, distances and structures, with market *size* effects necessarily being correlated with (neo-classical) *price* effects: the position taken here is that the market size effects are the more fundamental ones of the two. It was stressed that the model must allow for some important parameters to be different (possibly even as to their signs) for different sizes and different phases of development: this is facilitated by considering two types of regions and, in each case, two size ranges—dummy variables making it unnecessary to test non-linear and non-monotonous size-growth rate functions. The model may be applied in various steps whose results may then be combined. The basic approaches thus remain simple and should guard the model from being rejected by poor tests. Indeed, applications to metropolitan areas and their hinterlands have, though in a somewhat different context, yielded some encouraging results. But obviously the methods of regional growth analysis constitute only one of many possible avenues of further research in this field.

REFERENCES

von Böventer, Edwin (1962)
Theorie des räumlichen Gleichgewichts, J. B. C. Mohr, Tübingen. French translation as: Théorie de L'Equilibre en Economie Spatiale, Série Espace Economique 7, Paris 1966.

von Böventer, Edwin (1962)
Die Struktur der Landschaft. Versuch einer Synthese und Weiterentwicklung der Modelle J. H. von Thünens, W. Christallers und A. Löschs, in: Optimales Wachstum und Schriften des Vereins für Socialpolitik, N. F. Band 27, 77-133.

Kariel, Herbert G. and Vaselenak, Michael J. (1973)
Waves of Spatial Diffusion Reconsidered. *Journal of Regional Science*, 13 (2), 291-296.

Morrill, Richard L. (1968)
Waves of Spatial Diffusion. *Journal of Regional Science*, 8, (1), 1-18.

Morrill, Richard L. (1973)
Waves of Spatial Diffusion: A Reply. *Journal of Regional Science*, 13 (2), 297-298.

Muth, Richard F. (1968)
Differential Growth Among Large U.S. Cities, in: Quirk, J. P. and Zarley, A. M., eds. (1968). *Papers in quantitative economics*. Lawrence: University of Kansas, 311-355.

Richardson, Harry W. (1973).
Regional Growth Theory. London.

[23] Again, only 'abnormal' changes count—second derivatives matter.

ADDENDUM

3 Whether in an anlysis of growth in space, one obtains balanced growth or cumulative growth depends very much on the mobility of the factors of production over space. If mobile natural resources play an important role, then the adaptation of production and its spatial distribution to the given distribution of these natural resources is subject to diminishing returns for the mobile factors: in many cases this will (depending on the type of technological advance) yield balanced growth. By contrast, if natural resource sites are less significant and the other factors of production are mobile, it is much more likely that cumulative growth will follow: if many, or most, of the factors of production may *move together*, they are less likely to run into diminishing returns (or will much later do so) and more likely to generate cumulative growth than is the case under the limited-mobility assumptions of neo-classical theory (in particular as based on traditional foreign trade theory).

[19]

THE COSTS AND RETURNS OF HUMAN MIGRATION[1]

LARRY A. SJAASTAD
University of Minnesota

MIGRATION research has dealt mainly with the forces which affect migration and how strongly they have affected it, but little has been done to determine the influence of migration as an equilibrating mechanism in a changing economy. The movements of migrants clearly are in the appropriate direction, but we do not know whether the numbers are sufficient to be efficient in correcting income disparities as they emerge.[2] There is a strong presumption that they are not.

The central purpose of this paper is to develop the concepts and tools with which to attack the latter problem. I propose to identify some of the important costs and returns to migration—both public and private—and, to a limited extent, devise methods for estimating them. This treatment places migration in a resource allocation framework because it treats migration as a means in promoting efficient resource allocation and because migration is an activity which requires resources. Within this framework, my goal will be to determine the return to investment in migration rather than to relate rates of migration to income differentials.

I. MIGRATION: TOO MUCH OR TOO LITTLE?

Economists and others are generally dissatisfied with the past performance of migration in narrowing geographic income differentials, in spite of the tremendous amount of internal migration taking place in the United States.[3] During the twelve months preceding the 1950 Census of Population, 5.6 per cent of the United States population moved to a different county and 2.6 per cent to a different state.[4] Accordingly, there were enough interstate migrants to replace the population of Delaware every month and even that of mighty New York within twenty-one months. Nevertheless, Delaware's per capita personal income continues to be two and one-half to three times that of Mississippi. How can these large income differences persist in the face of such massive movements?

Part of the answer lies in the fact that these movements are *gross* rather than

[1] I wish to acknowledge discussion and comments on an earlier draft by Anthony M. Tang and John C. Hause. In addition, I am indebted to T. W. Schultz for extensive comments and aid in revision. Remaining errors and omissions are, of course, my sole responsibility.

[2] A substantial number of highly creditable studies on the nature and strength of the forces affecting human migration have been completed; the earliest of these was published more than seventy-five years ago (see E. G. Ravenstein, "The Laws of Migration," *Journal of the (Royal) Statistical Society*, Vol. XLVIII [June, 1885]). The main concern of economists has been with the response of individuals to economic opportunity at a distance. Harry Jerome's *Migration and Business Cycles* (New York: National Bureau of Economic Research, 1926) leaves little doubt that international migration is influenced by the business cycle, and more recent work indicates a parallel relation for internal migration. Moreover, recent statistical studies have revealed a relationship between internal migration and income differentials as well.

[3] On this point see George H. Borts, "The Equalization of Returns and Regional Economic Growth," *American Economic Review*, L, No. 3 (June, 1960), 319–47.

[4] United States Bureau of the Census, *1950 Population Census Report*, P-E, No. 4B (Washington: Government Printing Office, 1956), p. 13, Table 1.

net migration rates, and that the gross migration rate at the state level is typically several times the net rate. But this fact raises an even more perplexing problem: why is gross migration in one direction the best single indicator of the amount of backflow, as appears to be true? For example, the Census estimates that 62,500 persons migrated from Mississippi in the year preceding the 1950 count; but it also estimates that 51,900 migrated into that state during the same period.[5] If people insist upon migrating into the lowest income state in the union at such a rate, how are economists to rationalize their behavior—much less prescribe the remedy for their alleged sorry earnings? If we take the out-migration of 62,500 persons as evidence that Mississippi is a low earnings area, we must by the same token accept the 51,900 as counter evidence that it is indeed a good place to earn a living. The simple majority favors the out-migrants, but this majority is unimpressively small put alongside the income statistics. It is one thing to find lack of mobility the culprit that prevents spatial equalization of incomes; it is quite another to suggest that a lot of mobility in the wrong direction may be the cause!

These remarks, of course, beg the question. Mississippi's per capita income may have risen as much from the 51,900 influx as from the 62,500 outflow. Men are not created equal, nor would they be likely to stay so if they were. A 10 per cent in-migration of highly skilled persons (with few children) may improve Mississippi's per capita income more than a larger but less selective outflow. One can conceive of conditions which would cause incomes to rise faster the smaller is net migration.

How may one explain Mississippi's migration pattern (which, incidentally, is typical of that of most states)? The year 1949 was one of recession, which generates an increase in return migration. Moreover, Mississippi is homogeneous neither in occupations nor in industries. The out-migrants may have left declining industries and may not have been qualified for employment in the expanding ones. Or, some or all of the in-migrants may have been disillusioned out-migrants of previous years. There are also retirements. Retired persons may seek places where labor is cheap, whereas employed people are attracted to areas where it is dear; or people who are retiring return to communities in which they were reared and spent the earlier years of their lives.

Whatever may be the best hypothesis for this seemingly paradoxical behavior, three related points become clear: (1) Net migration is not necessarily a useful measure for testing the labor market's ability to remove earnings differentials. (2) Disaggregation of both the migrant and parent population by at least age and occupation may be required to confirm (or deny) the alleged failure of migration to achieve a reasonably equal income distribution over space. (3) The "perverse" behavior of gross migration is consistent with observed income differentials being generated by occupational as well as geographic immobility. Let me add that the somewhat paradoxical relation between gross in- and out-migration may be substantially an aggregation problem, as I have argued elsewhere.[6]

II. DIFFERENCES IN EARNINGS

Migration poses two broad and distinct questions for the economist. The

[5] United States Bureau of the Census, *op. cit.*, p. 32, Table 8.

[6] See my "Migration in the Upper Midwest" in "Four Papers on Methodology" (an unpublished manuscript of the Upper Midwest Economic Study, University of Minnesota).

first, and the one which has received the major attention, concerns the direction and magnitude of the response of migrants to labor earnings differentials over space. The second question pertains to the connection between migration and those earnings, that is, how effective is migration in equalizing inter-regional earnings of comparable labor? The latter question has received much less attention than the former. It is also the more difficult of the two.

Most studies concerned about the first question have focused upon *net* migration to or from various geographic areas or between pairs of such areas. Most of them have found a relationship between income or earnings and migration, and usually in the expected direction (that is, high earnings are associated with net *in*-migration, low earnings with net *out*-migration). The qualifications, however, are numerous; and the observed relationship is usually quite small and weak. My study of interstate migration, for example, shows that over the 1940–50 decade, an increase in per capita labor earnings of $100 (1947–49 dollars) induces net in-migration or retards net out-migration by only 4 or at most 5 per cent of the population aged fifteen to twenty-four years at the end of the decade.[7] The percentage was lower for other ages and hence lower for the total population. This modest response of net migration to earnings differentials implies that per capita earnings must be low indeed for net out-migration to overcome natural increase and effect a local population reduction. My study indicates that during the1940's the earnings level in a particular state would need to be roughly one-half the national average in order for migration from that state to offset completely the natural increase, thus leaving a static population.

But as was suggested earlier, net migration alone is not the only mechanism for removing earnings differentials; one should also consider gross migration. Presumably, net migration is required only from those industries (or occupations) with locally depressed wage rates. If low earnings characterize all or most industries in a particular area, net out-migration is required; and it should bring about an increase in the wage rate relative to the case without out-migration. If some industries in the area, however, are paying higher wages than elsewhere, and the workers leaving the low-wage industries are unqualified and cannot easily become qualified for employment in the high-wage industries, in-migration should also occur. But this diversification among high- and low-wage industries is almost certain to *weaken* the expected relation between average earnings levels and net migration, although there remains a strong presumption that low average earnings will induce net out-migration.

Occupational composition can account for some, but not all of the differences in earnings among states. The results of Frank Hanna's admirable study show that: (1) the low income states are dominated by occupations with relatively low earnings at the national level, and (2) the earnings within particular occupations in low-income states tend to be lower than the national average.[8] Opposite relationships characterize the high-income states. Hanna's study, together with the observed relation between income and net migration, supports the hypothesis that

[7] Larry A. Sjaastad, "Income and Migration in the United States" (unpublished Ph.D. dissertation, University of Chicago, 1961), p. 38.

[8] Frank A. Hanna, *State Income Differentials, 1919–1954*, (Durham, N.C.: Duke University Press, 1959), p. 128.

migration does constitute a response to *spatial* earnings differentials; moreover, this evidence is consistent with the hypothesis that migration is a search for opportunities in *higher-paying occupations*. Both hypotheses are reassuring to the economist.

Although the studies of net migration to date partially reveal the functioning of the labor market, they tell us little more than the fact that net migration is in the "right" direction. The estimated response magnitude of net migration to gaps in earnings is of little value in gauging the effectiveness of migration as an equilibrator. There are, however, several alternative approaches. One simple approach is to compare rates of (gross) migration with changes in earnings over time. Numerous compositional corrections would be necessary, and this approach would still have to answer the difficult question of how much equalization of earnings should be brought about by a given amount of migration. Moreover, it is possible that the impact of migration can be offset by further changes in the economic forces which originally generated the earnings differentials.

A better alternative, at least analytically, is to cast the problem strictly as one of resource allocation. To do this, we treat migration as an *investment increasing the productivity of human resources*, an investment which has costs and which also renders returns.

Treating migration as an investment removes one of the difficulties inherent to the first approach; there exists a ready-made criterion to test the effectiveness of migration in reducing earnings differentials over space. That criterion is, of course, the rate of return on resources allocated to migration. The difficulty of the method is that it is necessary to identify and measure the costs as well as the returns to migration; its credit is the possibility of meaningful comparisons between migration and alternative methods of promoting better resource allocation.[9]

III. THE PRIVATE COSTS OF MIGRATION

The private costs can be broken down into money and non-money costs. The former include the out-of-pocket expenses of movement, while the latter include foregone earnings and the "psychic" costs of changing one's environment. Each of these is treated in turn below.

1. THE MONEY COSTS

There are no data to my knowledge on the expenses incurred by migrants in the course of moving. Although these data could be collected only from the migrants themselves, these costs could, no doubt, be estimated reasonably well for given distances (and number of dependents, if one treats migration of families). Such estimates have been made, but I suspect they are quite conservative.[10] Nevertheless, since the money costs one ought to include are only the *increase* in expenditure for food, lodging, transportation (for both migrants and their belongings), etc., necessitated by migration, the order of magnitude of these costs is surely sufficiently small that it cannot account for the large earnings differentials encountered in the data (even after taking into

[9] Obviously, complete or perfect spatial equalization of earnings is ruled out (other than by chance) so long as migration involves costs to the migrant.

[10] James G. Maddox, for example, estimates "that many farm people can travel as far as five hundred miles from their home, take ten days to find non-farm jobs, and wait a week for their first paycheck after they start work with a nest egg of no more than $100 per person" ("Private and Social Costs of Movement of People out of Agriculture," *American Economic Review*, L [May, 1960], p. 393). Note that this is an estimate of capital requirements as opposed to money costs, since Maddox does not take account of what it would cost to live without migrating.

account foregone earnings). Moreover, the results of my study of internal migration in the United States, 1949–50, suggest that the marginal costs associated with additional distance are considerably higher than could be attributed to the costs considered in Maddox's estimate. The migration variable was defined as the number of (net) migrants going from state i to state j as a fraction of all (net) migrants from state i. Regression coefficients obtained indicate that the attractiveness of a given destination was unaffected by a 10 per cent gain in annual per capita labor earnings *and* a simultaneous 16 per cent increase in distance.[11] At the mean of the income and distance variables these percentages imply that the typical migrant would be indifferent between two destinations, one of which was 146 miles more distant than the other, if the average annual labor earnings were $106 (1947–49 dollars) higher in the more distant one.[12] Marginal costs per mile of migration would have to be high indeed to reconcile this negative effect of distance with the present value of the earnings differential even at very high discount rates, particularly since the persons involved are already migrants and only their allocation over space is in question. Moreover, this result cannot stem from migrants moving in a series of short jumps. That explanation would be plausible if the allocation of gross migrants were being studied; in the case under question, however, the variable is net migration. One is strongly tempted to appeal to market imperfections such as the lack of information to explain the apparently high distance cost of migration. Unfortunately, no simple way has been devised for testing that hypothesis—although attempts have been made.[13] Even so, the migration-impeding effects of uncertainty remain to be measured.

2. THE NON-MONEY COSTS

The non-money considerations involved in migration are surely significant, probably far more so than the money costs. The first non-money costs to consider are opportunity costs—the earnings foregone while traveling, searching for, and learning a new job.[14] Part of these foregone earnings will be a function of the distance of migration. In addition the time required to find a new job is presumably affected by the level of unemployment. Clearly one should be able to estimate these components. The costs of learning a new job (on-the-job training) are treated in detail by Mincer in another paper in this Supplement. As Mincer demonstrates, these costs are subject to measurement. Since they are reflected by reduced earnings, these costs are to be taken into account by choosing the appropriate expected earnings stream (after migration) for comparison with the expected stream had the migrant not moved.[15]

[11] Sjaastad, "Income and Migration in the United States," p. 63.

[12] These estimates are partial regression coefficients and since an occupational mix variable was also present, it is assumed that the occupational mix is either constant or changes such that average earnings of the labor force remain constant if each member earns the national average within his occupation. The occupational mix correction is that devised by Hanna and called "rate constant earnings" (*op. cit.*, chap. v).

[13] In particular, see Philip Nelson, "A Study in the Geographic Mobility of Labor" (unpublished Ph.D. dissertation, Columbia University, 1957).

[14] One could include in opportunity costs the entire earnings stream the migrant is expected to earn had he not migrated, and then include in returns the expected earnings stream after migration. The alternative followed in this paper is to look only at the increment to costs and earnings associated with migration.

[15] Risk and uncertainty "costs" can be treated in a fashion similar to on-the-job training costs; that is,

A second form of non-money costs must be considered. Since people are often genuinely reluctant to leave familiar surroundings, family, and friends, migration involves a "psychic" cost. It would be difficult to quantify these costs; moreover, if they were quantified, they should be treated quite differently from the costs previously considered. The costs treated above represent real resource costs; however, the psychic costs do not. Rather they are of the nature of lost consumer (or producer) surplus on the part of the migrant. Given the earnings levels at all other places, there is some minimum earning level at location *i* which will cause a given individual to be indifferent between migrating and remaining at *i*. For any higher earnings at *i*, he collects a surplus in the sense that part of his earnings could be taxed away and that taxation would not cause him to migrate. The maximum amount that could be taken away without inducing migration represents the value of the surplus. By perfect discrimination, it would be possible to take away the full amount of the surplus, but in doing so leave resource allocation unaffected (other than through distributive effects). Hence, the psychic costs of migration involve no resources for the economy and should not be included as part of the investment in migration.

Although the psychic costs involve no resource cost, they do affect resource allocation. Very likely, more migration would take place if psychic costs were zero for everyone. In addition, even if knowledge were perfect, psychic costs could explain the existence of earnings differentials larger than those implied by the money and opportunity costs of migration. However, these excessive differentials would not represent resource misallocation. The optimal allocation of resources must take tastes as given, and will differ accordingly if people prefer familiar over strange surroundings. Migration incentive transfers to compensate for these psychic costs would be as inappropriate as transfers to render people indifferent among occupations even though strong preferences may exist. To compensate for psychic costs would result in resources being used for migration to obtain earnings with a lower value than those received before. To draw upon an old example, because the public hangman earns a high income owing to his distasteful job, it does not necessarily follow that welfare would be improved with more hangmen!

Although we should not treat psychic costs as a component of the costs of migration, they pose a problem for the analysis of rate of return. To the extent that some part of existing earnings differentials represents tastes alone, the rate of return to resources allocated to migration is biased. One manner in which this problem can be partially circumvented is to consider only persons for whom the marginal psychic cost is zero. The allocation of actual migrants by distance migrated should be relatively free of the influence of psychic costs, although the percentage of all persons who become migrants is not. Using education as an analogy, this approach is similar to determining the rate of return on the *n*th year of schooling as compared to the rate on *n* years.

by an appropriate increase in the rate of discount for the increment to expected future earnings created by migration. Moreover, the adjustment in the discount rate need not be made explicitly if internal rate of return calculations are made.

IV. THE PRIVATE RETURNS TO MIGRATION

For any particular individual, the money returns to migration will consist of a positive or negative increment to his real earnings stream to be obtained by moving to another place. This increment will arise from a change in nominal earnings, a change in costs of employment, a change in prices, or a combination of these three. Money returns so defined are sufficiently general to encompass not only those returns stemming from earnings differentials between places, but also the returns accruing to the migrant in his capacity as a consumer. Both of these returns are net gains; increased efficiency in consumption is logically equilavent to increased efficiency in production. In addition, there will be a non-money component, again positive or negative, reflecting his preference for that place as compared to his former residence.[16] Finally, there is pure consumption. The pure consumption return should be regarded as the satisfaction or dissatisfaction the migrant receives in the course of his actual travel. This is analogous, again in the case of education, to the satisfaction the student experiences merely from being on campus, quite apart from the non-marketable satisfactions he may obtain over his life span as a result of his education.[17] The non-money returns will be examined first.

[16] Preference for familiar versus strange surroundings are included in psychic cost and are excluded here. Preference at this point refers to such factors as climate, smog, and congestion. It is assumed that the individual's production and consumption occur at the same place; if that were not true, his preferences would be reflected in the amount of cost he is willing to bear to consume at one place and to be employed at another.

[17] The consumption-investment dichotomy I have in mind is based strictly upon the point in time at which the migrant actually receives the satisfactions. An outlay made to increase future productivity is usually called an investment; an outlay for immediate satisfaction is labeled consumption. Moreover, if a person uses some of his resources to increase future satisfactions, it should not matter whether or not the increase is reflected in future market transactions. From this point of view, there is no logical difference between a consumer or producer durable; I choose to call them both an investment.

1. THE NON-MONEY RETURNS

Earlier it was found that we can safely ignore psychic costs of migration since they involve no resource cost; likewise, we should ignore non-money returns arising from locational preferences to the extent that they represent consumption which has a zero cost of production. Some people, for example, may be indifferent between earnings at one level in Minnesota and a lower level in California owing to a preference for the latter's climate. If a large portion of the population showed this preference, California would have a locational advantage, and industry would migrate in that direction to enjoy the resultant lower labor costs. In a world of perfect competition and resource mobility no earnings differentials arising from these preferences would remain in final equilibrium; if discrimination were perfect, the existence of the preferences would be totally reflected in rents earned by factors (land) specific to the climate. Moreover, the pure rents so paid should not be treated as costs of employment since they arise from tastes for location rather than differences in productivity.

Even in a world of perfect competition and resource mobility there can be earnings differentials arising from variations in costs of employment (which must be offset by corresponding differentials in productivity). Larger cities typically reveal higher earnings within occupations than smaller cities. Costs of employment are higher in larger cities due to additional transportation, rent, etc., which are compensated by higher earnings. If one includes the former as a return to migration to the larger city, he should deduct the latter as additional cost of employment. Locational preferences pose a problem in estimating the return to migration to the extent that they can give rise to rents not to be counted as costs of employment; but additional costs arising from the superior productivity of a specific location are to be deducted. Although a distinction between those returns to migration which represent higher productivity and those which are merely consumption of zero cost goods is analytically useful for considering the returns to migration arising from increased efficiency, it is of no practical use. Final spatial equilibrium in the real world would permit variations in earnings (within occupations) resulting from non-labor resource immobility (particularly natural resources) and from lack of competition as well as from differentials in cost of employment and labor immobility. Moreover, since discrimination in the land market is not perfect, persons can and do receive windfalls by moving to a place of their preference. Private non-money returns to migration may very well exist and influence behavior; and they cannot be separated from those private returns reflecting higher productivity alone. Even in a world of perfect competition, of resource mobility, and of discrimination according to preference it would not be feasible to classify costs of employment into the two categories outlined above. For practical purposes, the only alternative appears to be the unrealistic assumption that variation in tastes permits a spatial distribution of persons such that no rents arise from differences in amount and composition of natural amenities, and that this distribution does not seriously differ from the "optimal" distribution from the viewpoint of resource allocation.

2. THE MONEY RETURNS

It is obviously not sufficient simply to compare labor earnings over space and assume that any observed differences arise from disequilibrium in the labor market. Hanna's study reveals that occupational composition explains a significant portion of earnings differentials among states.[18] Other variables such as age and sex affect earnings within an occupation.[19] However, assuming occupation, age, and sex to be the more important compositional variables affecting earnings, first estimates of the return to migration is the difference in earnings within occupations, ages, and sexes, and between all places. These estimates would almost surely be underestimates because they fail to take into account possible disequilibrium between as well as within occupations and because a change in occupation may necessitate migration. The more relevant alternatives for migrants may be *among* rather than *within* occupations. While one may be able to show that the Alabama farm laborer can improve his earnings on an Iowa farm, his prospective opportunities may be far more in an urban area and occupation.

If the return to migration can be increased by occupational upgrading, the problem in estimating the return becomes far more complex. In this context it is particularly useful to employ the human capital concept and to view migration, training, and experience as *investments in the human agent.* These investments, specific to the individual, are subject to depreciation and deterioration both in a physical and an economic sense. If market forces reduce the relative wages of a particular occupation, practitioners of that occupation suffer a capital loss and are faced with the alternatives of ac-

[18] *Op. cit.*, p. 121.

[19] The value of leisure is also neglected when comparing earnings. If the individual labor supply function is not backward bending, smaller earnings will necessarily be accompanied by larger amounts of leisure time, which should not be valued at zero. Thus one should look at hours of work as well as earnings. There remains the problem of the value to impute to an hour's leisure. While an imputation probably cannot be accurately made, this omission should be borne in mind.

cepting the lower earnings or making additional investments in themselves to increase their earnings in a more favorable market. If the relative wages in an occupation are adversely affected locally, migration alone is sufficient; if the adverse effect is national, such as the earnings in agriculture, the entire occupational earnings structure is under stress and migration is feasible only if new skills are acquired by the migrant. Whether or not the additional investment is worthwhile depends crucially upon the age of the individual. Young persons will typically have made only a small investment in themselves through training for and experience in a specific occupation and a relatively large one through formal education; whereas a larger portion of the investment in older persons presumably arises from skill and experience specific to a particular employment.[20] For the former group, obsolescence is a far smaller threat; moreover, their longer life expectancy increases the present value of the returns to additional investment relative to the older group.

Since the age-income relation within an occupation is at least partially due to the accumulated experience (on-the-job training), older persons entering a given occupation even after minimal training are likely to receive lower earnings than persons of similar age but well experienced in that occupation. Hence, comparisons across occupational groups but within age groups lead to overestimates of the rate of return to migration alone. The return so estimated is to be attributed to *both* the migration investment and the investment in on-the-job training, as well as costs of pre-employment training. Estimates of the return to migration alone must be preceded by an explanation of the age-earnings relation so that earnings representing equal experience are compared.

If it is true that complementary investments are required to make migration feasible, particularly among the older migrants, one must be extremely careful in making broad comparsions of earnings and, upon finding significant differences over space, in concluding that voluntary migration is incapable of efficient allocation of labor resources. It is clearly possible that the migration mechanism could be working extremely well in the sense that the marginal return to additional migration is not "high," but that substantial differentials in earnings may persist. I strongly suspect, for example, that the lack of relevant alternatives for older farmers in non-farm occupations may go a long way in explaining why off-farm migration has not increased relative earnings in agriculture so that "comparable" factors receive comparable returns. The point is that factors are not really comparable, having had different occupational histories.

I have estimated net migration rates from rural areas in the upper Midwest which sharply reveal the age selectivity of net migration from agricultural areas.[21] These are presented in Table 1.[22] Although nearly half of the persons, aged 10–14 years in 1950, migrated from the

[20] In the United States, the difference in this intangible "portfolio" is exaggerated by the secular increase in levels of formal education attained.

[21] The upper Midwest includes the following states and parts of states: Montana, North and South Dakota, Minnesota, northwestern Wisconsin, and Upper Michigan. The migration rates are estimated by the census-survival rate method using 1950–60 census-survival rates developed by the author in connection with his research on the Upper Midwest Economic Study.

[22] Since these migration estimates are from rural areas only, the problem of the difference between net and gross migration is less serious than suggested earlier. The rural areas of a given region are likely to be quite homogeneous, so only a small amount of cross-migration is anticipated.

rural areas during the 1950–60 decade, less than one in ten of the persons 20 years of age and over in 1950, migrated. Although one might plausibly argue that both money and non-money costs of migration increase with age, it seems doubtful that the increase in these costs as initial age rises from 15–19 to 20–24 can be sufficient to reduce the out-migration rate from over 30 per cent to less than 10 per cent. If increases in costs reduce rural out-migration as age increases, the same cost increases should be borne by all migrants. Table 1 also presents gross migration in 1949 for the United States as a per cent of parent population. The age-migration pattern there is quite different. However, the data are not comparable since the age range for 1950–60 upper Midwest migrants differs, for example, 0 to 4 in 1950 is from 0 through 14 over the decade. The data are reorganized in Table 2 for identical age groups, and the pattern is similar. Although the migration rate falls 70 per cent in the upper Midwest as one goes from age ranges 15–29 to 20–34, it remains constant for the United States. Although not conclusive, the evidence for the United States strongly suggests that little of the decline in migration rates as age increases can be explained by associated increases in the money or non-money costs of migration.

TABLE 1

1950–60 NET OUT-MIGRATION FROM RURAL AREAS, UPPER MIDWEST, AS A PER CENT OF 1950 POPULATION, AND GROSS MIGRATION RATES, UNITED STATES, 1949

1950 Age	Upper Midwest Per Cent Out-Migration Rate	United States Per Cent Gross Migration*
0–4	13.7	7.0†
5–9	25.1	5.0
10–14	44.5	4.0‡
15–19	30.6	6.9§
20–24	9.1	11.3
25–29	10.4	9.4
30–34	10.7	6.7
35–39	9.8	4.7
40–44	8.6	
45–49	9.2	3.0
50–54	7.5	
55–59	9.4	
60–64	8.8	
65+	1.8	2.6

* Source: Bureau of the Census, *1950 Population Census Report*, P-E, No. 4D, Tables 1 and 2.
† Aged 1–4 in 1950.
‡ Aged 10–13 in 1950.
§ Aged 14–19 in 1950.

TABLE 2

COMPARISON OF RURAL OUT-MIGRATION, UPPER MIDWEST, WITH GROSS MIGRATION RATES, UNITED STATES

Age Range	Average of Range	Upper Midwest Per Cent Out-Migration Rate	United States Per Cent Gross Migration
0–14	7.5	13.7	5.5*
5–19	12.5	25.1	5.4
10–24	17.5	44.5	7.6
15–29	22.5	30.6	9.1†
20–34	27.5	9.1	9.1
25–44	35.0	10.5	6.5
35–44	40.0	10.0‡	4.7
45–64	55.0	8.4	3.0
65+	....	1.8	2.6

* Aged 0–13.
† Aged 14–29.
‡ Approximate.

As age increases, of course, there is a shortening of the time period over which the migrant expects to recapture these costs; but again it seems unlikely that this effect can so sharply reduce the migration rate. If retirement comes at age 65 to 70, the group aged 15 to 19 in 1950 will have about 45 years, on the average over the decade, remaining in the labor force—as compared with 40 years for those initially aged 20 to 24. At a discount rate of 10 per cent, the present value of an additional dollar per year for the former group is \$9.89; for the latter group it is \$9.82, a mere 7 cents less. The dispersion in cost of migration would have to be fantastically small if a reduction in present value of returns by less than 1 per cent (owing to the shortening of the amortization period) would reduce the migration rate by 70 per cent. Neither increasing costs of migration nor reduction in the amortization period alone can explain the age-migration relation observed in the upper Midwest.[23]

However, if substantial additional costs of retraining for a new occupation must be borne by these rural out-migrants, the age-migration pattern displayed in Table 2 becomes more comprehensible. The majority of the rural out-migrants from the upper Midwest will necessarily be changing occupations. Clearly they come from agricultural occupations but are entering urban occupations. New skills must be acquired. Only a smaller portion of the gross United States migrants, however, need to change occupations; much of this mobility can be merely geographic and not occupational. For the latter group, the total costs to the individual for migration and acquiring new skills can be much smaller than for the former.

The sharp reduction in rural out-migration at relatively early ages and its near constancy thereafter suggests that (*a*) the investment in skills in rural occupations is concentrated in early years, and (*b*) consequently, the rural age-earning relation should rise sharply as returns to this investment are realized. Both of these propositions can be tested by the analysis developed in Mincer's paper. Moreover, this hypothesis implies that the degree of disequilibrium may differ among age groups—being largest for the young and less for the older persons. Differences in earnings could, of course, become larger for the older persons; but this is not inconsistent with efficient resource allocation. These older people may have suffered a capital loss, and their remaining lifetime is too short to justify large additional investments in themselves. To the extent that the above characterization is true, such disparities in earnings become a question of social policy rather than one of resource allocation.[24]

If, as I suggest, interoccupational earning differences may be the more relevant ones in dealing with migration, but if there is as yet no way of making sense out of these differences in terms of actual incentives offered migrants of different ages, some alternative approach to estimating the rate of return on migration is necessary. Fruitful lines of attack may be to focus upon migrants only or to make comparisons between migrants and nonmigrants of similar age.[25] Conceptually,

[23] Suppose that the distribution of costs, as well as the present value, of returns to migration for all potential migrants is normal, mean C and PV, respectively; variance S^2 and zero, respectively, and that costs and returns are independent. For the 15–19 age group, $C = C_1$, $S^2 = S_1^2$, $PV = PV_1$; for 20–24, $C = C^2$, $S^2 = S_2^2$, $PV = PV^2$; assume a discount rate less than 10 per cent so that $PV_2 = 0.99PV_1$. For 30.6 per cent of the persons aged 15–19, $PV_1 \geq$ cost; for 9.1 per cent of those aged 20–24, $PV_2 \geq$ cost. At the margins, $PV_1 = C_1 - .5S_1$; $PV_2 = C_2 - 1.3S_2$. Let $C_1 = C_2 = C$; $S_1 = S_2 = S$; then $S/C = 0.0135$. The implied coefficient of variation is a mere 1.35 per cent. More reasonable coefficients of variation for both costs and present values are possible if there exists a strong positive correlation between these two variables. Some positive correlation is expected.

[24] For a bold approach to the social policy question posed by persons "locked-in" their historic occupations, see T. W. Schultz, "A Policy To Redistribute Losses from Economic Progress" (prepared for a labor mobility conference, Iowa State University, November, 1960) (mimeographed). In this paper Schultz argues that since the losses to individuals from economic progress are much more narrowly distributed than are the gains, a case can be made for redistributing those losses over a larger group.

[25] By focusing upon migrants only it would be possible to eliminate the effects of differences in psychic costs, as was mentioned above.

there is no problem in determining whether and by how much a migrant's earnings are altered by his move. Cross-classified data concerning vital characteristics of migrants such as age, occupation, earnings before and after migration, etc., are a prerequisite to a thorough study of return to migration along these lines. Fortunately, substantial data of this sort will be available in the 1960 *Population Census Special Reports* and will cover a five-year period; the negative transitory effect of migration upon the earnings of migrants should largely disappear. As far as I know there will be no earnings data for migrants before migration, but cross-classification may permit use of earnings of comparable non-migrants as a substitute.[26]

V. PRIVATE VERSUS SOCIAL COSTS AND RETURNS

Does the migrant bear all the costs of migration and receive the total reward for his activity? The obvious answer is probably not. Migration will typically involve costs (and rewards) to non-migrants as well as migrants; the relative prices seen by the migrant are likely to be at variance with transformation rates for the economy as a whole. Divergences between social costs and returns arising from externalities pose knotty analytical problems; those arising from market imperfections and institutional factors are somewhat easier to examine and are my main concern here. The cases considered are illustrative rather than exhaustive; consequently, the omissions may be the more important.[27]

The above discussion of private costs and returns places voluntary migration in the general framework of a competitive economy satisfying the minimal requirements permitting an "optimum" allocation of resources. Among other features, wages must be freely determined and there must be no barriers to the free movement of labor and other inputs among industries or across space.[28] Even if wages are freely determined and equal marginal product, differences in the relation between wages and, for example, retained earnings in different areas will cause private returns to differ from social returns. Consider the case of local differences in the degree of progression in income taxation; migration redistributes resources in a fashion to equate earnings over space *subject to the taxation structure*, a process which may indeed be detrimental to resource allocation.

Divergence between private and social costs of migration can also occur when the charges for services collectively provided (such as schools) are based upon the per capita cost rather than the actual

[26] If a study of the returns to migration were carried out along these lines, one additional factor must be considered. I have assumed that migration is mainly in response to differences in earnings over space. In the case of off-farm migration, however, rising unemployment in the non-farm sector has been observed to attentuate sharply the outflow from agriculture even though we may assume earnings differentials (for employed persons) to remain relatively stable. If unemployment is high, the probability of the off-farm migrant obtaining a job at a given level of earnings is reduced, perhaps much more than rates of unemployment would indicate, owing to seniority rules and the like. Observed earnings differentials must be further discounted for the risk of unemployment and the appropriate discount rate may be very high, as imperfections in the capital market may prevent potential migrants from assuming this risk during periods of moderate to heavy unemployment. The logical choice in this circumstance is to defer the move until more favorable labor market conditions prevail.

[27] This section draws heavily upon the comments of Anthony M. Tang on an earlier draft.

[28] We must also require that product prices also be freely determined and barriers to free trade nonexistent.

marginal cost of providing those services to migrants. However, capital losses imposed by migrants upon the privately held fixed assets of non-migrants in an area experiencing a population decline generally cannot be admitted as an excess of social over private cost. These losses involve no resource cost; persons presumably will not migrate until their productivity elsewhere is sufficiently high to compensate for rent differentials.

Another source of an excess of social over private returns to migration arises from a failure of migrants to consider the returns to their progeny from the resulting change in the latter's (initial) location. By assuming the current change in market conditions to continue indefinitely into the future, a crude first approximation of this excess is possible. Suppose the migrant includes as private return the additional earnings obtained by himself and his immediate family but excludes any return to unborn children. The rate of interest, compounded instantaneously, is assumed to be 10 per cent per year; and the rate of population increase at 1.5 per cent per year. If his first as-yet-unborn child enters the labor market in twenty years, and if earnings differentials are and remain the same for all occupations (since there is no certainty that the migrant's progeny will enter his occupation), each dollar of his (uniform) earnings stream for a forty-five year participation in the labor force has a present value of $9.90. The present value of a permanent income stream of $1.00 beginning in twenty years and growing at the rate of 1.5 per cent per year (due to natural population increase) is about $1.62. The first figure is the present value of the return to the migrant aged twenty years of each dollar of earnings differential; the second is the present value of the return to the stream of unborn children he will generate.[29] If the migrant neglects the latter completely, the social return to migration will be 16.4 per cent in excess of the private return; if the private rate of return is in fact 10 per cent, the additional social rate of return will be 1.164 per cent. For older migrants the excess of the social return over the private will approach zero (they are less likely to have more children); and for younger migrants the social rate also approaches the private rate because a longer period will elapse before their children enter the labor market. For all migrants the excess of the social over the private rate of return is less than the estimate made above.

VI. CONCLUDING COMMENTS

My effort in this paper has been to place human migration in an investment context and in so doing to formulate testable hypotheses germane to observed migration behavior. My main conclusion remains that migration cannot be viewed in isolation; complementary investments in the human agent are probably as important or more important than the mi-

[29] The present value of the income stream of the migrant of $1.00 per year is computed as

$$\int_0^{45} e^{-rt}dt = 9.90$$

when $r = 0.10$. It is assumed that the migrant's children will realize an equal gain per year, and that the first child will not enter the labor force until twenty years in the future, their number growing continuously at 1.5 per cent per year thereafter. The present value of one income stream of $1.00 per year but which grows in number at 1.5 per cent per year and which will not begin for twenty years is

$$\int_0^{\infty} \frac{(e^{nt})\,e^{-rt}}{(e^{20r})\,dt},$$

which reduces to

$$\left(\frac{1}{e^{20r}}\right)\frac{1}{(n-r)\,e^{-(r-n)t}}\Bigg]_0^{\infty}.$$

If r is greater than n, the expression is finite and equal to 1.62 for $r = 0.10$ and $n = 0.015$.

gration process itself. As I have indicated, cognizance of, and attention to, these additional investments offer a promising clue to observed immobility in the face of large differentials in *current* earnings. In addition, only the estimation of the direct as well as associated costs of migration together with returns can reveal the extent of resource misallocation created by the frequently alleged barriers to mobility.

Costs and returns to migration have been consistently viewed in a real resource sense. Our tools of analysis are applicable only when costs and returns are so restricted; measures of psychic cost of migration, for example, are hard to come by. As I have suggested at various points, indeed the very need for these measures can often be circumvented.

Although my discussion provides only a sketchy framework for further empirical study of migration, the following additional conclusions are relevant to empirical undertakings. (1) Gross rather than net migration is a more relevant concept for studying the returns to migration as well as the impact of migration upon earnings differentials. (2) Migration rates are not an appropriate measure for estimating the effect of migration. (3) Age is significant as a variable influencing migration and must be considered in interpreting earnings differentials over space and among occupations. (4) The relation between private and social costs of, and returns to, migration at best depends upon market structure, resource mobility in general, and revenue policies of state and local governments.

[20]

Regional Studies, Vol. 19.2, pp. 95–110.

The Cyclical Sensitivity of Regional Employment and Unemployment Differentials[1]

IAN R. GORDON

Urban and Regional Studies Unit, University of Kent at Canterbury, Canterbury, Kent CT2 7NF, UK.

(Received November 1983; in revised form March 1984)

GORDON I. R. (1985) The cyclical sensitivity of regional employment and unemployment differentials, *Reg. Studies* **19**, 95–110. This paper examines inter-regional variations in the cyclical sensitivity of employment and unemployment in the UK over the past thirty years. It shows that the patterns for employment and for unemployment are quite different. The cyclical sensitivity of unemployment is greatest in the high unemployment regions while that for employment is greatest in the more industrial regions. It is argued that the primary reason for differences in the sensitivity of unemployment is not demand-side factors but cyclical variations in labour mobility between regions. Lower mobility in periods of high unemployment reduces the effectiveness of inter-regional supply adjustments and increases the variance of unemployment rates.

Cyclical sensitivity   Regional employment   Regional unemployment   Migration

GORDON I. R. (1985) Variation conjoncturelle des écarts de l'emploi et du chômage régionaux, *Reg. Studies* **19**, 95–110. Cet article examine les variations conjoncturelles inter-régionales de l'emploi et du chômage au Royaume-Uni sur les trente dernières années. Il démontre que les tendances relatives à l'emploi et au chômage sont tout à fait différentes. La variation conjoncturelle du chômage est la plus élevée dans les zones à forte intensité de chômage, tandis que la variation conjoncturelle de l'emploi est la plus élevée dans les zones à caractère industriel. On affirme que la raison primordiale susceptible d'expliquer la variation de l'emploi n'est pas l'influence des facteurs sur la demande, plutôt les variations conjoncturelles de la mobilité inter-régionale de la main-d'oeuvre. Une mobilité faible en période de chômage élevé réduit l'impact des ajustements inter-régionaux côté offre, et augmente la variance des taux de chômage.

Variation conjoncturelle   Emploi régional
Chômage régional   Migration

GORDON I. R. (1985) Die konjunkturrhythmische Empfindlichkeit regionaler Beschäftigungs- und Arbeitslosigkeitsgefälle, *Reg. Studies* **19**, 95–110. Diese Abhandlung untersucht zwischenregionale Abweichungen in der konjunkturrhythmischen Emfindlichkeit von Arbeitseinsatz und Arbeitslosigkeit im Vereinigten Königreich während der letzten dreissig Jahre. Es erweist sich, dass die Muster für Arbeitseinsatz ganz verschieden sind von denen der Arbeitslosigkeit. Die konjunkturrhythmische Empfindlichkeit der Arbeitslosigkeit ist in den Gebieten hoher Arbeitslosigkeit am grössten, während diejenige des Arbeitseinsatzes in den stärker industrialisierten Gebieten am grössten ist. Es wird festgestellt, dass der Grund für die unterschiedliche Empfindlichkeit der Arbeitslosigkeit in erster Linie nicht in den Faktoren seitens der Nachfrage zu suchen ist, sondern in konjunkturrhythmischen Abweichungen in der Mobilität der Arbeitskräfte zwischen den Regionen. Geringere Mobilität zu Zeiten hoher Arbeitslosigkeit setzt die Wirksamkeit zwischenregionaler Angebotsanpassungen herab und vermehrt die Varianz der Arbeitslosigkeitsraten.

Konjunkturrhythmische Empfindlichkeit
Regionaler Arbeitseinsatz
Regionale Arbeitslosigkeit   Wanderung

INTRODUCTION

Studies in several industrialized countries—for example, THIRLWALL, 1966, on the UK; VAN DUIJN, 1975, on the Netherlands; and HEWINGS, 1977, on Canada—have noted a tendency for wider cyclical fluctuations in unemployment rates, in absolute terms, in those (usually more peripheral) regions which suffer from higher unemployment throughout the business cycle. This pattern is generally assumed to reflect regional differences in the cyclical sensitivity of demand for labour and given a longer term significance as indicative of the marginality of these regions, the vulnerability of their industrial structures and/or the use of their labour force as a reserve army for the metropolitan economies. In this paper we shall argue that the basic assumption is incorrect at least in the British case—i.e. that the greater cyclical sensitivity of unemployment in peripheral areas is not a reflection of wider fluctuations in labour demand—and that more attention needs to be given, in both long and short term perspectives, to the role of supply side factors including the behaviour of migration. Elsewhere (GORDON, 1985a) we have provided evidence, from a time series study for one region, that cyclical variations in the responsiveness of migration to economic incentives can account for regional differences in the amplitude of fluctuations in unemployment. This case study showed that in periods of economic growth and high levels of activity, migration tended to be a very effective equilibriator of regional unemployment disparities but that the efficiency of this adjustment mechanism is much more limited in periods of recession, whether relatively short as in the 1950s and 1960s or protracted as in the 1970s, when workers are less willing and able to move to areas of relative advantage.[2] In this paper we show that the relationship across regions between the cyclical sensitivity of employment and unemployment also supports this explanation of regional variations in the sensitivity of unemployment.

In fact, past studies have not been entirely consistent in associating greater cyclical sensitivity with the peripheral regions of generally high unemployment. BRECHLING's, 1967, study, in particular, is frequently cited as exhibiting the reverse pattern, i.e. wider cyclical swings in the low unemployment regions. The basis of comparison in such studies is, however, the *proportional* rather than the *absolute* fluctuation in unemployment rates. This may be a somewhat arbitrary measure of cyclical sensitivity since equal proportional fluctuations in employment would produce equal *absolute* fluctuations in the unemployment rate and the circumstances which would generate proportionately equal fluctuations are quite unclear. However, it is notable that analyses in different countries and time periods appear quite consistently to show both smaller proportionate fluctuations in the high unemployment regions and larger absolute fluctuations there. In addition to the studies already cited, this is the case with the data of OKKO, 1981, and GARCIA DE BLAS, 1981 on unemployment trends in Finland and Spain, respectively, during the 1970s and the analysis of SUM and RUSH, 1975, of the distribution of unemployment between US regions between 1961–73: an Israeli study (MUSHKAT, 1974) which lacks data on absolute fluctuations also shows that proportionate fluctuations are greatest in the regions of high demand. The generality of this pattern of cyclical variability between different sets of regions suggests that adequate explanations are not to be found in purely local factors or the specific circumstances of particular booms or recessions but rather that there are some systematic links between the causes of cross-sectional differentials in unemployment rates and variations in cyclical responsiveness.

One such link which has been implied in some discussions of the development of regional problems, though never apparently formalized, assumes the existence of a ratchet process whereby the peculiar vulnerability of peripheral regions to cyclical fluctuations produces a progressive attrition of their economic base during successive recessions which accounts in part at least for their generally higher levels of unemployment. This is, of course, a one-sided account of cyclical sensitivity, focusing on trends during downswings in economic activity, whereas the standard measures of cyclical sensitivity give equal weight to relative performance during periods of expansion. The greater cyclical sensitivity of unemployment attributed to peripheral regions in studies using the absolute measure of fluctuations implies that these regions not only suffer more during recessions but also recover more markedly during the upswing, although their actual unemployment rate tends to remain higher than in the core regions. In fact, the conventional measurement techniques, which we shall also employ, maintain an independence between the cyclical and secular elements in regional unemployment and the evidence which they yield can thus have no bearing on the 'ratchet' hypothesis. However, the time trends estimated as part of the measurement process, in the next section do not suggest that there has been any general tendency over the past thirty years to divergence in UK regional unemployment rates, at a given level of national unemployment, as would be required by the 'ratchet' hypothesis.

In this paper we treat cyclical fluctuations throughout the past three decades as essentially temporary and reversible phenomena, superimposed on secular trends in regional employment, migration and unemployment, and do not distinguish between the quite regular fluctuations of the 1950s and 1960s and the more irregular and unbalanced changes in unemployment levels during the 1970s (see FROST and SPENCE, 1981b). So far as regional differentials are concerned, despite the significant changes in particular regions associated with the development of oil extraction and the decline of the motor industry, we shall emphasize the essential continuity in the patterns and relationships during this extended period. The focus will thus be on identifying general explanations for the varying cyclical sensitivity of the British regions, rather than on charting the causes and effects of particular fluctuations.

At this level of generality, attention in previous studies has been concentrated almost exclusively on fluctuations in unemployment with negligible attention to actual changes in employment or labour supply. Until recently cyclical fluctuations in migration levels—the major influence on regional labour supply changes—have been ignored, pardonably since very little time series data has been available except for indirect estimates of net movement of suspect quality. The lack of attention to employment fluctuations at the regional level is more curious but it has been generally taken for granted that these are more or less a mirror image of the unemployment changes with the implication that the primary cause of regional variations in the cyclical sensitivity of unemployment must be differences in the sensitivity of employment. These presumed differences in employment sensitivity have in turn been commonly attributed either to the effects of industrial structure or the likely vulnerability of employment in the branch plants of peripheral regions. Since BROWN, 1972, a number of studies (notably BELL, 1981) have emphasized the greater significance of labour hoarding in regions of high labour demand. Something rather similar is implied in VAN DUIJN's, 1975, explanation in terms of the constraining effects of capacity ceilings on the amplitude of cycles. The weakness of such demand side explanations in the case of British regions is, as shown later, the lack of any evidence that employment is actually more cyclically sensitive in the high unemployment regions. This has not generally been the case for any of the reference periods considered in the studies of unemployment fluctuations. Thus it is not surprising to find that industrial or occupational composition, which would have to work *via* employment levels, do not directly account for much of the regional variation in the cyclical sensitivity of unemployment (DIXON and THIRLWALL, 1975; VAN DUIJN, 1975; GILLESPIE and OWEN, 1981). Similarly despite its *a priori* plausibility (LOASBY, 1967), the evidence for the particular vulnerability of branch plants in peripheral areas seems very weak (TOWNROE, 1975; ATKINS, 1973; O'FARRELL, 1976; CLARKE, 1976). The part of Brown's thesis concerned with differential labour hoarding would also fall foul of the apparent relative insensitivity of employment in the high unemployment regions.

The principal alternative to these demand-side explanations has been couched in terms of the role of unregistered labour reserves as a factor tending to reduce fluctuations in measured unemployment in the regions of high labour demand. For example, ELIAS, 1979, argues that the propensity of unemployed men to register with employment exchanges, and thus to qualify for the regular statistics, is higher in the regions of low labour demand with the implication that regional variations in cyclical sensitivity of unemployment are basically a measurement phenomenon. However, the evidence cited relates only to average propensities, reflecting a fairly constant rate of unregistered unemployed men, and the marginal propensity to register appears to be close to 100% for males, thus allowing no significant regional variations (GORDON, 1980). A broader version of this argument is presented by BROWN, 1972, who suggests that in the high demand regions fluctuations in employment are achieved largely by drawing into the labour force during booms marginal workers who drop out again spontaneously in times of slump. As for VAN DUIJN, 1975, the scale of fluctuations in registered unemployment is effectively constrained in the high demand regions. In both cases the assumption is apparently that in the short time-scale of employment fluctuations regional labour markets are effectively closed, although in the longer run at least net migration is clearly the principal adjustment mechanism for changes in employment. Brown's conclusions are actually based on a set of time series regression analyses, for each region, of the response of unemployment to short term variations in employment 'corrected to allow for purely demographic changes'. The basis of this correction is not specified and thus it is unclear to what extent it controls for any short-term adjustments in labour migration. Brown, however, takes the view that marked disparities between the peripheral and central regions in the responsiveness of unemployment to employment changes reflect their varying use of alternative reserves of indigenous labour supply to accommodate these fluctuations. Since such reserves of marginal workers would be preponderantly female, on this assumption we should expect to find that regions also differ significantly in the distribution of employment fluctuations between males and females, with male employment being more sensitive in the peripheral regions and female employment more sensitive in the central regions. Such a pattern is not apparent, however, and the results of MOLHO, 1983, suggest that there are no significant regional variations in the response of female participation rates to unemployment changes.

In this paper the patterns of cyclical sensitivity in *unemployment* are first re-examined in the light of a longer period of experience than has previously been examined and alternative indicators of sensitivity. In the following section the demand-side explanations of inter-regional variations in cyclical behaviour are reviewed and related to estimates of the cyclical sensitivity of *employment*. Finally, the relationship between employment and unemployment changes is investigated in relation to the varying efficiency of migration as an equilibriating mechanism.

UNEMPLOYMENT

Past studies have variously made use of two alternative measures of the cyclical sensitivity of regional unemployment which give quite contradictory impressions. THIRLWALL, 1966; and BROWN, 1972, concentrate on *absolute* differences in unemployment rates between regions and over time, whereas BRECHLING, 1967; ELIAS, 1978; and BELL, 1981, take as their point of comparison *proportionate* variations in unemployment rates. From a normative standpoint the former comparison seems rather more appropriate and natural. The analytic usefulness of the alternative measures depends however on whether there are any prior grounds for expecting equal sensitivity for different regions in either absolute or proportionate terms, and/or, from an inductive standpoint, on whether one or other of the formulations yields a pattern of variation which is more readily explained. GORDON, 1980, argued that the null hypothesis of equal absolute changes was consistent with a simple model of equilibrium regional unemployment levels whereas the hypothesis of equal proportional changes was not. At this stage, however, it would be appropriate to consider both approaches in examining the pattern of regional variation over the past thirty years.

The basic method used as in earlier studies involves a set of time series regressions in which the regional unemployment rate (an annual average) is related to the corresponding national rate and to a polynomial time trend. With untransformed unemployment rates the coefficient on the national rate provides a measure of cyclical sensitivity in absolute terms; with logged rates the same coefficient indicates the relative sensitivity in proportional terms. The time trend is intended to control for non-cyclical trends or fluctuations affecting either labour supply or demand in particular regions. The time trends are significant in each of the regional equations, although much less important than the national unemployment variable, but for simplicity (since seven terms are involved) these have been omitted from the results presented in Table 1 which includes only the coefficient on the cyclical variable.

The OLS results show that the linear formulation provides the better fit in all but one case, although R^2 values are always high, and the residual variance is typically about one third less than with the non-linear specification.[3] It can also be seen that whereas four of the nine regions' unemployment rates seem to move in parallel with national trends on the absolute measure, this is only the case for one region on the proportional measure. The most striking feature of the results is, however, as suggested by the conflicting evidence of earlier studies, the negative correlation between the two alternative indicators of cyclical sensitivity.[4] For example Northern Ireland is clearly the most sensitive region in terms of absolute variations but also clearly the least sensitive in terms of proportional variations. On some intermediate formulation it is likely that most regions would emerge as about equally sensitive, as can be seen by considering the geometric averages of the two measures. On the latter basis the principal variations would appear to be between the industrial regions of the Midlands, Yorkshire and the North West with an above average cyclical sensitivity, and the rest of the country.

However, the fact that there is a negative correlation between the two traditional measures also implies that both of these are related to the prevailing unemployment levels in the regions concerned. It can indeed be seen from Table 1 that the high unemployment (Development Area) regions show above average cyclical sensitivity on the absolute measure and below average sensitivity on the proportional measure.

Table 1. OLS regression of regional on national unemployment rates, 1949–80

	Linear regression (absolute variations)			Log-linear regression (proportionate variations)		
	Coefficient on national unemployment	R^2	*DW*	Coefficient on national unemployment	R^2	*DW*
South East and East Anglia	0·744 (5·8)	0·992	1·59	1·064 (1·1)	0·989	1·77
South West	0·979 (0·2)	0·988	1·43	0·849 (1·6)	0·980	1·52
West Midlands	1·033 (0·3)	0·984	1·53	1·290 (1·6)	0·957	1·78
East Midlands and Yorkshire and Humberside	0·963 (1·1)	0·998	2·40	1·311 (4·8)	0·993	1·76
North West	1·228 (2·3)	0·990	2·19	1·195 (1·8)	0·978	2·09
Northern	1·093 (0·5)	0·966	1·79	0·740 (2·0)	0·945	1·79
Wales	1·155 (1·8)	0·990	1·52	0·796 (2·7)	0·978	1·65
Scotland	1·238 (1·8)	0·974	1·08	0·753 (3·2)	0·970	1·13
Northern Ireland	1·733 (3·6)	0·939	2·24	0·621 (7·0)	0·950	2·48

Notes: 1. All regressions also include a seventh order time trend and are based on annual data ($N = 32$).
2. Bracketed values are *t* statistics relating to the difference from 1·0.
3. All unemployment rates are from published DoE statistics and relate to monthly averages of registered male and female unemployed each year as a proportion of the mid-year estimate of insured employees (employed plus unemployed).

Inspection of the Durbin Watson statistics in Table 1 shows no general tendency for serial correlation in the residuals, either positive or negative: the DW values for Scotland are rather low but inside the lower limit at the 5% significance level. Re-estimation of the regressions using the Cochrane-Orcutt iterative correction yielded only minor changes to the coefficients, of no more than 1% or 2%. These ordinary least squares estimates may not, however, provide entirely reliable measures of the degree of cyclical sensitivity of unemployment in particular regions since they ignore the possibilities *both* of significant lags in the relationship *and* of the dependence of national unemployment on regional unemployment levels.

BRECHLING's, 1967, original study suggested that individual regions may tend to lead or lag behind national changes in unemployment by a quarter or so but even with quarterly data the correlations were not greatly altered by ignoring these lags. A more exhaustive study by FROST and SPENCE, 1981b, with data at sub-regional and Travel-to-Work Area levels found no evidence to suggest that any area shows consistent tendencies for the timing of its unemployment responses to be different from that of other areas. There are reasons for expecting a more complex distributed lag in the relationship between national and regional unemployment rates, since this is, at best, a reduced form of a system of equations involving national and regional output, employment, migration and commuting (see BELL, 1981; GORDON, 1985b). DUNN, 1983, shows empirically that this lag distribution may involve negative as well as positive terms.

As BELL, 1981, implies, however, these questions can only adequately be investigated within the context of a properly specified set of structural equations, whereas regressions of regional on national unemployment can aim only at description and comparison of the consequent changes in the regional distribution of unemployment over the course of a cycle of some years' duration. For this purpose, there is no reason to believe that the omission of possible lagged effects involves significant biases in the estimates of cyclical responsiveness.

Even at the descriptive level, however, there appear to be real risks of bias in treating national unemployment rates as an independent variable in regressions with regional unemployment since the national rate is simply a weighted average of the regional rates. The identification problem was pointed out by Webb and Harvey (reported in CHISHOLM *et al.*, 1971) while JOHNSTON, 1979, showed that the definitional link between sub-national and national rates limited the likely variability of conventional estimates of cyclical sensitivity for the larger urban or regional units. Because of this factor he suggested that relatively small deviations from a coefficient of 1·0 for the more populous areas should be treated as more significant than some larger deviations recorded for minor towns or regions. His discussion of the issue, however, tends to elide two quite different points. Firstly there is the fact that areas accounting for a significant proportion of national employment will tend to deviate less, in all respects, from the national average for definitional reasons as well as on account of the law of large numbers. Estimates of cyclical sensitivity are not thereby biased but have to be interpreted in the light of this tendency *or* of the relevant causal variables, such as industrial structure, which are themselves likely to approximate the national pattern. The second and more problematic issue, however, is whether regression estimates of relative cyclical sensitivity for the larger areas reflect the effect of regional unemployment on national unemployment as well as *vice versa*, i.e. whether they are subject to simultaneous equation bias. The issue is problematic since the conventional regression equation is based on no explicit causal model and, when the regional-rational identity is set alongside it, the system is apparently quite unidentified. With the simple model sketched in a later section of this paper, in which regional unemployment depends on national unemployment and regional *differentials* in employment growth rates, national unemployment would be causally independent of regional unemployment, despite the identity which links them. The validity of this hypothesis requires testing, however, and it seems appropriate to re-estimate the regression of regional on national unemployment by instrumental variables. For this purpose, national unemployment a year previously, employment growth rates in each region and the polynomial in time were used as predictors of the current national unemployment rate.

The results from the two-stage least squares estimation showed some non-trivial differences from the OLS estimates, although individually none of these differences appear statistically significant.[5] Systematic comparison with the OLS estimates suggested that there was no evidence of simultaneous equation bias in the former. Assuming that differentials in regional unemployment rates had a *positive* effect on national unemployment rates, particularly in the case of the larger regions, we should expect to find that the variance in the estimated cyclical coefficients was larger in the two-stage than in the OLS estimates. More specifically, if this assumption were correct, the OLS estimates should be biased upwards for values of below 1·0, particularly for the larger regions: for values above 1·0 predictions are less clear cut but the bias should be downwards for the higher coefficients in the smaller regions. In fact, the linear equations show a similar range of variation in the two sets of estimates while the variance in the log-linear coefficients is about one sixth less with the two-stage estimates. The one really substantial change, a lower coefficient for Northern Ireland in the linear estimates, is in the reverse direction to that hypothesized. We conclude that there is no evidence of bias in the OLS estimates and that these are to be preferred, on grounds of efficiency, to the alternative estimation procedure.

Although the period analysed here is significantly longer, the pattern of variation between regions broadly follows that identified in earlier studies, but the range of variation appears substantially reduced. In terms of the linear measure, for example, DIXON and THIRLWALL, 1975, report a range for the period 1951–72 between 0·54 (in the South East) and 1·39 (in Wales), while for the log-linear measure BRECHLING, 1967, reports a range for the 1952–63 period between 0·77 (in Scotland) and 1·43 (in the West Midlands): both studies omit Northern Ireland. In the period considered here the range of national unemployment rates has gone much higher than those included in the earlier studies and over this extended range it is quite likely that the linearity assumptions in the relationship between regional differentials and national rates would no longer hold. To test this explanation, annual data for the 1949–80 period on the weighted standard deviation in regional unemployment rates was included in regression analyses with a polynomial time trend and a series of monotonic transformations of the national unemployment rate.[6] Cochrane-Orcutt iterative technique was used for estimation. The final regression, with *corrected t* statistics in brackets, was:

$$SD_u = 1{\cdot}00 f_1(t) + 1{\cdot}0 f_2(U_n)$$
$$(6{\cdot}1) \qquad (11.3)$$

$$\text{with } R^2 = 0.88 \quad DW = 1{\cdot}80$$
$$SE = 0{\cdot}12 \quad N = 31, \ \rho = 0{\cdot}324$$

where: SD_u = the standard deviation of regional unemployment rates, weighted by numbers of employees, about the national average

t = time

The time trend showed a secular convergence in regional unemployment rates over the period 1957–73 followed by a sharp divergence after 1975. The stronger influence, however, is that of national unemployment rates which show a positive but markedly non-linear relationship with the regional deviation. There is a quite sharp kink in this relationship around a 2½% level of national unemployment which accounts for the recorded narrowing of the range of cyclical sensitivities in the 1970s. With national unemployment rates over about 2½%, the tendency for inter-regional variations to widen is quite substantially reduced, so that neither the linear nor log-linear formulations of the cyclical sensitivity indicator provide an adequate description of the whole range of experience.

The explanation for this non-linearity in the unemployment function is discussed in a later section. At this point, however, we may simply note that whatever the causes of regional variations in cyclical sensitivity are, they do not operate in a uniform, or linear, fashion at high and low levels of unemployment. This is the case, whether the relationship between regional and national rates is specified in linear or log-linear form. As we have noted, the linear function appears to fit the time series significantly better and it is also preferable in terms of its ease of interpretation, being related much more directly to numerical changes in the number of unemployed and to changes in employment. If we thus choose to use the absolute magnitude of fluctuations in the unemployment rate as the measure of cyclical sensitivity, the clear tendency over three decades has been for unemployment in the peripheral or Development Area regions to be more sensitive than average and for South East England alone to have a significantly lower sensitivity.

EMPLOYMENT

Regional differences in the cyclical sensitivity of *employment* may be expected for at least three reasons. *First*, and most obviously, regions differ in the extent to which they specialize in products with a particularly cyclical pattern of demand. Sectors producing capital goods would be particularly exposed to the effects of acceleration and deceleration in aggregate demand. In terms of employment the impact of most fluctuations during this period had been principally concentrated in manufacturing activities, particularly the metal and engineering industries, textiles and building materials, with both primary and service activities being relatively unaffected. Thus proportionately larger cyclical changes in employment would be expected in the West Midlands, which has much the greatest share of employment in manufacturing, and rather smaller swings in employment in South East England and the South West. A version of this hypothesis has been tested in several previous studies (e.g. DIXON and THIRLWALL, 1975; GILLESPIE and OWEN, 1981) with negative results but these have all sought to account for the sensitivity of unemployment not employment.

Secondly, as BELL and HART, 1980; and CHESHIRE, 1981a, have argued, we should also expect variations between regions in the extent of labour hoarding during recessions as a reflection of the differing costs of rehiring (or failing to rehire) the necessary labour force in the external labour market if and when demand picks up again. Thus there may be differing rates of adjustment of actual to required levels of employment, according to the expected tightness of the relevant labour market during the next up-swing, which will alter the amplitude of fluctuations in employment. More particularly, it is predicted by

BELL and HART, 1980, that adjustments in terms of employment, as distinct from labour services, will be slower in regions with a relatively skilled labour force, while CHESHIRE, 1981a, argues that they should also be slower in low unemployment regions (and periods). Bell and Hart also suggest that employers in the high unemployment (Development Areas) regions may find it difficult to finance labour hoarding during a downswing while those in the low unemployment regions have difficulty in attracting labour in the upswing.

These arguments perhaps require some qualification. Firstly they tend to underplay the extent to which employers accomplish adjustments in their labour force by variations in hiring, rather than firing, rates. MACKAY *et al.*, 1971, show for Birmingham and Glasgow that market separation rates actually tended to be significantly lower during times of high unemployment, because the great majority of separations were voluntary. Clearly there will be much less reason for employers to hoard labour where this involves earlier re-hiring (with its attendant fixed costs) rather than deferred redundancy. MACKAY *et al.*, 1971, did show that average redundancy rates tended to be lower in Birmingham than Glasgow, particularly for skilled men, but they found no evidence of hoarding of skilled men in Glasgow, although this was the case in the much smaller labour market of North Lanarkshire. We may speculate that in the latter case, which is not untypical of peripheral regions, redundant workers are much more likely to migrate and thus be unavailable for re-hiring if they are not hoarded, which would be less likely to happen in metropolitan regions. Skill alone does not seem to be the determinant of hoarding unless combined with either general labour market tightness or the threat of migration. And, since redundancy has usually been the minor element in employment reductions, while upswings do not necessarily affect the same firms as preceding downswings, it may still be the case that cyclical adjustments in employment levels are most rapidly accomplished in large metropolitan labour markets (such as that of the West Midlands) with their high rates of voluntary movement.

The *a priori* arguments do not yield simple predictions about likely variations between groups of regions in the speed of adjustment of employment to changing demands for labour. However, BELL and HART, 1980; and BELL, 1981, appear to have found clear evidence in two independent analyses that mean adjustment lags for manufacturing employment are relatively shorter in the Development Area regions in general, in the former case, and in Scotland in particular in the latter case. In both studies estimates of the mean adjustment lag are derived from the coefficient on the lagged value of the dependent variable in an employment equation. BELL and HART, 1980, obtain values of seven years and eleven years respectively for the Development Area and Non Development Area regions from a pooled cross-section/time series analysis for 1970–5. BELL, 1981, obtains estimates of 0·6 years and 2·1 years respectively for Scotland and for the UK as a whole from time series analyses for 1961–76. In each case the difference is significant at about the 5% level (t = 1·8 and 1·6 for the two analyses). The actual lag estimates are clearly much less plausible in the former case, and generally incompatible with other studies. The problem appears to be that in pooling observations from the five Development Area (DA) (and the five non DA) regions with quite different industrial structures, in a single equation including no dummy variables, the lagged dependent variables pick up most of the effects of omitted regional variables and the coefficients on them are biased sharply towards one. Certainly it is notable that these lagged variables account for the bulk of the explanation in each equation (with t values of 46 and 72). The difference between the two coefficients may simply reflect the fact that the non DA regions (accounting for about 60% of national employment) vary rather more than do the DA regions.

Such problems are not involved in the BELL, 1981, analysis which is based on quite adequate time series data and which yields entirely plausible results for both Scotland and the UK. There is, of course, the usual econometric problem in identifying the coefficient on the lagged dependent variable exclusively with the stock-adjustment relationship as distinct from serial correlation and it may be doubted whether this assumption is equally appropriate for two 'regions' which differ so markedly in scale. Certainly it is notable that the UK employment equation is better determined (R^2 = 0·97 compared with 0·93), principally because of a much stronger relationship with lagged employment. In this case also there may thus be some ambiguity about whether the results signal a real difference in employers' willingness or ability to adjust employment levels which would be reflected in the cyclical sensitivity of employment.

Thirdly, regions will differ in the incidence of industrial restructuring in terms of the replacement of old and unprofitable production with new and probably less labour-intensive plants. Restructuring is not intrinsically a cyclical process but the timing of openings and closures will tend to reflect demand cycles. Thus regions which are disproportionately involved in the restructuring process whether because of a concentration of less profitable establishments *or* because they are particularly attractive sites for the new capacity will tend to display more marked cyclical fluctuations as well as secular losses or gains in employment. As MASSEY and MEEGAN, 1979, have shown, the regional re-allocation of employment, within a diminishing total, as a result of restructuring activities may take a rather complex form involving a new spatial division of labour. The aggregate implications of such organizational changes are by no means clear but we might expect the combination of job loss plus job creation to be relatively more important in the DA regions than elsewhere.

Despite this variety of possible explanations, previous studies have not actually demonstrated that there are any consistent regional variations in the cyclical sensitivity of employment. In order to test this hypothesis we need to look at the changing regional shares of employment during the course of a number of successive cycles. For nine regional groupings in the UK comparable data series on employment can be derived for the years 1951–80 and these form the basis for the regression analyses reported in Table 2. The regressions related the regional share of employment in each year to national employment, expressed as an index, and to a polynomial time trend, included to control for secular changes in a region's relative performance during this period which might otherwise be confounded with its cyclical sensitivity. After experiment in which a varying number of terms proved significant, the order of this time trend was fixed at seven for each of the regressions. Although these time trends always accounted for at least 80% of the variation, the coefficients are not reported in Table 2 which focuses on the single cyclical relationship with which we are concerned in this paper.

Since it was possible that national employment could be affected by exogenous fluctuations in the

Table 2. Regressions of regional shares on national employment, 1951–80

	Coefficients on UK employees in employment index (1965 = 1·0)	Constant term	R^2	*SE*	*DW*
South East and East Anglia	−0·057 (3·9)	0·420	0·995	0·00070	2·15
South West	0·004 (0·6)	0·052	0·991	0·00032	1·79
West Midlands	0·030 (2·5)	0·068	0·870	0·00058	2·00
East Midlands, and Yorks. and Humberside	0·018 (2·1)	0·130	0·927	0·00041	1·93
North West	0·004 (0·5)	0·123	0·998	0·00032	2·17
Northern	−0·005 (0·6)	0·060	0·918	0·00040	1·84
Wales	0·001 (0·3)	0·040	0·950	0·00024	1·75
Scotland	0·004 (0·4)	0·087	0·985	0·00045	1·61
Northern Ireland	0·000 (0·1)	0·020	0·968	0·00018	1·97
Development Area regions	0·000 (0·0)	0·207	0·986	0·00064	1·78

Notes: 1. Bracketed coefficients are *t* values
2. The Development Area regions are the North, Wales, Scotland and Northern Ireland
3. The time trend variables have been omitted

employment levels of the larger regions (and thus by their share of national employment) two-stage least squares estimates were again computed for comparison, with employment changes in each other region included as instruments. The results, however, provided no evidence at all that national employment was dependent on any regional share and we conclude that there are no grounds for using two-stage least squares in preference to OLS.

The results reported in Table 2 show clearly for six of the nine regions that their share of national employment has over this long period been quite independent of changes in the level of national employment. In other words the amplitude of fluctuations in employment have tended not to be significantly different from the national pattern. The only exceptions to this norm are South East England, where cyclical fluctuations seem to have been much less marked throughout the period, and the two Midland regions (here incorporating Yorkshire and Humberside) where fluctuations have tended to be correspondingly larger. The DA regions as a group (Northern, Wales, Scotland and Northern Ireland) seem to have moved almost precisely in line with the national average over the cycles of this thirty-year period. This may not have been the case in each and every up- and down-swing when particular factors may have produced better or worse outcomes for individual regions. Clearly, however, there has been no general tendency over this period for cyclical fluctuations in employment to be wider (or narrower) in the peripheral regions.

In fact, of the three sets of potential explanations of regional variation in the cyclical sensitivity of employment which we have discussed, only the first, based simply on regional differences in industrial structure, appears to be supported by these indicators of employment sensitivity. As Table 3 shows there is, with one exception (the South West region), a close correspondence between the rankings of regions in terms of the observed cyclical sensitivity of their employment, on the one hand, and of the proportions in the most cyclically sensitive groups of industries, on the other hand. The simple correlation between the two measures ($r = 0{\cdot}83$) is significant at the 0·5% level and even the discrepancy in the South West case may not be significant in relation to the standard errors of the cyclical sensitivity estimate. Otherwise, the only regions with markedly above or below average proportions of employment in the 'cyclical' industries are the West Midlands and, to a lesser extent, the East Midlands/Yorkshire, both with more employment in these industries, and the South East, with less: these are also the three regions where actual employment displayed significantly greater (in the first two cases) or less (in the third) cyclical sensitivity.

At this level of analysis the regional employment data will clearly not support any more complex

Table 3. Cyclical sensitivity of regional employment and employment structure

	Index of cyclical sensitivity 1951–80	% employed in manufacturing 1966	% in cyclical industries 1966
South East	84	32·3	24·4
South West	108	29·9	23·9
West Midlands	131	52·3	46·3
East Midlands, and Yorks. and Humberside	112	42·6	34·5
North West	103	44·8	32·4
Northern	91	34·9	28·1
Wales	103	32·8	29·3
Scotland	104	34·1	29·3
Northern Ireland	102	37·6	31·9

Notes: 1. The index of cyclical sensitivity, with a value for the UK of 100, is calculated as $100\ (1 + \lambda\bar{E}_r/\bar{E}_n)$ where λ is the regression coefficient of the region's share of national employment on the national employment level (from Table 3) and $\bar{E}_r/\bar{E}_n$ is the region's average share of national employment.
2. The 'cyclical' industries are defined here as: metal manufacturing, engineering, ship-building, vehicles, other metal goods, textiles, building materials and construction.

Table 4. Cyclical sensitivity and unemployment rates by region

	Employment sensitivity (UK = 100)	Unemployment sensitivity (UK = 100)	Average unemployment rate (%) 1951–80
South East and East Anglia	84	74	1·8
South West	108	99	2·7
West Midlands	131	103	2·3
East Midlands, and Yorks and Humberside	112	97	2·3
North West	103	122	3·3
North	91	109	4·2
Wales	103	116	4·1
Scotland	104	121	4·4
Northern Ireland	102	172	7·9

Note: The measure of unemployment sensitivity included here relates to absolute variations and derives from the linear regressions in Table 1.

hypothesis in terms of labour hoarding, the vulnerability of branch plants or industrial restructuring.[7] It is perhaps fair to suggest that the majority of these hypotheses were developed in order to account for a pattern of regional differentation in cyclical sensitivity suggested by the unemployment data, namely a contrast between the peripheral and central areas, but which does not in fact characterize the employment data. A partial exception is BELL's, 1981, study which referred to a period (1961–76) when for specific reasons Scottish employment did appear to be particularly cyclically sensitive: this period was not typical of Scottish performance in the longer run, however, and Scotland was not typical of the peripheral regions in that particular period.

THE RELATIONSHIP BETWEEN EMPLOYMENT AND UNEMPLOYMENT SENSITIVITIES

As we have noted, the implicit or explicit assumption of most previous work has been that cyclical fluctuations in unemployment in particular regions must reflect quite directly the fluctuations in employment—and thus that inter-regional variations in the cyclical sensitivity of unemployment reflect underlying variations in the cyclical sensitivity of employment. A comparison of the sets of estimates derived in the two previous sections, reveals no simple correspondence, however, but suggests that the cyclical sensitivity of unemployment, whether measured in absolute or proportionate terms, *is* related to average unemployment levels in the regions concerned (see Table 4). The two hypotheses have been tested by running OLS regressions with the alternative measures of unemployment sensitivity in each region as a function of the measure of employment sensitivity and the average unemployment rate over the whole period. The two regressions obtained were (with *t* statistics in parentheses):

$$UC_A = 9{\cdot}4 + \underset{(11{\cdot}1)}{14{\cdot}4\bar{U}} + \underset{(2{\cdot}6)}{0{\cdot}48EC}$$

with $R^2 = 0{\cdot}954$

where: UC_A = cyclical sensitivity of unemployment (absolute measure)
$\bar{U}$ = average unemployment rate in the region 1949–80
EC = index of cyclical sensitivity of regional employment 1951–80

$$UC_p = 58{\cdot}9 - \underset{(3{\cdot}2)}{9{\cdot}9\bar{U}} + \underset{(1{\cdot}6)}{0{\cdot}70EC}$$

with $R_2 = 0{\cdot}708$

where: UC_p = cyclical sensitivity of unemployment (proportional measure)

It is notable that the regression with the *absolute* measure of cyclical sensitivity is much more significant, confirming that this is the more useful measure. However, in both cases the results show that there *is* a positive association between unemployment and employment sensitivities when regional differences in average unemployment levels are controlled for. The regression coefficients are well below one, however, and the equation for the absolute measures (UC_A) in particular indicates that on average only about half the differences in cyclical sensitivity of employment are transmitted to unemployment. The shortfall must be principally attributable to the role of inter-regional migration which tends to absorb much the greater part of regional differences in employment growth rates. If this is in fact the case, we should expect to find that the link between fluctuations in unemployment differentials and relative employment growth will be weakest in small and/or central regions which are highly open to migration and strongest in large and/or peripheral regions with lower migration potentials.

The major implication of these two regression equations, however, is that differential changes in regional unemployment are to be expected during the course of an employment cycle even if there are *no* differential employment changes. For some reason, differences in the cyclical sensitivity of unemployment appear to depend primarily on longer term differences in the prevailing rates of unemployment.[8] To investigate this relationship further, a series of time series regressions were run in which biennial *changes* in regional unemployment rates were related to the corresponding changes in national unemployment rates and to differential rates of employment change in the region concerned. The results, presented in Table 5, confirm that, when relative employment changes are held constant, changes in national unemployment rates on their own produce rather larger changes in the North West and Development Area regions and smaller changes in the South East. The coefficient on national unemployment (in column 1) may be thought of as a slightly purer estimate of the sensitivity of unemployment and is also strongly correlated with the region's average unemployment rate over the period.

The relationship with differential employment growth is also significant in most regions but for the average region this amounts to only 21% of the employment change. At the national level by contrast unemployment has tended to account for about half of the effect of cyclical changes in employment, as can be seen from a regression of two-year changes in the national unemployment rate (over the same period) on employment changes and a time trend:

$$\Delta U_n = \underset{(6\cdot 9)}{-0\cdot 517}\,\frac{\Delta E_n}{E_n} + \underset{(4\cdot 7)}{1\cdot 0T} + 0\cdot 326$$

with: R^2 = 0·72
U = unemployment rate
E = employment
T = a 5th order time trend (with 1965 = 0)

The remaining 48% or so of the employment adjustment nationally is accounted for by changes in participation rates, unregistered unemployment and net international migration.[9] Some or all of these factors could be more important in some regions than others (see ELIAS, 1979) although there appears to be no direct evidence of such variations and they could not account for the generally lower proportion of differential *regional* employment changes accounted for by changes in registered unemployment. The latter must be attributed to the greater potential for inter-area adjustment processes at the regional level, notably through induced (or deterred) labour migra-

Table 5. Regressions of regional unemployment changes on national unemployment changes and differential employment growth, 1951–80

	National unemployment change	Differential employment growth	Time	Constant	R^2	*DW*	*SE*
South East and	0·804	−0·257	−0·0223	0·1111	0·960	1·58	0·16
East Anglia	(5·2)	(3·5)	(2·9)	(2·3)			
South West	0·942	−0·283	−0·0153	0·3572	0·858	1·44	0·42
	(1·0)	(4·2)	(0·5)	(3·3)			
West Midlands	1·032	−0·145	−0·0091	0·1074	0·868	1·21	0·45
East Midlands, and Yorkshire	(0·3)	(1·7)	(0·5)	(1·2)			
and Humberside	0·936	−0·133	−0·0059	0·0520	0·973	1·53	0·17
	(2·0)	(2·3)	(1·0)	(1·6)			
North West	1·182	−0·091	−0·0117	−0·0917	0·947	1·54	0·30
(1953–80)	(2·9)	(0·7)	(0·8)	(0·6)			
Northern	1·095	−0·200	−0·0151	0·0663	0·752	1·86	0·69
	(0·6)	(1·7)	(0·7)	(0·5)			
Wales	1·150	−0·164	−0·0153	−0·0296	0·928	1·66	0·35
	(2·1)	(2·3)	(1·1)	(0·4)			
Scotland	1·218	−0·312	−0·0152	−0·2231	0·880	1·51	0·48
	(2.2)	(2·5)	(0·7)	(1·8)			
Northern Ireland	1·504	−0·308	−0·0492	−0·1074	0·871	1·77	0·70
	(3·5)	(3·4)	(2·3)	(0·7)			

Notes: 1. Employment and unemployment changes are both measured on a biennial basis in order to minimize the effects of measurement errors in the data and any short adjustment lags. Unemployment data are averages for calendar years while employment data relate to mid-year. Estimates for the North West are based on 1953–80 only to exclude an anomalous observation for 1952.
2. Bracketed values are *t* statistics: those in column 1 refer to the significance of deviations from a value of 1·0.
3. The regressions have been estimated via the Cochrane-Orcutt technique.

tion and possibly some more limited changes in the balance of commuting across regional boundaries. Confirmatory evidence for this interpretation can be found from the varying regional coefficients on the differential employment growth variable (column 2 of Table 5) which show the strongest effects in the least 'open' regions to migration flows (Scotland and Northern Ireland) and the weakest in the two Midland regions. Regressing these coefficients on measures of inter-regional migration potential[10] yields an equation:

$$\frac{dU}{d\hat{E}} = \underset{(7{\cdot}3)}{0{\cdot}460} - \underset{(4{\cdot}1)}{0{\cdot}384}\, POT$$

with $R^2 = 0{\cdot}704$
$N = 9$
$SE = 0{\cdot}048$

where: $\hat{E}$ = differential employment growth rate
POT = migration potential of region as proportion of the maximum value for a labour market area

predicting a maximum coefficient of 0·460 for a region completely closed to inter-regional migration (i.e. the nation as a whole) and a minimum of about 0·075 for the most accessible local labour market area. The upper end of this range is consistent with the time series estimates presented above of the proportion of national fluctuations in employment growth accounted for by unemployment changes. The lower end of the range is not significantly different from zero, and implies that in the most open labour markets local employment fluctuations would have no significant impact on local unemployment.

This relationship between differential employment growth and *changes* in regional unemployment is essentially a short-term, disequilibrium, phenomenon. In the long term, when unemployment differentials and inter-regional migration are in equilibrium, relative unemployment *levels* only should be affected by employment growth rate differences (Burridge and Gordon, 1981). Changes in unemployment rates would thus be better expressed in terms of the difference between relative employment growth in the current period and an appropriately weighted moving average (to reflect lags in the adjustment of migration) of relative employment growth rates in the past. To approximate this formulation, the regressions in Table 5 may be re-expressed with the employment growth variable measured as a deviation from its mean for the period as a whole. The variance of the constant terms around zero is significantly reduced in this re-arranged version of the results, although they are apparently significant (at the 5% level) in two regions—the East Midlands where the constant term is positive and Northern Ireland where it is negative.

The results show clearly, however, that it is not responses to differential employment growth (i.e. demand-side factors) which are the direct cause of inter-regional differences in cyclical sensitivity since the latter, represented here by the coefficients on national unemployment change, persist when the employment growth differences are controlled for. But it is also clear from the results that any cyclical factors which altered the relative proportions of differential employment growth in any region which were, on the one hand, accounted for by induced net migration *or*, on the other, transmitted to regional unemployment—causing fluctuations in the coefficients on relative employment growth—could have a major effect on the cyclical sensitivity of regional unemployment. Hart, 1975, argued that, in the face of increasing uncertainty, labour mobility should tend to fall in periods of recession, and we have found strong evidence in time series data for Scotland, covering the period 1952–81, to support this hypothesis (Gordon, 1985a). More generally, Ogilvy, 1979, has shown how the volume of long-distance migration in Britain has fallen during the current recession. In fact, it is not strictly necessary for actual rates of migration to fall as unemployment rises for wider cyclical fluctuations to be induced in the high unemployment regions. It would be sufficient for the rates of movement associated with given unemployment differentials to be cyclically sensitive. In this case, as unemployment rises, more of the continuing differential in rates of employment growth (less natural increase of labour supply) will get transmitted to regional unemployment, thus widening the variance in regional unemployment rates. The cyclical sensitivity of regional unemployment would thus depend primarily on long-term sources of disparities in regional unemployment and only secondarily on the cyclical sensitivity of employment itself. This is essentially the pattern which we find empirically for the British regions over the past three decades.

If the strength of inter-regional migration as an adjustment mechanism is the crucial factor affecting the cyclical behaviour of regional unemployment it is not only *current* rates of migration which are significant. Regional unemployment rates *may* thus depend not only on current but also on past national unemployment rates, according to how close the distribution of regional unemployment rates is to equilibrium. This will in turn be a function of the level of national unemployment, as a determinant of the general level of mobility. At high levels of unemployment the equilibriating process, in terms of inter-regional migration, is not only weaker it also becomes more protracted. The variance of regional unemployment rates thus comes to depend not only on the level of national unemployment but also on how long it has persisted. At low unemployment rates by contrast the system should always be close to equilibrium, particularly if lags in the migration function are short, and regional unemployment rates should depend more straightforwardly on current national unemployment rates.

This point can be illustrated with a simplified model of the migration-unemployment relationship. Suppose that all people of working-age are either employed or unemployed and that the rate of natural change in this working-age population is everywhere constant. Then changes in relative unemployment rates can be represented by the identity:

$$\Delta(U_r - U_n) \equiv M_r - \hat{E}_r \quad (1)$$

where: M = net inter-regional migration of working-age

Let us further suppose that the differential employment growth rate for any particular region is stable over time but that net migration varies with national economic conditions *and* relative unemployment rates, e.g.:

$$M_r = f(U_n)\ (U_r - U_n) \quad (2)$$

where: $f(U_n)$ = a mobility factor dependent on national unemployment levels
$f(U_n) < 0\ f'(U_n) > 0$

If there are no lags in this relationship the system moves directly to an equilibrium in which the ranking of regional unemployment rates is the inverse of their relative employment growth rates and their variance is a direct function of national unemployment rates:

$$(U_r - U_n)_t = \frac{\hat{E}_r}{f(U_n)} \quad (3)$$

In this case net migration becomes a constant, independent of the mobility factor:

$$M_r = \hat{E}_r \quad (4)$$

since variations in the mobility factor will be exactly off-set by induced changes in differential unemployment rates. This is also the equilibrium to which the system tends in the presence of lags in the migration function (equation (2)) when national unemployment rates remain relatively constant over some period of time.

The long-run elasticity of unemployment differentials with respect to the mobility factor ($f(U_n)$) is thus -1. The short-run response to variations in the mobility factor can be seen if a simple lag is inserted in equation (2), making migration in a period dependent on unemployment differentials at the start of that period:

$$M_{rt} = f(U_{nt})\ (U_r - U_n)_{t-1} \quad (5)$$

The short-run (single period) elasticity of unemployment differentials with respect to the mobility factor can then be derived, from equations (1) and (5), as:

$$\frac{d(U_{rt} - U_{nt})}{f'(U_{nt})} \cdot \frac{f(U_n)_{t-1}}{(U_r - U_n)_{t-1}} = (U_r - U_n)_{t-1} \cdot \frac{f(U_n)}{(U_r - U_n)} = f(U_n) \quad (6)$$

The absolute value of this expression also represents the proportion of the long-run response to changes in the mobility factor, resulting from changes in national unemployment, which occur in the first period following the change. It can be seen that the speed of adjustment is itself a negative function of the level of national unemployment. At high unemployment rates therefore regional differentials are likely to be not only large but increasing, since they will be approaching the equilibrium only slowly. By the same token it follows that actual net migration rates are likely to fall initially when national unemployment rises, with a slow subsequent recovery as regional disparities in unemployment increase.

These qualitative results, which will hold also for more sophisticated formulations of the unemployment change identity and of the migration function, help to account for two important features of the results reported earlier at the end of the second section. The first of these relates to the diminishing effect of increases in national unemployment on regional variations in unemployment rates once national unemployment had passed 2½–3%. A fundamental reason for this pattern, it can now be seen, is the lengthening lag at higher levels of unemployment between changes in 'mobility' and their full effects on regional differentials. Secondly, it was suggested that, for given levels of national unemployment, there was a strong tendency towards divergence in regional unemployment rates from the mid-1970s onwards. At least part of this divergence, it would now appear, is to be attributed to the delayed effects of high national unemployment rates which are a cause of *continuing* divergence in regional unemployment.

This analysis suggests an alternative formulation of the regression model to account for the changing deviations in regional rates in stock-adjustment terms. Adapting equation (3) above, equilibrium unemployment differentials at any point in time would be represented as functions of a time trend and the national unemployment level:

$$(U_r - U_n)^{\star}_t = \frac{f_e(t)}{f_m(U_n)} \quad (7)$$

where the superscript ★ denotes an equilibrium value.

Changes in unemployment differentials in any period would, however, following equation (6), be a variable proportion of the difference between this equilibrium value and the observed differential at the start of the period:

$$(U_r - U_n)_t = (U_r - U_n)_{t-1} + [(U_r - U_n)^{\star}_t - (U_r - U_n)_{t-1}]\, f_m(U_n)$$

$$= f_e(t) + (U_r - U_n)_{t-1}\,(1 - f_m(U_n)) \quad (8)$$

This simple model suggests a more meaningful basis for the decomposition, attempted at the end of the second section, of changes in the regional variance of unemployment rates into secular and cyclical components. The reformulated regression equation takes the form:

$$SD_{ut} = \alpha_1 SD_{ut-1} + \alpha_2 f_1(t) - \alpha_3 f_2(U_n)\,(SD_{ut-1}) + \varepsilon_t \quad (9)$$

where the time function is now taken to represent the secular trend in the variance of pressure of demand for labour between regions and the function of national unemployment to represent the cyclically variable mobility factor, and hence the rate of adjustment towards equilibrium regional unemployment rates. The period length, and thus the lag in the migration equation, is set at a year on the basis of the analysis of Scottish migration series (GORDON, 1985a). The coefficient on the lagged dependent variable is expected to be unity. The two variables expressed as generalized functions are intrinsically non-linear, and estimated in the same fashion as before (see earlier and note 6): the coefficients in the estimated equation are purely conventional and their form is best seen graphically (Figs. 1 and 2). Once again the Cochrane-Orcutt iterative technique has been employed to reduce the effect of serial correlation in the disturbances: the final regression estimate, with corrected t statistics in brackets, was:

$$SD_{ut} = \underset{(15{\cdot}00)}{0{\cdot}9994 SD_{ut-1}} + \underset{(7{\cdot}3)}{1{\cdot}0 f_1(t)} - \underset{(10{\cdot}8)}{1{\cdot}0 f_2(U_n)}\,(SD_{ut-1})$$

$$\text{with } R^2 = 0{\cdot}9924 \quad DW = 2{\cdot}22 \quad \rho = -0{\cdot}434 \quad SE = 0{\cdot}110 \quad N = 31$$

It can be seen that the strongest relationship is with the lagged dependent variable and that the coefficient on this variable is very close to the hypothesised value of 1·0. This result and the acceptable Durbin-Watson statistic suggest that the assumption of a single year lag in the migration relationship may not be a bad approximation. Both the time trend and the mobility factor are also clearly significant but it is the latter which contributes more to the explanation. The form of the time trend (in Fig. 1) again shows a tendency for regional convergence, particularly in the period 1963–75, with a marked divergence after 1977, although the latter tendency now appears much less extreme. In broad terms it appears that regional differences in pressure of demand for labour tended to narrow during the period of active regional policy but that they have increased again quite sharply during the *current* recession, which seems to have had an unusually strong effect on the peripheral regions and the West Midlands (MARTIN, 1982). The estimates of the mobility factor (in Fig. 2) show a five-fold difference between the levels of mobility to be expected at the highest and lowest levels of national unemployment observed in this period. The mini-

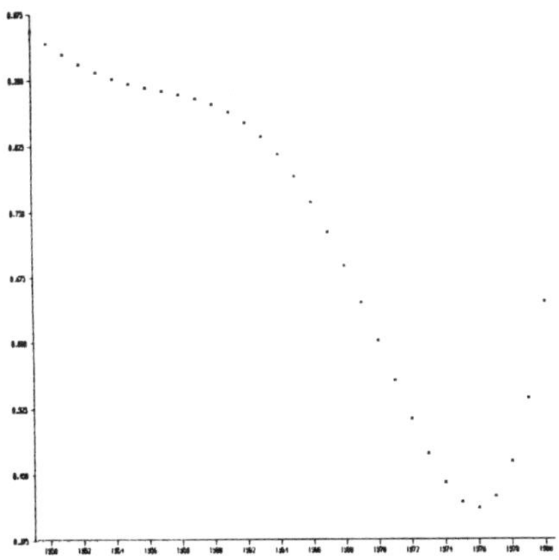

Fig. 1. Time trend in the SD of regional employment rates

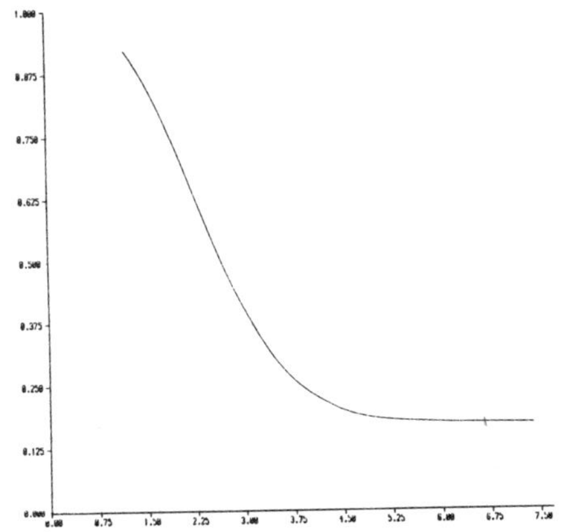

Fig. 2. Mobility factor as function of national employment rate

mum level of mobility appears to have been approached by the time national unemployment has passed 4%, however, and increases beyond this point have much less effect. This indirect estimate of the mobility function[11] is very similar to that derived from a time series analysis of Scottish migration (GORDON, 1983): the respective coefficients of variation of the two estimates over the observation period are 0·442 and 0·483 and the simple correlation coefficient between them is 0·979.

Values of this factor can also be interpreted as the proportion of regional adjustment towards equilibrium which would be realised in a one-year interval: over the observed range of national unemployment this is estimated to vary between 92% at the lowest levels of unemployment and 17% at the highest. During the 1950s and 1960s, therefore, regional unemployment differentials are likely to have been consistently close to their equilibrium values but by the late 1970s they are likely to have been well away from equilibrium. In 1980 for example when the actual standard deviation in regional rates was some 2·3% the predicted equilibrium differentials would have involved a standard deviation of about 3·8%. Neither the effects of the shrinkage in labour mobility nor of the unequal regional job losses during the recession had by then been more than partially reflected in the spread of regional unemployment rates. Even without further change in either factor, continuing divergence in regional unemployment rates would be expected into the later 1980s as the partial adjustments work their way through.

SUMMARY

Following THIRLWALL, 1966, and BRECHLING, 1967, a considerable number of studies have examined the cyclical sensitivity of regional economies in terms of the behaviour of their unemployment rate series. These have generally been assumed to reflect the pattern of employment fluctuations but the actual cyclical behaviour of employment has not been examined. In this paper we have shown that inter-regional variations in cyclical sensitivity are actually quite different for employment and for unemployment. For unemployment, the difference is essentially between the high and low unemployment regions, with the former displaying absolutely larger (though proportionately smaller) fluctuations. For employment, the difference is essentially between the more and less industrial regions, with larger fluctuations in those regions which specialize in the more cyclically sensitive sectors (notably the metal trades). The two patterns of variation are completely uncorrelated.

The link between employment and unemployment changes is comparatively weak because the greater part of the unemployment variations consequent on a regional employment change is not found in the region concerned but is transmitted elsewhere as a result of induced labour migration. The extent to which this occurs, however, varies both between regions, according to how open they are to migration (which depends on their size and accessibility), and over time, according to whether there is a high level of economic activity (favouring inter-regional mobility) or not. This cyclical variability in mobility is the primary reason for the observed pattern of regional variation in the cyclical sensitivity of unemployment both in Britain and elsewhere. Its significance tends to hide the smaller variations associated with differences in the cyclical responsiveness of employment.

This paper has sought to use the longest time series available to establish 'normal' patterns of cyclical behaviour for the British regions. It has thus not distinguished between the cycles of the 1950s and 1960s and the recessions of the 1970s. It is clear, however, that the conventional measures of cyclical sensitivity of unemployment become less appropriate when applied to the wider range of unemployment rates experienced in recent years. Previous studies have used either absolute (linear) or proportionate (log-linear) measures of sensitivity. On both conceptual and empirical grounds the absolute measure is preferable but even this measure is clearly sensitive to the range of unemployment rates over which it is applied. At high levels of national unemployment—over about 3%—the tendency for regional unemployment rates to diverge starts to weaken, since inter-regional mobility is approaching its minimum. Moreover, the process of adjustment towards equilibrium becomes a much more protracted business. Thus measures of cyclical sensitivity with a more recent base period tend to show a smaller variance even though nothing fundamental may have changed either in the relationships or in the relative employment performance of the regions. This 'normal' (but non-linear) pattern of response needs to be controlled for in order to discern any more fundamental changes. When this has been done it seems that regional disparities have tended to widen significantly since the mid-1970s in a fashion which had not characterized previous downswings. Because of the slowing down in mobility the effects of this experience have not yet worked themselves through into unemployment differentials which are likely to continue to diverge for several years still, even if nothing else changes. If the real concern is with the cyclical behaviour of labour demand in the regions, however, a simpler approach is to monitor changes in regional shares of employment rather than to infer such changes from the unemployment series.

Acknowledgement—I am grateful to members of the SSRC Urban and Regional Economics Study Group and also to Tony Thirlwall, Ian Molho and an anonymous referee for comments on earlier versions of this paper.

NOTES

1. An earlier version of this paper was presented to the SSRC Urban and Regional Economics Study Group at Glasgow University in September 1981.
2. CHESHIRE, 1981b, also argues that the efficiency of the adjustment process varies positively with excess demand because of the effects on migration and job mobility.
3. The appropriate log-likelihood test for non-nested hypotheses indicates that neither formulation is consistently better than the other, however.
4. There is a significant negative correlation at the 5% level between the linear coefficient and the log of the coefficient in the log equation ($r = -0{\cdot}61$, $t = 2{\cdot}0$, $DF = 7$).
5. In addition to the polynomial time trend, the instruments employed in the estimation procedure were national unemployment lagged one year and the employment growth rates in each region. The latter were only available from 1951, requiring the first two observations to be omitted.
6. The unemployment function was estimated with a three-step procedure. Firstly, a polynomial function of national unemployment was included in the regression equation. Then the best fitting monotonic approximation to this polynomial was found by experiment. Finally, this approximation was reinserted in the regression alongside the composite time trend.
7. The results for individual industries presented by ELIAS and KEOGH, 1979, Table A2, suggest that only in the South East region is there a significant tendency for particular sectors to be either more or, in this case, less significantly sensitive in employment than at the national level. In the South East, eleven of twenty-four sectors for which results are obtainable were significantly less sensitive (at the 95% confidence level) compared with one which was more sensitive. For the four main DA regions *taken as a group* there was apparently some tendency for primary and secondary industries to be more cyclically sensitive than the corresponding industries nationally: nineteen sectors, out of fifty-nine, appeared significantly more sensitive and six significantly less (at the 95% level).
8. FROST and SPENCE, 1981b, report a similarly strong relationship at the sub-regional level between the sensitivity of male unemployment and its average level for all but ten of the sixty-one sub-regions. These exceptions, in the West Midlands, Yorkshire and Lancashire, are accounted for by their specialization in cyclically sensitive manufacturing industries.
9. Most of the unemployment effect in the past has related to males, and most of the residual to females. Estimates for the years 1959–75 suggest that changes in unemployment accounted for about 77% of the effects of cyclical changes in employment for males compared with about 20% for females. In recent years, however, the registration propensity of the female unemployed has increased significantly.
10. Defined as $\Sigma_j E_j f(D_{ij})$, where $f(D_{ij})$ is a distance function calibrated on long-distance (employment) migration streams (GORDON, 1982).
11. The equation of the plotted function is:

$$f(U_n) = 1{\cdot}0612 - \frac{0{\cdot}0267}{(0{\cdot}030 + \exp(-1{\cdot}52U_n))}$$

REFERENCES

ATKINS D. H. W. (1973) Employment change in branch and parent manufacturing plants in the United Kingdom, 1966–71, *Trade and Industry* **12,** 437–9.

BELL D. N. F. and HART R. A. (1980) The regional demand for labour services, *Scot. J. Pol. Econ.* **27,** 140–51.

BELL D. N. F. (1981) Regional output, employment and unemployment fluctuations, *Oxf. Econ. Pap.* **33,** 42–60.

BRECHLING F. (1967) Trends and cycles in British regional unemployment, *Oxf. Econ. Pap.* **19,** 1–21.

BROWN A. J. (1972) *The Framework of Regional Economics in the United Kingdom.* Cambridge University Press, Cambridge.

BURRIDGE P. and GORDON I. R. (1981) Unemployment in the British Metropolitan Labour Areas, *Oxf. Econ. Pap.* **33,** 274–97.

CHESHIRE P. C. (1981a) The regional demand for labour services: a suggested explanation for observed differences, *Scot. J. Pol. Econ.* **28,** 95–8.

CHESHIRE P. C. (1981b) Labour market theory and spatial unemployment, in MARTIN R. L. (Ed.) *Regional Wage Inflation and Unemployment,* pp. 189–207. Pion, London.

CHISHOLM M., FREY A. E. and HAGGETT P. (Ed.) (1971) *Regional Forecasting.* Butterworths, London.

CLARKE U. E. G. (1976) The cyclical sensitivity of employment in branch and parent plants, *Reg. Studies* **10,** 293–8.

DIXON R. J. and THIRLWALL A. P. (1975) *Regional Growth and Unemployment in the United Kingdom.* Macmillan, London.

DUNN R. (1983) Spectral analysis and distributed lags in geographical studies of local unemployment: 2. distributed lags, *Environ. Plann. A* **15,** 1,043–55.

ELIAS D. P. B. (1978) Regional unemployment elasticities: further evidence, *Scot. J. Pol. Econ.* **25,** 89–96.

ELIAS D. P. B. (1979) Regional unemployment elasticities: migration or registration, *Scot. J. Pol. Econ.* **26,** 103–6.

ELIAS D. P. B. and KEOGH G. T. (1979) Structural change in regional employment in the UK, 1965–1985, Discussion Paper 6, Manpower Research Group, University of Warwick.

FROST M. E. and SPENCE N. A. (1981a) Unemployment, structural economic change and public policy in British regions, *Progr. Plann.* **16,** 1–103.

FROST M. E. and SPENCE N. A. (1981b) The timing of unemployment responses in British regional labour markets, 1963–1976, in MARTIN R. L. (Ed.), *Regional Wage Inflation and Unemployment,* pp. 208–31. Pion, London.

GARCIA DE BLAS (1981) The regional unemployment and industrial crisis in Spain 1976–1980, paper presented to the European Congress of the Regional Science Association, Barcelona.

GILLESPIE A. E. and OWEN D. W. (1981) Unemployment trends in the current recession, *Area* **13,** 189–96.
GORDON I. R. (1980) Regional unemployment differentials: migration not registration, *Scot. J. Pol. Econ.* **27,** 97–102.
GORDON I. R. (1982) The analysis of motivation-specific migration streams, *Environ. Plann. A* **14,** 5–20.
GORDON I. R. (1985a) The cyclical interaction between regional migration employment and unemployment: a time series analysis for Scotland, *Scot. J. Pol. Econ.* **32** (forthcoming).
GORDON I. R. (1985b) Distributed lags in local responses to fluctuations in unemployment *Environ. Plann. A.* **17** (forthcoming).
HART R. A. (1975) Interregional economic migration: some theoretical considerations (part II), *J. Reg. Sci.* **15,** 289–305.
HEWINGS G. D. (1977) *Regional Industrial Analysis and Development.* Methuen, London.
JOHNSTON R. J. (1983) On the symmetry of leads and lags in studies of regional unemployment, *Reg. Studies* **17,** 105–12.
LOASBY B. J. (1967) Making location policy work, *Lloyds Bank Rev.* **83,** 34–47.
MACKAY D. I., BODDY D., BRACK J., DIACK J. A. and JONES N. (1971) *Labour Markets Under Different Employment Conditions.* George Allen and Unwin, Hemel Hempstead, Herts.
MARTIN R. L. (1982) Job loss and the regional incidence of redundancies in the currrent recession, *Camb. J. Econ.* **6,** 375–95.
MASSEY D. B. and MEEGAN R. A. (1979) The geography of industrial reorganization: the spatial effects of the restructuring of the electrical engineering sector under the Industrial Reorganisation Corporation, *Prog. Plann.* **10,** 155–237.
MOLHO I. I. (1983) A regional analysis of the distribution of married women's labour force participation rates in the UK, *Reg. Studies* **17,** 125–33.
MUSHKAT M. JR. (1974) Interregional variations in cyclical sensitivity to unemployment in Israel, Victoria University of Wellington (mimeo).
O'FARRELL P. N. (1976) An analysis of industrial closures: Irish experience, 1960–73, *Reg. Studies* **10,** 433–48.
OGILVY A. (1979) Migration—the influence of economic change, *Futures* **11,** 383–94.
OKKO P. (1981) The regional structure of labour markets and the adjustment problem in the 1970s: Finnish experiences, paper presented to the European Congress of the Regional Science Association, Barcelona.
SUM A. M. and RUSH T. P. (1975) The geographic structure of unemployment rates, *Monthly Labor Review*, March, pp. 3–9.
THIRLWALL A. P. (1966) Regional unemployment as a cyclical phenomenon, *Scot. J. Pol. Econ.* **13,** 205–19.
TOWNROE P. M. (1975) Branch plants and regional development, *Tn. Plann. Rev.* **46,** 47–62.
VAN DUIJN J. J. (1975) The cyclical sensitivity to unemployment of Dutch provinces, 1950–72, *Reg. Sci. Urban Econ.* **5,** 107–32.

[21]

A REGIONAL TEST OF THE HECKSCHER-OHLIN HYPOTHESIS

JOHN R. MORONEY AND JAMES M. WALKER*
Michigan State University and Florida State University

I. INTRODUCTION

THERE are currently two important theories of comparative advantage as a basis for international or interregional trade. The first to be developed is the classical doctrine of comparative costs, which stems from Ricardo (1951, chap. vii) and Mill (1929, pp. 574–606).[1] More recently, the so-called Heckscher-Ohlin Theorem has received extensive study as an alternative theoretical basis for trade (Heckscher, 1919, 1949; Ohlin, 1933).[2] Regarded as empirical propositions potentially useful for predicting the course of a nation's (region's) development, the two theories diverge because they offer different explanations of the basis for comparative advantage.[3] Specifically, the comparative-cost doctrine holds that a country (region) possesses a comparative advantage in producing those commodities in whose production its "real" labor costs (in the sense of the inverse of average productivity of labor) are relatively lower than those of other countries.[4] On the other hand, the Heckscher-Ohlin theory of comparative advantage depends upon (*a*) different productive factor endowments among countries and (*b*) different factor intensities of production processes for different goods.[5]

This paper is concerned with the empirical content of the Heckscher-Ohlin

* This study was supported by a Florida State University Graduate Research Council award and by a grant from the Relm Foundation. We are pleased to acknowledge the constructive comments received from C. E. Ferguson, Marshall R. Colberg, and M. L. Greenhut.

[1] An excellent review of the literature on comparative costs appears in Caves (1960, pp. 6–22). More detailed discussion is found in Mason (1926), Taussig (1927, esp. pp. 43–68), and Viner (1932, 1937).

[2] The Heckscher-Ohlin theory is succinctly treated in Caves (1960, pp. 23–30). Geometrical and algebraic versions of the two theories of trade appear in pp. 30–57 of this work. Further discussion of the classical and Heckscher-Ohlin theories is found in Bhagwati (1964).

[3] The two theories are discussed in a developmental context by Chenery (1961).

[4] Capital costs were largely ignored or were accorded secondary importance in most treatments of comparative costs. Similarly, international wage differentials that might serve to offset international labor-productivity differentials were generally regarded as unimportant in explaining patterns of commodity trade. Caves points out that the schism between "real" labor costs and money costs, especially predominant in the work of Mill and Marshall, bothered Cairnes and certain continental economists (see Caves 1960, p. 13). Nevertheless, the classical emphasis on "real" costs, construed as the inverse of labor productivity, continued through the writings of Taussig and Viner. Yet Viner seems to feel that several classical predecessors abandoned the simple labor-cost theory of value in favor of money costs of production in order to explain the actual course of trade (see, for example, Viner, 1936, p. 6). In empirical tests of the classical labor-cost theory, the studies by MacDougall (1951, 1952), Kravis (1956*a* and *b*), and Balassa (1963) tend to confirm the primary importance of labor-productivity differentials and the secondary role of wage differentials in explaining international trade. On the contrary, the study by Forchheimer (1947) finds relative wage differentials to be a somewhat more important determinant of comparative advantage in selected industries. See particularly his discussion on p. 24 (Forchheimer, 1947).

[5] It should be noted that Heckscher did not regard his contribution as a radical departure from the classical theory but rather as a modification and addendum to the classical labor-cost theory. Ohlin (1933, pp. 33–34) disagrees, contending, "As a matter of fact, I do not think it [Heckscher's paper] can be fitted into the labour cost theory at all."

hypothesis applied to regional manufacturing in the United States. The empirical framework of our test is new, yet it relies on most of the traditional Heckscher-Ohlin postulates. We feel that our framework is preferable on four grounds to most tests conducted with international data: (1) It avoids the assumption that production coefficients are fixed and identical in the two trading areas. (2) It avoids the assumption that demand functions for all commodities are identical in the two trading areas. (3) It utilizes regional data in the United States. These data are more likely than international data to reflect common industry production functions, an essential condition for meaningful interpretation of results. (4) It avoids the problem that actual international trade is obstructed by tariffs.

Section II briefly reviews tests of the Heckscher-Ohlin hypothesis using international data, Section III presents the basis of our tests using regional data, Section IV suggests some advantages in testing the hypothesis with regional instead of international data, and Section V presents the test results.

II. INTERNATIONAL TESTS OF THE HECKSCHER-OHLIN HYPOTHESIS

The purpose of reviewing international tests is twofold: first, to indicate the controversial status of the hypothesis tested with international data and, second, to provide the background for criticisms of international tests and to show why our regional tests seem preferable.

MacDougall (1951, 1952) was the first economist to test empirically the Heckscher-Ohlin hypothesis. Using horsepower as an index of capital, MacDougall postulated that the United States had more capital per worker than the United Kingdom. According to the hypothesis, then, the United States should have a larger relative share of exports in the world market for capital-intensive goods. MacDougall, however, found no such systematic relationship; consequently he rejected the hypothesis as an explanation of comparative advantage.

Kravis (1956*b*) also tested (indirectly) the Heckscher-Ohlin hypothesis. He showed that wages are high in U.S. export industries relative to import-competing industries. If these high wages stemmed from relatively much capital per unit of output (and presumably per worker) in these industries, this finding would be consistent with the hypothesis. Kravis, however, was unable to find any relationship between capital per unit of output and exports.

A third study bearing on the hypothesis was conducted by Tarshis (1959). Instead of studying exports in the light of factor endowments, Tarshis focused on relative internal commodity prices within nations. He found that price ratios of capital-intensive goods relative to labor-intensive goods were lower in the (presumably capital abundant) United States and were higher in less capital-abundant countries. Consequently his results, although not a direct test of the hypothesis, are consistent with its implications.

The most extensive tests of the Heckscher-Ohlin hypothesis are those of Leontief (1953, 1956). Given that the United States has more capital per unit of labor than any country with which it trades, the hypothesis asserts that the United States has a comparative export advantage in capital-intensive goods and should import labor-intensive goods. To test the hypothesis, Leontief assumed that both U.S. exports and imports are reduced by one million dollars. He reasoned that the export reduction should release relatively more capital and relatively less labor than would be absorbed (assuming fixed capital-labor input coefficients) by import-replacement industries.

Surprisingly, Leontief found that "an average million dollars' worth of our exports embodies considerably less capital and somewhat more labor than would be required to replace from domestic production an equivalent amount of our competitive imports. America's participation in the international division of labor is based on its specialization on labor intensive, rather than capital intensive, lines of production. In other words, this country resorts to foreign trade in order to economize its capital and dispose of its surplus labor, rather than vice-versa" (1953, p. 343).

Instead of interpreting his results as inconsistent with the relative-factor-proportions hypothesis, Leontief contended that in fact the United States is *relatively labor abundant* in the sense that U.S. labor is roughly three times as efficient as foreign labor. Thus, the U.S. labor force can be multiplied by three to yield internationally comparable labor efficiency units; labor becomes the relatively abundant productive factor in the United States; and the Heckscher-Ohlin hypothesis is saved because the United States exports labor-intensive goods, which is consistent with the prediction of the hypothesis.[6]

An alternative resolution of the so-called Leontief Paradox is suggested by a few economists, including Ellsworth (1954), Becker (1962), Colberg (1963), and especially Kenen (1965). Each of these writers feels that U.S. exports have been improperly identified by Leontief as "labor intensive." Instead, they contend that these commodities are "material capital plus human capital" intensive; therefore, the U.S. export mix is consistent with the factor-proportions hypothesis. Although the papers of Ellsworth, Becker, and Colberg are only suggestive on this point, Kenen skilfully analyzes the material- and human-capital content of U.S. exports in drawing this conclusion.

Four further studies in the spirit of Leontief's work should be mentioned. Using a 1951 input-output table for Japan, Tatemoto and Ichimura found that "an average million yen's worth of Japanese exports embodies more capital and less labor than would be required for the domestic replacements of competitive imports of an equivalent amount" (1959, p. 445). If one postulates that Japan is relatively labor abundant, this conclusion is consistent with the Leontief Paradox and inconsistent with the Heckscher-Ohlin hypothesis. However, the authors were able to dispel the paradox by a more careful examination of Japanese exports and imports. First, they observed that Japan's capital-labor endowment is intermediate between advanced and underdeveloped nations. Consequently, she

[6] Leontief presents no evidence that three is the correct index of U.S. labor efficiency compared to foreign labor. Moreover, he contends that the relatively greater efficiency of U.S. labor cannot be attributable simply to greater capital per man in the United States. Instead, he asserts that the probable explanation lies in the area of "entrepreneurship and superior organization" but recognizes that this explanation is not wholly convincing since these forces also tend to increase the efficiency of U.S. capital (Leontief, 1953, pp. 334–45). The recent empirical study by Kreinin (1965) indicates that U.S. labor may be 1.2 or 1.25 times as efficient as foreign labor but that Leontief's multiple of three is much too high. Two other studies are pertinent. The international study of Diab (1956) tends to confirm Leontief's assertion that the United States is relatively labor abundant. Diab estimated capital-labor ratios in several countries using a Cobb-Douglas production function and assuming capital productivity is equivalent in all nations. On the other hand, Bhagwati (1963) used Diab's procedure but assumed that *labor* productivity is comparable across nations and found that the United States is relatively *capital* abundant.

should have a comparative advantage in labor-intensive goods when trading with the former and in capital-intensive goods when trading with the latter. Then they observed that 75 per cent of Japan's exports were to underdeveloped countries, the remaining 25 per cent going to advanced countries. Since they found that Japan's exports to the United States were indeed relatively *labor* abundant and her exports to countries other than the United States were relatively *capital* abundant, their results are consistent with the Heckscher-Ohlin hypothesis. Their paper is the first of four more "specific" than Leontief's in the sense that each one studies more carefully the destination of exports.

Stolper and Roskamp (1961) conducted an input-output study of East German trade. They found that exports are capital intensive and imports labor intensive. They concluded that this finding is consistent with the hypothesis since three-quarters of East Germany's trade is with the Communist bloc, among whose countries she is probably the most capital intensive.

Wahl (1961) conducted a similar study for Canadian industrial products. He found that Canadian exports in 1949 "embodied more capital and less labour than would have been required to replace an average million dollars' worth of total Canadian competitive imports with domestic production" (p. 353). Since this finding pertains to trade specifically with the United States as well, it is presumably inconsistent with the hypothesis.

Finally, the study by Bharadwaj (1962) of Indo-U.S. trade yielded results inconsistent with the hypothesis, since it found Indian exports to the United States to be capital intensive and imports from the United States to be labor intensive.

It is clear that international tests of the Heckscher-Ohlin hypothesis have displayed mixed success. The tests by MacDougall, Kravis, Leontief, Wahl, and Bharadwaj have, on balance, been negative, while those by Tarshis, Tatemoto and Ichimura, and Stolper and Roskamp generally have been consistent with the hypothesis.

It should be recalled that the tests by MacDougall, Kravis, and Tarshis were not "direct" tests of the hypothesis. On the other hand, those by Leontief and several others were. Leontief's test procedure, incorporated in several of the above studies, has evoked a barrage of criticisms. Since a number of these criticisms are questionable and irrelevant to our test, we shall not repeat them. However, a number of comments on Leontief-type studies merit consideration, since they bolster the case for regional tests of the hypothesis. These comments are discussed in detail in Section IV.

III. BASIS FOR REGIONAL TESTS

International trade theory is generally based on the assumption that productive factors are imperfectly mobile. Indeed, the lack of factor mobility gives rise to comparative advantage in the Heckscher-Ohlin framework. If factors were fully mobile among nations, they would migrate so that in general competitive equilibrium the ratios of marginal physical products to factor-price ratios would be equal in all nations. If all nations used similar production techniques, they would have the same comparative costs for all goods and there would be no basis for trade.

The theory of trade resting on imperfect factor mobility among nations is equally applicable to regions in the United States because productive factors have never been fully mobile among regions. If full factor mobility among regions occurred, factor-price equalization would result. Some evidence on the absence of factor-price equalization is presented in the remaining part of this section.

The hypothesis we propose to test might be regarded as the simple factor-proportions view of comparative advantage. In particular, we shall first test the null hypothesis that there is no correlation between relative regional factor endowments and regional location of manufacturing in the southern and non-southern regions of the United States. Our second test concerns regional factor endowments and relative regional *growth* of manufacturing. The basis for our tests is that the South (that is, the East South Central, South Atlantic, and West South Central census regions) is relatively labor abundant, while the non-South is relatively capital abundant.

Evidence of the relative labor abundance in the South may be found in the wage differentials between the South and non-South. We computed an index of this differential using data from the *Census of Manufactures, 1958* (U.S. Bureau of the Census, 1961). The average hourly wage of production workers in the South was 78 per cent of the non-South average. Similarly, average annual non-production worker salaries in southern manufacturing were 87 per cent of the corresponding non-South average. These differentials are consistent with the results of the studies by Fuchs and Perlman (1960) and by Gallaway (1963).

The wage differential is explained, according to the Heckscher-Ohlin hypothesis, by different relative regional supplies of labor (factor endowments). It is possible, however, that the lower southern wage rates are attributable to lower demand schedules for labor relative to the non-South. Presumptive evidence indicates that differences in regional supplies of labor may be the more important explanation. In particular, Hanna (1957) found that unexplained interstate differences in hourly earnings in manufacturing industries "stem chiefly from differences in pay rates for similar skills" (p. 152). Moreover, Gallaway (1963, pp. 269–70) tentatively rejected the hypothesis that observed regional wage differentials were attributable to dissimilar regional demand schedules for labor. Indeed, he concluded that "by implication it has been established that the capital-labor ratio of the South is less than that of the North" (p. 270). The only circumstance under which the South might be relatively capital abundant is if the relative cost of capital in the South were even lower than the relative cost of labor. This seems to be most unlikely since casual inspection of regional interest rates indicates that, if anything, the absolute (and therefore relative) cost of capital tends to be higher in the South than in the non-South.

IV. ADVANTAGES OF REGIONAL TESTS

In theory, the Heckscher-Ohlin Theorem depends fundamentally on the assumption that any commodity is produced according to a single, linearly homogeneous (constant-returns-to-scale) production function common to all countries.[7] Leontief's (and others') input-output analyses presume this is so. Obviously, it would be impossible to identify a nation's relatively abundant factor of

[7] We think it is fair to conclude that both Heckscher and Ohlin regarded this as a reasonable approximation to reality, although both recognized the possibility of intercountry differences in efficiency (see Heckscher [1949, esp. pp. 277–79] and Ohlin [1933, pp. 14–15, 29–30]). Ohlin also recognized the possibility of production indivisibilities and economies of scale, particularly in his discussion on pp. 52–58.

production in terms of *observed* capital and labor data if its factor efficiencies were different from those in another nation. Valavanis-Vail (1954, p. 528) commented on this point: "When technologies are very different, no simple relationships hold between [relative factor endowments]. . . . In this case relative endowments have little meaning, for the transformation curves themselves tell us all there is to know about both the endowments and the technologies."[8] It is significant, therefore, that two recent studies of capital-labor substitution using international data found that different countries producing the same International Standard Industrial Classification three-digit product operate with different levels of (neutral) technology, that is, on different production functions (Arrow, Chenary, Minhas, and Solow, 1961, esp. pp. 242–43; Fuchs, 1963). The interpretation of the results of tests of the factor-proportions hypothesis that use international data consequently seems hazardous. On the other hand, our application to regional data may be more appropriate since it seems plausible that regional production functions in the United States are similar.[9]

A second objection to international studies of the factor-proportions hypothesis involves "factor-intensity reversal." If two trading areas each produce two commodities with either Leontief fixed proportions or Cobb-Douglas production functions, it can be demonstrated that, if one commodity is produced with a higher capital-labor ratio than the other at any set of factor prices, it is so produced at all sets of factor prices. This is Samuelson's (1948, 1949) so-called strong factor-intensity assumption. If, however, the relevant production functions are of the constant-elasticity-of-substitution form (with different elasticities of substitution in the two industries), relative capital-labor intensities (that is, equilibrium capital-labor ratios) for two commodities may reverse as relative factor prices change. If such reversals in factor intensities are empirically important, one is unable to classify (and consequently to rank) commodities as uniquely capital or labor intensive since relative factor intensities may switch with changes in relative factor prices. Indeed Minhas (1962; 1963, chap. iv) raised this specific objection to the traditional Heckscher-Ohlin hypothesis.[10] He argued that if factor-intensity reversal is *unimportant* empirically there should be a strong positive rank ordering of capital-labor ratios by industry in different countries. He performed a rank correlation test for twenty industries common to both Japan and the United States. He obtained a Spearman ρ of $+0.328$ using direct plus indirect capital in his capital-labor ratios. On the other hand, he found ρ to be $+0.730$ using only direct capital in computing capital-labor ratios. The first value is not significantly different from zero at

[8] Although the implications for the hypothesis of dissimilar production functions have not been fully explored, some are discussed by Laursen (1952, pp. 556–57), Robinson (1956*a*, pp. 173–74), and Laing (1961).

[9] Although there have been no extended studies covering this proposition, Gallaway (1963) rejected the hypothesis of dissimilar regional production functions in U.S. census regions as an explanation of regional wage differences.

[10] Although Lerner (1952) did not utilize the constant-elasticity-of-substitution (CES) production function, he was perhaps the first to recognize the possibility of factor-intensity reversal in a paper written in 1933 but not published until 1952. Further discussion of factor intensity reversal appears in Pearce and James (1951–52) and the subsequent paper by Samuelson (1951–52). Although he did not use the CES production function explicitly, but specifically recognized differences in "facility in substituting capital for labour" among industries, Johnson (1957) also demonstrated theoretical factor-intensity reversal.

$P \leq .10$, and the second is judged to be sufficiently different from unity "to provide room for reversals in relative capital-intensity to take place" (Minhas, 1962, p. 148). Consequently, Minhas rejected the strong factor-intensity hypothesis; by doing so, he rejected one of the bases of the Heckscher-Ohlin hypothesis. Minhas' conclusion, however, is open to serious criticism. In the first place, his test data are taken from input-output tables that, *in pure theory*, do not permit factor-intensity reversal. Our judgment is that his data are not suitable for the test he performs and that they actually indicate only that Japanese and U.S. industries operate on different production functions. In the second place, Leontief (1964) feels that some of Minhas' other data may be used to support the strong factor-intensity hypothesis. Ball (1966), on the other hand, feels that Minhas' tests neither support nor refute the strong factor-intensity hypothesis.[11]

Nevertheless, since factor-intensity reversal might vitiate the meaning of our regional test of the hypothesis, we ranked the 1958 two-digit-industry capital-labor ratios given by Ferguson (1964, pp. 429–33) for the South and non-South.[12] Kendall's τ is $+0.78$, significantly different from zero at $P \leq .00001$. Apart from its statistical significance, we feel that this value is very high considering the gross nature of the capital-labor ratios from which it is computed. Therefore, we cannot reject the strong factor-intensity hypothesis and we feel that factor-intensity reversal should not obscure our test results.[13]

A third objection to international tests of the Heckscher-Ohlin hypothesis concerns the assumption that the countries under observation have similar demand functions for the commodities traded. If demand functions are different between the two trading areas so that one country demands relatively more commodities whose production requires much of its relatively abundant factor, then trade may fail to occur as predicted by the hypothesis. Valavanis-Vail (1954) aptly describes this possibility as a country's *physically* abundant factor being *economically* scarce.[14] Since our study concerns comparative advantage in terms of production *location* and does not specifically identify regional *trade* (that is, commodity flows) of manufactured goods, it avoids this fundamental criticism of international tests.

[11] Ball (1966) shows that, by removing the agricultural and foodstuffs industries from Minhas' tests, the rank correlation between factor intensities of Japanese and U.S. industries increases appreciably. He further argues that these industries *should* be deleted from the tests and that the strong factor-intensity hypothesis remains neither rejected nor accepted on the basis of these tests.

[12] It should be noted that the regional capital estimates in this study were estimated by use of the CES production function which *specifically allows* for reversal of factor intensities. "Southern" capital-labor ratios were weighted averages of South Atlantic, East South Central, and West South Central ratios given by Ferguson. "Non-southern" capital-labor ratios were weighted averages of those in the remaining regions.

[13] Although the strong factor-intensity hypothesis is accepted in this regional test, factor reversals remain an empirical possibility at the international level. Mordechai Kreinin suggested to one of us that factor reversals are less likely to occur in regional than in international tests because of relatively smaller variation in relative factor prices in the former.

[14] Robinson (1956*a*, pp. 184–87) demonstrated that "biased "demand functions are not a necessary condition that a country export its scarce factor-intensive commodity. It is only necessary that countries have different income levels and nonlinearly homogeneous utility functions. As a historical point, frequently overlooked, it should be noted that Ohlin (1933, pp. 16ff.) recognized that different regional demand conditions could cause differences in "relative scarcity" of similar physical endowments of "industrial agents."

V. STATISTICAL TESTS OF THE HYPOTHESIS

As framed in Section II, the Heckscher-Ohlin hypothesis predicts that the South will specialize in the production of goods requiring relatively much labor because such goods can be produced at lower money cost in the South than in the non-South.

As an empirically testable proposition, the hypothesis implies that commodities requiring in production a relatively low capital-labor ratio are concentrated more heavily in the South than industries requiring in production a relatively high capital-labor ratio. To test this hypothesis, one must develop a measure of relative concentration of southern manufacturing industries and obtain estimates of the capital-labor ratio in each industry.

Capital-labor ratios for 1957 were computed from the capital and employment estimates given in the *Census of Manufactures, 1958* (U.S. Bureau of the Census, 1961). The Census capital-stock data were obtained from a sample survey of manufacturing establishments to determine accumulated depreciation and the gross book value of depreciable and depletable assets as of December 31, 1957. The gross book value of such assets is available by two-digit industry and was used as the numerator in the capital-labor ratios.[15] The labor input used as the denominator is full-time equivalent man years of employment. Employment data for 1957 are given in the *Census of Manufactures, 1958* (U.S. Bureau of the Census, 1961). Although the capital-labor ratios are national, not regional, estimates, their rankings are maintained in the South and non-South because of the strong factor-intensity hypothesis.

For the same two-digit industries, a measure of regional output concentration was computed for 1949 and 1957 by dividing per capita value added in the South for each industry by per capita value added in the nation for each corresponding industry.[16] If the resulting quotient is greater than 1, per capita production concentration is greater in the South than in the non-South. If the quotient is less than 1, the converse holds.

The industry capital-labor ratios and location quotients used for the statistical tests appear in Table 1. Before we proceed to tests of the hypothesis, a few comments on the test data are in order. First, one notices that in 1949 the South had location quotients exceeding 1 in only four industries. In 1957 this was also true in four industries. The South obviously had less than its per capita "share" of total U.S. manufacturing. As one might expect, however, the South increased its per capita "share" of manufacturing in every industry under review with the single exception of industry 24, as shown by the pervasive increases in industry location quotients during 1949–57.

Because of the so-called lag in Southern economic development, particularly in manufacturing, one should not really expect the South to have a location quotient greater than 1 in all industries in which it possesses a comparative advantage. A more reasonable expectation, in light of the different development stages

[15] Net-capital-stock figures could have been used. The gross figures seem preferable, however, because net capital stocks partially reflect legal (as opposed to economic) depreciation rates. Accordingly, gross capital stocks may be the better choice as proxies for services of capital.

[16] Regional value added was taken from the 1949 and 1957 *Annual Surveys of Manufactures* (U.S. Bureau of the Census, 1952, 1959). Regional population figures were obtained from *The Statistical Abstract of the United States, 1954* and *1964* (U.S. Bureau of the Census, 1954, 1964).

between the South and non-South, is that the South possesses *comparatively* larger location quotients (although these quotients may be less than unity) in those industries in which it enjoys a comparative advantage.[17] An empirical test of the Heckscher-Ohlin hypothesis may be deduced from the following theorem developed by Jones (1956–57, p. 6): "Ordering the commodities with respect to the capital/labor ratios employed in production is to rank them in order of comparative advantage" (1956–57, p. 6). Because of the theorem's rank-ordering nature, rank-correlation tests seem more suitable than parametric ones. Accordingly, with reference to the data in Table 1 we test the following hypothesis: *Hypothesis 1: There is an inverse rank ordering between capital-labor ratios and location quotients.*

[17] This formulation also permits the South to have commodity demand functions different from the rest of the nation. This represents a distinct advantage over international tests performed from input-output tables. For example, the test in this paper does not attempt to identify southern *exports* or *imports;* instead, it identifies only the relative concentration of industry location. As mentioned before, Valavanis-Vail (1954) suggested that dissimilar commodity demand functions between two trading regions might cause a region to *import* a good requiring in production much of its relatively abundant factor provided its demand were biased in favor of the good in question. Consequently he suggested that the Heckscher-Ohlin hypothesis be reworded to read: "A country tends to *produce* relatively more of the product that uses relatively more of its abundant factor" (p. 525). Our test conforms to this suggestion.

TABLE 1

CENSUS CAPITAL-LABOR RATIOS: 1957; INDUSTRY LOCATION QUOTIENTS: 1949, 1957; PERCENTAGE CHANGES IN LOCATION QUOTIENTS: 1949–57

Industry*	1957 Capital-Labor Ratios (Dollars/Man Year)	Location Quotients		Percentage Change in Location Quotients (1949–57)
		1949	1957	
20 Food and related products	6,952	0.6173	0.7236	+ 17.22
21 Tobacco products	4,535	2.4543	2.8359	+ 15.55
22 Textile products	5,039	1.4312	1.8176	+ 27.00
23 Apparel	796	0.3919	0.6144	+ 56.77
24 Lumber	4,518	1.0997	0.9780	− 11.07
25 Furniture	2,777	0.6026	0.9101	+ 51.03
26 Paper and pulp	12,718	0.6958	0.8628	+ 24.00
27 Printing and publishing	4,267	0.3806	0.4434	+ 16.50
28 Chemicals	17,308	0.9592	1.1447	+ 19.34
29 Petroleum and coal	42,770	1.1047	1.4482	+ 31.09
30 Rubber products	6,858	†	†	....
31 Leather and leather products	1,290	0.2794	0.3533	+ 26.45
32 Stone, clay, and glass products	9,804	0.6327	0.6738	+ 6.50
33 Primary metal products	13,624	0.4442	0.4564	+ 2.75
34 Fabricated metal products	5,131	0.3006	0.3806	+ 26.81
35 Machinery (except electrical)	5,521	0.1930	0.2800	+ 45.08
36 Electrical machinery	3,771	0.1312	0.2480	+ 89.02
37 Transportation equipment	4,893	0.2583	0.3697	+ 43.13
38 Instruments	4,111	0.0240	0.0600	+150.00
39 Miscellaneous	4,012	0.0908	0.1640	+ 80.62

* Two-digit industries listed in the *Census of Manufactures, 1958* (U.S. Bureau of the Census, 1961).
† Information insufficient to develop a location quotient.
Source: U.S. Bureau of the Census (1952, 1954, 1959, 1961, 1964).

Kendall's τ was computed between industry capital-labor ratios and corresponding location quotients for 1949 and 1957. In the first case τ is +.3216; in the second, +.2865. In neither case is τ significantly different from zero at $P \leq .05$. Nevertheless, τ is significantly positive in the first test at $P \leq .06$ and in the second at $P \leq .10$. However, τ is of the "wrong" sign. That is, the data display a *positive* rank ordering between capital-labor ratios and location quotients. The main reason is that three of the most capital-intensive industries (petroleum and coal, chemicals, and paper products, ranking 1, 2, and 4 in capital-labor ratios) are relatively highly concentrated in the South (ranking among the seven most concentrated in terms of location quotients).

One might argue that these industries, along with tobacco, are based on "natural resources" more than other industries are (see, for example, Fuchs, 1962, pp. 250–54). Consequently, their location might be more influenced by availability of natural resources than by relative abundance of capital and labor as defined in this study. We removed these four industries from the sample and recomputed τ. Using 1949 location quotients τ is +.2000, and using 1957 location quotients τ is +.1429. Thus, even after arbitrarily removing these industries from the sample, τ is still of the "wrong" sign. But in neither test is τ significantly different from zero at an acceptable level of probability.[18]

As an auxiliary test of hypothesis 1, we performed rank correlations between location quotients in Table 1 and capital-labor ratios computed from the 1953 capital and employment estimates of Creamer, Dobrovolsky, and Borenstein (1960, pp. 270–73).[19] These capital-stock data include the book value of owned land, buildings, and equipment based primarily on original cost less depreciation. They differ in detail from the *Census of Manufactures, 1958* (U.S. Bureau of the Census, 1961) data mainly on two grounds. First, the Creamer *et al.* estimates are net capital stocks while the Census estimates are gross. Second, the Creamer *et al.* estimates are derived from corporate *firm* reports collected by the Internal Revenue Service and reported in *Statistics of Income* (U.S. Treasury Department, 1955), while the Census data are collected from a sample of *establishments* (plants) which may be only subsidiary components of multiplant firms. The Creamer *et al.* employment figures do, however, correspond to the Census employment estimates in that they cover all employees measured in man-years.[20]

The rank correlation between the Creamer *et al* (1960) capital-labor ratios and industry location quotients is +.1667 using 1949 location quotients, and +.2000 using 1957 location quotients. Neither of these values is statisti-

[18] Certain "market-oriented" industries (for example, food and related products, primary metals, and fabricated metals) were also removed from the sample, but positive rank correlations (not statistically significant) were still obtained.

[19] These capital-labor ratios are not given in detail in this paper but are available from us on request.

[20] The Creamer *et al.* (1960) employment data group together industries 24 and 25 (lumber and furniture) and industries 33 and 34 (primary and fabricated metals). Furthermore, Creamer *et al.* have no employment estimates for industry 38 (instruments). Thus, Creamer *et al.* group four two-digit industries into two classifications (24 and 25 and 33 and 34) and exclude industry 38. To test for consistency between the two sets of capital-labor ratios, we grouped industries 24 and 25 and 33 and 34 and excluded industry 38 from the Census data. We then computed the rank correlation between the Creamer *et al.* capital labor ratios and comparably classified Census capital-labor ratios. Kendall's τ was +0.5000, significant at $P \leq .01$. Therefore, the *rankings* are reasonably consistent, although the *magnitudes* of the capital-labor ratios differ because of reasons mentioned in the text.

cally significant. Moreover, both have the "wrong" sign, as did the values of τ computed from Table 1. The Heckscher-Ohlin hypothesis, tested by hypothesis 1, clearly must be rejected on the basis of either the Census or the Creamer *et al* (1960) capital-labor ratios.

The foregoing tests of hypothesis 1 are conducted in a static framework. That is, the tests are performed with static capital-labor ratios and location quotients at two different dates. In the comparative static sense, the widespread increase in southern location quotients was mentioned. Thus, within a *developmental context* the Heckscher-Ohlin Theorem implies that those industries in which the South has the greatest comparative advantage should be developing relatively more rapidly in that region. Using data in Table 1 we test this corollary: *Hypothesis* 2: *There is an inverse rank ordering between capital-labor ratios and* percentage changes *in location quotients.*

We calculated the rank correlation between capital-labor ratios and percentage changes in location quotients listed in the last column of Table 1. Industry 24, the only one showing a *decrease* in the magnitude of its location quotient, was ranked last in terms of percentage change. The calculated value of τ is $-.3216$, significantly different from zero at $P \leq .06$. Thus τ is not only significant at an acceptable level of probability but is also negative as the hypothesis predicts. There is some evidence, therefore, that the South tended to attract more strongly the relatively labor-intensive industries during the period under review.[21] This result is consistent with Fuchs' study (1962, pp. 124–25), which found that during 1929–54 the South attracted comparatively low-wage four-digit industries in which the wage bill was a significant part of value added (that is, industries that were labor intensive).

Hypothesis 2 was also tested using the Creamer *et al.* (1960) capital-labor data. The rank correlation between capital-labor ratios and percentage changes in location quotients is $-.0667$, negative as the hypothesis predicts but not statistically significant. We regard the test using the Census data as preferable to that using the Creamer *et al.* data because of more complete and accurate industrial coverage in the former.

VI. CONCLUSION

It is emphasized that the hypothesis tested in this paper is of course not fully comparable to the factor-proportions theorem attributable to Heckscher and Ohlin. Specifically, the model tested includes as productive factors only labor and material capital. Heckscher, on the other hand, included as "factors of production" not only broad categories of land, labor, and capital but different *qualities* of each. Similarly, Ohlin envisioned mineral deposits, land suitable for growing particular products, and climate as contributing to different factor endowments. Thus, the full-dress Heckscher-Ohlin Theorem is far more comprehensive in its inclusion of "productive factors" than our hypothesis. It is conse-

[21] This conclusion, of course, rests on statistical tests using percentage changes in location quotients. Regional scientists often criticize the use of location quotients because, for example, location quotients usually change if the comparative "base" changes. Although this criticism is justified in certain cases, it seems less applicable in the present one. Either relative per capita value added or regional share of value added (value added in South/value added in nation) seems to be the most appropriate base for testing the Heckscher-Ohlin hypothesis. Although the location quotients do indeed change if the regional share base is used, the *rankings* and *rankings of percentage changes* are identical for both bases. Since our conclusions rest *only* on rankings and on rankings of percentage changes, they are not affected by the change in base. Nevertheless, the percentage changes in location quotients refer to the period 1949–57 and might be altered somewhat if different dates were used.

quently more elegant and at the same time more tautological. For if all of the "productive factors" contemplated by Heckscher and Ohlin are accounted for, the theorem becomes an exhaustive description of trade conditions; it is no longer a potentially fruitful hypothesis capable of empirical refutation.

Framed as an empirically testable proposition, hypothesis 1 fails to predict the areas of manufacturing where the South's comparative advantage lies, at least in terms of homogeneously defined capital and labor alone. Indeed, there is some indication that the South experiences a comparative advantage in relatively *capital-intensive* industries.

The truth seems to be that natural resources as well as capital and labor "endowments" represent an important determinant of comparative advantage.[22] Petroleum, chemicals, tobacco, and paper products cannot be produced in areas lacking the natural resources (including climate) necessary for their production. Therefore, the complete Heckscher-Ohlin Theorem properly "predicts" that the South possesses a comparative advantage in producing those commodities requiring in production an abundance of "southern conditions." These conditions apparently include much more than a relative abundance of labor.

[22] This is one of the principal points made by Kravis (1956*b*, esp. pp. 148–50) and by Vanek (1963). Viner (1937), of course, feels that natural resources may be even more important than relative abundance of capital and labor in determining comparative advantage (see, for example, pp. 503 ff.).

Once the basic structure of comparative advantage is determined in view of climate and availability of natural resources, as well as in view of capital and labor "endowments," a corollary of the Heckscher-Ohlin Theorem seems to be supported. Specifically, hypothesis 2, tested with Census data, indicates that the South tends to attract more strongly the relatively more labor-intensive industries, as the theorem implies.

The combined results of testing hypotheses 1 and 2 indicate that perhaps the initial endowment of natural resources may be more important than relative abundance of material capital or labor in determining the *initial structure* of comparative advantage. After this initial structure is established, however, relative endowments of material capital and labor are important in influencing the pattern of industrial growth. Finally, as certain natural resources are depleted and new ones are discovered, and as capital and labor migrate in response to regional factor-price differentials, the concept of "initial endowment" loses meaning. Consequently, modifications in the over-all structure of regional comparative advantage might be expected in the long run. Nevertheless, the Heckscher-Ohlin hypothesis seems to have some value in predicting regional patterns of industrial development.

REFERENCES

Arrow, K. J., Chenery, H. B., Minhas, B. S., and Solow, R. M., "Capital-Labor Substitution and Economic Efficiency," *Rev. Econ. and Statis.*, XLIII (August, 1961), 225–50.

Balassa, Bela. "An Empirical Demonstration of Classical Comparative Cost Theory," *Rev. Econ. and Statis.*, XLV (August, 1963), 231–38.

Ball, David Stafford. "Factor-Intensity Reversal in International Comparison of Factor Costs and Factor Use," *J.P.E.*, LXXIV (February, 1966), 77–80.

Becker, Gary S. "Investment in Human Capital: A Theoretical Analysis," *J.P.E.*, Supplement (October, 1962), 9–49.

Bhagwati, J. N. "Some Recent Trends in the Pure Theory of International Trade," in Roy Harrod and Douglas Hague (eds.).

International Trade Theory in a Developing World. New York: St Martin's Press, 1963.

———. "The Pure Theory of International Trade: A Survey," *Econ. J.*, LXXIV (March, 1964), 1-84.

Bharadwaj, R. "Factor Proportions and the Structure of Indo-U.S. Trade," *Indian Econ. J.*, X (October, 1962), 105-16.

Caves, Richard. *Trade and Economic Structure.* Cambridge, Mass.: Harvard Univ. Press, 1960.

Chenery, H. B. "Comparative Advantage and Development Policy," *A.E.R.*, LI (March, 1961), 18-51.

Colberg, Marshall R. "Human Capital as a Southern Resource," *Southern Econ. J.*, XXIX (January, 1963), 157-66.

Creamer, Daniel, Dobrovolsky, Sergei, and Borenstein, Israel. *Capital in Manufacturing and Mining.* Princeton, N.J.: Princeton Univ. Press, 1960.

Diab, M. A. *The United States Capital Position and the Structure of its Foreign Trade.* Amsterdam: North-Holland Publishing Co., 1956.

Ellsworth, P. T. "The Structure of American Foreign Trade: A New View Examined," *Rev. Econ. and Statis.*, XXXVI (August, 1954), 279-85.

Ferguson, C. E. "The Elasticity of Substitution and Regional Estimates of Capital and Capital Ratios in American Manufacturing Industry, 1954-1958," in Melvin L. Greenhut and W. Tate Whitman (eds.). *Essays in Southern Economic Development.* Chapel Hill: Univ. of North Carolina Press, 1964.

Forchheimer, Karl. "The Role of Relative Wage Differences in International Trade," *Q.J.E.*, LXII (November, 1947), 1-30.

Fuchs, Victor R. *Changes in the Location of Manufacturing in the United States since 1929.* New Haven, Conn: Yale Univ. Press, 1962.

———. "Capital-Labor Substitution: A Note," *Rev. Econ. and Statis.*, XLV (November, 1963), 436-38.

Fuchs, Victor R., and Perlman, Richard. "Recent Trends in Southern Wage Differentials," *Rev. Econ. and Statis.*, XLII (August, 1960), 292-300.

Gallaway, Lowell. "The North-South Wage Differential," *Rev. Econ. and Statis.*, XLV (August, 1963), 264-272.

Hanna, Frank A. "Analysis of Interstate Income Differentials: Theory and Practice," in Conference on Research in Income and Wealth, *Regional Income* ("Studies in Income and Wealth, Vol. XXI.) Princeton, N.J.: Princeton Univ. Press (for the National Bureau of Economic Research), 1957.

Heckscher, Eli. "Utrikeshandelns verkan på inkomstfordelningen," *Ekon. Tidskrift*, XXI (1919), 1-33.

———. "The Effect of Foreign Trade on the Distribution of Income," in H. S. Ellis and L. A. Metzler (eds.). *Readings in the Theory of International Trade.* Homewood, Ill.: Richard D. Irwin, Inc., 1949.

Johnson, Harry G. "Factor Endowments, International Trade, and Factor Prices," *Manchester School Econ. and Social Studies*, XXIV (September, 1957), 270-83.

Jones, R. W. "Factor Proportions and the Heckscher-Ohlin Theorem," *Rev. Econ. Studies*, XXIV (1956-57), 1-10.

Kenen, Peter B. "Nature, Capital, and Trade," *J.P.E.*, LXXIII (October, 1965), 437-60.

Kravis, Irving B. "Wages and Foreign Trade," *Rev. Econ. and Statis.*, XXXVIII (February, 1956), 14-30. (*a*)

———. " 'Availability' and Other Influences on the Commodity Composition of Trade," *J.P.E.*, LXIV (April, 1956), 143-55. (*b*)

Kreinin, Mordechai. "The Leontief Scarce-Factor Paradox," *A.E.R.*, LV (March, 1965), 131-39.

Laing, N. F. "Factor Price Equalization in International Trade and Returns to Scale," *Econ. Record*, XXXVII (September, 1961), 339-51.

Laursen, Svend. "Production Functions and the Theory of International Trade," *A.E.R.*, XLII (September, 1951), 540-57.

Leontief, Wassily W. "Domestic Production and Foreign Trade: The American Capital Position Re-examined," *Proc. American Philosophical Soc.*, XCVII (September, 1953), 332-49.

———. "Factor Proportions and the Structure of American Trade: Further Theoretical and Empirical Analysis," *Rev. Econ. and Statis.*, XXXVIII (November, 1956), 386-407.

———. "An International Comparison of Factor Cost and Factor Use," *A.E.R.*, LIV (June, 1964), 335-45.

Lerner, A.P. "Factor Prices and International Trade," *Economica*, XIX (February, 1952), 1-15.

MacDougall, G. D. A. "British and American Exports: A Study Suggested by the Theory of Comparative Costs" (Part I), *Econ. J.*, LXI (December, 1951), 687-724.

———. "British and American Exports: A Study Suggested by the Theory of Comparative Costs" (Part II), *ibid.*, LXII (September, 1952), 487–521.

Mason, Edward S. "The Doctrine of Comparative Costs, *Q.J.E.*, XLI (November, 1926), 63–93.

Mill, J. S. *Principles of Political Economy.* Edited by W. J. Ashley. New York: Longman's, Green & Co., 1929.

Minhas, Bagicha S. "The Homophypallagic Production Function, Factor-Intensity Reversals, and the Heckscher-Ohlin Theorem," *J.P.E.*, LXX (April, 1962), 138–56.

———. *An International Comparison of Factor Costs and Factor Use.* Amsterdam: North-Holland Publishing Co., 1963.

Ohlin, Bertil. *Interregional and International Trade.* Cambridge, Mass.: Harvard Univ. Press, 1933.

Pearce, I. F., and James, S. F. "The Factor-Price Equalisation Myth," *Rev. Econ. Studies*, XIX (1951–52), 111–20.

Ricardo, David. *The Principles of Political Economy and Taxation*, in *The Works and Correspondence of David Ricardo.* P. Sraffa (ed.). Cambridge: Cambridge Univ. Press, 1951.

Robinson, Romney. "Factor Proportions and Comparative Advantage," (Part I), *Q.J.E.*, LXX (May, 1956), 169–92. (*a*)

———. "Factor Proportions and Comparative Advantage" (Part II), *ibid.* (August, 1956), 346–63. (*b*)

Samuelson, Paul A. "International Trade and Equalisation of Factor Prices," *Econ. J.*, LVIII (June, 1948), 163–84.

———. "International Factor Price Equalisation Once Again," *ibid.*, LIX (June, 1949), 181–97.

———. "A Comment on Factor Price Equalisation," *Rev. Econ. Studies*, XIX (1951–52), 121–22.

Stolper, W., and Roskamp, K. "An Input-Output Table for East Germany with Applications to Foreign Trade," *Bull. Oxford University Institute Statis.*, XXIII (November, 1961), 379–92.

Tarshis, Lorie. "Factor Inputs and International Price Comparisons," in *The Allocation of Economic Resources.* M. Abramovitz *et al.* (eds.). Stanford, Calif.: Stanford Univ. Press, 1959.

Tatemoto, Masahiro, and Ichimura, Shinichi. "Factor Proportions and Foreign Trade: The Case of Japan," *Rev. Econ. and Statis.*, XLI (November, 1959), 442–46.

Taussig, F. W. *International Trade.* New York: Macmillan Co., 1927.

U.S. Bureau of the Census. *Annual Survey of Manufactures, 1949 and 1950.* Washington: Government Printing Office, 1952.

———. *The Statistical Abstract of the United States. 1954.* Washington: Government Printing Office, 1954.

———. *Annual Survey of Manufactures, 1957.* Washington: Government Printing Office, 1959.

———. *Census of Manufactures, 1958.* Washington: Government Printing Office, 1961.

———. *The Statistical Abstract of the United States. 1964.* Washington: Government Printing Office, 1964.

U.S. Treasury Department. *Statistics of Income.* Washington: Government Printing Office, 1955.

Valavanis-Vail, Stefan. "Leontief's Scarce Factor Paradox," *J.P.E.*, LXII (December, 1954), 523–28.

Vanek, Jaroslav. *The Natural Resource Content of United States Foreign Trade, 1870–1955.* Cambridge, Mass: M.I.T. Press, 1963.

Viner, Jacob. "The Doctrine of Comparative Cost," *Weltwirtschaftliches Archiv*, XXXVI (1932), 356–414.

———. "Introduction: Professor Taussig's Contribution to the Theory of International Trade," in *Explorations in Economics.* New York: McGraw-Hill Book Co., 1936.

———. *Studies in the Theory of International Trade.* New York: Harper & Bros., 1937.

Wahl, D. F. "Capital and Labour Requirements for Canada's Foreign Trade," *Canadian J. Econ. and Polit. Sci.*, XXVII (August, 1961), 349–58.

[22]

JOURNAL OF REGIONAL SCIENCE, VOL. 25, NO. 4, 1985

REGIONAL DEVELOPMENT ANALYSIS AND POLICY*

Charles L. Leven†

1. INTRODUCTION

Regional development is concerned with levels and changes over time in population, work force, capital-labor ratios, and in rates of return to land, labor, and capital in geographically bounded, generally contiguous territories. Here we are unconcerned with the use of *space* and/or variations in rates of return *within* such a contiguous territory, essentially the province of urban economics, although we are concerned with *distances* to be overcome for transactions in real goods to take place *between* territories [Isard (1954)]. Similarly, regional analysis is focused not on where among a set of spatially separated regions a given economic unit, be it household or firm, would locate (these are the concerns of migration models and location theory) but rather on the aggregate of activities to be found *at a given node* (here regarded as spaceless) *in a set of spatially separated nodes*. In that sense we are concerned with the macro-economics of what has or might locate in a region as an aggregate (sometimes small or sometimes large) as opposed to the micro-economics of the locational choice of a particular decision unit [Aganbegyan (1981), Needleman (1968)].

The connections between urban and regional analysis and location and migration theory in reality are not completely separable [Greenwood (1978)]. Prospects for growth in population or per capita income at a particular location depend on the location of people and firms there or at other points, more rather than less proximate to that location [Nicholson, Brinkley, and Evans (1981), Yamamura and Iwasa (1984)]. Ability of a region to compete for external markets would depend on factor productivity in that region, which in turn would depend on the efficiency of internal space use, since the costs of internal movement, congestion, and public service delivery ultimately must be borne by production units in the region either directly or via higher labor supply price. But here we abstract from those interconnections, partly because there is little, if any, literature treating of spatial equilibria at that level of generality [Isard and Ostroff (1960)], and perhaps even more because none of that literature has been able to go beyond simple formal description [Lefeber (1958)].

Defined as above, we can characterize the literature on regional development as relatively recent in historic terms, although it is fairly extensive in terms of general theory and methodology, as well as in applied studies of particular places or the effects of particular interventions [Kresge and Seiver (1978); Kuklinski (1978);

*The author wishes to thank Philip Braun for his help in developing the bibliography.

†Professor of Economics and Director, Institute for Urban and Regional Studies, Washington University, St. Louis, Missouri.

Moore and Rhodes (1974); Rich (1980); Widner (1973)]. It is concerned with differentials in levels of activity, growth, and rates of return across a number of, although not all, social dimensions (i.e., age, sex, race, occupational or industrial category, and region). What distinguishes the dimensions of differential performance in which we are interested is that they reflect aspects of individuals' statuses which may be more or less immobilizing [Kuklinski and Lambooy (1983)]. For example, we care about differential rates of return to men and women since discriminatory or demand-induced differentials cannot be eliminated by intergroup migration. We do not care about differences between Republicans and Democrats, not because they might not exist—in fact, they probably do—but because anyone disadvantaged beyond their nonpecuniary returns by that assignment could change if they desired. Differences in rates of return by region fall somewhere in between these two extremes. While individuals can move from an area where rates of return are low to one where they are higher, substantial economic as well as psychic cost could be involved [Beaumont (1976), Hansen (1977, 1980)].

Through most of history interregional differentials in rates of return were not a matter either of intellectual interest or practical concern. Differences between national states were, and substantially still are, regarded as legitimate artifacts of the territorially sovereign property rights of legitimate national governments. Where workers were indentured, interregional differences could be regarded similarly as reflecting legitimate rights of personal inheritance. Historic location of population and production obviously affected rates of return of land differentially, but those differences were outcomes of prior decisions on capital investment, land utilization, or inheritance. Therefore, questions such as how many people ought to be at a particular location and/or how capital could be redirected so as to achieve more equitable capital-labor ratio differences, although of private interest, were not an object of public concern [Callahan and Hutchinson (1980)].

With the coming of the Industrial Revolution the number of people potentially immobilized by their location grew dramatically, but individual adjustment through migration was seen either as an easily achieved outcome of personal choice, or was just not feasible. Throughout the nineteenth century there were a number of development policy interventions that had highly differential impacts on different regions, but their geographic dimensions were largely incidental. Major policies impacting on regional differentials in the U.S. included river improvements, canals, and railroads, the Homestead and Morrill Acts, farm-to-market roads, and eventually a national highway system [Cumberland (1973)]. The impact of such interventions on labor demand, population holding capacity, and productivity of capital varied greatly from region to region, but these were after-the-fact aspects of interventions undertaken for the benefit of the nation as a whole, or perhaps to address the needs of a particular segment of society or branch of industry.

Unintended but highly uneven geographic outcomes were the source of substantial interregional strife in Europe and North America in the nineteenth and early twentieth century, of which the American Civil War is perhaps the most dramatic example. Notwithstanding the growth of regionalism from at least the beginning of the nineteenth century, examples of explicitly regional policy prior to the Great Depression are almost nonexistent [Riefler (1979)]. Strange as it might seem today, even a regional phenomenon as dramatic as the Potato Famine in Ireland failed to evoke any explicitly regional policy for offsetting its effects [Gallagher (1982)].

One of the very few examples of concern with region, per se, from a national viewpoint was the question of settlement policy for Australia in the mid-nineteenth century [Senior (1831)]. In that case, explicit attention was given to incentives to labor and capital by way of infrastructure and transport subsidy, marking a departure from a simple policy of land grants to private developers as in Canada and the pre-Revolutionary U.S. In fact, from the start of European colonization in the sixteenth century territorial development was a concern, but except for Australia it was carried out almost entirely by concession, so that regional analysis and/or regional policy per se did not emerge until well into the twentieth century. In the U.S. too, while all through the nineteenth century there were many policies dealing with sectoral or distributional disadvantage which had differential spatial impacts, policies aimed at *spatial* disadvantage or dislocation per se have emerged only in the past 50 years or so [Kerr and Williamson (1970)].

Proprietary concern of its inhabitants with population and rates of return in a particular region have a long-established tradition, probably even antedating the Industrial Revolution, but it is the concern of the larger society for spatial dislocation either as a shortage of jobs or of capital relative to its resources, location, and constrained factor mobility that concerns us here [Needleman and Scott (1964)]. These proprietary concerns, however, are only one of three broad kinds of concern which we will consider here. The others are the *national interest* in intervention in interregional allocation for equity and for efficiency, although as we shall see later on, efficiency cannot be so neatly factored out of national equity concerns as might appear at first glance [Gordon and Lande (1977)].

In the next section we review the literature on theories, models, and policies related to proprietary concerns with region. Sections 3 and 4 will cover the same ground with respect to national welfare and economic efficiency considerations, respectively. In Section 5 we consider the impact of recent changes in the regional allocation process and implications for future research.

2. REGIONAL DEVELOPMENT AS A PROPRIETARY CONCERN

Concern of residents and property owners with their region's economic prospects in a sense is inherent in the concept of region itself [Evenden (1980)]. While the literature involved with regional definition is considered elsewhere in this issue, it is worth noting here the connection between definition and the perspective one would take in viewing regional development [Isard (1956)]. Since a fundamental characteristic of a region is commonality of interests (i.e., transactional interdependence), we can take as axiomatic that individuals within a region have an interest in aggregate regional performance greater than their interest in randomly selected aggregates to which they belong, much as firms in an industry or individuals in an occupation have a particular interest in economic performance of industry or occupational aggregates [Fox (1984)].

The self-interest of residents stems from the demand as inputs to production for factors which they control and/or the prices which they as consumers must pay for goods and services purchased or distributed through the local public sector. But there really are no policies aimed at a more efficient interregional allocation of local public expenditures, since the prevailing theoretical view is that migration yields at least close to a market efficient solution [Tiebout (1956)]. Similarly, while spatial monopolies or oligopolies surely can extract rents, their magnitude probably is pretty limited by threatened entry, as in local retail stores, or by regulation where potential entry really is limited as in many transport or public utility services [Greenhut, Norman, and Hung (forthcoming)].

So what we come down to as the major focus of proprietary concern over a region's well-being is demand for its inputs. This is most readily articulated in conventional economic base theory. Presuming a relatively low elasticity of substitution of labor for capital in the aggregate, if interregionally competitive rates of return are to be maintained for both factors, this comes down to explaining the level of some convenient metric of total output [Andrews (1953)]. More to the point, the theory maintains that factor input demand can expand only via an increase in demand for produced output; but output for the local (nonbasic) market can increase only if local income increases, and the latter can increase only if total demand for produced output rises so that exogenous change necessarily cannot occur except in the export sector [Blumenfeld (1955)]. As the Tiebout-North controversy made evident [Friedmann and Alonso (1964)], this ignores import substitution as a development stimulus, but otherwise is surely valid as a tautology. In equilibrium, spontaneous expansion of the import substitute sector would call for technological advances in local production of locally consumed goods. In equilibrium, however, it would require technical advance to expand the basic sector too; it would have to be at some other region's expense. Just why it is that local developers see breakthrough as possible in finding new basic opportunities but not in nonbasic goods has appeared somewhat curious to many observers [Tiebout (1962)]. Perhaps local "movers and shakers" believe that if there were a better way of serving local demand they surely would already have thought of it, while better ways of serving distant and perhaps unknown external markets might require external observers to identify them; in any event there is almost no literature on how to identify gaps in local supply of household demand or intermediate inputs.

So, finally we come down to economic base theory as the guiding conception behind a proprietary perspective on regional development. In a national context it is simply mercantilism, a powerful idea still with us in squabbles over American-Japanese trade restrictions and in current proposals of the Tory Government for cutting industrial money wage rates in Britain, the first as a defense against long-run job loss, the second as a means of recovery. At a regional level the critical role of basic vs. nonbasic, town-building vs. town-filling, or export vs. local activity had its explicit origins in a study of the growth of the New York area in the late 1920's [Haig (1928)], although it has gone through a variety of refinements. Early squabbles concerned the appropriate unit of measurement [Leven (1954)] and specification of the aggregate [Hochwald (1961)]. Later efforts took account of interindustry linkages in deriving sectoral multipliers—sometimes broadly [Leven (1963)], sometimes in great detail [Isard and Langford (1971)]. The equivalence of the basic-nonbasic ratio to the foreign trade multiplier was shown [Tiebout (1960)] and concern over estimation techniques and technical refinement continues [Koropecky (1972); Kuklinski (1974); Perloff and Leven (1964)]. But the motivating idea is ever the same; expansion of demand in a region's export bill of goods is the *only* theoretical basis for an increase in local demand for factors leading to expansion of employment.

The interests of wage earners in this process are ambiguous. On the one hand, even in the face of a competitive local labor market and wage elastic in-migration, a continually expanding labor demand would lower job search costs and/or reduce transitional unemployment [Khaitun (1980)]; and with imperfect local labor markets and/or sluggish migration response [McCulloch and Yellen (1977)], the advantages to entrenched workers could be even greater [Chalmers and Greenwood (1985)]. On the other hand, scalar growth is likely to bring increased real prices of goods with a significant land-input component, like housing [Muth (1969)], or of nontraded goods subject to scale diseconomy, like local government services [Hirsch (1965)].

Owners of land unambiguously would benefit from regional scalar expansion as would owners of capital sunk in production of local goods, especially if they were goods subject to barriers to entry and/or increasing returns to scale. Owners of capital sunk in production of export goods should be largely indifferent. On the one hand, scalar expansion might afford them some agglomeration economies, but dynamic adjustment of wage rates and/or higher equilibrium land prices could increase the real supply price of labor [Ghali, Akiyama, and Fujiwara (1978)].

Thus, within an economic base conception this leaves prospective owners of new capital as the critical determiners of regional growth, so it is not surprising that area growth policies focus largely on incentives to them [Malizia and Reid (1976)]. Neither is it surprising that local real estate and construction interests and major suppliers of nonbasic goods are in the vanguard of local campaigns for regional development, with wage earner and export goods producer interests in the role of passive approvers [Rasmussen, Bendick, and Ledebur (1984)]. About the only source of antigrowth advocacy is concern over an excessive burden on the physical environment, but these concerns are more likely to be manifest at geographic aggregations larger or smaller than a functional economic region [Fox and Kumar (1965)]. An SMSA, for example, seems too small to intrude seriously on macro-environments and too big to be contaminated by point sources of pollution that could affect an individual neighborhood or subdivision.

Accordingly, we find owners of land and fixed capital and operators of decreasing-cost, nonbasic industries pretty much unopposed in their advocacy of export base expansion as the target for regional development [Mansell and Wright (1978)]. The derivative policies mainly consist of expanded markets for existing basic producers, but even more, attraction of new investors in job-creating production facilities for new basic output; historically, these have been seen as manufacturing enterprises [Ashcroft and Taylor (1977)]. This approach to regional development essentially denies efficient competitive spatial allocation markets.

For the economic base argument to be valid, either external markets for locally produced goods or profitable local investment outlets for external capital must be unrealized essentially through information failure or discontinuities leading to nonprofitability of investment below some threshold, or it could be contingent on failure of complementary investments to agglomerate [Corden and Findlay (1975)].

This leads to information, promotion, and/or capital subsidies as policy instruments [Pascal and McCall (1980)]. But although there is a good deal of nonacademic literature about promoting the economic base, there is almost no academic literature on the actual effects of such attempts. The reason for this seems clear, namely, the absence of operational multiregional (even if for only two regions) models, with aggregate or multisector production functions allowing for the impact of *changing* input ratios on production [Stevens (1958)]. As argued more than 15 years ago [Leven, Legler, and Shapiro (1970)], the data base for such analyses simply did not exist; it still does not.

The popularity of base-expanding policies to local leaders is not hard to understand. Those that involve only information or promotion are inexpensive and claims of their effectiveness are hard to refute; they are the most common form of locally funded effort. Direct subsidies to investors are more expensive and less commonly funded locally, especially in forms other than tax abatement, construction, and lease-back of production facilities, or write-downs of land acquisition cost. These devices as well as operating subsidies such as wage subsidies or low interest rate loans are typical of state policies [Woodward (1974)] and some federal initiatives [Graham and Martin (1980)].

The particular federal policies most consistent with local base expansion per se are preferential award of government contracts or below-market-rate loans to businesses establishing production facilities in areas eligible according to a formula based on relative per capita income and level and persistence of above-average unemployment [Miernyk (1980)]. These initiatives began in the 1950's under the Area Redevelopment Administration and continued under the Economic Development Administration, although there is no substantial use of them currently. Most of the federal policies aimed at regional development, however, have not been aimed directly at adding to export demand or subsidizing new business capital formation, but rather have been aimed more at indirect expansion via infrastructure that could improve the status of troubled regions as places to work and live, outside as well as in the U.S. [O'Farrell (1980); Richardson and Richardson (1975); Vermot-Desroches and Joyal (1979)]. This leads to a second kind of concern with regional development and a second theoretical conception.

3. REGIONAL PRODUCTIVITY AND REGIONAL DEVELOPMENT

Inherent in an economic base conception is the notion of disequilibrium in interregional allocation as the norm; either potential demands are unrealized or capital is not in its most profitable location [Engle (1974)]. In contrast is the notion that regional differentials in real rates of return to labor stem from differences in productivity [Dienes (1972)] for reasons more fundamental than a disequilibrium capital-labor ratio per se [McDermott (1977)]. In particular, a low capital-labor ratio could stem from a lower rate of return to private capital because of environmental or infrastructure deficiencies, or there could be a low rate of return to labor for similar reasons [Batra and Scully (1972)].

This view essentially sees regions as being poor not because of bad luck or market failure, but rather because of low factor productivity. In a sense one could describe this as a migrational disequilibrium [Fielding (1966)]. While this is possible, it also could be that investing in the region's infrastructure could increase rates of return more than would be achievable by migration at finite cost and/or there could be a national welfare interest in maintaining some rather than other population distributions [Vitebskii (1979)].

Essentially, it is this view that lies behind a national interest in ameliorating regional disadvantage or promoting particular regional settlement [Leven (1969)]. Here we refer to something much more specific than the incidental differential regional impact that necessarily affects almost any policy impacting on resource availabilities or on factor-neutral productivity change. Settling of the West was an object of federal policy in the nineteenth century [Legler and Davis (1966)] and by definition had a differential regional impact on the marginal efficiency of capital. But its object was to exploit previously inaccessible resources that just happened to be somewhere in particular, the West, rather than everywhere in general. Similarly, agricultural policies of the 1930's benefited midwesterners disproportionately, but the purpose was aid to distressed farmers without respect to location. Most particularly, characteristics of particular regions, as opposed to people, were not taken as criteria for eligibility.

Federal appropriations for developmental projects at specific locations do have a long history, particularly military and civil functions of the defense departments, but here the ostensible criterion was the convenience of the federal government. Interregional competition for locks, dams, and army depots notwithstanding, the benefits to the directly affected region were not an admissible criterion prior to the Flood Control Act on 1936 [President's Water Resources Council (1962)].

That Act for the first time made it legitimate for the federal government to fund projects, in this case navigation and flood control projects, wherein the benefits, to whomsoever they might occur, exceeded the costs. In a sense, the resultant geographic impact was incidental in that the motive was to provide protection to citizens. It also became a way of altering a region's productivity by opening up lands on flood plains to more dependable agricultural or industrial use. Analyzing the developmental impacts, however, can pose complex analytical problems, especially in the protection of urban flood plains where relevant land supply itself and, hence, intraregional spatial assignment can be affected [Greenberg, Leven, and Schlottman (1974)].

At least until the 1960's the pork-barrel tradition, while by definition aimed at developing specific geographic places, was responding not to a national interest in regional well-being or efficiency per se, but simply used regions as proxies for political trading groups whose spatial relationships, one to another, was of no special analytic significance [Fahle and Rauner (1971)].

The Tennessee Valley Authority (TVA) probably is the first example of a specific national interest in the well-being and productivity of a *particular place* [Martin (1956)]. The rationale for the TVA reflects the notion that the nation itself was losing out due to the low rates of return in the mid-south area TVA was organized to serve. Somehow it was believed that the enhancement of the region's infrastructure not only would raise the market rates of return to private factors, but also could add to the nation's product, conceivably in excess of the cost of providing the infrastructure [Martin (1979)].

The older theoretical argument for such an intervention has been reviewed [Richardson (1978)] and debated more recently by others [von Böventer (1975), Richardson (1975)]. Essentially, this perspective sees regional output per capita as a function of the size and quality of its labor force and its stock of private and public capital, given its resource base and location relative to other regions. Except for market information failure, this view would see total labor supply or private capital stock adjusting pretty much by themselves or in response to the more modest promotional policies or subsidies associated with economic base theory. Even in equilibrium a region could still be poor due to low quality of its labor force, shortcomings in its public capital, or limited resource endowment that would not necessarily be eliminated even with competitive factor markets with full information [Barth, Kraft, and West (1975), Dahlberg (1978)].

In actual practice, limits to resource availability are not necessarily fixed. New resource stocks can be discovered as an outcome of investment in exploration; productivity of existing resources can be improved via investments in research; and the effective availability of resources at any given location can be increased by improved interregional transport links [Spiegelglas (1960)]. While there is a considerable literature on the economics of resource discovery and/or extraction and the economics of technical change, in general, there is almost no theory or analysis of either process, specifically in a regional context [Ewers and Wettman (1980)]. Perhaps this is because the technology of resource discovery makes it inefficient to look for resources in general in a bounded territory, and the economics of discovery make it difficult to appropriate geographically the proprietary rights to new knowledge. In any event, while its position in the transport network can be a major focus of a region's developmental policy concern, there are few examples of regional investment in resource discovery or technological change.

The rationale for regional investment in education of individuals is well documented in the economics of education and will not be summarized here. The essential point for a region's productivity over and above private gains to the individual lies in the notion of complementarity of different labor inputs. Despite the apparent stake in its work force's education, as witnessed by substantial public spending on education (even post-secondary education) at a regional level, there are really no definitive studies of payoffs of improved human capital to the investing region or of policies to promote entrepreneurialism per se [Leahy and McKee (1972)].

For the most part, policies designed to enhance regional productivity focus on infrastructure investments aimed at improving the marginal efficiency of private capital investment [Lande (1978)]. The theoretical rationale for the effectiveness of infrastructure lies in an aggregate production function conception of regional productivity [Leven, Legler, and Shapiro (1974)]. At a locally financed level these could include such things as servicing of industrial subdivisions, city streets, storm water drainage, and special police and fire protection facilities. State initiatives could include environmental management policies or business services such as provided by state university bureaus of business research [Mulkey and Dillman (1976), Sazama (1970)]. Federal initiatives could include funding of local or state initiatives or direct funding by the federal government as in regional power administrations and/or water transport, irrigation, flood control, or water recreation. Somewhat less specifically aimed at regional objectives as such would be land management and forest development activities.

Here too, the literature evaluating the effectiveness of such interventions is remarkably sparse, mainly due to the absence of a data base appropriate for testing the impact of long-run changes in capacity (regional development) in contrast to the substantial literature on the impact of short-run—i.e., with fixed or infinitely elastic capacities—changes in regional final demand [Leven and Read (1971)]. In fact, in the late 1960's and early 1970's the development of just such a data base was a major concern of the Committee on Urban Economics [Hoch (1969)], but despite specific attempts to specify data system characteristics [Hirsch (1969)], their development has not been forthcoming.

There are relatively few applied studies about a particular region's low productivity, and the few examples that can be found tend to be speculative and anecdotal rather than analytical and statistical [Maddox (1968)]. As we have said, part of the difficulty is in the available data base, but even more it may lie in a logical inconsistency between an economic base conception and an aggregate production function conception of long-run growth [Andrikopoulos (1980)]. The economic base perspective is the underlying rationale for believing that information failure or possibly infant-industry discontinuity is the fundamental barrier to regional development [Leone and Struyk (1976)]. In essence, it argues that the region's equilibrium level of production is higher than observed. Claims that it was actually in a low-output, low-productivity equilibrium would invalidate the rationale for economic base-related policies and could even be seen by regional proprietors as actually disloyal and counter-productive of area promotion or industrial recruiting campaigns. In short, one is unlikely to stress the shortcomings of a regional economy as part of a program to attract outside investment. At the same time, it is difficult to identify gaps in a region's infrastructure if one maintains that the major barrier to growth is limited information or a poor image.

Why, we might ask, though, is it that economic base theories and derivative policies occupy so much of the literature and aggregate production function notions so little? Since available data bases do not really permit robust empirical comparisons, the explanation cannot be better explanatory power. In a logical sense, of course, both are valid explanations, although both tell only part of the story. In fact, it would seem that the major basis for adopting one perspective or the other would lie in the alternative implications for policy.

On the one hand, those with proprietary concerns are likely to be predominantly the owners of fixed factors in the region (land and to a partial extent capital) whose rate of return is likely to be determined mainly by the aggregate demand for inputs, much more than by the productivity of complimentary variable inputs, such as labor. Accordingly, their interests would be served much more by simple expansion of aggregate demand so they would focus on the number of jobs rather than per capita income. For local goods producers there could be a positive feedback from higher wage rates per se, but at best this would only be limited, since the community's marginal propensity to consume out of an increased number of workers would approximate the community's average propensity to consume; and that would generally exceed the average value of the marginal propensity to consume out of wage rate increases [Miernyk et al. (1967)].

Owners of fixed factors used in export production in principle should be neutral with respect to increased regional employment, although to the extent that growth of employment puts short-term or (via congestion diseconomies) long-term pressure on money wage rates, they could be expected to be less than enthusiastic about base expansion, in general. Also, while they might benefit from higher labor productivity if achieved by public policy not financed by them, the fact that labor markets are generally more competitive than product markets would dissipate part of such benefits [Lever (1980)].

In contrast, those having a strong interest in increasing the average product of labor would almost entirely be workers themselves, with lower-skilled workers generally having more to gain from public intervention than higher-wage workers. What this means is that so far as local and state initiatives are concerned, we should expect them mostly to reflect an economic base conception of regional development. Moreover, those policies are also likely to be much cheaper to implement, i.e., promotional brochures and advertising are cheaper than worker-retaining or redesign of the local transit system. Not surprisingly, they would be more sympathetic to policies consistent with an aggregate production function conception, such as improvements in education, health, housing, transport, etc., especially where provided by the federal government. So long as employers were not paying for them in other than an incidental way, we should not expect any local resistance to federal policies aimed at improving worker productivity, and positive enthusiasm for federal policies that added to the region's physical infrastructure, like waterway improvements, federally financed highways or mass transit demonstration programs [Chinitz (1966), Hale and Walters (1974)].

A variant of an aggregate production function perception sees the problem as not necessarily inadequate infrastructure or human capital, but regional deficiency in technological knowledge per se. Here we refer to the potentially limited knowledge of those in the region concerning technology and markets outside, not limited information about the region possessed by outsiders as posited by an economic base perception. Where this might be so, one can view a region's development as importantly affected by the spread of technological knowledge [Alves and Morrill (1975)]. The perception that technological knowledge emerged disproportionately in selected locations has been understood for some time [Hoover and Vernon (1959)] as has the notion that it takes time for that knowledge to spread to the hinterlands [Lasuen (1962)]. Mainly, the spread of innovation as a determinant of differentials in regional growth has been emphasized in developing countries [Gunasekera and Codippily (1977)] but has been noted as a factor in developed countries as well [Biehl, Hussmann, and Schnyder (1975)].

Related to the spread of information is the diffusion of investment itself. A question of particular interest in this regard is whether significant discontinuities could be expected at particular locations; rather like an infant industry argument expressed spatially rather than sectionally [Caceres and Seninger (1980)]. If so, then investment in response to disequilibria (in particular, interregional shift in location over time) would occur only at particular critical scales of regional activity when they achieved status as growth poles [Perroux (1950)]. Their status as growth poles, however, would depend not just on size, but also on a center's sectoral composition, its siting in the transport network, and its distance from other centers, especially the primate city [Kuklinski (1972), Lewis and Prescott (1972)].

4. MARKET EQUILIBRIUM AND REGIONAL DEVELOPMENT

In a sense, the perspective on regional development to be discussed in this section could be described as a nonperspective. Its theoretical basis was first elucidated more than 20 years ago [Borts and Stein (1964)] although subject to later refinements [Romans (1965), Smith (1974)]. The theoretical key to this perspective lies in the belief that product markets, at least in traded goods, are sufficiently competitive so that export producers in general face infinitely elastic demands for their output. Under this condition, if it were allocationally efficient, all employment could be absorbed in the export sector with all local consumption coming out of imports. In cases of extremely isolated regions with unusually harsh environments this literally could be true [Anderson (1976)]. More commonly, a region would have a comparative advantage in some import-substitute production at whatever money wage was established by the opportunity wage available in the export sector. That wage, in turn, would depend upon money wages available nationally plus a local cost-of-living differential due to higher labor supply costs either from regionally specific differences in inputs to the household production function (more fuel needed in colder climates), or higher land costs from increased congestion and/or higher local transport costs due to greater regional scale [Greytak (1975)].

The foregoing could lead to regional differences in money wage rates even in competitive equilibrium, but only to the extent that resource or scale economy differentials offered corresponding advantages to the marginal efficiency of capital [Sveikauskas (1975)]. Regionally specific production advantages also could arise in production of goods for local consumption vis-à-vis imports, and likely would be even more pervasive there than in the export sector. In fact, in equilibrium most regional economies would have more of their production in nonbasic than in basic employment, especially as the population scale of the region grew, providing more opportunity for realizing scale economies in the nonbasic sector [Golladay and Sandoval (1972)].

Strictly speaking, within a market equilibrium perspective one cannot really talk about regional development, only growth [Olsen and Garb (1965)]; growth would depend on special environmental advantages either for consumption or production. For example, superior amenities (i.e., sunshine, oceans, etc.) could lead to workers willing to work at the same money wages as in other regions even though part of their wages would be bid away by the higher rents commanded by owners of access to the amenities [Cebula and Vedder (1973)]. Starting at any equilibrium, an increase in amenities would attract in-migrant workers only up to the point where the value of the amenities was equal to the rent paid for them, which would increase as the number of in-migrants increased. Alternatively, excess rents could be avoided by in-migrants settling at increasingly distant residential location; but again, the increasing transport costs associated with increasing population would limit the number of attracted in-migrants.

Growth could also be stimulated by a region-specific amenity that increased output-input ratios in basic production activities. Here too, unless the amenity were a purely public good, the increased quantity of labor demanded in the basic sector again would be bounded. Short of this, since the additional workers would have to live somewhere, the increased costs of housing or transporting them ultimately would limit growth [Evans (1972)].

As in other conceptions of regional development, a market equilibrium perspective can be associated with a particular kind of interest and associated policies. The major constituency for a market equilibrium perspective would be producers serving national as opposed to local or regional markets [Courbis (1979)]. For them, increased purchasing power or market scale in one region at the expense of another is essentially a zero-sum game. True, a more technically efficient national allocation would represent aggregate efficiency growth in which they might have an interest, and to the extent that a region's economic-base promoting policies accomplished this, they would be consistent with improved market equilibrium. But the specific regional dimension of such policies would be subsumed by a general interest in improvement of information that would follow from a market equilibrium perspective. The same sort of relationship would apply to the market equilibrium perspective on infrastructure. True, it would admit of public sector investments positively affecting the productivity of particular enterprises, and such enterprises could be expected to lobby for such, but while the public facilities that would provide net excess benefits to such enterprises might commonly lie in the same region, any resultant correspondence would be incidental [Liu (1977)].

Thus, the policies that stem from a market equilibrium perspective essentially are aimed at reducing market imperfections or achieving generalized increases in factor productivity [Miernyk (1979)]. Obviously, these could include the whole range of standard industrial organization measures to establish ease of entry and exit into industries and occupations, diffusion of knowledge concerning markets and technology, and even antimonopoly and antidiscrimination measures [Pal (1963)]. Of special interest here would be interventions to remove barriers to spatial mobility [Pfister (1961)].

Traditionally, its relative absence of barriers to spatial mobility has been an important distinguishing characteristic of the U.S. economy so that, to a considerable extent, a market perspective on regional development in the U.S. leads to nonpolicy; for the most part, what would be done to promote regional efficiency is already contained in whatever would be done to promote economic efficiency, in general. In other countries regional efficiency per se may be seen as more of a problem [Tooze (1976)] and may emerge in the form of restrictions on migration [Buck and Atkins (1976)]. In other developed countries it is limits on housing exchange that most commonly pose a barrier to interregional migration—perhaps due to nontransferability of rights to public housing as in Britain [Edwards and Posnett (1980)], perhaps due to very high housing transaction costs as in Japan [Mills and Ohta (1976)]. In the third world, cultural and linguistic differences or simply limited information are more likely to pose the critical limits [Lefeber and Datta-Chaudhuri (1971)].

In one sense, a market equilibrium perspective adds little even to a general theory of regional development, since it leads to policies which are analytically noncontroversial. On the other hand, it provides a theoretical basis for a sometimes partisan urging of the dismantling of specific regional policies as themselves introducing barriers to competitive adjustment [Cumberland (1975)]. For example, for at least the past two decades, whether there should be an urban policy or not has remained a controversial issue [Mills (1972)]. What was at stake was not urban policy in the sense of how public service delivery was accomplished *within* urban areas, but rather how economic activities, population, infrastructure, and ability to finance local services was distributed *among* metropolitan economies, seen as spatially separated points [Wingo (1972)]. Perhaps this debate reached its culmination in the presidential commission on urban policy in the Carter administration [U.S. Department of Housing and Urban Development (1978)] and its failure to result in the National Urban Policy that was intended. That policy would have focused on specifically urban questions, but would have had interregional allocation as an important concern [Perloff (1973), Thompson (1972)].

Frankly, it seems hard to believe that the debate over this issue was so recent that as late as 1980 a volume resulted from a major initiative with respect to estimating urban impacts of federal policy [Glickman (1980)]. Since that time it would seem that a market equilibrium perspective has pervaded federal policy. While EDA programs continue, their funding has been drastically reduced, and community block grants, mass transit demonstrations, subsidies to interregional transport, and most federal housing programs have all but disappeared and the Small Business Administration seems likely to be abolished.

The only federal initiative which continues to have political support is Urban Development Assistance Grants (UDAG), and even there funding reduction has occurred. The UDAG program is closer to a market equilibrium perspective than most other initiatives in that it provides supplemental financing for otherwise private initiatives, the theoretical justification being the overcoming of bottlenecks to private investment from prisoner's dilemma situations.

Here too, the issue is not really whether a market equilibrium perspective is correct or not. Rather, what is of interest is its relevance to policy consistent with particular interest positions [Williams (1983)]. In an abstract sense it is certainly the case that market imperfections lead to allocational inefficiency in the same sense that it is true that an increase in a region's export bill of goods would have a multiplier effect on its economy, or that enhancement of its infrastructure would increase the productivity of complementary inputs. On the other hand, while both market equilibrium and aggregate production function perspectives are equilibrium concepts, the economic base perspective is a disequilibrium concept. Accordingly, there have been some attempts to evaluate empirical distinctions between economic base and market equilibrium explanations of regional change [Freund (1973)]. An economic base concept argues that observed disequilibria stem from a failure of capital to adjust while a market equilibrium perspective sees disequilibrium as caused by the failure of labor to adjust [Mazek (1969)].

While quality-of-life indices are not part of the scope of this review, it does seem of interest to note, at least in passing, a logical inconsistency between a market equilibrium perspective and quality-of-life indices as ordinarily formulated. Clearly, there are amenity differences between areas—sunshine, mountains, wild life, zoos, symphonies and libraries, etc.—so that meaningful physical amenities indices certainly could be constructed [Dale (1980)]. On the other hand, most of the quality-of-life indices include economic return variables such as wage rates, unemployment, per capita income, and prices as components of the quality of life even though, if labor markets adjust efficiently, interregionally we should have the result that the quality of life so measured necessarily would be the same in all locations except for barriers to migration.

5. A CHANGING ENVIRONMENT FOR REGIONAL DEVELOPMENT

The discussion up until now has assumed that from one or another of three perspectives, a region's development necessarily is tied up with an expansion of its export base, perhaps in a simplistic mercantilist way, perhaps through a more subtle and complex connection from investment to productivity to absolute advantage to higher exports, or perhaps from import substitution. The literature related directly to forecasting models stands apart from this conception and from our interest here, but essentially it is neutral in regard to regional development per se [Czamanski (1965), Smith (1961)]. Also, within a Borts-Stein view we could conceive of development without an increase in exports, or indeed without growth, simply from capital deepening (human or otherwise), but it would require a very peculiar combination of inelastic substitutability of labor for capital and/or specificity of increases in capital stock for scalar growth in the work force not be to accompanied by scalar growth in a region's exports.

Against this background we have the peculiar phenomenon, since perhaps as long ago as 1950, of regional growth accompanied by apparent contraction not expansion of basic employment. Nationally, for example, manufacturing employment has declined fairly steadily from about 35 percent to a little over 20 percent of total employment from 1950 to 1984. What this means is that, on average, many regional economies must have had increasing nonmanufacturing employment while their manufacturing employment was falling. However, as economic base theory usually is interpreted, declines in manufacturing employment should lead to a *decline* in nonmanufacturing.

In part, this contradiction may be only apparent rather than real, since substantial segments of nonmanufacturing always have been exportable, such as retail goods and services sold to visitors, and some manufacturing is nonbasic, like bottling plants and bakeries. Also, even if the contradiction is real, to some extent it may be nominal; that is, the substitution of off-site producers of intermediate service inputs (e.g., robot programming) for on-site production workers (e.g., assemblers) in the production of conventional manufactured goods [Macrae (1978)]. Finally, part of the apparent switch in final household consumption away from tangible goods (relatively easy to ship) to intangible services (relatively hard to transport) may be simply a consequence of the supposed higher income elasticity of demand for services than for goods as postulated long ago in the literature on economic development, in general [Rostow (1965)]; and personal services have gone from about one-fourth to one-third of U.S. personal consumption expenditures since about 1965.

The spatial impact of the switch from goods to services is compounded by the falling cost of shipping intangibles via new information technologies. Note, if we assume that within-establishment scale economies generally are more substantial for tangibles than intangibles, we are led to the theoretical conclusion that there should be an evening out of the equilibrium size distribution of production agglomerations and moving to that new equilibrium would require precisely the kind of metro-nonmetro reversal in population that we have observed in the U.S. since about 1970 [Burns and Van Ness (1981)]. Moreover, the notion that this shift is fundamentally technological in origin and not just an artifact of sociological decay of the American inner-city is buttressed by the emergence of a similar regional demographic dynamic in Canada as well as the U.S. [Todd (1978)], in West Europe as well as North America [Aydalot (1984), Keeble, Owens, and Thompson (1983)] and even emerging in East Europe [Demko (1984)] and perhaps at its first stages in developing countries [Rondinelli (1983)].

How the geography of regional and urban activity is itself being transformed is a topic of considerable interest in its own right, but it is more properly a concern of the articles in this issue dealing directly with location theory and migration. What concerns us here are its implications for regional development analysis [Fuchs and Demko (1977)]. In that regard it is central that we understand the forces producing this very dramatic turnaround [Alonso (1978)]. The problem in this regard is not that there is no explanation, but rather that there seem to be too many.

One possibility is that what we are observing somehow or other is a manifestation of household preferences for environmental amenities. Without reciting the long litany of the Sunbelt-Frostbelt issue [Arnold (1980)] it seems difficult to view it as more than a minor theme in a much more fundamental spatial realignment. True, there has been a major shift of population to the Sunbelt from the Frostbelt, but most of the recent increase is due to the recent obsolescence of very large metropolitan regions [Brown and Kneese (1978)]. A shift-share analysis of regional population has shown a shift component from the Northeast and Midwest to the South and West operating quite consistently for at least the last century, but a share component turning precipitously in favor of Sunbelt states only since 1970 [Sheppard and Leven (1984)]. Accordingly, macro-regional preferences do not really explain much of what we see as recent sharp breaks in long-term trends. Even to the extent that they are operative, they may be as much a very long-term response to uneven original settlement, with corresponding lower supply prices of land inputs in the South and West, than to any underlying climatic differences per se [Malecki (1983)].

In principle, of course, one could test for the importance of environmental and amenity pull (i.e., supply-side) explanations as opposed to changes in demand for labor in the export sector as the critical exogenous factor. If it were the former, one would expect owners of fixed resources to extract location rents from in-migrants so that real wages in equilibrium would be lower where nonreproducible amenities were higher. If environmental factors were unimportant, however, one would still expect to see differentials in real as well as money wages at a point in time, i.e., one would expect convergence in the money cost of labor over time [Coelen (1978)]. Note that the required test would be convergence of the unit money cost, not the wage rate of labor, and we simply have no way of observing that. We cannot assess the cost of labor without determining its average product, which in turn cannot be determined without knowing the stock of capital at a regional level.

Two other explanations for an apparent increase in nonbasic/basic ratios relate to the consumption or production of services. The more common of these explanations is simply the high income elasticity of demand for services as opposed to goods, indicated above. However, while services have increased as a percentage of personal consumption, we do not know if they still are as less transportable than goods as in the past. Casual observation suggests this may be so, but it is easy to think of many services which have become more transportable with modern communication technology. Accordingly, if we were to validate increased importance of service consumption as the major explanation, we would have to know, at a regional level, the distribution of personal consumption expenditures between imported and locally produced services; there is no ready source of these data, even in cross section, much less over time.

On the other hand, the observed increases in services relative to goods output could be consistent with a very different explanation of recent trends in regional development, namely, that services themselves increasingly have become basic rather than nonbasic outputs, so that the seeming decrease in the manufacturing/nonmanufacturing ratio may be a simple consequence of the composition of the basic sector itself becoming more heavily weighted in services.

If we had data on the geographic distribution of service outputs we could distinguish between these two explanations of the causes of the rise in the relative importance of the service sector. Also, we should note that depending on which explanation emerged as valid, the consequences for regional development policy would be very much different. In the first case, we would look to exploiting increasing service demand by local residents as a way of achieving growth through import substitution; what we should be studying is the economics of local consumption. If the second explanation were valid, the indicated strategy would be trying to capture relatively footloose producers of exportable services, leading to the need for research on the economics of location (at a macro-regional scale) of service activities.

A final explanation for recent trends that should be considered is that it may have relatively little to do with changes in either the demand or the transportability of services per se, but rather that it originates in changes in the nature of production functions for conventional goods, in particular changes which make production more information intensive. A fairly dramatic illustration of the impact of the new information technology on production is found in the recent history of the Chrysler Corporation. Only a few years after being given government guaranteed loans to insure solvency, it managed not only to repay them ahead of schedule, but to provide substantial wage increases to its workers. Part of this success story was the restoration of the level of output of automobiles to levels approximating those prior to decline, but it should be stressed, with employment only about half what it had been initially. This was not, however, a reflection of a doubling of the productivity of labor per se. In fact, without more adequate measures of changes in capital stock we could not really tell what changes in labor productivity had occurred; but clearly, it could not have been of that magnitude in that short a time. What had happened was a change in production techniques to a much more automated, robotized scheme, with many fewer on-site production workers required, with the drop in on-site workers all or partly made up by a rise in employment in other establishments directly and indirectly providing the information control inputs.

A very dramatic aspect of this change is that many workers who formerly were linked to other steps in production in ways requiring them to be working at the same time and in the same place as other workers, can now perform their work separated both in time and space from each other. To the extent that this is so, this would represent a very powerful dilution of the forces producing industrial agglomeration both within and between establishments at a given location [Carlino (1980)]. In turn, weakening of this link makes disagglomeration of certain steps in production possible so that higher congestion costs can be avoided [Bergsman, Greenston, and Healy (1972)]. It really should be stressed that much as we might suspect that changes in production processes like those outlined above were underway, we could only validate this by determining what had happened to input coefficients for information related activities going into conventional goods production. Even if we had more up-to-date interindustry accounts than presently available, and even if they were available at a regional level, the nature of conventional sectoral definitions would make it very difficult to determine whether this was so.

The problems in the interindustry accounts are two-fold. First, there is simply much less detail in the service industry than would be required for a rigorous look at what has happened to information inputs. The second problem is that many workers in goods-producing establishments themselves might be service workers, even if classified as production rather than administration employees. In fact, the general problem is that sectors in interindustry analysis are classified according to the tangibility of the product being produced, whereas what we really need is sectors classified according to the tangibility of inputs. Ideally, we should want workers classified exhaustively into four basic sectors depending on whether their actual work involved processing of materials, moving of materials, processing of information, or moving of information. Each of these sectors might then be divided in two depending on whether they were in an establishment producing a tangible or an intangible output. Clearly, we are a long way from having a data flow that would permit this kind of analysis.

As somewhat of an aside, we note that the recent decline in federal policy for providing resource intervention into regional development has been accomplished by a remarkably rapid apparent adjustment of regional differentials in factor returns. Only a few years ago places like Pittsburgh and St. Louis were thought to have serious obsolescence and very grim futures. Currently, at least one set of quality-of-life indicators [Rand McNally (1985)] rates them as the first and seventh most livable cities in America. Whatever methodological sense that may or may not lie behind these indicators not withstanding, it is clear even by casual observation of the apparent levels of private capital formation that real turnaround in these SMSA's has occurred and occurred very rapidly. Does this leave any room for future concern with regional development? It would seem that the conclusions of this paper are strongly that it does [MacKay and Thomson (1979)].

First of all, a good deal of disadvantage and economic wastage was and still is involved in the transition of older northeastern industrial areas so that a better understanding of the dynamic could have saved substantial resources and inequity and it could still lead to more efficient adjustment in Europe [Thirwall (1974)]. Accordingly, just what it is that determines the rate of convergence to a new interregional allocation equilibrium would seem important for public and private sector planning, even in the absence of substantial intervention in the form of publicly-funded infrastructure. To accomplish this we really need to make some headway on the research suggested by our discussion of the possible sources of the apparent recent shift in nonbasic/basic ratios.

To summarize the research needed for sorting out that change: (1) what is the spatial distribution of sales of different kinds of service activities; (2) what determines the location by region of service establishments selling in a nonlocal market; and (3) what has happened to the information intensity of production functions for goods and how is that connected to changes in agglomeration economies? Perhaps we may hope that there will be an article in the 50th Anniversary issue of this *Journal* describing the substantial progress on these three topics that had been made in the preceding 25 years. It may take that long.

REFERENCES

Aganbegyan, A. G. (ed.). *Regional Studies for Planning and Projecting.* The Hague: Mouton Publishers, 1981.

Alonso, William. "The Current Halt in the Metropolitan Phenomenon," in C. L. Leven (ed.). *The Mature Metropolis.* Lexington, MA: Lexington Books, 1978, pp. 23–41.

Alves, William R. and Richard L. Morrill. "Diffusion Theory and Planning," *Economic Geography,* 51 (1975), 290–304.

Anderson, F. J. "The Effects of Remoteness and Size on Regional Real Wage Determination," *Regional Studies,* 10 (1976), 223–231.

Andrews, Richard B. "Mechanics of the Urban Economic Base," *Land Economics,* 29 (1953), 161–167, 263–268, 343–350; 30 (1954), 52–60, 164–172, 260–269, 309–319.

Andrikopoulos, Andreas A. "A Synthesis of the Production Function and the Shift-Share Model," *Regional Science and Urban Economics,* 10 (1980), 539–560.

Arnold, Victor (ed.). *Alternatives to Confrontation.* Lexington, MA: Lexington Books, 1980.

Ashcroft, Brian and Jim Taylor. "The Movement of Manufacturing Industry and the Effect of Regional Policy," *Oxford Economic Papers,* 29 (1977), 84–101.

Aydalot, Philip. "The Reversal of Spatial Trends in French Industry Since 1974," in J. G. Lambooy (ed.), *New Spatial Dynamics and Economic Crisis.* Tampere, Finland: Finnpublishers, 1984, pp. 41–62.

Barth, James, John Kraft, and Philip West. "A Portfolio Theoretic Approach to Industrial Diversification and Regional Employment," *Journal of Regional Science,* 15 (1975), 9–15.

Batra, Raveendra and Gerald W. Scully. "Technical Progress, Economic Growth, and the North-South Wage Differential," *Journal of Regional Science,* 12 (1972), 375–386.

Beaumont, Phillip B. "Assisted Labour Mobility Policy in Scotland 1973–1974," *Urban Studies,* 13 (1976), 75–79.

Bergsman, Joel, Peter Greenston, and Robert Healy. "The Agglomeration Process in Urban Growth," *Urban Studies,* 9 (1972), 263–288.

Biehl, Dieter, Eibe Hussmann, and Sebastian Schnyder. "Determinants of Regional Development Potential," *The German Economic Review,* 13 (1975), 117–134.

Blumenfeld, Hans. "The Economic Base of the Metropolis," *Journal of the American Institute of Planners,* 21 (1955), 114–132.

Borts, George H. and Jerome L. Stein. *Economic Growth in a Free Market.* New York. Columbia University Press, 1964.

Brown, Lee and Allen V. Kneese. "The Southwest: A Region under Stress," *American Economic Review,* 68 (1978), 105–109.

Buck, T. W. and M. H. Atkins. "The Impact of British Regional Policies on Employment Growth," *Oxford Economic Papers,* 28 (1976), 118–132.

Burns, Leland S. and Kathy Van Ness. "The Decline of the Metropolitan Economy," *Urban Studies,* 18 (1981), 169–180.

Caceres, Luis Rene and Stephen F. Seninger. "Endogenous Change in an Interregional System of Growth Centers: An Application to the Central American Common Market," *Regional Studies,* 14 (1980), 1–13.

Callahan, Colleen M. and William K. Hutchinson. "Antebellum Interregional Trade in Agricultural Goods: Preliminary Results," *Journal of American History,* 40 (1980), 25–31.

Carlino, Gerald A. "Contrasts in Agglomeration: New York and Pittsburgh Reconsidered," *Urban Studies,* 17 (1980), 343–351.

Cebula, Richard J. and Richard K. Vedder. "A Note on Migration, Economic Opportunity, and The Quality of Life," *Journal of Regional Science,* 13 (1973), 205–212.

Chalmers, James A. and Michael J. Greenwood. "The Regional Labor Market Adjustment Process: Determinants of Changes in Rates of Labor Force Participation, Unemployment, and Migration," *Annals of Regional Science,* 19 (1985), 43–58.

Chinitz, Benjamin. "Appropriate Goals for Regional Economic Policy," *Urban Studies,* 3 (1966), 1–7.

Coelen, Stephen P. "Regional Income Convergence/Divergence Again," *Journal of Regional Science,* 18 (1978), 447–458.

Corden, W. M. and R. Findlay. "Urban Unemployment, Intersectoral Capital Mobility and Development Policy," *Economica,* 12 (1975), 59–78.

Courbis, Raymond. "The Regina Model—A Regional-National Model for French Planning," *Regional Science and Urban Economics,* 9 (1979), 117–139.

Cumberland, John H. *Regional Development: Experiences and Prospects in the United States.* The Hague: Mouton Publishers, 1973.

———. "Current Issues in Regional Development Theory and Practice," *Economic Applications,* 28 (1975), 361–377.

Czamanski, Stanislaw. "A Method of Forecasting Metropolitan Growth by Means of Distributed Lags Analysis," *Journal of Regional Science,* 6 (1965), 35–50.

Dahlberg, Åke. "Changes of Investments in Publicly Owned Social Overhead Capital in Connection with Labor Migration," *Journal of Regional Science,* 18 (1978), 195–202.

Dale, Britt. "Subjective and Objective Social Indicators in Studies of Regional Social Well-Being," *Regional Studies,* 14 (1980), 503–515.

Demko, G. (ed.). *Regional Development, Problems and Policies in Eastern and Western Europe.* London: Croom Held Ltd., 1984.

Dienes, Leslie. "Regional Variations of Capital and Labor Productivity in Soviet Industry," *Journal of Regional Science,* 12 (1972), 401–406.

Edwards, Chris and John Posnett. "The Opportunity Cost of the Sale of Local Authority Rented Accommodation," *Urban Studies,* 17 (1980), 45–52.

Engle, Robert F. "A Disequilibrium Model of Regional Investment," *Journal of Regional Science*, 14 (1974), 367–376.

Evans, Alan W. "The Pure Theory of City Size in an Industrial Economy," *Urban Studies*, 9 (1972), 49–77.

Evenden, L. J. "Regionalism and the Cognitive Hierarchy of Towns," *Regional Studies*, 14 (1980), 473–490.

Ewers, H. J. and R. W. Wettmann. "Innovation-oriented Regional Policy," *Regional Studies*, 14 (1980), 161–179.

Fahle, Vernon L. and Robert M. Rauner. "National Policy for Regional Economic Development," *Growth and Change*, 2 (1971), 9–15.

Fielding, A. J. "Internal Migration and Regional Economic Growth—A Case Study of France," *Urban Studies*, 3 (1966), 200–214.

Fox, Karl A. "Behavioral Settings and Eco-Behavioral Science: A New Arena for Mathematical Social Science Permitting a Richer and More Coherent View of Human Activities in Social Systems," *Mathematical Social Sciences*, 7 (1984), 117–165.

Fox, Karl A. and T. K. Kumar. "The Functional Economic Area: Delineation and Implications for Economic Analysis and Policy," *Papers, Regional Science Association* 15 (1965), 57–85.

Freund, James B. "A Note on Short Period Changes in Earned Income in Manufacturing Among Urban Areas," *Journal of Regional Science*, 13 (1973), 279–289.

Friedmann, John and William Alonso (eds.). *Regional Development and Planning*. Cambridge, MA: The M.I.T. Press, 1964.

Fuchs, Roland J. and George J. Demko. "Spatial Population Policies in the Socialist Countries of Eastern Europe," *Social Science Quarterly*, 58 (1977), 60–73.

Gallagher, Thomas M. *Paddy's Lament: Ireland 1846–47*. New York: Harcourt Brace Jovanovich, 1982.

Ghali, Moheb, Masayuki Akiyama, and Junichi Fujiwara. "Factor Mobility and Regional Growth," *Review of Economics and Statistics*, 60 (1978) 78–84.

Glickman, Norman J. (ed.). *The Urban Impacts of Federal Policies*. Baltimore, MD: The Johns Hopkins University Press, 1980.

Golladay, Fredrick L. and A. David Sandoval. "Optimal Development Policy in an Open Regional Economy: A Programming Analysis," *Journal of Regional Science*, 12 (1972), 185–198.

Gordon, Peter and Paul S. Lande. "Regional Growth in the United States: A Re-examination of the Neoclassical Model," *Journal of Regional Science*, 17 (1977), 61–69.

Graham, Robert E., Jr. and Randolph C. Martin. "The Impact of Economic Development Administration Programs: Some Empirical Evidence," *Review of Economics and Statistics*, 62 (1980), 52–62.

Greenburg, Edward, C. L. Leven, and A. Schlottman. *Analysis of Theories and Methods for Estimating Benefits of Protecting Urban Flood Plains*. Springfield, VA: National Technical Information Service No. IWR 74-14, 1974.

Greenhut, Melvin, George Norman, and Chao-shun Hung. *Imperfect Competition: A Spatial Approach*. New York: Cambridge University Press, forthcoming.

Greenwood, Michael J. "An Econometric Model of Internal Migration and Regional Economic Growth in Mexico," *Journal of Regional Science*, 18 (1978), 17–32.

Greytak, David. "Regional Consumption Patterns and the Heckscher-Ohlin Trade Theorem," *Journal of Regional Science*, 15 (1975), 39–45.

Gunasekera, H. A. deS. and H. M. A. Codippily. "Employment Creation Through Regional Development: Recent Experience in Sri Lanka," *International Labour Review*, 116 (1977), 35–52.

Haig, Robert. *Regional Survey of New York and Its Environs*. New York: Committee on Regional Plans of New York and Its Environs, 1928.

Hale, Carl W. and Joe Walters. "Appalachian Regional Development and the Distribution of Highway Benefits," *Growth and Change*, 5 (1974), 3–11.

Hansen, Niles. "The Economic Development of Border Regions," *Growth and Change*, 8 (1977), 2–8.

———. "Dualism, Capital-Labor Ratios and the Regions of the U.S.: A Comment," *Journal of Regional Science*, 20 (1980), 401–403.

Hirsch, Werner Z. "Cost Functions of an Urban Government Service: Refuse Collection," *Review of Economics and Statistics*, 47 (1965), 87–92.

———."Regional Information Design for Public Decisions," *Review of Income and Wealth*, 15 (1969), 369–380.

Hoch, Irving. *Progress in Urban Economics: The Work of the Committee on Urban Economics 1959–1968 and The Development of the Field*. Washington, D.C.: Resources for the Future, 1969.

Hochwald, Werner (ed.). *Design of Regional Accounts*. Baltimore, MD: The Johns Hopkins University Press, 1961.

Hoover, Edgar M. and Raymond Vernon. *Anatomy of a Metropolis*. Cambridge, MA: Harvard University Press, 1959.

Isard, Walter. "Location Theory and Trade Theory: Short-run Analysis," *Quarterly Journal of Economics*, 68 (1954), 305–320.

———. "Regional Science, the Concept of Region, and Regional Structure," *Papers, Regional Science Association*, 2 (1956), 13–26.

Isard, Walter and David J. Ostroff. "General Interregional Equilibrium," *Journal of Regional Science*, 2 (1960), 67–74.

Isard, Walter and T. W. Langford. *Regional Input-Output Study: Recollections, Reflections and Diverse Notes on the Philadelphia Experience*. Cambridge, MA: The M.I.T. Press, 1971.

Keeble, David, Peter L. Owens, and Chris Thompson. "The Urban-Rural Manufacturing Shift in the European Community," *Urban Studies*, 20 (1983), 405–418.

Kerr, Alex and Robert B. Williamson. "Regional Economics in the U.S.," *Growth and Change*, 1 (1970), 5–19.

Khaitun, A. "Interregional Utilization of Labor Resources," *Problems of Economics*, 22 (1980), 3–19.

Koropeckyj, I.S. "Methodological Problems of Calculating National Income for Soviet Republics," *Journal of Regional Science*, 12 (1972), 387–400.

Kresge, David T. and Daniel A. Seiver. "Planning for a Resource-Rich Region: The Case of Alaska," *American Economic Review*, 68 (1978), 99–104.

Kuklinski, Antoni (ed.). *Growth Poles and Growth Centers in Regional Planning*. The Hague: Mouton Publishers, 1972.

———. *Regional Information and Regional Planning*. The Hague: Mouton Publishers, 1974.

———. *Regional Policies in Nigeria, India, and Brazil*. The Hague: Mouton Publishers, 1978.

Kuklinski, Antoni and J. G. Lambooy (eds.). *Dilemmas in Regional Policy*. The Hague: Mouton Publishers, 1983.

Lande, Paul S. "The Interregional Comparison of Production Functions," *Regional Science and Urban Economics*, 8 (1978), 339–353.

Lasuen, Jose-Ramon. "Regional Income Inequalities and the Problems of Regional Growth in Spain," *Papers, Regional Science Association*, 8 (1962), 169–188.

Leahy, William H. and David L. McKee. "A Schumpeterian View of the Regional Economy," *Growth and Change*, 3 (1972), 23–25.

Lefeber, Louis. *Allocation in Space: Production, Transport and Industrial Location*. Amsterdam: North-Holland, 1958.

Lefeber, Louis and Mrinal Datta-Chaudhuri. *Regional Development Experiences and Prospects in South and Southeast Asia*. The Hague: Mouton Publishers, 1971.

Legler, John B. and L. E. Davis. "The Government in the American Economy, 1815–1902: A Quantitative Study," *Journal of Economic History*, 26 (1966), 514–552.

Leone, Robert A. and Raymond Struyk. "The Incubator Hypothesis: Evidence from Five SMSAs," *Urban Studies*, 13 (1976), 325–331.

Leven, C. L. "An Appropriate Unit for Measuring the Urban Economic Base," *Land Economics*, 30 (1954), 369–371.

———."Regional and Interregional Accounts in Perspective," *Papers, Regional Science Association*, 9 (1963), 127–144.

———. *Development Benefits of Water Resource Investments*. Springfield, VA: Clearinghouse for Federal Scientific and Technical Information, No. IWR 69-1 and IWR 69-1-A, 1969.

Leven, C. L., J. Legler, and P. Shapiro. *An Analytical Framework for Regional Development Policy*. Cambridge: The M.I.T. Press, 1970.

Leven, C. L. and R. B. Read. *A River, A Region and A Research Project*. Springfield, VA: National Technical Information Service No. IWR 76-1, 1971.

Lever, W. F. "Manufacturing Linkages, Industrial Dynamics and the Transmission of Growth," *Regional Science and Urban Economics*, 10 (1980), 491–502.
Lewis, William C. and James R. Prescott. "Urban-Regional Development and Growth Centers: An Econometric Study," *Journal of Regional Science*, 12 (1972), 57–70.
Liu, Ben-Chieh. "Local Government Finance and Metropolitan Employment Growth—A Simultaneous-Equation Model," *Southern Economic Journal*, 43 (1977), 1379–1385.
McCullouch, Rachel and Janet L. Yellen. "Factor Mobility, Regional Development, and the Distribution of Income," *Journal of Political Economy*, 85 (1977), 79–96.
McDermott, Philip J. "Capital Subsidies and Unemployed Labour—A Comment on the Regional Production Function Approach," *Regional Studies*, 11 (1977), 203–210.
MacKay, R. Ross and Lydia Thomson. "Important Trends in Regional Policy and Regional Employment—A Modified Interpretation," *Scottish Journal of Political Economy*, 26 (1979), 233–260.
Macrae, Norman. "Tomorrow's Agglomeration Economics," in C. L. Leven (ed.), *The Mature Metropolis*. Lexington, MA: Lexington Books, 1978, pp. 131–145.
Maddox, James G. (ed.). *Growth Prospects of the Piedmont Crescent*, Papers presented at conference in Charlotte, NC. Raleigh, NC: The Agricultural Policy Institute, North Carolina State University, 1968.
Malecki, Edward J. ""Technology and Regional Development: A Survey," *International Regional Science Review*, 8 (1983), 89–125.
Malizia, Emil and Dianne Reid. "Perspectives and Strategies for U.S. Regional Development," *Growth and Change*, 7 (1976), 41–47.
Mansell, Robert L. and Robert W. Wright. "Evaluating Large-Scale Investment Impacts on the Regional Economy," *Growth and Change*, 9 (1978), 23–30.
Martin, Randolph C. "Federal Regional Development Programs and U.S. Problem Areas," *Journal of Regional Science*, 19 (1979), 157–170.
Martin, Roscoe C. (ed.). *TVA: The First Twenty Years: A Staff Report*. Knoxville, TN: University of Tennessee Press, 1956.
Mazek, Warren F. "Unemployment and the Efficacy of Migration: The Case of Laborers," *Journal of Regional Science*, 9 (1969), 101–107.
Miernyk, William H. "A Note on Recent Regional Growth Theories," *Journal of Regional Science*, 19 (1979), 303–308.
———. "The Tools of Regional Development Policy," *Growth and Change*, 11 (1980), 2–6.
Miernyk, William H., E. R. Bonner, J. H. Chapman, Jr., and K. Shellhammer. *Impact of the Space Program on Local Economy*. Morgantown, WV: West Virginia University Library, 1967.
Mills, Edwin S. "Welfare Aspects of National Policy toward City Sizes," *Urban Studies*, 9 (1972), 117–124.
Mills, Edwin S. and Katsutoshi Ohta. "Asia's New Giant: Urbanization and Urban Problems," in Hugh Patrick and Henry Rosovsky (eds.), *Asia's New Giant: How the Japanese Economy Works*. Washington: Brookings Institution, 1976, pp. 673–751.
Moore, Barry and John Rhodes. "Regional Policy and the Scottish Economy," *Scottish Journal of Political Economy*, 21 (1974), 215–235.
Mulkey, David and B. L. Dillman. "Location Effects of State and Local Industrial Development Subsidies," *Growth and Change*, 7 (1976), 37–43.
Muth, Richard F. *Cities and Housing*. Chicago: University of Chicago Press, 1969.
Needleman, L. (ed.). *Regional Analysis*. Baltimore: Penguin Books, 1968.
Needleman, L. and B. Scott. "Regional Problems and Location of Industry Policy in Britain," *Urban Studies*, 1 (1964), 153–173.
Nicholson, B. M., Ian Brinkley, and Alan W. Evans. "The Role of the Inner City in the Development of Manufacturing Industry," *Urban Studies*, 18 (1981), 57–71.
O'Farrell, P. N. "Multinational Enterprises and Regional Development: Irish Evidence," *Regional Studies*, 14 (1980), 141–150.
Olsen, Bernard M. and Gerald Garb. "An Application of Factor Analysis to Regional Economic Growth," *Journal of Regional Science*, 6 (1965), 51–56.
Pal, M. N. "A Method of Regional Analysis of Economic Development with Special Reference to South India," *Journal of Regional Science*, 5 (1963), 41–58.

Pascal, Anthony H. and John J. McCall. "Agglomeration Economies, Search Costs, and Industrial Location," *Journal of Urban Economics*, 8 (1980), 383–388.

Perloff, Harvey S. "The Development of Urban Economics in the United States," *Urban Studies*, 10 (1973), 289–301.

Perloff, H. and C. L. Leven. "Toward an Integrated System of Regional Accounts: Stock, Flows, and the Analysis of the Public Sector," in W. Hirsch (ed.), *Studies in Regional Accounts*. Baltimore, MD: The Johns Hopkins University Press, 1964, pp. 175–210.

Perroux, Francois. "Economic Space: Theory and Applications," *Quarterly Journal of Economics*, 64 (1950), 89–104.

Pfister, Richard L. "The Terms of Trade as a Tool of Regional Analysis," *Journal of Regional Science*, 3 (1961), 57–66.

President's Water Resources Council. "Policies, Standards, and Procedures in the Formulation, Evaluation, and Review of Plans for Use and Development of Water and Related Land Resources," Washington, D.C., U.S. Senate Doc. 97, 87th Cong., 2nd Session, 1962.

Rand-McNally. *Places Rated Almanac*. Skokie, IL: Rand-McNally Publishers, 1985.

Rasmussen, David W., Marc Bendick, Jr., and Larry C. Ledebur. "A Methodology for Selecting Economic Development Incentives," *Growth and Change*, 15 (1984), 18–25.

Rich, D. C. "Locational Disadvantage and the Regional Problem: Manufacturing Industry in Scotland, 1961–1971," *Regional Studies*, 14 (1980), 399–417.

Richardson, Harry W. "Regional Growth Theory: A Reply to von Böventer," *Urban Studies*, 12 (1975), 31–35.

———. *Regional Economics*. Urbana: University of Illinois Press, 1978.

Richardson, Harry W. and Margaret Richardson. "The Relevance of Growth Center Strategies to Latin America," *Economic Geography*, 51 (1975), 163–178.

Riefler, Roger F. "Nineteenth-Century Urbanization Patterns in the United States," *Journal of Economic History*, 39 (1979), 961–974.

Romans, J. Thomas. *Capital Exports and Growth Among U.S. Regions*. Middleton, CT: Wesleyan University Press, 1965.

Rondinelli, Dennis A. *Secondary Cities in Developing Countries—Policies for Diffusing Urbanization*, 145, Sage Library of Social Research. Beverly Hills, CA: Sage Publications, Inc., 1983.

Rostow, W. W. *The Economics of Take-Off Into Sustained Growth*. New York: St. Martin's Press, 1965.

Sazama, Gerald W. "A Benefit-Cost Analysis of a Regional Development Incentive: State Loans," *Journal of Regional Science*, 10 (1970), 385–396.

Senior, Nassau William. *Three Lectures on the Rate of Wages*. London: Murray, 1831.

Sheppard, Steven and C. L. Leven. "Changing Structure of the Metropolitan Dimension of the U.S. Population," St. Louis, MO, Washington University, Institute for Urban and Regional Studies Working Paper RPS 5, 1984.

Smith, Donald Mitchell. "Regional Growth: Interstate and Intersectoral Factor Reallocations," *Review of Economics and Statistics*, 56 (1974), 353–359.

Smith, Paul E. "Markov Chains, Exchange Matrices, and Regional Development," *Journal of Regional Science*, 3 (1961), 27–36.

Spiegelglas, Stephen. "Some Aspects of State to State Commodity Flows in the United States," *Journal of Regional Science*, 2 (1960), 71–80.

Stevens, Benjamin H. "An Interregional Linear Programming Model," *Journal of Regional Science*, 1 (Summer 1958), 60–98.

Sveikauskas, Leo. "The Productivity of Cities," *Quarterly Journal of Economics*, 89 (1975), 393–413.

Thirlwall, A. P. "Regional Economic Disparities and Regional Policy in the Common Market," *Urban Studies*, 11 (1974), 1–12.

Thompson, Wilbur R. "The National System of Cities as an Object of Public Policy," *Urban Studies*, 9 (1972), 99–116.

Tiebout, Charles M. "A Pure Theory of Local Expenditure," *Journal of Political Economy*, 64 (1956), 414–424.

———. "Community Income Multipliers: A Population Growth Model," *Journal of Regional Science*, 2 (1960), 75–84.

———. *The Community Economic Base Study.* New York: Committee for Economic Development Supp. Paper 16, 1962.

Todd, Daniel. "Regional Intervention in Canada and the Evolution of Growth Center Strategies: Reply," *Growth and Change*, 9 (1978), 50–52.

Tooze, Michael J. "Regional Elasticities of Substitution in the United Kingdom in 1968," *Urban Studies*, 13 (1976), 35–44.

U.S. Department of Housing and Urban Development. *The President's National Urban Policy Report.* Washington: U.S. Department of Housing and Urban Development, 1978.

Vermot-Desroches, Bernard and Andre Joyal. "The State of Regional Economics: A Note on the French Contribution," *International Regional Science Review*, 4 (1979), 41–46.

Vitebskii, R. "Regional Differences in Expenditures on the Infrastructure," *Problems of Economics*, 21 (1979), 40–57.

von Böventer, Edwin. "Regional Growth Theory," *Urban Studies*, 12 (1975), 1–29.

Widner, Ralph R. "Evaluating the Administration of the Appalachian Regional Development Program," *Growth and Change*, 4 (1973), 25–29.

Williams, Daniel G. "Regional Development as Determined by Alternative Regional Goals," *Growth and Change*, 14 (1983), 23–37.

Wingo, Lowdon. "Issues in a National Urban Development Strategy for the United States," *Urban Studies*, 9 (1972), 3–28.

Woodward, Robert S. "The Effectiveness of Intra-Island Industrial Incentives in Puerto Rico," *National Tax Journal*, 27 (1974), 261–273.

Yamamura, Etsuo and Masaaki Iwasa. "Quantitative Model Analysis of the Regional Population and Economic Changes Arising from the Industrial Development," *Environmental Science, Hokkaido*, 7 (1984), 133–239.

[23]

Environment and Planning C: Government and Policy, 1987, volume 5, pages 197-218

Regional development: the Reagan-Thatcher legacy

M Chisholm
Department of Geography, Downing Place, Cambridge CB2 3EN, England
Received 9 May 1986; in revised form 26 August 1986

Abstract. During the 1950s and 1960s, it seemed that our understanding of regional growth processes had progressed far enough for confident policy prescriptions to be advanced. From the vantage point of the 1980s, that assurance seems to have been misplaced. The paper contains a review of the debate on regional growth processes and the policy implications, in the context first of Britain and then more generally. It is shown that there has been a strong move away from the advocacy of traditional redistributive, and essentially zero-sum, policies to the view that intraregional policies to foster the supply potential are more appropriate. This shift in emphasis is partly attributable directly to the current high rates of unemployment. Probably more important has been the associated emergence of the monetarist/supply-side challenge to Keynesian demand-management orthodoxy. This macroeconomic debate is briefly reviewed and the implications for regional policy indicated. In the concluding section, an outline is provided of the supply-side approach to regional development that seems relevant for the foreseeable future, not as a replacement for traditional redistributive policies but as a necessary, and hitherto somewhat neglected, complement.

1 Introduction

In regional development theory and practice, the 1960s were a golden age. It seemed that our theoretical understanding of regional growth processes had become sufficiently sophisticated that good policy prescriptions could be made. Furthermore, the skill of governments appeared to be adequate, so that practical policies as implemented seemed to be making tangible progress. From the vantage point of 1987, that confidence, however appropriate two decades ago, now seems questionable, if not misplaced. On any reading of the literature and of events, one must conclude that scholars and practitioners alike are now casting around to understand what it is that drives regional development, and hence to derive appropriate goals and instruments for public policy.

There are several reasons for this rather remarkable change, reasons that are in part interrelated. Ever since 1973/74, when the first major jump in oil prices occurred, the world economy has been sluggish, and in most developed nations unemployment has been unwontedly high (though the 1986 slump in oil prices raised hopes of higher growth rates). At least in Britain, serious doubts have emerged concerning the efficacy of traditional regional policy, especially the small number of jobs actually diverted to the Assisted Areas, and the high public cost for each job so shifted (Moore and Rhodes, 1982; Moore et al, 1983). Another obvious fact is the change in political stance and rhetoric that occurred with the advent of Mrs Thatcher in 1979 as Prime Minister in Britain, and of Mr Reagan in 1980 as President of the United States of America. In both cases, the rhetoric has emphasised the virtues of government disengagement from intervention and the merits of a 'new' approach to macroeconomic management; however, rhetoric and action do not always coincide. A further point to be noted in the present context is the growth, at 'grass roots' level, of locally based development efforts—local authority initiatives, enterprise trusts, locally based programmes of regional development agencies, etc. In part, these developments reflect despair that national programmes can be adequate to fulfill local aspirations; in part, also, they are a response to changing perceptions regarding the nature of regional growth processes in developed economies.

These themes are reflected in the debate that is currently going on in the regional development literature, as well as in the literature in macroeconomic theory. In this paper, both debates are reviewed, and the links between them are demonstrated. Underlying the whole discussion, however, are three issues of fundamental importance for the way we perceive regional development in the more advanced nations, and it is these themes that will form the warp and woof of the remainder of this paper. They will be stated rather baldly now, and will be elaborated as the discussion proceeds.

1. In traditional regional growth theory a region is envisaged as subject to exogenous, mainly demand, impulses. Endogenous, or supply-side, issues have been very largely neglected.

2. An orientation to exogenous demand implies that, in policy terms, regional development will be seen as largely a zero-sum problem, a matter of reallocating a given demand (stock of firms, jobs) in space. The utility of such an approach is clearly questionable at a time of high general unemployment.

3 Twenty years ago, it seemed that the future could be predicted with reasonable confidence. For example, 'growth' industries could be identified (for example, vehicle manufacture) and their location patterns manipulated in order to foster development in desired locations. With market saturation for some products, more intense international competition, and rapid technological change, the future is now more generally perceived to be uncertain rather than certain (Piore and Sabel, 1984).

Figure 1 summarises some of these points. If we start from the apex, the national economy and its growth rate, the left-hand side and middle of the diagram represent 'traditional' approaches to regional growth processes and policy, whereas the right-hand side portrays aspects which hitherto have been relatively neglected. The bottom line distinguishes between economic and social justifications for regional policy. The traditional zero-sum view leads one to consider that, in a time of high

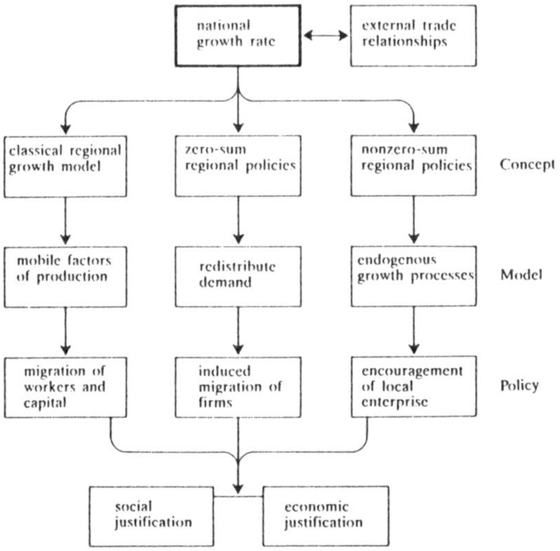

Figure 1. Schematic representation of regional policy options.

unemployment, economic and social considerations will probably be pulling in opposite directions. In contrast, following the right-hand side of figure 1, we may properly conclude that in many cases they will point in the same direction.

In this paper, some of the more important issues that have been raised in the preceding paragraphs will be examined. Two major topics will be addressed in turn: the current debate in the regional development literature in Britain and more generally; and the macroeconomic debate between Keynesian and monetarist protagonists. These sections pave the way for reconsidering the purpose of regional policies and the appropriate instruments. First, however, let us consider the regional policy debate in Britain, and then more generally.

2 Regional policy debate, with special reference to Britain

In a period of high general unemployment and sluggish economic growth, there is no doubt that the best regional policy is in fact a policy for national recovery (Moore and Rhodes, 1982; Wilson, 1982). The open nature of regional economies in Britain, and even in the USA, means that all regions will share, even if unequally, in any resurgence of economic activity. However, although this point would be generally accepted, there is considerable disagreement concerning the measures that it is appropriate for governments to take at the macroeconomic level in order to achieve faster growth, a matter to which I will turn later.

Pending national economic recovery, the question remains, as Rees (1985, page 471) puts it: "Is there still a national economic case for regional policy?" Note the emphasis on the *economic* case, as distinct from the social case, for conventional regional policy. In the present context, the social case may be set aside, for the following reason:

> "however much regional policies of the conventional type are strengthened, if they are pursued against a background of continued unfavourable macroeconomic conditions, their 'social' role will be largely limited to simply spreading the misery of mass unemployment more 'fairly' around the country while providing little boost to total economic activity or employment" (Martin and Hodge, 1983b, page 319).

In contrast, if there is 'full employment' in some regions but not in others, a regional policy which is redistributive in form will not be zero-sum in practice. If steps are taken to encourage the movement of firms from the regions with a 'high pressure of demand' to regions where labour resources are surplus, either of two things may be achieved. For a given level of national output, the rate of inflation will be lower than would otherwise be the case. Or, at a given rate of inflation, a greater national output could be achieved. In practice, the net addition to output that was possible in Britain in the 1960s amounted to only about 1%, or the national growth that could be achieved in three or four months (Wilson, 1979, page 81). In the absence of even this benefit, Rees (1985) identifies two possible economic justifications for a redistributive, initially zero-sum, regional policy.

In the context of recent economic thinking, which may be variously labelled as 'new right', monetarist, or supply-side (though these terms are not strictly synonymous), the concept of a 'natural' rate of unemployment has gained some support. If this concept is accepted, then it may be argued that the long-run national 'natural' rate of unemployment will be somewhat lower if regional disparities in unemployment are reduced. In the long run, this would enable the economy to perform at a somewhat higher level of output than might otherwise be possible at a given rate of inflation. This argument is difficult to distinguish from the more conventional argument for reducing regional unemployment differentials, in that any benefit to total output must wait on an upturn in the economy and the reappearance of pressure on labour supplies.

An alternative economic justification for regional policies of a redistributive character would exist if some clear link could be established between the proportion of the working population in a given area that is unemployed and attitudes to work, the level of crime, etc. If a positive link exists, the equalisation of regional unemployment rates might have a significant beneficial economic effect in both the short run and the long run. However, although it is likely that some link does exist, the nature of the association has not been established in an unequivocal fashion. Therefore, this justification for redistributive regional policies is hard to sustain.

Consequently, thoughts have been turning to an alternative concept of the purpose of regional policy. Two lines of thought may be identified, one that may be described as pessimistic, the other as essentially optimistic. The pessimistic view has been advanced by Wray (1983), writing from his experience in Merseyside. He starts from the premises that further absolute decline in some major centres, of which Merseyside is one, is inevitable; that past regional policies oriented to *areas* have failed; and that for the future a new orientation is required, to helping *people* in less fortunate regions cope with the problems they face. Wray identifies four major ingredients of future regional policy. First, he identifies the need for greater labour mobility, both sectorally and geographically, and the consequential need to examine the operation of the housing market, the availability of training facilities, and the need for migration assistance. Second, investment in human capital, in the form of assistance for individuals setting up businesses and incentives for firms which are human-capital intensive to establish/expand in the less prosperous areas, is needed. More generally, the supply of entrepreneurial talent needs to be expanded. His third point is the need consciously to plan for contraction, which implies making the best use of existing social capital rather than earmarking land for grandiose new projects which are unlikely to materialise. The fourth and last suggestion is for 'cost-effective' job creation. Wray notes the high cost of 'creating' a job in manufacturing by traditional regional policy means and compares this with the much lower (net) costs of providing jobs for "housing improvement and insulation, energy conservation, re-cycling, waste reclamation and environmental improvement" (page 470). Although job creation of this kind is likely to improve a region's long-term attractiveness and hence potential for prosperity, these cost-effective jobs are temporary, in the sense that to maintain a given number of jobs in an area, continuing expenditure is required.

Although one must accept the general thesis that the relative importance and prosperity of major cities will vary over time, and although there are some optimistic elements in Wray's arguments, the general line of reasoning he advances is to the effect that Liverpool, and other major cities, must be assisted in a major downward adjustment of population and activity. That degree of pessimism seems to be unwarranted, and is in any case potentially explosive politically.

A small number of scholars have been arguing that the emphasis on redistributive regional policies is misplaced, and that regional policy should be regarded as part of a general approach to growth. Wilson (1979) has noted the massive scale of inter-regional transfers that takes place in a modern economy, transfers that can be and are used to reduce income disparities, even if not to achieve complete income equality. Given that this is the case, Wilson concludes that regional policy, viewed in the most general sense, should be conceived as "assistance with regional economic development ... by making the less prosperous regions more efficient" (pages 106–107). Even in a period of severe recession, such a policy is in the national interest, since an important factor in overcoming national recession must be a general increase in efficiency in order to compete in foreign and domestic markets (see Chisholm, 1985).

In one of the most thoughtful contributions to date, Martin and Hodge (1983a; 1983b) see a clear economic case for public intervention in the space economy, with the primary aim of fostering 'indigenous' (local) development which would represent net additions to the national economy, not just a redistribution of the existing stock of jobs. They advocate two major lines of policy to achieve this end: first, better targeted, more selective, and coordinated instruments of central government intervention, through investment grants, etc; second, the fostering of local initiatives in the form of enterprise trusts, county council involvement in employment promotion, and the like. In addition, they emphasise the need to provide adequate training facilities to 'reskill' the labour force (see also Wilson, 1982) and the need for greater labour mobility. In essence, the policy prescription is to foster local growth by a combination of central and local initiatives working in harness, the local initiatives focusing specifically on the role of local authorities—counties and districts.

This conclusion is consistent with evidence presented by Fothergill and Gudgin (1979) that, at least in Britain, regionally differentiated rates of employment growth are due primarily to differing performances of 'indigenous', as distinct from immigrant, firms. Their evidence shows quite clearly that influencing the location choices of mobile firms, however significant as an instrument of policy in the immediate post-war period, had by 1966-71 ceased to be the major factor affecting employment change in regions generally regarded as in need of assistance. It follows that if regional employment change is to be affected beneficially, the greater part of the influence must be via existing firms—assisting them to maintain and expand employment—and the formation of new ones. At a time when the relocation of firms is essentially a zero-sum game, emphasis on indigenous firms (existing or potential) clearly offers hope of expanding total (national) activity and employment in the short to medium term, at the same time as expanding the long-term supply capacity of the economy. Such an emphasis puts the spotlight on innovation in general and new-firm formation in particular (Armstrong and Taylor, 1985).

At the most general level, such an approach requires three strands of policy to be implemented, over and above any policy there may be for continuing redistributive action. First, national and regional agencies, such as the Manpower Services Commission (MSC) and the Scottish Development Agency (SDA), should be aware of locally differing needs and be organised to respond thereto. Whereas the SDA has in recent years been implementing an imaginative series of locally based development initiatives, regrettably the MSC appears not to have grasped the need, let alone begun to devise a proper package of locally based policies. Second, local bodies, whether county and district councils, enterprise trusts, etc, need active encouragement; and consideration needs to be given to changes in their powers that might be desirable. Yet, however well national and local agencies may work together, a necessary condition of success is the third ingredient. Certain national policies may have quite serious local consequences in inhibiting useful development. For example, the fact that derelict and vacant land is exempt from rates implies that there is little incentive to bring the land back into use. The bizarre situation can arise that up to 10% of the land in inner cities is idle (Chisholm, 1983)—even, as in the Glasgow Eastern Area Renewal (GEAR) district of Glasgow in 1976, as much as 18% (Leclerc and Draffan, 1984). Or consider the housing stock. It is clearly much easier, subject to planning regulations under the 1947 and subsequent Town and Country Planning Acts, to start a small business in an owner-occupied dwelling than in a rented one, and in a two-storey house than in a high-rise flat. The nature and distribution of the housing stock must have some impact on the supply of entrepreneurs. Both the land and the housing questions involve government departments—the Department of the Environment in both cases—and policy at the national level which may have regionally differentiated effects. Until these are examined in a systematic way, and action taken to remove local supply bottlenecks, the fostering of indigenous enterprise is likely to be unnecessarily uphill work.

One of the more elegant and direct expressions of the need for a new approach to regional policy is the 1979 essay by Segal, with reference to less prosperous regions whose former prosperity rested on coal and/or heavy manufacturing industries, typically supplying capital goods. Segal notes the traditional view that their present problems reside in deficient demand, which causes high unemployment. However, he argues that this is only half the explanation:

> "The real questions to be answered are: (a) why have the regions' specialist industries failed to benefit from *growing but changing* markets in their own and related industries? and (b) why have the regions failed to generate new and different activities on a sufficient scale to compensate for the decline in the traditional industries?" (Segal, 1979, page 213).

For, as he points out:

> "The key feature of a strong regional economy is its ability to adapt—to adapt its attitudes, skills, products, supporting institutions and infrastructure in response to constantly (but unpredictably) changing economic circumstances" (page 212).

In considering the 'supply response' or 'supply capability' of a region, we must also consider the nature of the historical legacy, which is region-specific, and consider four lines of policy that may be pursued. The focus is upon the need to encourage entrepreneurial activity, to diversify regional economies, to improve social overhead capital in order to attract and retain senior personnel, and to review institutional arrangements of all kinds.

Within the conventional approach to regional policy, as portrayed by the middle of figure 1, the major supply-side variable that has been considered is labour, but only in the rather restricted sense of the contrast between work to the workers and workers to the work, that is, the question of labour migration. The supply-side ideas emergent in the British debate on regional policy go far beyond this rather crude dichotomy, to emphasise a whole suite of supply-side considerations focused on the operation of the multiplicity of locally articulated markets. This is a view that I have advanced for a number of years (Chisholm, 1974; 1976; 1983; 1984; 1985). But it is also a view that has been severely criticised.

The view, as Richardson (1984b, page 276) has put it, that "the local development process must be *endogenized*" has come under attack from several quarters. Before proceeding with the main argument of this paper, some consideration must be given to these criticisms. The most extreme viewpoint is the 'uneven development' school, exemplified by two collections of essays, one edited by Carney et al (1980), and the other by Anderson et al (1983). Uneven development is visualised as a process characterising 'capitalist' economies, in which 'monopoly capital' can operate at will across geographical space in its search for maximum profits. In doing so, capital is viewed as 'hypermobile', that is, as facing low, nearly zero, costs of relocation; therefore, so it is argued, monopoly capital may move into an area and then abandon it within the space of a few years. As Richardson (1984a, page 16) observes:

> "A central proposition of the uneven regional development theorists is that regional growth differentials do not reflect the net result of the operation of abstract and impersonal market forces but the purposive actions of the capitalist class. Moreover, as long as capitalism survives, intervention to correct regional inequalities will be ineffectual because the state is merely the coercive instrument of capitalist class interests".

If the problem of regional development is viewed from this perspective, the following conclusion is offered by Damette (1984, page 78):

> "The central problem in spatial planning is to offer monopolies the optimal spatial conditions for maximising profits".

Looked at from the viewpoint of particular localities, Morgan and Sayer (1983, page 46) assert:

> "parochial solutions to regional problems ... are not solutions at all. This is not to say that nothing can be done at the local level, but that most of what can be done will have to be in alliance with other areas as part of a wider strategy to wrest economic power from the divisive control of capital".

This last statement implies a form of 'socialist' revolution, and is predicated on a number of assumptions, of which two are worth particular attention. First is the idea that in a 'capitalist' economy regions are in thrall to exogenous forces, embodied in 'monopoly capital', and have no control over their destiny. The second point, made explicitly by Morgan and Sayer, is that if one region becomes more competitive (more efficient), then "other regions would become less competitive" (page 44). This implies a wistful, but unrealistic, desire to opt out of technical and economic change.

A somewhat different critique has been mounted by Holland (1976). He focuses attention on the mesoeconomic sector, and the role of large multiplant multinational companies. He views these as the dominant element in national and regional development, able to pursue their own goals—profit maximisation—with relatively little control by national governments. In Holland's view, government strategy should be based on the old adage, "if you cannot beat them, join them". New public enterprises should be set up, giving the state control of the location of investments; planning agreements should be reached with the large private-sector companies to regulate their location choices; subsidies should be given to growth sectors investing in lagging regions; and, if necessary, direct control should be imposed on the large companies. By these means, Holland believes the mesoeconomic sector could be harnessed, and the otherwise inevitable concentration of activities into a few regions reversed, to the benefit of lagging regions.

Holland does not address the following question. If the mesoeconomic sector can obtain greater profits by locating in a prosperous ('central') region than in a lagging ('peripheral') one, what would be the magnitude of the profits foregone were the package of policies he advocates actually implemented? It is that loss which would represent the direct cost of his policy prescription, on his premises. It can also be noted that, as with the uneven development school, Holland views regions as having no control over their destiny.

This last point has been addressed by Massey (1979) and Massey and Meegan (1978). Their central thesis is that if an area (region) is identified as presenting 'problems'—for example, high unemployment—it is incorrect to look for the causes in the same area (region). This is because the local symptoms arise from the operation of national or international processes; in the context of the two papers mentioned, these were processes of 'restructuring' during a period of severe recession. Massey and Meegan are right to point out that national and international processes are important, though this is hardly a novel observation. They are equally right to point out that these large-scale processes intersect with the cost surfaces which face firms. However, it seems odd to argue, as they do, that the sole source of change is the former, the latter remaining static and unchanging. Purely in cost terms, it seems likely that local action—not just by local authorities—may have some impact: land costs are affected by planning controls, rates and local taxes are influenced by local expenditure programmes, etc. Equally important, though, is the influence that local action may have on the more general perception surface facing firms in their location choices.

Therefore, although Massey and Meegan are clearly right to argue that local problems cannot be solved only by local action, they are surely mistaken to suggest that there is nothing local communities can do, with or without outside assistance, to help themselves.

This discussion of changing ideas about regional development processes in Britain indicates a considerable divergence of viewpoints. At the most general level, it is clear that traditional zero-sum redistributive policies are not appropriate for present-day circumstances, if ever they were appropriate. A major strand in the debate, however, is awareness that locally based development must be considered, at least as a partial solution for areas of high unemployment. However, it is also clear that this view has not achieved full acceptance, and it is clear that so far these ideas have emerged without full articulation to wider debates in the field of economics. Nevertheless, similar ideas are being expressed in the more general literature about regional development, as will be shown in the following section.[8]

3 A more general view of the regional growth debate

The wider debate on regional growth processes encompasses several major themes, and, broadly, may be characterised in the following way. Neoclassical regional growth theory postulates a tendency toward equilibrium in which the returns to labour and capital will be equalised among regions. In contrast, the disequilibrium models of Myrdal (1957) and Hirschman (1958) present a mechanism that may lead to prolonged disequilibrium, with continuing or accentuated disparities in income, employment, etc. This second view is paralleled by the Keynesian income multiplier approach to regional growth processes. On the whole, the disequilibrium views have seemed to provide a more accurate description of reality than does the neoclassical formulation. In face of the seemingly permanent nature of regional disparities, despite substantial government intervention in many countries, four reactions can be identified in the literature:

1. the invocation of further factors, such as the product/income cycle, to explain the failure of development to produce regional income and employment equality;
2. the postulated need for even greater government intervention to correct the perceived inequalities;
3. despair that regional (national) prosperity can be achieved in the absence of partial, if not complete, insulation of the region (nation) from the wider national (international) economy;
4. an interest in the processes of change and adjustment within regions, with a view to identifying and remedying the bottlenecks and deficiencies.

These themes will be briefly considered in the paragraphs that follow.

"Neoclassical models have dominated regional growth theory" (Richardson, 1973, page 22), or had certainly done so at the time Richardson wrote. If we postulate homogeneous linear regional production functions, and the free mobility both of goods and of the factors of production other than land, then it is not difficult to develop a model in which labour will migrate from low-wage (low-productivity) regions to high-wage ones. Capital will move in the opposite direction, as entrepreneurs seek maximum rates of return. Such a model is, in essence, a model for the reallocation of resources in conformity with comparative advantage as formulated by Hecksher and Ohlin, rather than a model of growth in a strict sense. It is this model which Borts and Stein (1964) set out to test with long-run data for the states of the USA. Although their results do not yield high levels of association between the variables they were able to use, the general run of their findings is that, between the late nineteenth century and the 1950s, factor migration was a significant element in the income convergence that occurred.

The Borts and Stein study took a long-run view of a single economy. Experience elsewhere led other observers to conclude that permanent or quasi-permanent disequilibrium characterises the regional development process. Myrdal in 1957 and Hirschman a year later both advanced the idea that once an initial impetus has been experienced in one or more regions, the marginal return both to capital and to labour will be higher in that region (those regions), leading to a cumulative migration of both factors into the favoured region (regions). A polarisation of development will thus occur, in which regional economic and social disparities will increase. Both Myrdal and Hirschman emphasised that in time some of the development should spread from the initially favoured centre(s). Two main mechanisms can be envisaged which would have this effect:

1. the demand generated by the favoured centre(s) for food and raw materials will trigger a cumulative development process in previously lagging regions;
2. diseconomies of scale—pollution, traffic congestion, land prices, etc—will erode the initial advantage of the favoured region(s) and ultimately lead to an expansion of the developed area.

Williamson (1965) compiled evidence consistent with the disequilibrium model, showing regional income disparities widening during the early stages of development and then narrowing. However, for most observers the closure phase has seemed either so far removed in future time or so mild in its effects that the second part of the Myrdal/Hirschman model has appeared to be an article of faith rather than a probable outcome. In any case, the Keynesian income multiplier has given a strong intellectual boost to the cumulative causation model.

It was North (1955) who formulated and popularised the idea of the export base as the foundation for regional prosperity, though the idea had previously been in circulation, having, for example, been used by Innis (1930; 1936) as an explanatory framework for his studies of Canadian economic history. North expressed the role of exports in terms of a 'stages' approach to the sequence of events in the development process. A more general formulation, derived from national income concepts in the Keynesian tradition, may be expressed as

$$Y = \frac{1}{m} X ,$$

where Y is regional income, X is regional exports, m is the propensity to import, and $1/m$ is the export multiplier.

As Kaldor (1970, page 342) observed, in such a formulation "the rate of economic development of a region is fundamentally governed by the rate of growth of its exports". In addition to the direct mechanism embodied in the above identity, Kaldor emphasised two additional factors that will ensure the cumulative growth of regions initially blessed with a strong demand for their exports:

1. increased export activity implies an enlargement of the regional economy and the attendant economies of scale to which Young drew attention in 1928;
2. capital investment to match higher output implies the embodiment of 'best practice' technology, so that the productivity of labour in the prosperous region will rise faster than in slow growing regions.

On the assumption that wages rise more slowly than does productivity, the 'efficiency wage' of the prosperous region(s) will fall, and it (they) will be able to capture an ever larger share of export markets (the Verdoorn effect). This reasoning leads one to believe that once a region gains a lead it will be able to maintain and enlarge its advantage (see Armstrong and Taylor, 1985).

Kaldor's formulation of the Keynesian income multiplier in regional terms provides powerful intellectual reasons for the maintenance of regional income disparities or their enlargement (however, see Chisholm, 1985). This theory of regional development seemed to accord with the experience of a number of countries, Britain included. Furthermore, during the 1970s it began to appear that the forces generating regional disparities were far too strong for the policies that were in place in various countries with the aim of reducing/eliminating spatial inequalities. The apparently inexorable relative growth of the more prosperous regions led to a number of divergent conclusions.

The first of these divergent lines of enquiry relevant in the present context may be labelled as the search for yet further mechanisms that reinforce the tendency for success to breed success. Perhaps the most notable is the product cycle hypothesis (Steiner, 1985), which has been generalised as the profit cycle by Markusen (1985). Briefly, it can be argued that individual industries experience a 'cycle' from initial technological development, through maturity, to senescence, which is associated with changes in the rate of profit. If a region's economy is dominated by an oligopolistic industry, a period of declining regional prosperity will, in this formulation, inevitably follow after a period of rapidly increasing relative wealth. On the other hand, a region which has a large number of firms operating in competitive markets will enjoy the benefit of nonsynchronous profit cycles, and therefore will be able to maintain its prosperity. Markusen seems to regard the theoretical and empirical evidence on profit cycles as providing a clear affirmation that there is an historical inevitability about the process, though at one point she does indicate that this inevitability might be tempered:

> "The point is that the rise and decline of a region's economic base are predictable developmental events. This is not to say that all communities are equally vulnerable to the passage of industries through profit cycles. ... The long-term development potential of any community or region does appear to depend on its ability to attract newer sectors to supplant (*sic*) job losses in the older ones" (Markusen, 1985, page 279).

In contrast, Steiner is more explicit about the possibility of a region breaking out of the development sequence that history might appear to ordain. Nevertheless, the general thrust of the product/profit cycle approach is to underline the strength of the economic forces with which regions have to contend, and thereby to reinforce the sense of despair that present policies of government intervention can redress the balance.

That sense of despair has led observers to two contrasting conclusions. Holland's views on the need for more government intervention, especially in relation to the mesoeconomic sector, have already been summarised (page 203). However, since the mid-1970s, nationalised industries around the world have been caught up with the problems of recession and capacity reduction, along with firms of all sizes, and it is not clear that the 'control' envisaged by Holland is in fact practicable in an interdependent world economy. Furthermore, one of the world-wide growth industries in recent years has been the privatisation business, actually reducing the power of governments to intervene directly in the spatial disposition of manufacturing resources. This experience over the past decade lends some support to an alternative approach to the problems posed for lagging regions by the apparent inability to control their destinies.

A passionate plea for development from below has been made by several authors, most notably by Friedmann and Weaver (1979), Stöhr (1981), Chambers (1983), and Weaver (1984; 1985). This literature is primarily concerned with the less developed nations, the Third World, and includes several common themes.

First, the authors are concerned that development should serve social goals and therefore, as Stöhr puts it, the criteria for evaluation of policies must differ from pure efficiency considerations. In the second place, the aim is to mobilise local resources and local initiatives, instead of relying on external development impulses. This implies a major change in perception and motivation on the part of the inhabitants. To achieve this mobilisation, it is contended that a higher degree of 'self-reliance' must be achieved, that is, greater autarky or partial system closure. This view is based on the belief that the present national and international arrangements serve to drain resources from the poor to the rich regions, a belief shared by the 'underdevelopment' school of economists in their consideration of national development processes, for example, Frank (1964; 1966; 1967) and Furtado (1964). Underlying this belief is the concept of 'unequal exchange' (Johnstone, 1980), which is derived from Marxian thinking about the working of 'capitalist' economic systems, a concept which I find impossible to accept (Chisholm, 1982). That aside, the logic of the unequal exchange thesis leads to the conclusion that a deliberate rupture in the exchange (trade) relationships is a necessary condition for the development of less prosperous nations or regions, the 'delinking' advocated by Fishlow et al (1978), or system closure, in part or in full.

This bundle of ideas, applied to regions within a nation, appears to be utopian and impractical, if only because deliberate system closure is not a policy option open to regions within a nation. One conclusion that might be drawn is that the inhabitants of less fortunate regions (nations) should "create spatially conscious counterstrategies at all geographical scales" (Soja, 1985, page 188). Although this may be a desirable thing to happen, it does not directly further our understanding of the processes of spatial growth and change; it is in fact a declaration of faith concerning the way in which society as a whole should be organised.

The last response to be noted may be described as attempts to probe the processes of regional development in order to gain a better understanding of what actually happens, why it does so, and hence the extent to which intervention may be possible. The first major statement of the theory of adjustment in a spatial context has been provided by Clark et al (1986). In brief, they argue that the concept of equilibrium is inappropriate and that by definition any spatial system which approximates reality will embody major imperfections, such that the study of adjustment is a necessary starting point for any examination of real regional systems. A major subset of this general theme is provided by the considerable amount of work that has been done in recent years on the location of 'high tech' industry and the role of innovations in regional development (for example, Ewers and Wettmann, 1980; Hall and Markusen, 1985; Meyer-Krahmer, 1985; Keeble and Kelly, 1986; Stöhr, 1986). Although it would be premature to claim that we have gained a sufficient insight into the mechanisms of adjustment and the reasons why innovations occur in a localised fashion, and therefore do not have a detailed prospectus of how to intervene, nevertheless the basic characteristic of this approach is clear. Instead of stressing exogenous (mainly demand) influences, emphasis on adjustment and innovation puts the spotlight on supply responses and the supply side generally.

The force of this assertion is vividly illustrated by Breckenfeld in Perry and Watkins's book *The Rise of the Sunbelt Cities* (1977). Most of the older industrial cities in the USA have lost very large numbers of people; eight had lost at least one-fifth of their 1950 total by 1975. As a result, the central areas were run-down and partially abandoned, a blight that exacerbated the loss of inhabitants and workers. Faced with these problems, the city administrators in New York, Cleveland, St Louis, and Detroit followed inept policies that compounded the difficulties, in

New York's case leading "to the thinly camouflaged state-federal receivership imposed in June 1976" (Breckenfeld, 1977, page 243). (Compare New York with Liverpool in 1986.) Philadelphia and Boston flirted with similar policies but pulled back, and subsequently have achieved a remarkable turnaround. In contrast, both Pittsburgh and Baltimore have been blessed with able leaders, who read the signs correctly and, over an extended period, have succeeded in transforming their cities. Both are cities which, on a 'product cycle' analysis, would be in irreversible decline; in fact, despite population loss, they remain vital cities, clearly viable for the foreseeable future. No better illustration would be possible to show that it is feasible for a city (region) to avoid terminal decline, and to do so largely by local effort, and thereby reverse "the triumph of misguided altruism over economic common sense" (Breckenfeld, 1977, page 251).

From this very brief discussion, it is evident that the regional policy debate in Britain has mirrored a much wider debate. In the wider arena as in the smaller, the last decade or so has seen the emergence of much greater interest in the mechanisms of regional adjustment and of endogenous endeavour, and what may be done to foster them, than has hitherto been the case. This trend in the regional policy literature is, in turn, but part of a wider debate couched in macroeconomic terms.

4 Macroeconomic debate

Any noneconomist who has attempted to follow the discussions concerning the nature of macroeconomic processes and the role of governments is likely to be as much confused as enlightened, for a combination of reasons. With voluminous and influential writers, whether Marx, Keynes, or anyone else who is no longer alive, there is a major problem to determine precisely what it is they did think, and to systematise those ideas into a consistent system. This problem is compounded by the natural tendency of contemporaries and successors to develop their own extensions and variants of fundamental doctrine. For example, Crotty (1980) identifies neo-Keynesian and post-Keynesian Keynesians, and Tobin (1981) recognises both monetarism 1 and monetarism 2. Perhaps mischievously, Meade (1981) believes that there are four kinds of macroeconomist, with real practitioners of the first three kinds; the fourth, being an empty box, contains no actual specimens:
1. non-Keynesian monetarists,
2. Keynesian monetarists,
3. Keynesian nonmonetarists,
4. non-Keynesian nonmonetarists.

To compound our problem even further, we must distinguish very carefully between the rhetoric of governments (the claims they make to be pursuing specified economic doctrine) and what they do in practice. The divergence can be disconcertingly large. Finally, given the fundamental theoretical differences that have emerged in the last one to two decades, "even where the protagonists can agree on which are the crucial variables to be tested and how to match the theoretical concepts with empirical constructs, the economic system does not stand still" (Deane, 1978, page 222), with the result that empirical testing of theory is difficult, if not impossible.

Some very important ideas are embodied in the discussion among economists, and it is the purpose of the ensuing paragraphs to identify some that have a relevance for regional growth theory. In a short space, it will be possible only to sketch the relevant issues. This will be done as undogmatically as possible, in an attempt to tease out issues of enduring importance that will outlive any present-day polemic.

With the publication of his *General Theory* in 1936, Keynes launched a revolution in economic thinking. Instead of microeconomic problems of price and equilibrium, he focused on macroeconomic matters and the then evident disequilibrium of the Great Depression (Harcourt, 1972; Deane, 1978). During this period, the 'impossible' had occurred—massive and sustained unemployment at a time of falling prices (and wages). This situation was 'impossible' within the framework of the then current orthodoxy, which, embodying Say's Law, expected supply to be matched by the requisite demand. Keynes's insight was that "employment was determined by effective demand rather than the state of confidence" (Bleaney, 1985, page 32), and furthermore: "He demonstrated in a way that had never been so dramatically and clearly brought out before, the dependence of aggregate expenditure on itself in its income-generating capacity" (Deane, 1978, page 183). In addition, Keynes showed that governments could intervene to manipulate the level of demand in the economy, with the aim of achieving full employment. A cardinal assumption of Keynes and his followers is that changes in aggregate demand will be matched by changes in aggregate supply, without variation in price level, within the bounds set by 'full employment'. Consequently, the task of governments is to adjust total demand, in response to changing circumstances, to maintain the requisite employment level.

The starting point for these ideas is the now-familiar, then novel, national income identity:

$$Y = C+I+G+X = C+S+T+M$$

where Y is gross national product (GNP), C is consumption, I is investment, G is government expenditure, X is exports, S is savings, T is taxes, and M is imports.

By definition, the above identity must be true for past periods of time. However, for future states of the economy, expectations may differ from realisations; this is a fundamental problem facing any policymaker but one that for the moment we will set aside.

In the short run, the population and the labour force in a country may be taken as given. Therefore, total employment will be a function of Y, which is a measure of total activity in the economy. The problem facing a government is to manipulate Y to achieve the desired level of employment. Two items in the above identity are directly under the control of governments (or are perceived to be), namely, government expenditure (G) and the amount raised in taxes (T). Changes in taxation also have a fairly direct impact on private consumption (C). In addition, governments have considerable control over interest rates, and it was (still is) thought that the interest-rate level controls (strongly influences) the level of investment (I) in the economy. In this formulation, the supply of money is regarded as unimportant, productivity is assumed to look after itself if demand conditions are appropriate, and supply is assumed to adjust to demand without price inflation, within the boundary set by 'full employment'. Consequently, it is further assumed that, for the purpose of economic management, it is immaterial whether demand consists of consumption or investment, etc, except that certain forms of investment (public works) are under the direct control of governments.

One must hasten to note that most, if not all, of these assumptions are patently unrealistic in some degree and it is unlikely that anyone, let alone Keynes himself, has ever conceived of an economy working in such a simple way. However, much of the elaboration in Keynesian economic thinking can fairly be described as the incorporation of constraints (for example, balance of payments) and complications (for example, the role of expectations) to make the underlying conceptual framework more 'realistic', or practically functional. The basic assumptions were not widely challenged, though Friedman fired his opening salvo in 1956 and Hazlitt mounted a blistering attack on Keynes in 1959; more moderate critiques of Keynesian thinking also appeared, for example, Wright (1962) and Patinkin (1965). Nevertheless, the 1950s and most of the 1960s witnessed remarkable rates of economic growth worldwide, the apparent abolition of cyclical depression, and the general acceptance that Keynesian policies of demand management worked. That consensus began to collapse in the early 1970s, with the emergence of a new phenomenon, 'stagflation', which, according to Keynesian orthodoxy, was 'impossible'.

This new 'impossibility' was the phenomenon of high and rising levels of unemployment coupled with accelerating inflation which, at various times in several countries, threatened to run out of control. Orthodox opinion held that if there were excess demand in an economy, this would call forth the requisite supply of goods and services until full employment was achieved. In practice, at much less than 'full employment', demand was being translated into price increases, independently of the oil price increases imposed by the nations of the Organization of Petroleum Exporting Countries in 1973/74 and again in 1979. This widespread experience among the industrial nations forced commentators to ask what was wrong with a theory that manifestly was yielding incorrect predictions?

Two aspects stand out. The first is associated in particular with Friedman (1985) and his concern with the quantity theory of money, which, to his disgust, is generally known as monetarism. The essential point of this concern is that money can be regarded as a commodity which is subject to supply and demand, and its 'price' depends on their relationship. Therefore, on this reasoning, the 'money supply' should be subject to regulation, with the aim of achieving a stable rate of growth commensurate with other economic targets; in other words, in contrast to the previous orthodoxy, money does matter.

The second manifest lesson is that, within the limit set by full employment, the supply of goods and services cannot be assumed to adjust quickly and properly to changes in aggregate demand. This adjustment process is itself, therefore, problematic, a fact which focuses attention on actual or potential supply bottlenecks, and raises the question of how government could and should intervene to eliminate, or at least reduce, the ill effects of supply deficiencies.

If we return to the national income identity on the previous page, we can see how it is that monetarist/supply-side economists part company from their Keynesian colleagues. Two main points are relevant. First, unlike Keynesians, supply-side economists regard the distinction between consumption (C) and investment (I) as being very important, and that therefore aggregate demand is not in fact homogeneous. The basic reason for this is that investment adds to the long-term capacity of the economy to produce goods and services, whereas consumption does not. Therefore, the ratio between the two is important, and it is not sufficient to rely on interest rates and aggregate demand to regulate the level of investment. In the second place, supply-side economists give much more attention to the incentive effects of tax regimes than do Keynesian economists, and indeed the arguments may be totally inverted. In the very short run, an increase in taxes may increase the incentive to work, as income earners struggle to maintain their accustomed standard of living. Simultaneously, as it is generally the case that individuals have a higher propensity to save than do governments, higher taxes will increase aggregate demand. Contrary to these Keynesian arguments, supply-side economists point to the long-run disincentive effects of high tax regimes, especially direct taxes, and to the necessity for a high level of savings to match a high level of investment. These issues have been thoughtfully discussed by Ture (1982).

In its most doctrinaire form, the counterrevolution to Keynesian thinking emphasises, almost to the exclusion of everything else, just two things: the necessity for governments to control the supply of money in order, primarily, to regulate the rate of inflation; and the benefits to be had from reducing rates of personal taxation, to foster the incentive to work. Such a view of the economy is every bit as simple as the basic Keynesian schema outlined above. In practice, supply-side economists are interested in the whole range of supply constraints and what might be done to ease bottlenecks—by deregulation in labour markets, land markets, etc (Drucker, 1981; Laidler, 1981). Underlying this interest is a concern with the long-run productive capacity of an economy, and deep scepticism that 'economist kings' can actually make the right decisions to fine tune an economy. The fundamental stance, therefore, is the belief that governments should use monetary weapons to establish a predictable environment in which individuals and firms can make sensible judgments about the future and act accordingly, subject to constraints on that behaviour deemed to be in the public interest, expressed in part by fiscal means.

The above account of the recent major debate in economics does scant justice to the range and complexity of the issues. It has been framed to show both the following features: the common starting point for the Keynesian and monetarist/supply-side protagonists in the national income identity; and the divergent emphasis given to different elements in that identity. However, as one attempts to refine either doctrine, one is driven to incorporate elements that are akin to the other doctrine, until something approaching an amalgam is developed. During the early 1980s, at the height of the Thatcher-Reagan attempt to shift the locus of economic management, newspaper headlines proclaiming that "we are all monetarists now" were not uncommon (for example, *The Times*, 1985). It would have been equally true to aver that we are all Keynesians:

> "Keynesianism, monetarism, and supply-side economics are not conflicting theories of how the economy works, but limited perspectives stressing different factors" (Greenhut and Stewart, 1983, page 263).

Whether or not a true integration of these perspectives is either possible or desirable (Matthews, 1981) is not particularly relevant in the present context. The issue of key importance for regional growth theory is the following. Until the political rhetoric of the Thatcher-Reagan era captured public imagination in the late 1970s and early 1980s, the supply-side perspective had been given a good deal less attention than it warrants. It seems likely that when Mrs Thatcher and Mr Reagan have quit the public stage, whatever the political complexion of succeeding administrations, there will be continuing recognition of the role of supply-side issues. However, it does appear that undue attention may have been given to the role of taxes in affecting personal incentives, and not enough to the wider range of supply-side issues. This is with reference to national policy questions. So far as I am aware, no attempt has yet been made to consider formally what a supply-side view of regional development processes implies, in contrast to the exogenous (demand) orientation of conventional regional growth theory. The need for such a framework of theory has been clearly shown in the debates on regional growth in Britain and elsewhere that have been summarised above. In approaching this task, we should carry in our minds the following observation by Drucker (1981, page 14), whose views are not dissimilar to those of Pratten (1985):

> "The next economics ... will require a theory that aims at optimizing productivity".

5 Implications for regional growth theory

Given the situation described in preceding sections, we must now consider what light the supply-side view can throw on regional growth processes, not with a view to suggesting that this will yield *the* answer, but as an elaboration of a perspective.

As a start to this exploration, evidence concerning the sources of *national* growth is briefly reviewed; this evidence has been summarised elsewhere (Chisholm, 1982).

Until relatively recently, it was widely believed that the long-term rate of growth of national economies was some function of the flow of capital investment. Rostow published his *The Stages of Economic Growth* in 1960. This book triggered a debate about the stages concept, but initially the *apparent* Rostow thesis, that the transition into self-sustained growth depended on a marked increase in the volume of investment as a share of GNP, was widely accepted. In fact, Rostow argued that such an increase could not take place prior to radical changes in socioeconomic ideas and habits in the Third World nations. Equally important, in major studies by Kuznets (1966; 1971) and Denison (1967), offering measurements of the contribution to increased output arising from labour supplies and capital stock changes, it was found that the *measurable* contribution of these factors was surprisingly small. This finding was summarised by Kuznets (1971, pages 306–307) as follows:

> "The rise in productivity amounts to at least eight-tenths of the rise in per capita product in several countries ... improvements in quality of labor and capital—improvements not caused by any extra input of resources—were responsible for the high rate of growth of per capita product so characteristic of modern economic growth. These 'costless' improvements are connected with the tremendous increase in the stock of useful knowledge, much of it traceable to growth of science viewed as a social institution devoted to the production of new tested and hence potentially useful knowledge."

A rather similar view, based on the available empirical work of Denison, Kuznets, and others, has been propounded by Schultz (1961; 1981). He argues that both in the less developed and in the more developed nations, it is human capital which is the main determinant of growth rates, not changes in the stock of conventional capital.

This view of the growth process clearly emphasises something that is completely outwith the arithmetic of national income identities. Equally clearly, the idea of human capital sits more easily with the long-term view which is characteristic of supply-side thinking. Indeed, the very concept of 'costless' productivity changes implies supply-side changes—in work practices and attitudes to new technology, the introduction of new products previously not imagined, etc.

If this is true at the national level, is it also true for regions within nations, at least in part? And, if it is, what does this imply for policy?

Traditional industrial location theory emphasises the location of raw materials, of labour supplies and of markets, and the costs of transporting inputs and outputs (Isard, 1956; Smith, 1971). This view is relevant for industries such as steel manufacture, but even for industries of this kind little or no attention is given to sources of variation in production costs that are attributable to managerial efficiency, capital productivity, etc, except for the limited case of variations in labour costs because of wage rate differences, unionisation, etc. One reason for the limited view taken in the location literature is that variations in efficiency—in effect, unit labour costs—are not very obviously linked to 'permanent' and spatially organised variables, like the location of markets. Yet, if the evidence of Denison, Kuznets, and others is accepted at the national level, it is probable that it is precisely the less traditional factors which are now the most important for many, if not most, location decisions—in other words, that the prosperity of a region depends on its human capital as much as, if not more than, on attributes of location, natural resources, etc. That in turn implies that maintaining the prosperity of a region depends on maintaining, and preferably improving, the quality of its human capital relative to the quality elsewhere. The reason why this is an ongoing competitive situation can be readily demonstrated.

During the last 150 years, several major industrial powers have emerged on the world scene; additional giants such as China, India, and Brazil are on the move (however hesitatingly); and significant Newly Industrialising Countries, such as Taiwan and Korea, have made their presence felt. No country now dominates the world industrial scene in the way that Britain did in the nineteenth century. As a consequence, any country that allows its productivity to slip behind that of its rivals, and allows its rate of product innovation to lag, will find its standard of living will increase less rapidly than the standard in other countries. If a nation does opt out of the productivity and innovation competition, the price will be relative, and possibly even absolute, decline in *per caput* income. This fact is inescapable.

Only if a short-term static view is taken could it be said that this competition is only a zero-sum game, in which any gain to one nation will be at the expense of another. Given the dynamic characteristics of the world economy, the post-1979 recession notwithstanding, the reality is that some change will have zero-sum characteristics and some will not. From a national perspective, it does not matter what the proportions of the two elements are.

When we consider a region within a nation, the same general point holds. A region, especially the industrial sector of a regional economy, is in competition with other regions within the nation, and with regions/nations abroad. To the extent that this competition is a zero-sum game, from the viewpoint of any one region this may be so either with other regions in the same country or with overseas competitors, or some combination of both. But some part of the competition may also be nonzero-sum in character. Viewed from the national perspective, it is desirable that as much regional growth as possible, summed across all regions, be nonzero-sum in character, or, if it is zero-sum, it is so with overseas competitors, not with other regions within the nation. Whether or not the competition is zero-sum in character, it is desirable that it be won on the basis of general efficiency—high productivity, good marketing, and appropriate innovation. In addition, governments may offer firms incentives, in the form of investment grants, etc, that may attract internationally mobile investment, but such assistance either is self-defeating (if everyone joins the game) or is apt to leapfrog upwards.

From the perspective of an individual region, the problem of maintaining competitiveness may be resolved into the following components. The ideal situation is that the existing firms, and the flow of new firms, together maintain their competitive position and are sufficiently numerous to provide (regional) full employment. This implies continuous productivity improvements, continuing change in work practices, product innovation, a supply of entrepreneurs, etc. In the absence of this ideal situation, if population and employment are to be maintained, a region may need one of two things. It may need to increase its stock of firms; or it may need to improve the business 'climate' through improvement to the physical environment and changes in local attitudes/supply bottlenecks. Often, both sets of changes are needed, and in many cases some form of help from the central government may be essential to enable a region to make the necessary changes.

However one looks at the mechanism of regional growth, in the context that has been outlined it is evident that considerable importance attaches to two things. First, the quality of the human resources and their ability, or inability, to enter the competitive game. Second, supply bottlenecks that might arise from a mismatch of skills required and skills available, an inadequately working land market (perhaps due to national legislation concerning the taxation of properties or controls on land use), etc. In both cases, central government may have to intervene to help, but such help ought to be viewed as 'temporary' and designed to reestablish a regional economy that can engage in the long-term competitive race.

Given the wide range of circumstances in different countries, it is impossible to specify a set of concrete policies that ought to be generally applied. However, it is possible to formulate a few general principles as a guide to the way supply-side policies should be formulated.

The initial proposition is that regions should be expected to help themselves, and that the primary purpose of external intervention (by central or federal government, for example) should be to help regions in the task of helping themselves. A first requirement is awareness on the part of government of the implications for regions of national policies and laws, and a willingness either to amend provisions or deliberately to exploit them in order to foster desired objectives. This implies a clear awareness of the fact that the national geographical space is not homogeneous, so that national actions have geographically differentiated effects, both on the demand side and on the supply side. With respect to the supply side, it is not sufficient to think in terms of aggregate labour or capital or land; the markets are highly differentiated geographically, so that what is a bottleneck in one place is not in another. For example, in Britain it seems that the land markets operate much less effectively in the conurbations than in smaller cities, with the implication that any policy intervention ought, perhaps, to distinguish between settlements by size.

If regional supply responses are improved, the possibilities of attracting mobile investment will be enhanced. In addition, though, attention must be given to fostering indigenous enterprise. To some extent this is a matter of national legislation, affecting taxes, conditions of employment for workers, etc. In part, though, it is a matter of identifying specific local impediments. One that has become evident in Britain in the last decade or so is the lack of suitable 'starter' premises for firms setting up in business, and agencies such as English Estates have been consciously attempting to rectify the deficiency. Another problem for small firms has been access to capital, and it is striking how in recent years local enterprise trusts have been established to improve the situation.

Finally, there is the role of agencies of all kinds. Local government administrations appear to be taking a much more active role in economic development than was customary two decades ago. In addition, most developed countries have national agencies involved in regional development, such as English Estates for the provision of factories, and one or more regional agencies (Yuill, 1982). A point not brought out by Yuill is the widely differing styles of regional development agencies, and changes over time in these styles. In the British context, the Mid Wales Development Board takes a traditional planner's view of development as a top-down process; at the other extreme, the Development Commission (operating in rural England) works with maximal involvement of local interests, on whom the onus is placed to suggest developments appropriate for their area. And the Highlands and Islands Development Board, which was initially highly centralised at Inverness, has in recent years taken pains to establish a much more locally based administrative system, better geared to engaging local energies.

It seems evident that the Reagan-Thatcher legacy will be considerable, in the sense that they have helped to reestablish the idea that, at least nationally, supply-side issues do matter. It seems likely that this will be an enduring feature for the years to come. In a 1982 study for the Council of Europe, Robert argued that improved economic circumstances for the disadvantaged regions of Europe depend on developing the material and human resources of the regions:

"Methods for mobilising the indigenous potential of disadvantaged regions include modernising the technologies used in industry, especially in independent small and medium-sized firms, providing the workforce with better vocational training, increasing the profitability of agricultural industries, developing rural tourism and exploiting renewable sources of energy. To take effect, these measures require a new form of physical planning, more broadly based and closer to the grassroots, which should involve integrated local development schemes aimed at developing all mobilisable resources and encouraging the synergy on which the revival of these regions depends" (Robert, 1982, page 3).

Acknowledgements. A version of this paper was given at the annual conference of the Association of American Geographers, held in Minneapolis in May 1986. I am grateful to those conference participants who commented on that paper. I have also benefitted from the opinions of several people in particular, in the form of comments on the AAG paper or in general discussion: Professor G C Cameron and Dr R L Martin, University of Cambridge; Mr N Segal of Segal Quince Wicksteed, Cambridge; Dr R R Mackay, University College of North Wales; Dr J B Parr, University of Glasgow; and Dr R W Vickerman, University of Kent. In addition, anonymous referees made helpful suggestions for the partial rewriting of part of the paper. To all of the above, and to others as well, I am indebted for stimulus and help. However, they cannot be blamed for any errors or omissions that there may be. The figure was drawn by Mr I Gulley, Department of Geography, Cambridge.

References

Anderson J, Duncan S, Hudson R (Eds), 1983 *Redundant Spaces in Cities and Regions? Studies in Industrial Decline and Social Change* (Academic Press, London)

Armstrong H, Taylor J, 1985 *Regional Economics and Policy* (Philip Allan, Oxford)

Bleaney M, 1985 *The Rise and Fall of Keynesian Economics* (Macmillan, London)

Borts G H, Stein J L, 1964 *Economic Growth in a Free Market* (Columbia University Press, New York)

Breckenfeld G, 1977, "Refilling the metropolitan doughnut" in *The Rise of the Sunbelt Cities* Eds D C Perry, A J Watkins (Sage, Beverly Hills, CA) pp 231-258

Carney J, Hudson R, Lewis J (Eds), 1980 *Regions in Crisis. New Perspectives in European Regional Theory* (Croom Helm, Beckenham, Kent)

Chambers R, 1983 *Rural Development. Putting the Last First* (Longman, Harlow, Essex)

Chisholm M, 1974, "Regional policies for the 1970s" *Geographical Journal* **140** 215-231

Chisholm M, 1976, "Regional policies in an era of slow growth and higher unemployment" *Regional Studies* **10** 201-213

Chisholm M, 1982 *Modern World Development. A Geographical Perspective* (Hutchinson, London)

Chisholm M, 1983, "City, region, and—what kind of problem?" in *The Expanding City* Ed. J Patten (Academic Press, London) pp 39-76

Chisholm M, 1984, "Regional policy for the late twentieth century" *Regional Studies* **18** 348-352

Chisholm M, 1985, "De-industrialisation and British regional policy" *Regional Studies* **19** 301-313

Clark G L, Gertler M S, Whiteman J, 1986 *Regional Dynamics. Studies in Adjustment Theory* (George Allen and Unwin, Hemel Hempstead, Herts)

Crotty J R, 1980, "Post-Keynesian economic theory: an overview and evaluation" *American Economic Review. Papers and Proceedings* **70** 20-25

Damette F, 1984, "The regional framework of monopoly exploitation: new problems and trends" in *Regional Development. Problems and Policies in Eastern and Western Europe* Ed. G Demko (Croom Helm, Beckenham, Kent) pp 76-92

Deane P, 1978 *The Evolution of Economic Ideas* (Cambridge University Press, Cambridge)

Denison E F, 1967 *Why Growth Rates Differ: Postwar Experience in Nine Western Countries* (Brookings Institution, Washington, DC)

Drucker P F, 1981, "Toward the next economics" in *The Crisis in Economic Theory* Eds D Bell, I Kristol (Basic Books, New York) pp 4-18

Ewers H-J, Wettmann R W, 1980, "Innovation-oriented regional policy" *Regional Studies* **14** 161-179

Fishlow A, Díaz-Alejandro C F, Fagen R R, Hansen R D (Eds), 1978 *Rich and Poor Nations in the World Economy* (McGraw-Hill, New York)
Fothergill S, Gudgin G, 1979, "Regional employment change: a sub-regional explanation" *Progress in Planning* **12** 155–219
Frank A G, 1964, "On the mechanisms of imperialism: the case of Brazil" *Monthly Review* **16** 284–297
Frank A G, 1966, "The development of underdevelopment" *Monthly Review* **18** 17–31
Frank A G, 1967 *Capitalism and Underdevelopment in Latin America: Historical Studies of Chile and Brazil* (Monthly Review Press, New York)
Friedman M, 1956, "The quantity theory of money—a restatement" in *Studies in the Quantity Theory of Money* Ed. M Friedman (University of Chicago Press, Chicago, IL) pp 3–21
Friedman M, 1985, "Monetarism in rhetoric and in practice" in *Monetary Policy in Our Times* Eds A Ando, H Eguchi, R Farmer, Y Suzuki (MIT Press, Cambridge, MA) pp 15–28
Friedmann J, Weaver C, 1979 *Territory and Function. The Evolution of Regional Planning* (Edward Arnold, London)
Furtado C, 1964 *Development and Underdevelopment* (University of California Press, Berkeley, CA)
Greenhut M L, Stewart C T, 1983 *From Basic Economics to Supply Side Economics* (University Press of America, Lanham, MD)
Hall P, Markusen A (Eds), 1985 *Silicon Landscapes* (George Allen and Unwin, Hemel Hempstead, Herts)
Harcourt G C, 1972 *Some Cambridge Controversies in the Theory of Capital* (Cambridge University Press, Cambridge)
Hazlitt H, 1959 *The Failure of the "New Economics". An Analysis of the Keynesian Fallacies* (Van Nostrand, Princeton, NJ)
Hirschman A O, 1958 *The Strategy of Economic Development* (Yale University Press, New Haven, CT)
Holland S, 1976 *Capital Versus the Regions* (Macmillan, London)
Innis H A, 1930 *The Fur Trade in Canada: An Introduction to Canadian Economic History* (Yale University Press, New Haven, CT)
Innis H A, 1936 *Settlement and the Mining Frontier* volume 9, part 2 of *Canadian Frontiers of Settlement* Eds W A MacKintosh, W L Joerg (Macmillan, London)
Isard W, 1956 *Location and Space-Economy. A General Theory Relating to Industrial Location, Market Areas, Land Use, Trade, and Urban Structure* (Technology Press of the Massachusetts Institute of Technology and John Wiley, New York)
Johnstone M A, 1980, "Unequal exchange and the flow of surplus in the world capitalist system" in *An Introduction to Marxist Theories of Underdevelopment* Ed. R Peet, Publication HG/14, Department of Human Geography, Australian National University, POB 4, Canberra, ACT 2601; pp 145–160
Kaldor N, 1970, "The case for regional policies" *Scottish Journal of Political Economy* **17** 337–348
Keeble D, Kelly T, 1986, "New firms and high-technology industry in the United Kingdom: the case of computer electronics" in *New Firms and Regional Development in Europe* Eds D Keeble, E Wever (Croom Helm, Beckenham, Kent) pp 75–104
Keynes J M, 1936 *The General Theory of Employment, Interest and Money* (Macmillan, London)
Kuznets S, 1966 *Modern Economic Growth: Rate, Structure and Spread* (Yale University Press, London)
Kuznets S, 1971 *Economic Growth of Nations: Total Output and Production Structure* (Harvard University Press, Cambridge, MA)
Laidler D, 1981, "Monetarism: an interpretation and an assessment" *Economic Journal* **91** 1–28
Leclerc R, Draffan D, 1984, "The Glasgow Eastern Area Renewal Project" *Town Planning Review* **55** 335–351
Maclennan D, Parr J B (Eds), 1979 *Regional Policy. Past Experience and New Directions* (Martin Robertson, Oxford)
Markusen A, 1985 *Profit Cycles, Oligopoly, and Regional Development* (MIT Press, Cambridge, MA)
Martin R L, Hodge J S C, 1983a, "The reconstruction of British regional policy: 1. The crisis of conventional practice" *Environment and Planning C: Government and Policy* **1** 133–152

Martin R L, Hodge J S C, 1983b, "The reconstruction of British regional policy: 2. Towards a new agenda" *Environment and Planning C: Government and Policy* **1** 317-340
Massey D B, 1979, "In what sense a regional problem?" *Regional Studies* **13** 233-243
Massey D B, Meegan R A, 1978, "Industrial restructuring versus the cities" *Urban Studies* **15** 273-288
Matthews R C O, 1981, "Comment on the papers by Professors Laidler and Tobin" *Economic Journal* **91** 43-48
Meade J E, 1981, "Comment on the papers by Professors Laidler and Tobin" *Economic Journal* **91** 49-55
Meyer-Krahmer F, 1985, "Innovation behaviour and regional indigenous potential" *Regional Studies* **19** 523-534
Moore B, Rhodes J, 1982, "A second depression in the UK regions: can anything be done?" *Regional Studies* **16** 323-333
Moore B, Rhodes J, Tyler P, 1983, "The effects of government regional economic policy" Discussion Paper series, Department of Land Economy, 16-21 Silver Street, Cambridge CB2 9EP
Morgan K, Sayer A, 1983, "Regional inequality and the state in Britain" in *Redundant Spaces in Cities and Regions? Studies in Industrial Decline and Social Change* Eds J Anderson, S Duncan, R Hudson (Academic Press, London) pp 17-49
Myrdal G, 1957 *Economic Theory and Underdeveloped Regions* (Gerald Duckworth, London)
North D C, 1955, "Location theory and regional economic growth" *Journal of Political Economy* **63** 243-258
Patinkin D, 1965 *Money, Interest and Prices. An Integration of Monetary and Value Theory* second edition (Harper and Row, New York)
Perry D C, Watkins A J (Eds), 1977 *The Rise of the Sunbelt Cities* (Sage, Beverly Hills, CA)
Piore M J, Sabel C F, 1984 *The Second Industrial Divide. Possibilities for Prosperity* (Basic Books, New York)
Pratten C, 1985 *Applied Macroeconomics* (Oxford University Press, Oxford)
Rees R D, 1985, "Is there still a national economic case for regional policy?" *Regional Studies* **19** 471-475
Richardson H W, 1973 *Regional Growth Theory* (Macmillan, London)
Richardson H W, 1984a, "Approaches to regional development theory in Western market economies" in *Regional Development. Problems and Policies in Eastern and Western Europe* Ed. G Demko (Croom Helm, Beckenham, Kent) pp 4-33
Richardson H W, 1984b, "Regional policy in a slow growth economy" in *Regional Development. Problems and Policies in Eastern and Western Europe* Ed. G Demko (Croom Helm, Beckenham, Kent) pp 258-281
Robert J, 1982, "Mobilising the indigenous potential of disadvantaged regions. A new dimension of regional planning" European Regional Planning, study series number 40 (mimeo), Council of Europe, F-67006 Strasbourg, Bas-Rhin
Rostow W W, 1960 *The Stages of Economic Growth: A Non-communist Manifesto* (Cambridge University Press, Cambridge)
Schultz T W, 1961, "Investment in human capital" *American Economic Review* **51** 1-17
Schultz T W, 1981 *Investing in People. The Economics of Population Quality* (University of California Press, Berkeley, CA)
Segal N S, 1979, "The limits and means of 'self-reliant' regional economic growth" in *Regional Policy. Past Experience and New Directions* Eds D Maclennan, J B Parr (Martin Robertson, Oxford) pp 211-224
Smith D M, 1971 *Industrial Location. An Economic Geographical Analysis* (John Wiley, New York)
Soja E W, 1985, "Regions in context: spatiality, periodicity, and the historical geography of the regional question" *Environment and Planning D: Society and Space* **3** 175-190
Steiner M, 1985, "Old industrial areas: a theoretical approach" *Urban Studies* **22** 387-398
Stöhr W B, 1981, "Development from below: the bottom-up and periphery-inward development paradigm" in *Development from Above or Below? The Dialectics of Regional Planning in Developing Countries* Eds W B Stöhr, D R F Taylor (John Wiley, Chichester, Sussex) pp 39-72
Stöhr W B, 1986, "Territorial innovation complexes" DP-28, Interdisziplinares Institut für Raumordnung, Wirtschaftsuniversität, A-1090 Vienna, Augasse 2-6 (mimeo)
The Times 1985, "Editorial" 3 October

Tobin J, 1981, "The monetarist counter-revolution today—an appraisal" *Economic Journal* **91** 29-42
Ture N B, 1982, "The economic effects of tax changes in neoclassical analysis" in *Supply-side Economics: A Critical Appraisal* Ed. R H Fink (University Publications of America, Washington, DC) pp 33-69
Weaver C, 1984 *Regional Development and the Local Community: Planning, Politics and the Social Context* (John Wiley, Chichester, Sussex)
Weaver C, 1985, "Romance of the roses: a discourse on the path to regional reconstruction" *Environment and Planning D: Society and Space* **3** 239-258
Williamson G, 1965, "Regional inequality and the process of national development. A description of the patterns" *Economic Development and Cultural Change* **13** 1-84
Wilson T, 1979, "Regional policy and the national interest" in *Regional Policy. Past Experience and New Directions* Eds D Maclennan, J B Parr (Martin Robertson, Oxford) pp 81-108
Wilson T, 1982, "The macro-economic background to regional policy" *Regional Studies* **16** 383-389
Wray I, 1983, "Planning for declines? An unconventional regional policy for the 1980s and 1990s" *Regional Studies* **17** 467-471
Wright D M, 1962 *The Keynesian System* (Fordham University Press, New York)
Young A A, 1928, "Increasing returns and economic progress" *Economic Journal* **38** 527-542
Yuill D (Ed.), 1982 *Regional Development Agencies in Europe. An International Comparison of Selected Agencies in Europe* (Gower, Aldershot, Hants)

[24]

Scottish Journal of Political Economy, Vol. 32, No. 3, November 1985

REGIONAL POLICY AND THE INTERREGIONAL MOVEMENT OF MANUFACTURING INDUSTRY IN GREAT BRITAIN*

JIM TWOMEY AND JIM TAYLOR

Manchester Polytechnic

University of Lancaster

INTRODUCTION

Evaluating regional economic policy in Britain has proved to be an extremely difficult task. A House of Commons Accounts Committee recently observed that "the limitations of . . . analytical techniques and the quality of data prevented any precise indication of the positive benefits to the assisted regions . . ." (*House of Commons Paper 206*, 1981, pvi). The present paper is concerned with the first part of this statement. Specifically, our aim is to devise a satisfactory method of measuring the impact of regional policy on the movement of manufacturing establishments between each pair of G.B. regions.

The approach taken in this paper differs from earlier work in two major respects. Firstly, it provides estimates of the effect of regional policy on the movement of industry between each pair of G.B. regions. This contrasts with earlier work which provides estimates only of the aggregate movement of industry into the assisted areas (Moore and Rhodes, 1976; Department of Trade and Industry, 1983; Ashcroft and Taylor, 1977, 1979). Secondly, our empirical analysis follows recent work by Flowerdew and Aitkin (1982), who demonstrate the superiority of the Poisson distribution over the log-normal distribution in modelling interregional migration.

Since information on location controls prior to 1960 is not available for individual regions, and since there is a considerable lag in the compilation of movement of industry data, the empirical analysis is confined to the period 1960–77. The analysis is based upon data published in *Regional Trends* covering three six-year time periods: 1960–65, 1966–71 and 1972–77. These three periods were determined by data availability, but it turns out that they are convenient for examining the effect of changes in

* We are grateful to Harvey Armstrong, Robin Flowerdew, Murray Aitkin and an anonymous referee for considerable help at various stages in the work reported in this paper. We are also grateful to the ESRC for their support under the research-linked studentship scheme and to the Department of Industry for supplying data relating to Industrial Development Certificates.

Date of receipt of final manuscript: 14 May 1985.

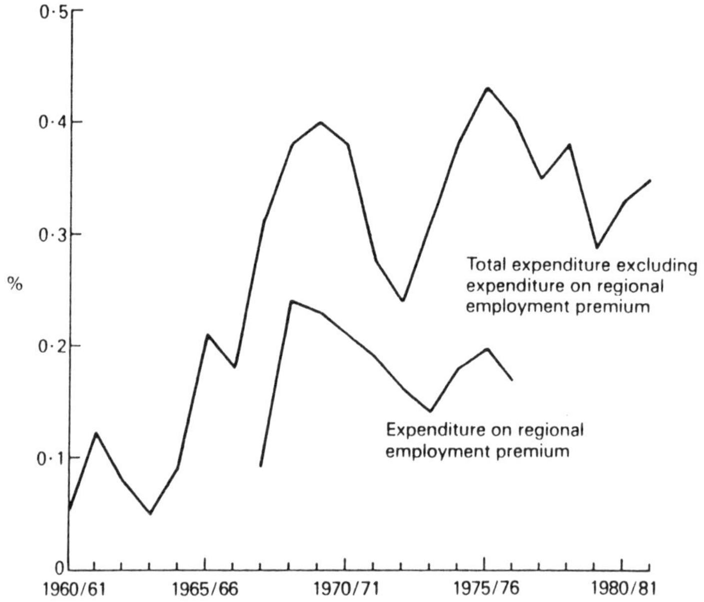

Figure 1. Regional policy expenditure as a percent of GDP (at market prices): 1960–81

regional policy on the movement of industry during 1960–77. The first period (1960–65), for example, was marked by low expenditure on regional policy (see Fig. 1) coupled with tight controls on the location of industry. Evidence that location controls were stringently applied during 1960–65 is provided in Figure 2, which shows that the early 1960s were marked by a much higher refusal rate for industrial development certificates than was the case in later years. Regional policy expenditure rose sharply during the second period (1966–71), but this was accompanied by a less stringent location controls policy. Finally, during the third period (1972–77), regional policy expenditure was maintained at a relatively high level whilst the location controls policy continued to decline in importance.[1]

The remainder of this paper is in five sections. Section I briefly discusses the broad trends in industrial movement in G.B. during the study period. Section II examines the factors that may be expected to have had an effect on the movement of industry in G.B. and this is followed in Section III by a discussion of the Poisson probability model. Section IV discusses the results of the empirical analysis and these are used in Section V for estimating the impact of regional policy on the movement of industry between each pair of G.B. regions during 1960–77.

[1] See McCallum (1979) for a detailed discussion of the historical development of regional policy in the U.K.

Figure 2. Refusal rate for industrial development certificates: 1960–77

I

THE INTERREGIONAL MOVEMENT OF INDUSTRY IN G.B. (1960–77)

Data describing the interregional movement of industry in the UK first became available in 1968 (Howard, 1968) and are now published regularly in *Regional Trends* (with a lag of about four to five years). These data refer to manufacturing units which opened in specified sub-divisions of Great Britain and which survived to the point of data collection.[2] Establishments which close during the periods in question are therefore excluded from the empirical analysis by the data collection methods and not by choice. Ideally, non-surving moves should be included in the movement data.

To qualify as a move, an establishment must employ at least 10 persons and the firms concerned must not currently have any producing units in the specified sub-division. Each move can be the result either of a complete transfer of an existing producing unit or the opening of a new branch plant by firms located in another sub-division. Finally, moves that cross a standard regional boundary are defined as *inter*regional moves. The remaining *intra*regional moves are not considered in the present paper.

The broad trends in the movement of manufacturing establishments can be seen in Table 1, which shows that all regions experienced both an

[2] See the appendix to Ashcroft and Taylor (1979) for a detailed discussion of the industrial movement data.

TABLE 1

The movement of establishments between Great Britain regions: 1960–65, 1966–71 and 1972–77

Region	Number of moves out of region					Number of moves into region					
	1960–65	1966–71	1972–77	1960–77	%	1960–65	1966–71	1972–77	1960–77	%	Net inflow
North	7	16	14	37	1·6	68	115	67	250	10·7	+213
Yorkshire & Humberside	33	55	41	129	5·5	27	41	75	143	6·1	+14
East Midlands	46	79	58	183	7·8	44	80	127	251	10·7	+68
East Anglia	10	15	26	51	2·2	81	158	120	359	15·3	+308
South East	330	535	477	1342	57·3	12	69	43	124	5·3	−1214
South West	17	24	34	75	3·2	86	152	95	333	14·2	+258
West Midlands	96	18	72	286	12·2	19	13	39	71	3·0	−215
North West	40	72	70	182	7·8	85	67	65	217	9·3	+35
Wales	6	9	5	20	0·9	79	148	104	331	14·1	+311
Scotland	11	14	13	38	1·6	95	94	75	264	11·3	+230
Total	596	937	810	2343	100·0*	596	937	810	2343	100·0	0

* Error due to rounding.

Source:
Howard (1968) and *Regional Statistics*.

TABLE 2

The interregional movement of manufacturing establishments: matrix of surviving moves 1960–77

Origin region	Destination region N	YH	EM	EA	SE	SW	WM	NW	WAL	SC	Total
N	—	7	4	3	5	0	1	5	2	10	37
YH	35	—	39	4	16	3	2	13	3	14	129
EM	22	33	—	16	19	15	22	16	20	20	183
EA	6	5	6	—	11	1	2	6	7	7	51
SE	118	62	152	319	—	262	27	117	141	144	1342
SW	3	2	7	3	15	—	5	7	25	8	75
WM	23	7	28	6	27	32	—	44	84	35	286
NW	30	23	11	5	18	15	10	—	45	25	182
WAL	2	0	0	1	6	3	2	5	—	1	20
SC	11	4	4	2	7	2	0	4	4	—	38
Total G.B.	250	143	251	359	124	333	71	217	331	264	2343

Note: N = North, YH = Yorkshire and Humberside, EA = East Anglia, EM = East Midlands, SE = South East, SW = South West, WM = West Midlands, NW = North West, WAL = Wales, SC = Scotland.
Source:
Howard (1968) and *Regional Statistics*

outflow and an inflow of industrial movement during the three periods discussed in the introduction. The most outstanding feature of Table 1 is the large proportion of industrial movement that originated in the South East region (57 per cent). The West Midlands also contributed substantially to industrial movement (supplying 12 per cent of the total moves) whereas the three main assisted areas (Scotland, Wales and the North) contributed only 4 per cent between them. As far as the destination of moves is concerned, only 8 per cent of total moves went to the South East and West Midlands whereas 36 per cent went to Scotland, Wales and the North. Closer scrutiny of the interregional movement data reveals that 43 per cent of the total moves out of the SE ended up in East Anglia and the South West during 1960–77 whereas only 30 per cent ended up in the three main assisted regions (see Table 2).

II

Modelling Industrial Movement

Central to our explanation of industrial movement is the proposition that the industrial location decision is determined primarily by economic factors. Specifically, we argue that the interregional movement of industry is responsive to regional disparities in expected rates of return on investment, subject to any constraints that may be operative (such as the costs of moving or the imposition of government controls on industrial location).

Various approaches can be taken to constructing an interregional movement model. One obvious starting point is the gravity model, which has been used extensively in studies of population migration. The basic assertion of the gravity model is that the interaction between any pair of regions is positively related to their magnitude and inversely related to the distance between them. The magnitude of regions in the present case is measured by the stock of establishments since the movement of industry variable is itself measured as the number of establishments moving between regions. We can therefore write:

$$E(M_{ij}) = \beta_0 S_i^{\beta_1} S_j^{\beta_2} d_{ij}^{\beta_3} \quad (\beta_0, \beta_1, \beta_2) > 0, \quad \beta_3 < 0 \tag{1}$$

where:

M_{ij} = number of establishments moving from i to j ($i \neq j$)
S_i = stock of plants in i
S_j = stock of plants in j
d_{ij} = distance between the main industrial centres in i and j
β_i = parameters to be estimated.

The simple gravity model given by equation (1) can be justified as follows. The distance between i and j is a proxy for movement costs, which can be expected to exert a negative effect on industrial movement, hence the negative sign hypothesized for β_3. The stock of plants in the origin region (S_i) is essentially a scale variable. The more plants there are in the origin region, the greater will be the potential for generating movement. The sign of β_1 is therefore expected to be positive. Finally, according to the gravity model, the size of the destination region can be expected to exert a positive influence on M_{ij}, presumably because of the presence of agglomeration economies. But this ignores the possibility that large regions may suffer from agglomeration diseconomies, in which case the role of S_j is uncertain, and so therefore is the sign of β_2.

The gravity model can now be extended to allow for the influence of factors that are likely to affect the relative economic attractiveness of regions. Heron's (1981) review of industrial location surveys, for example, indicates that factors such as labour availability and regional policy instruments have had a significant effect on location decisions. In view of this, equation (1) can be modified as follows:

$$E(M_{ij}) = S_i^{\beta_1} S_j^{\beta_2} d_{ij}^{\beta_3} f(\mathbf{X}_{ij}) \tag{2}$$

where $f(\mathbf{X}_{ij})$ is simply a function containing a vector of additional variables. Some of these additional variables reflect the influence of regional disparities in economic attractiveness. Others reflect the influence of constraints on the re-location of industry.[3]

[3] Ashcroft and Ingham (1982) develop a stock-adjustment model to explain the movement of industry over time. This approach can be adapted to explain the interregional movement of industry at a "point" in time (or during a given period of time such as those used in the present paper). When adapted in this way, their model explains two aspects of movement: transfer of existing plant (stock adjustment) and the movement of new capital stock (flow adjustment). Unfortunately, the movement data do not distinguish between transfers and new stock. In addition, their model requires investment data by region. Future work along these lines will therefore require a more adequate data base.

The next step is to specify the variables that we might expect to determine regional disparities in the economic attractiveness of regions. The factors determining re-location costs also need to be specified. According to surveys of industrial location, the three factors that have had the greatest influence on the location decision are the availability of labour, regional investment incentives and controls on the location of industry (Heron, 1981). In view of the criticisms often levelled against business surveys, it is prudent to investigate the influence of other variables that may be expected *a priori* to have an effect on the interregional movement of industry. These may be expected to include regional disparities in labour costs and regional disparities in the growth of markets. Finally, movement between regions is not costless and is likely to be positively related to the distance between the origin and destination regions. In the simple gravity model (given by equation (1)) a smooth non-linear relationship is assumed to exist between industrial movement and the distance moved to reflect the non-linearity in the movement cost function. The possibility that there exists a sharp discontinuity in movement costs (between "short" and "long" distance moves), however, can be allowed for explicitly in the extended gravity model.

Before the effect of these various explanatory variables on the movement of industry can be estimated, it is necessary to describe each variable in detail and to specify an explicit functional form for the estimating equation. The variables in the simple gravity model have already been discussed. The additional variables are expressed as differences between the destination region and the origin region since we assume that location decision-makers will be interested primarily in the net advantage of moving from one region to another. The variables are as follows:

1. *The female participation rate* ($FPR_{ij} = FPR_j - FPR_i$)

Regional disparities in the female participation rate (viz. the per cent of females of working age who are economically active) are used as a measure of labour availability in preference to regional disparities in the unemployment rate since the unemployment rate was found to be highly collinear with the regional policy variables (to be discussed below). There are inevitably problems of interpretation associated with this variable, however, since it is influenced by a host of factors such as historical and industrial work patterns. Nevertheless, the dramatic changes which have occurred in the labour market over the last two decades suggest that female labour market variables may well prove to be more sensitive indicators of labour availability than their male counterparts. A negative relationship is expected between FPR_{ij} and M_{ij}.

2. *Average male earnings* ($AME_{ij} = AME_j - AME_i$)

The influence of regional disparities in labour costs on industrial movement is reflected by the inclusion of regional differences in the average weekly earnings of male manual workers. Furthermore, the potential impact of the Regional Employment Premium (a labour subsidy) on industrial movement is taken into account by adjusting male earnings in those regions receiving the subsidy. A negative relationship is expected between AME_{ij} and M_{ij}.

3. *Output growth* ($GY_{ij} = GY_j - GY_i$)

To the extent that firms are market-orientated, they can be expected to move towards those regions with the fastest rate of output growth. One problem with this variable, however, is that fast-growing regions may generate more movement than slow-growing regions with the result that regions growing slowly may experience little out-migration of capital. The expected effect of GY_{ij} on industrial movement is therefore uncertain.

4. *Regional investment incentives* ($II_{ij} = II_j - II_i$)

If regional investment incentives are successful, they should induce industry to move into those regions offering the most lucrative incentives.[4] These incentives are measured in the present paper by the present value of the subsidy available to each region (see appendix). This variable takes into account the varying subsidies available in different types of assisted area, which include Special Development Areas, Development Areas and Intermediate Areas in the second and third periods. For regions with a range of subsidies available, a weighted average was calculated using employment weights (see appendix). A positive relationship is expected between II_{ij} and M_{ij}.

5. *Controls on the location of industry* ($LC_{ij} = LC_j - LC_i$)

Previous work on the movement of industry has suggested that location controls have had a substantial effect on the movement of industry in G.B. (Moore and Rhodes, 1976; Ashcroft and Taylor, 1977, 1979). As in earlier work, the strength of location controls has been approximated by using the refusal rate for Industrial Development Certificates. A negative relationship is expected between II_{ij} and M_{ij}.

6. *Spatial contiguity* ($CONT_{ij}$)

Movement costs may be subject to a threshold effect with short-distance moves being highly attractive compared to moves over longer distances. A spatial contiguity variable is therefore included in the model

[4] Other regional policy measures, such as the advance factory building programme and the provision of financial support to grant-awarding agencies (the Highlands and Islands Development Board, the Scottish and Welsh Development Agencies) have been ignored in the present study since expenditure by these agencies has been small in relation to expenditure on capital and labour subsidies. This is not to argue, however, that such agencies have not affected the movement of industry.

to reflect this threshold effect. It takes on a value equal to the length of the common boundary between *i* and *j* if the regions are contiguous and a value of zero if they are not. This variable is preferred to the conventional zero-one dummy since the latter is a particularly crude measure of contiguity which fails to take account of the different degrees of access associated with varying boundary lengths. $CONT_{ij}$ is included with the intention of reflecting those factors that are likely to make short-distance movement more attractive than movement over longer distances. These include the need to maintain regular and close links between plants both within the organisation and with suppliers or buyers located in the region of origin.

These additional variables can now be incorporated into the extended gravity model (equation (2)) once a suitable functional form has been specified. Computational convenience has dictated the mathematical form of our estimating equation, which is as follows:

$$M_{ij} = S_i^{\beta_1} S_j^{\beta_2} d_{ij}^{\beta_3} \exp(\beta_0 + \beta_4 FAR_{ij} + \beta_5 AME_{ij} + \beta_6 GY_{ij} + \beta_7 II_{ij} + \beta_8 LC_{ij} + \beta_9 CONT_{ij} + \varepsilon_{ij}) \tag{3}$$

where ε_{ij} is the error term and the β_i's are parameters to be estimated. Taking the natural logarithms of all variables in equation (3), we obtain:

$$\ln M_{ij} = \beta_0 + \beta_1 \ln S_i + \beta_2 \ln S_j + \beta_3 \ln d_{ij} + \beta_4 FAR_{ij} + \beta_5 AME_{ij} + \beta_6 GY_{ij} + \beta_7 II_{ij} + \beta_8 LC_{ij} + \beta_9 CONT_{ij} + \varepsilon_{ij} \tag{4}$$

The method used to estimate the parameters (β_i) is discussed in the next section.

III

Selecting an Appropriate Probability Model

Flowerdew and Aitkin (1982) have shown that the choice of probability model is critical to the statistical analysis of migration data. They show, for instance, that it is not appropriate to fit a log-normal model to a variable which has a high concentration of zeros and which has no negative values. The assumption of log-normality is not sustained by the data. In addition, a serious problem with the log-normal approach arises as a consequence of the requirement that a constant has to be added to the dependent variable when the latter includes zeros, as is the case with the movement of industry data. The problem arises as a result of the sensitivity of the estimated parameters of the model to the choice of constant (which is usually a small number between 0·1 and 1·0).[5]

Flowerdew and Aitkin show that it is more appropriate to fit a Poisson

[5] Preliminary work using the log-normal model indicated substantial variations in the estimated coefficients when the constant added to the dependent variable was changed from 0·1 to 1.

model to migration data than a log-normal model. As they observe, migration is a non-negative integer and it is therefore appropriate to treat migration as a random variable with a discrete probability distribution. Furthermore, provided there is only a small probability that any individual establishment in region i will move to region j (i.e. the stock of establishments in i is large relative to the movement of establishments from i to j), and provided each move is independent of all other moves,[6] then the number of establishments moving from i to j will have a Poisson distribution with a mean of λ_{ij}. The probability that k establishments will have been recorded as moving from i to j is given by:

$$\Pr(M_{ij} = k) = \frac{\lambda_{ij}^{k} e^{-\lambda_{ij}}}{k!} \quad (3)$$

The relationship between M_{ij} and the range of variables specified above can now be investigated by estimating the relationship between λ_{ij} (the mean of the Poisson) and these explanatory variables.[7] It is assumed that the parameter λ is logarithmically linked to a linear combination of the independent variables by the following function:

$$\lambda_{ij} = \exp(\beta_0 + \beta_1 \ln S_i + \beta_2 \ln S_j + \beta_3 \ln d_{ij} + \beta_4 FPR_{ij} + \beta_5 AME_{ij} + \beta_6 GY_{ij} + \beta_7 II_{ij} + \beta_8 LC_{ij} + \beta_9 CONT_{ij}) \quad (4)$$

IV

Results

In any model fitting process, it is necessary to have some method by which it is possible to assess the extent to which the model fits the data. The most obvious method is to compare the values predicted by the model with the actual values. A second approach is to calculate the standard errors of the estimated coefficients of each explanatory variable in order to estimate whether the estimated coefficient is significantly different from zero. The procedure is straightforward when the error term is normally distributed since the estimated coefficient divided by its standard error has a t-distribution. For the Poisson model, however, there are no hard and fast rules. Baker and Nelder (1978) suggest that any parameter value greater than three times its standard error can usually be regarded as significantly different from zero (using asymptotic theory). A third method, preferred by Baker and Nelder, is based on a

[6] It is conceivable that the movement of a major industrial plant to a particular region will induce other plants to move to the same region to benefit from external economies. We have no information to support or refute this hypothesis.

[7] For a full discussion of the technical aspects of the estimation procedure, see Nelder and Wedderburn (1972) and Baker and Nelder (1978). See Flowerdew and Aitkin (1981) for a discussion of the application of the Poisson model to migration data.

statistic referred to as the deviance.[8] This statistic can be estimated for each alternative specification of the model in question, the simplest being the Null model, which contains no explanatory variables and uses only the mean of the dependent variable in the model fitting process. All the variation in the dependent variable in this case is assigned to the random component. Adding a set of explanatory variables to the model will lead to a reduction in the deviance. The resulting reduction in the deviance relative to the deviance of the Null model is then used to indicate the extent to which the model fits the data. Whether any individual variable has a significant role to play in the model is therefore judged on the basis of the extent to which the deviance increases when the variable in question is excluded from the model. All three approaches are used in this section.

A number of equations were estimated for each of three periods. Some of these equations are reported in Table 3. The first equation in each case is the simple gravity model, the second is the full model and the third includes only those variables with estimated coefficients which have the hypothesized sign and which have t-ratios of at least 2.

The overall fit of the model can be judged by comparing the deviance of the Null model with the deviance of each equation. Although the simple gravity model can be seen to fit the data reasonably well (at least 71 per cent of the deviance being explained by LS_i, LS_j and LD_{ij}), the inclusion of additional explanatory variables raises the percentage of the deviance explained by the model to at least 85 per cent. The effect of amending the gravity model formulation to incorporate factors which affect the relative economic attractiveness of regions (including regional policy instruments) is to improve the fit of the model. This is achieved, however, at the expense of two of the explanatory variables in the simple gravity model. Specifically, the variables LS_j and LD_{ij} lose their significance (in the 1960–65 and 1972–77 periods) when other variables are added to the model.[9] This result is not surprising in the case of LD_{ij} since the contiguity variable (CONT_{ij}) is highly correlated with LD_{ij} and can therefore be regarded as a substitute for it in the extended equation.

Two variables had a predominating effect on the movement of industry

[8] Nelder and Wedderburn (1972) suggest that the fit of a model can be measured by a statistic called the deviance. The lack of fit of any model to the data is measured as minus twice the maximum log likelihood and the deviance of any model is the difference in this value between the model used and the complete model. For the Poisson model, the deviance is given by:

$$-2\left[\sum_{\substack{i \\ i \neq j}}^{n} \sum_{j}^{n} M_{ij} \ln\left(\frac{M_{ij}}{\hat{\lambda}_{ij}}\right) - \sum_{\substack{i \\ i \neq j}}^{n} \sum_{j}^{n} (M_{ij} - \hat{\lambda}_{ij})\right]$$

[9] The irrelevance of LS_i and LD_{ij} as explanatory variables suggests an alternative approach. With $\beta_1 = 1$ and $\beta_2 = \beta_3 = 0$, the model reduces to an explanation of M_{ij}/S_i, which expresses movement from i to j as a proportion of the stock of plants in i. Modelling this as a binomial process, we found that the estimated parameters on the regional policy variables were very similar to those obtained from the Poisson model.

TABLE 3

Estimated equations: dependent variable = M_{ij}

Explanatory variables	1960–65			1966–71			1972–77			
Constant	−8·98 (10·5)	−8·55 (6·1)	−8·41 (13·0)	−6·12 (8·5)	−14·77 (13·5)	−11·26 (12·7)	−7·32 (9·5)	−7·99 (6·2)	−11·6 (22·4)	−10·1 (10·6)
LS_i	1·469 (26·1)	1·046 (13·4)	1·033 (14·7)	1·517 (33·7)	0·852 (10·4)	1·043 (14·3)	1·543 (31·2)	1·207 (11·8)	1·436 (26·5)	1·27 (20·6)
LS_j	−0·278 (4·9)	−0·081 (0·6)		−0·426 (8·5)	0·718 (5·5)	0·351 (3·2)	−0·225 (4·3)	−0·085 (1·0)		
LD_{ij}	−0·068 (0·9)	0·149 (1·3)		−0·397 (6·0)	0·371 (3·7)		−0·580 (8·3)	−0·158 (1·5)		
FPR_{ij}		0·020 (1·4)			−0·073 (5·5)	−0·037 (3·1)		−0·062 (2·1)	−0·115 (4·3)	−0·052 (2·1)
AME_{ij}		−0·025 (0·3)			0·262 (4·6)			−0·061 (1·4)		
GY_{ij}		0·498 (1·0)			2·021 (5·6)	1·107 (3·7)		−4·02 (3·4)	−5·17 (4·8)	−2·82 (2·9)
II_{ij}		17·33 (4·3)	19·30 (5·3)		4·61 (5·3)	4·29 (5·3)		1·12 (1·6)	2·549 (5·1)	
LC_{ij}		−0·116 (4·1)	−0·113 (7·5)		−0·209 (6·4)	−0·087 (4·9)		−0·141 (3·3)		−0·198 (6·3)
$CONT_{ij}$		0·057 (8·4)	0·051 (10·5)		0·073 (13·3)	0·059 (14·3)		0·054 (8·8)	0·059 (13·2)	0·059 (13·5)
Null deviance	1262	1262	1262	2067	2067	2067	1644	1644	1644	1644
Deviance of model	367	155	161	528	253	283	339	219	242	255
% of deviance explained by model	71	88	87	74	88	86	79	87	85	86

Estimated coefficients (all columns)

Note: ( ) = estimated coefficient divided by its standard error.

All estimated equations are based on the Poisson probability model and were estimated by the procedures described in Baker and Nelder (1978) using GLIM at the University of Lancaster Computer Centre.

between the G.B. regions during all three periods: the size of the origin region (LS_i) and the spatial contiguity variable ($CONT_{ij}$). Thus, the "largest" regions are seen to generate the most moves and a large proportion of these moves end up in contiguous regions. Of the two labour market variables in the model (FPR_{ij} and AME_{ij}), only the variable reflecting the influence of regional differences in labour availability (FPR_{ij}) helps to explain M_{ij}. There are two possible reasons why regional disparities in male earnings fail to help in explaining M_{ij}. Firstly, regional wage differentials may not be large enough to have an effect on M_{ij}. Secondly, the variable used to measure regional wage differentials does not allow for regional disparities in the occupational mix of regions. This could mean that the variable used to measure regional wage differentials (AME_{ij}) does not measure the true disparities. Finally, regional disparities in output growth had an effect on M_{ij} during 1966–71 and 1972–77. The direction of this effect, however, is reversed between these two periods, which suggests that the market-attraction effect outweighed the generation of moves during 1966–71 but that the reverse occurred during 1972–77.

With one exception, the estimated coefficients on the two policy variables were found to be significantly different from zero and were of the expected sign.[10] The exception occurs in the period 1972–77. Only when LC_{ij} is excluded from the equation is the estimated coefficient on II_{ij} significantly different from zero. This problem occurs because of the (negative) correlation between II_{ij} and LC_{ij}. The fact that expenditure on investment incentives was as high (in real terms) on average during 1972–77 as during 1966–71 is indicative that investment incentives continued to have an effect on M_{ij}. In view of this, the effect of investment incentives and location controls were estimated from two separate equations (with LC_{ij} omitted from the first and II_{ij} omitted from the second).

Although the extended gravity model fits the data quite well (in terms of the deviance explained by the model), an examination of the prediction errors suggests that the explanatory variables have failed to reflect the influence of all the forces that have been at work in determining M_{ij}. Table 4 contains the main prediction errors derived from the extended gravity model for each period. Some interesting results emerge from an examination of these prediction errors. Firstly, most of the main prediction errors occur in the interindustry flows from the South East to other regions. The errors are particularly large for the estimated moves from the South East to East Anglia, suggesting that the

[10] It should be noted that the relative impact of the two policy instruments cannot be assessed by comparing the size of the estimated coefficient between the three periods. The policy variables were constructed separately for each period. Thus, during 1960-65 II_{ij} ranges from 0·452 to 0·488 whereas during 1972–77 it ranges from 0·363 to 0·568. The much lower magnitude of the estimated coefficient on II_{ij} in 1972–77 is therefore a consequence of the greater variation in II_{ij}.

TABLE 4
Main prediction errors for each period

	Prediction errors ($\hat{M}_{ij} - M_{ij}$) 1960–65	1966–71	1972–77
(i) *over-prediction* ($\hat{M}_{ij} > M_{ij}$)			
YH → N		15	
SE → YH	16	13	
SE → SW		11	
SE → W Midlands		18	23
SE → Scotland			14
NW → YH		11	
WM → EM		10	
(ii) *under-prediction* ($\hat{M}_{ij} < M_{ij}$)			
SE → E Midlands			−29
SE → E Anglia	−19	−40	−21
SE → NW	−18		
SE → Wales		−13	−11
SW → Wales			−11
NW → Wales	−10		

Notes: 1. This table includes prediction errors below −9 and above 9.
2. The arrow indicates movement from region *i* to region *j*.
3. The prediction errors were obtained from the extended gravity model in each period.
4. Of the 90 prediction errors, 77 were between ±4 during 1960–65. The corresponding numbers for 1966–71 and 1972–77 were 64 and 70.

model fails to accurately reflect the attractiveness of East Anglian locations for firms located in the South East. A similar result is obtained for moves from the South East to the East Midlands during 1972–77. Secondly, moves from the West Midlands (and to a lesser extent Yorkshire and Humberside) are significantly overestimated. This may be due to the fact that location controls were more stringently applied in these two regions than is indicated by the location controls variable (LC_{ij}).

IV

Estimating the Effect of Regional Policy Instruments on the Movement of Manufacturing Establishments Between Regions

The effect of investment incentives and location controls on the movement of industry can be estimated by utilizing the equations given in Table 3. The estimated effect of each policy instrument is obtained by "switching off" one instrument at a time. Thus, taking the estimated equation for any given period, the actual value of each of the explanatory variables is substituted into this equation except for the policy instrument under scrutiny, which is given a value of zero. This procedure produces an estimate of the movement that would have occurred (between each pair of regions) if the policy instrument in question had not existed. Subtracting this value from the value predicted by the complete equation (i.e. when the actual values of all variables are substituted into the estimated equation) provides an estimate of the effect of the policy instrument in question on M_{ij}. This is not an entirely satisfactory mode of operation since it relies upon the estimation of a hypothetical situation. It is not possible to say what *would* have happened in the absence of policy since the world was such that policy did, in fact, exist. If the policy had not existed, the world would have been a different place and other influences may have played an entirely different role. Nevertheless, this approach has the advantage that both non-policy influences have been jointly modelled and provided there is no reason to expect the non-policy effects on movement to have been significantly different in the absence of policy, simulating a non-policy situation is in our view a plausible approach.

It should be noted that this procedure carries with it the implicit assumption that investment incentives and location controls have operated independently of each other. This assumption can be challenged on the grounds that the existence of a location controls policy has the advantage of forcing expanding firms to contact the Department of Industry, which then has the opportunity to expound the advantages of regional investment subsidies. The success of investment subsidies may therefore be dependent (to some extent) upon the existence of location controls. Experiments with an interaction term in the regression model (i.e. $II_{ij} \times LC_{ij}$) proved to be unsuccessful. This does not necessarily mean, however, that investment incentives and location controls did not have a joint influence on the movement of industry. It may simply mean that we have been unable to detect such interaction with the available data.

The estimated effect of location controls and investment incentives on M_{ij} (during 1960–77) is given in Tables 5 and 6. Similar tables are available for each of the three periods. The main results are as follows:

(i) Of the 2343 moves that occurred during 1960–77, 678 were the result of location controls and 299 were the result of investment incentives. Regional policy instruments were therefore responsible for about 42 per cent of the total moves during 1960–77.

(ii) Of the 678 moves attributed to location controls, 504 (74 per cent) originated in the SE, with the bulk of the remainder coming from the West Midlands (18 per cent).

(iii) Of the 678 moves attributed to location controls, only 290 (43 per cent) ended up in the three main assisted areas (Scotland, Wales, and the North).

(iv) Of the 504 moves from the SE induced by location controls, 210 went to East Anglia and the SW, both of which are contiguous to the SE. A major effect of the location controls policy was therefore to divert expanding manufacturing firms from the SE to its immediate neighbours.

(v) More than half of the 299 moves attributed to investment incentives originated in the SE and about one-fifth originated in the West Midlands.

TABLE 5

The estimated effect of location controls on the movement of manufacturing establishments 1960–77

Origin region	Destination region N	YH	EM	EA	SE	SW	WM	NW	WAL	SC	Total
N	0	0	0	0	0	0	0	0	0	0	0
YH	1	0	0	0	0	0	0	0	0	1	2
EM	4	11	0	6	0	2	0	4	5	7	39
EA	0	0	0	0	0	0	0	0	0	0	0
SE	55	48	27	95	0	88	9	47	60	75	504
SW	1	1	0	0	0	0	0	1	1	2	6
WM	13	10	6	9	0	10	0	13	42	17	120
NW	2	1	0	0	0	0	0	0	2	2	7
WAL	0	0	0	0	0	0	0	0	0	0	0
SC	0	0	0	0	0	0	0	0	0	0	0
Total	76	71	33	110	0	100	9	65	110	104	678

Note: These estimates were obtained from the "reduced" equations given in Table 3 (i.e. the third equation for 1960–65 and 1966–71 and the third and fourth equations for 1972–77).

(vi) The main beneficiaries of regional policy were Scotland, Wales, the North, the SW and East Anglia in that order. Regional policy accounted for around $\frac{2}{3}$ of the total moves into the SW and East Anglia. The results are given for all regions in Table 7.

It is interesting to compare the effect of regional policy on M_{ij} across the three time periods. The estimates given in Table 8 indicate that the effectiveness of location controls declined during the period and that investment incentives had their greatest impact during 1966–71.

The estimated effect of investment incentives and location controls

TABLE 6

The estimated effect of investment incentives on the movement of manufacturing establishments 1960–77

Origin region	Destination region N	YH	EM	EA	SE	SW	WM	NW	WAL	SC	Total
N	0	0	0	0	0	0	0	0	0	2	2
YH	19	0	0	0	0	0	0	5	2	8	34
EM	3	2	0	0	0	0	0	2	3	7	17
EA	2	0	0	0	0	1	0	0	1	1	5
SE	37	5	0	0	0	14	0	16	27	66	165
SW	2	0	0	0	0	0	0	0	1	2	5
WM	9	1	0	0	0	1	0	6	22	16	55
NW	7	0	0	0	0	0	0	0	1	7	15
WAL	1	0	0	0	0	0	0	0	0	0	1
SC	0	0	0	0	0	0	0	0	0	0	0
Total	80	8	0	0	0	16	0	29	57	109	299

Note: See note to Table 5.

TABLE 7

The estimated contribution of Regional Policy Instruments to the movement of industry into each region 1960–77

Region	Number of moves into region	Number of moves due to regional policy	Moves due to regional policy as a % of total moves into region
Scotland	264	213	81
Wales	331	167	50
North	250	156	62
S West	333	116	35
E Anglia	359	110	31
N West	217	94	43
Yorks & Humb	143	79	55
E Midlands	251	33	13
W Midlands	71	9	13
S East	124	0	0
Total (G.B.)	2343	977	42

Note: These estimates were obtained from Tables 1, 5 and 6.

TABLE 8

The estimated effect of regional policy on the movement of manufacturing establishments 1960–77

Policy instrument	Estimated effect of policy instrument 1960–65	1966–71	1972–77	1960–77
Investment incentives	80	124	95	299
Location controls	254	230	194	678
Total	334	354	289	977

Note: These estimates were obtained from a period breakdown of Tables 5 and 6.

obtained from the cross-section model of movement in the present paper can be compared with estimates recently obtained from a time-series model of industrial movement by Moore, Rhodes and Tyler. Their approach is described in detail in an earlier paper (Moore and Rhodes, 1976). Comparison between these two sets of estimates is impaired somewhat since the estimates in the present paper are for the standard regions, whereas those produced by Moore, Rhodes and Tyler are for the Development Areas. Moreover, Moore, Rhodes and Tyler use openings as a measure of movement whereas only surviving moves were available for the cross-section model. Table 9 does suggest, however, that the two sets of estimates produce a similar overall picture of the effect of regional policy on the movement of industry.[11]

[11] Moore, Rhodes and Tyler (see Department of Trade and Industry, 1983) argue that the Regional Employment Premium also had a substantial effect on the movement of industry into the Development Areas. We discovered no such effect in the present paper. This result relies, however, on the assumption that AME_{ij} adequately measures regional disparities in labour costs.

TABLE 9

The estimated effect of investment incentives and location controls on the movement of industry in three time periods: comparing time-series and cross-section estimates

	Moves to assisted areas estimated to have been caused by regional policy as a % of total moves to the assisted areas					
	Time-series estimates			Cross-section estimates		
Policy instrument	1960–65	1966–71	1972–77	1960–65	1966–71	1972–77
Investment incentives	0·20	0·32	0·42	0·27	0·30	0·30
Location controls	0·65	0·43	0·24	0·52	0·26	0·28
Total	0·85	0·75	0·66	0·79	0·56	0·58

Note: The time-series estimates were obtained from B. Moore, J. Rhodes and P. Tyler of the University of Cambridge. These estimates are likely to differ from the cross-section estimates for three reasons: (1) the time-series estimates are based on openings of new manufacturing establishments whereas the cross-section estimates are based on surviving moves; (2) the time-series estimates refer to moves into the U.K. Development Areas (including N. Ireland and parts of the NW and SW) whereas the cross-section estimates refer to moves only to Scotland, Wales and the North; (3) the methods of estimation differ.

Conclusion

Previous work on estimating the effect of regional policy on the movement of industry in G.B. has concentrated on providing estimates of the effect of individual policy instruments on the aggregate number of moves, such as the number of moves into the assisted areas resulting from investment incentives and location controls. The present paper has extended this earlier work by estimating the effect of policy instruments on the movement of industry between each pair of G.B. regions. This more detailed approach has the distinct advantage that it permits the estimation of the effect of policy instruments on the overall spatial pattern of industrial movement rather than focussing simply on the effect of these instruments on the movement of industry into the assisted areas. Thus, it is possible to estimate the effect of location controls on the movement of industry from the South East and West Midlands into *all* regions and not simply into the assisted areas.

As far as the effectiveness of regional policy is concerned during the period 1960–77, the results obtained in this paper indicate that both location controls and investment incentives had a significant impact on the movement of industry in G.B. We estimate that of the 2,343 moves during 1960–77 nearly 1,000 were a result of regional policy measures. Moreover, of the 845 moves to the three main assisted areas in G.B. (Scotland, Wales and the North), 536 were the result of regional policy. As far as individual policy instruments are concerned, location controls appear to have been much more effective in inducing industrial movement than were investment incentives. Approximately 70 per cent of all the moves estimated to have been caused by regional policy were due to restrictions on the location of industry. What is even more surprising, however, is that a major effect of location controls was to divert establishments from the South East to non-assisted areas rather than to assisted areas. This presumably unwanted side-effect of regional policy has not been previously quantified. It raises the question of whether policymakers, in their attempt to divert establishments from the South East to the assisted areas, should also have done more to prevent expansion in contiguous regions. It is particularly pertinent to note that both East Anglia and the South West performed extremely well in terms of employment growth compared to the assisted areas during the 1960s and 1970s. Location controls therefore appear to have done as much to enhance the growth prospects of regions contiguous to the South East as to improving the economies of the assisted areas. It is impossible, of course, to say whether a more restrictive policy in regions contiguous to the South East would have stimulated more moves to the assisted areas. Nevertheless, if the aim of regional policy was to promote relocation to the assisted areas then consistency alone required that the intensity of location controls did not differ considerably between the South East and its non-assisted area neighbours.

Our final conclusion relates to the method of estimating the effect of regional policy on the spatial pattern of industrial movement used in the present paper. In our view, the value of this approach would be enhanced if the movement data were made available for sub-regional units. Further spatial disaggregation is especially necessary for those cells in the movement matrix which contain a substantial number of moves. This would help to provide more detailed estimates of the effect of regional policy since greater disaggregation would make it unnecessary to treat an entire region as a weighted average of different types of assisted areas. In addition, further disaggregation should help to identify the non-policy influences on industrial movement more accurately, such as the effect of the urban/rural shift (Fothergill and Gudgin, 1982).

REFERENCES

ASHCROFT, B. and TAYLOR, J. (1977). The movement of manufacturing industry and the effect of regional policy, *Oxford Economic Papers 29*, 84–101.

ASHCROFT, B. and TAYLOR, J. (1979). The effect of regional policy on the movement of industry in Great Britain, ch. 2 in *Regional Policy: Past Experience and New Directions*, edited by D. Maclennan and J. B. Parr, Martin Robertson: Oxford.

BAKER, R. J. and NELDER, J. A. (1978). *The GLIM System Release 3, Generalised Linear Interactive Modelling*, Rothamstead Experimental Station, Harpenden, England.

BEGG, H. M., LYTHE, C. M., SORLEY, R. and MACDONALD, D. R. (1975). Annual expenditure on special regional assistance to industry in Great Britain 1960/61–1971/73: A note, *Economic Journal 85*, pp. 884–887.

DEPARTMENT OF TRADE AND INDUSTRY (1983). *Regional Industrial Policy: Some Economic Issues*, Department of Trade and Industry, London.

FLOWERDEW, R. and AITKIN, M. (1982). A method of fitting the gravity model based on the Poisson distribution, *Journal of Regional Science 22*, pp. 191–202.

FOTHERGILL, S. and GUDGIN, G. (1982). *Unequal Growth: Urban and Regional Employment Change in the U.K.*, Heinemann.

HERON, F. (1981). Post Industry Act (1972). Industrial movement into, and expansion in, the assisted areas of Great Britain, *Government Economic Service Working Paper 46*, Department of Industry.

HOWARD, R. S. (1968). *The Movement of Manufacturing Industry in the U.K. 1945–65*, HMSO: London.

MCCALLUM, D. (1979). The development of British regional policy, ch. 1 in *Regional Policy: Past Experiēnce and New Directions*, edited by D. Maclennan and J. B. Parr, Martin Robertson: Oxford.

MELLIS, C. L. and RICHARDSON, P. W. (1976). Value of investment incentives for manufacturing industry 1946 to 1974, in *The Economics of Industrial Subsidies*, edited by A. Whiting, HMSO: London.

MOORE, B. and RHODES, J. (1976). Regional economic policy and the movement of manufacturing firms to Development Areas, *Economica 43*, pp. 17–31.

NELDER, J. A. and WEDDERBURN, R. W. M. (1972). Generalised Linear Models, *Journal of the Royal Statistical Society, Section A, 135*, Part 3, pp. 370–384.

APPENDIX

Definition of variables and data sources

Investment incentives (II)

The investment incentive variable was calculated from the formulae given in Mellis and Richardson (1976). The net present value of investment incentives per £100 expenditure was calculated separately for plant and machinery and for buildings, which were then combined into a single figure using the standard 4:1 ratio. Since various changes in tax rates, grants and allowances occur at different times during any given year, the net present values were annualised before being averaged over each five year period. In addition, the net present value figure for each region is a weighted average of the figures calculated for each type of assisted area. The weights were based on employment data.

The net present value of the investment incentives were calculated as follows:

(i) plant and machinery

$$1963\text{–}65: \quad \mathrm{NPV} = \frac{T}{(1+r)^L}[(1+V)(1-G)] + \frac{G}{(1+r)^G}$$

$$1966\text{–}70: \quad \mathrm{NPV} = \frac{T}{(1+r)^L}\left[\frac{d(1-G)}{d+r}\right] + \frac{G}{(1+r)^G}$$

$$1970\text{–}72: \quad \mathrm{NPV} = \frac{T}{(1+r)^L}$$

$$1972\text{–}77: \quad \mathrm{NPV} = \frac{G}{(1+r)^G} + \frac{T}{(1+r)^L}.$$

(ii) buildings

$$1963\text{–}77: \quad NPV = \frac{T}{(1+r)^L}\left[(V+R+d) + d\left(\frac{(1+r)^N - 1}{r(1+r)^N}\right)\right]$$

where

$$N = \left[\frac{100 - R - d - G}{G}\right]\frac{1}{100} \quad \text{for 1963–72}$$

and

$$N = \left[\frac{100 - R - d}{d}\right]\frac{1}{100} \quad \text{for 1972–77.}$$

Key to variables:

T = tax rate on business income (per cent)
R = initial allowance (per cent)
V = investment allowance (per cent)
d = statutory annual reducing balance writing down allowance (per cent)
r = rate of discount (using annual average per cent redemption yield on long-dated British government stocks)
L = time lag in tax payment = 1·75 years
G = grant (as per cent of capital costs).

Industrial Location Controls (*LC*)

Data were obtained from the Department of Industry on the number of applications for Industrial Development Certificates that were approved and refused. These data were available for each G.B. region 1960–77.

Female Participation Rate (*FPR*)

Data obtained from *Regional Statistics*.

Growth in Regional Manufacturing Output (*GY*)

The following data were used:

(i) 1960–65 period: regional output growth in manufacturing 1958–63. Source: Census of Production (1963).
(ii) 1966–71 period: regional output growth in manufacturing 1963–71. Source: Census of Production (1971).
(iii) 1972–77 period: regional output growth in manufacturing 1971–76. Source: Central Statistical Office.

Average Male Earnings (*AME*)

Data obtained from *Employment Gazette*, April 1979.

Distance Between Regions

The following locations were used to measure the main road distance between each pair of regions: Newcastle (North), Leeds (Yorkshire and Humberside), Nottingham (East Midlands), Norwich (East Anglia), London (South East), Bristol (South West), Birmingham (West Midlands), Manchester (North West), Cardiff (Wales), Glasgow (Scotland). For 1960–65, Bristol to Cardiff was measured via Gloucester.

Name Index